PRAISE FOR

"In a world of too much information, *Good Enough Parenting* teaches parents how to *meet core needs*, and, at the same time, how to avoid passing down their own dysfunctional behaviors. Schema Therapy has been successful with adults, but I have always wanted to see someone do something on preventing schemas, or Lifetraps, in children, and here it is!"

— **Dr Jeffrey Young**
Dept of Psychiatry, Columbia University, New York
Founder, Schema Therapy

"This ground-breaking book will help parents raise healthier children, and when they grow up, healthier and more successful adults. I highly recommend it."

— **Charles L Whitfield**, MD
International bestselling author, "Healing the Child Within";
"Wisdom to Know the Difference: Core Issues in Relationships, Recovery and Living"

"Some experts propose that the best gift we can give to our children is a healthy parent. *Good Enough Parenting* offers us the opportunity to peer into the complexities of our own personalities, life traps, and coping styles, to discover those unique challenging moments in parenting…the ones that can activate longstanding personal struggles as well as amazing strengths. In addition to providing clear and accessible information, along with powerful tools for effective parenting, John and Karen Louis invite the reader to experience an investigative journey into the "personal" trappings and triggers that occur under the condition of being a parent. You will find step-by-step strategies for overcoming some of the most difficult obstacles, not the least of which is learning how to eliminate the unhealthy distraction of critical self-judgments in favor of harnessed responsibility and joyfulness, and managed expectations. Grounded in the robust foundational work of the evidenced-based Schema Therapy approach, *Good Enough Parenting* will be a valuable asset to your library."

— **Wendy Behary**
Author, "Disarming the Narcissist…Surviving and Thriving with the Self-Absorbed"
President, International Society of Schema Therapy (ISST)

"In *Good Enough Parenting*, John and Karen Louis put powerful new understandings and tools into parents' hands and show them, with an engaging blend of clarity, authority, warmth, openness and humility, exactly how to use these to transform the quiet day to day moments, common challenges and emotional crises of parenthood into opportunities to set their children on the path to flourishing as adults. In this first of its kind guide, John and Karen integrate the insights and strategies of an important new approach to meeting core emotional needs, Schema Therapy, with central principles of Christianity and the latest research related to parenting. They do so in a way that makes clear their extensive experience in helping parents, as church leaders and as parents; doing full justice to the complexity and challenges of parenting and yet keeping it simple and clear enough to be of immediate and practical relevance. Parents and professionals helping parents should read this book."

— **George Lockwood**, PhD
Director, Schema Therapy Institute Midwest
Representative for Public Affairs, International Society of Schema Therapy (ISST)

"This handbook bridges the gap between a scientifically based schema perspective and a deeply rooted Christian attitude towards life. It is impressive in its detail, and the theoretical knowledge is linked with expressive examples from everyday life (including examples from the authors' own family) plus vivid cartoons. The tone of the book is always non-judgmental, warm and encouraging. The title 'good enough parenting' cautions us against unrelenting standards."

— **Eckhard Roediger**, MD
Secretary, International Society of Schema Therapy (ISST) Frankfurt

"The heart of practicing Schema Therapy is healing the wounds and trauma created in childhood as parents fail to meet the core emotional needs of their children. With characteristic humor, insight and commitment to Christian life, John and Karen Louis address a need of Schema Therapy in offering a practical guide for raising children with an understanding of core emotional needs and what is required to meet them. They combine experience as parents, therapists and church leaders to offer a valuable perspective on raising happy and emotionally healthy children."

— **Catherine Amon**, MSW, Mdiv.
Cognitive Therapy Center of New York

"*Good Enough Parenting* is a valuable addition to a long list of credible books on raising children. John and Karen Louis have given us Biblical principles and truths uniquely blended with scholarly studies which validate and illuminate these principles and truths. The result is a work that enables parents to confidently follow God's guidelines without having to apologize or defend them to those who would promote methodology based on the current 'worldly wisdom' of the day. We highly recommend this book."

— **Dr Al Baird and Gloria Baird**
Elder and Women's Ministry Leader, Los Angeles

"John and Karen dig deeply! An informative and enlightening look at parenting that will help you connect more profoundly with your kids."

— **Sam and Geri Laing**
Elder and Women's Ministry Leader, South Florida
Authors of five books on marriage and parenting

"In the former Soviet Union, we are facing first generation Christianity, challenged with the liberalism of Europe, and we find the task of equipping parents to be overwhelming! The children growing up in our churches can be surrounded by religion and never really connect with God or their parents. We are personally indebted to the Louis family for their love and example. We are grateful that when it comes to their teaching on parenting, they do not leave it up to chance or base it on personality. Instead, they have put in hundreds of hours of research and come up with deep convictions and detailed practicals to give us every opportunity to lay a foundation of love in the hearts of our children! This book is a great guide for any family, and any minister, to help us connect to God, to one another, and to our children."

— **Shawn and Lena Wooten**
Evangelist and Women's Ministry Leader, Kiev

"*Good Enough Parenting* is a book to be studied and not just read. John and Karen Louis have created a valuable resource to help parents recognize and understand the core emotional needs of their children and how to meet those needs. John and Karen have a unique gift of being able to blend solid biblical teaching with the latest scientific research. The material presented in these pages is extraordinary and profound. If you want to sharpen your parenting skills, drink deeply from these waters."

— **Dr G. Steve Kinnard and Leigh Kinnard**
Adjunct Professor of Bible, Lincoln Christian University
Teacher / Evangelist and Women's Ministry Leader, New York

"Linda and I found the Louis' book to be full of deep, well researched wisdom. This book will help you to understand your children and yourself, as well! John and Karen were vulnerable in their personal examples, witty in their illustrations, and comprehensive in the scope of parenting issues addressed."

— **Ron and Linda Brumley**
Ministry Leaders, San Diego

"Beginning with the scriptures, John and Karen do a masterful job of opening our hearts and minds to parenting in a way that points us to God's heart and intent. With depth, but also simplicity, they use Scripture, research, various illustrations and real life examples to teach us about ourselves, our marriages and our parenting. We learn through the pages of this book that when we as parents better understand ourselves, and learn to more carefully understand our children, we can better know how to build healthy interactions and "deep-down" security. However, this book not only espouses this noble concept, but also provides practical examples and exercises to teach and train us how to actually change. Our belief is that many families can find direction for healing through the lessons taught. Every parent would do well to not only read this book, but to take time to discuss it with their spouse and others in their lives. It is well worth the time and can give hope to our families and friends. Share it all around. After all, what is more important to us than our children?"

— **Wyndham and Jeanie Shaw**
Elder and Women's Minister, Boston

"A very insightful and practical parenting book that transcends race and culture! A must read for all parents with kids of any age. It has opened our eyes to a healthier way of communicating with our children to make sure we meet their needs and stay connected to them. The changes in them and us have been dramatic. Thank you so much!"

— **Dr Mark Timlin** MBChB, MPH, MBE **and Vicki Timlin**
Melbourne

"Many parenting books today paint the picture of how to be the perfect parent. Finally, a book is available to equip parents to be good enough. John and Karen's writing style captures your attention while explaining in detail strategies necessary to cope with parenting. The authors have compiled a revolutionary book that provides biblical principles, practical application and real life stories to guide parents. I particularly found the inclusion of Master Class refreshing. It was reassuring to read the stories of those who have gone before us. *Good Enough Parenting* is rich in insight, direction and provides great hope for parents everywhere; …every parent should have it in their library."

— **Michael and Laura Fix**
Evangelist and Women's Ministry Leader, New Hampshire

"Every parent should study *Good Enough Parenting* to help them fully understand and visualize the effects of their parenting. The Good Enough Parenting workshop by John and Karen was the most helpful one we have ever attended. We were greatly inspired by their in-depth research, biblical wisdom, and years of practical application. Parents should put their strategic principles into practice because they work."

— **Dr Turner Sinn and Dr Elizabeth Sinn**
Senior Pastor / Elder and Women's Ministry Leader, Hong Kong

Good Enough Parenting

A Christian Perspective on
Meeting Core Emotional Needs and
Avoiding Exasperation

John Philip Louis & Karen McDonald Louis

LCTS
Louis Counselling & Training Services Pte. Ltd.

All rights reserved. No part of this publication may be reproduced, stored in a retrieval system, electronic or transmitted, in any form or by any means, electronic, mechanical, photocopying, recording or otherwise, without the prior written consent of the publisher.

Copyright © 2012 by Louis Counselling & Training Services Pte. Ltd.

Website: http://www.gep.sg

Email: johnlouis@louiscts.com

All scriptures quotations, unless otherwise stated are from the Holy Bible, New International Version®, NIV®. Copyright © 1973, 1978, 1984, 2011 by Biblica, Inc.™ Used by permission of Zondervan. All rights reserved worldwide. www.zondervan.com The "NIV" and "New International Version" are trademarks registered in the United States Patent and Trademark Office by Biblica, Inc.™

First Edition Printed in Singapore

First Edition

National Library Board, Singapore Cataloguing-in-Publication Data

Louis, John Philip, 1963-
Good enough parenting / John Philip Louis & Karen McDonald Louis. -- Singapore : Louis Counselling & Training Services Pte. Ltd., c2012.
p. cm.
ISBN : 978-981-07-1971-5 (pbk.)

1. Parenting--Religious aspects--Christianity. 2. Parent and child--Religious aspects--Christianity. I. Louis, Karen McDonald,d1962-   II. Title.

BV4529
248.845-- dc23   OCN808056821

Previous ISBN: 978-981-07-1971-5

Second Printing

Copyright © 2014 by Louis Counselling & Training Services Pte. Ltd.

American Edition ISBN: 978-1-939086-84-6. Distributed in association with IP Books.

Illumination Publishers, 6010 Pinecreek Ridge Court, Spring, Texas 77379

Available at www.ipibooks.com. **New ISBN: 978-1-939086-84-6**

Good Enough Parenting by John & Karen Louis
Chief Illustrator: Sher Lee Wee
Assisted by: Tan Beng Hwa

TABLE OF CONTENTS

Acknowledgements and Dedication i
Preface iii

Section One: Introduction to Good Enough Parenting

Introduction: Parenting Matters 3
    Master Class – An Introduction to Our Panel of Elders and Their Families 7

Chapter One: The Case for Core Emotional Needs 13
    Lifetraps and Coping Styles 13
    The Foundation of Core Emotional Needs 18
    How Marriage Affects Parenting 24
    Schema in the New Testament 32

Chapter Two: The Frustration of Core Emotional Needs 41

Chapter Three: Exasperation Interactions 49

Section Two: The Core Emotional Need for Connection and Acceptance

Chapter Four: Connection and Acceptance 65

Chapter Five: What's at Stake? 75
    Basic Safety 92
    Connection and Acceptance among the Patriarchs 97

Chapter Six: Quality Time Takes Time 103
    Commit to a Regular One-on-One Time with Each Child 103
    Commit to Regular Gatherings around the Table 105
    The Importance of Early Attachment 109

Chapter Seven: Empathy and Validation of Feelings 139
    What Makes it Hard for Parents to Show Empathy to Their Children? 140
    Processing Emotions 147
    Accepting Behaviour vs. Accepting Feelings 158

Section Three: The Core Emotional Need for Healthy Autonomy and Performance

Chapter Eight: Healthy Autonomy and Performance 163

Chapter Nine: What's at Stake? 169
    Basic Safety 187
    Healthy Autonomy and Performance among the Patriarchs 190

Chapter Ten: Age-Approriate Empowerment 197

Section Four: The Core Emotional Need for Reasonable Limits

Chapter Eleven: Reasonable Limits 209

Chapter Twelve: What's at Stake? 217
    Reasonable Limits among the Patriarchs 229

Chapter Thirteen: Avoiding Bottlenecks and The Vortex 233
    Basic Safety..236
    The Vortex of Conflict Escalation..................................242

Chapter Fourteen: Avoiding the Vortex......................................253

Section Five: The Core Emotional Need for Realistic Expectations

Chapter Fifteen: Realistic Expectations.....................................275

Chapter Sixteen: What's at Stake?..285
    Realistic Expectations among the Patriarchs...................295

Chapter Seventeen: An Asset or a Liability?............................301
    Basic Safety..301

Section Six: The Plus-One Core Emotional Need for Spiritual Values and Community

Chapter Eighteen: Spiritual Values and Community 333
    Dysfunction in the Patriarchs..342

Chapter Nineteen: Spiritual Values..349

Chapter Twenty: The Power of Community 379
    Spiritual Values and Community for Different Age Groups..............387
    Unleashing the Power of Community............................393

Section Seven: Final Thoughts

Chapter Twenty-One: Fatherhood 399
    The Impact Fathers Can Have......................................402
    Stay Involved Through Thick and Thin..........................407
    Know the Father's Unique Contribution 411

Chapter Twenty-Two: Repair and Reconnect 423
    Healing Comes from Being Vulnerable..........................425
    How To Be Vulnerable..428
    Principles that Parents Should Consider When Repairing Parent-Child Relationships 430

Epilogue..434

Appendix 1 Exasperation Interactions Worksheet...................435

Appendix 2 Exercise on Processing Difficult Emotions 436

Appendix 3 Exercise on Connecting with Your Child 437

Appendix 4 Exercise on the Vortex of Conflict Escalation......443

Appendix 5 Exercise on Being Vulnerable 447

Notes 463

Bibliography 483

Index...502

ACKNOWLEDGEMENTS AND DEDICATION

First and foremost, **thanks to God**, who is not just a good enough parent, but the ultimate parent: *Thank you, Heavenly Father, for giving us all things for life and godliness and for meeting our core emotional needs.*

To **Dr Jeffrey Young**, the founder of schema therapy, whose influence is felt on every page: *We appreciate so much the time you set aside to give us valuable consultation on this topic. We are grateful for encouragement from a world-class clinician to follow our dream.* To our assistant and Movie Therapy partner, **Pat Sim,** who, while spinning many different plates, managed to troubleshoot in all sorts of situations, often working into the wee hours of the morning: *Pat, we so appreciate our friendship over the last two decades and our partnership in helping parents. We literally couldn't have pulled this off without you.* **To the Master Class church elders and their families who took time away from their busy schedules to help us:** *Thank you all so much for sharing your lives with us. Thank you for inspiring us as parents and helping literally thousands of others with your wisdom.*

TO OUR DEDICATED RESEARCH TEAM

Dr George Lockwood, who spent many hours with me (John) over Skype: *Thank you for reading chapters, hashing things out with me, and expressing yourself so clearly. You helped me to crystalize my thoughts and findings.* **Dr Harold Sexton**, a seasoned researcher in the field of statistics who used his expertise to double-check our findings and refine our data: *Thank you for leaving no stone unturned and for always replying to us promptly with feedback and insights. I (John) have learnt a lot from you.* **Dr Asle Hoffart,** another important research partner: *Thank you for your consultation as you watched us churn out the results in the midst of your busy schedule.* **Yuao Hu and Wayne Chong:** *Thank you for helping me (John) with the statistical analysis of my data even though you were both busy with your PhD programme and other important work.* **Teo Yig Zern (Yiren)**: *Thank you for helping us collect the raw data and consolidate it in a manner that helped the researchers analyse it without difficulties.* **The Singapore National Council of Social Services (NCSS)**: *Thank you for giving us the grant that helped to partially finance this research.* **The Management Committee and members of the Central Christian Church** who volunteered their time to fill up questionnaires: *We really appreciate you taking the time to fill out the incredibly long personal inventories without which we could not have done our initial research. May God bless all of your families.* **The entire staff of the Central Christian Church**, who sorted data, did emergency editing from time to time, and provided encouragement all of the time: *Thank you all, especially Patrice, Wai Yee and the student interns, for your suggestions and service.*

TO OUR DYNAMIC EDITING TEAM
Dr Shirlena Huang, a friend of almost 25 years, who read our manuscript when she really had absolutely no time to do so: *Your astute editing skills helped us to notice what might have otherwise been overlooked with a manuscript of this size.* **Dr Randy Janka**, who deserves our utmost thanks for setting aside time to help us edit such a huge number of pages in painstaking detail: *Your truthful feedback written in love helped our work to be much more readable.* **Catherine Amon**, who understands the connection between schema therapy and spirituality as few others do: *Thank you so much for editing one huge section of this book. We appreciate our common work in schema therapy and are grateful for our friendship.* **Dr Mark and Vicki Timlin**, who are not only extremely intelligent and energetic, but also willing to travel over land and sea both to get help for their young family and to help other families: *We are grateful for your editorial feedback and for being there when John needed a doctor!* **Paul Ramsey, Mark Templer**, and **Lisa Laoye,** who each did a read through and gave us meaningful and helpful feedback: *Thank you—you really made a difference!*

FINAL THOUGHTS
Thank you to **Sher Lee Wee,** our artist, whose cartoons are a huge addition to this work: *Thank you for sharing your gift and for working with us on this project.* **Tan Beng Hwa**, who worked on the graphics: *We changed our design so many times and your patience is something we appreciate a lot.* **Abraham Augustin**: *Thanks for helping us with the formatting of this script.*

We are also grateful for **the Sims, the Salims and the Ngs,** who are our partners in church ministry and leadership in this part of the world: *We could not have asked for better peers and colleagues to work with. Thank you for loving us enough to seek our highest good, for loving our children, for loving people, and for loving God.*

Thank you to **our parents,** who, in both visible and unseen ways, are incredibly supportive of the work we are doing: *You left us big shoes to fill and we are grateful for the ways you helped to meet our core emotional needs. And you are awesome grandparents, as well!*

Finally, we want to thank our children, Sonia, now 20 years old, and David, 18: *This book is dedicated to you. We cannot imagine being happier with our children than we are with the two of you. We respect you for being the young woman and young man that you have become and are becoming. We derive so much joy from just being with you; spending time with you is one of our favourite things to do on the planet! We know that you both will continue to grow and become a much more improved version of us. Thank you for your friendship, honesty, and partnership in the gospel, and for showing us so much forgiveness in our journey to become Good Enough Parents.*

PREFACE

We approached the writing of a parenting book with fear and trembling, so we feel a little compelled to explain what brought us here, as a justification for what may seem like the hubris of such an undertaking. Why the need for yet another parenting book? What makes this book unique is that it is a combination of the old and the new—on the one hand, we are basing our work on very old school (as in Ancient!) Biblical principles, combined with real-life wisdom from respected elders and their families; on the other hand, we are making use of the latest scientific research available to help parents prevent dysfunction in their children. The short version of how our Good Enough Parenting workshop and ultimately this book came to be is that in October 2007, we attended a workshop called "An Introduction to Schema Therapy" by Dr Jeffrey Young, the therapy's founder. During a Q & A session, one of the participants asked Dr Young, "If your theory is correct and people develop these 'schemas' (automatic negative thought memories) in childhood, has anyone considered coming up with a schema prevention programme for parents?" Half in jest, Dr Young replied that his life's work had been coming up with the therapy, but that no one had ever worked on any prevention, and please feel free to do so. We privately expressed interest, telling Dr Young about our parenting presentations that used movie scenes to give parents awareness. Our lessons seemed to align with what Dr Young said would prevent the development of schemas. He encouraged John to train with him in Manhattan, and by May 2008, Dr Young gave our schema prevention prototype the green light. In the autumn, we conducted the first run of our Good Enough Parenting workshop in the church we help to lead in Singapore, with hundreds of friends from the community joining our congregation. Over the next two years, we conducted training sessions for over 700 church staff and lay leaders from around the world. At each turn, we were asked, "When are you going to write a parenting book to go with the workshop?" Because we feel strongly that the best gift parents can give their children is to love each other, we first developed a marriage workshop with an accompanying book, *I Choose Us*, as a kind of prequel to this book—*Good Enough Parenting* is really Volume II. Eventually we set aside a year to work on this tome. So now you know how this book came about. Please receive it in the spirit with which it was written, from two Christian parents who understand only too well that we are not perfect! We hope you will be able to use it throughout your parenting journey as a guide to being "good enough".

John and Karen Louis, Singapore, November 2012

Authors' notes regarding SPELLING, GENDER, & CONFIDENTIALITY:
- Because this book is being printed in Singapore, a member of the British Commonwealth, we have used British spelling and punctuation. The name "Good Enough Parenting" appears in italics when referring to the title of this book (*Good Enough Parenting*) and in regular font when referring to the name of our workshop or the parenting concept itself.
- We tried to avoid a gender bias when talking about children, mostly by employing plural nouns that call for gender-neutral pronouns, such as they/them/theirs. In some cases we used "he/him/his" in one chapter, and "she/her/hers" in the next, and in other situations, we alternated genders within the same chapter.
- All "case studies" are true stories of parents and/or children from within our family of churches who either we have counselled personally or whose counselling we have supervised in our youth and family ministry. The names and some details have been changed to protect confidentiality. In the case of stories made up for the sake of illustration, we have labelled them "vignettes".

SECTION ONE

Introduction
Good Enough Parenting

So what on earth is

Good Enough Parenting?

INTRODUCTION

Parenting Matters

While putting together a workshop for Singapore's Health Promotion Board on the topic of building self-esteem in children, I (Karen) solicited help from our then 11-year old son, who had (and still has) a good sense of self-worth. Our conversation went something like this:

Karen : (*sitting next to David on the sofa*) Hey, sweetie, I need some help for a presentation I am working on. May I ask you some questions?

David : Sure, Mum.

Karen : Ok, just out of curiosity, what would you do if a *kid* in your school told you that you were stupid?

David : (*confidently*) I'd tell him that *he* was stupid!

Karen : Ok… and just out of curiosity, what would you do if one of your *teachers* told you that you were stupid?

David : (*thoughtfully and with a smile*) Well, I probably wouldn't *tell* them they were stupid, but I would *think* it!

Karen : One more question…what would you do if *I* told you that you were stupid?

David : (*slowly, with a bit of sadness*) Well, I would probably get angry, (*pause*) but I might believe *you*.

Parenting matters. Don't let anyone tell you that parenting is not important. It is the most significant job that you will ever do, with far-reaching consequences.

Modern research has found that, in general, teens who have good relationships with their parents do better at school, have more friends, imitate their parents' good values, and stay out of trouble. We distilled a painstakingly long and detailed study summarising over 1000 parenting articles into two sentences:

- Teens whose parents are supportive and caring, but who also consistently monitor and enforce family rules, are more likely to be motivated and successful at school, as well as psychologically and physically healthy.
- In contrast, adolescents whose parents are overly strict and do not give them any independence, as well as those with parents who are warm but permissive, are more likely to be impulsive and engage in risky behaviour.[1]

> ◁ **RESEARCH REVEALS** ▷
>
> **RR0.1:** *Adolescent Well-Being Is Strongly Related to the Quality of the Parent-Child Relationship*
>
> In 2002, Child Trends looked at 1,100 research articles to identify what promotes positive adolescent development. They found that the parent-child relationship is strongly related to adolescent well-being. Here were their four key factors:
>
> 1. Relationships – Teens who have warm, involved, and satisfying relationships with their parents are more likely to do well in school, be academically motivated and engaged, have better social skills, and have lower rates of risky behaviour than their peers.
> 2. Modelling – Teens whose parents demonstrate positive behaviour on a number of fronts are more likely to engage in those behaviours themselves.
> 3. Monitoring / Awareness – Parents who know about their children's activities, friends, and behaviour and monitor them in age-appropriate ways have teens with lower rates of risky physical and sexual behaviour.
> 4. Approach to Parenting – Teens whose parents are supportive and caring, but who also consistently monitor and enforce family rules are more likely to be motivated and successful at school, as well as psychologically and physically healthy. In contrast, adolescents whose parents are overly strict and do not give them any independence are more likely to engage in risky behaviour. Similarly when parents are warm but permissive, adolescents tend to be impulsive and engage in more risky behaviour.[2]

These findings are not really surprising; they kind of sound like common sense. Parents should be close to their teens, avoid hypocrisy, and not be too controlling or permissive. However, the following bit of research is more startling: A study of almost 600 families in New York lasting for 18 years found that the occurrence of mental illnesses in children was related to unhealthy parenting, regardless of whether or not the parents themselves suffered from mental illness. Parenting matters!

> ◁ **RESEARCH REVEALS** ▷
>
> **RR0.2:** *Unhealthy Parenting Promotes Mental Illness*
>
> A group of researchers looked at 593 families and their children from two counties in the state of New York in 1975, 1983, 1985 to 1986, and 1991 to 1993, made up of parents with and without mental illness. Their aim was to examine the association between parents' mental health, unhealthy

> parenting behaviour, and off-spring mental health. One of their findings was that the children who developed mental illness (depression, anxiety disorder, substance abuse, personality disorder, ADHD, panic disorder, social phobia, OCD, antisocial personality disorder and PTSD) did so primarily because of unhealthy parenting, not because of their parents' mental illness. Thus, the higher the level of unhealthy parenting, the higher the frequency of mental illness in their children.[3] Most parents would probably assume that mental illness passes down genetically, but that is not always the case. Dr. Charles Whitfield highlighted this and many similar studies, done primarily since the 1980s, asserting that the devastation of unhealthy parenting has only surfaced by way of empirical evidence as time moves on.[4]

We recognize that most parents are trying their best to love their children, and that their mistakes are usually *subtle* and *unintentional*. And while there is no such thing as a perfect mum or dad, parents can learn to be "good enough". (We didn't make up that phrase—English paediatrician and psychoanalyst Donald Winnicott wrote about the "good enough mother" over a half-century ago.[5]) Good Enough Parenting takes being intentional, and it takes training.

Allow us to illustrate this principle with a story from Karen's extended family in Texas. The McDonalds play a card game called Liverpool Rummy. They see every holiday as an excuse for a tournament; three tables or more of six players is not an uncommon sight at any gathering. While new family members struggle to learn the intricacies of the game with its idiosyncratic rules, after a few Thanksgivings and Christmases they begin to pick up the skills needed and pretty soon they start winning, or at least not coming in last place. (They learn not to sit behind the uncle who buys *everything*, to beware the aunt who always plays low, and to not be surprised when a certain cousin breaks into song if he loses!) The outcome of the game is determined partly by the cards one is dealt, but also very much by how one plays the game. Some players moan about their bad luck, and eventually make excuses about why Liverpool is not their game. Others hone their skills, year after year, and get better and better. We feel that parenting is very similar. When prospective parents combine their gene pools, part of the excitement of having a child is to discover what characteristics have been "dealt," if you will. Their temperaments are inborn, and we do not get to decide that. That is the "nature" side of things. But there is also the "nurture" side, and that is where our part comes in. We can be trained. We can learn strategies. We can study our children and know which one "plays low", and which one is likely to "break into song". We may not win every hand, but we can improve with time, and get better and better. *That* is Good Enough Parenting.

Why is Good Enough Parenting effective? Good Enough Parenting helps parents meet what we call "the core emotional needs" and will:
- Equip parents to raise emotionally healthy and autonomous children who will make a positive contribution to their world
- Prevent parents (as much as possible) from passing down their own dysfunctional attitudes and behaviours
- Guide parents so that they will be able to connect emotionally with all of their children and share values, including passing their torch of faith to the next generation
- Give step-by-step advice, in the case of teenagers or adult children, on repairing and reconnecting.

In *Good Enough Parenting*, we explain the importance of core emotional needs, define and describe them, and discuss the long-term problems that come from *not* meeting them. We give parents practical instruction about how to meet the different core needs, share insights from over 30 counselling cases, and suggest exercises and activities. We guide parents of teenagers and adult children through the process of repair and reconnection, and offer a chapter on fatherhood. With our children's permission, we have also sprinkled the book with stories from our family; we have nicknamed each of those sections "Louis Lowdown". We also gathered a number of testimonials from various church elders and their families with the moniker of "Master Class" (see the next page for an introduction to all the families highlighted). In addition, most chapters contains several "Research Reveals" sections, which you can either read to your heart's content or skip altogether. For those who are able to attend the accompanying Good Enough Parenting workshop, we hope that the combination of movies, instruction, and interaction is a blessing to you in your parenting journey.

We wish we could give you a formula, but even though we use scientific research and methods, children are not science projects—there is no equation that works with every child. Sam and Geri Laing, one of our Master Class couples, told us that they put so much time into "studying" each of their four very different offspring that they had the equivalent of a PhD in each child! That attitude is necessary if we want to be Good Enough Parents, because parenting is as much of an art as it is a science, with each child his own priceless masterpiece.

Parents need to know the difference between teaching discipline and not being harsh, being affectionate without being enmeshed, being involved but not creating dependence, showing empathy but not being permissive, showing healthy indignation at times while not sinning in anger, and having healthy standards but not showing conditional love. This balance calls for training, as well as a lot of grace. Lack of training, plus ignorance and discouragement, are the main reasons that parents who love their children do not break the unhealthy cycles that they themselves have inherited.

Warning: *Good Enough Parenting* is not for the faint hearted or the lazy. This is not a "feel-good" book. Practicing the principles of Good Enough Parenting takes courage, passion, and perseverance, or as some have said, blood, sweat, and tears. But the joy and satisfaction that come when you are emotionally connected with your child, when you share many values, when he is functioning at a healthy level in his world, when she loves being with you but is successful when apart, when you see them thriving in relationships, and when you are eventually united in Christ, make Good Enough Parenting worth every minute.

Maybe that's just what Solomon meant when he penned these verses:

My son, if your heart is wise, then my heart will be glad;
my inmost being will rejoice when your lips speak what is right.
Listen to your father, who gave you life,
and do not despise your mother when she is old.
The father of a righteous man has great joy;
he who has a wise son delights in him.
May your father and mother be glad;
may she who gave you birth rejoice!
My son, give me your heart and let your eyes keep to my ways…
(selected verses from Proverbs 23)

Master Class – An Introduction to Our Panel of Elders and Their Families

We have known these eight elders and their wives for over two decades; some even attended our wedding in 1987 or gave us pre-marriage counselling, and all of them have given us parenting advice over the years. Their lives are a testimony to family, both their own families and the family of God. We wrote to these friends to ask for their favourite parenting memories, knowing that what they or their children might share would be inspiring. What we received from them exceeded our expectations. Throughout every section of this book, readers will see real life examples of how these God-fearing families very intuitively put the principles in this book into practice. We call their reflections "Master Class".

The loving leaders prefaced any thoughts on parenting with a declaration of what contributed most to the blessings in their family—the mercy and grace of a very forgiving and loving heavenly Father. One of the brothers wrote, *"God would be totally justified in striking us deaf, dumb and blind if we didn't give Him all the credit and honour He is due. Neither our kids nor we would have made it into the Kingdom of God without the rather obvious intervention of God on numerous occasions."* With that as a foundation, below, in alphabetical order, are the elders and their wives and families who shared specific memories so that they might be of some encouragement to others who are in the process of becoming Good Enough Parents.

Al and Gloria Baird began their married life with their hearts on the mission, and nothing has changed since then—they have spent their lives advancing the cause of Christ and tirelessly strengthening disciples on just about every continent. In fact, we cannot think of another couple who has tried to help more families and resolve more conflicts than the Bairds. Now in their 70s, they live half the year in LA, and divide the rest of their time between traveling to various spots around the world, maturing the next generation of elders and families, and visiting their three wonderful daughters, three awesome sons-in-law, and nine delightful grandchildren. Al and Gloria got advice about their parenting from Gloria's mom and dad, and are now seeing their own children put those things into practice. When asked what he thinks is the number one stumbling block that keeps "church kids" from following Jesus as teens, Al stated, *"I think the overriding cause is parents not living radical, sold out lives that their kids can tell they enjoy."*

Ron and Linda Brumley have two sons, two daughters and many grown-up grandchildren! They live and work with a congregation in Seattle, but have served God in every part of the USA. Like the Bairds, they are spending their "retirement" helping others spiritually, including brothers and sisters on the other side of the globe. When asked about their parenting memories, Ron was his usual positive self, *"Linda and I feel like the most blessed people in the world! When we started on life's journey together some 51 years ago, we began praying to God that He would bless us with healthy, faithful children. We prayed that He would make up the difference (rather huge at times) between what our kids needed from us and what we were able to give them spiritually. God has always been so faithful. As we look back over our 49 years as parents, we concluded that we could never be perfect parents but we could strive to fill our house with love, gratitude, joy and faith."*

Walter and Kim Evans come from a legacy of sacrifice and have led churches in the USA plus been missionaries in the UK. Walter currently serves as lead evangelist in a church in Philadelphia, and Kim serves the women while also having a big heart for youth outreach. They have a son and two daughters—one is still in college, and the older two have recently married. Their parenting wisdom includes an interesting analogy: *"We visualise parenting to be kind of like a novice chef baking a cake—no one knows what it's going to look like when it comes out of the oven. Parents can carefully put in the ingredients but what the children take away is sometimes recognizable and sometimes not. The God-given personality of each member of the family is unique and brings a chemistry to the family unit that is very individual. When the five members of our family answered the question, 'What has been most helpful and important in our parenting?' there were five completely different answers—you wonder if we were all in the same house! The beauty of family is that there is not just one recipe—every family's cake looks different; the starting point for parents is to think about what is most important to them, to pray, and to watch what God and the Holy Spirit bring out of the oven."*

Mike and Terrie Fontenot know a lot about girls—they have three daughters and seven granddaughters! Mandy, Megan and Michelle and their husbands are all in the full-time ministry, and are happy serving God in the USA, in Australia, or anywhere that God calls them. Mike serves as an evangelist in Virginia, and he and Terrie work side by side in overseeing a huge family of churches. At the time of this writing, they are taking their zeal and wisdom on the road, helping to mature leaders in the UK and other countries. They feel that parenting is really about the parents being like Jesus, and then helping their children to become like Jesus. *"Being a disciple of Jesus means 'living' with Him in order to become like Him. The inner transformation we so desperately desire can only be achieved over time, and can only happen if we maintain a constant close connection with God. As we 'abide' with Jesus, we watch and learn and imitate how to live a life of self-denial and love. As our children live with us, they also watch and learn and imitate. Kids are amazing mimics, and they will become like us. Our children should gain wisdom for living by absorbing it from those closest to them. Because of this, we must constantly be evaluating our values. We are continually going to the scriptures to be sure we are being transformed consistently in our discipleship. In order to grow and mature as disciples of Jesus, we must learn from Him about the deep things of God. The alternative is to live in perpetual childhood, remaining immature and condemning ourselves to a wasted, frustrating life. We can apply this same principle in our parenting as we raise young disciples in our family. It takes study, thoughtfulness, prayer, instruction, correction, observation, humility and consistency that can only be achieved over time. There are no 'quick-fixes', only a lifetime laid down and devoted to discipleship. God has blessed our efforts, answered many prayers and been very gracious to us as parents so far and we rely on His continuing mercy."*

Bill and Sally Hooper serve in the full-time ministry in a church in Dallas, along with their daughter and her husband. Their older son and his wife serve as lead evangelist and women's ministry leader in a congregation in Austin and younger son and his wife also serve in the church in Dallas. Bill worked for years in aerospace engineering and Sally enjoys planning tours to the Holy Lands. They have also been very active over the years helping out many churches in the countries that make up the former Soviet Union. When asked about what helped their parenting to be successful, they replied, *"We have been married for 45 years and God has blessed us with six children (three by birth and three by marriage) and nine grandchildren (the two oldest have already made Jesus their Lord). Parenting is not easy and we realized after studying the Bible and becoming Christians that there was a lot we needed to learn in order to raise our children to love God. We prayed every day that they would grow up to be strong Christians and marry strong Christians, and we sought advice from other parents who had already raised their children to love God; when it came to seeking out input, no matter was too small or insignificant."*

Sam and Geri Laing currently live in South Florida and serve in a church there, although they have worked in churches up and down the east coast for almost 40 years. They have four children; all are married and serve in various capacities in churches around the United States. Not only are Sam and Geri both excellent teachers, they are also published authors and have written three books on parenting and many other books on marriage and various aspects of godliness. Their eldest child, Elizabeth Laing Thomson, is also an accomplished writer, having published three books to date: a book for "kingdom kids" called *Glory Days*, a book for mothers of toddlers called *The Tender Years* and a fun novel for young teen girls called *The Thirteenth Summer*. Sam prefaced his entries for this book with the following, *"Here are three simple but profound lessons that made a huge difference in building our family. We hope they help you as they did us."* You'll have to keep reading to find out what they are!

John and Nancy Mannel have been indefatigable servants in a church in Los Angeles since the early '90s. Their children are great disciples of Jesus and are raising their own young families to be the same. Not only have the Mannels helped out with many marriages in the United States, they have also had a heart to help out in Russia and surrounding countries. They bring a slightly different experience to their parenting and outreach than the other couples mentioned here. John and Nancy write, *"In March of 1978 we were baptized into Christ. As exciting as that was, an unavoidable reality remained before us—a severely damaged and broken marriage complete with three children. By way of an opening statement, to figure out how to rebuild, we knew our relationship with God had to be of first importance. Having others in our lives to teach us to become like Jesus, which we refer to as discipling or being discipled, is also vital, ("teaching them to obey everything I have commanded you" Mt 28:20). Roger and Marcia Lamb studied the Bible with us and taught us about God and His church. They taught us how to love each other and love our children. They instilled in us the need to put God first in our lives, in our jobs and schedules, in making choices about school activities for our children. They gave us particularly good advice about being careful in the area of after-school competitive sports, which could possibly have an adverse effect on our time together as a family and faithful attendance to meetings of the body. We have come to believe that these spiritual priorities are a crucial foundation for any Christian family. We stand before you today by the grace of God as an elder and women's counsellor in the Los Angeles Church of Christ. God has given us an amazing marriage and children who are disciples, now raising their children to be disciples. We worked to spend quality and quantity time with our family to rebuild what was broken, and are grateful for God's grace."*

Wyndham and Jeanie Shaw are adopted New Englanders, and serve in a church in Boston, along with one of their daughters and her husband who lead a thriving campus ministry. They have not only worked with unflagging zeal in the full-time ministry for decades, they have also been very active in coordinating efforts with the less fortunate in many parts of the United States, and have given passionately to furthering the work of the gospel in Europe. Wyndham and Jeanie have each published several books and are gifted teachers. They have four adult children and many young grandchildren, and have this to say by way of introduction: *"As parents, nothing was more important to us than passing on to our children the vision of Mighty God, Wonderful Counsellor, Everlasting Father and Prince of Peace. We wanted our children to see God interwoven throughout the threads of our thoughts and actions, and to learn how to apply His love and His words to their everyday life. We hoped that they would be equipped for hardships and injustices as well as blessings. While we enjoyed their participation in academics, sports and extracurricular activities, it was much more important to us that they grew in their characters as they practiced and learned the true meanings of the fruit of the spirit…love, joy, peace, patience, kindness, gentleness, goodness, faithfulness and self-control. Nothing brings our hearts more joy today than seeing our three oldest children parent their own children, teaching them to love God and each other. Our youngest, who is 25 years old, has been a part of our family since he was a pre-teen, having spent the first twelve years of his life in an orphanage. Learning how to reach his heart and build connection in different ways has been a wonderful journey that has made us more loving as individuals and as a family."* In addition, Jeanie shares wonderful memories of her parents' faith—her father was an elder in a congregation in Florida. Jeanie says, *"I had the joy and privilege of being raised in a Christian home and deeply appreciate the legacy of faith my parents left for me. The way they lived their life spoke louder than anything they may have missed in the way of parenting. I followed the path they began, because their faith made me want to find my own faith. I saw my parents live their convictions about God to their last breath."*

*Why are
core emotional needs
so important and
how did you
come up with them?*

CHAPTER ONE

The Case for Core Emotional Needs

Water, sunlight, air and nutrients are the core needs for plant life. In the same way, human beings must have their core emotional needs met in order for them to be mentally and emotionally healthy. And just as brown petals or wilted leaves are the first signs that a plant is not thriving, so, too, there are signs when core emotional needs are not being met adequately in children, leading to a broad range of dysfunctional patterns later in life. Meeting the core emotional needs is not a nice tip for parenting, or a quaint suggestion to improve behaviour, but an absolute necessity for raising healthy and happy children. After two and a half decades of ministry work in many different cultures, being therapists, and being parents ourselves, we are convinced that helping children function and thrive in an adult world comes down to the parents meeting the core emotional needs of their children. If these are not met, children will internalise these frustrating and painful experiences and struggle to cope. This imprint and this struggle leads to the development of what Dr Jeffrey Young calls "lifetraps" or early maladaptive schemas. Dr Young developed Schema Therapy to help adults change these patterns which otherwise repeatedly play themselves out throughout one's life.[1] One of the exciting purposes of *this* book is to prevent schemas from forming in the first place!

Lifetraps and Coping Styles

Think of lifetraps/schemas like this: we all develop certain thinking patterns during our childhood. For example, the first born child in a family where the breadwinner is struggling to make ends meet might develop a greater sense of responsibility than the last born in a family of four with an upper middle class income. In the same way, a child who has been brought up in a neighbourhood which values athletic achievement might develop differently if he suddenly moves to a place which values academics.

Unfortunately, influences on a child are not always so benign. A child who is sexually molested by a relative might think that he cannot trust any authority figure. A child who is bullied at school might begin to think she is unlovable. A child who is berated by his parents might come to believe he is worthless or that he will never measure up. These toxic experiences lead to the development of negative patterns of thinking, feeling and behaving; conscious and non-conscious memories; and beliefs about ourselves and others that carry over into our adulthood, into our marriage and into our parenting! The beliefs about ourselves, others and the world that are part of a lifetrap are *distorted*. The *stronger* our lifetraps, the more *distorted* our view (see Figure 1.1). We all develop lifetraps in childhood, partly due to inborn temperament, and partly due to enviornment. *However, the number and strength of our lifetraps increases to the extent that our core emotional needs are not met.* Perhaps we tried gaining attention or love from our caregivers. Perhaps our number one goal was to avoid being shamed. Perhaps we had an early sexual experience or were held to a very high standard. If we were abused, abandoned, shamed, or deprived of love by our parents, siblings, or peers, we almost certainly would have developed some corresponding lifetraps.

Figure 1.1: Lifetraps (Schemas) Distort Views about Ourselves and Others

Part of the dysfunction is the lifetrap. The other part of the dysfunction is the way we cope when these lifetraps get triggered. When our core emotional needs are not met as children, we get exasperated and subconsciously develop a way to cope with the pain of the unmet need. The way that we cope (e.g. to run away or fight back) has a lot to do with our temperament. We bring these coping styles into our adult life. These efforts may lessen the pain in the moment, but invariably perpetuate or intensify the lifetrap in the long run and leave our deeper needs unmet. There are three ways we cope with our lifetraps when they are triggered: surrender, avoidance, or overcompensation, sometimes also referred to as counterattacking. (Eighty years ago, Walter Cannon first identified fight and flight as common responses to stress; combined with fright, these correlate to the three coping styles.[2])

Surrender (Fright)

The surrender coping style is based on a fear of what we believe is the truth the lifetrap tells about us. We react from a negative and fearful place where the lifetrap is in control of what happens to us. The message of this coping style is, *"What my lifetrap is telling me about myself is true and I am powerless to change it."*

Children with the surrender coping style believe in their own distorted diminished view of themselves. They then act in ways to confirm this distorted view. If a father says something rude, for example, that the child is ugly or stupid, the child agrees with him in her heart—she really believes that she is dumb and stupid. Children who surrender to these kinds of critical messages will have a low opinion of themselves. This causes them to have a distorted view of others, and a distorted notion of how others view them. They tend to blame themselves, comply and give in when something goes wrong. The voice in their heads says, "It is my fault." Surrendering types (see Figure 1.2) who face criticism and blame usually:

- Feel inferior to others
- Think others are better
- Accept all criticism
- Expect people to be critical
- Look for events to confirm that "it is their fault"
- Put the needs of others before their own.

Examples of "surrender behaviour" associated with criticism and blame:

- Giving in to others during arguments
- Being overly apologetic
- Compliantly keeping rules
- Being drawn to others who are more confident.

Figure 1.2: Surrender (Fright) Coping Style

There are many other types of toxic experiences to which children surrender (e.g. deprivation and neglect, being excluded from a group, physical abuse) and each leads to its own pattern of beliefs, feelings and behaviours.

Avoidance (Flight)

The avoidance coping style is based on flight from the pain associated with the lifetrap. We react by avoiding situations and interactions that lead to the lifetrap being triggered. The message of, or underlying belief associated with, this coping style is, *"It is too painful and uncomfortable to hear or feel my lifetrap. I must keep myself separate and distracted so I am not aware of this painful truth about myself."*

When their needs are not met or when their lifetraps get triggered, children with this coping style will move away from disappointment and pain. Sometimes they feel powerless. They bypass situations that could be painful and trigger their lifetrap. They delay thinking about the situation. They circumvent conflict and intimacy by distracting themselves. Avoiders are prone to addiction, and often try to forget their pain by drinking excessively, taking drugs, being involved in promiscuous sex, overeating, or other self-destructive behaviour. Some will not go to such extremes, choosing instead to immerse themselves in schoolwork or a hobby. They usually do not want to talk about their issues and will come up with excuses. The voice in their head is "I will avoid emotional pain at all costs." Sometimes they are not able to remember much from the past, and draw a blank when the past is questioned or explored because it hurts too much to remember. Children with the avoidance coping style often struggle with being deceitful, and are sometimes uncomfortable with eye contact. Avoiding types (see Figure 1.3) tend to:

- Be out of touch with their own feelings
- Dampen their feelings with substances (food, alcohol, drugs) or activities (gambling, sex, workaholism)
- Act like they do not have a problem
- Avoid intimate relationships
- Walk around numb
- Avoid confronting problems.

Those who cope by avoiding often spend an inordinate amount of time engaged in the following activities:

- Reading newspapers and magazines
- Surfing the net
- Cleaning their room
- Checking their Facebook account

Figure 1.3: Avoidance (Flight) Coping Style

- Monitoring their favourite sport or team
- Running or playing a team sport
- Watching television
- Drinking alcohol
- Talking on the phone.

Overcompensation (Fight)

The overcompensation coping style stems from the desire or need to fight what we believe is the underlying truth the lifetrap holds about us. We react by behaving in a way designed to create the opposite effect of the lifetrap. The message of or underlying belief associated with this coping style is, *"I must fight as hard as I can to think and act as though what my lifetrap says about me is not true."*

When their lifetraps get triggered, children with this coping style who have been treated harshly and criticised, for example, will feel attacked, and they will attack back in order to prove that the negative feeling they have about themselves is not true. They will lash out in anger and attack the source of the negative message. Those who have been abused will abuse others or fight for justice when they feel unsafe; those who have been deprived of love and affection will convince themselves and others they are tough and do not need others in this way.

Overcompensation can take many forms, depending upon what painful message and experience the individual is fighting against. Those with this coping style often overreact to small slights or disappointments and can come across as, for example, rude, insensitive, and demanding or aloof and above it all. Someone who is overcompensating (see Figure 1.4) may:

- View disagreements as a threat, going out of their way to prove that others are wrong
- View feedback as criticism, going out of their way to prove that the opposite is true
- Appear strong, but actually be fragile
- Not care who gets hurt in the process of proving themselves to be right
- Isolate themselves and not be intimate
- Prioritise protecting their image over intimacy
- Put their own needs first over the needs of others
- Constantly bring up their unhappiness about others' annoying traits while acting as if they themselves are perfect
- Not wait for a suitable time to talk; wanting it done there and then
- Throw tantrums and abuse others with name-calling
- Make unhealthy comparisons with others during quarrels
- Criticise and have no qualms about getting involved in long, drawn out fights
- Become an over-achiever and be unusually driven in work or projects outside of normal working hours.

Figure 1.4: Overcompensation (Fight) Coping Style

⟨ LOUIS LOWDOWN ⟩

Anyone who knows us knows that John is an overcompensator (counterattacker), while Karen is an avoider. Our first-born tends toward an overcompensation coping style in keeping with her temperament; our son tends toward avoidance. The four of us understand that we all cope with conflict and stress differently and we work hard to be sensitive to and navigate our various styles.

Now that you have been introduced to new terms like schemas, lifetraps, and coping styles, take some time out to think about what your predominant coping style may be. If you are so inclined, you might want to fill out a schema inventory to learn more about your own possible lifetraps. Visit www.schematherapy.com for more information. When we parent our children from a "self-awareness" point of view, we will have more empathy and be better equipped to meet their core emotional needs.

The Foundation of Core Emotional Needs

Abraham Maslow was the first to write prominently about our needs as humans. He taught about five sets of needs: physiological essentials, safety, belongingness, esteem, and self-actualization. Maslow arranged them into a hierarchy—once the most basic need is satisfied, another emerges. He qualified that this does not mean each need has to be satisfied 100% before moving on to the next need, since most people are satisfied with their needs being partially met. Some of these needs are more often unconscious than they are conscious.[3] Physiological and safety needs are more likely to be conscious, identifiable and more easily measured than psychological needs. Physiological needs include, among other things, the body's effort to remain a constant normal state, such as water content of the blood, salt content, oxygen content, constant temperature of the blood, etc. Safety needs include the need for security, stability, dependency, protection and freedom from fear, anxiety, and chaos, as well as the need for structure, order, law, and limits. When we live in environments where these are satisfied, these needs no longer act as a primary motivator. However, if a war breaks out or if there are natural disasters, we unconsciously revert back to the earliest needs in the hierarchy such as physiological essentials and safety. They now become our primary motivators.[4]

If, on the other hand, people live in an environment where these basic levels of needs are met, humans will then move up Maslow's hierarchy and be motivated by the next level of needs. These involve love, affection and belonging. Of necessity, these higher needs are not as tangible and easily measured as the safety needs. When we are hungry, we physically feel the gnawing at our insides and we are driven to eat. When we are thirsty, we crave a drink. When subjected to extreme temperatures, we seek relief instantly. But even though the needs higher up in the hierarchy are not as tangible and identifiable, they are every bit as real. For example, if a child in primary school were left out of games during recess and not allowed to be part of a group, the child would probably feel hurt, but she might not be able to identify that she felt pain because her need for acceptance and connection was not getting met. However, that would not make the pain any less real. We have as much of an insatiable thirst and hunger for the core emotional needs to be met as we do for food, clothing and shelter. Core emotional needs are as real as our physical needs. They may have been identified in the twentieth century by therapists and psychologists, but they have existed as long as man has; when deprived of such needs, humans are less healthy. In the words of Maslow, "Who will say that a lack of love is less important than a lack of vitamins?"[5]

Definition of a "Core Emotional Need"

We would like to draw from Lockwood and Perris' criteria of what constitutes a core emotional need:

1. Meeting or not meeting this need should lead to an increase or decrease in well-being, and it should affect more than psychological functioning alone. It should result in an impact on such things as brain function, bodily functions, and family functionality.
2. Each proposed core need should make its own contribution to well-being and not be derived from or overlap with any other core need.
3. The core need must be evident universally across cultures.[6]

This desire to have our core emotional needs met began when we came out of the womb. As we grew, we learned to cope in different ways when our needs were not adequately met. As children, we were not able to look at our parents (or others in authority) and think, "Oh, they had a rotten childhood, so I am sure they don't really mean what they say." We could not help but take their words (or lack of words) personally. We internalised their messages, so much so that those messages became part of our makeup. We formed distorted views about ourselves and others, and we acted on them. We heard a distorted voice in our head, though there may have been little or no truth in it. This voice may have tried to convince us that:

People I love will eventually leave me.
If they really knew me, they would know that I am worthless.
People cannot be trusted.
Something bad is bound to happen.
I just can't get close to other people.
Dad was right—I'll never amount to anything.
Showing emotions is weak.
I should be punished.

This voice sometimes stays with us into adulthood. For many of us, this distorted voice is so strong that it still has power over our behaviour and decision making process. The more we counsel people, the more we have come to realise the power of not having our core emotional needs met in childhood. Both of us have seen the strong correlation between early experiences and current unhealthy behaviour and thinking. For some of us, our lifetraps are so prevalent and strong that they become a roadblock to us becoming healthy adults. They also become a barrier in our relationships with others, including our spouses.

We should pause for a moment here to encourage the reader to go through our marriage book, *I Choose Us*[7]. As a companion to this book, it will help you to identify and begin working on your own lifetraps, and move toward Love Connection, the first step in being a Good Enough Parent.

MASTER CLASS

> Wyndham and Jeanie Shaw asked their eldest son, Sam, what helped him from their parenting and this was his reply, "The older I get the more I appreciate the way my parents raised me. They never assumed to know what I was feeling in a certain situation, but took the time to draw me out. This was especially important since I had, and still have, a difficult time understanding my own feelings. To me, sorting through my feelings was painstaking and complicated. I preferred to stow them away and focus on simple things like watching sports or funny movies. Drawing me out took time. My parents made the time to do this and convinced me it was worth it."

Jeffrey Young's theory is that when children's core emotional needs are not met, and/or when they undergo trauma, they experience frustration and develop active "schemas" or "lifetraps" and a "coping style" that complements

their inborn temperament.[8] While some parents think that their duty is solely to provide for their children's basic necessities (food, clothing, shelter, etc.), one of the main purposes of this book is to help parents gain awareness about the ways they discourage their children by not meeting their core emotional needs. (From here on, we will use the terms "frustration of core emotional needs" and "trauma" interchangeably with "exasperation"). Drawing from our own research and that of others, we have identified four core emotional needs, and they are:
- Connection and Acceptance
- Healthy Autonomy and Performance
- Reasonable Limits
- Realistic Expectations

──────────────── ◈ RESEARCH REVEALS ◈ ────────────────

RR1.1: *The Origin of the Four Plus One*

Over the years, Young developed a set of questionnaires known as the Young Schema Questionnaire (YSQ). As of 2011, the latest version is called the YSQ-S3[9]. The majority of the studies done on this questionnaire found that the schemas clustered together into four categories, or schema domains. All these studies were done in Western cultures. We decided to administer this questionnaire to our own church members, an Asian sample in Singapore, to see if we would find the same results. Around 650 questionnaires were filled out and handed back. Our results concurred with the studies done in Western cultures. Four domains were found in the USA,[10] Australia,[11] and Norway,[12] and the same four schema domains appeared in our Singapore sample. As we worked with Dr Jeffrey Young, we labelled these domains as follows:

- Disconnection and Rejection
- Impaired Autonomy and Performance
- Impaired Limits
- Exaggerated Expectations.

We took these four domains of early maladaptive schemas (groupings of lifetraps) and changed their names to reflect what a child needs to prevent these negative patterns from forming and, better yet, to develop positive and life affirming patterns (early adaptive schemas). These became the "four core emotional needs":

- Connection and Acceptance
- Healthy Autonomy and Performance
- Reasonable Limits
- Realistic Expectations.

If the empirical results show four major categories, then why do we speak of "four plus one core emotional needs"? While the four domains were backed up by research, we felt the need for a spiritual component. Wisdom found in the Scriptures has been helping God's people for millennia. And scientists are starting to admit what people of faith have known all along— research shows that people of faith enjoy better physical and mental health and live longer.[13] For example, numerous studies have found that adolescents with higher levels of spirituality and religiosity are less likely to engage in risky behaviour, substance use, and are more likely to have better mental health outcomes.[14] Thus the "four plus one" core emotional needs are Connection and Acceptance, Healthy Autonomy and Performance, Reasonable Limits, Realistic Expectations, and Spiritual Values and Community.

THE FOUR PLUS ONE
Connection and Acceptance
Healthy Autonomy and Performance
Reasonable Limits
Realistic Expectations
Plus one… Spiritual Values and Community

Understanding needs makes a huge difference in our parenting. Think about young children. They may not know what to say when they are needy emotionally or psychologically. They are aware when they are hungry or thirsty, but what about their unseen needs? Unconsciously, in order to get those invisible needs met, they will act out, and they will not even know it.

We sometimes do the same as adults. We have unconscious feelings and thoughts, unconscious reactions and unconscious behaviour. There are times when our automatic reactions take control and moments later we wonder why we acted in a certain manner; we shout or cry, and do not know why.

If parents are educated about children's core emotional needs, then they will be in a much better position to respond and meet needs, rather than react to their child's misbehaviour, end up in conflict, or worse still, deprive them further of having these needs met. Understanding which feelings are underneath empowers parents with knowledge of what is lacking and enables them to take the appropriate steps to meet the unmet needs. This takes practice, but when we are able to master it, our parenting skills will greatly improve simply because we will be better able to meet our children's core emotional needs.

On the contrary, when we do *not* meet our children's core emotional needs, they will be frustrated and maybe even traumatised. They will become exasperated and discouraged, and develop schemas/lifetraps and coping styles in accordance with their temperament. In the following chapters we will learn more about what we call "exasperation interactions": how parents (usually unintentionally) frustrate their children by not meeting these core emotional needs, and ways parents can avoid the "exasperation pathway" (see Figure 1.5).

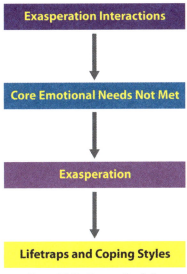

Figure 1.5: The Exasperation Pathway

Throughout this book we will follow the steps listed below:
- Parents need to be attuned to what core emotional needs are not being met when there is a pattern of misbehaviour.
- Parents need to see how their children are getting exasperated or discouraged and how this is being acted out.
- Parents then need to take steps to meet these core emotional needs as best as they are able.
- Parents need to come up with a routine and lifestyle where these needs are being met consistently.

One caveat—when rushing to meet the core emotional needs, we have to be careful to not go to extremes. For example, while we need to connect, we should avoid being enmeshed. While we need to have healthy standards and limits, we cannot go to the other extreme and be neglectful and permissive. Good Enough Parenting is about not giving too much and not giving too little. It is about meeting these needs in a balanced and satisfactory way. Many of us grew up on the receiving end of at least one of these extremes. Some of us have been under parented; our parents were not there for us emotionally or even physically, and we were emotionally deprived. We wonder where they have been all these years, and feel that we missed out on the love and guidance that we needed.

This often leads to feeling alone and empty and needing to be stoic and fend for oneself on an emotional level. If our parents have been overly critical we will be left with a sense of shame, rejection and defectiveness. These bad feelings often contribute to a complicated mix of hate, love, gratitude and resentment. On the other hand, some of us were so enmeshed with our parents that we did not know where they ended and we began. This can leave us feeling, even as adults, like we are not free to go out into the world and pursue our own path and dreams, separate from our parents.

The main premise of Good Enough Parenting is that if we, as parents, meet the core emotional needs adequately, we greatly increase the possibility of a healthier outcome. Conversely, if our children experience repeated exasperation interactions during their childhood, the risk of a less healthy outcome is high. And even if children end up on a less favourable pathway, we can correct it if we make amends, repair, reconnect and tap into the power of the community (see Figure 1.6).

How Marriage Affects Parenting

Many parents believe, "It does not matter if my spouse and I do not get along, as long as we are there for the children." Parents who have this philosophy have forgotten what it was like for them when they were growing up, when the two people they loved most in the world were not getting along. They have forgotten how it hurt them emotionally, and how much insecurity was bred into them by the lack of stability and the level of conflict in their parents' marriage.

An overwhelming amount of research over the last 20 years has surfaced showing a correlation between the quality of one's marriage and the quality of one's parenting. In other words, the emotional and psychological development of a child is related to the intensity of the conflict between his parents. All parents will have conflict at one time or another. Cummings and Davies have arguably done the most work on the effects of marital conflict on the child's development process. They define marital conflict as "any major or minor inter-parental interaction that involved a difference of opinion, whether it was mostly negative or even mostly positive."[15]

Based on this definition they wrote about conflicts being either constructive or destructive. How conflicts are handled makes a huge difference as to their effect on children. They concluded that conflict which gets resolved "may have relatively benign effects on children."[16]

The Case for Core Emotional Needs ■ 25

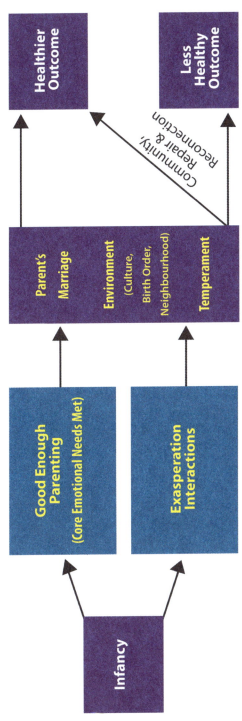

Figure 1.6: Good Enough Parenting Model – The Interplay of the Different Factors on the Outcome of Parenting

LOUIS LOWDOWN

We have been married for almost 25 years. How many conflicts have we had? We can't really count. While we can't boast of having less conflicts than most, we can say that we have tried to resolve issues quickly, as the Bible calls us to do. This has really helped us stay connected as a couple. On one occasion when our children were about eleven and nine years old, I (Karen) walked down the street to buy milk after dinner, and the kids asked to go with me. Once we were on our way, their mission became clear—our children suspected that all was not well between Mum and Dad and wanted to gather information. I said that everything was okay, but they would not relent. Finally I admitted that, yes, we had just had words before dinner, but that all was still fine because we would solve it easily as soon as I got back home and, by the way, how did they even know, since the atmosphere at dinner had been as cheerful and upbeat as usual. The little detectives explained that they had noticed that we had been speaking only to them, not to each other, and I was shocked at how attuned their antennae had been! The conversation continued...

Mum : Honestly, kids, don't worry, it was a small thing; we will sort it out as soon as I get back to the house.

Kids : What were you fighting about anyway?

Mum : You're rather nosy, aren't you?

Kids : Mum—out with it!

Mum : Well, the short version is that Dad did something helpful but instead of saying thank you, I blurted out how he could have done it a bit better, so Dad felt disrespected and unappreciated.

Kids : MUM! That's terrible! You shouldn't do that!

Mum : I know, it was really stupid and I regretted saying it as soon as it left my mouth...

Kids : Well, didn't you apologise???

Mum : Well, yes, but-

Kids : What?! You apologised and he didn't forgive you? He's the leader of the church—he tells everyone else to forgive! What a hypocrite!

Mum : Guys, hold on here, your Dad didn't even have time to do anything. I said what I said right after I put the dinner on the table, so there wasn't time to sort anything out before we ate. We will be alright—as soon as I get home, we will talk and everything will be okay, I promise.

Kids : We will sort it out Mum, cause we are going to go in and talk to Dad first.

Mum : That's really not necessary.

Kids : It's okay, we got it...

> As soon as they reached home, the kids left Karen in the living room and walked into the office area where I (John) was doing some paper work.
>
> Kids : Dad, Mum said she was disrespectful to you.
>
> Dad : Yes kids but don't worry about it—we will have a talk in just a minute.
>
> Kids : But Dad, didn't she already apologise to you?
>
> Dad : Well, erm, yes, but…
>
> Kids : So shouldn't you forgive her? You always say that if someone says "sorry"…
>
> Dad : Hey kids, you're right. Thank you for calling me out on this. I will talk with Mum right now. I love you.
>
> Kids : We love you, too, Dad.
>
> The kids left my room with huge smiles on their faces, knowing that Karen and I would once again be reconciled. And I was convicted and full of remorse for not forgiving my wife immediately. (And I, Karen, was full of remorse for being a know-it-all.) After we made up, we all had a nice laugh, and we marvelled at how God gave us two kids who would never let us get away with anything!

While this is a rather simple and light-hearted example, it does show how sensitive children are when their parents are at odds with each other. Children pick up on a lot more than we realise. They internalise our silent messages to our spouse, and then slowly over a period of time if the tension is repeated and not resolved satisfactorily, their well-being is affected. One argument will not do that, but a pattern of repeated arguments over time will. Mistakes made by one spouse or the other, if repaired soon and amicably, will not have much of a negative effect on the children, but a lifestyle of unresolved conflicts between the parents will eventually take its toll on them.

◇ **RESEARCH REVEALS** ◇

RR1.2: *Marital Conflict and Children*

Cummings and Davies have found that marital conflicts affect on children is not based on a one-time argument, but rather over a period of time. They wrote:

> …However, the risk factor operates over time and insidiously, by altering family and child functioning over time.[17]

Arguments that are repaired satisfactorily and amicably with both parents being happy with the outcome actually have a positive impact on the children because it models for them how conflicts should be resolved. These are called constructive conflicts. However, the types of arguments that will have a much more negative impact on the children are those that are left unresolved over long periods of time, repeated heated and aggressive type of conflicts, and conflicts where one parent is being subjugated by the other. These are called destructive conflicts.

Unfortunately, sometimes we are not the best judge of whether our conflicts with our spouse are constructive or destructive. Often we lack the awareness to know how we come across to our children. As parents we tend to underestimate the effect of our conflicts with our spouse. *Cummings and Davies' research found that the children's evaluation and response to a conflict is the best way to determine whether a conflict is constructive or destructive.* Children's responses include their emotional reactions as well as their coping mechanisms. So if a conflict is producing more positive responses than negative responses, then it is fair to classify it as constructive. If it is producing more negative responses than positive responses, then it would fall in the category of a destructive conflict. Based on this research, the following kinds of conflict have been found to be destructive.[18]

a. Physical aggression, involving swearing, insulting, throwing or smashing, or threatening to hit.
b. Verbal hostility, which includes yelling as well as verbal threats.
c. Non-verbal hostility, which includes withdrawal by husbands and/or wives, i.e., giving each other the silent treatment. This has been reported to have a negative effect on children's behaviour and state of mind, including causing distress. One study showed that the children's reactions to verbal conflict were similar to their reactions to non-verbal conflict. In fact, parents' non-verbal reactions of fear caused more distress in the children than heated arguments.[19]

One study showed that if apologies were accompanied by negative emotions, then it had a negative effect on the children.[20] Another study found that children's feelings of distress diminished when conflicts were resolved at an emotional level.[21] Another finding notes that conflicts which were not resolved but which were portrayed by parents to have been okay were found to have not been so beneficial to the children.[22] Lastly, insecurity in children was caused equally by both a father and mother's behaviour during conflict.[23]

There are many ways a poor marriage can influence a child's well-being, and it begins with destructive conflict. Some might ask, just how does destructive conflict interfere with our parenting? The research team of Cummings and Davies have devoted decades to analysing how instability in the marriage causes children's well-being to decline. By drawing heavily on their work and also on the research of others, combined with our own experiences as counsellors and parents, we believe that poor marriages cause harm to children both directly and indirectly.

Destructive conflict *directly* affects the child's emotional security, which is linked to the child's confidence in the parents' ability to handle the conflict and to maintain family stability. In the case of destructive conflict, children become concerned about preserving emotional security, even getting involved in the conflict, as well as becoming emotionally distressed, and almost always interpret their parents' interaction negatively.[24]

Destructive conflict also *indirectly* affects the quality of the parent-child relationship. It is very common for parents who are in conflict to become depressed, which over time affects the attachment quality of their relationship.[25] Marital conflict discourages the parents, so that the parents then have less energy to manage their children with adequate supervision, open communication, and enforcement of rules for appropriate child conduct. Marital conflict also negatively affects the teamwork needed for parenting.[26]

❧ MOVIE MOMENT — *When a Man Loves a Woman*[27] ❧

> One of the subplots of the movie, with Andy Garcia and Meg Ryan, is the impact of their unstable and failing marriage on their daughter's well-being. Meg Ryan portrays an alcoholic who is struggling to keep her life together, while Garcia plays her husband, a busy airline pilot who is becoming increasingly troubled by the wife's alcoholism. One night, during a loud disagreement, the husband violently overturns the coffee table. This is followed by lots of yelling and shouting from both parties. The conflict ends with Garcia's character deciding to move out of the house. When the wife goes to her room alone to gather her thoughts and smoke a cigarette, her daughter gets of out bed and goes to her with a fearful and distressed look on her face. The first words out of her mouth are, "You guys were really loud." Her mother responds, "Oh, I'm sorry..." While the focus of the husband and wife's conflict was each other, the effect of their repeated unresolved hostility was to create a sense of instability for their daughter, depriving her of sleep and causing her great emotional suffering.

It is true that some destructive conflicts may have a benign effect on children. There are children whose temperaments are able to block out these negative effects. The poor quality of their parent's marriage may have minimal impact on them. Some children have resilient temperaments that also cushion the blow.[28]

However, this is more the exception than the norm. When the quality of our marriage is poor, with a pattern of destructive conflict, we are putting our children at risk of being negatively affected. Many parents erroneously assume that since they were not affected by their parents' quarrels, their children will not be impacted by theirs. This view does not take into account the fact that their children might have a more sensitive temperament and, therefore, be more susceptible to damage by the same type of conflict. Parents need to realise that the way they conduct themselves during a conflict is important and that reaching a satisfactory resolution will go a long way to reducing the typical child's level of distress.

So what do we do when there is tension between parents? Cummings and Davies' research points us toward biblical forgiveness and reconciliation (see Chapter Nineteen), because children's levels of distress reduce to the extent that the parents conflicts are resolved satisfactorily. This means that conflicts between mums and dads need to be genuinely resolved, at an emotional level, not just at a rational level. Children need to see their parents resolving issues in a healthy way. This is beneficial not only to the parents themselves, but also to the children, who feel healed and resolved when they see their parents working out conflict fairly. However, if one parent is subjugated to the other during the conflict, then although the parents may *feel* that it is resolved, a "forced-submissive" kind of resolution is seen as one parent "winning"; this does not sit well with the kids.[29] The resolution between parents has to be genuine and complete at an emotional level, not white-washed or faked, or with one parent always capitulating and the other always getting their way. Children can tell the difference between genuine reconciliation and reconciliation that is superficial.

When parents resolve their conflicts constructively, they are being good role models and their children will then learn how to handle such conflicts themselves.[30] Parents who do not get along should consider what kind of example they are setting when it comes to how they should get along with others. How sad if parents give their children the impression that hostility, aggression and withdrawal are acceptable ways to overcome problems.

◁ LOUIS LOWDOWN ▷

Looking back, there is one particular incident of which I (John) am really not proud, where I clearly had a negative effect on my daughter. I was upset with Karen about something (neither of us remembers what it was) and I was stubborn and refused to get reconciled with her. In the evening, when Karen and I were in the bedroom with the door closed, I raised my voice. Sonia happened to be doing late night homework at the dining table located at the foot of the stairs, and she heard everything. The next day, we all went to church as usual, and I saw Sonia talking with one of our best friends, who also happens to be the adult with whom Sonia is closest in the whole church outside of Karen and me. I saw out of the corner of my eye that Sonia was sobbing. My friend approached me and let me know what was troubling Sonia. I assumed that my daughter was feeling anxious about something at school, but it turned out that she was feeling bad about her parents not getting along. Karen and I usually resolve our conflicts quickly but, to my shame, I had let that particular situation drag on longer than it should have. I felt so bad and had no idea that our lack of harmony was having such an effect on Sonia. That was enough. I went back that afternoon and talked with my wife, and quickly got the issue resolved. We then let both of our children know of the positive outcome of our reconciliation, and also shared about what had caused the conflict in the first place, though not in great detail. Sonia welcomed the resolution, I apologised to her for being so unspiritual, and we got back on track. It was a painful lesson that I will not forget. (I am thankful to the community of people who care enough to look over our interests, I am thankful to my daughter for her courage to tell someone who could help, and I am thankful to God for bringing me to my senses so I could repent and be resolved with my wife.)

In summary, the effects of a poor marriage on the child are a lot more severe than people realise; on top of the emotional side-effects already mentioned, school performance, sleep, and peer relationships also get affected.

◈ RESEARCH REVEALS ◈

RR1.3: *Affects of Marriage on a Child's Well-Being*

Marital conflicts diminish children's school performances by undermining their capacity to sustain attention.[31] When marital conflict increased, children's emotional insecurity about inter-parental relations also increased and children's sleep was disrupted.[32] Sleep problems were related to children's behavioural, emotional and academic problems.[33] Marital conflicts also caused disruptions in the children's peer relationships, physical ailments, internalizing problems (such as kids becoming anxious, depressed, introverted and withdrawn) and externalizing problems (such as kids acting out, delinquency).[34]

Children show responses to parental anger as early as 6 months old.[35] Gottman says that the stress of living with parental conflict can affect the development of an infant's autonomic nervous system, which, in turn, has an impact on the child's ability to cope. While it is true that babies do not know the content of the parents' arguments, they are able to sense that something is wrong.[36]

Hetherington describes the first two years following a divorce as a time of serious disruptions to parent-child relationships. Divorce and conflicts leading up to a divorce can cause parents to be depressed, distracted and exhausted, which can prevent them from being effective disciplinarians.[37] Difficulty controlling and monitoring children's behaviour is the most sustained parenting problem faced by divorced mothers.

Please refer to the introduction of our marriage book, *I Choose Us*, for more information about the effects of marriage on parenting.[38]

Many career-driven parents cope with their lack of marriage satisfaction and problems with their children by being detached and focusing more on their work or some other activity, which short-changes their kids. But children are not the only ones who suffer—a poor marriage also affects parents' health and productivity at work.

Studies have shown that a person's work environment affects his or her marriage. A poor working environment causes stress to build up, and many working parents bring their burdens home, along with unrealistic expectations imposed on them by their bosses. Relationships within the family get compromised as a result. *But it also works the other way round.* Studies show that the quality of a person's marriage has a significant impact on his health and how he functions at work. So, while seeking refuge at work from a poor marriage or distressed family relationships may provide relief in some ways, problems at home will eventually have a negative impact.

RESEARCH REVEALS

RR1.4: *How Marriage Affects Work*

In a study done on a sample of 1,026 married workers in Singapore, it was found that marital distress was a significant predictor of depressive symptoms, health and work satisfaction. Marriage affects work in that it distresses the employees and causes work absenteeism and underperformance, which is common and costly. Therefore, addressing such issues makes good business sense.[39]

We end this section on marriage with a Cummings and Davies' analogy. To convey the effects of marriage on a child's well-being, they compare a healthy marriage to a strong bridge:

> When the marital relationship is high-functioning, a secure base is provided for the child. Like a structurally sound bridge, a positive marital relationship supports the child's optimal functioning in the context of potentially threatening conditions, fostering explorations and confident relationships with others. When destructive marital conflict damages the bridge, the child may become hesitant to move forward and lack confidence, or may move forward in a dysfunctional way, failing to find the best footing in relations with others or within the self.[40]

Schema in the New Testament

Getting back to the topic of lifetraps and coping styles, some Christians have asked, "Is any of this schema stuff in the Bible?" While schema therapy is something that is relatively new, the concept itself is ancient. The English word schema actually comes from the Greek word, σχημα (schema), which means, "form, in appearance, in fashion" (Strong Number 4976). It appears in the New Testament several times and some of the usages are similar to the way we are using it in this book.

We are fortunate in the 21st century to be able to benefit from advances in modern medicine. There are cures for cancer this decade that did not exist 20 years ago. Treatments for diabetes, heart disease, and other life threatening illnesses have extended life expectancies around the developed world. Similarly, we are blessed that professionals in the field of mental health have used their God-given talents to identify specific schemas that are common to all people, which are detrimental to emotional health. Learning about them, while not a matter of salvation, serves to help us move forward spiritually and emotionally, and frees up our hearts to be able to love others. This is essentially what biblical schema therapy is about—identifying our prevalent unhealthy thinking patterns or lifetraps that are tripping us up so that we might be able to have breakthroughs in our worldly and unhealthy thinking, throw off everything that hinders, be more like Christ, and help others to know Him as well.

RESEARCH REVEALS

RR1.5: *"Schema" in the New Testament*

(Thanks to Dr. G. Steve Kinnard, a Teacher and Evangelist with the New York City Church of Christ and also the Adjunct Professor of Bible at Lincoln Christian University, who helped to make sure our Greek references passed muster.)

The first place schema appears in the New Testament is in 1 Corinthians 7:31,

Those who use the things of the world should not become attached to them. For this world <u>as we know</u> it will soon pass away. (NLT)[41]

and those who use the world, as though they did not make full use of it; for <u>the form</u> of this world is passing away. (NAS)[42]

καὶ οἱ χρώμενοι τὸν κόσμον ὡς μὴ καταχρώμενοι· παράγει γὰρ τὸ σχῆμα τοῦ κόσμου τούτου. (NT Greek)[43]

Dr. Kinnard suggests one possible way of rendering the second part of this verse:

for the <u>schema</u> of this world is passing away.

Another example of a derivative of the word *schema* being used to convey the idea of "in form" or "in appearance" can be found in Philippians 2:7-8,

Instead, he gave up his divine privileges; he took the humble position of a slave and was born as a human being. When <u>he appeared</u> in human form, he humbled himself in obedience to God and died a criminal's death on a cross. (NLT)

> ...but emptied Himself, taking the form of a bond-servant, and being made in the likeness of men. Being found <u>in appearance</u> as a man, He humbled Himself by becoming obedient to the point of death, even death on a cross. (NAS)
>
> ἀλλὰ ἑαυτὸν ἐκένωσεν μορφὴν δούλου λαβών, ἐν ὁμοιώματι ἀνθρώπων γενόμενος· καὶ <u>σχήματι</u> εὑρεθεὶς ὡς ἄνθρωπος ἐταπείνωσεν ἑαυτὸν γενόμενος ὑπήκοος μέχρι θανάτου, θανάτου δὲ σταυροῦ· (NT Greek)

Dr. Kinnard offers:

> *"and being discovered in <u>schema</u> as a man."*

The Holy Spirit wanted to convey something to the effect of how, even though Jesus is so amazing and is the name above all names, he was willing to take "the humble position of a slave and be found in appearance or in form as a human being," and more than that, die on the cross for us.

A variation of the noun σχῆμα (schema) is the Greek verb συσχηματίζομαι (syschematizomai), which means to conform one's self (i.e. one's mind and character) to another's pattern (fashion one's self according to), or to be conformed (Strong Number 4964). This word first appears in Romans 12:2a,

> <u>Don't copy the behaviour and customs</u> of this world, but let God transform you into a new person by changing the way you think... (NLT)
>
> And <u>do not be conformed</u> to this world, but be transformed by the renewing of your mind... (NAS)
>
> καὶ μὴ <u>συσχηματίζεσθε</u> τῷ αἰῶνι τούτῳ, ἀλλὰ μεταμορφοῦσθε τῇ ἀνακαινώσει τοῦ νοός... (NT Greek)

Here the English phrase, "copy the behaviour and customs of" in Greek comes from the word "syschematizomai", which means "be conformed", taken from the root word σχῆμα or schema.

It can be inferred that the text says that disciples have a choice whether to follow the behaviour/customs/schemas of the world or to be transformed into new people by letting their minds be renewed by God and His word.

Dr. Kinnard gives a possible translation for Romans 12:2a as:

> *And do not be "<u>schema-tized</u>" to this world, but be "<u>meta-morphed</u>" by the renewing of the mind...*

Steve coined the word "meta-morphed" here which is the transliteration of a Greek word and means transformed. Steve says he uses it because "people tend to understand what metamorphosis is—for example, the changing of the caterpillar into a butterfly. This is what Jesus does for us."

> The second place the verb form of schema appears is in 1 Peter 1:13-14,
>
> > So think clearly and exercise self-control. Look forward to the gracious salvation that will come to you when Jesus Christ is revealed to the world. So you must live as God's obedient children. <u>Don't slip back into your old ways of living</u> to satisfy your own desires. You didn't know any better then. (NLT)
> >
> > Therefore, prepare your minds for action, keep sober in spirit, fix your hope completely on the grace to be brought to you at the revelation of Jesus Christ. As obedient children, <u>do not be conformed</u> to the former lusts which were yours in your ignorance... (NAS)
> >
> > Διὸ ἀναζωσάμενοι τὰς ὀσφύας τῆς διανοίας ὑμῶν, νήφοντες τελείως, ἐλπίσατε ἐπὶ τὴν φερομένην ὑμῖν χάριν ἐν ἀποκαλύψει Ἰησοῦ Χριστοῦ. ὡς τέκνα ὑπακοῆς, μὴ συσχηματιζόμενοι ταῖς πρότερον ἐν τῇ ἀγνοίᾳ ὑμῶν ἐπιθυμίαις... (NT Greek)
>
> Dr. Kinnard gives the following possible translation:
>
> > As obedient children, do not be 'schema-tized' in your former lusts/desires, which were in ignorance.
>
> Just as Paul had written to the church in Rome, Peter was conveying in his letter that Christians should take care not to be conformed to the world, not to "slip back into (our) old ways of living" (not to "syschematizomai" in Greek), but to rather "gird up the loins of our minds" (KJV),[44] i.e., get rid of any mental flabbiness and prepare our minds for action. Why? Because the negative thinking patterns of the world (and the automatic reactions they teach us to have) are worldly, ungodly and unhealthy.

Dr Jeffrey Young and his team were able to identify a total of 18 schemas/lifetraps. Knowing them helps to put a specific label on different kinds of unhealthy thoughts or behaviours. This greater precision can be helpful in developing a better understanding of the nature and origins of these patterns. Using accurate labels helps us develop a more nuanced language to share in working to change these patterns. You may wonder why we would need such accurate words. Perhaps you have fellowshipped with someone who ascribed all relationship conflict to "pride" "hard heartedness", "lack of brokenness", or "insecurity". We believe that, although there is a time and place for such terms, they are too often used as a default when the speaker is not aware of more specific terms. Being accurate helps people to feel fully listened to and clearly understood.

Once Christians learn the biblical basis of these principles, the next step is for them to investigate which unhealthy thinking patterns of the world are negatively affecting their spirituality. If we then attack these schemas with the goal of weakening them, this will take our spirituality higher and help us to be more Christ-like. In essence, we will be doing exactly what Paul asked us to do in Romans 12:2a, not copying *the behaviour and customs [or schemas] of this world, but [letting] God transform [us] into a new person by changing the way [we] think...* (NLT)

Which can only be a good thing, right?

> *And we, who with unveiled faces all reflect the Lord's glory, are being transformed into his likeness with ever-increasing glory, which comes from the Lord, who is the Spirit.* (2 Corinthians 3:18)

We close the first chapter with a sneak peak into our study of the patriarchs. Inside each section of this book, we have placed a study based on the lives of Abraham and his descendants to illustrate how the core emotional needs were met or not met in their lives, and how the dysfunction passed down from generation to generation.

Right from the book of Genesis, we are able to read the dynamics within the families of our patriarchs. The Bible devotes so many chapters to their lives; God obviously wants us to learn from them. One of the beautiful aspects of Genesis is that it is full of characters we can all relate to, even though these events took place thousands of years ago. The common struggles between husbands and wives, parents and children have not changed over the millennia. As we glean through the pages of the Old Testament, we will see that the core emotional needs of children—to be connected, accepted, and loved by their parents—have always existed. Children will go to the ends of the earth to please their parents and vice versa. Sibling rivalry often comes between children and parents trying to meet these objectives. These kinds of dynamics have occurred in every generation between parents and children. This is not a new phenomenon that has sprung up in recent centuries. These dynamics are as old as the hills.

In the days of the patriarchs, one of the reasons children would strive to be in good standing with their parents was because they wanted to be "blessed" by them. The word "to bless" means "to bow the knee" in Hebrew. This makes sense visually, since when someone was being blessed, they often kneeled in respect. However, the personal blessings given in the book of Genesis meant more than just a physical bending of the knee—they also carried the weight of bestowing a great honour, of recognition and value. In biblical times, receiving a blessing was arguably one of the most special points in a person's life. The blessing was sometimes mandated by God and was prophetic—in other words, when a patriarch pronounced a blessing on his son, it would come true! (Gary Smalley and John Trent wrote about this extensively in their book, *The Blessing*.[45])

These special blessings encouraged the children who received them, and made them feel valued and accepted. They also conveyed God's protection and assurance that their future would turn out well (in most cases). Since this was evidently a part of their culture, the children growing up in that region would have naturally looked forward to this deciding point of their lives with great anticipation, hoping to hear positive, heart-felt words from their parents. Conversely, missing out on getting the blessing would have certainly led to confusion and hurt, and possibly to anger, resentment, bitterness, avoidance and many other unhealthy attitudes.

A common misconception that people have is that only the eldest son could be blessed or that the eldest son inherited blessings that were far superior to that of his younger siblings. We feel that this is an exaggeration, since all children could be blessed by their father regardless of their birth order. As for Old Testament teaching on the eldest son, Deuteronomy 21:17 reads:

He must acknowledge the son of his unloved wife as the firstborn by giving him a double share of all he has. That son is the first sign of his father's strength.

The right of the firstborn belonged to him. The eldest son had the right to a double share in comparison to the other siblings. Thus being a firstborn gave him an edge over the other younger siblings, but this did not mean that the other younger siblings were excluded from being blessed abundantly too.

Deuteronomy 5:16 mandates:

Honour your father and your mother, as the LORD your God has commanded you, so that you may live long and that it may go well with you in the land the LORD your God is giving you.

As long as children honoured their parents, regardless of their birth order, they would be blessed in return by God. Thus having a healthy, respectful relationship with one's parents in the Old Testament actually had repercussions later on in their adult lives.

Unfortunately, we do not see this scenario playing out when we read about the dynamics within families in the Old Testament. Instead, intense rivalry developed between siblings in their pursuit for the blessing. Parents often took sides, showing favouritism, and during this process the core emotional needs of the children were deprived.

In the pages that follow, as we examine each core emotional need, we will also immerse ourselves in the stories of Isaac, Esau and Jacob, along with their wives and sons. We will walk through these stories, reflect on them, ask questions, and see how the lack of blessing played a part in the lives of this family. We will examine their captivating stories. We will see their ups and downs, their sufferings and blessings, their interactions with one another, and learn from their good and bad examples. On the one hand, we will be encouraged to see how real they were, how they struggled with the real life issues of envy, greed, deception, acceptance, love, fear, and worry, to name a few, and how, if God could use them to do great things, He can surely use us! On the other hand, we will be grateful that we can learn parenting lessons that they did not know, so that we will hopefully be better equipped to meet our children's core emotional needs and prevent our dysfunction from passing down. No matter where we are, we can get the help to break unhealthy cycles, so that we will be able to do a better job raising a healthier generation. Hopefully, in just the same way that computers and mobile phones are always being "upgraded", our children will be, for the most part, the new and improved version of us!

*Would you please

explain more about

this exasperation concept?*

CHAPTER TWO

The Frustration of Core Emotional Needs

This concept is so central to Good Enough Parenting that we wanted to give it its own chapter. As we said before, the basic premise of Good Enough Parenting is that as parents we must adequately meet the core emotional needs of our children. If we do not, they will be at risk of facing frustrative and traumatic experiences, i.e., exasperation.

What does the Bible have to say about this concept? Interestingly, there are not many passages in the New Testament that specifically address parenting, but in two of the verses that do, both happen to warn against exasperating or discouraging your children! We will now look at these two passages from several different translations/versions.

> *Fathers, do not exasperate your children; instead, bring them up in the training and instruction of the Lord.* (Ephesians 6:4, NIV)
>
> *Fathers, do not embitter your children, or they will become discouraged. (Colossians* 3:21, NIV)
>
> *Fathers, don't exasperate your children by coming down hard on them. Take them by the hand and lead them in the way of the Master. (Ephesians 6:4, The Message)1*
>
> *Fathers, do not exasperate your children, so that they will not lose heart. (Colossians 3:21,* NAS)

We are using the word exasperation interchangeably with the idea of frustrative and traumatic experiences. However, when we speak about the frustration of core emotional needs, we have to distinguish between the frustration that comes as a result of not having core emotional needs met and the frustration that just comes normally from time to time. No doubt, experiencing frustration is part of life. All children will face frustration in different shapes and forms throughout life—losing a favourite toy, not being able to reach something, getting knocked down by the family dog, being disappointed by a friend at kindergarten, not receiving the gifts they had their heart set on, and so forth. This kind of frustration is normal, and if children do not experience this kind of frustration at all, that will cause a different kind of exasperation, because they will become entitled. (We digress!)

Experiencing normal frustrations in life is different than the *repeated frustration and trauma (exasperation) that takes place when core emotional needs are not met.* This continued state of exasperation eventually shapes a child's worldview and affects his way of thinking. The child's thoughts about himself and others becomes distorted.

It is important to point out that most parents love their children and want to be the best parents they can be. These parents are not trying to deprive their children of anything; the mistakes they make are usually *subtle* and *unintentional*. While there are instances when parents' mistakes are overt and obvious, such as yelling in anger or name-calling, or even worse, with beatings and physical violence, not to mention sexual abuse, there are many more times when the mistakes are just not that obvious. Further, they may very well stem from well-meaning intentions and objectives. However, whether mistakes are made overtly or subtly, there are still consequences.

We have noticed that some parents think that by depriving their children purposefully, even of core emotional needs, they are preparing their children well for later on in life. Please do not buy into the philosophy that depriving children of the core emotional needs will make them become tough and more resilient adults. In fact, the outcome of this kind of twisted logic is that often the children turn out to be just the opposite; they are insecure, fearful, not trusting, and with a low sense of self. Such children will grow up not knowing how to handle disappointments and frustration because of their insecurity and fear. They may be tense and constantly on guard. The stakes are high because causing exasperation, even accidentally, brings much harm to children.

◁ MASTER CLASS ▷

> Ron and Linda Brumley on how to not exasperate your teenagers, "We strongly believe (and we had to learn this over time) that parents of teens must be very expressive of praise *to* them and *about* them. Our teens, male and female, need our hugs and kisses. They need to be held and affirmed and reassured of how awesome they are and how much their parents like and love and treasure them. The world may be telling them quite the opposite, but it won't matter nearly as much if they hear and feel all this good stuff from mom and dad."

We will illustrate how parents may be subtly (or not so subtly) exasperating their children with the following vignettes:

One-year-old Alan is not around his parents much during the day. His mother's house cleaner brings him to a day care centre in the morning, then leaves him at his grandparents' house in the afternoon, and feeds him his dinner in the early evening. Both of Alan's parents work, and often come home late because of the demanding nature of their jobs. It is not unusual for Alan to cry and not be easily contented even when comforted by others. What is the underlying reason? His core emotional need for **Connection and Acceptance** has not being adequately met. If Alan were experiencing physical discomfort such as an earache, a sore throat, or a headache, he would cry and be uneasy and difficult to soothe until someone tended to that need. The same goes for his emotional needs. What makes it difficult is that these emotional needs are not apparent and obvious. Whenever Alan reacts from a deprivation of these core emotional needs, his parents put it down to something else, such as him being difficult, hungry, thirsty, sleepy, or catching a cold, but they do little to meet the child's core emotional needs.

Children do not have the words to express these needs but will react when there is deprivation nonetheless. How can we expect children to make known these emotional needs when even adults are largely ignorant? If Alan's parents were to be asked, they might say that they have to focus on their respective careers because they want their children to be taken care of financially. These are good and well-meaning parents; the harm that they are causing is unintentional and subtle. Yet the consequences can be grave, especially to children with a very sensitive temperament. Parents must therefore be attuned to the subtle and unintentional ways that they are not meeting the core emotional needs of their children. This is not a nice parenting tip, but an essential need.

Sarah is five years old. She is curious and wants to play with the toys she received last Christmas, but her mother has other ideas. A highly-controlling woman, Sarah's mother decides what clothes Sarah should wear, what books she should read, and when and where she will play with her friends, without giving Sarah any choice in the matter. Sarah is not allowed to play in others' homes or have sleepovers like her other friends. Her mother dictates all matters. Sarah depends on her mother for everything. She is not comfortable being on her own and making choices that others her age are making. She gets frustrated easily, cries and becomes angry, so her mother disciplines her for not being good mannered, which then frustrates her even more. Sarah becomes angry because her core emotional need for **Healthy Autonomy and Performance** is not being adequately met. Her mother is completely oblivious to this and focuses on Sarah's outward behaviour. She thinks that her highly-controlling nature will help steer her daughter in the right direction while in reality, Sarah's frustration will continue and she will develop an unhealthy way of coping. If Sarah's mother were to be asked why she is so controlling of her daughter, she probably would say that she is trying to be thorough, and that she wants to be there for her daughter. Subconsciously Sarah's dependence probably makes her feel useful as a mother. The mother would never want to cause harm to her daughter, but is doing so, subtly and unintentionally.

Simon, a first grader, is energetic, highly curious, and wants to explore every new thing he comes across. His parents are around but they do not know how to set proper limits to his behaviour. Simon does not obey rules in class and is bossy when he is with his friends. When he does not get his way, he displays his anger by hitting other children. His aggressive behaviour has caused him to be disliked and as a result he does not have many friends. Adults often stare disapprovingly when Simon misbehaves in public places. If this continues, he will realize that he is not well-liked, adding to a poor sense of self, which will cause frustration to develop, and over time, this will cause him to become even *more* aggressive. If his parents continue to fail in providing adequate guidance and do not expect him to obey some **Reasonable Limits**, his frustration will continue as others give signals that he is not pleasant to be around. He will also feel frustrated at the lack of guidance from his parents. If we were to ask the parents why they were not more involved, they might chalk it up to not wanting to be too controlling or say they are too busy. They would have never meant to cause harm, but overly permissive parenting results in children paying a high price.

Maria is only four years old and is already being sent to a kindergarten that prepares children to excel in math and science. Her mother, who directs her to do extra work so that she can score well in these subjects, often interrupts Maria's playtime. She also limits her daughter's time with friends, and often nags Maria about doing better at school. Maria gets frustrated, though she does not know the word for that feeling. She looks unhappy and sullen much of the time. She daydreams a lot and does not concentrate on her schoolwork, which is already excessive. Her mother puts this down to laziness and lack of focus. Her demands are extreme—she is definitely not meeting the core emotional need for **Realistic Expectations**. Maria feels exasperated and frustrated most of the time. She is becoming rude to her mother and has started angrily lashing out at her friends in kindergarten. Her mother feels that she is a good mum, looking out for her daughter. Little does she know how much frustration Maria is experiencing. Again, the mother would probably say that her expectations are for Maria's own good, but she has little idea of the unintentional harm and exasperation that she has caused her daughter to experience through her repeated unrealistic expectations.

Ben is a fourteen-year old boy who finds it difficult to fit in. He is not into sports like the other boys in his class. He feels ashamed of his acne, his oily hair, and his looks in general. Ben avoids interacting with others and often feels left out. He spends most of the time after school in his room alone. His parents on the other hand are pleased with this behaviour since they feel that he is a "good boy" who does not mix with the "wrong" crowd. Further, since he is good student, they are proud of his progress at school and boast about him incessantly, thinking that will build up his self-esteem, but it makes him feel guilty instead. Ben appears to get along well with others, but does not actually connect well and feels lonely. He often goes to bed crying, longing to have a best friend. He does not feel that he fits in anywhere. As his loneliness increases, he starts to surf the Net to soothe his pain, and becomes addicted to Internet pornography. His parents are completely unaware since he gives the impression that he has not yet noticed girls. All they seem to be concerned with is how well he is doing at school. Ben's loneliness is causing him frustration. He feels lousy about himself and knows deep down that he is headed in the wrong direction. He resents his parents for not understanding his challenges, but he is also afraid to tell them so. His parents continue to be oblivious to his need. They have no idea what he is feeling. They mean absolutely no harm, but as unintentional as it is, harm is still being caused. Imagine if Ben were part of a functional community, where he felt accepted, loved, guided and challenged? His feeling of loneliness might very well be reduced, at least to a degree. His close relationships with peers and adult friends would foster spiritual values and this would help him deal with his porn addiction. **Spiritual Values and Community** makes a huge difference in people's lives. We are made to connect. The two institutions that God created for us are the family and a functional community like the church, and God intends for us to connect with one another in these two institutions.

Back to exasperation—since it usually takes place *subtly* and *unintentionally*, parents must take stock of how they might be accidentally sabotaging their own parenting. Sometimes this happens as they *imitate behaviours from their own parents* that they observed growing up. Sometimes it can be the exact opposite, *an overreaction to what they experienced growing up*. And sometimes it stems from *fear of what their children may become* if they keep heading a certain direction; perhaps their child reminds them of Uncle Ned, the bankrupt womaniser who could not hold a job. It can even be a *caving-in to parental peer-pressure*, worried about what other parents could be thinking. Or it can occur because of a *reaction to something they have read or heard* in the media, or even heard in a sermon.

We cannot end this introduction to exasperation interactions without pointing out that many of the issues about which parents and children argue are matters of opinion and preference. Parents who refuse to be dragged into "disputable matters" and focus their energies on truly important issues have a greater chance of helping their children to be morally and emotionally healthy and avoiding exasperation interactions.

On this note, we believe that the research of Dr Larry Nucci,[2] an education expert in children's social and moral development, sheds light on what kind of issues should carry more weight than others. He put different ways of looking at right and wrong into "domains", and found that all cultures have a common idea of "right and wrong", encompassing concepts such as fairness, justice, and honesty. According to Nucci, a five-year-old boy, regardless of where he is raised, knows it is never right for a big kid to hit a smaller child or keep all the candy for himself. Dr Nucci calls this the **Moral Domain**, and says it is pretty much the same across the world, whether you are talking about Singapore, South Africa or Scandinavia.

The **Conventional Domain** deals with issues that tend to be arbitrary, it exists through the social agreement of people who are part of a social system. For example, in some cultures it is perfectly fine to address another person by their given name, but in other cultures this would seem very informal, and in some places, downright rude. Burping aloud at the table is condemned in some countries but seen as a compliment to the chef in others. A third domain he labels as the **Personal Domain**, which deals with matters of privacy and personal preference, such as a person's style of dress or hairstyle. As a child grows this domain will also increase with their autonomy. Finally, there is the **Prudential Domain** involving safety and well-being and pertaining to rules associated with things like the consumption of alcohol, using drugs, smoking and driving.

Of all the above domains, which should be the main focus—Moral, Conventional, Personal or Prudential? When discipline is being administered, should one domain take precedence over another? Disciplining and training children about issues within the Moral Domain which are truly about right and wrong is central to their development. However, when parents argue with and discipline their children for "offenses" within the conventional and personal domains, children, especially adolescents, will often infer hypocrisy and rebel. As parents argue with their children about the arbitrary and personal choice issues that are not truly a matter of right and wrong, their children will become exasperated and will experience frustration of their core emotional needs.

Understanding the above will help parents know where their focus primarily should be, when they should make something a big deal, when it is acceptable to occasionally be indignant—and over what issues.

Important Qualifier: Repeated frustrative and traumatic experiences are *not* the same as occasional mistakes by parents. It has been said before that having children changes parents. Most of us, if we persevere and continue to grow as individuals, and are willing to be humble and learn, will change for the better. However, during this journey we will all make mistakes, whether it be losing our cool, being forgetful, getting frustrated ourselves, and perhaps even being a little too intrusive, too demanding, or overly permissive. However, it is important to note that there is a big difference between *repeated* frustrative and traumatic experiences that a child goes through and the occasional mistakes made by parents here and there but who generally do a great job meeting these core emotional needs. If parents are "good enough" then mistakes made now and then will not cause harm. Such mistakes can be repaired easily, by gaining awareness, getting feedback from our spouse and from our children. What we are talking about are the kind of dynamics that have become a part of normal interactions and part of the family culture. Parents that cause repeated frustrative and traumatic experiences by not meeting the core emotional needs will facilitate the development of maladaptive schemas/lifetraps and unhealthy coping styles. It is important to distinguish the difference between the two types of parenting mistakes just discussed—the occasional mistakes made by "good enough parents" who are meeting their children's core emotional needs, and the ones who *repeatedly* exasperate their children, even though it is not intentional.

*So exactly how

do we exasperate

our children?*

CHAPTER THREE

Exasperation Interactions

Have you ever said, "That really pushes my buttons"? We all have trigger points, situations that cause us to feel exasperated. As counsellors, church leaders, and certainly as parents, we have observed that there are specific interactions that seem to always cause exasperation in children. This exasperation eventually leads to the children experiencing a frustration of core emotional needs (their core emotional needs repeatedly not being met) and later in adulthood may be remembered as trauma. We call these "exasperation interactions". The individual interactions that we are identifying in this chapter were confirmed during our research using the Young Parenting Inventory (YPI)[1] from the schema therapy model. They are Belittling, Perfectionistic and Conditional, Controlling, Punitive, Emotionally Depriving and Inhibiting, Overprotective, Pessimistic, and Overly Permissive. Being on the receiving

---
◁ **RESEARCH REVEALS** ▷

RR3.1: *What Exasperates Children*

In 2011, the Singapore National Council of Social Services (NCSS) awarded John Louis and his team from HOPE *worldwide* (Singapore) a grant that partially financed the research on the association between past negative parenting experiences as a child and the severity of schemas as an adult.[2] This research set out to confirm an earlier study on past parenting experiences conducted by Sheffield, in London in 2005.[3] The earlier work of Sheffield was based on a sample of 422 university students and found nine different parenting scales. Our Singapore sample was made up of over 600 members of the Central Christian Church from many ages and nationalities. The results confirmed the same nine scales found in the UK, thus supporting the stability of the nine scales across cultures. However, in our study, two of the scales, namely Perfectionistic and Conditional/Narcissistic had a very high correlation with one another, as did the scale of Emotionally Depriving with the Emotionally Inhibiting scale. Thus we combined the four into two scales and these two were re-worded and called the *Emotionally Depriving and Inhibiting* scale and the *Perfectionistic and Conditional* scale. This reduced the number from nine to seven scales in total. While an *Overly Permissive* scale did not appear strongly in our sample, other works by Baumrind,[4] a pioneer in identifying parenting styles, proved the existence of a *Permissive* parenting scale. This was supported by many other researchers, who also identifed a permissive parenting style. However,

> given that some parents might overreact to the word "Permissive" and then not meet the core emotional need for healthy autonomy, we decided to re-word the scale and call it *Overly Permissive*. This scale was added to the others we found in our research and in total form the basis of the different exasperation interactions that are used throughout this book.

end of any of these interactions blocks children's core emotional needs from being met.

Let us now go through each research proven frustration and trauma-causing interaction specifically.

Belittling

When parents make fun of their children, call them names, make derogatory remarks about things that are important to their kids, disparage their looks, or humiliate them in any way, children will feel belittled. This will lead to other emotions and a negative view of themselves such as feeling put down, flawed and or rejected. Parents sometimes poke fun at their children for their preferences. They belittle them about decisions on issues that are not life-threatening in nature, such as school subjects, sports, choice of friends, clothes, hair style, music, table manners. Some parents' philosophy is that humiliating their children will induce them to change their "inappropriate" behaviour. Even the *emotions* of the children are not viewed in a positive light, let alone their choices and decisions—these parents dislike the expression of feelings, particularly so for boys. Children in such an environment quickly shut down. They are afraid to voice any of their preferences and feelings. Parents who belittle often have a narrow way of thinking about feelings. These parents usually have deep pain or hurts themselves that have not been dealt with properly. They are angry most of the time, and have little or no positive outlook on life. They think that humiliation is the best way to bring about change in their children. They may put their children down because of the way the children look or act, for their grades or their lack of achievement—usually it is something that is triggering the parents' own feeling of defectiveness. The overall effect is that children who feel belittled and rejected become exasperated and are eventually traumatised.

Examples:
(from parents to a son)
> *If you were not such a sissy you would take up a real sport instead of ballet.*
> *What kind of dumb hairstyle is that? You look like a girl. I should call you by a girl's name.*
> *Big boys don't cry. Stop being a girl. Only girls cry.*

> *There is something wrong with you. Why are your feelings all over the place all the time? It is time to grow up.*
> *Let's see you cry like a baby (then parent mimicking the child cry…)*
> *Learn to take hits like a man. Stop being a wimp.*

(from parents to a daughter)
> *We were expecting a boy, not a girl!*
> *Remember that your brother gets the first choice in everything.*
> *You're a girl—why do you look like your dad?*
> *You are trying to manipulate me with your feelings, aren't you? I am not going to fall for it.*
> *Here we go again, is this your monthly woman thing? Why can't you think straight?*
> *You look so fat. How about losing some weight?*
> *If you knew how to cook, maybe you could get a boyfriend.*

(from parents to either sons or daughters)
> *If you don't improve your grades, how will you fit in with our family?*
> *If you don't shape up you will bring shame to the family name.*
> *If you don't make the cut, I don't know how to face the relatives.*
> *I know you like to focus on the Arts, but I want you to focus on Science. Please don't bring shame on us by going against our wishes.*
> *How can you be from our genes and look like this?*
> *I wish I never had you.*
> *Second place is a disgrace to our family.*
> *Where is your brain, stupid?*
> *You think they will let you into kindergarten if you can't even tie your shoes?*
> *If you keep getting these kinds of grades you will end up being a loser. Do you get that?*
> *Hey, butterfingers, no coach in his right mind would let you be on his team.*
> *You have the table manners of a pig.*
> *Why did you have to make such a stupid mistake on your exam?*
> *What's wrong with you?*

Children who regularly hear such comments are not likely to feel accepted and connected with their parents, nor will they readily be in a position to get their other core emotional needs met in other ways.

A study done jointly by Harvard Medical School and McLean Hospital in Boston, USA, published in 2006, highlighted that demeaning or belittling words contribute more to the maladjustment of children than harsh physical punishment.[5] This is consistent with our own counselling experiences involving adults whose greatest pain revolves around early memories of the hurts caused by words from their parents; they carry wounds from "put-downs" for years afterwards.

> **◊ LOUIS LOWDOWN ◊**
>
> One of my (Karen) least proud parenting moments happened when David was in kindergarten. We lived on the 10th floor of an old apartment building with very slow elevators. On one particular day, I had not helped David to get ready in time to catch the school bus without rushing. Instead of making sure his shoes were on well in advance, I suddenly called out, "David, we need to go now!" He was struggling to get his shoes on (as five year olds sometimes do) so I impatiently told him that he could finish putting on his shoes outside of our apartment while we waited for the elevator door to open. The poor guy then sat down on the ground and began to try once again to get his shoes on. However, as luck would have it, the doors opened immediately, and there were people inside, which meant that we either would wait several minutes to get another lift down, or we would have to get in while David was still putting his shoes on. We scrambled into the elevator, and I remember feeling embarrassed in front of the other lift passengers. Why? Because my weird ego was somehow interpreting that they were judging my parenting and I was coming up short. (Who cares, right?) Even though David could hear me, I made excuses to the other elevator riders, "Look how slow and disobedient my son is. So sorry. I hope he learns his lesson." When we exited the elevator, I already felt like a world-class jerk. Thankfully, the school bus wasn't even there, which gave me time to say sorry for my rudeness as a parent. I sat down with David on the curb, apologised profusely for the belittling words and asked his forgiveness. David was able to go to school happy after all, if not slightly confused at his mother's strange behaviour. If I had not apologised immediately, David would have gone off to school exasperated. Repeat this episode a few more times, and my son would have learned to steer clear of Mum!

Perfectionistic and Conditional

Children will be exasperated by their parents when they feel they can never measure up to a perfectionistic ideal. Parents who cause this kind of frustration usually care very much about how they are perceived by others, how they look in society. They demand perfection and are only satisfied when things go a certain way (and children rarely match these kinds of expectations). These demands put an incredible pressure on the children who become frustrated and sometimes traumatised, and their core emotional needs are therefore not met.

Parents who have such a philosophy about perfection and about looking good care little that their children are feeling sad, disappointed or fearful. Such parents even think of themselves as good parents, who do everything for their children. *Parents who come across conditional in the love and acceptance of their children are often driven by how they are viewed by others.* They are highly competitive—when *their children* perform well, because they view their children as an extension of themselves, they feel that *they* have performed well. They may brag about their kids, in subtle or not-so-subtle ways. Some of them are reserved and withhold encouragement for fear that it will demotivate their child. Conversely when their child does not "do well", they feel it deeply and take it out on the child. They are driven by how others perceive their chld's "failure", and, when disappointed, it shows up in the way they treat their child. They withhold affection and love as a result of their disappointment, seen in their body language and with their words as well. Life for the child is constantly filled with criticism. Even when the child becomes an adult, the parents also have this misguided notion that they always know what is best for the child, and have a sense that they are superior to the child.

Celebrative emotions that come with achievements should be welcomed, but those will come few and far between. Or perhaps one child is a super achiever, so the sibling gets compared and criticised for not being as good. The children's preferences, decisions and emotions are not treated as being as important as those of the parents. What parents feel about a certain achievement is more important than how the children feel. The parent's shame about a certain achievement not being met is more important than the children's feelings. As a result, the children feel unhealthy guilt and shame; over time, this becomes a frustrative and traumatic experience, and can cause a lot of anxiety and fear. The following words might be heard during these interactions:

> *I hope you see that your grades are terrible. Do you have any idea how this makes us feel?*
>
> *How dare you embarrass us with your behaviour!*
>
> *You are too easily satisfied. This is your problem.*
>
> *If you are not baptised, how will that make us look?*
>
> *Do you have any idea how much we have sacrificed for you? Do you know how we feel when you don't score top grades? (or come in first at the swimming competition or whatever)*
>
> *Stop feeling great when what you did was average. Look at your older/ younger sister/brother (or cousins or others that the children are compared to). You should feel terrible about what you did.*
>
> *The Bible says children should bring honour to their parents, and when you act like this, you don't.*
>
> *Stop wasting time going out with your friends or having sleepovers. Get serious with your tennis (or soccer/ballet, etc) and be productive.*
>
> *Maybe everyone else in the class did well, too, or maybe you were lucky. So, don't get comfortable. Keep pressing on. You may not be so lucky next time.*

Honey if you could just recite all the books of the Bible from memory like the Smith boys, then I would be happy.

When you don't look your best, you make us look bad.

Work a bit harder to lose weight—you can never be too rich or too thin.

Once your braces are off, then for your 16th birthday, you can have a nose job.

⟨ LOUIS LOWDOWN ⟩

I (Karen) will share another cringe-worthy parenting story—this one is even more embarrassing, but then, we are talking about exasperation interactions! I will preface it by giving my theory on why parents have "freak-out moments": I think it is when a fear gets triggered. Fear that the kids will not be good enough in something, fear that they won't turn out alright, fear that they will be just like us in some area that we hate about ourselves, fear that they will have the pet sin or weakness that we detest, or fear that they will become just like that person we don't really like very much. On one particular weekend when Sonia was eleven, she had been planning a sleepover with a girl from her Sunday school class, someone she often stayed with. At the last minute, Sonia told me that the plans had changed, and then asked me if she could stay overnight with a school friend instead. It was with a family I knew well and trusted, but they didn't have the same spiritual values that we did, so I wasn't that happy about Sonia switching the plan at the last minute. Then for some reason, I asked my daughter if she had read her Bible or prayed yet that morning. (It was around 10am on a Saturday.) When she replied that she had not, I suddenly was filled with panic that my child was going to the dark side. I cannot explain it (PMS?) but I just blurted out, "OK, then, don't become a Christian! See if I care!" My wonderfully expressive daughter looked me right in the eye and said, "Who are you?" That made me immediately broken and I sat down and apologised and told her that I was sorry and not sure what had come over me. Then I asked God to help me never do that again!

Controlling

Parents who control and exasperate their children in this way are driven by a variety of factors, one of which is the enmeshment lifetrap. They are enmeshed with their child/children. They will not permit their children to feel differently from them. They also force their children to be privy to age inappropriate information, such as the deteriorating relationship with their marriage partner, their own loneliness, sometimes even their sexual frustrations. Such parents do not let children express their own feelings but rather dictate how their children should feel and think. Enmeshed parents instil a strange kind of loyalty in their children. They deprive their children of their own emotions and instead expect them to think about the needs of the enmeshed parent most, if not, all of the time.

Apart from enmeshment, some parents are controlling because of fear that their children will make wrong decisions and use bad judgement. This fear drives the parents to micro-manage their children's affairs and as a result, children feel that they have little freedom of choice. They also feel that they cannot rely on their own decision or judgement; eventually they will not develop their own sense of direction because they feel that their parents are such strong individuals. Similar to those with the enmeshment lifetrap, these children will not grow up with individuality and a sense of separateness from the parents.

Children with such experiences do not feel that they have room to be themselves, which creates frustrative experiences growing up, especially in the case of mothers who are enmeshed with her children. The messages that children hear from their enmeshed parent, either explicitly or implicitly, are exasperating statements such as:

> *I need to teach you to think and feel like me. Then you'll learn and grow up.*
>
> *There are no secrets between us, ok? Tell me everything.*
>
> *You need to be loyal, so stop thinking and feeling differently, and do as I say. (Pulling out the loyalty card frequently).*
>
> *You need to think about how I feel before you make decisions, and not just think about your feelings!*
>
> *Let me tell you about how I am feeling about your father.*
>
> *I don't want you to be with your friends even if this is how you feel. Stay home with me. I am your mum and I need you, so stop thinking about yourself.*
>
> *Let me decide which extra curricular activity you should sign up for. I know what is best for you, so do what I tell you.*
>
> *If you are feeling bad, talk to me, not to your father. We are best of friends.*
>
> *Don't worry about how you feel towards your father. You will always have me. (Some children are distant from their fathers and their enmeshed mothers encourage the disconnectedness.)*

Mothers who are enmeshed are usually clueless about how their interactions exasperate their children. They think they are close to their child, but often their child feels exasperated, although the child eventually gets used to it and then starts to become overly dependent on the mother.

Punitive

Parents who exasperate their children in this way most likely grew up in such an environment themselves. Examples of the punitive exasperation interaction are children being punished for *every little thing* that they do wrong, or for displaying certain emotions, or for infractions that are conventional in nature, as opposed to moral (see Chapter Two), or being made to feel guilty for past mistakes. Parents who treat their children this way show very little grace. They emphasise "justice" and "truth" rather than mercy, and put their kids "in the dog house" every time they feel a sin has occurred. Words that come out from them may include:

I heard that you were told off by your teacher for not doing well in your exams. That will be nothing compared to what I will do to you.

You did not clean your room well enough—you're grounded!

You deserve to be punished; it is the only way you learn.

If you start crying, I will send you to your room.

If you can't express this without being angry, then stand in the corner until you are able to do so.

I will never trust you again after what you did.

If you get emotional, there will be consequences; you have no idea how this reflects on you.

Do you really think one apology is good enough?

Just stop being sad. I hate it. It is not good for you. I am not going to allow any sad people in this house.

If you are afraid to do this, then I am not going to communicate with you on this anymore.

Stop crying and get happy now or else I will spank you! Now!

If you are going to be quiet and sad, then go to your room and forget about having dinner together. Come out when you are happy.

Emotionally Depriving and Inhibiting

Parents who are successful at work and seem all together can end up accidentally exasperating their children by emotionally depriving them of empathy, comfort and guidance. Parents who fall into this trap often want their children to learn how to behave and be calm. They do not particularly like passion, including children crying. Their philosophy is, "Children are to be seen and not heard". They feel uncomfortable with both the high and low emotions—they do not encourage children to laugh out loud, play loud games, or have friends over often, and they certainly are not comfortable when their children like talking about heart-felt issues, their low times, disappointments, and sadness. These parents maintain an even keel in their homes. Noise is just a nuisance, whether stemming from joy, happiness, pain or hurt. These parents will talk about anything rather than emotions and feelings. Most parents who exasperate their children in this manner were treated similarly growing up, so this kind of coping mechanism is now familiar to them, and as a result, this is what they re-create in their own home. Statements like the following are frequently made to their children:

Don't be so complicated. Just listen to what we have to say and be logical.

We know best. So just listen and obey.

If you are going to talk about your feelings, then just go to your mother.

Get that sad look off your face. Don't you know that the Bible says to rejoice in the Lord always?

Take life as it comes. Life is like that unfortunately. These things happen.

Just forgive people when they hurt you. It is not a big deal.

Why are you so excited? Calm down.

What did you do wrong first? Admit that before anything, otherwise let's not talk about your feelings.

If you let your feelings bother you, they will bother you. If you don't bother with your feelings, then they will not bother you.

I am not emotional like other people. I am a rational, logical person, so let's talk about this logically.

Let's talk about something helpful rather than focusing on your feelings.

You are losing it. When you are calm, then we can talk. Until then please don't say anything.

Can we all be calm here? There is too much noise. (Even when it does not happen frequently).

Please play quietly.

Stop laughing so loud when you watch TV.

I am not the type to listen to feelings. Can we get straight to the point?

I may not show you a lot of affection, but I do care about you.

Let's only talk about the positives. I want a positive atmosphere in the home.

Sometimes parents emotionally deprive their children by being too busy for them. When both parents have demanding jobs, there can be a problem with setting aside time for their kids. Children are raised more by their grandparents or by a hired caregiver/day care service, and they grow up not being emotionally close to their own parents. More affluent parents may see going on elaborate holidays as a way of making up for a lack of time spent with the kids but quality does not make up for quantity and the children feel a lack of empathy, nurturing and guidance. Working late hours day after day takes its toll; the years go by quickly and before they know it, the children are at an adolescent stage and already exasperated.

There are other reasons why parents may emotionally deprive their children. Some adults are incapable of being warm, affectionate, nurturing and showing empathy because of their own upbringing. Sometimes they have little mental and emotional capacity to give to their children. Some parents go through such difficult times in their marriage that they are consumed with their problems and have little left over to give to their children. Harm is done regardless of the reason, and the children grow up with frustration of not having their core needs met. Another very important aspect of this kind of interaction is when parents do not provide their children with helpful and age-appropriate guidance. This is the opposite of the next type of interaction where parents go to the other extreme.

Overprotective

Parents who are overprotective are excessively worried about their children for the smallest of issues, such as them being hurt while playing at the playground, or them being sick when caught in a light rain. They convey unrealistic expectations to their children, and at best, they react in a way that is very out of proportion to the actual situation, so much so that even onlookers will notice. Eventually their children may become like them and over-react, too. Children often feel frustrated when exposed to such constant signals from their parents. Kids from such families eventually prefer hanging out with their friends, or they surrender to their parents' fears and become stay-at-home worry warts.

> *I can't believe that your friends hurt you. Who do they think they are? I will deal with them. Give me their phone numbers.*
>
> *I don't want you to play sports because you will hurt yourself. How about joining the reading club?*
>
> *I can't believe they let that boy with a cough stay at day care. Now you are going to get sick. Rest at home tomorrow and I will speak to them, or maybe we'll just change centres.*
>
> *I know that you are old enough to travel by yourself, but it might rain, and I don't want you to catch a cold.*
>
> *Looks like you are sad. Well, let's go to the doctor tomorrow, cancel school, and get something for your depression. Don't do anything else and go to bed early.*
>
> *I can't believe that the person who served you food at the school cafeteria was rude. I will go there tomorrow and give him a piece of my mind.*
>
> *It is hard for me to stand here and do nothing when you are sad that*

your teacher gave you a lower grade then you deserve. I will see him tomorrow myself.

Pessimistic

Children become exasperated when they repeatedly hear that the glass is always half empty, not half full. If you were to ask the parents why they were being negative, their first reaction would be that they do not want their children to be unrealistic about life. The reality is that these parents probably grew up in a negative environment in which they were afraid of making mistakes. Taking risks was never encouraged. So, fuelled with a desire to not make mistakes and to make sure that things do not go wrong, they decide that it is easier to not be hopeful at all, and hence become negative. Children will feel down talking to their parents and often feel frustrated being at home, and would rather go elsewhere.

Some remarks from parents who interact with their children in this way might be:

Don't admire anyone. They will end up disappointing you.

There is no point getting sad about relationships. Relationships will always disappoint you, so I never have hope in them.

It is dangerous to talk about feelings, so let's not do it.

This world is a sick place, so don't expect to be happy.

I don't know why you are excited about entering that contest. What's the point?

I just don't want you to be terribly disappointed.

I know you are positive about taking up that sport. But it is rough and you will get injured and then your life will collapse.

Why are you sad? The world is a horrible place, so get used to it and get over your emotions.

Overly Permissive

Parents who are overly permissive are not available, or too busy doing their own thing. Sometimes the parents feel guilty for not getting involved with their children, so they overreact by not expecting the kids to respect boundaries or learn proper discipline. They are not there to talk about the difficult issues that their children are going through. In order to distract their kids from their emotions, they let them watch loads of TV and spoil them with goodies. The parents themselves are uncomfortable getting involved in their children's lives, perhaps for fear of bad news, or perhaps they do not like talking about emotions and so they avoid them by not being available or taking their focus away from their emotions. As a result, children begin to think that it is wrong to talk about their emotions. They also do not take the time to guide them through issues. They allow their children to get away with a lot of mischief before they even say anything. Eventually when children do not feel guided by their parents, this can cause them to feel insecure about the direction they are heading, and they may turn to their peers instead.

Sorry, I am too busy. You need to learn to deal with your ups and downs yourself. You are a grown up.

If you are feeling angry, just let it all out. Then you will feel better.

I am sorry you feel that way. It is my fault. I am a lousy parent. (Or parents thinking this instead of saying it.)

If you just leave your feelings aside, they will go away. Time will heal your wounds.

Sorry, you feel sad. Want to watch TV? There's something really fun on now.

Have some ice cream. That is the best way to take your sadness away and make you feel better.

You're emotional. I think I will leave you to be by yourself.

Children whose parents are overly permissive feel that their parents are just not there for them and are too busy doing their own thing, leaving them to figure out how to manage and control their lives. This can easily cause them to not feel connected with their parent and create resentment and frustration in them, especially when their parents give them advice and finally, on the very rare occasion, decide to talk to them about sensitive issues. As mentioned, parents will make mistakes, but this is very different and separate from the repeated pattern of negative experiences that becomes the norm rather than the exception in the parent-child interaction.

☙ RESEARCH REVEALS ❧

RR3.2: *Traumatic Experiences during Childhood Cause Lifetraps*

Our own research, consistent with the findings of others, has found that frustrative and traumatic experiences during childhood are associated with the development of lifetraps.[6] In turn, lifetraps are related to the development of other dysfunctions, such as a tendency to: be victimized or aggressive;[7] have depression and anxiety;[8] have an increase in body mass index;[9] be involved in conflict;[10] and be affected by adulthood attachment issues.[11]

Why Are Lifetraps (Schemas) a Big Deal?

As we explained in Chapter One, lifetraps are memories, cognitions and emotions stored in our brain that are triggered when we are presented with familiar situations later on in life. All of us have lifetraps, since none of our "growing up" environments were perfect. We have all had unpleasant experiences and also positive ones growing up. The positive ones help us to move forward in life in the face of adversity or challenges. The strongly negative ones affect our self view and our relationships with people and we may get stuck with this over and over again, unable to break completely free and start over. Remember the figure of the woman looking into the mirror (see Chapter One, Figure 1.1)? It shows a young woman whose traumatic experience of verbal abuse from her father shaped her view of herself. She has the lifetrap of defectiveness—she feels there is something wrong with her, that she is not "good enough"; as a result, her self-image is distorted, which is seen in the mirror's reflection. (For more on this subject, see Chapter Three of our companion volume *I Choose Us*.[12])

⊰ MOVIE MOMENT – *Taare Zameen Par*[13] ⊱

Watch this Bollywood movie to see examples of almost all of the exasperation interactions. Ishan, a little boy with dyslexia, experiences interactions that are belittling, emotionally depriving and inhibiting, perfectionistic and conditional, punitive, and pessimistic at the hand of his father. Ishan turns selectively mute but eventually, salvation comes in the form of an art teacher. We highly recommend that this film be watched together as a family for entertainment and to lead into discussions of any number of topics, including exasperation, helping others, having empathy, and what to do when people are different.

While we believe that everyone who has had his sins forgiven by God is saved, not all of us are equally healed emotionally. Most of us are happy as young Christians regardless of our childhoods, simply because we are so grateful for our new lives in Christ. And that is a good thing! However, after ten or twenty years as disciples of the Master, it is not unusual to hit some bumps. We may be stuck spiritually (hence the name "lifetrap") and not be able to overcome bitterness, or an habitual sin, or figure out why the same issues keep coming up in our relationships. At the end of the day, life as a Christian sometimes requires dealing with past emotional hurts as we strive to become more like Christ, in order for our hearts to be free to give to others. Our spirituality and relationship with God and with those in the church community are the best way to move forward. While we continue our journey as saved individuals, we need to strive for as much healing as possible in order to limit the transfer of our dysfunction to our children and affect other important relationships negatively. This is where understanding our past and gaining awareness is so helpful. We put the pieces together, experiencing many "aha" moments along the way. Hopefully, this self-awareness helps us to avoid exasperating our children and to better meet their core emotional needs.

> **❖ RESEARCH REVEALS ❖**
>
> **RR3.3:** *Relevance between People's Present Lifetraps with Pathologies*
>
> A plethora of research has shown links between people's present strong, active lifetraps with the following pathologies:
> - Personality disorders, such as paranoid personality disorder, dependence personality disorder, obsessive compulsive disorder, borderline personality disorder, and narcissistic personality disorder[14]
> - Psychiatric symptoms[15]
> - Depression among adolescents[16]
> - Depression and anxiety among adults[17]
> - Job burn-out among public school teachers[18]
> - Bulimic eating disorder[19]
> - Anorexia nervosa eating disorder[20]
> - Romantic jealousy[21]
> - Alcohol dependency[22]
> - Depersonalization disorder.[23]
>
> The fact that lifetraps are associated with early parenting experiences and with the disorders and pathologies mentioned above again highlights how crucial it is for us as parents to know how to satisfactorily meet the core emotional needs of our children. The stakes are high. The way our children perceive their early experiences with us makes a huge difference, including possibly whether or not they embrace the values that we are trying to pass on to them.

Our Singapore research uncovered that frustrative and traumatic experiences during childhood are associated with the development of lifetraps. However, some of these exasperation interactions are more harmful in relation to certain core emotional needs. In particular, when considering the core emotional need for connection and acceptance, we found that, in order of severity, Belittling, Controlling, Emotionally Depriving and Inhibiting, and Overprotective are most harmful. When considering the core emotional need for healthy autonomy and performance, the most harmful exasperation interactions are Controlling, Overprotective, Belittling, and Pessimistic. When it comes to the core emotional need for reasonable limits, Punitive and Pessimistic turn out to be the most harmful. Lastly, when considering the core emotional need for realistic expectations, we found that the Perfectionistic and Conditional, Pessimistic and Overprotective interactions are the most harmful. Typically, a parent falls into a combination of these interactions; they are even more harmful when combined.[24]

SECTION TWO

The Core Emotional Need for
Connection and Acceptance

So what is

the first core

emotional need?

CHAPTER FOUR

Connection and Acceptance

The Core Emotional Need for Connection and Acceptance can be defined as the state our children live in when they feel completely attached to their parents in a healthy way, that they belong, and that they are accepted and loved unconditionally. When this need is being met to a satisfactory degree, children will *consistently* and *on an emotional level* hear and believe the following messages about their parents:

They are playful with me and spend time with me.

They miss me when I am not around.

They care about deep feelings, both mine and theirs.

They are proud of me even with my flaws.

They think I am special.

They talk to me in a respectful way.

They are honest with me.

They believe in me and guide me.

Denise, 37, grew up in a home where she was made to feel stupid, ugly, fat, and unwanted. Her parents had wanted a boy for their first born, and she was reminded of that fact frequently. They also had high hopes for her academically, even though they themselves had only finished elementary school. When she did not "excel" in kindergarten, they called her mean names like "idiot" and "retard" and made it no secret that they wished she had not been born. She was beaten for the slightest offence, and when she was sexually abused by a relative, no one cared. Locked out of the house for minor infractions such as laughing too loudly, she quickly learned to stay in the background. When her brother arrived a few years later, Denise's only value to the family was as a caretaker. In every possible way, her parents did not meet Denise's core need for connection and acceptance, nor any of her other needs, for that matter. This lonely child did poorly in almost every subject, and did not even pass high school. Denise has been hospitalised for suicidal tendencies, and constantly struggles with relationships, finances, depression, boundaries, and self-esteem issues. It does not take a psychiatrist to see that Denise's issues are directly related to her childhood and it is no wonder that she continues to have trouble *connecting* with others and *accepting* herself.

On the other end of the spectrum, Caroline, 32, was never beaten or sexually abused. Her family went on nice holidays. She had lots of friends, attended a posh private school, and excelled in her favourite hobbies. Although her parents both found it hard to express their feelings and had very high unrelenting standards, they believed in being firm but kind, valued discipline, trying one's best, being humble, and showing respect. Her mother had a flexi-hour job so that she could be at home with the children whenever possible; her father worked long hours as a lawyer. Her older sister was "a handful" and seemed to get the brunt of the discipline, while her younger brother was sickly, so the parents spent most of their time worrying over Caroline's siblings. In this environment, Caroline was overlooked and did not *feel* her parents' love. As a teenager, she yearned to break free from and rebel against the disapproving oversight of her fairly strict and emotionally inhibited parents. Although her siblings are doing well in their careers, Caroline never graduated from college, and has many boundary issues. Like Denise, she has also been on suicide watch at times, and finds it hard to hold a job or keep a long-term relationship. Many people would look at her parents and family and think that she had the ideal home, but her core need for connection and acceptance was not met, and she has trouble feeling *connected* to her family and *accepting* herself or others. What do these two women from very different families have in common? Their basic core emotional need for connection and acceptance was not met by their parents, and now, even though these two women should be able to function as successful adults, their struggle is immense.

Real connection with our children is when the sharing of emotions takes place in both directions; parents to children and children to parents, such that a healthy affectionate bond and an empathic understanding develop between the two sides and they both feel positive at an emotional level. The result is that the children feel that their thoughts and ideas, hurts and feelings, and victories and defeats have a place in their parents' hearts and vice versa. Acceptance with our children is when the children feel that their parents value them for who they are, with their strengths and weaknesses, flaws and all, and regard them as a blessing in their lives at an emotional level. Unconditional love and acceptance makes home a safe place.

These two constructs go hand in hand. It is impossible to get connected to a child at an emotional level and at the same time not accept them. When a child gets connected, the acceptance comes with it; connection and acceptance are interwoven. The reverse is also true; where there is disconnection there is also a sense of rejection. Children will then feel exasperated and discouraged and their behaviour will reflect these feelings. When this core emotional need is met well, it lays the foundation for a lifelong enjoyable and fulfilling relationship between parent and child.

Children must feel a deep emotional connection with their parents in order for them to mature into healthy adults, and they must feel accepted by their parents if they are going to develop self-esteem. In our opinion, much of the harm in today's world is caused by this core emotional need not getting met. Oh, that parents would take heed of the absolute necessity of meeting this need!

◈ MASTER CLASS ◈

> Sam and Geri Laing say that one of the three most important lessons they would want parents to learn is for them to connect with their children by communicating on a heart level. Their favourite verse on the subject is Proverbs 23:26 *"My son, give me your heart and let your eyes keep to my ways…"* Sam says, "Talking *at* our children is not the same as talking *with* them. Sometimes we feel that because we have communicated the information our kids need to hear, our job is done. The fact is, until they understand on a mental and emotional level what we mean, and until we have heart-connection, our words may not be getting through. This takes time and patience, but the rewards are invaluable."

Of all the "four plus one" core emotional needs, connection and acceptance is probably the need in which emotions play the keenest part. Meeting this need cannot be done if parents insist on staying in rational or logical mode. If parents are going to connect with their children and help them feel accepted, they must interact with them on an emotional level. And that does not mean that family interactions will then be characterised by screaming, temper tantrums and crying. It does mean that parents must deal with theirr own hesitation to have anything to do with emotions. (For help on learning to accept the whole spectrum of emotions, from anger, fear, sadness, embarrassment and shame, to joy, peace, contentment, hope and gratitude, see Chapter Seven on empathy.)

As we think of the importance of emotions in parenting, we should note that our emotions get communicated through many different means, even when we think we are keeping our emotions in check. Experts teach that we communicate not just with words but also through non-verbal means, such as body language, tone of voice, demeanour and gaze. Albert Mehrabian is the originator of the often quoted "7%-38%-55% Rule"; back in the late 1960s, his experiments led to him assert that words account for only 7% of what we ultimately communicate, tone of voice accounts for 38%, and body language accounts for a whopping 55%! His work particularly points to the importance of congruence—that if our words are saying one thing and our tone another, our listeners will believe the tone.[1] So, when we think we are not being emotional, we might just be telling our child that we do not care about them with our logical and non-feeling eyes and tone of voice. When we say the "right" words but our voice and body language convey disdain or disapproval, our child may be experiencing an exasperation interaction and the connection will be harmed. Working on our tone, body language or eye contact when speaking with our children is not just a good suggestion, it is crucial to meeting our children's need of connection and acceptance!

When we do meet the core emotional need for connection and acceptance, both parents and children experience satisfying emotions, and the "positive vibrations" are almost palpable. The atmosphere in the home is better; parent and child are free to be vulnerable and childlike with each other. This experience is very fulfilling and creates joy in parenting. When the opposite takes place and both sides feel disconnected and rejected, raising children feels more like an obligation and an exhausting chore. Satisfying the core emotional need for connection and acceptance makes a very big difference.

We notice in the parenting sections of bookshops that most titles tend to be about changing children's behaviour, e.g., how to help them be more disciplined, more respectful, more serious in their academics, fight less with their siblings, have better values, and avoid undesirable behaviour. Very few books teach parents how to develop a meaningful and enjoyable connection with their children, yet having such a connection with them is probably the most important need they have as they grow up.

Some parents feel connected to their young children but find that they are not as connected to their teens. Ideally, as their children's level of autonomy increases (see Chapters Eight to Ten), parents should maintain the connection *as well as* successfully make the transition from leading by authority to leading by relationship/influence[2]. This is where many parents err; they allow the connection level to deteriorate with the increase in autonomy, thinking that this is part and parcel of their child growing up. They need to fight hard to ensure that their children make room for them in their lives. If parents are nonchalant about this gradual separation, they will end up forfeiting a valuable on-going connection which teens need as they make the transition from childhood to adulthood. While autonomy (the second core emotional need) is increasing, the connection must be maintained.

Some parents are worried that if they have a strong emotional connection with their children, it will *prevent* them from guiding and teaching their kids and helping them to shoulder responsibilities effectively. This is not true; in fact, it is just the opposite. We all want our children to grow up and become responsible, but they probably will not be that open to learning from us about responsibility until they feel accepted by us and connected with us. *Gottman's research into what he calls "emotion coaching" led him to conclude that the more a child is emotionally connected with his parents, the more likely the child is to accept his parent's values.*[3] When the level of connection is high, the ability of the parents to influence them is also high. One study has even shown that the number one influence in the lives of teenagers is not their friends, but their parents (see Research Reveals).

─── ❖ **RESEARCH REVEALS** ❖ ───

RR4.1: *Teens Secretly Want Parents in Their Lives*

From the book *Soul Searching*, "One of the key themes in this book is that parents are normally very important in shaping the religious and spiritual lives of their teenage children, even though they may not realize it…Many parents come to the conclusion that they have lost their influence in shaping the lives of their teenage children, that they no longer make any significant difference. But for most, this conclusion is mistaken. Teenagers' attitudes, verbal utterances, and immediate behaviours are often not the best evidence with which to estimate parental influence in their lives. For better or worse, most parents in fact still do profoundly influence their adolescents—often more than do their teenage peers—their children's apparent resistance and lack of appreciation notwithstanding. This influence often also includes parental influence in adolescents' religious and spiritual lives. Simply by living and interacting with their children, most parents establish expectations, define normalcy, model life practices, set boundaries, and make demands—all of which cannot help but influence teenagers, for good or ill. Most teenagers and their parents may not realize it, but a lot of research in the sociology of religion suggests that the most important influence in shaping young people's religious lives is the religious life modelled and taught to them by their parents."[4]

It is amazing what good connection does for children—and for parents! When babies are born prematurely and need to live in incubators, hospitals know that the children will thrive only if exposed to human touch. If physical connection helps to determine the physical health of a baby, it seems natural that emotional connection would be vital for mental health. The power of

─── ❖ **RESEARCH REVEALS** ❖ ───

RR4.2: *Changing the Protocol for Premature Babies*

Tiffany Field, who gave birth to a premature baby, realised that incubators did not allow parents to touch their babies. She later invented an incubator that helped parents touch their new-born. The research that put Field and her organisation on the map showed that massage caused premature infants to gain more weight than their non-massaged peers—thereby improving the infants' health and potentially saving millions of dollars each year in health-care costs. That study was published in 1988. Today, more than 100 studies and 350 medical journal articles later, Field is recognized as the premier expert in touch research and advocate for touch therapy.[5]

touch and connection is incredible. Humans were created to connect with one another, especially with loved ones; children need the affection of their parents constantly, not just when they are first born. Even Harvard graduates do better when they have a connection with their parents—only 25% of Harvard graduates from the 1950s who reported a close relationship with their parents had major illnesses 35 years after graduation, compared with 87% of those who said their relationship with their parents was strained and cold. While many academically ambitious parents fight tooth and nail to get their kids into Ivy League schools, how many of them put in the same effort to be connected and to show acceptance?

◁ RESEARCH REVEALS ▷

RR4.3: *Honouring Your Parents Really Does Bring Long Life!*

Students who attended Harvard University between the years 1952 and 1954 were asked whether their relationship with their mother and with their father was "very close", "warm and friendly", "tolerant", or "strained and cold". Thirty-five years later when the participants were middle-aged, their medical records were collected. Results showed that 87% of students who rated their mothers and fathers low in parental caring had been diagnosed with diseases such as coronary artery disease, hypertension, duodenal ulcers and alcoholism in midlife, whereas only 25% of those who rated both their mothers and fathers high in parental caring had diagnosed diseases. This research took into account the family history of illness, smoking behaviour, the death and/or divorce of parents and marital history of the students.[6]

This reminds us of something God says about parent-child relationships, which is a quote from the Ten Commandments:

Children, obey your parents in the Lord, for this is right. "Honour your father and mother"—which is the first commandment with a promise—"so that it may go well with you and that you may enjoy long life on the earth." (Ephesians 6:1-3)

Researchers a few millennia later have learned what God had already told us and recorded for us in His word about the benefit of good relationships between parents and children, which is specifically about meeting the core emotional need for connection and acceptance.

What does it take for our children to feel connected to us and accepted by us to an adequate degree? Certainly it seems logical that we should ask ourselves whether or not our children think that we like them! In the quiet recesses of their minds, do our children sense that we *like* to be with them? We will only be able to meet the need for connection and acceptance if our children sense that we as parents enjoy being around them as people. For many parents, their hearts are so consumed by their worries that they either do not have room in their lives to connect with their children or they actually see their children as being in the way of meeting other goals.

◁ MASTER CLASS ▷

Walter and Kim Evans shared their memories of what they thought was most important about their parenting. Kim says, "The most important thing for me as a Mom was that connection was built and maintained. I knew that I had to keep the kids talking. All three tended to talk at different moments of the day and that was something I prayed about and studied in each child. Our son was most forthcoming while riding alone with one parent in the car and those situations needed to be created and capitalized on. Our youngest like to talk the moment she walked in the door after school. If the moment was missed, it could not be recreated and we would have to wait until the next day for the opportune time. Our middle child talked right before bed. Extra time needed to be planned and not rushed because like no other time of the day, the truths would roll out from her as she lay in bed. Keeping each child talking was the name of the game for me."

Wyndham and Jeanie Shaw echoed the Evans' sentiments. "Each of our four children (presently aged 26-34) is quite different from the other. We prayed and worked hard to understand and draw them out individually. This took much prayer, learning and listening. We strove (and still strive) to be avid learners, reading about parenting and asking advice of those who had gone before us."

We would like to end this chapter by sharing the findings of some of the most intuitive family educators over the last 50 years. See if you can spot a pattern, a common thread that runs through their parenting philosophies:

Haim Ginnot was a clinical psychologist and therapist who wrote a best selling book called *Between Parent and Child*. He said that parents should accept the feelings of the children but not necessarily their behaviour. He also felt very strongly that parents (and to an extent, teachers) should be connecting with and accepting of their children, which is one of the core emotional needs. He states:

> I am a child psychotherapist. I treat disturbed children. Supposing I see a child in therapy one hour a week for a year. Her symptoms disappear; she feels better about herself, gets along with others, even stops fidgeting in school. What is it that I do that helps? I communicate with her in a unique way. I use every opportunity to enhance her feelings about herself. *If caring communication can drive sick children sane, its principles and practices belong to parents and teachers.* While psychotherapists may be able to cure, only those in daily contact with children can prevent them from needing psychological help. [7]

Rudolf Dreikurs, a student of Alfred Adler, wrote *Children: The Challenge*. Here are two of his well-known principles explaining misbehaviour and the importance of non-verbal communication:

> A misbehaving child is a discouraged child...In a thousand subtle ways, by tone of voice and by action, we indicate to the child that we consider him inept, unskilled and generally inferior...[8] Parents many times do not know how they go about discouraging their children, starting in very subtle ways, both verbally and with tone and body language.[9]

David Elkind is a professor emeritus at Tufts University, Massachusetts, and wrote several best sellers, including *The Hurried Child*. Elkind has this to say about how pushing children to learn academically and hurrying them to grow faster than their natural pace puts them in harm's way:

> The abuse of hurrying is a contractual violation. Contractual violations are experienced as exploitative and stressful by children because the implicit contracts between parents and children are the fundament of the children's sense of basic trust, a kind of standard against which the children's social interactions are measured. Two different types of contractual violations and exploitations can be identified. One is qualitative and might be called calendar hurrying. It occurs whenever we ask children to understand beyond their limits of understanding, to decide beyond their capacity to make decisions, or to act wilfully before they have the will to act. But children can also be hurried quantitatively, and this might be called clock hurrying. We engage in clock hurrying whenever, through our excessive demands over a short period of time, we call upon children to call upon their energy reserves.[10]

This Elkind quote deserves extra attention:

> In effect, adolescents pay us back in the teen years for all the sins, real or imagined, that we have committed against them when they were children.[11]

Adele Faber and Elaine Mazlish co-authored a ground breaking book entitled, *How To Talk So Kids Will Listen and Listen So Kids Will Talk*, and echoed the principles taught by Ginnot. They wrote:

> If our attitude is not one of compassion, then whatever we say will be experienced by the child as phony or manipulative. It is when our words are infused with real feelings of empathy that they speak directly to the child's heart.[12]

John Gottman's "emotion coaching" helps children deal with their emotions in an empathetic and guiding way that contributes to connection between parent and child. He and his team at the University of Washington conducted in-depth research with 119 families to see how parents and children interact with each other, following children from the age of four until adolescence. His conclusion was that:

> Children whose parents consistently practiced emotion coaching have better physical health and score higher academically than children whose parents don't offer such guidance. These kids get along better with friends, have fewer behavioural problems, and are less prone to acts of violence. Overall children who are emotion coached experience fewer negative feelings and more positive feelings. In short they are healthier emotionally.[13]

Gottman believes that when a parent coaches a child's emotions, he helps the child to deal with uncomfortable feelings like guilt, regret and sadness. The child then feels more supported. He goes on to say:

> If children are emotion coached from a young age, they become well practiced at the art of self-soothing and they can stay calm under stress, which also makes them less likely to misbehave.[14]

Gottman's research demonstrates that the practice of empathy by parents makes children feel supported; they feel like their parents are their allies, and they are much more likely to accept the parents' values.

This is the common thread running through all of the excellent parenting philosophies above—that parents must connect with their children empathically, and not cause exasperation. **This is not just a good idea; it is the foundation of effective and healthy parenting; it is the bedrock of Good Enough Parenting.**

What are the lifetraps

associated with this

core emotional need?

CHAPTER FIVE

Connection and Acceptance: What's at Stake?

Advantages of Meeting this Need

When parents meet the core emotional need for connection and acceptance, the child will develop some or all of the following traits and beliefs: trust, self-acceptance and openness, emotional fulfilment and intimacy, belonging and affinity, emotional spontaneity and expressiveness, and mastery and success.

Trust

Children who have had the core emotional need for connection and acceptance met trust others. They naturally have thoughts such as *"I generally expect others to treat me in a fair, considerate and just manner, especially those with whom I have a close relationship"*, *"Under normal circumstances, I do not expect to be hurt, lied to, taken advantage of, or manipulated"* and *"Most of the time, I take others at face value, and I expect others to do the same with me."* Children *should* be able to trust their parents. The world makes sense when children are able to trust their parents implicitly. When trust is proven over and over again, children will instinctively trust people; they will feel in their gut that, in general, the world is a trustworthy place. They will feel positively disposed toward others unless given a reason not to. This attribute is not the same as being naïve, gullible, or easily taken advantage of. Trust enables children to make friends readily and to have an easier time navigating relationships as they get older. To facilitate connection and the trust that comes from it, parents should first and foremost expect the home to be a safe haven free from abuse. They should also be mindful of not making promises they cannot keep, and of having an expectation that the home will be a place where one's yes is expected to mean yes, and one's no means no.

Self-Acceptance and Openness

Children who have had the core emotional need for connection and acceptance met feel good about themselves; they have a healthy sense of self-acceptance and are open to new experiences and people. Their worldview is, *"Deep down, I am okay the way I am. I am not perfect but I am basically a good guy. Anyone who truly knows me would love me, or at least like me."*

When children are given acceptance and treated by their parents as if they matter and are important, they begin to think of themselves the same way. They are self-assured but not to the point of being cocky. They genuinely feel that, despite their shortcomings, they are good on the inside, and that most reasonable people will like them and get along with them. They feel that they are valuable to their significant others, and that their contributions to the world around them matter.

Emotional Fulfilment and Intimacy

Children who have had the core emotional need for connection and acceptance met will be able to achieve emotional fulfilment and intimacy as they get older. They will naturally take the position that, *"I expect others to be supportive of me and care about what I need"* because they have been adequately nurtured, guided, and directed, and feel that their parents empathise with them. Children who have been loved, nurtured, guided, and treated with affection will feel a sense of connection and attachment with their parents that is especially reassuring. They will not doubt or second-guess their friends, since they will believe that their friends genuinely like them and that they are likeable. They will feel supported and understood, and not feel neglected. They will feel listened to and empathised with and will in turn be able to do the same with others. Having grown up in a safe and understanding environment, they will more easily feel connected to the world.

Belonging and Affinity

Children who have had the core emotional need for connection and acceptance met have a sense of belonging and affinity. They naturally feel, *"I am similar to most people around me, and I feel that I 'belong' and fit into a group and/or community."* Children who have a circle of friends with whom they have much in common will generally be confident that their friends care for them and that normally they will be included in activities. They will feel as if their friends treat them as equals. They will not feel weird or different (other than the way that all kids feel weird at times) and they will not feel alone.

Emotional Spontaneity and Expressiveness

Children who have had the core emotional need for connection and acceptance met in their lives will have the capacity for emotional spontaneity and expressiveness. They will feel comfortable telling themselves, *"I am free to be me; I feel safe expressing myself and showing my emotions and passions."* When children feel connected and accepted by their parents, they will naturally feel that they are free to be themselves and to act like children. As they grow up seeing people they are close to being spontaneous and having fun, they learn to be the same. Therefore, they will even feel comfortable expressing different types of emotion along with sharing joy and excitement with their parents, without fear of being belittled or ridiculed.

Mastery and Success

Children who have had the core emotional need for connection and acceptance met in their lives are able to develop a sense of mastery and success. They approach challenges with attitudes such as, *"I am fundamentally competent in the areas which I have chosen to master,"* and *"Generally speaking, I am as talented and successful as most of my peers. I can be proud of what I have achieved and I have vision for future success that is not a pipe dream."* These children may or may not be academically gifted, but in the face of adversity, they will not feel like failures; rather, they will have confidence in their own personal strengths.

Disadvantages of Not Meeting this Need

To the extent that parents do not meet the core emotional need for connection and acceptance, their children will be at risk of developing some or all of the following lifetraps: mistrust, defectiveness, emotional deprivation, social isolation, emotional inhibition, and failure.

The Lifetrap of Mistrust / Abuse

The core message of the mistrust lifetrap is, *"I cannot expect others to treat me in a fair, considerate or just manner. I should expect to be hurt (emotionally or even physically), lied to, taken advantage of, and manipulated. Others always have their own agenda."*

Children who are abused or who have witnessed abuse will almost always develop the lifetrap of mistrust. When their caregivers, especially their parents, are not trustworthy, children receive a very damaging message. When the abuse happens repeatedly, children will of necessity stop trusting. They become wary and have a much harder time bonding, making friends, and accepting help. They look for the "agenda" in people and will often read something negative into others' actions and doubt their motives, feeling that others are out to take advantage of them or cause them harm. They are constantly on the alert. They carry pain and mistrust into their adult relationships and interactions, frequently misconstruing others' words. They have a hard time giving the benefit of the doubt, and easily fall into labelling or judging others. As crusaders for justice, they often try to expose others' duplicity, even though there may not be any. They frequently have a low opinion of others, including those who are loving and caring but weak in a "pet" area that they think is very important. People with the lifetrap of mistrust see the world in black and white and think that everyone falls into two categories—those who can be trusted and those who cannot—instead of understanding that people's motives lie somewhere in a range. They tend to give people "tests", but no one knows they are being tested, and of course, eventually, all their friends will fail one of the tests. This lifetrap can also develop from witnessing abuse done to others (see Figures 5.1 and 5.2).

78 ■ Good Enough Parenting

Figure 5.1: The Lifetrap of Mistrust / Abuse (Alastair as a child)

A quick glance at what might have happened to an adult with this lifetrap during childhood:

- The child was abused verbally, physically and/or sexually, by a parent, a relative, a teacher, a classmate, or any combination of the above. (When speaking with someone who is opening up about their abuse for the first time, the listener should be patient and understanding, giving the speaker time to speak in an unhurried environment.)
- The child's siblings fought with him constantly and his parents allowed it and did not protect him.
- There was tension in the child's home; e.g., he witnessed his father abusing his mother.
- The child grew up in an environment where the abuse was not done to him directly, but to others, and he observed the abuse. For example, perhaps a sibling was ill-treated, or the child knew that one of his friends was being abused, or he saw peers in school being bullied by fellow students or abused by teachers.

Connection and Acceptance: What's at Stake? ■ 79

Figure 5.2: The Lifetrap of Mistrust / Abuse (Alastair as an adult)

Exercise: Please refer to the Exasperation Interactions worksheet (Appendix 1) and identify the exasperation interaction(s) in Figure 5.1.

Case Study

When Kathy was younger, her mother was going through a difficult time in her marriage. She expected Kathy to take her side and hate her dad. Kathy kept quiet because her mother would rave and rant if she spoke up. Today, Kathy resents her mother and feels used. Even though she does not outwardly retaliate, she rebels by doing things behind her mother's back just to get even. She has trouble trusting anyone because she feels like people will just use her.

On top of inappropriately telling her daughter her marriage woes, Kathy's mum was very controlling, which caused more exasperation. She is now working on repairing the relationship by backing off, supporting her daughter financially in an overseas university, and making an effort to connect in a healthy way, while Kathy is seeking to grow in her trust.

The Lifetrap of Defectiveness / Shame

The core message of the defectiveness lifetrap is, *"I am not good enough. I am inherently flawed. Anyone who truly knows me could not love me."*

When children hear over and over from their parents (or siblings or teachers) that they are stupid, ugly, good-for-nothing, etc., they start believing it. Do you know smart people who do not think they are intelligent, and attractive people who do not think they are nice-looking? Those ideas did not come out of nowhere—they heard them for many years. People with this lifetrap feel that something is wrong with them—that they are strange, stupid, short, fat, inept, or just plain lousy. They are over-sensitive to their weaknesses, with an unjustified fear of exposing themselves to others. They do not take compliments well, and feel that they do not deserve praise. They get jealous and competitive as well as insecure around those whom they perceive as being better than they are. They make a lot of comparisons, even in common interactions. When their lifetrap is very strong, they become consumed with status and position, and they overvalue success, such as academic or athletic achievement. Even though they may *appear* highly successful, deep down they do not think they have "made it". Because they feel defective, they are

Figure 5.3: The Lifetrap of Defectiveness / Shame (Sharon as a child)

never satisfied with the present state of affairs. Nothing they accomplish makes them feel "good enough". They have not yet learnt to accept themselves, flaws and all, and celebrate their strengths and accomplishments with confidence. Instead, they push themselves all the time, to the point that their closest relationships get hurt along the way. If they happen to have the overcompensation coping style, they will be easily offended, and when they sense a "put-down" coming, they will put the other person down first! They are more concerned about proving they are not defective than they are about meeting the needs of their significant others. They also subconsciously fear that their defectiveness will get exposed and they will be shamed—this lifetrap is rooted in shame (see Figures 5.3 and 5.4).

Exercise: Please refer to the Exasperation Interactions worksheet (Appendix 1) and identify the exasperation interaction(s) in Figure 5.3.

A quick glance at what might have happened to an adult with this lifetrap during childhood:

- The child was compared to others (siblings, relatives, and peers) and felt that her parents were disappointed with her.

Figure 5.4: The Lifetrap of Defectiveness / Shame (Sharon as an adult)

82 ■ Good Enough Parenting

- The child was frequently blamed, possibly unfairly, for mistakes.
- The child was criticised by her parents for being the "black sheep" of the family—for being useless, slow, dumb, clumsy, ugly, stupid, etc.
- The child was not favoured in the family.
- The child's parents constantly talked about their definition of a successful person and how their girl did not make the cut.
- The child always felt that she did not quite measure up (not good enough in studies or in sports, or that she was not pretty enough or talented enough, and so forth).

Case Study

Danna grew up in a home where the atmosphere was full of belittling and constant comparisons of one sibling to another. She would put in hours of work to complete a school project, only to have her dad pick it apart and point out how it was not as good as what he could do. Danna was frequently told that she had no talent and that she was not as smart as her older siblings. She now has a very high defectiveness lifetrap and, not surprisingly, a lack of connection with her whole family. This led Danna to feel that she has to fight for her rights at every chance. Even though her mum has learnt a lot

Figure 5.5: The Lifetrap of Emotional Deprivation (May Lee as a child)

Connection and Acceptance: What's at Stake? ■ 83

and grown in her parenting, Danna, at 20 years old, still feels that life is unfair. She continues to struggle with having a victim mentality at home, in school and with her friends. She throws tantrums, fears that she is inferior to her siblings, and often feels unloved. Danna has shared that she longs for positive recognition. However, she takes no responsibility for her behaviour. She was exasperated growing up, and now she is causing exasperation to her parents.

The Lifetrap of Emotional Deprivation

The core message of the emotional deprivation lifetrap is, *"I cannot expect others to be supportive of me and care about what I need."* Emotional deprivation is about insufficient empathy, nurturing, and/or not receiving guidance and direction.

Children will eventually develop the emotional deprivation lifetrap if they do not feel emotionally close to their parents when they are growing up. This may or may not involve physical separation from their parents, but it definitely involves emotional distance. When children are deprived of love or left to themselves in their formative years, they become angry and lonely.

Figure 5.6: The Lifetrap of Emotional Deprivation (May Lee as an adult)

This will carry over into adulthood, and they will fear that the same thing will happen—that they will never be loved enough. They yearn to be loved but feel that they are neither loved nor understood. They seem to have a bottomless pit—no matter how much love is shown to them, it is never enough to satisfy them. Even in marriage, people with this lifetrap frequently feel lonely and feel that no one is there to have care and concern for them. They might not feel a deep friendship with people even though the other parties feel close. They combat constant feelings of never having enough love (see Figures 5.5 and 5.6).

Exercise: Please refer to the Exasperation Interactions worksheet (Appendix 1) and identify the exasperation interaction(s) in Figure 5.5.

A quick glance at what might have happened to an adult with this lifetrap during childhood:

- The child did not have loving and nurturing parents; there were not many kisses or hugs, and not much physical touch. Although the child's parents were physically there, no one was very warm to her, or remembered and celebrated special days, like birthdays.
- The child's parents were emotionally absent and may have had someone else raise her. She seldom went to them for love and affection, of if she tried, it didn't go well.
- The child's mother had a busy schedule (this lifetrap may have more to do with lack of maternal closeness, rather than paternal), and was focused on her own career or social life and did not have time for the child. She may have been ill and not able to meet the child's needs for a legitimate reason.
- Even when the child did open up to her parents, they did not know how to empathise with her. So, the child grew up feeling like her feelings were not important or understood.
- The child was given material things and vacations, perhaps even spoiled, but she felt that little interest was expressed in her and what was going on in her life.
- When the child had problems, her parents were not there to listen and advise her.

☽ MASTER CLASS ☾

> Megan Fontenot Bliley wrote a letter to her mother, expressing how she felt extremely connected to her parents when she was growing up, including feeling very nurtured and guided. "I remember lots and lots and lots of one on one talks—about my heart (I now understand why), my character, my interests, fears, joys, etc. I remember the talks not just from you, but also from Dad. As I got to the preteen stage, I remember you trying to help me figure out my feelings by asking me lots of questions. Those questions still

> ring in my mind when I am feeling something today and I can't figure out what is wrong. I also remember you supporting me in situations at school, during conflicts, and with standing up for God. That helped me feel like you were connected to my personal world. I have a vivid memory of my first violin recital which you had to miss because you were out of town. You surprised me and gave me a cross that used to be yours so that I could wear it while I performed. I remember wearing it proudly, feeling like I had a piece of you with me...If you had to be absent, you always made an effort to connect in other ways—postcards from your trip, gifts from your travels, and letters left for me to read while you were gone."

Case Study

Bill's parents are committed Christians who always dreamed that he would be as devoted to God as they are. Sadly, his mother's busy lifestyle left little time for affection and closeness. Instead, she constantly nagged him about what he should and should not do, and told him to be a good example. Bill felt that his parents did not try to understand him, and that they withdrew their affection whenever Bill did not comply. He felt they were only interested in him when he was doing the "right thing". He longed to talk deeply with his parents but when he would try, his dad would tell him that he had no time for emotions. Bill felt exasperated by his emotionally depriving and inhibiting parents, and also chafed at the frequent comparisons with his older brother, "Mr. Perfect". Bill craved connection. When he did not get it at home, he searched elsewhere and eventually joined a gang. No more a teen, he does not speak to his parents unless absolutely necessary and rebuffs them when they reach out to him. Needless to say, their relationship is very tense. His parents have been advised to spend time with him to try to begin repairing the connection; they have a long road ahead of them.

The Lifetrap of Social Isolation / Alienation

The core message of the social isolation lifetrap is, *"I am different from other people and do not fit in."* The feelings of isolation and being alone stem from feeling apart from any group or community, and too different to belong.

Children who develop this lifetrap feel different from other people and feel that they do not fit in. They may avoid social gatherings because they do not like to mix with others, and if they do join, they feel out of place. They may even feel singled out since they *feel* that they are different and not part of the group. What makes them feel different is not necessarily negative; they may be more educated, have more money, or come from a highly talented family. Ultimately, when they look at those around them, they feel that they are the odd one out. Adults with this lifetrap focus more on what makes them different and set apart from others than on what they have in common, and

Figure 5.7: The Lifetrap of Social Isolation / Alienation (Chitra as a child)

consequently they end up isolated and lonely. They exaggerate differences between themselves and others rather than focusing on what they have in common with friends, family and colleagues. Although it is related to the lifetrap of defectiveness, it is different from defectiveness. Someone with defectiveness feels inferior on the inside, but people with the social isolation lifetrap feel out of place because of external factors. It is possible to have both (see Figures 5.7 and 5.8).

Exercise: Please refer to the Exasperation Interactions worksheet (Appendix 1) and identify the exasperation interaction(s) in Figure 5.7.

A quick glance at what might have happened to an adult with this lifetrap during childhood:

- The child felt different from others and felt that he did not fit in.
- The child's friends were of a different race, spoke a different language, or were perceived as being more intelligent than he.
- The child's friends may have been way behind him in school or sports or in some talent, which still may have given the child the feeling that he was the odd man out.

Figure 5.8: The Lifetrap of Social Isolation / Alienation (Chitra as an adult)

- The child felt that his family was weird or that something was really wrong with them. This could result from problems in his family, or other factors, real or imagined, including being from a rich and powerful family or being exceedingly gifted at studies or athletics.
- The child's parents were divorced, but his friends' parents were not. Or the child's school friends lived in a nice neighbourhood, but he did not, or the other way round.
- One of the child's parent's jobs resulted in the family having to move a lot so the child felt different from everyone wherever he went.

Case Study

When Cindy's parents go to restaurants, they silently sit in the corner and people-watch. When Cindy was younger, her parents didn't let them mix with friends from church. The children pretty much grew up with their parents at home, alone. The parents had no other friends, nor did they do any fun activities. They went to church but skipped the marriage and parenting classes. Cindy's father seldom spent time with the kids, and usually pursued his own interests. Cindy's parents were very strict about what food the children were allowed to eat; when the kids were young, they were only allowed to eat home-cooked food. Cindy became exasperated by her parents' inhibiting and overprotective ways. She developed the social isolation lifetrap—she does not feel close to kids in church, and struggles to go to the teen class. She is always quiet, not able to mix around or talk with other kids. Her social isolation causes harm at school where she is bullied by classmates. Now she is very stubborn, rebellious, and argues frequently with her mother. What's more, whenever she attends parties, she snatches food aggressively as if afraid there will be none left. Cindy always feels the other teens at church don't like her, and she only feels close to one other child at school.

The Lifetrap of Emotional Inhibition

The core message of the emotional inhibition lifetrap is, *"I should not express myself or show my emotions. I should always be in control."*

When children are not allowed to be themselves, or made to feel that their emotions are wrong, and belittled for feeling excited or joyful or angry, they are at risk for developing the schema of emotional inhibition. These children

Figure 5.9: The Lifetrap of Emotional Inhibition (Amir as a child)

receive a message that it is safer in their family to not stand out or draw attention to themselves. Some children are even made to tiptoe around the house so as not to offend a highly sensitive parent who does not want to be "disturbed". Adults with this lifetrap are often seen by others as having no emotions. They value being rational as a superior disposition. They do not like anything too loud, too spontaneous, too noisy, or too passionate, though it may not be perceived as such by their spouses or other people. They see such behaviour as being ill-mannered, inappropriate, and very much out of place.

In some cases, people from upper middle class backgrounds have been brought up to think this way. In other cases, it may be a cultural issue, associated with ethnicity. Certain societies tend to feel that emotions should be contained; in fact, they are not to be shown. This becomes damaging because even intimacy has to be "appropriate". Any emotion or opinion forthcoming is viewed as being too aggressive. People with this lifetrap struggle to get intimate and are usually unaware of the lack of connection felt by their loved ones. It is difficult for them to share what is heartfelt. What lurks beneath the surface is fear of shame if they were to let out their

Figure 5.10: The Lifetrap of Emotional Inhibition (Amir as an adult)

true feelings or emotions. People with the lifetrap of emotional inhibition are tempted to think that it is weird to laugh loudly, cry, or express affection because they were looked down upon for being expressive when they were younger. As adults, they have learned to hold things in, rather than seeing emotional expression as being healthy (see Figures 5.9 and 5.10).

Exercise: Please refer to the Exasperation Interactions worksheet (Appendix 1) and identify the exasperation interaction(s) in Figure 5.9.

A quick glance at what might have happened to an adult with this lifetrap during childhood:

- The child's parents hardly talked when they were at home, even when they were having a meal together.
- One or both of the child's parents looked down on him or his siblings for displaying emotions.
- The child's parents believed in the old sayings, "Children are to be seen and not heard" and "Big boys don't cry".
- The child was prevented from being childlike. He had to temper his excitement about normal things and control his emotions so as to not bother his father or mother.
- Noisy, excited behaviour was deemed unacceptable.
- The child had to walk on eggshells when he was in the home. Loud conversations were viewed as shouting.

Case Study

Ever since Sam can remember, his parents chose everything for him. They told him what song to sing in the Christmas concert, what subjects to take in school, and where he should go to college. Sam's parents' overprotective and controlling parenting style led to the core emotional need for connection and acceptance not being met and the development in Sam of the emotional inhibition lifetrap. Sam is very subdued, not only around his parents but also around his peers. He has a very hard time expressing his opinion to anyone. He is friendly, and will say "Yes" to a task or responsibility, but will not always do it. He lacks confidence and defers to others very easily. He gives the proper response but is not in touch with his own emotions.

The Lifetrap of Failure

The core message of the failure lifetrap is, *"I am fundamentally incompetent and have failed, am failing, and will fail again in the future. I am less talented and successful than other people."* The focus of this lifetrap is on achievement and external status symbols of success, rather than on the internal feeling of shame and inferiority that is present in the case of the defectiveness lifetrap.

Some children have a harder time than others in school, which may make them susceptible to developing this schema. Some children may actually excel at many things, but not in the one area their parents value, or they may excel in a field their parents disdain. When these children become adults, they will feel down on themselves compared to their peers. Others may tell them that they have done a great job, but they will not believe it. Instead, they will feel like a failure, in relation to their accomplishments, wealth, status, or academic pursuits. Whatever success they have managed to achieve they will attribute to luck. They will believe that the people giving them encouragement are mistaken. People with this lifetrap believe they have failed and are destined to fail, and often do not try very hard to succeed. They make unfair comparisons with others about where they are in life. Some people will not be as successful as others financially, and everyone has limitations in some areas. In fact, it is good for people to be sober about where they are, but people with this lifetrap need to not go to the other extreme (see Figures 5.11 and 5.12).

A quick glance at what might have happened to an adult with this lifetrap during childhood:

- The child's parents emphasized success in something that was not her strength. For example, they (or society at large) may have focused on the sciences, but she may have been good at the arts.
- When the child did not succeed, her parents (or other authority figures) were harsh with their criticism and called her a failure.
- The child's parents focused attention on what she could not do, and not on the ways she achieved success.
- The child did not receive much encouragement from her parents about her strengths, and was constantly trying to get their attention.
- The child's parents compared her with siblings or cousins or she may have heard how much they bragged about them but not about her, so she lost motivation to give her best.
- Friends, teachers or peers looked down on the child due to racism or other reasons, and she may have believed them.

Exercise: Please refer to the Exasperation Interactions worksheet (Appendix 1) and identify the exasperation interaction(s) in Figure 5.11

Case Study

Martina is from a very pessimistic family. Her father doubts her ability to achieve success every time she tries to do anything. Martina is a responsible eldest child. She is quite determined to excel in school but the family environment has been one in which there was no encouragement. Her parents are particularly negative about projects she attempts. Her efforts are never encouraged. Both of her parents frequently and repeatedly warn her that she better not be hopeful as she will probably fail. Martina has very little confidence about what she can do even though she tries very hard. She is

Figure 5.11: The Lifetrap of Failure (Gunther as a child)

down on herself and does not know how to accept compliments since she finds it hard to believe that others would love and accept her. A teen mentor from the church she attends is trying to help her with these issues.

Basic Safety

Basic safety for this core need revolves around protecting your children from abuse for many reasons, including to avoid the development of the mistrust lifetrap. Children need to be protected from all kinds of abuse—emotional, physical, sexual, and the abuse of neglect.

Having counselled hundreds of people who have experienced emotional abuse, some of them discussed in these pages, we find that it is just as harmful if not more so than physical abuse. Having said that, there is absolutely no excuse for physical abuse. It is illegal and in most countries will either land the parent in jail or warrant the child being removed from the home altogether. Neglect is another kind of abuse. In the United States, parents who neglect their children out of ignorance or because of extreme

Figure 5.12: The Lifetrap of Failure (Gunther as an adult)

poverty, addiction, criminal activity, or any other reason make up the largest number of abusers, estimated to be as high as 78% of all reported cases.[1] Physical abuse is rampant, and sexual abuse continues to threaten children around the globe. In America, one out of every four girls, and one out of every six boys will be sexually abused by their eighteenth birthday. Affecting all races, cultures, religions, and socioeconomic groups, sexual abuse is a scourge of our modern world.[2]

It is a given that parents should not abuse their children. Meet the core emotional needs and you will not! In addition, in order to provide basic safety, parents must also ensure that their kids are not abused by others. This involves monitoring your children's moods when they play with others and when they come home from school, along with getting to know your children's friends and being involved at school. Specific signs of sexual abuse can be difficulty while walking or sitting, genital pain, excessive aggression, seductiveness, early sexualisation, difficulty in eating and sleeping, crying and feeling sad to the extreme, and avoiding communication with others.

Don't forget to protect your child from sexual abuse on the Internet. (This will be discussed more in Chapter Thirteen.) Also, pay attention when someone shows greater than normal interest in your child. Adults should be attentive and caring towards kids, but not overly attentive, so beware. Parents can help by being active in prevention services like public education activities, family support programs, parent education classes, or classes held in local places of worship.

⟨ RESEARCH REVEALS ⟩

RR5.1: *Dealing with Sexual Abuse*

Do not be angry with your child or even surprised if they do not talk to you when they have been abused. The US-based National Center for Victims of Crime reports that there are many reasons why children are hesitant to disclose instances of abuse:[3]

Child Sexual Abuse Reporting

Children may *resist* reporting sexual abuse because they are afraid of angering the offender, they blame themselves for the abuse, or they feel guilty and ashamed. Children are *more likely to reveal* sexual abuse when talking to someone who appears to "already know" and is not judgmental, critical or threatening. They also tend to disclose when they believe continuation of the abuse will be unbearable, they are physically injured, *or when they receive sexual abuse prevention information.* Other reasons may be to protect another child or if pregnancy is a threat.[4]

Once a child discloses the abuse, an appropriate response is extremely important to the child's healing process. The adult being confided in should encourage the victim to talk freely, reassure the child that he or she is not to blame, and seek medical and psychological assistance. Family members may also benefit from mental health services.

Adult Survivors of Child Sexual Abuse

Survivors of child sexual abuse use coping mechanisms to deal with the horror of the abuse. One such mechanism known as protective denial entails repressing some or all of the abuse. This may cause significant memory gaps that can last months or even years. Victims also use dissociative coping mechanisms, such as becoming numb, to distance themselves from the psychological and physiological responses to the abuse. They may also turn to substance abuse, self-mutilation and eating disorders. In order to recover, adult survivors must adopt positive coping behaviours, forgive themselves, and relinquish their identities as survivors.[5] The healing process can begin when the survivor acknowledges the abuse. When working with adult survivors of child sexual abuse, therapists should consider the survivor's feeling of security and the personal and professional ramifications of disclosure, especially if the abuse involved a family member.

Societal influences play a big role in the recovery process. Although males may have been raised to "be tough" and shoulder responsibility for whatever happens to them, male victims need to understand that the victimization was not their fault. Only then can they begin to accept that they were not responsible for the abuse.[6]

Cycle of Violence

Children who are abused or neglected are more likely to become criminal offenders as adults. A National Institute of Justice study found "that childhood abuse increased the odds of future delinquency and adult criminality overall by 40 percent".[7] Child sexual abuse victims are also at risk of becoming ensnared in this cycle of violence. One expert estimates that 40% of sexual abusers were sexually abused as children. In addition, victims of child sexual abuse are almost 30 times more likely than non-victims to be arrested for prostitution as adults.[8] Some victims become sexual abusers or prostitutes because they have a difficult time relating to others except on sexual terms.

Stopping the Cycle of Violence

With early detection and appropriate treatment, society can prevent some victimized children from becoming adult perpetrators. Parents must be on the alert, since abuse occurs at every socioeconomic level across ethnic and cultural lines within all religions and at all levels of education. Most importantly, **in order to intervene early in abuse,** parents should educate their children about appropriate sexual behaviour and how to feel comfortable saying "No".[9]

According to the US based National Child Abuse Statistics in Childhelp, founded in 1959 by Sara O'Meara and Yvonne Fedderson:[10]

- A report of child abuse is filed every ten seconds.
- More than five children die every day as a result of child abuse.[11]
- Approximately 80% of children that die from abuse are under the age of four.[12]
- It is estimated that 50 to 60% of child fatalities due to maltreatment are not recorded as such on death certificates.[13]
- More than 90% of juvenile sexual abuse victims know their perpetrator in some way.[14]
- About 30% of abused and neglected children will later abuse their own children, continuing the horrible cycle of abuse.[15]
- About 80% of 21 year olds who were abused as children met the criteria for at least one psychological disorder.[16]
- The estimated cost of child abuse and neglect in the United States for 2008 was $124 billion.[17]
- 14% of all men in prison in the USA were abused as children.[18]
- 36% of all women in prison were abused as children.[19]

- A child who experiences child abuse and neglect is 59% more likely to be arrested as a juvenile, 28% more likely to be arrested as an adult, and 30% more likely to commit violent crime.[20]
- Abused children are 25% more likely to experience teen pregnancy.[21]
- Abused teens are less likely to practice safe sex, putting them at greater risk for STDs.[22]
- One-third to two-thirds of child maltreatment cases involve substance abuse to some degree.[23]
- Children whose parents abuse alcohol and other drugs are three times more likely to be abused and more than four times more likely to be neglected than children from non-abusing families.[24]
- As many as two-thirds of the people in treatment for drug abuse reported being abused or neglected as children.[25]

We highly recommend the four-book series by Stan and Brenna Jones called *God's Design for Sex*.[26] These books are for different ages and are to be read with the children up until ten or eleven years old. The final book in the series is for teens to read on their own. This series is excellent. We were fortunate to discover them when our kids were five and three. We followed this series to the letter and found that it led to deep and extremely helpful discussions with our children. The authors also have a parents' manual called *How and When to Tell Your Kids About Sex: A Lifelong Approach to Shaping Your Child's Sexual Character*.[27]

◁ LOUIS LOWDOWN ▷

We informed our kids early on about "private parts", and how those parts were special, "just for you and one day just for your spouse", "no one, outside of Mummy and Daddy giving you a bath, is supposed to see or touch them". We explained how they should tell us if that happened and not be ashamed. We celebrated God's creation—we didn't want them to be ashamed of sex or of their bodies, but we did want them to understand the concept of modesty. We didn't let Sonia wear halter-tops, spaghetti straps or bikinis when she was young because we didn't want her wearing those when she was older, and we wanted to be consistent. We would ask the kids in a very nonchalant way every so often if anyone had tried to touch their private parts, not wanting to freak them out but wanting to provide protection. And we were careful about who spent time with the kids when we were not around, although in hindsight, we should have been more careful. Over the last ten years, we have heard many stories of children being sexually molested by neighbours, relatives, and kids at school. These stories may have caused us to be a bit hyper-vigilant, but these days, it's better to be safe than sorry.

◇ THE CORE EMOTIONAL NEED FOR CONNECTION ◇
AND ACCEPTANCE AMONG THE PATRIARCHS

Now that we have examined the advantages of meeting the core emotional need of connection and acceptance, as well as the dangers that come from not meeting this need, let us study out how the core emotional need of connection and acceptance was not met in the family of the patriarchs in Genesis 25:19-34.

Questions for Discussion

- What were the strengths and weaknesses of both Esau and Jacob?
- In Genesis 25:28, how much do you think that favouritism from the parents by Isaac and Rebekah on Esau and Jacob, respectively, affected the relationship between the two sons?
- How did Esau feel about looking so "red"? Did he feel accepted by Rebekah, or perhaps flawed in the inside? Did he feel like he "fit in"?
- How did Jacob feel not being able to match up to his brother's hunting skills and adventurous spirit? Did he feel accepted by Isaac, or perhaps flawed inside?
- How much was the subject of the blessing to the eldest son, or birthright, discussed and talked about among the two brothers when they were growing up?
- Considering Jacob's relationship with Isaac, which of Jacob's core needs were probably not met by his dad?
- How may this have affected Jacob as a teenager growing up, and later on as an adult?
- Considering Esau's relationship with Rebekah, which of Esau's core needs were probably not met?
- How may this have affected Esau as a teenager growing up and later on as an adult?

Insights

While not stated explicitly in the text, it appears to us that this family had a problem with favouritism: it sure looks as if Isaac gravitated towards Esau while Rebekah gravitated towards Jacob. One can only imagine the relationships among the four family members. How much connection and acceptance did Jacob receive from Isaac? Likewise, how much of this did Esau receive from Rebekah?

It can also be speculated that if Isaac and Rebekah had been better partners in raising their children together, they may have been able to help each other be more connected to the child with whom they weren't naturally close. Rebekah might have been able to help Isaac be more connected with Jacob by encouraging them to go out hunting together. Jacob may not have turned out to be as skilful as Esau in this area, but their relationship would have likely been in a better place. If Isaac had continually reassured Jacob that he would also be blessed although he was the younger of the twins, maybe Jacob would not have been so competitive with Esau, especially to the point of resorting to scheming and trickery in order to deceive his brother. Likewise, if Isaac had helped Rebekah to connect with and accept Esau, there is a very good chance that the relationship between mother and elder son would have been healthier. In the parenting of their children, one parent could have observed and given valuable feedback on how the other parent was being perceived by the children and vice versa. As partners, both of them could have worked together to help meet their twins' core needs for connection and acceptance better. This would have had a profound impact on both parent-child relationships growing up.

As a result of favouritism, each of the sons developed his own skewed rationale, his own damaged "world view". And since Rebekah was a shrewd woman, if she had had a decent relationship with Esau, she probably could have influenced him to not marry the Hittite women (Genesis 26:34-35). She could have balanced out Isaac's parenting, who alone seemed to influence Esau. Instead, Isaac was practically Esau's only parent, and Isaac had a blind spot with his favourite son! It seems sad that growing up, Esau probably did not feel that he was special in the eyes of his mum. Did Esau ever feel that Rebekah was proud of him? Did Rebekah tell Esau what she liked about him? Did Rebekah miss Esau when he was gone hunting for several days? When he came back, was it perhaps business as usual? Did she celebrate when he had a good hunt? Was Isaac the only one to provide encouragement?

Since Isaac comes across as having been a bit unperceptive, he may not have been able to see trouble coming until it was too late. It is evident that, even though Isaac was godly, he was not able to pass his godliness down to his son. What got passed down to Esau instead was this lack of perception, since he only learned that his mum was not happy with the Hittite women *after* he married them (Genesis 28:8). So much for Isaac and Esau having a good father and son talk about the important things in life. Assuming that Isaac did not make it a priority, or maybe never even spoke to talk to Esau about who he should marry (maybe he never even talked to him about it at all), then how many deep talks about other subjects did he and Esau have? Did Esau feel guided by his parents? There is little evidence of that, other than in the matter of hunting. Needs were not met, and it is obvious that favouritism was not helpful to their family!

Jacob, on the other hand, felt distant from Isaac. Did Isaac miss Jacob when Isaac was away with Esau? Again, it is hard to picture that this actually was the case. The subject of the birthright must have been very predominant because as soon as Jacob had a chance to have Esau pass it down to him, he seized it. Jacob must have felt a bit cheated, being labelled the second born even though he was born only minutes apart from Esau. It is very conceivable that Jacob never felt accepted by Isaac and that his skills were unappreciated by him. For example, did Jacob feel that what he did around the tent as a boy was valuable in Isaac's eyes? Did he feel like he was developing a useful skill, or did he feel useless? Did he feel accepted and valued as the second born? It is likely that he felt looked down upon by Isaac as being a "Mummy's boy". There may have been subtle or not so subtle belittling interactions between them. One can imagine how these kind of messages could have come up in casual conversations when they were all at home. A little here, a little there and eventually the children's mind sets about themselves slowly were altered.

On the other hand, Rebekah was enmeshed with Jacob. They hung out in the home together. She taugh skills in relation to managing the home, from cooking to cleaning. She probably also discussed with him, as they got closer, how to "steal" the birthright from his older twin.

Esau, likewise, heard from his own mother how inadequate he was. Right from the start she may have labelled him as being an outdoor-type. He was with his dad much of the time and they went out hunting a lot. Imagine if she had understood him at a deep level, perhaps he would have talked about how he felt flawed being so hairy and red looking. Did he feel like he fit in with the community looking like that? If his mother had been empathetic about his issues, this would have helped him a great deal. It seems that Esau was never close to his mother. More and more research is now showing that lack of an early attachment to one's mother even during infancy has serious repercussions as one grows up and eventually becomes an adult. Esau must have suffered from his lack of attachment to his own mother.

What was the level of trust between Esau and his mother? Whenever Esau talked about Jacob, Rebekah must have thought, "I wonder what he is up to? What are Esau's real motives?" His moves were watched because she was protective of Jacob. Imagine how this would have dissipated if Rebekah and Esau and Isaac and Jacob got individual quality time together frequently? How close would they have been as a family? Isaac likewise could have learned to understand Jacob and his less adventurous spirit. They would have been able to communicate that one personality was not necessarily better than the other, but that each of the brothers had strengths and weaknesses and that they could compensate accordingly. But this was not to be. Esau was probably told over and over again about the privilege he had for being the firstborn, and from this, he knew he had an advantage over his younger brother. There was probably much bragging and gradually the rivalry grew between the two. All of such opportunities for brotherly love and mutual respect got lost in the midst of the rivalry and mistrust.

In the end, both of them heard how special they were, but only from one parent. They also heard the opposite. While they felt encouraged by the positive feelings from the parent that favoured them, they felt the opposite from the other. Both of them could also tell that their parents were not united in their views, and this would have deepened their hurts and affected their relationship even more. Did this unfairness get addressed? Did Jacob receive any blessing from Isaac? Did Esau receive anything from Rebekah?

Favouritism also blocks effective communication at the heart level. It prevents people from being vulnerable with each other about their feelings when they feel disliked, or that they have fallen out of favour. For this patriarch's family, much was lost in the early years. They lost out on what might have been fantastic times together. They could have had so many great memories together as a family. Each of the sons could have turned out much more well-rounded if they had tapped into the strengths of both of their parents. In the end, favouritism blocked Isaac and Rebekah from meeting the core emotional need for connection and acceptance in Jacob and Esau. At most, they got it from one parent only. Favouritism breeds jealously and results in arguments with and resentments toward our siblings, which in turn, creates scars and gets carried into adulthood.

How DO

we connect?

CHAPTER SIX

Quality Time Takes Time

> **◆ MOVIE MOMENT** – *Divine Secrets of the Ya-Ya Sisterhood*[1] **◆**
>
> In this movie, Sandra Bullock's character and her father's character, played by James Garner, are having a meaningful discussion about their relationship with the woman who is her mother and his wife. She asks him, "Daddy, did you get loved enough?" He replies with a wry smile, "What's enough?" Then he gently looks into her eyes and asks, "My question is, 'Did you?'" The daughter's eyes fill slowly with tears. She silently shrugs her shoulders as if to say, "I don't know, Daddy, I don't know…" He holds her lovingly and says, "It's never too late." The comforting embrace lasts for a few more seconds, and then they walk hand in hand back to the house. All parents invariably make mistakes and come up short, but we hope that by explaining how to meet the core emotional need for connection and acceptance, our children in adulthood will feel they were "loved enough" and we can take advantage of "never too late" to do any needed repair.

So here is the first all-important practical step in order to meet the core emotional need of connection and acceptance: Spend time with your children!

Commit to a Regular One-on-One Time with Each Child

One way parents can spend more time with their children is to commit to a regular one-on-one time with each child. Most parents do not have a scheduled alone time with each child. Their interactions tend to happen on an *ad hoc* basis, i.e., when they go shopping, when they are on a holiday together, when they are driving together after school, and other such times. While these are all great times to talk, and while these times have tremendous value in themselves, we believe that most children need more. When parents go the extra mile to set aside one-on-one time for each child, the child receives a loud and clear message, "You are more important to me than anything else right now. You have value and are worth my time." The busier the parents are, the stronger this message comes across to the children. Children know how busy their parents are. Children themselves are also busier than they have ever been, considering the pressure to perform academically and athletically, but that is for a later chapter! Suffice it to say, children understand what it means to be busy. And they absolutely know what their parents value and what they make time for. So, when a parent sets aside individual time to spend with each child, it has a great impact.

❧ LOUIS LOWDOWN ❧

Here are four of my (John) favourite stories about my regular time with Sonia and David. Sonia and I had been having "dates" together off and on ever since she was in primary school, which usually consisted of me taking Sonia to a mall for a "bubble tea" or something like that. One day I asked Sonia what she wanted to do and my nine year old daughter replied, "Draw." "Draw?" I repeated back to her in a panic, "I can't draw!" Karen smiled at us and said, "You asked! Here are the coloured pencils…" When I inquired about what we would be drawing, Sonia replied, "Come here, Daddy. Sit on the balcony with me, and let's draw what we see." I was in uncharted waters, but that didn't matter. My daughter thoroughly enjoyed herself, and it moved us just that much closer in our connection.

The next memory happened several years later. I had allowed myself to get too busy with things and neglected our weekly time for a few months. I tried to "reboot", and put the suggestion to Sonia, but she didn't see the need to pick up where we left off! "I want to be close to you", I pleaded but she replied, "We are already close." Then I bribed her by offering to take her to her favourite café, Secret Recipe, and told her she could order whatever she wanted. That did the trick. I listened to the latest updates on her friends, and what was important to her at that time. The next week, I brought her to a CD shop where we shared headphones and listened to her favourite music; this helped me to get further into her world. I don't know what kind of impression it made, but I remember trying, and in the end, we got our routine back and reconnected.

When Sonia was in high school, we changed our regular time to be early in the morning before school. I had to wake up earlier, but it was worth it. Sonia and I had many short talks, about half an hour to forty minutes. Conversations were sometimes light hearted, but many times, she would open up about how she was feeling. Then we would say a prayer and off she went to school. It didn't take much time, but our connection became very deep.

When David and I spend time together, we call it "our time" rather than a "date"—it's a guy thing. David and I try to go out for breakfast together once a week before school, and we enjoy praying together. However, our real connection is when we play badminton, which is a very competitive sport in Southeast Asia. In the past few years, David and I have played roughly every other week. Somehow when we are both covered in sweat, after getting out all of that aggression through sports, we have the deepest talks! Sins get confessed, attitudes get resolved, dreams get divulged—there is a real connection. I wouldn't trade those times for anything, and I pray we will always stay connected.

Commit to Regular Gatherings around the Table

The Putting Family First community polled a nationwide sample of American teens in the year 2000. *In a surprising discovery, 21% of the teens rated not having enough time together with their parents as one of their top two concerns.*[2] They also found that from 1981 to 1997, American families had dinner together less often, spent less time talking as a family, took fewer vacations together, and participated together in religious observances less often. By the end of the twentieth century, fewer than one third of US families were eating dinner together regularly, which is too bad, since having more meal times together is the single strongest predictor of better achievement scores and fewer behavioural problems (see next two Research Reveals).

❖ **RESEARCH REVEALS** ❖

RR6.1: *Important Aspects of Family Time*

The report published in 2008 by the US-based Society for Research in Child Development, authored by Barbara Fiese and Marlene Schwartz,[3] suggests that infrequency of family mealtimes, a negative climate during shared mealtimes, and poor quality food choices are related to children's health issues such as depression, worry, fear, self-injury, social withdrawal and poor academic achievement.[4] Specifically regarding regular family dinners and nutrition, the two wrote:

> A medical study of children ages nine to fourteen found that children who have more regular dinners with their families and have more healthful dietary patterns, including more fruits and vegetables and less saturated and trans fat, fried food and soda, have better mental health and are less likely to suffer from pediatric obesity. (Findings held up after statistical controls for household income, maternal employment, body mass index, physical activity, and other factors.)[5]

The report also stated that conflicting schedules is the number one reason for not sharing a meal.[6] Another study found that on days when adults felt hassled and stressed, they consumed more high fat/sugary snacks and spent fewer minutes having regular meals.[7] Given that more households are now two income households, less time is available to plan and cook healthy meals. Since meals at home are lower in calories and fat than meals in restaurants, the nutritional value of family meals has degraded.[8] For example, kids' menus usually offer hamburgers, hot dogs, grilled cheese sandwiches, deep-fried meat dishes and sugar heavy desserts.

The environment of the mealtime is also a predictor of a child's well-being, the report said. The absence of television is significantly related to the child's well-being. When the family comes together at the table, there should be a certain expectation to serve, listen and give to each other, not just to eat. Families that communicate in a considerate, direct, and clear manner during

> mealtimes are also less likely to have children with internalizing symptoms, such as depression, worry, fear, self-injury, and social withdrawal.[9]
>
> Finally the report revealed that parents giving attention to their children, responding to questions from their children, and keeping everyone's behaviour at the table well regulated is associated with enriched language development and academic achievement.[10] However, if either parent employs one or more of the various exasperation interactions, then the mealtime will serve as an example of an unhealthy parenting experience for their children, i.e. the process will backfire.

Since almost half of US families reported having a TV in their dining area, parents should note that researchers found watching television during mealtimes is *not* helpful for overall family well-being. One reason is that some families turn their television on as a way to avoid further conflict in the family.[11] Another reason is that eating in front of the television is associated with significantly greater caloric intake in children and adults, partly because food ads cue eating behaviour.[12] The most obvious reason is that television impairs connection between family members. We strongly recommend that family members share their highs and lows during mealtimes, be attentive to one another and not be distracted by media.

All in all, good enough parents should take meal times seriously and not abandon the ritual to gather around the table as a family. For most families, no other shared activity is done with such regularity as a family meal. If a family spends a mere 20 minutes together during dinnertime, for example, then in a given week, that's more than two hours, with no agenda besides fun, (healthy) food, and fellowship. Such regular connection building leads to many positive benefits for all family members, particularly the children. Can't do it every night? Shoot for five nights a week. We are pretty insistent on this whenever we do marriage and family counselling or workshops, without apologies.

◁ RESEARCH REVEALS ▷

> **RR6.2:** *Decline in Time Spent between Parents and Children*
>
> Take a look at the general trend of the amount of time between parents and children over the years in America, which is probably also the case in many first world nations. These findings are taken from a wonderful website resource for parents called "Putting Family First"[13] (http://www.puttingfamilyfirst.org), which was created by William Doherty and Barbara Carlson. In a detailed article highlighting some very important trends related to the lack of connection that is all too common in America in recent years, the authors note the following:[14]

(Findings from national time diary surveys conducted in 1981 and 1997 by the Survey Research Center at the University of Michigan.[15] All findings reported below are from this study unless otherwise footnoted.)
1. A major decline in the free time of children ages three to twelve between 1981 and 1997.
   - Free time: A decline of twelve hours per week in overall free time for children
   - Play time: Decreased by three hours per week (a 25% drop from about sixteen hours to about thirteen hours for the whole group—less than nine hours per week for older children)
   - Unstructured outdoor activities: Fell by 50% (includes activities such as walking, hiking or camping).
2. A decline in family and religious participation time.
   - Household conversations: Dropped by 100%, which means that in 1997 the average American family spent no time per week when talking *altogether* as a family was the primary activity. (The 1981 baseline was already low.) Overall, children in 1997 averaged about 45 minutes per week in conversation with *anyone* in the family, when the conversation was the primary activity.
   - Family mealtime: Declined by nearly an hour per week from 1981 to 1997, from about nine hours per week to about eight hours per week.
   - Family dinners: A 33% decrease over three decades in families who say they have dinner regularly. (This finding is from repeated annual surveys of American families.[16] In a 1995 national poll, only one-third of U.S. families said they "usually have their evening meal together on a daily basis.")[17]
   - Vacations: A 28% decrease over the past twenty years in the number of families taking a vacation (from annual surveys of American families).[18]
   - Religious participation: A decline of 40% in hours per week in children's (ages three to twelve) religious participation time from 1981 to 1997[19]; and a decline of 24% of high school students with weekly religious attendance (from 40% in 1981 to 31% in 1997, based on annual surveys of high school students).[20]
3. A major increase from 1981 to 1997 in children's time spent on:
   - Structured sports: Doubled from 2 hours and 20 minutes per week to 5 hours and 17 minutes per week. Boys and girls increased equally in structured sports time, but boys still spent twice as much time as girls in sports.
   - Passive, spectator leisure (not counting television or other forms of "screen time"): A fivefold increase from a half hour per week to over three hours per week. This includes watching siblings play structured sports.

- Studying: Increased by almost 50% from 1981 to 1997.

The same research also highlighted the value of family time in raising well-adjusted children, which is shown below:

- Mealtime: More mealtimes at home was the single strongest predictor of better achievement scores and fewer behavioural problems. Regular mealtimes were far more powerful than time spent in school or studying, at church, playing sports, and doing art activities. Results were statistically controlled for age and gender of child, race and ethnicity, education and age of the head of the family, family structure and employment, income, and family size.[21]
- Regular family dinners and teen adjustment: The largest ever federally funded study of American teenagers found a strong association between regular family meals (five or more dinners per week with a parent) and academic success and psychological adjustment, as well as lower rates of alcohol use, drug use, early sexual behaviour, and suicidal risk. (After controlling for social class factors, results held for both one parent and two parent families.)[22]
- Teens' concerns: In a national YMCA poll of a representative sample of American teens in 2000, 21% rated "not having enough time together with parents" as one of their top two concerns. (The other was "educational worries".)[23]

We can see from the studies mentioned in the Research Reveals section above that lack of time spent with our children has a detrimental effect on our children's emotional and intellectual well-being. It is ironic that parents from affluent societies push their children to be accepted into the best schools, require their children to attend extra classes, sign them up for rigorous competitive sports, not to mention extracurricular activities such as art, music, dance, debate, and acting, while neglecting that which is most important—spending time! It is no wonder that children today do not have much time to connect with their parents. Many of these affluent parents travel for work or are consumed with work, and are not available to the family. They are considered successful in society but they have little or no connection with their children, which begs the question, "Are they *really* successful?" Interestingly, after we began writing this book, we found a book which actually has the title, *The Price of Privilege: How Parental Pressure and Material Advantage Are Creating a Generation of Disconnected and Unhappy Kids.*[24] We read it, but we did not need to read it to know we would agree with it!

Hasn't our society got this backwards? When social scientists study our cities a thousand years from now and examine the post World War II era, will they think, "That's weird. Wonder why they didn't do anything to stop the decline? Wasn't it obvious that a lack of parenting was causing it?" Imagine the well-being of a nation if it were largely made up of emotionally healthy families with high quality relationships between husbands and wives, parents and children—in the long run, families would be happier, economies would improve and nations would turn around for the better, as several studies have indicated.[25] The unrelenting standards of societies, seen both in affluent nations as well as developing ones, are driving parents to push themselves and their children with one devastating consequence: Poor parent-child, marriage and family connection! The stakes are so high—future generations are depending on us to get this right!

By the way, we are not saying that getting involved in sports or being concerned with academic success is wrong *per se,* but when it is done at the expense of the parent-child connection, it is harmful to the family. There is no substitute for spending undivided time connecting and talking with our kids. Their emotional health depends on it.

In counselling sessions, when we highlight a need for family time, some parents say they are not into quantity but rather quality time; that it's not how *much* time they spend with their child, but what they *do* with them that counts. Not really. Quantity is part of quality when it comes to our children. When no structured time is set aside for family interactions and one-on-one time between parent and child, we believe that children will internalize the message that they are of little worth.

⟨ MASTER CLASS ⟩

When Bill and Sally Hooper asked their kids what they remembered about their parenting, their daughter Leigh Ann replied, "Presence—they were available. Mom was home every day when we returned home from school. We had family dinners, family nights and family vacations. Dad worked a full-time job, but when he was home, he was present and available for time with each of us."

The Importance of Early Attachment

The way in which a parent connects with a child varies greatly from stage to stage in the child's development. We have included these stages here, with explanations and suggestions about connecting for each. However, before we discuss how to foster connection and acceptance with a child at the infancy stage, we feel it is necessary to give some background information on the subject and history of "attachment formation", which just means how babies get connected to their parents.

While it may be common sense today for parents to be close to their infants, this was not always the case even up to half a century ago. After the Second

World War in England, conventional wisdom was that children were attached to their mothers for two reasons. One was food. The other was "dependency".[26] In other words, the thinking of that day was that if young children were allowed to be too close to their mothers, they would be spoiled. As a result, it was the norm for mothers to not spend "too much time" with their infants. It is hard to believe that this was the mind-set only sixty years ago.

John Bowlby changed this thinking. His study of ethology, psychology and other related fields revealed results that went against mainstream thinking and challenged this view. He hypothesised that infants would experience loss and suffering when separated from their primary caregivers, and as a result of his own observations, put forward the theory of the importance of attachment of infants to mothers from birth. His writings were influential and caused many changes in hospitals and in the childcare practises of his day. Mary Ainsworth was a student of Bowlby and later became his colleague. She studied the nature of infant separation in Uganda and came up with a method of research used for identifying different attachment styles between mothers and infants. In short, Bowlby's findings stressed that children below two and a half years old become secure when they form special attachments to familiar caregivers. These attachments are an indicator of future social behaviour; e.g., interrupted attachment can cause long-term negative effects.[27]

⋖ RESEARCH REVEALS ⋗

RR6.3: *Attachment Research and Connection*

Children between six and 30 months are very likely to form emotional attachments to familiar caregivers, especially if the adults are sensitive and responsive to child communications.

The emotional attachment of young children is shown behaviourally in their preferences for particular familiar people, their tendency to seek proximity to those people (especially in times of distress), and their ability to use familiar adults as a secure base from which to explore the environment.

The formation of emotional attachments contributes to the foundation of later emotional and personality development, and the type of behaviour toward familiar adults shown by toddlers has some continuity with the social behaviours they will show later in life.

Events that interfere with attachment, such as abrupt separation of the toddler from familiar people or the significant inability of caregivers to be sensitive, responsive or consistent in their interactions, have a short-term and possible long-term negative impact on the child's emotional and cognitive life.

Attachment according to Bowlby is defined as, "Lasting psychological connectedness between human beings".[28] This means an affectionate bond or tie between an individual and an attachment figure, usually the parents.

> Such bonds may be reciprocal between two adults, but between a child and a caregiver, these bonds are based on the child's need for safety, security and protection, all of which are paramount in infancy and childhood.[29]
>
> Other research stemming from attachment theory has shown that a child's development is also affected by the quality of earlier bonds and relationships with caregivers.[30] We know from the principles and empirical evidence mentioned earlier in the book that early and later experiences will also shape a person's view of him or herself and that of others. Here are some important broad findings on the importance of early attachment:
>
> - Secure infants are more likely to become socially competent than are insecure ones.[31]
> - Insecure infants are placed at risk of developing future pathology such as mental health issues.[32]
>
> In 1991, the US Department of Health and Human Services posted these findings regarding early attachment between infants and caregivers:[33]
>
> - Children with secure attachments have more basic trust than those whose attachments are insecure and marred by anxiety.
> - Children with secure attachments have more ego resiliency through early and middle childhood, meaning their self-esteem will be healthier, unless they experience significant negative changes. They can also cope with setbacks and recover more quickly.
> - Securely attached children have more flexibility in processing current information and in responding appropriately in new situations and relationships.

According to the research above, children with secure attachments have better self-esteem, are more trusting and more resilient during difficult times, handle relationships better, and are more flexible learners.

Tiffany Field has shown that mothers who are negative and who do not respond to their babies by connecting to them emotionally will end up passing these traits down to their children—even at this age! The infant grows up following suit and becomes depressed as well, with low energy, anger, and irritability. Further, if the mother's depression continues for a year or so, the baby will show lasting delays in growth and development. This highlights the need for parents to guard their own mental wellness.

Children need to learn to relate in an emotional way to a person, and the level of attachment is a powerful motivation for them to learn. Susan Anderson is a professor of psychology and says that when attachment is not satisfactorily achieved, children will become concerned about it; but when it is satisfactorily achieved, then the issue of attachment falls to the background.[34] In other words, when a child is securely attached, he is free to focus on learning and exploring. The child will be eager to explore his new world. Having a healthy connection with the parents, especially the mother at this stage, is crucial. When a child is not securely connected, he ends up getting discouraged and exasperated because his needs are not met. The child then seeks ways to adapt to the mother instead of the other way around. As a result, a false self, as Winnicott calls it, emerges.[35] Later on in life this develops into what we call a coping style. This is also a period when a sense of trust is being built. Elkind says that this sense of trust develops when the primary caregivers are consistent and dependable, which will gradually instil in the child the sense that the world is the same; that it is consistent and dependable and can be trusted. On the other hand, parents who inconsistently spend time with their children, and are always busy with something else, cause their children to not be trusting of the world, and this carries through into their adult lives.[36] We have borrowed from David Elkind, who wrote about the three inborn drives that power human thought and action, and we will refer throughout this book to the concepts of "Connect, Work and Play".[37] To put things simply, having the right balance of connection, work and play helps us on our journey to be good enough parents as we learn to meet the core emotional need of connection and acceptance without neglecting the other core emotional needs.

⸹ RESEARCH REVEALS ⸺

RR6.4: *Elkind's Belief in Play*

In his book *The Power of Play*, Elkind introduces what he says are the three inborn drives that power human thought and action: Love, work and play.[38] We are borrowing this idea from him with one exception. While we agree with him wholeheartedly, we want to replace the word "love" with "connect", simply because the word "love" in the English language is too broad. (Karen loves Indian food, John loves badminton, we love our children, etc.). We feel that "connect" gets the message across better. It also fits squarely with the description of the first core emotional need, and that is "connection and acceptance". Thus, we will refer throughout this book to the concepts of "connect, work and play".

Connection with the parents from infancy is crucial, and it is not something that parents should wait and focus on only after the child is able to talk and reason. Parents must start building the connection right when their children are born. At birth, play and connection are so intertwined that it is hard to separate the two. In fact, every time we play with an infant, we are connecting. Usually when infants are about three months old, parents are able to hold their attention. They use a high-pitched voice and talk slowly and repetitively and this type of tone often gets a response and conveys connection with the baby. The baby now is developing a strong healthy connection with the parents.

Connect, Work and Play Through the Ages

The meaning of connection in our book was described earlier (see Chapter Four), the idea being that when children connect with their parents it means that sharing of emotions takes place in both directions; parents to children and children to parents, such that a healthy affectionate bond, and an empathic understanding, develops between the two sides and they both feel positive at an emotional level.

◁ RESEARCH REVEALS ▷

RR6.5: *Connect, Work, Play Defined*

Connect

Connect, in the context of this book, is closely related to the concept of attachment, defined by Bowlby as a "lasting psychological connectedness between human beings".[39] However, most people refer to Bowlby's use of the word attachment as the bond from the child to the parent, rather than the other way round. Even Bowlby, when he first formulated his theory, was more focused on the child's perspective toward the parent. However, when we use the word *Connect*, we want the focus to be bi-directional, from parents to children as well as from children to parents.

Work

For the definition of *Work*, we shall borrow Elkind's, which is: "Our disposition to adapt to the demands of the physical and social worlds".[40] "Play is the work of the child", said Maria Montessori.[41] According to her, you cannot separate these two concepts. They both go hand in hand for a child. Yet parents often think that if children are left to play, they are wasting their time; they should buckle down to "work", for example, learning timetables or memorizing words for a spelling test. Scientists now know that when children play, they are also "working" many parts of their brain, exercising them and stretching them like a muscle. So, in the context of a young child, work is being done when a child engages in an activity that the child likes. As the child get older, work will take on different aspects.

Play

Accoring to Elkind, "play is our need to adapt the world to ourselves and create new learning experiences".[42] Children learn best when they create their own learning experiences, making up rules as they go along either playing with other children or on their own. Enlightened education philosophies reflect this approach in pre-schools, where children are allowed to work on their own, using their own imaginations and creativity. Mostly unstructured, the children are in charge of their own activity, and their teachers direct, facilitate, and observe. This is so different from the structured agenda that many teachers have in kindergartens or childcare centres, standing over

114 ■ Good Enough Parenting

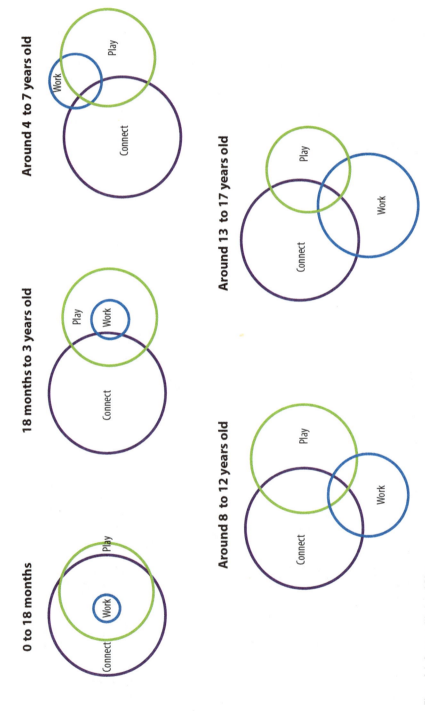

Figure 6.1: Connect, Work and Play

> children during mathematics drills and giving spelling tests at a young age, to the detriment of the youngsters' development.

As Elkind did,[43] we also believe that connect, work and play function together, but in the course of time they become increasingly separate. We would like to build on what Elkind mentioned, and be more specific about the way these three drives evolve with age, as we talk about meeting the core emotional need for connection and acceptance (see Figure 6.1).

Infancy

At the infancy stage (see Figure 6.1: 0 to 18 months), connect and play are dominant. Work is done as the child grows, from his five senses, but nothing intentional. Parents should not stress themselves out reading mathematical equations aloud so that their children will be good at the subject when they get older, or playing classical music for them in the womb to make them into geniuses; those theories have turned out to be more urban legend than good science. From what we could gather, listening to classical music may soothe your baby and turn her into a classical fan later in life, but it won't make her smarter. (Researchers at Appalachian State University believe that they have debunked what has been called the "Mozart effect", i.e., a temporary increase in intelligence experienced after listening to a piano sonata written by the famed composer.[44])

Infants cry in order to get their needs met. They are not being manipulative at this stage; there is no need for discipline. Their cries are for care, and parents need to respond appropriately. Infants are learning to trust the parents; this comes as parents respond to their baby's cries.

When parents are spending time with their infants, they should hold them gently and look at them lovingly. Feeding time can be a special bonding time, since babies are able to respond to facial expressions and even imitate them. How fun when babies smile back—and it's not just gas! Parents can see smiles at around two months and by the second year, sustained joy.

Parents should talk to their babies, describing all they are doing and seeing. This communication helps babies feel nurtured and loved. Mothers should encourage them with a gentle and nurturing voice, which sometimes has to be pitched higher than usual (fathers please take note), as babies respond better to such sounds. This involves lots of affection, such as holding, kissing and cuddling.

And parents should sing to their babies! By all means, play classical music if you enjoy it! Play fun baby sing-a-long songs as well. Any music that promotes a healthy atmosphere is helpful, whether it's Bach, Beatles, Bluegrass, Bollywood, or Brazilian samba! Did you ever hear the old adage,

"You don't sing because you're happy, you're happy because you sing"? I (Karen) find that singing calms me down when I am in stressful situations. How nice for children to be surrounded by song.

We have talked a lot about play. Babies love playing. And certainly babies do not need to work! Young babies, however, can only handle a certain amount of play, and then they will turn their head away and will not be interested anymore. Do not pursue further, since overstimulation may cause distress.

Parents must provide consistent nurturing and care. We recommend that mothers stay at home with their children until the kids begin to attend school, or at the very least stay home with their infants for a year, and ideally, when they must go back to work, get a flexi-hour or part-time job. There are many alternatives. Perhaps the parents can hire temporary help for household chores so that the mother's attention can be devoted to the baby as well as her part-time job, or maybe she can work-at-home, or have a flexi-hour job. Perhaps two couples can live in the same home and share more of the load so that they can save on bills and the mums can be full-time with their babies, or they can help look after each other's infants when the other needs to work. This calls for creativity and flexible thinking. We know that this is not a politically correct recommendation to make, but for the sake of seeing a generation of children whose parents met their need for connection and acceptance, we are willing to stick our necks out and say it.

❖ LOUIS LOWDOWN ❖

Having said that, I (Karen) know some mothers who have no choice but to go back to work full time when their babies are small, and they have mixed emotions. This is not meant to make them feel like second-class mothers. I also know some mothers who are so miserable not working that they do not enjoy staying home and then they bring down the atmosphere in the home. So, if there is such a thing as women's liberation, surely it is that we are liberated to make the best choices we can make for our babies and ourselves and we do not have to do what society or anyone else pressures us to do. Speaking of freedom, in my opinion, it is not very liberating to work outside the home in a full time job, spend an hour commuting and picking up your baby from a childcare centre, come home exhausted from giving your best at work, then do all the housework, laundry and cooking, even if you have a husband who will do half, and have little or no energy or time left to work on connection with one's own children. I benefitted enormously from living in Asia when my children were born. In many countries outside of the US, Britain and Australia, it is not unusual to be able to hire help at a relatively low cost. Since I was working what I would call a flexi-hour job, I spent most of my free time with my babies, but was able to pay someone to do many of the household chores. Maybe I am just weak, but I cannot imagine working as a mother any other way.

Nigel Barber's research on the windows of opportunity in brain development found that emotional security in future close relationships is determined by their first birthday! Parents, this means that you would be giving your child a head start in having good friendships and a great marriage by connecting with them in the first year of their lives! Even more shocking is Barber's finding that intelligence, the kind that is developed while feeling secure, and exploring and bonding with parents (not from rote learning) is determined in the first two years.[45] So rather than spend all that money worrying about how to pay for some supersonic daycare, why not spend two years looking after your baby, giving them meaningful intelligence? You will see the benefits later.

Babies become very attached to their primary caregivers after about six to eight months. (But oddly enough, babies will not have figured out that they are completely separate people until they are around eighteen months old!) If they are crawling, they will enjoy moving away from their parents, empowered by their new skill, but then they will want to come back to when they realise "I'm too far". When that happens, parents should receive their new explorer with open arms and a big smile, "Where did you go just now?" (Of course mothers are actually watching to make sure the babies are fine; the babies just don't know it!) Some parents want to teach autonomy too soon and get angry that the child isn't more independent, and make statements like, "You are big enough" or "Just stay there!" Do not rush—they will get independent soon enough! Parents may also be frustrated when their babies are very clingy. After all, before entering into this stage, babies will usually go to strangers and can be left in the dark without fear, but around eight months or so, they will start showing signs of separation anxiety, such as fear of going to strangers. It is normal. Enjoy this while it lasts—all too soon, babies grow up and the parents are the ones with separation anxiety!

Securely attached babies have mothers who respond quickly to their signals. The need for attachment is a natural part of an infant's development. Mothers should not get irritated at this need. It is normal for mothers to need to leave the baby's room for a while, but being enthusiastic upon returning is important. Many parents do not understand that babies need to *learn* that their parents are dependable and predictable. If parents are unreliable, this makes the baby feel insecure, and this lack of confidence may facilitate the development of lifetraps such as emotional deprivation and abandonment later in life.

Parents should beware of arguing with each other or with their in-laws in front of the baby, thinking the baby is too young to notice. Infancy is the time when pathways of a child's autonomic nervous system are developing (see Chapter One). Gottman says, "Whatever happens to a child emotionally during this first few months may have a significant and lifelong effect on the child's vagal tone; that is the child's ability to regulate the nervous system… which makes a difference in a baby's long term ability to respond to stimuli, to calm herself and recover from stress." [46]

A definite routine for babies is important, especially when it comes to time to sleep. A bedtime ritual is one of the fondest memories for connection that a parent can build with a child. Here are some recommendations that parents can adopt in putting their babies to bed (you will probably experiment with many options but these are some that worked for us).

In keeping with our belief in talking constantly to your baby, parents should begin by telling their baby that it is time to have a bath and go to bed. This gets parents into the habit so that when the child is in the toddler stage, the parents are accustomed to alerting them that bedtime is coming. Parents can give the baby a bath, including brushing their teeth, or rubbing their gums, and get them into their pyjamas, a clean nappy/diaper, and sing lullabies during the final feed, all in a comfortably darkened room and relatively quiet environment. (Of course, with tiny babies, they fall asleep frequently for short spurts of time and it is not really your choice when!) Normally, parents will rock and sing to the baby until the baby is asleep, then they will place the baby into a safe crib with walls so that there is no chance of the baby falling, crawling or jumping out in the middle of the night. With new-borns, it is not uncommon for parents to put their babies to sleep in a bassinette, or a Moses' basket, that is set up in the parents' bed room, which makes night feeds easier and puts parents at ease.

Once a healthy baby is over three months old, it is our opinion that parents can feel comfortable leaving the room even when the baby is awake. As long as the mother is bonding all day long and responding to the child at other times, the baby will not suffer if left to cry himself to sleep. In our opinion, helping babies learn to fall asleep on their own and stay asleep through the night is crucial for four reasons:

- Without it, the baby may not get enough sleep, and will not thrive
- The mother will not get enough sleep, and will not be able to meet her baby's needs properly during the day
- The parents' Love Connection, especially their physical intimacy, will suffer, paving the way for all sorts of other problems
- When babies do sleep on their own and sleep through the night, and when mummies get enough sleep, then mummies are happy and excited to see their babies the next morning—they actually miss them rather than resent them.

In the beginning, most children will cry when left on their own before they go to sleep. Eventually they will come to accept that the separation will be only temporary and that the parent will be there when they wake up. When the mother sees the baby the next morning, it is important that she greet the child enthusiastically to show that separation is only temporary and that mummy can be counted upon to come back. This repeated pattern is important to the child's sense of security.

When the core emotional needs are met adequately during the first stage of life, children will be much less likely to act out in aggressive ways towards other children or to get attention from their parents in order to have their needs met.

All of this takes energy, so we must also share the following—*parents must get help when fatigued*. This is very important to prevent depression, neglect, and abuse.

◁ LOUIS LOWDOWN ▷

When Sonia was about two months old, there were quite a few nights when she slept for ten hours straight—which was a miracle! However, she was only going to sleep at around 3am, and then sleeping until 1pm. I (Karen), on the other hand, was getting completely exhausted, because even though I tried, I couldn't sleep that well in the day. John and I took turns playing with her at night, and, since we had rented out a room to two single friends, even they got in on the midnight fun from time to time. When Sonia was about four months old, after seeking advice from friends who had older children, John and I decided to start adjusting her sleeping habits. Our first goal was to stop her from sleeping in the late afternoon. That took about a week and was not very difficult once we put our minds to it. The second goal was to make sure she went to bed at 8pm, not 3am. This part was harder but still not that difficult, since she had stopped the late nap. The third stage was the hardest—we had been rocking and singing her to sleep, at night, and we decided it was time for her to be put into the crib while not yet asleep, and to go to sleep on her own. This took exactly four days. The first night, we did our bath and lullaby and prayer routine, then said, "Ok sweetie, now Mummy is going to go to sleep in her room, and you are going to stay here. I love you, precious." There was a dim nightlight, her nappy had been changed, she was fed and burped, and intellectually I knew she would be fine. However, when I left the room, she started to wail, and I was imagining her thoughts, a la *Look Who's Talking*, "You guys are leaving me here alone? What in the world? I'm a little baby for crying out loud—get back in here and rock me to sleep! Mummy, Daddy, how can you be so cruel?" John and I sat in bed and had tears running down our faces, but we knew that it was for her best in the long run, so we let her cry for a whole hour. She fell asleep exhausted…I went in at around 5am when I heard the first little peep from her, and I was so happy that she was so happy. The second night we repeated the routine and the wailing only lasted 40 minutes, the third night it lasted 20, and the fourth night, she smiled at me as I left her in the bed and all was well. The last stage of sleep training was when Sonia was seven months old and no longer being breastfed. She would wake up for milk in the middle of the night. By this time I was putting her to sleep around 7pm, then I would get her out of

> bed at 11pm (I was a flexi hour working mum, remember, so I would work after she went to sleep), take off her pyjama bottoms, change her nappy, give her a bottle, sing softly, all of this in a fairly dark and quiet room, and she mostly slept through the whole thing. She would then go back to bed, hardly knowing what happened, and would sleep until 6 or 7am. Amazing! One more trick—when Sonia could comfortably pick up and hold her own bottle, maybe at eight or nine months, I would leave a bottle of milk in her bed at 11pm when I was ready to go to sleep. This milk was made with water at room temperature, not warm, so that it would not go 'off', plus her bedroom was air-conditioned. I no longer had to go through the midnight nappy change, and she would just wake up and drink by herself and then go back to sleep. I know this routine isn't for everyone, and maybe it would not work for all babies, but it worked for both of mine, and made life much easier and I believe the kids had better sleep because of it.

The Toddler Years

Of the three drives, play and connect are still the most dominant (see Figure 6.1: 18 months to 3 years old). Work will start to be introduced, but in small doses, like putting dirty clothes in a hamper, books back in the shelf, etc. The work component is therefore a little bigger than the previous stage. As Elkind said, the more that their work resembles play and is in the form of play, the better it will go down with young children. It is not necessary to expand on the work drive too early. Many societies are pushing children to learn at a younger age than in previous generations, even though much research has shown that this can do more harm than good. Yet parents out of ignorance and fear are frantic about finding the most effective preschools to prepare their children for the future.

On this note, we quote Dr Sharon Kagan, co-director for the US-based National Center for Children and families who works in a leadership capacity on children's issues with Columbia and Yale. She had this to say about sending children to school too soon:

> There is simply no evidence to show that preschool would help very young children more than the care of a loving, dedicated parent. When children are young they need intimacy, they need the nurturing of caring adults, they need to be held. Society doesn't necessarily benefit from having children be required to go to an institution when they are very, very young.[47]

So while there may be a rush to get young children educated and exposed to math and in-depth reading, resist going with the flow. Parents should focus on connecting, not work. And play is the best way for a parent to connect; play and connection go very much hand in hand at this stage.

During these years, parents have virtually all the say and can indeed be directive in areas that include selecting activities, the topics of conversations, kinds of toys, and choices of playgrounds. However, parents need to ensure that the child can be himself, expressing his feelings and thoughts, not just following "rigid" instructions of "yes" and "no". Parents should make full use of the opportunity to interact with their toddlers, and continue talking about surroundings, including colours, numbers, emotions, and so forth.

Kagan also addressed the danger of very young children being given access to technology too soon:

> There needs to be some preparation, but at the age of two or three, that is too young...A child that age needs to first pick up interaction skills, which can happen only if adults actively engage them in conversation.[48]

Erik Erikson, an influential developmental psychologist, said that during this period, a balance has to be struck between a child's sense of autonomy and his sense of shame and doubt.[49] What this means is that when toddlers are curious and ask all kinds of questions, and their parents do not respond, or respond reproachfully, a sense of shame and guilt can result. Kagan says that parents should be careful to ask open-ended questions at this stage instead of closed-ended questions that demand only a yes or no answer. Otherwise children can become reluctant to initiate and can become withdrawn and these traits could be carried on into their adult lives.[50]

Children enjoy make-believe, and a great way to connect with them is by participating in their fantasy play. Kids enjoy making forts and tree houses, playing dress-up, and pretending to be superheroes on their own, but also have fun when parents join in sometimes. (Please note that we are not saying parents have to play for hours on end everyday.)

Fathers, take the initiative. More and more research is now showing how crucial fathers are in the lives of children at this age. While we included a whole chapter on "Fatherhood," later in the book, we feel that when it comes to meeting this core emotional need, we must emphasise the relationship between fathers and play specifically. Here are some important findings on the impact that fathers have on their young children:

- One study that began in 1950 showed that children whose fathers were involved in their lives from the age of five grew up to be more empathetic and compassionate than those whose fathers were absent. The children also ended up having better social relationships and as a result they tended to have better marriages, better relationships with their own kids and were more likely to engage with others in recreational activities later in life.[51]
- In a study published in 1986, conducted by Parke and MacDonald, researchers from California State University and University of Illinois respectively, showed that children who had the best relationships with their

peers were those whose fathers engaged in high levels of physical play and who were affirming verbally. Children whose fathers were authoritarian and critical had the worst peer relationships, regardless of amount of physical play.[52]

Gottman states:

> Many psychologists believe that dad's raucous style of 'horseplay' provides an important avenue for helping children learn about emotions. Imagine a daddy 'scary bear' chasing a delighted toddler across the yard, or lifting and twirling the child over his head for an 'airplane ride'. Such games allow the child to experience the thrill of being just a bit scared, but amused and aroused at the same time...Having roughhoused with dad, the child knows how to read other people's signals when feelings run high. He knows how to generate his own exciting play and react to others in ways that are neither too sedate nor spinning out of control. He knows how to keep his emotions at a level that's optimal for fun-filled play.[53]

In other words, playing fathers build the parent-child connection, improve their children's social skills, and give their kids a work-out!

⟨ MASTER CLASS ⟩

> John and Nancy Mannel's oldest child, Jeff, is an evangelist and presently leads the Greater Saint Louis Church of Christ with his wife Lori. He comments on his parents, who understood the importance of play, "Growing up in our house was fun. I didn't feel our home was stressed or that Mom and Dad felt burdened by life or the responsibilities they had with their secular jobs or with the responsibilities they had in the church."

When spending time with your children at this age, try to really enjoy it, and let go of your inhibitions. The house will get messy but that's ok—connection is getting built! This is a good alternative to electronic gadgets. Avoid prolonged time spent on computers, tablets, etc. Parents in dual income households are usually challenged to find time to engage in rough and tumble activities with their children. In this day and age, many parents buy their kids electronic devices to keep them occupied. Interacting consistently and personally with your children is not something that can be replaced by expensive toys. There really is no substitute. The most important focus at this stage is learning to interact and socialise. Playing on a computer does not particularly help a child to accomplish that. (A wise parent we know said that the best "**soft**ware" for teaching a child how to read is a parent's lap!)

Playing is extra fun if the siblings are close in age, i.e., one to two years apart. However, if the age gap is larger, then some playing may need to be done separately. The kind of activities will determine when they should be combined. Again, at this stage of a child's life, play and connect are the most dominant.

As parents, we sometimes get bored with repetition, but children at this age do not get tired of the same old "hide and seek". It is amazing how much they even like to hide in the same place! Do not get put off by this; see it as part of the makeup of this stage of child development. Here is the challenge: Learn to enjoy it as much as they do! They will be able to read your face and know if you are engaged as much as they are.

If fathers struggle with being competetive, they should remember that this is not a competition. Dads should balance out who wins and loses, occasionally winning to see their reaction, which helps kids learn to be gracious losers. With siblings, take turns and help them all win. Even if one may not be the fastest runner, you as a father can work it out to help the weakest child win. This helps everyone to feel confident and also to feel that playtime is fair.

Parents do not need to spend loads of money on equipment—they can make use of playgrounds in the neighbourhood. Swings, seesaws and slides are tools to help children's emotions go through a roller coaster ride of ups and downs. Fathers should not just leave them to play by themselves; they should get involved, making the play more exciting for the child. When parents play hide and seek, this is a good time to chase, make them feel scared or anxious and then victorious when they win. Experiencing all these emotions, as mentioned earlier, is very helpful for their mental health. Playing computers in their bedroom while parents are reading the newspaper does not bring out these emotions. It takes fathers getting involved and mothers encouraging such activities to ensure that the emotional core need for connection and acceptance is met.

Mothers need to be supportive about fathers roughhousing with the children. Many mothers often caution their husbands about what is or is not safe, which can put an unnecessary damper on the spirit in the home. If the house is too calm, other needs will not be met. Mothers should not overreact when there are small cuts and grazes. When a child falls, the mother's reaction often has a strong influence on the child's reaction. If the child is crying and the parents are calm, this will help the child to take the fall in his or her stride. Do not criticise the child, such as calling on him to be tough. Empathise, but at the same time, do not overreact. Accidents do happen, and in the course of their childhood, there will surely be the occasional split lip, broken arm, or gashed knee. Obviously parents should never be careless, and hopefully nothing serious will take place.

Mothers should find ways to spend enjoyable time with their toddlers—not just feeding or bathing them, but also playing and reading lots of storybooks to them. It is important that they make time for tasks such as putting together simple puzzles with them. Mothers should engage with their children in something that they like. It is tempting for working mothers to use fatigue as an excuse not to play, but if mums only give the leftovers of their energy to their children, then, in the long haul, the children's growth will be affected. We encourage mothers to make sure they are giving the best of their lives to their children and not their bosses. Meeting the core emotional need of connection and acceptance will pay far better dividends than any annual bonus.

Another important aspect of connection with children at this age is related to setting healthy limits. It is hard for children to develop a proper connection with anyone when they are moaning and whining due to lack of sleep. Sticking to regular bedtimes should be taken seriously. Children need to learn that sleeping times are not negotiable. Young children need to be in bed so they can get to sleep by about 7:00 or 8:00 p.m. They need lots of sleep (see Chapter Seventeen about the Basic Safety need for sleep). Boundaries should be drawn here not just for the good of the children, although that is the main reason, but also so that parents can devote time to each other in continuing to build their marriage, entertain, serve at church, keep fit, etc. Over and over again in counselling situations, we find that marriages get compromised because young children have not been trained to go to bed at a certain time. This infringes on the time parents need for each other, and over time this can damage the parents' marriage. A poor quality marriage will end up hurting the children.

Here are some recommendations for putting toddlers to bed:

Parents should give about fifteen minutes' notice to their children that it is time to begin the bedtime ritual, which would include giving them a bath, brushing teeth, and so forth. At this age, they will still enjoy lullabies, but also bedtime stories. Connection is being built when parents enthusiastically and lovingly read stories with lots of pictures and colours. Toddlers will enjoy books about hugs and kisses and falling to sleep, or even pop-up books, and parents should read in a position that enables lots of cuddling and affection. In addition, at 18 months, children may be able to fill in words as parents read along in a picture Bible or book. This kind of repetition is helpful for their cognitive development. Parents can end with a short prayer and say "goodnight" with kisses and cuddles.

Some children love to talk just before they go to bed while some do not, depending on their "unique wiring". Parents should not be too busy and get impatient if their child is a talker and needs some time in order to have healthy closure for their day. It is not helpful for children's emotional security if a parent sends the message that putting them to bed is a nuisance. They will at this stage be deliberately disobedient and difficult in order to get attention from their parent(s). They would rather face the consequences of being disobedient than not having their core emotional needs met, especially of connection and acceptance. They need lots of cuddling, affection and a feeling that they are special, even if they make mistakes.

⟨ LOUIS LOWDOWN ⟩

> From the time they were small, we taught our children to stay in bed and not come out of their rooms after bedtime unless it was really important. This had to be repeated often, and eventually they learned these limits and adhered to them—well, most of the time. This gave us more time for our ministry work, which often included evening appointments. When they were younger, we would put them to bed by 7:00 p.m. By the time they were in primary school, we usually had them to sleep by 8:30 p.m. until third grade; in fourth and fifth grade they were in bed usually by 9:00 or 9:30 p.m. (Bedtimes are a personal preference; see Chapter Seventeen which discusses the need for adequate sleep.) During the spring of 2003, our church held extra small group meetings, and we both needed to be available almost every night for the month of April. I told the kids that I (Karen) needed to move the bedtime routine up by an hour so that I could finish by 8:30 p.m. and get to the special meetings. In this way, I would still be able to read to them and have a chat while putting them to bed. (John and I met with family groups, men and women separately, at two different homes around the city every night at 9 p.m.) We got a trustworthy sitter, and since it was just for a month, the kids were fine with it. By the way, in those days, our reading was quite fun. Except for nights when John told stories, I usually read chapters from The Chronicles of Narnia or the Harry Potter series, and then I would spend time with David for a bit, before going in to talk to Sonia for a while. We still talk about the times that we read the Harry Potter books together!

Early Childhood

At this age, children generally are still more excited to play with their parents than with their peers. Connection and play are still very much a part of the same activity. Work can now be increased, but notice that it sits predominantly within play (see Figure 6.1, 4 to 7 years old). Good Enough Parents will avoid the panicked mind-set to rush their children and cram information, which does more harm than good. Children need to enjoy their childhood. We need to ensure that our children have time for organised play and free form play; both are important for healthy development.

For parents who are worried that playful children will be behind in school, the Prime Minister of Singapore, Lee Hsien Loong, recently voiced his concern about the phenomenon of "over-teaching" a child:

> Instead of growing up balanced and happy, he grows up narrow and neurotic. No homework is not a bad thing. It's good for young children to play, and to learn through play.[54]

Hot on the heels of the Prime Minister's comments, the Singapore paper,

The Straits Times, reprinted an article from *The New York Times*, entitled, "Simon Says Don't Use Flashcards". It reported:

> Parents who want to stimulate their children's brain development often focus on things like early reading, flashcards and language tapes. But a growing body of research suggests that playing certain kinds of childhood games may be the best way to increase a child's ability to do well in school. Variations on old-fashioned games like "Freeze Tag" and "Simon Says" require relatively high levels of executive function, testing a child's ability to pay attention, remember rules and exhibit self-control—qualities that also predict academic success. "Play is one of the most cognitively stimulating things a child can do", says Megan McClelland, an early childhood development researcher at Oregon State University who has led much of the research.[55]

◄ RESEARCH REVEALS ►

RR6.6: *Childhood Games Better Than Flashcards*

Researchers at Oregon State University have found that, rather than focusing on things like tuition classes, flashcards and math drills, playing typical childhood playground games may be the best way to help kids do better in school. A *New York Times* article, entitled "Simon Says Don't Uses Flashcards", states, "Variations on games like Freeze Tag and Simon Says require relatively high levels of executive function, testing a child's ability to pay attention, remember rules, and exhibit self-control—qualities that also predict academic success." Megan McClelland, who has led much of the research, says, "Play is one of the most cognitively stimulating things a child can do." One study of 814 children between three and six showed that "children who do well in Simon Says-like games do better in math and reading. A smaller study of 65 preschool children found that those who started the school year with low levels of self-control showed improvement after playing games in class, including a version of Red Light, Green Light." What makes the Oregon State study so exciting is that it was a longitudinal study that followed 430 subjects from preschool to the age of 25. "It turns out that a child's ability at age 4 to pay attention and complete a task, the very skills learned in game play, were the greatest predictors of whether he or she finished college by age 25."[56]

So parents need to play *with* their children and also facilitate their children having time to play, both free play and organised play.

At this age, children need to be exposed to a variety of activities so they can see if they have a natural flair. They are just starting to develop peer relationships, but usually at this stage these relationships are not strong. Gottman says that usually children at this age play best in pairs with another child,[57] but group play on the playground is also very helpful.

Parents should also take advantage of the fact that these are the years when children will not resist being with their parents. In fact they look forward to playing with the parents. These are the years that they think their parents are cool. If parents make sure they are spending lots of time with all the children together and also with them individually, it will serve as a good foundation for the years to follow. Parents finding ways to play and create laughter is absolutely crucial. Habits like spending time individually will be part of their long-term memories, and parents may be able to avoid a stage where their child does not want to speak with them at all. If done in the name of fun, parents, over time, will develop the connection with their children and also lay the foundation for their children to become healthy and capable adults.

Here are more pointers about spending time with children in this age:
- If parents have a certain passion about a sport or hobby, getting children exposed to this will allow them to also be part of their lives. However, this should not be taken to mean that children should just follow and observe the parent. Rather, individual time needs to be taken out to introduce these activities to them. As they get better and better, it may develop into a routine that both the parent and the child enjoy (or not!)
- At this age, they may or may not want to play the same old games over and over; if they like variety, work together to be creative. Some children will enjoy sitting and talking, others will not. In general, play is still the best way to connect. (And remember, children do not need expensive toys for creative play.)
- Having imaginary friends is not uncommon, especially when children may be going through a transition or feeling upset. Don't worry—one of the top-selling authors of all time recounted in her autobiography that many of her early memories involved imaginary friends, and she continued her conversations with some of them into adulthood—so who knows? You may be nurturing a budding best-seller!

⋲ LOUIS LOWDOWN ⋺

When our children were two and four years old, we found out that we would have to move to Australia from Jakarta for our work. I (Karen) prepared the children as best as I could, and neither of them seemed to mind that much. However, around that same time, Sonia started playing with imaginary friends, Noni and Toto (Indonesian names). She would tell me elaborate stories about these two friends. She talked to them and about them in many different ways, sometimes acting as if they were little children and sometimes as if they were adults. They were around most of the time. I would affirm her little buddies, and didn't argue with her or make a big deal out of the phenomenon. Our house we were to move into had already been chosen by our employers, so the day we moved to Sydney, we were able to go directly from the airport to our new home.

> The house looked out over what is known in Australia as "bush" so there were lots of trees and birds, and a backporch just off the kitchen, which the kids never had in Jakarta. Sonia was thrilled, and asked, "May I go look around by myself?" She ran excitedly throughout the whole place, up and down the stairs, looked in every room, and came back to the living room where I was standing by the window. With eyes as big as saucers, she happily announced, "Mummy, Noni and Toto are already here and they love this place!" And she never mentioned them again. With the benefit of hindsight, I guess the imaginary friends were her way of coping with the fear and uncertainty of moving to a new country and a new house!

Even though some children may not want to engage in long talks, parents can teach children to identify and be attuned to emotions such as sadness, joy, fear, excitement, disappointment, longing, or anger. This can be achieved by routinely asking about "highs and lows", and by using feelings charts, which parents can easily find on the Internet. (More on this in the next chapter.)

Remember that children need lots of affection. Many fathers at this stage withhold from kissing and hugging their children, but this is a mistake. Boys and girls both need this from their fathers.

Children should be encouraged to be involved in cooperative and competitive games, where they can be aware of how other people feel. For example, in a game if someone cheats, how would this make others feel? If someone wins all the time, how would this make others feel? If someone is not cooperative, how would this make others feel? As a parent on the playground with other children, you will be able to observe all of this taking place, and possibly even facilitate some of the games. If so, you can change the games in such a way that different children get to win, not just the fastest or strongest. If not facilitating, you can at least make use of question and answer later with your own children to draw out some of the lessons from what you observed. The single best childhood predictor of adult adaptation is *not* school grades, and not classroom behaviour, but a child's ability to get along with other children.[58] This should be given top priority. Principles such as give and take, trust, sharing, friendliness and selflessness should be taught over and over again so that they will be able to increasingly see things from other people's viewpoints.

It is important for parents to learn to encourage children by being specific about who did what well. For example, parents can be encouraging about the following:
- Who was cooperative?
- Who was honest?
- Who played hard?
- Who did not give up?

- Who was nice to others?
- Who had a good attitude?

So often encouragement goes to the person who won, or criticism goes to those who made mistakes. If parents make a big deal about winning, then children will follow suit. When winning does not become the parents' focus, then children will be more likely to focus on other people's feelings and not just their own. (Beware—sometimes the super-organised parents are too concerned about being efficient, and frustration builds up when activities are not going smoothly or on time. This is counter-productive to the main aim, which is to connect with your child!)

Do not choose a game where one child tends to lose continually, assuming the children are close in age, and roughly the same size, etc. This will affect their self-esteem and eventually they will not look forward to playing. It may cause them to be envious of siblings who always win. Parents can and should set it up where a different child wins, including the parents, and that the spread is fairly even, or at least not so skewed toward one family member.

◈ LOUIS LOWDOWN ◈

> Here's an example of how *not* to handle playing games with kids: During the time our children were in primary and middle school, we had our "family day" on Sunday afternoon from about 3:00 p.m. until bedtime. Sometimes we would dive into the shared swimming pool at our apartment complex and play pool games. Some weeks we would go for bike rides, or an inexpensive amusement park. One of our favourite activities was playing board games and card games as a family. When Sonia hit the preteen years, she became very distracted and for a few months, playing any sit-down game with her required restraint and patience. I (John) became frustrated and would reprimand her. My wife would politely signal to me to back off. She tried to explain to me that when I acted like this, it was defeating the very purpose of playing and having a good time as a family! I was too impatient and did not listen, and I ruined the atmosphere on more than one occasion. Thankfully, my better half pointed out the error of my ways, and I was able to prioritise having fun and connection over accuracy and efficiency. I am glad to say that my children forgave me, and now they often talk about our Sunday afternoon family times with great fondness. In fact, as young adults, they appreciate the fact that I chose to play hard and invest my time with them on a regular basis.

While play is still predominant, do set aside time to have more talks with them as well. At this age, try and read between the lines about why they are bringing up certain subjects, such as their concerns about moving to a different school, for example. Children experience a whole range of emotions and may need help to label their feelings as well as to process them. Discussing "highs and lows" at the dinner table is a great place to start, and it gets children into a healthy habit of having fun while being deep.

In terms of the three drives of connect, work and play, work will begin in more earnest at this stage. It is important for parents not to expose children to the pressure of learning at a level more than that for which they are mentally prepared. Connect and play will still be the largest of the three drives.

About playing and what children are able to learn when they mingle with others their age, Jean Piaget had this to say:

> It is through game playing, that is, through the give and take of negotiating plans, settling disagreements, making and enforcing rules, and keeping and making promises that children come to understand the social rules which make cooperation with others possible. As a consequence of this understanding, peer groups can be self-governing and their members capable of autonomous, democratic and moral thinking.[60]

It is important for parents to be creative and involved in their children's lives. This is helpful for all the reasons mentioned above, plus it builds fantastic memories. On this note, we recommend a great website that has all kinds of games parents can play with their children called "Games Kids Play".[61] We hope you enjoy looking over this website, and that you will play some of these games with your family. By all means, have fun, knowing that your child is developing as games are being played!

Elkind frequently speaks up about how parents today are hurrying children to grow up too fast. One of the obvious ways is by making them plunge into the learning of mathematics and advanced reading that is not appropriate for their age. In *The Hurried Child* he states:

> Advanced reading, like advanced number understanding, is quite different from beginners reading, although again our language provides no markers of the difference. We talk about children reading or not reading as if children either read or do not read. But there are many different levels of reading attainment. The young child who has memorised all of the words in a book has learned to sight read, but like learning the numbers two and three sight reading is a much easier mental activity than decoding new words using syntactic structure to infer meaning. That level of reading does not usually emerge until the age of six or seven. These levels of competence are often ignored when children are hurried…Mastering the basic skills means acquiring an enormous number of rules and learning to apply them appropriately. Hurrying children academically, therefore, ignores the enormity of the task that children face in acquiring basic math and reading skills. We need to appreciate how awesome an intellectual task learning the basics really is for children and give them the time they need to accomplish it well.[59]

Another negative impact of hurrying our children is that they miss out on popular stories and poems, such as those by Dr. Seuss, [62] that have been passed down for generations—hurried children are often deprived of this rich heritage.[63] There are other grave consequences when children are hurried into growing. Children who are confronted with demands to do math or to read before they have the requisite mental abilities may experience a series of demoralising failures and begin to conceive of themselves as worthless.[64]

Speaking of Dr Seuss, reading loads of books to and with children is a fantastic way to increase connection, teach values, and at the same time, help them academically (in a subtle way). Bedtime reading with such classics as *The Children's Book of Virtues*,[65] or children's Bibles or devotional books with pictures will provide hours of fun, bonding time, and help to set the tone for later years as they sow healthy seeds of spiritual values. When children are finished reading, and the kids are tucked in bed, this is a good time for parents to ask their children how they felt about the day, or repeat highs and lows. Bear in mind that even though this may have been shared during mealtimes, sometimes there are other lows that they would prefer talking about when alone with a parent, or they simply may have just forgotten to bring it up earlier.

Middle Childhood

During this age period, the shift among connect, work and play continues. Even though children are approaching adolescence, they still need to play, especially with their father (see Figure 6.1, 8 to 12 years old).

Here are some more points to take into account when meeting this core emotional need:
At this stage, work will now accelerate a little, especially at school and time for play will decrease correspondingly. Parents should take care that play is not eliminated. Some parents may want their kids to be so well equipped academically that they push them to study hard, even after school hours, with little time to play other than during recess time at school. No matter what, the connection must be maintained, which surely involves play.

Remember, children this age still really want your love and connection, but they may not want others to know it. They may resist open displays of affection and love. Boys especially would rather give high fives than kisses in public, but parents must not stop showing affection in private. Kids this age still love to have bed time reading along with mum or dad putting them to bed, believe it or not.

This is an age where many issues like winning, losing, looking bad, shame and fear will become real to them. When these emotions are discussed, children should be able to process their feelings and make sense of things without feeling weird. They will still need their parents to help them focus on other people so they understand that life is not just about them, or about them winning! Like we mentioned before, when watching children interact with other kids, or with family members, specific encouragement needs to be given in the same areas. We shall list them again for easy reference.

- Who was cooperative?
- Who was honest?
- Who played hard?
- Who did not give up?
- Who was nice to others?
- Who had a good attitude?

◆ LOUIS LOWDOWN ◆

> When Sonia and David were under ten years of age, the kids and I (John) frequently played our own version of hide and seek, which was fun for older children. I would count to twenty as both of my kids hid somewhere in the playground; if I saw them, I would chase them. If they ran to the base and touched it before I did, they would get one point. If I were quick enough to touch them before they hit the base, I would score a point. Since I could decide to run as fast or slowly as I wished, I could manipulate the scores between all of us so they would be close and most of the time I would let them win. This version enabled us to get lots of exercise, chase each other, plus provide the added excitement of running away from being caught, all of which got their adrenaline going. Our playtime caught the attention of the neighbours and soon other children joined us, which also helped me teach many lessons about empathy.

During this stage, play will gravitate more and more toward gender based activities. At the latter part of this stage (ten to twelve years of age), boys would rather play with boys and girls with girls. This would also be a good time for parents to watch team sports in which their children are involved. We are amazed at how competitive parents get on the side-lines, sometimes even more so than their children on the field.

Kids this age will also see their strengths and weaknesses more clearly. It is likely that they will talk more. They want and need their parents' constant encouragement and acceptance. If they are taking part in a sport or in a competition, and feel during the course of play that their parent does not value them, or that a parent is spending time with them out of a sense of duty, it will send the opposite message of connection and acceptance. So many times when a child does not win, a parent may say "Great job" or "It's okay, winning is not everything", but the tone of voice, facial expressions, and body language convey that winning actually mattered to him a lot. Most children can sense what the parent is really feeling; this sends a strong signal to the child about what their parent values the most.

In his book *No Contest: The Case Against Competition*, Alfie Kohn talks about the adverse effects of competition that many parents model for and breed in their kids.[66] He posed some of the following questions upon which parents would do well to reflect:

- Is competition more productive than cooperation?
- Is competition more enjoyable than cooperation?
- Does competition build character?

If not being the top or not winning gets in the way of cooperating, enjoying the game and/or building character, then how is competition helpful?

❖ LOUIS LOWDOWN ❖

> In the section on Realistic Expectations, we will share about dealing with competitiveness when our children played tennis. I (Karen) wanted to add here that when they were playing in tournaments, I would stand next to the court and smile at them for the entire match. This was not so much for the sake of connection as for acceptance. I didn't see any reason to be upset or disappointed with how they hit a ball, and I certainly didn't want them seeing disapproving expressions on my face. All they got from me were smiles, and of course, cheers for extra good shots. The kids appreciated it, and felt sorry for their friends whose parents barked at them from the sidelines. After winning a doubles match which put them into the finals of a national tournament, the father of Sonia's partner made several disparaging remarks to his daughter about her level of play, but told Sonia how wonderfully Sonia had played. My righteously indignant daughter looked him in the eye and said confidently, "Cathy played just as well or better than I did." I hope for his daughter's sake that he was listening.

To most parents, getting their children to succeed is about helping them to be more hardworking. However, while this may be the case, parents have no idea about the stronger message that is being sent to their children:

I am not good enough.

I am flawed.

I do not fit into my family.

I am a failure compared to my siblings and friends.

This develops the lifetraps of defectiveness, social isolation, and failure. Children who are internalising these messages may start to feel exasperated and discouraged, and when these feelings are not processed, may become resentful and then perhaps rebel in later years.

> ⋖ **LOUIS LOWDOWN** ⋗
>
> My (Karen's) father played every sport possible with my brother and me on our West Texas farm. He must have been patient, because I am not very athletic, but I ended up being reasonably decent at cycling, tennis, softball, basketball, and water-skiing; and I managed to get by in touch football and sailing. When I think back to those good old days, I don't remember any overly competitive spirit, insulting words, negative facial expressions or belittling tone of voice, and he certainly didn't act bored or like he wished he were somewhere else. I am so grateful for my dad's legacy, and the sense of fun and adventure that John and I have been able to pass on to our kids!

Adolescence

The adolescent period is described as being the years from puberty to adulthood. The American Academy of Paediatrics divides this period into three stages:[67] early adolescence, generally ages twelve and thirteen, middle adolescence, ages fourteen to sixteen, and late adolescence, ages seventeen to twenty-one.

Puberty is defined as the time when biological changes are taking place, and for many it takes place during early and middle adolescence. At this stage, adolescents tend to see things as black and white and are not able to set their sights on long-term goals or the consequences when they do something right or wrong. But by the time they hit late adolescence they are able to think in a far more complex and rational way. Recall the insights of Nucci[68] on the different kinds of morality (see Chapter Two). Some teens will resent parents insisting on adherence to certain rules if they feel that those rules are not truly important. In the interest of connection, parents should not make a big deal out of these things!

Adolescents care a lot more about their peers. Their social circle widens and they want to make their own decisions about who to spend time with and get close to. When they were younger their parents had more influence over these decisions, but at this stage they want to have more say. They are striving to have their own identity as a person yet at the same time they care a lot about what others think of them. Even though they will be somewhat less affectionate towards their parents, parents are still the primary influence in their lives, more than peers.

Children at this stage will appear childish at times, but react aggressively when parents do not give them the independence they crave. There is a tremendous amount of entitlement that creeps in but generally speaking, this type of entitlement is temporary, and eventually disappears as the teens mature, provided parents continue to adequately meet all their core emotional needs. As mentioned, while teens place a tremendous amount of emphasis on fitting in with their peers, deep down inside, they still care about what their parents think more than their peers. We strongly caution parents to avoid giving up spending time with their teenaged children because of the mistaken thinking that their adolescent children's peer relationships are more important than with their parents. Regular one-on-one time is crucial.

Adolescence has been seen as a transition point between childhood and adulthood. They still have their childhood ways, but at the same time, they are also striving to be an adult. More than any other stage, this is the time when they will start to pull away, and perhaps not want to be as attached to their parents. Even though they inwardly desire to know that they are loved by and close to their parents, teenagers will come across as if the opposite were true. So they will act like they do not need to connect, but parents need to persevere and find a way into their lives. It takes hard work and a lot of patience, but the end results are well worth the effort.

When children hit this stage, the interplay between connect, play and work will shift fairly dramatically (see Figure 6.1, 13 to 17 years old). They will find new interests and work at school will increase drastically. To parents, it seems like our teens suddenly have little or no time to "play" with their parents, but always manage to find time to play with their friends. Peer relationships are a huge part of an adolescent's life and will continue to be as they progress from being a young adolescent to an older adolescent. However, those who spent regular time in the preceding years with their parents and who still feel connected and accepted will continue to enjoy spending time with their family. Even then, they may resist at times. To that we say, persevere, persevere, and persevere!

Spending time with adolescents takes being very purposeful and intentional; it demands that we make our way into their schedule. Some parents have found it helpful to make the most out of the following opportunities:
- When their teens need to be driven somewhere
- When they need help with their school work
- When they need a ride to school—almost all teens would prefer to ride in the car with parents than take the school bus. (Of course, if they have a driver's license, they would really love to drive!)

So, in the end, the interplay of the three drives of connect, work and play changes as children move from one stage of growth to another. Parents should ensure that they maintain the connection with their children at all stages. Parents who do will never regret it.

We want to end this section on spending time by mentioning the importance of making memories. We learned from Mike Fontenot years ago about the need for creating positive milestones with our kids that we would always look back and remember fondly. Both our parents also had strong convictions about that; John's family has wonderful holiday memories of going to the beach in Penang, Malaysia, and Karen's family continues to holiday at the Gulf Coast of Texas, as well as having great memories of several trips in her teen and campus years.

No matter what stage of life your children are in, plan holidays with your family. Take pictures. Take the time to file them and create memories. As a family, look at them periodically. Place them in the house where they are accessible, in beautiful frames so that all can be reminded of the precious memories built over the years, adding new ones every so often. Going up and down the stairs of our home, we see photos like these that remind us of many great family times together. A momentary glance sometimes brings out a memory and it makes a difference to the home atmosphere. As you get older, sweet memories will flood your minds as you reminisce together. Not only will this benefit your family connection directly; this will give your children a blueprint of how they would also want to manage their respective families when they start to have their own in the years to come.

―――――――――――――― **◁ MASTER CLASS ▷** ――――――――――――――

> Mike and Terrie Fontenot asked their three daughters to share their memories about family connection. Mandy and her husband, Forest, have four children and have lead ministries in the USA and Australia. She wrote, "I remember family vacations, special days, celebrating birthdays, holidays, lots of laughter, fun, and games, family dinners, just spending time together; not forgetting talking through hard, challenging times." Megan and her husband have one daughter and lead a campus ministry in Virginia. Her thoughts are included in an earlier section, but in addition Megan told her parents, "One way I felt connected to you both is through having fun and making memories. Vacations, walks around the neighbourhood and the garden, playing Frisbee, decorating the tree...." Michelle and her husband have been serving in a church in Australia for the past few years, and before that, worked with youth in South Florida. Michelle wrote, "I remember games—we played cards as a family a lot and that was always a fun time just laughing and spending time together. I remember holidays—holidays were great! I remember food—we had some regular special places that we would go (in Australia it was Sizzler, the dim sum place, etc.) I remember sitting on your bed talking—seems like a lot of important conversations happened on a bed of some sort...hard things going on in life, confessions of sin, promptings to do something we didn't want to do, spilling of emotions; including the time that Forest (Mandy's husband) broke the bed when he got on, but at least he knew it was the place to be! Seems like computers in kids' rooms, TVs in kids' rooms, and iPods have really limited a lot of the family connections these days. It's so important to do lots together."

If spending time is the first "practical", what is the second?

CHAPTER SEVEN

Empathy and Validation of Feelings

Apart from play and spending special time, another paramount way we go about meeting our children's core emotional need for connection and acceptance is the way we draw out and process their feelings. Young children regularly go through all kinds of emotions—excitement, sadness, fear, anger, joy. When we empathise with them and help them understand and process their feelings, we will experience connection. However, in this fast-paced world, many parents do not attribute much importance to the feelings of their children; they allow their own agenda and worries to take over. Some parents are emotionally inhibited and regard feelings as being unhealthy; others just focus on doing what is right. In our Good Enough Parenting model, we believe that *not* empathising with our children's feelings and therefore *not* connecting with them at an emotional level leads to the exasperation interactions discussed in Chapters Two and Three.

Some may wonder what empathy has to do with parenting. Empathy is our heart-felt response to another's emotions. We get there by putting ourselves into the other person's shoes momentarily, then a response is made to convey these feelings accurately in a caring and respectful manner. Empathy can be compared to watching a movie about another person, immersing ourselves in their issues, and then reflecting back to that person his feelings and thoughts, with a sense of genuineness and care.

Think about it. Suppose you have a heated argument with your spouse just before leaving the house for work. Flustered, you decide to stop for coffee on the way to the office. What a surprise, while waiting in line, you meet a good friend. You are so happy to have someone to whom you can pour out your feelings so you just let it all out. How would you feel if, as soon as you finished your story, your friend replied by giving you a lecture about being a better wife or husband?! Or gave you advice? Or told you to stop worrying because you look nicer when you are smiling? Or minimised your feelings, or tried to psychoanalyse you? We bet you would not seek that friend out for a while, at least not when you had a problem! But isn't that what we sometimes do with our kids? What kind of listeners are we? Why do we struggle to show empathy to our children?

> *So in everything, do to others what you would have them do to you, for this sums up the Law and the Prophets.* (Matthew 7:12)

> *Therefore, as God's chosen people, holy and dearly loved, clothe yourselves with compassion, kindness, humility, gentleness and patience. Bear with each other and forgive whatever grievances you may have against one another. Forgive as the Lord forgave you. And over all these virtues put on love, which binds them all together in perfect unity. Let the peace of Christ rule in your hearts, since as members of one body you were called to peace. And be thankful. Let the word of Christ dwell in you richly as you teach and admonish one another with all wisdom, and as you sing psalms, hymns and spiritual songs with gratitude in your hearts to God. And whatever you do, whether in word or deed, do it all in the name of the Lord Jesus, giving thanks to God the Father through him.* (Colossians 3:12-17)

These verses are familiar Scriptures to all Christians. We know that we should strive to act like this in our interactions with others. Here are two challenges for all parents as we strive to meet our children's core need for connection and acceptance. The first is to make these verses alive in our hearts—to actually be this way, from the inside out, to feel for others in the way these verses characterise. That is what it means to clothe ourselves with love, as Paul wrote in Colossians 3 above. The second is to treat our *children* this way, to let them be the recipients of our compassion, kindness, patience, humility and gentleness, and do to them as we wish others would do to us.

MOVIE MOMENT – *The Great Santini,[1] East of Eden,[2] Freaky Friday,[3] North,[4] and Crammed[5]*

What makes it hard for parents to show empathy to their children?

1. Their Own Lifetraps are Getting Triggered

The apostle Paul understood the frustration of feeling "out of control":

> *We know that the law is spiritual; but I am unspiritual, sold as a slave to sin. I do not understand what I do. For what I want to do I do not do, but what I hate I do. And if I do what I do not want to do, I agree that the law is good. As it is, it is no longer I myself who do it, but it is sin living in me. I know that nothing good lives in me, that is, in my sinful nature. For I have the desire to do what is good, but I cannot carry it out. For what I do is not the good I want to do; no, the evil I do not want to do—this I keep on doing. Now if I do what I do not want to do, it is no longer I who do it, but it is sin living in me that does it. So I find this law at work: When I want to do good, evil is right there with me. For in my inner being I delight in God's law; but I see another law at work in the members of my body, waging war against the law of my mind and making me a prisoner of the law of sin at work within my members. What a wretched man I am! Who will rescue me from this body of death? Thanks be to God—through Jesus Christ our*

Lord! So then, I myself in my mind am a slave to God's law, but in the sinful nature a slave to the law of sin. (Romans 7:14-25)

This is probably the number one reason why parents struggle to have empathy, which is why we constantly bring up the need for parents to get in touch with their own issues. (Find out what triggers you by reading Chapters 3 of *I Choose Us*.) One of our favourite parenting movies is *The Great Santini*. The backyard basketball game between the Marine fighter pilot father and 18 year-old Ben is a great representation of a father's defectiveness lifetrap preventing him from connecting with his son.

2. They Have Their Own Agenda

Parents should make sure they are focusing on the real issue at hand and not something peripheral, otherwise they will be talking at cross purposes. For example, when a child has a hard day at school and comes home very upset and has used vulgar language, the parents may care more about "fixing" their child's embarrassing potty mouth than finding out why school was so difficult. In the 1955 James Dean classic, *East of Eden*, the father was very concerned with having financial integrity but did not see how his insistence on his interpretation of events was pushing his son away. Solomon wrote:

By wisdom a house is built, and through understanding it is established... (Proverbs 24:3)

It takes wisdom and understanding to focus on the root of the problem and not on our "pet peeves".

3. They Jump to Conclusions

Parents must take the time to really find out the whole story. Otherwise they risk falling into the trap described by wise King Solomon:

The first to present his case seems right, till another comes forward and questions him. (Proverbs 18:17)

The whole of the movie *Freaky Friday* is one gigantic lesson on the need to not jump to conclusions—a teenage daughter and her mother switch bodies and have to inhabit each other's lives until they can develop empathy for each other! Highly recommended.

4. They Think That One-Way Interaction is Conversation

How much exasperation is caused by parents not listening to their children...This is related to the emotionally depriving and inhibiting exasperation interaction, and brings to mind an old saying:

He who answers before listening—that is his folly and his shame. (Proverbs 18:13)

Some parents think that they *are* conversing with their children. The problem is, the parents are the only ones doing the talking. The movie

North, with Elijah Wood as the son and Jason Alexander and Julia Louis-Dreyfus as the parents, opens with the family dinner from hell. Both the mum and the dad are consumed with their own problems from work that day and talk non-stop at the same time without listening to or even acknowledging what the other is saying. The son wants to talk, but they don't pay any attention to him whatsoever. In fact, they don't even notice him until he passes out from a panic attack. This scene is an obvious exaggeration, but it sure gets the point across! As Grandma might say, "God gave us two ears and one mouth so we could listen twice as much as we talk." That applies in parenting as well as everywhere else.

5. They Are Too Tired and Burdened by Their Own Problems

We owe it to our families to take care of ourselves mentally, physically, and spiritually, so that we have the strength our loved ones need. And when we are stretched to capacity, we need to have friends and family upon whom we can rely.

Two are better than one, because they have a good return for their labour: If either of them falls down, one can help the other up. But pity anyone who falls and has no one to help them up. (Ecclesiastes 4:9-10)

How many times have we been short with someone because of lack of sleep? Or because something was bothering us or stressing us out? We can get away with this on occasion, but if this is more the norm than the exception, our children will not feel empathy from us. The mother in the Singapore short film, *Crammed*, was burdened and tired from work, a recent separation, and raising two young boys as a single mum. Unfortunately, tiredness led to tragedy.

The cost of living has increased to such a level that most families in the developing world now need two incomes in order to make ends meet, and in the so-called "first world", they need two incomes to keep up with housing, transportation, and credit card payments. (Obviously this is a generalisation—we know that there are some very wealthy folks in the developing world and some very poor individuals in developed societies.) One unfortunate consequence of this lifestyle is that these parents have a lot less time to spend with their children than families where only one parent is required to work. Moreover when they do reach home, and when parents should be focusing fully on their role as mums and dads after a full day at work, they often have very little energy left to give to their children. As a result, the quality of relationship between parents and children is on the decline. (That is why we are such big proponents of concepts such as downsizing so as to possibly not require two incomes, mums taking longer maternity leave or taking time out from their careers for several years when their children are born, and flexi-time work arrangements for mothers if not for fathers.)

On top of the economic pressure that adults are feeling, children are facing an increasing pressure to excel at school, which means more frequent exams and tighter deadlines. Both parents and children seem to be rushing from day to day in the pursuit of increasing academic intelligence, at the expense of other important areas of their lives. With less free time, parenting can become very productivity-minded, which leaves less time for play and drawing out feelings. As a result children do not give much importance to their feelings, or how to manage their feelings, which in turn has devastating consequences on their emotional intelligence. Children with poor emotional intelligence become adults with poor emotional intelligence who are not able to bond with important people in their lives, resulting in shallow relationships and little intimacy. Their marriages suffer, since they are less equipped to meet their spouse's needs. It is no surprise that divorce rates are rising sharply across the globe. Unhealthy marriages across the board will undoubtedly take their toll on parenting, and dysfunctional behaviour will keep on getting passed down to each successive generation. Gottman says:

> In the last decade or so, science has discovered a tremendous amount about the role emotions play in our lives. Researchers have found that even more than IQ, your emotional awareness and ability to handle feelings will determine your success and happiness in all walks of life, including family relationships.[6]

Gottman proved this by conducting research on families for over a decade. He monitored how parents dealt with their children's emotions, which included the parent's reaction to the children's emotional experiences, such as when their kids were angry, sad and fearful. He also measured the parent's awareness of the role emotions play in their own lives. Gottman's team followed these children from age four to adolescence. Their study found that when parents practised empathising with their children and validating their children's feelings, as well as helping their children to be emotionally intelligent, the children fared well in the following areas:

a. Emotional well-being – Children with emotional intelligence could regulate their own emotions, which means that they were better at soothing themselves when they got upset. They could also calm themselves down better and faster.

b. Physical health – As a result of being able to handle their emotions better, children with emotional intelligence had fewer illnesses.

c. Social competence – Children with emotional intelligence could relate to other people better, even in tough situations when they got teased. They also had better friendships with other children.

d. Academic performance – Children with emotional intelligence were better at focussing attention and performed better academically.[7]

This research highlights the importance of parents not ignoring their children's feelings, but valuing them by showing empathy and processing their emotions.

Simon Baron-Cohen has been studying empathy for thirty years, and recently published his findings with the eye-catching title, *Zero Degrees of Empathy*.[8] He believes that empathy varies in degrees; it is not an either-you-have-it-or-you-don't quality. In a normal population, people's different levels of inborn empathy will be reflected in a bell-shaped curve. Most people will be in the middle mark of having some empathy, but a small percentage will be in both extremes; one with a lot of empathy and the other with no empathy, or what Cohen refers to as "zero degrees of empathy".

Why do parents need to be concerned about this? Because what happens in childhood affects children's level of empathy. We agree with Cohen's belief that "empathy erosion" results when children's needs are not met over time. Cohen warns, "When empathy is switched off, people operate in the 'I' mode; their primary concern is about themselves," and they treat others as objects.[9] In the case of children whose empathy is being eroded over time, as they get older, they will develop a desire to protect themselves, then a desire for revenge, and later, blind hatred. Scary! Eventually, those with zero degrees of empathy cannot experience remorse or guilt because they do not or cannot understand what the other person is feeling. They lack awareness of how they *come across to others*, how they *interact with others*, and how to *anticipate others' feelings* or reactions. In addition, these individuals "believe 100% in the rightness of their own ideas and beliefs, and judge anyone who does not hold to their beliefs as wrong, or stupid."[10]

If you watch crime shows, you may have heard the terms "psychopath", or "malignant Narcissist" bandied about—these are the guys who cannot feel for others and only care about themselves. Guess what? They have "zero degrees of empathy". Cohen's research found that a huge percentage of adults with extreme personality disorders like those above have traumatic childhoods or experienced emotional neglect, indifference, deprivation and rejection.[11]

⋞ RESEARCH REVEALS ⋟

RR7.1: *Abuse in Childhood Increases Likelihood of Mental Disorders*

Simon Baron-Cohen found that, although not all abused children develop disorders such as Borderline Personality Disorders, many of them do. Between 40-70% of adults with Borderline Personality Disorder also had a history of sexual abuse, and between 60-80% also had a history of physical abuse, or early parental separation through divorce, or emotional neglect, indifference, deprivation and rejection.[12] He says that early negative experiences of abuse and neglect affect how the brain develops and causes abnormalities in the empathy circuit of the brain. He also identifies three types of personality disorders that reflect zero degrees of empathy: Borderline, Psychopathic and Narcissistic.[13]

We believe that when they are confident that their parents care about how they feel and will treat their feelings with respect, that children, rather than developing zero degrees of empathy, will go the other direction as they get more and more connected to their parents. *When the core emotional need for connection and acceptance has been met, children will naturally imitate their parents' values and this in turn will help them have the conviction to resist being drawn to unhealthy delinquent behaviours, beliefs and ideologies.*

But validating children's emotions and empathising with them does not come naturally for many parents. What comes naturally for parents is to respond with a coping style; i.e., to surrender, to avoid, to overcompensate, which inevitably leads to one of the exasperation interactions. When we were young, children on the playground said, *"Sticks and stones may break my bones but words will never hurt me."* Nothing could be further from the truth. Words have the power to divide nations, end friendships, wreck marriages, and do untold harm to children. Our choice of words, along with our non-verbal communication and our tone, make a difference to how well we meet the core emotional needs of our children.

When parents attempt to improve the behaviour of their child with harsh and disrespectful words, it leads to exasperation. They hurt the child's self-worth, making him feel rejected as an individual. This complicates the process of learning and awareness on the part of the child because the exasperation is separate and apart from the original act of misbehaviour. Eventually bitter roots begin to develop and rebellion will very likely follow in their adolescent years. In short, the child's core need for connection and acceptance is not met and he is in danger of developing the lifetraps highlighted in chapter five. But if the emotional connection is strong, then mild disapproval and mild anger will already be a form of discipline because the child cares about the relationship with his parents.[14]

The following story of Jesus and his disciples in Nain is one of my (Karen's) favourite passages illustrating Jesus' empathy for others:

> *As he approached the town gate, a dead person was being carried out—the only son of his mother, and she was a widow. And a large crowd from the town was with her. When the Lord saw her, his heart went out to her and he said, "Don't cry." Then he went up and touched the bier they were carrying him on, and the bearers stood still. He said, "Young man, I say to you, get up!" The dead man sat up and began to talk, and Jesus gave him back to his mother.* (Luke 7:11-15)

Common Feelings in Children

Sometimes parents do not think about the kind of feelings that their children experience. This is often related to the parents' lack of awareness about their own emotions. Parents who are not aware of their own feelings have a difficult time getting in tune with the feelings of their children. Children may not always openly show their feelings. Sometimes, they give out only subtle clues, but parents who are trained or intuitive will be able to read between the lines.

Children experience a myriad of emotions, such as anger, happiness, sadness, joy, shame, pride, humiliation, acceptance, guilt, confidence, abandonment, love, embarrassment, excitement, annoyance, contentment, to name a few. The more parents pick up on these feelings and learn how to process them with their child, the better the core emotional need for connection and acceptance will be met. However, parents react differently to the emotions experienced by their child. Many parents do not find talking about feelings or emotions attractive—they find ways to avoid talking about them. Some parents get triggered by certain emotions and respond in an unhealthy way, such as by putting the child down, being punitive, pouting, or blaming themselves silently. Parents who are able to gain awareness about how *they* respond to the feelings of their child will be off to a good start in trying to meet their child's core emotional need for connection and acceptance.

◁ LOUIS LOWDOWN ▷

> Sonia was always attuned to her own emotions and to everyone else's. When she was five years old, she could tell when I (Karen) was upset with her no matter how hard I tried to hide it. For example, if something happened right before bedtime, I might ignore it and try to do the normal bedtime routine, but Sonia would not have it. She would say, "OK, Mum, tell me what's wrong," and I would say, "Nothing's wrong, Sweetheart," because I had an appointment to get to and I really wanted her to go to sleep. And she would say, "Yes there is, I can tell. And the Bible says, 'Do not let the sun go down on your anger', so it's not right for me to sleep until it's settled." So even though it meant staying up later, we would sort it out. Usually it was me being a little irritated with her for something she had done and I would have been happy to bring it up the next day. However, when she even sensed the slightest thing, it was going to get dealt with right then. Sonia would always apologize for what she had done wrong, and we would finish with lots of cuddles and kisses and giggles and sometimes she would end by calling me on the carpet for not being open!

Exercise: Please go to Appendix 2 for a very important exercise on dealing with emotions.

⋖ LOUIS LOWDOWN ⋗

> When my kids were teenagers and became Christians, I (Karen) had some kind of parental Narcissism in that I subconsciously expected my children to react to situations the same way I would—and since I don't handle sadness so well, it became hard for me to help them deal with sadness. I wasn't as good a listener as I should've been when they were teens. On several occasions when they became sad and tried to get help from me, my avoidant coping style exasperated them, and they found that talking with John was more helpful. After John processed their emotions, he had to help reconcile me with the kids by acting as mediator, and I had to apologize for minimizing their sadness or not listening sensitively.

Processing Emotions

The three prominent parenting experts who we feel offer the most valuable insights in the area of how to process feelings with children in a healthy way are Ginott, Gottman, and the team of Faber and Mazlish.[15] The steps they advocate apply to both older and younger children. In summary these are:

1. Be aware that the child is experiencing emotions, and have an initial idea of which emotion(s) he might be feeling. This involves interpreting the verbal expressions, tone, and non-verbal expressions of the child.
2. See the child's feelings as an opportunity to connect with him at an emotional level. This will strengthen the bond between the parent and child. Parents should not rush into giving solutions. Both the tone of voice and body language is crucial in communicating this message.
3. Draw the child out verbally to be able to express these emotions or feelings, and to label these feelings or emotions correctly. This process will train the child (and in the beginning, the parent) to process his feelings, and thereafter cope in a healthy way.
4. Validate the emotion(s), then show empathy and compassion to the child. Again parents should not rush into giving solutions.
5. At a suitable time, collaborate with the child and help resolve the issue that triggered the child.

The manner in which the above principles are practised changes with the age of the children. For younger children, we echo and support the points below taken from the Faber and Mazlish book, *How to Talk So Kids Will Listen and How to Listen So Kids Will Talk*; this book has sold over 2 million copies in English alone and has been referred to as the parenting Bible. We found it to be invaluable to our parenting when our children were in elementary school. We have obtained permission from the authors to use their teaching points, but we have made up our own cartoons to accompany the steps below from Faber and Mazlish.[16]

1. Listen Quietly and Attentively

It is one thing to listen, it is quite another to listen attentively. Listening attentively with the right posture sends a very strong signal to our children that we care. If we multitask while they are talking about their emotions, we send the wrong message. If we stop whatever we are doing, give eye contact

Instead of...

Empathy and Validation of Feelings ▪ 149

and face them, we are conveying that we care about their feelings and that it matters to us more than our task at hand. This will help our children feel that home is a safe place emotionally (see Figure 7.1).

Try this...

Figure 7.1: Listen Quietly and Attentively

150 ■ Good Enough Parenting

2. Acknowledge the Child's Feelings with a Word

Parents tend to be quick in giving solutions, and sometimes this happens even before our children have finished talking about their issues. Keep in mind

Instead of...

the admonitions above, but instead of being completely silent, occasionally use words like "Aha", "Hmmm", "Right", which convey to children that their parents are engaged and not distracted (see Figure 7.2).

Try this...

Figure 7.2: Acknowledge the Child's Feelings with a Word

3. Give the Feeling a Name

In a given week, children experience a myriad of emotions. By helping the child to give the feelings a name, parents are validating and processing with the child, which will increase the child's emotional intelligence. It is tempting to jump the gun here, so ask questions and let them have their

Instead of...

say. This will prevent the parent from being judgmental and will help to meet the core emotional need for connection and acceptance in a powerful way (see Figure 7.3).

Try this...

Figure 7.3: Give the Feeling a Name

4. Give the Child his Wishes in Fantasy

Faber and Mazlish use humour in parenting. They advise parents to sometimes crack jokes, not at the expense of the child, but in a way that shows empathy (see Figure 7.4).

Instead of...

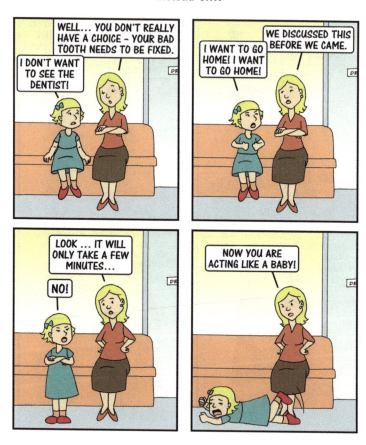

Empathy and Validation of Feelings ■ 155

Exercise: Refer to Appendix 3 and complete the exercise(s) that correspond(s) to the respective age of your child(ren).

Try this...

Figure 7.4: Give the Child her Wishes in Fantasy

◁ LOUIS LOWDOWN ▷

I (John) tended to get angry when the kids were disrespectful, which would sometimes happen if *they* were angry about something. So when they were young, and came to me and said something like, "I'm angry" or "So-and-so was mean to me today and I punched him in the nose", my first reaction was to say, "You shouldn't be angry", or "Don't be disrespectful!" or "Christians are not supposed to punch people!" or "Do you think Jesus would have punched someone?" Instead of empathising with them first, I would straightaway side with the other person's behaviour, and even sympathise with whomever had made them angry. That would upset them even more, which was not surprising. Mike Fontenot once said that children don't understand grace as much as they understand law, possibly because they do not feel the need for the blood of Christ, since they do not yet need to have their sins forgiven. I interpreted this to mean that it is not fair for us to force our children to have our faith or our level of commitment, or even understand grace the way we do. This would make them feel frustrated. In fact, the very way they will learn these exact things is for us to first validate their feelings! Fortunately when Sonia was about five years old, a couple with older kids confided in us that they had regretted telling their daughter, "You're not afraid, you're brave". That statement made me stop and think before dismissing my children's emotions. In the next few years, I read the Faber and Mazlish book, and I saw what I had been doing wrong. I really made a point to change and listen to and validate their feelings. Once I learned how to process the kids' emotions, I was able to say things like, "Sounds like you're really sad/angry/embarrassed" and then we could have a conversation from there.

Let us continue with a hypothetical situation: A mother has a five-year-old son. We'll call him Zane. He tells his mum that he punched someone and she replies, "Oh my, sounds like you were really angry," He continues with, "Yeah, I punched Jason because of what he did on the playground." Zane is able to say that because his mother does not jump in with a judgmental statement. She is now hearing new information—something happened on the playground. Perhaps her son was still in the wrong, but that is not the main issue. It is more important to find out why the emotions got triggered in the first place, then deal with the "what" later.

Zane's openness leads her to say, with a very sincere and caring tone, and with eyes wide with curiosity and concern, "Sounds like he did something on the playground that really made you upset." Now Zane feels free to keep going and tell her the rest of the story. Let's pretend he says: "Mum, you know how Daddy told me I had to be more responsible with my things? Well, that stupid Jason took my wallet and threw it up on the roof, and I was so mad! I didn't want Daddy to get upset and tell me I was not responsible, so I just punched him." Zane's mum consoles him, appreciates that his heart was in the right place about being responsible, and tells him that she would have been just as mad as he was if someone did that to her belongings. She might even add, "Boy, that Jason's mother must not have taught him about boundaries!" Then they have an after school snack, cool down, maybe listen to some music and do some homework, or play in the playground. Later Zane's mum has talk number two, and discusses how violence is not the answer when someone does something mean. She does a Bible study, and comes up with a suitable consequence, and they brainstorm a way for Zane to apologise and try to reconcile with the boy he punched. This might or might not involve talking to the teacher—depending on how big of an incident this was.

Now let's pretend that Zane punched Jason for a different reason altogether—maybe Jason scored a goal in the soccer game and Zane was jealous In this case, his mum would have to discuss that in more detail and in talk number two have more intense consequences, a very purposeful Bible study, and definitely contact the school. Or maybe Zane saw Jason abusing another child and he interrupted to intervene and help. In this case, the mum would congratulate Zane on having empathy, caring for the weak and helping those in need. Then she might explain that in the future he get a teacher involved because he might actually hurt someone or end up getting kicked out of school one day, even if he were theoretically in the right.

At the end of the day, when we talk with our children like this, and listen without being judgmental, our children feel connected and unconditionally accepted, and they also learn what they need to learn about their behaviour and their inner thoughts and beliefs. (Remember we should always show acceptance to them as our child and as a person but not necessarily show acceptance to their behaviour.)

Sometimes we can read their faces, and know from their tone of voice that all is not well. This is when as parents we need to start a dialogue, not a monologue or a lecture, but to listen and look at things from their point of view, and then offer guidance.

(Incidentally, one question some have asked is why teenagers usually like to talk at night. We do not really know the answer, but a good guess might be that they are busy during the day and have not had time to reflect; at night they finally slow down and become more ready to talk.)

> ### ⋖ MASTER CLASS ⋗
>
> This is Kim Evans conveying her middle child's opinion of what was helpful and important in Kim and Walter's parenting: "Her clear takeaway was that she could be herself and we would accept her. Of all five of us, she is the most unique in her makeup and thinking. In kindergarten she wore a dog hat to school that everyone teased her about. She came home in tears, but the next day put her dog hat on and headed for the bus. We asked her if she was sure that she wanted to wear the hat again. She said she loved her hat and she wasn't asking them to wear the hat and out the door she went. Within two weeks, moms were calling to ask where they could buy a dog hat. In our home of calm consistency and connection, she found a place to be herself and the strength to stand up to the world."

Accepting Behaviour vs. Accepting Feelings

Ginnot and Gottman also agree that as parents we should accept our children's feelings, but not necessarily their behaviour.[17] For many parents this is confusing. They think that the two are one and the same thing, but they are actually different. We connect with our kids when we empathise with their ups and downs. However, this does not mean that we will always agree with the behaviour accompanying their feelings. For example, a child may feel sad when left out of a game between his siblings, and respond by throwing a temper tantrum. The parents need to separate the feelings from the behaviour. They could process their son's feelings of rejection, and empathise with him, but they would also need to voice their disapproval of his *behaviour* (not him or his feelings), and apply an appropriate consequence. We need to communicate that there are some behaviours that are acceptable and there are some that are not.

In addition, we also believe that there will be times when it is inappropriate to get into a discussion about feelings.

a. When parents or children are in a hurry

Given the kind of schedule that people have today that involves rushing from one place to another, especially in the mornings, it is important to remember that sometimes when our kids are going through a difficult time, we need to schedule a separate time to deal with their emotions. If you try and empathise quickly, your child will notice that you are more concerned about something else, and this will be perceived as rejection. So, if you are in a rush, communicate that you will talk later in the day. However, do not wait too long before doing this. That might send the message that you forgot and did not care. (For very serious matters, you may want to cancel your next appointment and deal with it on the spot.)

◁ LOUIS LOWDOWN ▷

> As a person who prides himself in being efficient, I (John) have to deny myself and stop myself from bringing up issues when it is not appropriate. There have been many times when I wanted to bring up concerns as soon as the kids walked into the house from school. Most of the time, I bounced it off my wife, who then cautioned me to consider the issue of timing. Had it not been for her wise counsel, I surely would have exasperated them and caused many unpleasant encounters. This shows the importance of tapping into your spouse's strengths and allowing him or her to influence you, which I have to say has been an important learning path for me in my parenting. (Karen adds, "Ditto!)

b. When children are with their friends or in public

Children often feel shame when parents start to process their feelings in front of their friends or others. Either move somewhere private if the talk has to take place, or find a more suitable time. When children feel ashamed they will react negatively and this will invalidate the entire process.

c. When we are triggered either by our children or by other people

Sometimes as parents we are also not ready to listen and talk. Perhaps our child has just answered back with a rude and disrespectful tone. Perhaps we may have had a conflict with our spouse, or someone else, and right after getting triggered, our child comes in with his problems. How do we react? Ideally we will be self-controlled, separate ourselves from the emotions we are feeling personally, and help our child. However, sometimes the flood of feelings may overwhelm us and talking with our children may call for more self-control than we can muster. In that case, we should take an adult "time out", explaining that we need some space so that we have the mental and spiritual fortitude to deal with the issue at hand. This involves removing ourselves, and taking time to think, pray and/or be alone for a while. If it has nothing to do with our child, we can let him know that as well. However, children may panic when they think that their parents are in trouble, so we should not convey our worries in such a way that makes them upset. The choice of words is important. At the end of the day, our children will be proud of us and respect us for having self-control and relying on God.

d. When the offence is serious

When children go against the values of the family and do something unusually out of line, such as stealing, being extremely deceitful or disrespectful, hurting others, or destroying someone's property, the parents should express indignation. However, godly anger is not the same as rage or contempt or cynicism. Letting the children see actual indignation will wake them up to the seriousness of what they have done. This works well if you are in the habit of drawing out their feelings properly, in which case, (healthy) anger will be an exception, rather than the norm. Obviously, if anger is expressed frequently and disproportionately, then it will have little positive effect even when it is expressed the right way (see Chapter Nineteen).

e. When children are trying to manipulate with their feelings

Some children really know how to have things their way. They cry and manipulate; sometimes it is hard to know when it is legitimate and when it is manipulation. We believe that when parents are really listening and have done so frequently, they will be able to distinguish between the two. If a parent feels that their child is frequently being manipulative, we would say that this is a sign that there is an unmet need somewhere, in which case, parents need to, by way of respectful dialogue, uncover this unmet need. For example, perhaps there is a lack of connection due to not spending enough time together, or a lack of acceptance, or, very likely, a lack of limits. Apologise and meet the need adequately. As mentioned we will not get it right all the time, but we have to be "good enough".

f. When children are not prepared to talk and want some space first (this tends to apply to the adolescent stage)

There are times when children also need some space to be by themselves for a period of time. Parents need to respect this and not demand that all matters get settled there and then. While the Bible does encourage us to settle matters quickly, taking time and giving them space does not go against that principle. However, parents need to come back and continue discussing the unresolved situation and seek to bring it to closure. Our children will often be able to talk sense to themselves; when they talk to us at a later time, they will feel more resolved and their emotions will be much more subdued.

In conclusion, when you meet the core emotional need for connection and acceptance, and your connection is strong, then not only will your children love and respect you, but they will enjoy being with you. When the core emotional need for connection and acceptance has been met, children will naturally imitate their parents' values and this in turn will help them (eventually) have the conviction to resist being drawn to unhealthy delinquent behaviours, beliefs and ideologies. Therefore, if parents want their children to inherit their faith, it is imperative that they show empathy and learn to process their children's feelings! Spending time with your children, showing them empathy, and validating their feelings are the absolute most important ways to meet this need.

SECTION THREE

The Core Emotional Need for
Healthy Autonomy and Performance

All that lovey-dovey stuff sounds good, but won't it make our children too dependent on us?

CHAPTER EIGHT

Healthy Autonomy and Performance

The Core Emotional Need for Healthy Autonomy and Performance can be defined as helping our children develop their own personalities, abilities and self-confidence as they grow into separately functioning healthy adults. In order for the core emotional need for autonomy and performance to be met satisfactorily, children need to *consistently* and *on an emotional level* believe the following messages because of the actions and words of (and the atmosphere provided by) their parents:

I am my own person with my own identity.

I can do many things by myself.

I am free to chart my own direction with guidance from trusted advisors.

I am free to have a different opinion.

I am allowed to go places on my own as long as I conduct myself responsibly.

I think my parents worry about me when I get hurt or sick but not overly so.

My parents tell me they are proud of me.

My parents trust me to make wise choices and the trust grows each year as I prove myself in new situations.

Situations in life will turn out for the best, in general.

People who are close to me will not leave me unless there is an unforeseen tragedy.

If a child really believes those statements, how might that child feel? Confident, encouraged, secure and motivated are just some of the words that come to mind.

Desmond grew up an only child. Both of his parents worked in demanding professional jobs, and his mother was very strict with his schedule. As a child, he was not allowed to play at friends' homes, (might not be a good influence), not permitted to take the school bus (might not be safe), and not taught to ride a bicycle (might be dangerous). He never cleaned his room or made himself a meal, and his mother made sure she had the last word about what subjects he should take and which university he would attend.

When Desmond was in college, he was still expected to come home for dinner every night. If he made new friends, his mother became suspicious. In spite of all this, eventually he managed to get married. At first, his new wife thought his dependence on her was cute. "He needs me", she thought. Little did she know how much he needed her—he needed her for everything. Outside of the home this became an issue as well. When they tried to run a business together, he relied on her to do his share of the work, since he had no confidence in his own competence, and the wife finally had enough and gave him a "counselling or else" ultimatum.

Rick grew up in a family of sons. Their father was pretty much absent. Their mother, who was a housewife, lived for her sons. She did everything for them and was involved in every aspect of their lives. Rick was a bit shy, and was sometimes teased for being a "mummy's boy". When Rick and his brothers became successful and respected in their chosen professions, the mother beamed. But when he got married to a beautiful and successful young woman, his mother was not about to suddenly relinquish her role. She demanded to be in on every decision, and criticized the new wife for everything. After years of looking like the perfect couple on the outside, the wife had enough and walked out.

What do Desmond and Rick have in common? Their need for healthy autonomy and performance was not adequately met by their parents. One of the goals of parenting is to help our children at different points in their lives to make age-appropriate decisions and help them utilize their God given talents. If we guide and train them, then as adults they will be able to make such decisions themselves and achieve a sense of autonomy and competence without having to rely on their spouse or their parents in an unhealthy way. When children are very young, they make very few decisions about what to eat, what to wear, when to take a bath, and so on. However, as they get older, more and more age-appropriate decisions need to be entrusted to them. Unfortunately, many parents do not understand that helping them mature is a process. On the one hand, some parents feel the need to control every aspect of their child's life for as long as possible. On the other hand, some parents relinquish all control as soon as the kid enters secondary school, allowing their child to make many decisions that are not appropriate for their age, which causes just as many problems. As stated earlier, meeting the core emotional needs with Good Enough Parenting is about striking a balance.

When parents are over involved and too controlling, or under-involved and let go too soon, children do not develop healthy autonomy and do not become competent. From a child's perspective, when this core emotional need is not met, the child thinks and feels the following:

I don't feel that I am my own person nor do I have an identity.

I don't feel I can do anything right by myself.

> *I don't really have my own direction because my parent is such a strong person.*
> *I feel that if I make choices in life which are different from my parents' wishes it would hurt them. In fact, not only will it hurt their feelings, it will also get me in trouble.*
> *I feel that I cannot go anywhere or do anything responsible unless my parents are there with me.*
> *I think my parents worry excessively, especially when I get hurt or sick, and it's not even serious.*
> *I feel that when I make mistakes I should be punished, and my parents always make sure that happens.*
> *I will only be rewarded if I do what my parents want me to do, and do it well.*

When parents communicate any or all of the messages above, explicitly or implicitly, their children would probably feel exasperated. Discouraged, insecure and unmotivated are other words that come to mind. So many parents are not aware of the messages they convey when they are over-controlling and become over-involved. They think that they are being caring, thorough parents who are pouring time into their children, but the children perceive something totally different. These messages erode their children's self-esteem and facilitate the development of lifetraps. Consequently, there are very negative aspects that come with not allowing children to mature in their autonomy and performance, developing their own sense of competence.

What exactly is this sense of autonomy? The need for autonomy is the need to be self-determined and to have a choice in the initiation, maintenance, and regulation of an activity.[1] When older children and adults develop autonomy they feel their behaviour is truly chosen by them rather than imposed by some external source and their locus of initiation of their behaviour is within themselves rather than in some external control.[2] An expert in the field of human motivation, Dr Edward Deci is a psychology and social sciences professor at the University of Rochester, and is well known for his self-determination theory. He hypothesised that any occurrence which undermines people's feeling of autonomy and leaves them feeling controlled would decrease their inner, or *intrinsic,* motivation and very likely have other negative consequences. This was subsequently proven repeatedly by numerous studies conducted by him and his colleagues.[3] (See Chapter Seventeen for more on Deci's theories.)

Several other experts studied children whose parents and teachers used all sorts of strategies to motivate them, such as goals, deadlines, threats, and assessments, from the time they woke up till the time they went to bed. It was no surprise that they found this kind of hyper-control ended up having a negative impact on children's intrinsic motivation. Dr Mark Lepper and his team at Stanford University said that over-controlling kills children's sense of autonomy and takes away their inner motivation. Inner motivation is what we feel when we desire to do something out of passion or personal interest. When this is depleted because of over-controlling outward factors, children may be compliant for a while but later on become defiant.[4] Certainly this does not mean that children should be allowed to do only what they like and that discipline is not appropriate—limits and expectations are involved in the other core emotional needs. It is just that an overemphasis on discipline, rules and limits is counterproductive.

◁ LOUIS LOWDOWN ▷

> When Sonia and David were young teens, they gave me (Karen) input that sometimes my facial expressions could be extremely disapproving. I usually did a good job choosing my words carefully, but then I learned that words only counted for a small percentage of the message I was conveying. I saw that my tone was even, but my non-verbal expressions sometimes showed disapproval. After my kids' feedback, I literally began to "discipline my face" and force myself to maintain a neutral and non-judgmental demeanour even when I felt anxious.

When children are maturing in their autonomy and competence, accomplishing tasks that are age-appropriate will be a motivation unto itself. Children feel very satisfied when they are able to do certain things themselves. Each victory and new skill adds to their overall self-esteem and their intrinsic motivation. The more they accomplish by themselves, the more confident they will feel, and so a sense of competence will grow within the child. They will eventually believe that they are able to deal with life and the world in which they live. Of course the task cannot be too easy. The task must meet what Deci calls the "optimal challenge", which means that one does not need to be the best or get an "A", but need only to take on a meaningful personal challenge and give it one's best.[5]

When we are actively engaged in trying to train our children, sometimes there are simply too many things we have in mind that we want to teach them; maybe it's table manners, maybe it's how to dress, maybe it's personal hygiene, maybe it's hairstyles or something about tattoos or piercings, or who knows what. As a parent we want to have a say in how our kids behave and turn out. (We don't want our kids going over to someone's house, leaving things all over the place, and then hearing through the grapevine that people are asking if our kids were raised in a barn!) At the same time, as the kids get older, we have to be able to let go or at least communicate with them in a way that does not show disdain or disapproval when it's not a right or wrong morality issue. This will put us well on our way to meeting the core emotional need for autonomy and performance.

> ### ◁ MASTER CLASS ▷
>
> Ron and Linda Brumley had this to say about the core emotional need for autonomy and performance, "As with most families, our biggest challenges in child raising came when our kids were in the 12 to 18 age bracket. Prior to that, we were 'real experts' in raising kids. We had all the answers, or so we thought. We taught classes and workshops and came across as though raising children was a piece of cake. Then came the years of adolescence. One after the other, our four began to question our authority, our methods, and everything about our lives. They even began to question and doubt and struggle with the concepts of God, faith, righteousness, doctrinal issues, and on and on. Looking back on this period, we now realize how necessary and healthy it was for each of them. Each child had to experience this process to come out as a mature, adult believer who had his own faith, based on his own struggles with God. With each of our children, we went through periods of doubt, fear and heartache as to whether they would make it or not. We learned, often the hard way (through painful mistakes), that trying to control our teens bred frustration and rebellion in them. We came to realise, with the help of many people, that telling, demanding and lecturing seldom elicited a desired response. The very wise apostle Paul told fathers to 'encourage, comfort and urge' their children (see 1 Thessalonians 2:12). Affirming, praising, encouraging and not exasperating a teen will assist in meeting their need for autonomy, plus it is much more likely to get the behaviour you desire. Best of all, it will make you and your kids friends for life!"

*What are the lifetraps
associated with this
core emotional need?*

CHAPTER NINE

Healthy Autonomy and Performance: What's at Stake?

Advantages of Meeting this Need

When parents meet the core emotional need for healthy autonomy and performance, the child will develop some or all of the following traits and beliefs: confidence about safety and wellness, independence and competence, a sense of self that is differentiated and developed, security and stability, assertiveness and self-expression, and optimism.

Confidence about Safety and Wellness

Children who have had the core emotional need for healthy autonomy met feel confident about their own health and safety. They are not "worry warts", and generally live with the following worldview, *"Anything is possible but not everything is probable. I am confident that as long as I do what is reasonably in my power to do to protect my health and safety, I will be fine."* While not necessarily being adventurous, they are at least confident enough to try new experiences from time to time, and to not get bent out of shape when faced with an illness or a change of plans. They live happily, without worrying about their health or coming to harm. Ideally, children will assume that as long as they take proper precautions, they will be fine, and they are certainly in no more danger than anyone else.

MOVIE MOMENT – *Finding Nemo*[1]

One of our favourite children's movies is *Finding Nemo*, a pro-autonomy anecdote starring fish, turtles, and other sea creatures. The story begins when Marlin is knocked unconscious while trying to save his wife and her eggs from a predator. He awakes to discover that have all been devoured! However, one egg survives and Marlin makes it his goal in life to never let anything happen to his little son, Nemo. That means that Marlin will never let Nemo try anything, as well. Fortunately for the boy, Nemo is not influenced by his dad's lifetraps. He is able to function in a carefree manner, freely exploring the world around him, and gets himself into several exciting adventures, with a happy ending, of course. But don't be too hard on Marlin—we always say, you'd have lifetraps too if you saw your wife and kids get eaten by a barracuda!

Independence and Competence

Children who have had the core emotional need for healthy autonomy met feel independent and competent. They have thoughts such as, *"I can take care of myself"*, *"I do not need to rely on those around me in order to survive"*, and *"I can solve problems and make decisions on my own."* Children will develop independence and competence when they are encouraged to believe that they can do things on their own, when they are allowed to try and make mistakes, and allowed to fall down and sometimes get up by themselves. As they get older, they feel like their parents trust them to make day-to-day age-appropriate decisions and feel capable of handling normal responsibilities. They are able to do basic chores around the house and feel capable that they can manage on their own if they need to do so.

A Sense of Self that is Differentiated and Developed

Children who have had the core emotional need for healthy autonomy met feel a sense of self that is differentiated from their parents, and developed. They have the attitude that says *"I am my own person and can survive without constant contact and closeness with my parent or partner if I need to. I do not have to know what they think in order to be sure of what I think."* Children who are able to develop this way are allowed to disagree with their parents and not made to feel guilty about having their own opinions. They grow up seeing a healthy environment of respect for creative differences and they develop a sense of autonomy. They do not wait for their parents, caregivers, and significant others to make decisions for them, and are comfortable being alone if needs be.

Security and Stability

Children who have had the core emotional need for healthy autonomy met feel secure and stable. The way they feel about their parents, siblings and close friends is best summed up, *"I can count on my family and friends for consistent support, caring, and connection. I can count on the people I love and need to be there for me, just as I will strive to be there for them."* Children who feel this way have been raised in a secure and stable family atmosphere. They believe that the significant others in their life will always be there for them, regardless of what happens. They are not insecure about their connection with the people closest to them, and feel that they can depend on those connections in times of need.

Assertiveness and Self-Expression

Children who have had the core emotional need for healthy autonomy met are able to be assertive and confidently express themselves. While they may enjoy serving and pleasing others at times, they will also feel, *"My needs and desires are as important as the needs of others. I will choose relationships that are two-way rather than one-way, and I will not fear rejection or abandonment by people who are important to me. I have learnt to show my anger in a healthy way."* Children who are secure with their closest relations will feel that their opinion is valued. When they are allowed to disagree respectfully without feeling judged or pressured to conform to a parent's opinion, they will have the confidence to venture out on their own in an age-appropriate way. They will be able to express differences without fear, and be good at handling conflict and managing anger. They will feel comfortable both expressing their needs and meeting the needs of their significant others.

Optimism

Children who have had the core emotional need for healthy autonomy met have a sense of optimism. They may or may not be full-on optimists, depending on their temperament, but they will carry with them the belief that says, *"Deep down I believe that things generally go well, that one's outlook on life helps to make a difference to the outcome, and that, generally speaking, things will go well more often that go badly."* Children with a sense of optimism are at a supreme advantage in life. They are less likely to struggle with depression and will have an easier time getting a job and a spouse. Why? Because they believe genuinely that things will usually turn out all right in the end. They do not feel that the world is out to get them, nor are they great believers in Murphy's Law, although they may joke about it. They intuitively focus on what is going well, are solution-oriented, feel hopeful about the future, and try to make the most out of life when bad things happen.

Disadvantages of Not Meeting this Need

To the extent that parents do not meet the core emotional need for healthy autonomy and performance, their children will develop some or all of the following lifetraps: vulnerability to harm or illness, dependence, enmeshment, abandonment, subjugation, and negativity.

The Lifetrap of Vulnerability to Harm or Illness

The core message of the lifetrap of vulnerability to harm or illness is, *"Catastrophe is just around the corner. Something bad is about to happen and I am **powerless** to do anything about it."*

Children who end up with this lifetrap are made to live in fear that danger is imminent. They are taught to think that they will definitely contract a serious illness, lose money, be attacked, have an accident, or have some other bad thing happen to them. Their fear may become so exaggerated that it may manifest itself in the form of anxiety or panic attacks. They may go for medical check-ups over and over again. As adults, any sign of illness will be interpreted as something serious, like a heart attack. They are often able to function on a day-to-day basis but there is always a sense that danger is very close. Children with this lifetrap tend to be hypervigilant and go to great lengths to stop these things from taking place. Sometimes it may show up as excessive worry, such as trying to save large sums of money for the future

172 ■ Good Enough Parenting

Figure 9.1: The Lifetrap of Vulnerability to Harm or Illness (Shen as a child)

since they believe that they might be left stranded. This worry may then induce some form of actual stress-related illnesses, which will then confirm their fears, resulting in more worry. They get stuck in a cycle, and resort to all kinds of medications and rituals in order to be prepared when danger strikes. Adults with this lifetrap may have had a parent who obsessed about health and safety issues, had an exaggerated fear of being in danger, and who talked about tragedies not just as possibilities but as probabilities (see Figures 9.1 & 9.2).

A quick glance at what might have happened to an adult with this lifetrap during childhood:
- The child's parents lived out this lifetrap and he imitated it. They talked incessantly about illness, safety, about having no money or getting attacked, and they told him stories of other people's tragedies.
- The child's parents were excessively in control of his life, trying to make sure that he was not in danger.
- The child faced a traumatic event that rendered him unusually fearful.

Figure 9.2: The Lifetrap of Vulnerability to Harm or Illness (Shen as an adult)

- The child saw someone he loved die in an accident, or from an illness or tragedy and he internalized this and concluded that he should be on guard at all times.
- The child's home or environment was not a safe place for him or was unstable and unpredictable.

Exercise: Please refer to the Exasperation Interactions worksheet (Appendix 1) and identify the exasperation interaction(s) in Figure 9.1.

Case Study

Vickie's mother Samantha became a Christian when Vickie was ten years old. Her mother had a painful past, and came into the family of God with many bruises and scars. Even though Samantha tried her best with her young daughter, she ended up being very punitive with Vickie, often withholding affection when expectations were not met. Vickie endured her mother's frequent scolding and punishment, while trying not to notice her mother's complete lack of interest in her feelings. Exasperated at home, Vickie confides in her youth worker at church when she is stressed, upset, frustrated at taking care of her younger siblings, or even when she has accomplished something worthwhile. Vickie feels blamed for everything that goes wrong in the house, and has nowhere else to turn. This repeated exasperating punitive interaction has led to Vickie being susceptible to the lifetrap of vulnerability. She gets very emotional and dreams of her mother dying and of being left all alone to fend for the whole family. Vickie also struggles with emotional deprivation on all levels, approval-seeking behaviour, and other lifetraps.

The Lifetrap of Dependence / Incompetence

The core message of the dependence lifetrap says, *"I cannot take care of myself. I need to rely on those around me in order to survive. I cannot solve problems or make decisions on my own."*

Children who develop the dependence lifetrap have been treated as if they were not able to handle life with all of its responsibilities and tasks. They are not able to develop confidence in their own abilities and have the need for someone else to constantly be around. Left alone, they feel completely useless and feel that they will make wrong decisions. They feel that they do not have the skills to operate on their own, hence their dependence on others

Figure 9.3: The Lifetrap of Dependence / Incompetence (Sierra as a child)

Healthy Autonomy and Performance: What's at Stake? ▪ 175

to do things for them or to help them. They may vacillate and be double-minded about what to do, and worry about whether a previous decision was right. People with this lifetrap may function well in some settings, but be very dependent on others. Adults with the lifetrap of dependence do not know how frustrated others feel about their unhealthy reliance on them for daily tasks. They lack the confidence to be able to make decisions and take care of things by themselves. They think they are expecting normal support from their spouse and friends, and do not realise that they are actually unnaturally dependent on others (see Figures 9.3 & 9.4).

Exercise: Please refer to the Exasperation Interactions worksheet (Appendix 1) and identify the exasperation interaction(s) in Figure 9.3.

A quick glance at what might have happened to an adult with this lifetrap during childhood:

- The child's parents were overprotective, and did not allow the child to do things by himself that were age-appropriate. They were so cautious that they did not allow the child to develop a healthy autonomy. For example, when other children were allowed to travel by themselves, the child was

Figure 9.4: The Lifetrap of Dependence / Incompetence (Sierra as an adult)

not allowed to do so. When they were allowed to learn tasks, the child was not given the opportunity.
- The child's parents valued something (e.g., grades, music or sports), and allowed her to focus only on that. Consequently, the child never learned to do other tasks that her peers learned.
- The child was given unusually strict boundaries. She may not have been allowed to go out of the house, or participate in extracurricular activities, such as sports, and so she never developed a healthy autonomy.
- The child's parents made all decisions about her life, or she was "rescued" by one parent in many situations.
- The child's homework was done, or overly supervised, by one of her parents. When this was repeated many times, the child thought she couldn't do it anyway. She may have also developed a sense of laziness.
- The child was criticized for making bad decisions so she lost her confidence. Her parents gladly stepped in when she hesitated, therefore she never quite developed the confidence to act on her own.

Case Study

Kim lives at home, the oldest of three girls. Her father is an ex-Marine and runs his family like his own personal militia. Discipline is expected in all areas. Respect for your elders is a given. Talking back is not permitted. Showing weakness is not acceptable. Kim's father leads a small group at his church, and believes that leader's children should behave in a certain manner. He feels the need to look perfect to those outside, therefore, family problems "do not exist". In his perfectionism, Kim's father has also been punitive and has even slapped his teenagers. Kim has learned to behave outwardly in the expected manner and feels pressure to perform well on all fronts. It is no wonder she struggles to believe in herself and her own abilities. Spiritually, Kim also feels the pressure to become a follower of the Lord to please her parents, to meet up to their expectations and to set a good example for her younger sisters. She is torn between actually desiring to be a Christian and rebelling against her parents' values. If it were not for the support she is receiving in her church community, Kim feels she would probably surrender to her fears of not being good enough at anything and needing someone's help to do the smallest task. The good news is that Kim's parents are now getting help to repair the relationship.

The Lifetrap of Enmeshment / Undeveloped Self

The core message of the enmeshment lifetrap is, *"I cannot survive on my own without constant contact and closeness with my parent or partner. I need to know what they think in order to be sure of what I think."* This is about an underdeveloped sense of self as a separate person.

Children who develop this lifetrap are intertwined emotionally with one or both parents. For persons with the enmeshment lifetrap, it is hard to tell where one person ends and the other person begins. They are so closely interrelated with the other person that they are unable to tell themselves apart from that person. They feel empty and are often afraid of existing on their own. People can be enmeshed with their parents, their spouse, their children, a sibling, or their best friend. This becomes especially difficult when approaching or entering a marriage. If an adult female is enmeshed with a parent (usually her mother), she will communicate more with that parent than with her husband. Her mother will be the first to know about what names she likes for a future child, what kind of house she would like to buy, or which job she will possibly take. Enmeshed individuals feel the need to constantly talk and tell each other everything. There is a sense that the two of them are, in a strange way, one person. People with the enmeshment lifetrap have a hard time making decisions without first considering the opinions of the person with whom they are enmeshed. Enmeshed individuals do not learn healthy boundaries in childhood (see Figures 9.5 & 9.6).

Exercise: Please refer to the Exasperation Interactions worksheet (Appendix 1) and identify the exasperation interaction(s) in Figure 9.5.

Figure 9.5: The Lifetrap of Enmeshment / Undeveloped Self (Raj as a child)

Figure 9.6: The Lifetrap of Enmeshment / Undeveloped Self (Raj as an adult)

A quick glance at what might have happened to an adult with this lifetrap during childhood:

- There was a very close bond between the child and one of his parents. This happens almost exclusively between mothers and children. They were so close that they were able to easily read one another's non-verbal communication and know what the other person was thinking. The mother would also share her intimate issues with her child, such as the present state of her marriage. This kind of excessive attachment began very early on and continued into adulthood.
- The child's parents were very controlling and did not allow him to make decisions on his own.
- The child's parents were rigid in their thinking and opinions and did not allow for diversity of opinion.
- The child's parents were extremely over-protective.
- The child was taught to not set boundaries with the parents, and if he did, he would end up with unhealthy guilt.

Case Study

Susan is an only child. Her mother divorced Susan's father due to physical and verbal abusive. Susan's mum broke the news of the divorce to her one day and they never spoke about the issue again. Independent, strong and determined at work, Susan's mum climbed the corporate ladder and became the CEO of the company where she has worked for many years. At home, she pours all her energy and love into her daughter. Susan's mum's advice and opinion mean the world to her. If Susan is unsure about anything, she goes to her mum for comfort and assurance. Though now in her thirties and successful at work in her own right, Susan is very unsure when not with her mother or another strong figure. She lives under the shadow of her mum and also seeks the approval of her boss and friends. Susan is afraid of going though challenges in life because she feels she is fragile and incapable of handling difficulties, unlike her mother. Even after becoming engaged, she could not imagine being closer to anyone than her mother. Fortunately, Susan went for pre-marriage counselling, got married, and is working on her lifetraps.

The Lifetrap of Abandonment / Instability

The core message of the abandonment lifetrap is, *"I cannot count on anyone for consistent support, caring, and connection. I will be rejected; people I love and need will die; and people I love and need cannot be relied upon to be there when I need them."*

Children who are abandoned will almost certainly develop the abandonment schema. Virtually all children who are adopted will have this lifetrap, no matter how wonderful their adoptive home is. The fact is, they *were* abandoned, even if it was no one's fault. The extent that the adopted family meets their core emotional needs will go a long way in determining how easy it will be for adopted children to eventually come to terms with their abandonment, but it may take years. People who have the abandonment lifetrap fear that everyone they love will leave them. They believe that ultimately they will be alone, and that they cannot really count on people to be there for them. They constantly need to be reassured that they are loved, and that their close relationships will not leave them. If they are married, they expect their spouse to communicate undying commitment, without which they may become resentful. Underneath their anger and hurt, they do not feel secure and literally believe that they are destined for loneliness and have exaggerated feelings of instability in their closest relationships (see Figures 9.7 & 9.8).

Exercise: Please refer to the Exasperation Interactions worksheet (Appendix 1) and identify the exasperation interaction(s) in Figure 9.7.

Figure 9.7: The Lifetrap of Abandonment / Instability (Katya as a child)

A quick glance at what might have happened to an adult with this lifetrap during childhood::

- One of the child's parents left the home, died, or lived separately.
- The child was given up for adoption.
- The child was forced to live with someone other than her parents for a period of time during childhood, perhaps because of difficult circumstances.
- One of the child's parents was too ill to look after her.
- There was intense marital conflict between the child's parents.
- Someone else in the family took the attention away from the child (perhaps a sibling who was ill, or had special needs, or who was favoured).

Case Study

Nikko lives in a European city and is an only child. His mother has had many boyfriends, but never really settled down. When Nikko would get close to a father figure, it was time to either move or get a new boyfriend. Nikko's mother embraced Christianity when Nikko was a teen; she then married a

Healthy Autonomy and Performance: What's at Stake? ▪ 181

Figure 9.8: The Lifetrap of Abandonment / Instability (Katya as an adult)

man she met in church. When Nikko entered university, he began to have a hard time with his relationships there. He made friends easily enough, but if the other kids didn't respond the way he expected, he would stop talking to them. For example, if Nikko sent a text and the recipient did not respond right away, he would no longer send texts to him, or he would be cold in their next interaction. He also had a love-hate relationship with the kids at church that were his age. Nikko reached a breaking point when a girl he liked felt like they were rushing things in their dating relationship, after which he quit school, stopped all church involvement, and began taking drugs. He presently works part-time, is on his third girlfriend in as many years, and is having a hard time making new friends. Nikko's motto is, "I will leave them before they leave me."

The Lifetrap of Subjugation

The core message of the subjugation lifetrap is, *"I must submit to the needs and desires of others before my own or I will be rejected by the anger or abandonment of people who are important to me."* The internal slogan is

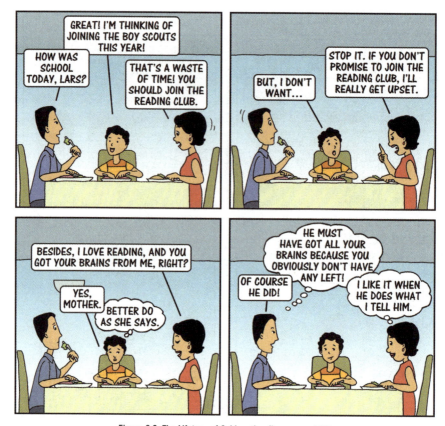

Figure 9.9: The Lifetrap of Subjugation (Lars as a child)

"I'm number two." Subjugation is about needs—not showing preferences, desires, decisions and opinions, or emotions—not showing feelings, particularly anger.

Children who develop the subjugation lifetrap will have been made to feel that their desires, needs and opinions are neither significant nor important. They will tend to repress expressing themselves, which leads to passive aggressive thoughts and behaviour, withdrawing, and ultimately to intense anger. They will believe they *have to* always put others' needs and opinions above their own. They will often neglect themselves and give in to others because they are extremely afraid of conflict, which they fear will lead to some kind of punishment or loss of love and affection. They will rarely express their own opinions, and even if they do, they will not treat their own opinion as being as important as others' opinions because of their fear of conflict or rejection.

One of the dangerous aspects of this schema is that after being subjugated for a while, feelings of anger and resentment will start to surface because they have not paid any attention to their own needs, and they have not

Figure 9.10: The Lifetrap of Subjugation (Lars as an adult)

asked others to meet their needs. They may feel very little excitement in life, because they have been too busy meeting others' needs. People around them will share that this is their strength, but it is actually a weakness. People with this lifetrap will not experience the kind of intimacy they want because all of their attention is focused on meeting their partner's needs and wants, with nothing left over for themselves. People who are subjugated put their needs at the bottom of the priority list for fear of conflict if they do not do what others want of them. When subjugated adults start feeling the need for self-care, they feel afraid that they will be rejected in anger or abandonment. They have not learned to draw boundaries with unhealthy people or say "No" to them. Eventually, people with this lifetrap will hit a wall. They may become depressed, or blow up and become aggressive, or focus on themselves to the point of selfishness. If married, the partner may think there is something wrong with his or her subjugated spouse. If the subjugated person swings to the other extreme, defies authority and refuses to follow any form of rules, the behaviour may be mistaken for the entitlement lifetrap (see Figures 9.9 & 9.10).

A quick glance at what might have happened to an adult with this lifetrap during childhood:

- The child's parents were upset when he did not yield to their wishes.
- The child's parents were over-controlling; with little autonomy, the child was not allowed to make his own decisions.
- The child saw one of his parents give in to the other and learned that it was the best way to keep the peace.
- The child was made to feel guilty if his needs were given attention.

Case Study

Nyah is one of eight children, the daughter of a second wife in a country where polygamy is legal. Her father, a local chief, lives with his first wife and his five children with her from Monday to Thursday, and lives with Nyah's mother and his three children with her Friday to Sunday. Nyah is in her teens, and yearns for her father's affection, but rarely gets to spend time with him. When Nyah asks to accompany him somewhere, he usually answers that he is too busy, working to provide for the family. She learned early on that her father values education, so she set out to achieve outstanding results academically hoping to gain his attention. Longing for connection, she now immerses herself in her studies and does whatever her father says. In fact, she is determined to be whatever her father wants her to be, including becoming a doctor one day. Even though she has her own dreams, she decided that she would study a field that her father thinks is good for her. Nyah feels sacrificing what she likes is not a big deal as long as her father is happy. On a positive note, because Nyah's mother was converted to Christianity when Nyah was young, the church community has actually helped to alleviate some of the other shortcomings of Nyah's childhood.

Exercise: Please refer to the Exasperation Interactions worksheet (Appendix 1) and identify the exasperation interaction(s) in Figure 9.9.

The Lifetrap of Negativity / Pessimism

The core message of the negativity lifetrap is, *"I am destined to make a serious mistake that will result in big problems. Things will inevitably go wrong. Bad things will happen to me."* The negative aspects of life are emphasised at the expense of those things which are positive and which will potentially bring joy.

Children who develop this lifetrap are made to feel that it is normal to feel down. Everything is seen and experienced with a negative spin on it. The cup is never half-full; it is always half-empty. Those who develop this lifetrap hate making mistakes and fear the supposed consequences that may arise. They worry about the loss and humiliation that may come from taking risks (and experiencing what they see as failure). They would rather be safe than sorry and take the path that would least expose them to such risks. Usually

Healthy Autonomy and Performance: What's at Stake? ■ 185

their negativity is not accurate but blown out of proportion. People with the lifetrap of negativity were made to feel ashamed of making mistakes and being wrong when they were growing up. As adults, they still do not realise that making mistakes is part of being human, and that part of learning comes from making mistakes. This often causes damage to relationships; for example, whenever their spouse or friends want to try something new, they will always be the "wet blanket" (see Figures 9.11 & 9.12).

Exercise: Please refer to the Exasperation Interactions worksheet (Appendix 1) and identify the exasperation interaction(s) in Figure 9.11.

A quick glance at what might have happened to an adult with this lifetrap during childhood:

- The child's parents talked about things from a negative point of view. Many times their answers would be "no" to the child's wishes or plans because they would assume the worst possible outcome. One of them may have painted such a negative picture of life that the child assumed that outlook as well.
- The child's parents went through very hard times, and so a strong signal

Figure 9.11: The Lifetrap of Negativity / Pessimism (Nicole as a child)

Figure 9.12: The Lifetrap of Negativity / Pessimism (Nicole as an adult)

was sent to avoid this fate at all costs, and to avoid making mistakes.
- The child actually experienced many negative events in her childhood, which reinforced what her negative parents told her about the world.
- The child has a more negative temperament, and her parents did not train her to be more positive.

Case Study

Suzette's parents were both from poor families in non-English speaking rural Asia, and were introduced to Christianity when they moved to their nation's capital. Straight A students who worked very hard for everything they got in life, they were content with very little in the way of possessions or stimulation. The couple were childhood sweethearts who planned for their one and only daughter to follow their faith, thinking they would then have the perfect Christian family. Unfortunately, they were also both extremely emotionally inhibited, and assumed that Suzette would be happy with their minimalist lifestyle. This frankly seemed boring to a child growing up in a thriving modern city. Suzette longed for emotional closeness with her parents but only got what she perceived as nagging—about schoolwork, housework, and holy behaviour. She became resentful at how unfair life seemed, and blamed her weird Christian parents for her unhappiness. Suzette became exasperated because of her parents' inhibition, and attributed a negative meaning to everything that happened in her life. She now rebels by keeping to herself and demanding her own way. She refuses to attend church services and only talks to her parents when absolutely necessary. Suzette has confided in others that she actually wants to become a Christian and has a mentor at church who she meets with secretly but she is so put off by what she senses as her parents' lack of love that it is very hard for her to get past the hurt. Suzette's parents are now getting help repairing their relationship, although they realise that it will take patience and understanding.

◈ MASTER CLASS ◈

> The Brumleys on being optimistic about the adolescent years, "Teens are fascinating, bright, talented and fun-loving creatures. Parents who are worried, fearful and uptight about their kids often don't see the goodness that is within them. We needed, and we believe most parents of teens need, others in the community of Christ who were much more objective and could help us see and appreciate and enjoy our children."

Basic Safety

Basic Safety for this core emotional need involves protecting your child from abandonment, which in practical terms means that parents need to protect their marriage. In our experience, the abandonment lifetrap is one of the harder ones to deal with, and we urge all parents to do their utmost to not inflict this on their children (see Research Reveals below for more details).

◈ RESEARCH REVEALS ◈

RR9.1: *Working on Marriage Benefits Children*

In our book on marriage, *I Choose Us*, we wrote about the problems that accompany abandonment or separation:[2]

- In Britain, less than half of the children in single-parent families see their fathers once a week. And 20-30% of non-resident fathers have not seen their children in over a year.[3] In the wake of divorce, it is common for the "leaving parent"—the one not getting basic custody, usually the father—to promise the children that he will always be there for them and will maintain a close relationship with them. Unfortunately, this promise is frequently not kept. Because of inconveniences arising from the divorce, and for other reasons, fathers often find it challenging to see their children. It should not come as a surprise then that many good intentions fall through on the part of both of the parents after the divorce. Generally speaking, the bond, especially between fathers and their children, deteriorates after a divorce.[4]

- Children in single-parent families receive about nine hours less from their mother per week than children from families where the parents were still married and living together.[5]

While no one sets out to get divorced, perhaps if parents knew the dire consequences of the alternative, they might take better care of their marriage!

Children learn from example, and imitate their parental role models more than parents realise. The lives of the parents provide a blueprint of how the children will probably lead their lives later on. Statistics show that the quality of the parents' marriage affects the quality of the children's relationships when they end up getting married. Our actions have consequences, the effects of which are felt in more than one generation.[6]

- Single mothers are twice as likely as two-parent families to live in poverty.[7]
- Single mothers are also eight times as likely to be without jobs and twelve times as likely to be on some form of government support.[8]
- Divorce causes the level of income for a middle-income family to decrease by 50%.[9]
- Single parents are also twice as likely to not have any savings.[10]
- Children in single-parent homes are 80% more likely to have health problems, such as pains, headaches, stomach symptoms, etc., than children from two-parent homes, even after taking into account economic hardship.[11]
- Divorce causes children to have more emotional distress and increases the risk of mental illness.[12] These symptoms do not disappear quickly. They linger on, in some cases for years.
- Children who live in a house with a stepfather, or a mother's boyfriend, are more likely to be abused than those living with their father or with a mother only.[13]
- Living with a step-parent has turned out to be the most powerful predictor of severe child abuse yet.[14]
- Young people are five times more likely to experience abuse if they grow up in a single home than if they grow up with parents whose marriages are still intact, according to the National Society for the Prevention of Cruelty to Children (NSPCC).[15]

The overwhelming evidence points conclusively to the fact that the state of marriages affects parenting, and has huge ramifications on children's relationships with their parents, economic well-being, physical and psychological health, protection from domestic violence, and the likelihood that these children in turn will stay together later on in their marriages.

In addition, Basic Safety for this core emotional need has to do with making sure children are not neglected and that their basic needs for shelter, food, clothing, and sleep are met. Parents should make sure that they know the basics regarding sleep, breastfeeding, proper nutrition, dealing with illnesses, and so forth.

Lastly, Basic Safety for this core emotional need also means ensuring that safety measures in and outside the home are put in place and that children are not allowed to be autonomous too soon. Inappropriate (too soon) autonomy can become neglect or can inadvertently promote abuse. Parents should familiarise themselves with childproofing measures so that their homes are safe. For example, poisonous substances should be kept locked away, and babysitter instructions and emergency numbers kept handy. Children need to learn to cook eventually, but they should not be using sharp knives on their own or operating stoves when they are too young. Children should eventually bathe themselves, but infants and toddlers should never be left alone around a pail of water, much less in a bathtub. School age children should be able to walk home from school or take public transport eventually, but not before they are capable. There are all sorts of ways that parents can protect their children under the auspices of meeting the core emotional need for autonomy.

One more thing—while it is perfectly normal to allow an elementary school aged boy to go to the restroom by himself in a public place, the sad fact of today's world is that sexual predators exist and they frequent places where young boys might be unattended. *The Straits Times* has reported several cases of boys under ten being forced to do unspeakable acts in public restrooms, even in a country as safe as Singapore.[16]

⋞ LOUIS LOWDOWN ⋟

When our son was young and needed to use a public restroom, my husband would accompany David if he were there, or I (Karen) would allow a trustworthy male friend to go along with David. If David and I were out on our own, before he started primary school, I just brought him to the women's room. However, once he hit about seven years old, he wanted to go into the men's room and I didn't blame him. However, I told him that the only way I would allow it is if he would keep a semi-running conversation with me while he was inside. I would walk up to the door of the men's room in such a way that I could not see inside, but as David walked in, I would shout, "David, I'm standing right by the door, ok?" He would answer, and I would ask another question about every fifteen seconds. I absolutely would have charged in if he hadn't answered me—luckily that never happened. Incidentally, when recounting this to my son as I was writing this book, he told me he had no memory of me standing guard anywhere, and congratulated me on keeping him safe while at the same time not making him paranoid.

⟨ THE CORE EMOTIONAL NEED FOR HEALTHY AUTONOMY ⟩
AND PERFORMANCE AMONG THE PATRIARCHS

Now that we have examined the advantages of meeting the core emotional need for healthy autonomy and performance, as well as the dangers that come from not meeting this need, let us study out how the core emotional need for healthy autonomy and performance was not met in the family of the patriarchs in the book of Genesis, chapters 27-35.

Questions for Discussion:
- In light of the fact that Rebekah favoured Jacob, what did she focus on as Jacob was growing up?
- In light of the fact that Isaac favoured Esau, what did he focus on as Esau was growing up?
- What could we speculate about Isaac and Rebekah's marriage relationship, given that each of them gravitated to Esau and Jacob, respectively?
- When Isaac saw Rebekah's focus on Jacob, what did he do or not do about it?
- When Rebekah saw Isaac's focus on Esau, what did she do or not do about it?
- Esau was known as a skilful hunter. How might he have felt as a teenage boy, not being acquainted with how to take care of himself around the house?
- Jacob was known as a quiet boy who stayed among the tents. How might he have felt as a teenager about going hunting?
- Do you think Jacob enjoyed being this way?
- How did Rebekah dictate what kind of decisions Jacob needed to make in his own life? Did he feel subjugated by her?
- Look in Genesis 27:5-13. Did Rebekah give Jacob any room for his own preferences and choices?
- Look again in Genesis 27:41-45. How did Rebekah come across to Jacob? Was there room for Jacob to make choices?
- How might growing up under a controlling mother have affected Jacob?
- Look in Genesis 29:14b-28. When Jacob was tricked, how did he respond to Laban's authoritarian and unfair dealings?
- Look in Genesis 29:28-30. Did Jacob resist being unfairly treated by a strong man like Laban?
- Did Laban sense that Jacob would be subjugated to his preferences while he was working with him for the first seven years?
- Might Jacob's demeanour have given Laban confidence to take advantage of Jacob, knowing he had problems having his own convictions of healthy autonomy?
- Look in Genesis 35:27-28. While Jacob was subjugated for years under Laban, was he ever able to see his mother, Rebekah, again?

- Did Rebekah perhaps reap what she had sown, the seeds of enmeshment and subjugation in Jacob?
- Look in Genesis 31:6-7. How many times did Laban take advantage of Jacob?
- Look in Genesis 31:20-38. Did Jacob finally have the conviction to do what he felt was right?
- Look in Genesis 31:42. Even though Jacob was subjugated to Laban, did he also grow in his trust in God?

Insights

Too fast, too quick. Hurry and grow up. Children are placed in situations where they are forced to learn skills that are beyond their age. Esau, right from the start, probably because of his appearance, was naturally seen as one who had a gift for the outdoors. So Isaac moved him in that direction. How did he feel not being close to his maternal parent, Rebekah? In today's context, perhaps she did not tuck him into bed and read him bedtime stories, like she did with Jacob. She was all too sensitive about how Jacob was feeling being the second-born and felt a tremendous need to compensate. Was Jacob really that disadvantaged? Did they possibly overvalue the rights of the firstborn (in hindsight, of course…)?

So as the years went by, it is probable that Rebekah never got close to Esau. We can surmise this partly from her plan to help Jacob deceive his older brother as recorded in Genesis 27:6-17. She had little empathy for Easu, but lots for Jacob. The closeness that developed between Jacob and Rebekah as they spent untold hours in the tent together while Isaac and Esau were out seems to have resulted in an enmeshed relationship between them. Jacob and his mother not only managed the household together, they must have also spent time planning and plotting to trick both Isaac and Esau, who were completely oblivious to this.

We wonder if Jacob enjoyed his teenage years, especially when he compared himself to his peers? Would Isaac perhaps have made suggestions for Jacob to go out and be exposed to other boys his own age? Did Jacob wonder if he was normal, like other boys? Did this sense of "protection" make him feel flawed or inadequate? Did it make him feel special or entitled? Was he made fun of by other boys, or even by Esau? Did he ever feel confident doing things on his own? Was he able to rely on his own judgment to make decisions on his own as he grew up?

Look in Genesis 27:5-13. Look at the similarity of her words in Genesis 27:13 and in Genesis 27:43. How did Rebekah come across to Jacob? "Do what I say…" Rebekah was more than just a little controlling of Jacob. He had to follow his mother's wishes. From the way she spoke to him, there was not much of a discussion. She was so direct and simply told Jacob what to do. Jacob did not put up much resistance. Why? From a young age he was subject to his strong mother's will. He complied, but in his heart he may have felt rotten. He probably knew that cheating his brother out of his birthright was wrong, but with a strong controlling mother's voice in his head, it eventually became part of his own inclination. Did he disagree with Rebekah at all as he was growing up? What would have been the consequences if he had? Was he ever allowed to say exactly what he thought to his controlling mother?

As it was, the plot to steal Esau's birth right originated from his mother, but Jacob went along with it. Did he agree in his heart that deceiving his brother was the right thing to do? Most probably he felt this to some degree. The overall effect was that he was not close to Esau but enmeshed with his mother. In fact, if he had gotten married nearby, there is a good chance that Jacob would have been closer to his mother than to his own wife, which is a recipe for a disastrous marriage.

When Esau heard about the way he was outwitted, he was enraged and wanted to kill Jacob. Again, what did Rebekah say to Jacob? She simply told him what to do. Here was a major life decision for Jacob and she basically told him to leave. Period. Jacob again did not put up much of a fight. Like an enmeshed son to his mother, he obeyed and went. He fled home at that moment because his controlling mother told him so.

If our speculations are correct, then all his life up to that point, Jacob lived in subjugation to his mother. Her preferences became his preferences. He would not dare to differ with her, or else he would be in trouble. Jacob's desires became secondary, and Rebekah's desires became primary. Such were Jacob's relationship dynamics with his mother.

After fleeing, he went to the home of Laban, which was where his mother told him to go. When Laban took Jacob under his wing by having Jacob work for him, do you think that Laban sensed that Jacob was a very compliant person? Could Laban sense that he could now manipulate Jacob?

Jacob, after leaving a strong mother, found himself in the hands of another strong person, Laban. Isn't that how it is with many of us? We leave the frying pan only to jump into the fire; we go from one strong person to another, and the strange thing is that we find ourselves very much at home when this happens. Why is that? Because we get drawn to the familiar much more than to the healthy. Jacob was so used to being subjugated by Rebekah that he naturally took the same role with Laban. Is it any surprise then that Laban used this compliant side of Jacob to his own advantage? Look in Genesis 29:14b-28. His plans worked. Jacob consented to working for him for another seven years, seen in Genesis 29:28-30. Jacob was not his own man. He never learned how to be autonomous in a way that was appropriate for his age. By this time in his life, Jacob was an adult and should have had a 100% say on whom he wanted to marry, but even in significant matters like this he was subjugated to another strong person. So, in the end, even though Jacob wanted to marry Rachel, Laban got Jacob to marry Leah instead, and then only gave Rachel to him in exchange for another seven years of labour. To us, this was completely out of line. However, to a subjugated person like Jacob, this was not injustice. In a strange way, Jacob was at home with a strong man who got his way all the time. Being with someone like Laban sat well with Jacob and his own lifetraps. So Laban killed two birds with one stone. Laban did not care about how marrying both of his daughters off to the same man would affect his daughters' relationship with one another. He was so self absorbed that all he cared about were his own plans and desires, regardless of how it made others feel. Laban kept using and manipulating Jacob. Looking in Genesis 31:6-7, we see how Laban cheated Jacob of his wages ten times. Again, Laban knew he could get away with it with a subjugated, compliant person like Jacob. Obviously, Laban was a pretty narcissistic individual.

Well, given that Jacob was subjected to Laban, did he ever see his mother, Rebekah again? It does not seem that he did. In fact, in Genesis 35:27-28, by the time Jacob had the next opportunity to come home, he arrived in time for his father's death. Nothing was mentioned about Rebekah, and so it is very likely that she died before Isaac. So, the price of an enmeshed mother–son relationship can sometimes be high. You reap what you sow. A child that does not enjoy healthy autonomy will eventually lead an unhealthy life. Such consequences often come back to haunt parents somewhere down the road.

In the end, subjugated people will come out of subjugation. God worked through Jacob and in Genesis 31:20-21 and 31:38; Jacob finally grew to develop and express his own convictions, then spoke up against Laban. He finally grew up! God was slowly working in his life during those years of being under Laban. Jacob finally broke ranks with Laban, took both his wives and fled from Laban. Good for him, but it took twenty years! When children's core emotional need for healthy autonomy is not met, they may take years to come out of this dysfunction. Some people never do, but some, through God's working, are able to break off from the heavy hand of their superiors.

Another issue at hand was the marriage relationship between Isaac and Rebekah. Could it be that it was because both of them were not meeting each other's needs that they found fulfilment in their respective favourite son? Rather than the marriage being a place for the two of them to parent their children together and meet each other's need of Love and Respect, they found solace in their favourite child as a substitute. As a result, a division rose between them, with Rebekah plotting how she could help Jacob without any due consideration for Esau. Isaac seemed clueless and simply went with the flow, not being in touch with the underlying currents of rivalry and jealously in the family.

Solomon said, "There is nothing new under the sun." In a parenting context, we can say that parents have been making the same kinds of mistakes for millennia. What Isaac and Rebekah no doubt wanted was a close and happy family. As we learn from the patriarchs, let us not pit our children against each other to satisfy our own dysfunctional needs, and let us meet our children's core emotional need for healthy autonomy and performance as we try to be Good Enough Parents.

*In that case,
how can I make sure
to meet this
core emotional need?*

CHAPTER TEN

Age-Appropriate Empowerment

Here are some ideas for how to adequately meet the core emotional need for autonomy and performance; for balancing between providing the right amount of protection with increasing freedom and empowerment.

Communicate Like You're on the Same Team

So often, the style of communication sends the wrong message. A parent may end up giving a choice to a child but may communicate it in a way that puts down the child, as opposed to letting the child feel like she is on the same team as her parents. Even when dealing with young children, the gentleness of a parent's tone and the words a parent uses are crucial.

For example, a parent may say in an authoritarian tone, "Today we are going to the park; decide quickly which toy you want to play with." This is giving the child a choice, but how exactly was it said? The harsh tone communicates that the child is secondary to the parent's agenda. As mentioned in Chapter Four, words only account for a small part of what we communicate to others; tone of voice, body language, and facial features are much more important. So a better way to talk to the child would be, "Hi sweetie, we are going to have fun today. Which toy would you like to bring to the park?" This conveys a vastly different message to the child. Or imagine a mum speaking with her very young child about having lunch. Instead of impatiently barking, "I want you to eat now. I will only let you go to the park if you finish eating." Would it not be better if the mum kindly but assertively beamed, "We will eat lunch first, and when we are finished, we can go to the park."

There is a world of difference between the two. Both are essentially spelling out a task but one is done in a way that shows both parent and child are friends and allies, not "I am up here" and "You are down there." (There are obviously times when a parent may have to raise his or her voice, such as when a child is in danger or about to hurt herself or another child. When we raise our voice only in *rare* circumstances, the child will know that something serious is being conveyed.) Making occasional mistakes do not cause harm, but repeat them day after day and you will eventually get exasperation. The temperament of the child will determine how long that will take, and in what way it will surface.

Provide Children with Age-Appropriate Choices

As part of Deci's research on motivation, he found that people who are given more choices regarding tasks showed more enthusiasm and spent more time doing tasks than those not given a choice at all.[1] They tested this by giving two groups a puzzle-solving experiment. One group was given a choice as to which puzzles they would work on and how long they would spend completing them. The other group was not given a choice but had the same amount of time spent at their disposal. As suspected, the group that was given a choice spent more time on the puzzles and reported enjoying the task more than the other group. Providing choices is a very important part in developing our children's autonomy. It draws them into the task and helps them to take more responsibility for it. But more than anything else, it shows our level of respect for them. (For this reason, for at least one quarter a year, our youth ministry offers several different classes to the teens so that they get to *choose* which midweek class to attend. It seems to generate much enthusiasm and participation.)

We urge parents to keep in mind that both children and adults feel more motivated and autonomous when they are given choices rather than having tasks be forced upon them. Therefore, rigidity and inflexibility will not help children to grow and may prevent the core emotional need for autonomy from being met, which in turn will eat away their inner motivation. At the same time, part of children becoming autonomous in a healthy way is knowing where their rights end and others' rights begin.[2] If children are old enough, parents should explain why certain behaviours are unacceptable. This will help them accept limits with a good attitude.

The following examples are not absolutes, as some children do mature quicker than others, but should be useful as general guideline.

Infancy

While it is helpful for babies to learn to be at ease around others, most parents are wise to not expose their new-borns to too many people for the sake of protecting them from germs. Once babies hit the stage where they are a bit clingy to mummy (see Chapter Six) parents can encourage their babies to not be fearful around others by holding their children securely in their arms while exposing them to other people. Parents should speak with a gentle and encouraging tone of voice, and never have an angry and disappointed tone if their babies are not yet ready to go to others.

From about three months onwards, babies can learn by being around other babies. There may not any adult-style communication taking place, but, especially after the babies can sit up, there can be interaction between the two. Babies should also learn to play alone and keep themselves occupied.

This is important for the building of their autonomy; many parents never allow their children out of sight at all. A child lying down can play with a mobile above the bed. A child who can sit up can play with safe and appropriate crib or play pen toys. Otherwise, these children will not be able to be by themselves at all when separated for only a few minutes. Parents should be able to leave their child for a few seconds at a time with toys and such, always ensuring that the baby is safe in the room. Parents can leave the door open and supervise without their children actually seeing them.[3] This in no way implies that parents are to ever leave a baby for more than a few seconds, and always within earshot, and not at all if they can crawl.

⟨ LOUIS LOWDOWN ⟩

> I (Karen) took my babies to church before they were two weeks old, but I purposefully arrived late, sat in the back, and left early so that they would not be swarmed by well-meaning friends with the flu! I also requested that visitors to our home wash their hands before holding Sonia and David, and even went so far as to ask folks to not come if they were unwell. (To this day, I always wash my hands before holding babies, and I will not visit any new-borns or new mothers when I have anything remotely contagious.) In spite of these precautions, I jumped at the chance to have others bond with my babies—I believe that getting them used to seeing different kinds of faces and being at ease with all sorts of people facilitates confidence in social interactions when they are older.

The Toddler Years

Children's brains develop faster in the first three years than at any other time—how exciting! Of course everyone has heard of "The Terrible Twos". Children at this stage want so desperately to do things themselves but they do not want to separate from their parents, so they are frustrated. They also do not know how to do many things and will have to learn and make mistakes, and this also frustrates them. There is a real desire for autonomy at this stage, to do things themselves. So, they should be allowed to explore their room, their toys, and other safe objects. Toddlers should learn to interact with their surroundings. Remember that parents are to provide "age-appropriate" autonomy, which means reasonable limits on one side and basic safety on the other. (We took advice from older parents and turned the terrible twos into the terrific twos by being *very firm* on a few important limits, providing lots of time for outdoor play, serving healthy meals, ensuring proper sleep patterns were followed, and being very connected.)

Play is the primary work for toddlers, up to six hours per day. They want to run, climb, and jump. Notwithstanding toddlers' love of repetition, when fathers are spending time at the playground with their children, they should ensure that their kids try a variey of physical movements. (As an aside, do not forget to capitalise on their love of repetition by repeating memory verses and spiritual principles during family devotionals.[4])

◈ LOUIS LOWDOWN ◈

> When Sonia was about a year old, I read a baby book that said when babies are able to sit up in a high chair comfortably that they should be able to start feeding themselves, and to not worry about the mess—put newspaper down under the high chair, and give them a bath afterwards, the book said. What the book did not say was to use common sense—that was probably implied! One day a friend came into town and we went to a restaurant for lunch—after fifteen minutes, the more experienced parent begged me to stop the madness. I proceeded to feed Sonia myself, helped the waitress clean up the disaster area, and waited a few more months before trying that again.

When providing choices, such as what type of toys to play with, which books to read and which playground to visit, keep in mind that children this age may be overwhelmed by too *many* choices. A parent may want to offer just two, e.g., "Darling, would you like to do some painting or read a book?" "Which video would you like to watch—*Busytown* or *Sing Along Songs*?" Different children will have different preferences. Our son couldn't care less what he wore at this age (in fact, he probably didn't care until he was sixteen!) whereas our daughter practically came out of the womb with an opinion about which hairclip she would use, and which dress she would wear. Meanwhile, our son was more concerned with which toy car he would carry around with him for the whole day.

Consider the options parents have when a child is struggling while putting a puzzle together. Some parents might intervene and start doing the puzzle for the toddler.

> Parent: No, that's not the right piece… You will never finish it if you do it this way. Let me show you. Pay attention.
> Child: OK…

Or parents could allow the child more leeway.

> Parent: Are you a bit stuck?
> Child: Yes.
> Parent: Well, do you see any pieces that look different from the others?
> Child: Here's one.

Parent: Excellent—that is called a corner piece. There are four corners in this picture—let's count together: *(mother pointing)* 1, 2, 3, 4. So how many corner pieces do we need? *(If child mimics mum and says 4, that's fine. Otherwise, just count to four again.)*

Parent: Can you find the other corner pieces? Now let's look at the picture to see where these might go. Very good. Keep trying, you're doing very well.

(The parent can then either watch the child finish up on his own or help with one or two pieces if necessary—depending on the child's age.)

Child: Finished!

Parent: Well done! I bet you are proud of yourself for doing this puzzle.

Again, we have to stress that these decisions need to be age-appropriate. Parents still need to make important decisions, and take charge in many areas, such as when to go to sleep, take a bath, eat, watch TV or be on a computer. Also, children should not get the impression that it is their right to choose everything; more on that when we discuss the next core need.

Early Childhood

By four to seven years of age, children are able to do many more things on their own. Some examples of tasks that children this age can do on their own, or with just a little help, are getting dressed, tying their own shoelaces, helping mother set the table before dinner, picking up their toys, packing their own bag, taking care of a pet and feeding it, and doing their own homework.

Parents will still need to take charge of, or at least monitor, the following areas:

- Going to bed and waking up on time
- Doing homework (done by the child, not the parents)
- Taking a bath (boys especially needs reminders at this age)
- Spending time with parents
- Having personal devotionals (or ensuring they are reading their children's Bibles, writing in a little prayer in a journal, or some such activity)
- Having family devotionals with them
- Facilitating other interests or activities, including "screen" time

In everyday situations, problems that they encounter should be brought out in the open for some discussion. At this age, parents need to be more directive, but whenever possible, they would do well to provide opportunities for their children to express their opinion, rather than always telling them what to do. Remember that play is still more important than work (e.g., if they are taking piano lessons, and you want them to practice a bit everyday, you may want to sit with them and make it into a fun activity or else it may become a battle which would be counterproductive).

Middle Childhood

Children who are at the pre-teen stage may develop strong tastes about their clothes or hairstyles. Allow them freedom in this area with only a bit of guidance (but parents should follow their own conscience—they do not have to let their daughter wear a micro-miniskirt just because the neighbour's kids are wearing them). Parents should encourage autonomy, allowing kids to do their own tasks without interfering, which will be a temptation for many parents. If some children act a bit younger than their peers, parents should not embarrass them but rather rejoice that they aren't growing up so fast.[5]

Examples of choices in this stage (with some limitations):
- What extracurricular activities to participate in (within budget)
- What kind of clothes to wear (within reason)
- What kind of music they would like to listen to (parents should still go through the lyrics to see what they are promoting)
- What kind of parties they get to have (also within reason)
- What they would like to do during "dates" with each parent
- Whether or not to have sleepovers (parents must ensure basic safety!)

Adolescence

As the child grows older and her need for autonomy increases, the need for parents to be directive decreases. When children encounter difficulties, parents should talk about the problem and ask them what choices they have about how to overcome them. Much guidance is still needed, but parents should draw out their children's opinions, not just lecture them and tell them what to do. For navigating autonomy and limits in the adolescent years, we were greatly helped by the book *Teen Proofing*. The author (John Rosemond) hits the nail on the head when it comes to figuring out the right balance.[6] On this topic, Rosemond echoes founder of Active Parenting, Dr Michael Popkin, who says, "Make the problem their problem."[7] And who could forget the quote from Spiderman's Uncle Ben, "With great power comes great responsibility."[8]

Parents Must Keep Their Own Agenda in Check

Sometimes we have underlying motives, not always obvious to us, that are pushing us to accomplish things through our kids. This motivation is so strong and forceful that it is done at the expense of our children's need for healthy autonomy and performance. It will help if parents ask themselves, "What is my agenda?" Here are some questions for further self-examination:

Do I feel that, come what may, my kids have to excel in their studies because I did not and I suffered because of it?

Do I live through my children?

Do I want to them to excel in sports or pageants or music so that I can look good through them?

Do I get over-involved with my kids because I am afraid that without my involvement they will not be as good as I need them to be?

Am I over-involved with them emotionally, talking with them constantly about everything, because I am lonely?

Do I feel the need to be ultra close to my children because of the poor quality of my marriage?

Am I trying to meet an underlying need in myself?

Do I feel the need to protect my children because in my heart I believe the world is a dangerous place?

Am I negative about them making any of their own decisions, be it about what to play or which book to read, because a pessimistic parent raised me?

Did I make a childhood vow such as "I will never be poor, and neither will my kid," or "No one will ever make fun of my son" or something to that effect?

❖ MOVIE MOMENT – *Akeelah and the Bee*[9] ❖

In this delightful Lionsgate film, Akeelah tries out for the spelling bee in her school, and ends up going to the National competition. Her nemesis has come in second place two years in a row, and the boy's father is desperate for the boy to finally take home the gold. As the two young teens talk, the boy reveals that the reason his father is so set on him winning is because he himself never came in first place in anything.

Please go through the questionnaires in Chapter Three of our marriage book, *I Choose Us*,[10] so that you can get an idea of the kind of lifetraps you have, and how they specifically relate to the meeting of the core emotional need for healthy autonomy and performance. Meeting this need will help to prevent the formation of the lifetraps discussed in detail in the previous chapter in your children (vulnerability to harm or illness, dependence, enmeshment, abandonment, subjugation, along with negativity.)

If you have any of these lifetraps to a strong degree, then there is reason to believe that your drive to be over-involved with your children is a result of your own upbringing and some unmet need. Parents who are able to gain awareness in these areas will be able to then identify their underlying unhealthy drive and motivation. Being aware is a huge first step. By being aware, you will know why you are triggered by certain behaviours in your children. For example, when they do not do as well in their school work as you think they should (e.g., if they scored a B instead of an A), when their efforts are never good enough for you, or when you seem to frequently be negative about your children's decisions.

During our workshops, we frequently say, "Dysfunction is the gift that keeps on giving." Here are three real life examples of parents whose own lifetraps caused them to pass down similar lifetraps to their children.

A mother enmeshed with her twins: Gayle had twin daughters. She doted on them and gave them every advantage she could, monetarily and in education. Gayle was also over-involved and controlling. She did not allow her daughters to do what normal teens do on their own and protected them from taking risks of any kind. In a city where kids either rode the school bus or took the subway, Gayle forbade her kids to do either. When it came time for the teens to go to university, they decided to live in different cities from their mother and each other. One of the girls was able to cope because of her temperament, but the other girl was not. Filled with fear, she had to drop out of school, move home, and was not able to go out alone. Now almost 30 years old, she is still dependent on others, is enmeshed with her mother, and frozen in fear. She is truly trapped by vulnerability to harm and illness.

A mother creating a mummy's boy: Augustina loved her only son and gave him everything she never had as a child. A working mum with a busy schedule, she hired a nanny to look after her son and make sure he was safe and secure. Like Gayle, she did not allow him to take public transport or even ride a bicycle. Her son became very dependent and had no sense of autonomy. About the time he got his first job, he began to attend church and made a commitment to God, and for the first time made some decisions on his own. However, he soon reverted back to his dependent behaviour with members of the church. He was dependent on the leader of his small group and when he got married he became dependent on his spouse, who eventually felt more like a babysitter than a wife. In counselling, he admitted that he did not feel confident. He developed the lifetrap of dependence and it carried all the way into his adult life. Augustina had meant well, and never intended for her son to end up this way; another example of parenting missteps happen subtly and unintentionally.

A father passing down negativity: Benjamin's son was all excited about entering an art competition. Although his son was good at drawing, Benjamin was not happy when he found out about it and completely berated and humiliated him. Benjamin barred his son from entering any such competitions because he thought they were a complete waste of time. The gruff father was so deeply filled with negativity that he could not imagine how anything good would come from such an attempt. This left a painful scar on his son emotionally. Sadly, Benjamin's son brought this pessimissim into his adult life when he became a father. He finds it difficult to encourage his own children, and still finds it hard to try anything new, as he constantly hears his father's voice, "It's no use, why bother, what's the point?"

When it comes to letting our children grow up, it is so tempting to hold on tightly, or to give up in despair. When we let our children make choices and give them age-appropriate freedom, we are meeting their core emotional need for healthy autonomy and performance. With autonomy on one side and connection on the other, we hope that our children will want to adopt our values. At the end of the day, we reason with them, plead our case, and even study the Bible with them, all the while showing them that we love them, trust them, respect them, and believe in them. The rest is in God's hands...

SECTION FOUR

The Core Emotional Need for
Reasonable Limits

*What if my child
is so confident
that he becomes
arrogant or insensitive?*

CHAPTER ELEVEN

Reasonable Limits

The Core Emotional Need for Reasonable Limits can be defined as giving our children an understanding of right and wrong, a sense of boundaries, the tools they need to get along in the world, and how to work well with others. In order for the core emotional need for reasonable limits to be met satisfactorily, children need to *consistently* and *on an emotional level* believe the following messages about their parents:

> They challenge me in a respectful and loving manner when I get out of control, such as when I am angry or impulsive.
>
> They guide and encourage me to persevere with a task even when I feel frustrated.
>
> They challenge me when I get out of line in my behaviour and words.
>
> They encourage me to consider multiple factors in order to avoid making a rash decision.
>
> They guide me when I do and say hurtful things.
>
> They say "No" when it is the best for me, firmly, but not harshly.
>
> They do not let me have my own way all the time.
>
> They expect me to be responsible and contribute to the well-being of our home, such as by doing chores.
>
> They expect me to be wise when choosing my closest friends, and to be able to say "No" to some of my friends when the need arises.

Carly's parents were not financially well off but they both worked hard and were able to get by. They looked forward to the birth of their first child so much that when little Carly was born, she was the apple of their eye. Other siblings followed, but she was always treated as special. To her mother, Carly was the smartest, prettiest, and most talented. She had a naturally friendly disposition, which drew her mother to her even more. When the parents would buy one toy each for the other children, Carly would get two. When her siblings got a single scoop ice cream cone, Carly would get a double scoop. The other children had a set bedtime with no television on school nights; Carly was allowed to stay up and watch TV as late as she wanted. Naturally gifted, she didn't have to work hard to stand out in class, and she was accepted into a university with no problems. However, once there, success did not come so easily. Shocked after being dumped by her boyfriend, she could not get out of bed to take some important exams.

Carly managed to graduate and even get a job, only to quit and drift from company to company, falling for "get rich quick" schemes along the way. A generous relative left her an inheritance so that she could buy a house and save for the future, but she lost everything at the casino and in the stock market, and had to declare bankruptcy. A few years after getting married, she had an abortion after committing adultery. Carly's husband eventually left her and she was fired from her last job. She now lives alone, bitter about how life has been unfair.

Peter was born into a wealthy family, surrounded by hired help. He had a nanny, a chauffeur, a cook, and a nurse to make sure he always had everything he wanted. The moment he cried, someone was there to offer him a cookie. The second he fell down, someone was there to coddle him. If he did not like his kindergarten, he was moved immediately. If he wanted the latest toy or a new pair of shoes like the ones he saw on television, he got them. Peter never heard the word "no" and never experienced frustration. All of this made Peter an insufferable bully on the playground, a shallow friend to the other kids at school, and an obnoxious older brother. The rest of the world wouldn't put up with his nonsense, and eventually, when faced with some frustrations at his first place of employment, he attempted suicide. After a stint in a mental hospital, he was able to get another good job, but so far he has never had the discipline or follow-through to get married or move up the corporate ladder.

Carly and Peter may have been from different socioeconomic backgrounds and raised in different countries, but they had the same kind of parenting— their need for Reasonable Limits was not met when they were growing up.

Limits and boundaries provide markers and guides so that children know what is acceptable and what is not. Merriam's dictionary defines a boundary as "a real or imaginary point beyond which a person or thing cannot go" as well as "the line or relatively narrow space that marks the outer limit of something".[1] In a very real way, both children and adults need boundaries to live in a world with others. Of course, everyone is different, and there will be some nuances that vary from family to family. (Some parents are comfortable with loud voices, messiness and spontaneity, others will more naturally opt for "inside voices", keeping the house tidy, having a strict schedule, etc.) The important thing is that parents should have conviction about their personal values, and their boundaries and limits should reflect their beliefs consistently. As with the other core emotional needs, the Goldilocks principle applies here: neither too many limits nor too few but just right. In other words, *reasonable* limits that are good enough.

There is no one in the world who likes to be around smart-alecky, whining, ungrateful children. Dr Phil, an American TV talk-show host and self-help guru, says that kids without limits become entitled, and feeling guilty about giving your child boundaries doesn't make sense. In fact, he says, "If you want to feel guilty, feel guilty for not teaching them to understand how the world works, that everyone goes on green and stops on red."[2] Psychoanalyst Dr Ruth Sharon co-authored the book *I Refuse To Raise A Brat*. She says that often when it comes to helping people have breakthroughs in therapy, the most difficult clients are *not* those who were disadvantaged and abused as children but rather the people who as children were pampered, over-indulged, and spoiled;[3] i.e., the ones who did not have their core emotional need for reasonable limits met. And we have all witnessed the fallout from the rise in entitlement—we will not mention any by name, but more than a few famous athletes, entertainers and politicians could have done with some reasonable limits when they were growing up!

This is not a new parenting need. Several thousand years ago, a well-known sage said, *"A wise son brings joy to his father, but a foolish son grief to his mother."* (Proverbs 10:1) In fact the whole book of Proverbs beseeches readers to exercise good judgment and live within healthy limits, and implores parents to teach their children to do this. *Meeting this core emotional need by teaching our children limits and expecting them to live within these limits is a very loving thing to do as a parent.* Children are not born programmed to learn to follow rules and to respect limits—it is the other way round. They are born without any knowledge of limits and rules. Children come into the world thinking that they are the centres of the universe. They love to explore, investigate and test the world, which seems so colourful, fun and inviting. However, at what point is it fine, or even safe, to go ahead, and at what point is it not wise to do so? Modern culture is confused on this point —many today mock limits and see restricting children as old fashioned and even cruel, others want to set boundaries but seem at a loss as to how to do so. Our children are certainly not going to learn reasonable and healthy limits in the world on their own. The only way we can make sure they learn is by meeting this core emotional need.

◈ **MASTER CLASS** ◈

> Walter Evans shares, "The most important thing to me was that our parenting was consistent and steady at all times, even during emotional trials. Our family routine was simple; there was nothing expensive or fancy about it. We had dinner at 6:00 o'clock most nights, family time on Monday nights that included dinner and a simple devotional, and Kim prayed each night with the kids before bed. Regardless of the circumstances, the illnesses (of which there were many), or the temper tantrums, the rules and routines remained the same. The emotional temperature and the volume were expected to remain under control. The 3 'dis'-es were the cardinal rules: disrespect, dishonesty and disobedience were not acceptable whether the kids were 6 years old or 16 years old. As far as I am concerned, when it comes to what was helpful in our parenting, calm consistency was the name of the game."

Just as important as ensuring that we convey limits is *how* we convey them. On the one hand, parents must ensure that they meet this need in a respectful and healthy way, lest they end up causing frustration and exasperation; on the other hand, *not* conveying reasonable limits with appropriate seriousness will bring problems of its own. Whatever happens, our children need limits if they are to grow up and become healthy adults.

Children who are not able to follow simple rules, be it in the classroom, in public places, or when they are at home, will face huge problems in life. They will cause burdens for others as well as bring heartache to the people who love them the most. There is a reason the Bible tells parents to ensure that their children honour and obey them. Paul quoted the Ten Commandments when he wrote:

> *Children, obey your parents in the Lord, for this is right. 'Honour your father and mother'—which is the first commandment with a promise—that it may go well with you and that you may enjoy long life on the earth.* (Ephesians 6:1-3)

On top of obedience, the Bible contains literally *hundreds* of verses about discipline and self-control. Modern research concurs, not surprisingly, that we are better off when we practice curbing our appetites. A study out of Stanford University in 1972 found that "…young children who were able to resist grabbing a fluffy marshmallow placed in front of them for 15 long minutes in order to get two of them later scored an average of 210 points higher on the SAT [an entrance exam for American universities which the kids took 12 years later] than kids who could not wait. About one third of the four to six year-olds studied were able to withstand the sweet temptation. Follow up was done 18 years later, and the kids with more self-control in the marshmallow trial had better life outcomes across the board."[4]

Parents often vacillate between extremes. Sometimes, they are very strict and rigid, while at other times, they rely on the children's sense of reasoning and are permissive. As a result, mixed signals are sent and both parents and children enter into a "Vortex of Conflict Escalation" where they trigger and re-trigger one another (see Chapter Thirteen). This gets repeated over and over again, and eventually, many parents end up losing their patience and resorting repeatedly to exasperation interactions, throwing their arms up in the air and giving up altogether, or tightening the screws and mandating strict obedience regardless of the state of their relationship, only to see resentment and rebellion down the road.

Our children were both fairly strong-willed and opinionated, so it is no surprise that we had to start saying "No" early on in their lives. We doubted ourselves as young parents do, wondering if we were being too strict. But

------ ✎ **MOVIE MOMENT** – *Willy Wonka and The Chocolate Factory*[5] ✐ ------

> In the wonderful 1971 movie based on Roald Dahl's classic children's book, Charlie and the Chocolate Factory, five children find Golden Tickets in their chocolate bars that enable them to be the first people to go behind the doors of the chocolate factory run by Willy Wonka. The eccentric inventor certainly understood the need for limits and let it be known that the parents of four out of the five children who won the tour did not know anything about them. One of the parents wouldn't stop her son from eating, one wouldn't stop his daughter from chewing gum, and another wouldn't stop her son from watching TV. The fourth, Veruka Salt, demanded that her father temporarily suspend his peanut factory so that his workers could "shell" chocolate bars instead, enabling her to "find" a Golden Ticket. "I want it now!" she demanded, and when he explained that they were working twelve-hour shifts, she shouted, "Make them work nights!" When Mr. Salt begged his daughter to be more understanding, she countered with, "I won't talk to you ever again! You're a mean rotten father and you never give me anything!" A few moments later, after a factory worker actually did find a ticket for her, Veruka's mother, who had been sitting in the corner knitting quietly, offered up, "Happiness is what counts with children, happiness and harmony." Unfortunately for Veruka, this misguided sentiment created a highly entitled child. Dahl's message: without reasonable limits, entitled children become entitled adults, and they will not have ended up that way by themselves!

we noticed a difference whenever we got soft and backed down from boundaries—chaos reigned, and the kids did not seem to be any happier for it! Limits and boundaries give children security and comfort because they know what to expect. They may try to fight them; they may even say they hate their parents, but they are secretly grateful. (And when they get older, they will tell you so!) Dr. Gary Solomon[6] calls it "CPR": parents who are *consistent*, *predictable* and *reliable* are more likely to produce children with good mental health.

Limits help kids to see that, contrary to every fibre of their young beings, they are *not* the centres of the universe and they must respect others if they expect to be respected. In essence, limits are a way of teaching children how to live out "The Golden Rule": *"So in everything, do to others what you would have them do to you, for this sums up the Law and the Prophets."* (Matthew 7:12) Unfortunately this does not exactly fit in with the direction the world is moving. The enlightening book, *Why Is It Always About You? : The Seven Deadly Sins of Narcissism* reports that entitlement is widespread and that an ever-increasing percentage of Americans are narcissistic![7]

⊰ LOUIS LOWDOWN ⊱

When our kids were around eight and six years old, an elder and his wife spent time with us during our travels, and we asked for input on our children toward the end of our time together. The elder's wife politely suggested that we buy the book, *Boundaries with Kids* by Cloud and Townsend.[8] This was a life-saving move, because it helped us greatly with our parenting and it also helped us in many other areas, including church leadership, as we read the other books in the series. As for our children, we looked up Bible verses containing the words boundary and boundaries and did a series of family devotionals about the different kinds of boundaries God wants us to have, such as personal space boundaries and possession boundaries. It made for very lively discussions and helped us to enforce agreed-upon household rules. Once when we left the children with a sitter, we came back to find our friend very curious. "What are you teaching your kids?" she asked. "What makes you ask that?" we nervously ventured. Her reply cracked us up; one of the kids had been annoying the other, only to be confidently rebuked by the offendee, "Remember your boundaries!" Speaking of Cloud and Townsend, I (Karen) found out later that my mother regularly buys *Boundaries with Kids* in bulk to give at baby showers. She hadn't given me a copy as she was trying to practice boundaries herself by not being an intrusive grandma!

What are the lifetraps associated with this core emotional need?

CHAPTER TWELVE

Reasonable Limits: What's at Stake?

Advantages Of Meeting This Need

When parents meet the core emotional need for reasonable limits, the child will develop some or all of the following traits and beliefs: reciprocity, fairness and equality, self-control and self-discipline, a sense of mutuality.

Reciprocity, Fairness and Equality

Children who have had the core emotional need for reasonable limits met know how to treat others fairly, they do not see themselves as better or worse than others but as equals. They believe in reciprocity, the "give and take" in relationships. Children who have had this need met would have an underlying approach to life that goes something along the lines of the following. *"I am a person of worth and value, but I am not better than others. The same rules that apply to others apply to me. Sometimes it is healthy to put others above myself, and it is certainly healthy to feel for others and try to put myself in their shoes. I do not need to control everything and everyone."* Children who have had this need met are kind, they feel for others, and they respect others' boundaries. They do not often purposely say things to hurt others, and if they do, they feel bad and apologise. They are not pushy and controlling, and naturally want to pitch in and do their share of work in projects. They know how to pursue their own happiness and desires without walking all over others.

Self-Discipline (Self-Control)

Children who have had the core emotional need for reasonable limits met are able to be self-controlled and self-disciplined, at least to an extent. Though it does not come naturally for most children, they will eventually be able to be grateful for the ability to limit themselves. They will have thoughts like, *"It is good to enjoy life but it is often necessary to do the hard things first, and to deny myself when I feel like giving in to potentially harmful emotions or desires. It is fair for me to get my way in relationships some of the time, but not necessarily all of the time. I feel a sense of satisfaction when I achieve goals I have set for myself."*

Children who develop this kind of thinking and inner motivation and discipline will be ahead of the pack in life—learning to delay gratification at an early age has proven to be an indicator of future success. A persuasive new study that followed 1,000 children from birth to age 32 found that "Children who showed early signs of self-mastery were not only less likely to have developed addictions or committed a crime by adulthood, but were also healthier and wealthier than their more impulsive peers...The new research confirms the findings of the famous Stanford marshmallow study"[1] (see Chapter Eleven).

There is a debate in some circles as to whether an emphasis on character is as necessary as an emphasis on IQ. Many parents push their kids to learn more and cram in extra classes so their children can increase their IQ, which will supposedly lead to better grades, better places in schools, and more success in life. Well, we saw earlier that a child's ability to pay attention, remember rules, and exhibit self-control also predict academic success (see Chapter Four). And two other studies revealed that (a) self-discipline predicted academic performance more robustly than did IQ, (b) self-discipline predicted changes in report card grades over time better than did IQ, and (c) IQ predicted changes in standardised test scores better than self-discipline.[2]

◁ RESEARCH REVEALS ▷

RR12.1: *Self-Discipline More Important Than IQ*

In summary, the study revealed the following regarding the effect of self-discipline:[3]

- Highly self-disciplined adolescents outperformed their more impulsive counterparts on every academic-performance variable, including report-card grades, standardized achievement-test scores, admission to a competitive high school, and attendance.
- Self-discipline measured in the fall predicted more variance in each of these outcomes: report-card grades, standardized achievement-test scores, admission to a competitive high school, and attendance, than did IQ, and unlike IQ, self-discipline predicted gains in academic performance over the school year.
- The correlation coefficients between self-discipline and most achievement indicators were significantly higher than and at least twice the size of correlations between IQ and the same outcomes.

It certainly seems clear that self-discipline has a bigger effect on academic performance than intellectual talent. However, who or what do parents blame when their children underachieve? Usually the school, teachers, lack of tutors, and large class sizes. While these are important factors, parents

> should also look closer to home—perhaps they failed to teach their children to make wise choices, to sacrifice short-term pleasures for long-term gains, and to pay attention to rules and remember instructions.

Ergo, there are loads of folks with high IQs who outscored others on their SATs but have not lived up to their potential because they did not learn self-discipline! In our opinion, societies, school systems and parents would be much better off if they all recognised the potential gains that could be made from teaching children the value of self-discipline.[4] It is doubtful if any child is born with these traits. Hopefully, parents can model and teach the value of doing the hard things first, of dealing with anger in a healthy way, of managing time and money well, of treating their body with respect, and of keeping their word (within reason, of course). If they can manage to do all that, they will have given their children a huge gift for which the next generation will forever be grateful.

A Sense of Mutuality

Children who have had the core emotional need for reasonable limits met will be secure enough to seek out relationships in which there is mutuality. Rather than being enslaved to others through people-pleasing, or even subjected to bullying, they will more than likely feel, *"I am confident in my own decisions and do not need to seek the approval of others. If other people do not approve of me, as long as I have acted in good faith, I know I have nothing to worry about."* Healthy children should care about what their parents think and they definitely will want their approval. However, parents give their children a real gift when they build their children's self-esteem to such an extent that their kids are able to be content with a decision that may not be exactly to the parents' liking. This may sound counter to what we have said so far about reasonable limits because surely we do not want to train our children to rebel. But if our kids are free to sometimes disagree with us because of what they have thoughtfully considered and are not just being contrary, and if they know that we will not reject them when this happens, it will strengthen them. It will build their confidence, give them self-worth, and make them feel more connected to us in the long run, which in turn helps them to choose our values anyway! Ultimately, we want our children as healthy adults to be able to say, "I am free to follow my own path in life, and I am able to both consider the feedback of others and maintain my decision." What does this have to do with limits? When parents are helping children to follow limits, they must ensure that the children are not just giving in to approval-seeking but genuinely understand that the limits are important. This is related to the first core emotional need for connection and acceptance and the second for autonomy, illustrating how intertwined the core needs are.

Disadvantages Of Not Meeting This Need

To the extent that parents do not meet the core emotional need for reasonable limits, their children will develop some or all of the following lifetraps: entitlement, insufficient self-control, and approval-seeking.

The Lifetrap of Entitlement / Grandiosity

The core message of the entitlement lifetrap is, *"I am special and better than other people. Rules should not apply to me. I should always come first."* This lifetrap is rooted in a desire for power and control.

Children with the entitlement lifetrap will grow up to believe that what they want or need should always be a priority. It is okay for them to cheat on tests or at sports, and they minimise it. They do not need to fasten the seat belt when the plane is taking off, they can drive while under the influence, and they generally get angry when they do not get what they want. Entitled individuals do not care if getting their way disadvantages others; they don't think twice about changing the rules when playing a game. As long as they win, that is what matters, and they do not have any awareness of the pain others feel. They have a warped sense of fairness, and may accuse others of being selfish instead. They rarely, if ever, put themselves in other people's shoes. They are usually not in tune with others' feelings, but are totally in tune with their own. When challenged about their behaviour, they often think that people should accept them the way they are.

Children develop the entitlement lifetrap in two ways. Being told that they are more special than other kids, having no limits, and never being made to take responsibility for their actions, words or moods produces "pure entitlement". These children will grow into pure narcissists, unable to be thoughtful of others. It is this kind of entitlement we are addressing when we talk about meeting the core emotional need for reasonable limits. The second way that entitlement is produced is a bit more complicated. This is called "fragile entitlement". This form of the lifetrap comes not from being spoilt, but is a *reaction* to unmet core emotional needs for connection and acceptance or realistic expectations, and is rooted in either the defectiveness lifetrap or the emotional deprivation lifetrap. When needs for caring and recognition are not met, a response of "I have to take it for myself" and "No one else is looking out for me" develops. The lifestyle and behaviour look the same as "pure entitlement", but it is important to understand that the behaviour of these narcissists is covering up a lot of pain from unmet needs.

Entitled children will often become leaders (at school, in sports, or in gangs) who boast about not taking "No" for an answer. Highly entitled individuals do not like to hear the word "No". They may even receive compliments for their natural leadership qualities and for being so determined in life. They do not like to work under others, since they do not like rules, but they do not mind enforcing rules with others. Adults with the entitlement lifetrap generally hate being vulnerable and sharing about their weaknesses, but they love to boast about their strengths. Because of their bullying, they have power, and they achieve results by infringing on others. Very few people with this lifetrap volunteer to seek help or see their need to change. Why? Life is good, since they get their way most of the time. Without intervention, entitled children who grow up to be entitled adults rarely get to the point where they can see that relationships are a two-way street, and that by becoming open and vulnerable, rather than being demanding, self-serving, or bullying, they are more likely to get what they *really need*—a satisfying and caring relationship.

Obviously as Christians we can repent of anything, and plenty of Christians have needed to repent of pride and arrogance. We should always believe that adults with narcissistic and entitled behaviour can change. However, it makes more sense to nip it in the bud when we see it in our children than trying to change them when they are older (see Figures 12.1 & 12.2).

Exercise: Please refer to the Exasperation Interactions worksheet (Appendix 1) and identify the exasperation interaction(s) in Figure 12.1.

A quick glance at what might have happened to an adult with this lifetrap during childhood:

- When the child did not get what he wanted, he threw a tantrum and the parents did little to set healthy limits.
- The child was shamed a lot growing up. To avoid feeling shame, he overcompensated and shamed others.
- There were no proper boundaries in his life early on. He set his own limits. Even if there were limits, they were few, and revolved around him achieving excellence in one or more areas.
- The child was allowed to throw tantrums and often got his way. His parents gave in because of his strong will. His anger was a manipulative tool to get what he wanted.
- The child was spoilt growing up. He got what he wanted and had an intimidating pout when he did not.
- The child was taught, either explicitly or implicitly by his parents, to not follow rules.
- The child was not taught to care about others. Parents often talked about achievement, status, and he did not want to go through the shame of not achieving these things.
- Insufficient attention was given to recognizing the child's accomplishments and he was unduly criticized. Attention was not paid to what he needed on a consistent basis; his core emotional needs were not met. His response was to become excessively demanding.

Figure 12.1: The Lifetrap of Entitlement / Grandiosity (Javier as a child)

Case Study

Hank grew up in poverty and was raised by strict parents who frequently belittled him. After his twins, Linda Lee and Laura Sue, were born, Hank's number one objective in parenting was that he wanted his daughters to know that he loved them. Consequently, he gave them everything they wanted all of the time. As children, Linda Lee and Laura Sue were the envy of their friends from Sunday School. They had the coolest toys, the nicest clothes, and the newest CDs. Even though Hank was not really that well-off, he spoiled the girls because he thought that this was the way to show love. To protect their self-esteen, Hank never raised his voice at the girls. His daughters did grow up with confidence, but it crossed the line and became sheer arrogance. Now that they are older, Linda Lee and Laura Sue don't care much for rules and have little empathy for others. On the one hand, they are confident of their father's love, but on the other hand, they have no fear of authority and do whatever they please. Sadly, Hank's daughters have confided with their youth workers at church that they are terribly confused and insecure about their future, and that they have messed up their lives with multiple

Figure 12.2: The Lifetrap of Entitlement / Grandiosity (Javier as an adult)

sexual partners, drunkenness, and the like. Hank is now trying to get help to undo the mistakes of the past and build connection instead of enabling entitlement before the twins move out of the home to go away for college. He is trying to get help for them now, before they expose themselves to even more dangerous situations with more serious consequences.

The Lifetrap of Insufficient Self-Control / Self-Discipline

The core message of the insufficient self-control lifetrap is, *"I should not be uncomfortable."* This lifetrap leads people to express their emotion negatively, avoid difficult tasks, and give in to temptation. This lifetrap interferes with healthy adult behaviour of reciprocity in relationships, and setting and achieving goals.

Children who are not given limits, who are given too much freedom, who are neglected or not given disciplined role models, will usually develop this lifetrap. Almost all children struggle with self-control growing up, which is normal. However, if they develop this lifetrap, then later as adults they may have difficulty controlling their impulses, such as losing their temper, sexual

Figure 12.3: The Lifetrap of Insufficient Self-Control / Self-Discipline (Young Jin as a Child)

promiscuity, over-eating, or other addictions. They also may have trouble sitting down and doing work for what others would consider a reasonable length of time because they feel it is boring. People with this lifetrap may set out to do a task, but then get easily distracted. If a task seems too difficult, they will give up after starting it.

Adults with the lifetrap of insufficient self-control have a hard time denying themselves, making themselves uncomfortable, or delaying gratification. When young, they did not learn the value of persevering and getting tasks accomplished, or the principle that in the long run, they would be much better off not giving into short-term pleasure. If they are in a position of authority, they will delegate more than others would delegate in their position. Discipline is a challenge for them. They often do not have a long-term view of things. Much of what they do is based on their desires, and they can be rash in their decision-making. Only when this lifetrap brings them to a low point in life will they start to realise that they have to deal with this problem. It is worth noting that people with this lifetrap are sometimes quite likeable because their spontaneous side is very attractive. This charm may carry them far, in spite of their lack of discipline (see Figures 12.3 & 12.4).

Figure 12.4: The Lifetrap of Insufficient Self-Control / Self-Discipline (Young Jin as an Adult)

A quick glance at what might have happened to an adult with this lifetrap during childhood:

- The child's parents were not very involved with her while she was growing up. Her parents left her to set her own limits when she was too young, such as when to sleep, how long to play, what to eat, how much TV to watch. Early on, she was allowed to act on her desires.
- No consequences were set when the child got out of line. Because the child's parents were not involved, they did not know what she was up to. They were too busy with their own work and schedules.
- Since the child's parents were busy, she was brought up by grandparents or by nannies, who spoilt her and gave her whatever she wanted.
- The child is naturally talented. She did not have to try that hard to succeed early on in life, and her parents did not sense the need to teach her perseverance. As life became more challenging, the child avoided pursuits that would require much perseverance.

Exercise: Please refer to the Exasperation Interactions worksheet (Appendix 1) and identify the exasperation interaction(s) in Figure 12.3.

Case Study

Jack has two little brothers, and his father, Frank, is also the eldest of three sons. Frank works in the construction industry and gets home late most nights. He expects his son Jack to be a good role model for his younger brothers. Over the years, Frank has been very controlling with Jack. He has imposed all sorts of rules on what Jack was allowed and not allowed to do. For many years, Jack was compliant. However, as he has gotten older, Jack has gradually felt more and more resentful. He is now in a stage of full-blown rebellion. Jack says he does not care at all about how his father feels. He acts as he wishes, including blatant acts of defiance, knowing that his father can no longer control his life. Jack has dropped out of school, goes nightclubbing, has several "body piercings", and turns a deaf ear to anything his conservative father has to say.

The Lifetrap of Approval-Seeking / Recognition-Seeking

The core message of the approval-seeking lifetrap is, *"I must seek the approval of others above all else. If other people do not approve of me, something is very wrong."* This pattern of thinking is about defining who we are through the eyes of others rather than paying attention to our own needs and desires.

Children who develop this lifetrap will struggle to form an opinion about themselves outside of what others think and feel about them. When push comes to shove, they are not secure enough to trust their own instincts. This lifetrap is not about achieving a self-imposed high standard, as in the case of unrelenting standards, or about feeling superior, as with entitlement. It is also not about compensating for defectiveness by pushing oneself to achieve. It is about craving other people's approval. If people's opinion of them is poor, they feel lousy about themselves.

People with this lifetrap feel that their world collapses when they sense that others do not think highly of them, but if they do, they feel elevated and happy about themselves. They put a lot of energy into drawing attention to their good deeds. Given how much they are controlled by what others think, they do not really develop an authentic sense of self with their own values and preferences. As a result, they cannot truly be fulfilled. At work, people with this lifetrap are constantly consumed with what their colleagues, and especially their boss, think of them. Even if they are doing a great job, it is the approval of others that will decide how they feel about themselves. They lack their own convictions and suppress their own preferences at the expense of being liked by others (see Figures 12.5 & 12.6).

A quick glance at what might have happened to an adult with this lifetrap during childhood:

- The child's parents emphasized the need for status, looking good, or recognition in such a way that it was part of their normal family conversation.

Figure 12.5: The Lifetrap of Approval-Seeking / Recognition-Seeking (Jono as a Child)

- The child's parents boasted about themselves. If they were praised by others (e.g., appearing in the papers or on TV), they trumpeted it to all.
- The child's parents bragged about their achievements and about knowing the "right people".
- The child's parents focused more on how things looked at home, rather than what was inside the hearts and minds of their children.
- Self-esteem had nothing to do with the child liking himself, and everything to do with others approval of him.

Exercise: Please refer to the Exasperation Interactions worksheet (Appendix 1) and identify the exasperation interaction(s) in Figure 12.5.

Case Study

Brian is a talented young man and an only child. When he was younger, Brian's father would tell him that he expected him to make it into a top high school. They would make plans about how the father would support him and how Brian would be a great achiever one day. Unfortunately, the young boy did not do as well as the father had hoped for on his high school entrance exams. The father was so devastated when he saw his son's report card

Figure 12.6: The Lifetrap of Approval-Seeking / Recognition-Seeking (Jono as an Adult)

that he refused to talk to him for weeks and their relationship was never the same again. Brian remembers the disdain in his father's eyes, and at only thirteen years old, Brian did not even dare approach his father for help when he applied for high school. Brian was accepted to a very good school, but not a *prestigious* school. When this happened, his father made him go to school on his own, because he was embarrassed to be seen bringing his son to that school. Brian became desperate for his father's approval, but he never won it again. He spent the next ten years of his life living a double life. He became addicted to pornography and having meaningless sex with various girls from high school and university, all the while trying to look good to his father and teachers. As he got older, he joined a church and also tried to impress everyone there with stories of his successes in life. Eventually Brian learned about what was causing him to seek approval and he is now getting help consistently to understand God's unconditional love and his worth as a person.

⟪ THE CORE EMOTIONAL NEED FOR REASONABLE LIMITS ⟫
AMONG THE PATRIARCHS

Now that we have examined the advantages of meeting the core emotional need for reasonable limits, as well as the dangers that come from not meeting this need, let us study out how the core emotional need for reasonable limits was not met in the family of the patriarchs in the book of Genesis.

Questions for Discussion:

Read the passages in Hebrews 12:14-17, and Genesis 26:34-35, 27:41-45, 28:6-9 and take some time to answer the following questions.

- What does the writer in Hebrews say about Esau?
- What did his parents do that prevented him from learning self-control?
- Did Esau learn to persevere with a task when it got too difficult?
- How many women did Esau simultaneously marry when he was forty years old? What does this possibly reveal about his character?
- How did Esau handle anger and conflict with his brother?
- Did Isaac pass down good moral values to Esau through the years?
- Esau was not that disturbed when he did not please his parents, seen in Genesis 26:34-35. How could this have come about? Could his lack of closeness to his mother and being outdoors a lot have contributed to this over the years?

Insights

While it is very likely that Rebekah was over-controlling of Jacob, it is also likely that Esau was allowed to wander around for days without guidance and had too much time on his hands. What did Esau do when he was outside alone, not hunting with his father? Who did he stumble into? Could it be that during his time outdoors, he became acquainted with the Hittite women? We know that Isaac and Rebekah were against him marrying the Hittite women, and we know that parents in Isaac's day were involved intimately in arranging the marriages of their children. We can look for clues in Hebrews 12:16, where we learn that that Esau was godless and sexually immoral. He acted on his desire as and when he wanted. He was impulsive and flared up in anger when he did not get his way.

We may also speculate that Isaac had not been deep with Esau, seeing as how Esau learned that his marriage to the Hittite women was displeasing to his parents only *after* the marriage occurred, Genesis 28:8-9. Then he tried to rectify it by acquiring another wife—what a solution!

It seems that Esau's upbringing lacked reasonable limits and boundaries. Little teaching seems to have come from his parents. He seems to have received very little guidance regarding his comings and goings, doing very much what he pleased, and in the end, he set his own limits. Since his parents did not set healthy limits, he did not learn to respect them, and he had no self-control. We all know the story of the birthright, where he apparently was so hungry that he was willing to negotiate part of his inheritance for a single meal (Hebrews 12:16-17). He had a hard time persevering with a task when it got difficult. He got pushy when he wanted his way. Did Isaac ever teach him to think things through carefully before making a decision? Did Isaac ever say "no" to him when he was growing up? Instead, Esau gave up when life got challenging. While Jacob experienced the unpleasantness of an over-protective and controlling mother, Esau grew up with a father that did not put reasonable limits in place for him. This was a huge need that was never met in Esau's life.

Why do I find meeting this core emotional need so difficult?

CHAPTER THIRTEEN

Avoiding Bottlenecks and The Vortex

We are beginning this chapter by sharing some reasons why setting healthy boundaries can be challenging for parents. Parents' emotional issues, as well as their own unmet childhood needs, can interfere, causing a "bottleneck" and preventing parents from meeting the core emotional need for reasonable limits. Below are some "bottlenecks" that we have come across frequently.

Parents feel guilty – They feel guilty that they are not perfect, guilty that they cannot buy everything for their family that they feel they deserve, guilty that they are not doing what all their neighbours are doing with their kids, guilty that they are not spending enough time with their kids, guilty about the shortcomings in their spiritual life. Whatever the reason for the guilt, when it comes to the crunch, guilty parents often give in to their children's complaints and excuses and do not follow through with previous agreements and enforcing family rules.

Parents overreact to their own childhood – Parents who grew up in a strict environment often hear a voice in their head reminding them how painful it was to live under rigid and strict rules. This is also true when a parent was subjected to a harsh schoolteacher or a harsh leader at church. In a noble effort to never emulate such treatment, parents go too far to the other extreme. Such leniency is a poor substitute for the effectiveness of establishing and enforcing limits.

Parents don't understand "grace and truth" – They focus too much on grace alone and not on obedience, truth and character. Some of the brattiest children have the sweetest and kindest parents. How can that be? Because the parents, who are genuinely good Christians, love their children so much that they cannot bear to say "No" to them at all. They serve their children unceasingly, and do not understand when the kids turn out entitled. They are sure that kindness and "turning the other cheek" are all that are needed to motivate their children to obey. The parents themselves often have compliant temperaments, are easy to get along with and would never hurt a fly, so to speak, so they do not understand that they need to actually discipline their innocent children in any way. This is not grace as defined by the life and death of Jesus; there is no substitute for the real thing.

Parents think their kids will develop limits by themselves – Some parents believe that their children will learn on their own when they are more mature. This is magical thinking. Children without limits become adults without limits. When they are not trained at a young age, it becomes harder and harder as they grow older. Adults with healthy limits are those who were trained to respect and obey healthy boundaries during every stage of childhood.

Parents want to avoid conflict – They are not ready to go "toe to toe" (meant figuratively!) with their own child. In an effort to make the home atmosphere more pleasant, some parents tend to avoid setting rules and talking about healthy limits, let alone confronting their children. These parents usually make excuses to other parents such as, "well, kids will be kids", or "these days, what's a parent to do?" Such short-term peace often comes with a huge price later on in the lives of their children when they have to face the consequences of their actions.

Parents want to be liked by their children – Most parents "hate being hated", but it is necessary at times to say "No". However, some parents cannot bear for thier children to be mad at them. They may regret not being close to their children. Emotionally inhibited, busy or neglectful parents are vulnerable to making choices to make their children like rather than respect them. Some parents, intentionally or not, may use the children to meet their own emotional needs. Perhaps they are unhappy with their spouse and feel lonely, or are divorced without much support, or are not connected to their church family. In their desire to be liked, they compromise and do not train their children to honour healthy and reasonable limits, which of course is unhealthy for the child. In the end, their children are not able to meet their needs so it is a lose-lose situation.

Parents are just too busy – This is probably the saddest one, but all too common these days. The amount of time many parents set aside today to spend time talking with their children is shockingly low. Schedules become packed and family time is not set aside as a priority. Often they wake up to a nightmare, surprised when they find out the ugly truth about what their children have been doing behind closed doors. ("We were so close when they were little...") The irony is, family crises take up far more time than simply nurturing good relationships in the first place.

❖ LOUIS LOWDOWN ❖

During the time we were living in Sydney, Australia, we had an afternoon play date with a family from our pre-school. It was the first and the last time that I (Karen) brought my children to this home. I should have known better, because my children had told me that the two boys were bullies. Still, because the mother was so nice, I had thought, "How bad can it be?" During the time we were there, my kids had to come to the kitchen for

> protection several times. The misguided mother would only shake her head helplessly as her children disobeyed her every word and ran riot throughout the house. Now my kids could be as naughty as the next child, and as we have said repeatedly, we are anything but perfect parents. But compared to what was going on in this woman's home, we could've been nominated for Family of the Year! I will never forget how dumbfounded I was when the mother uttered the following with complete wide-eyed sincerity, "I always thought that if I gave my children everything they wanted and never said 'No' to them, that they would be so happy they would obey me out of gratitude." Summoning all of my self-control, and trying not to sound shocked, I said, "Wow, that's an interesting parenting philosophy. My philosophy is a bit different. In fact, you might say that mine is kind of the opposite." At that moment, I truly thought the mother would say, "Oh please, tell me your philosophy; what do you do?" However, she just stared at me blankly, then smiled and said, "Oh well, I guess everybody has their own way." I almost fainted. A few minutes later my kids gave me a look that said, "Mum, we gotta get out of here!" Boy did we have lots to talk about on the way home!

Children who call the shots at home most of the time will believe that "rules do not apply to them". This is a breeding ground for the lifetrap of entitlement. Eventually children who are entitled will not have many friends, since most healthy individuals do not enjoy one-way relationships. They will not get along with their teachers or any other person who is in authority over them. They do not know how to progress if they are not in charge. Children may enjoy getting their way at times, but they neither remain happy nor feel safe if this is what they are experiencing.

When children know that their parents are in charge, it provides a tremendous amount of security and comfort. This feeling does a lot for their emotional well-being. Happy children are the ones who understand and adhere to healthy limits. Limits teach them to get along with others, especially those in authority, which helps them learn to be responsible and confident to face the world on their own. If limits are too strict, of course, it will backfire. We are talking about balance, and this balance does not come intuitively for many parents. Often, as with the other core emotional needs, their intuition is wrong, miscoloured by their own emotional needs and childhood experiences, and they have difficulty meeting this need adequately. Children raised to respect limits set by their parents are happy and fulfilled children.

MASTER CLASS

> The Evans asked their children, who all have a strong faith in God, what aspect of their parenting was most important to each of them. Walter reports, "Our oldest child said that us setting clear, unbending boundaries

> was the most helpful for him. The funny thing about that answer is that he struggled with the boundaries more than anything else, and didn't agree with many of the boundaries we set. For instance, 'no "R" rated movies until you are 18 years old' was an unbending rule at our house. It is amazing to us to hear him say that clear rules helped him the most because this was the very thing he seemed to dislike about growing up in our house." Kim continues:, "I am so thankful that Walter was clear-minded on consistency in emotional trials because with the flack that we got from our son about the rules, I might have been tempted to be soft. And I certainly would have never dreamed that when our son described his childhood, the words 'limits' and 'grateful' would be in the same sentence!"

Basic Safety

An extremely important component of Basic Safety for this core emotional need involves protecting children from the dangers of early/inappropriate exposure to sex and violence. In particular, this is related to dangers on the Internet (porn, revealing personal information on social networking sites, lurking paedophiles, scams, inappropriate YouTube videos, and the like), listening to inappropriate song lyrics, as well as inappropriate and sexually explicit books, movies, and TV shows.

Parents need to understand how using the Internet without limits, particularly in the case of pornography and games that emphasise violence and sexuality, can have dire consequences that may literally scar their children for life. In an age where two-year-olds surf the Internet on iPhones and tablets, how can parents realistically set healthy limits for their children? Given the devastation that the Internet can cause, this is not something that should be taken lightly.

The Influence of Media

Contrary to the opinion of those who argue that watching TV and playing violent computer games have little negative effect on children, there is overwhelming support that it is very harmful. From our own experience, we strongly believe that parents need to exercise control in allowing their children to watch unhealthy programmes on TV and play violent and inappropriate video games. *(Please note: a huge Research Revealed section stemming from multiple studies is placed at the end of this Basic Safety section filled with important facts and quotes.)*

For a start, children who play inappropriate video games and watch unsuitable TV programmes, YouTube videos and movies are exposed to thousands (maybe tens of thousands) of murders, along with hundreds of hours of vulgar language and unhealthy relationships. Even if children are not influenced to act out what they are watching, they risk a highly negative response in adopting a view that the world is a mean and a dangerous place. This inhibits their autonomy and interferes with forming healthy adult relationships.

Parents who doubt whether they should limit their children's "screen time" have to ask themselves if they are happy with their children being raised by "the other parent". *The Other Parent* is the title of a book authored by James P. Steyer and Chelsea Clinton;[1] it is their name for all the media our children are being exposed to. This "other parent" condones the following (indirectly and directly):

- Sex outside of marriage is fine, even without commitment
- Flirting is no big deal, even if you are married
- Children need to be allowed more freedom
- Strict parents are old-fashioned
- Material things buy happiness
- Looks are much more important than character
- Women are objects to be used and thrown away
- Drunkenness, drugs and the like are part of growing up
- Aggressive and violent behaviour is no big deal
- Killing people is part and parcel of everyday life.

Most experts advise parents to not allow children to have a TV or computer in their bedroom, as it is difficult to monitor and promotes isolation. They would also advise parents to not turn the TV on during meal times and when the family is talking together. Media experts also agree that parents should establish guidelines about how much TV should be viewed during school days, and talk about limits for holiday times as well.

We would add that parents should discuss what movies the children should watch, what to avoid and why. Parents would do well to make use of websites like www.kids-in-mind.com[2], which describes to parents exactly what sex, violence and vulgarities appear in each movie. There should be frequent discussions regarding gaming, TV and Internet content, and it should be a given that all computer, tablets and cell phones should have filters to avoid access to pornographic websites.

Parents should also help their children understand the importance of guarding the heart (Proverbs 4:23) and how what we watch and hear has a big impact on children and their future choices. Do not be permissive and do not underestimate the powerful influence of TV, computer games and the Internet. In the end, parents who take this kind of basic safety seriously and introduce these healthy limits will increase their chances of protecting their children, preventing many harmful outcomes.

⋖ LOUIS LOWDOWN ⋗

One of my (Karen) favourite children's songs that played on a cassette tape in our car back when the kids were little was sung to the tune of "If You're Happy And You Know It". The first verse was, "Oh be careful little eyes what you see. (repeat). For the Father up above is looking down in love, Oh be careful little eyes what you see." The verses that followed were "Oh be careful little ears what you hear…" "Oh be careful little mind what you think…" "Oh be careful little mouth what you say…" This is a good song to train the kids with when they are young. I wish we had sung it more often!

⋖ RESEARCH REVEALS ⋗

RR13.1: *An Extensive Look at Media and Youth*

The Kaiser Family Foundation undertook a comprehensive study on the use of media among American youth, entitled, "Generation M2, Media in the lives of 8 to 18-Year-Olds". The study was done on a sample of over 2,000 young people, from ages eight to eighteen, and was published in 2010. It covered a whole array of media such as TV, computers, video games, music, print, cell phones and movies. We extracted some of their *frightening* findings:[3]

- For purposes of comparison, young people were grouped into categories of heavy, moderate and light media users. Heavy users are those who consume more than 16 hours of media content in a typical day (21% of children from eight to eighteen); moderate users are those who consume from 3–16 hours of content (63%); light users are those who consume less than three hours of media in a typical day (17%).

- Nearly half (47%) of all heavy media users say they usually get fair or poor grades (mostly C's or lower), compared to 23% of light media users. Heavy media users are also more likely to say they get into trouble a lot, are often sad or unhappy, and say they are bored. Moreover, the relationships between media exposure and grades, and between media exposure and personal contentment, withstood controls for other possibly relevant factors such as age, gender, race, parent education, and single vs. two-parent households. This study could not establish whether there is a cause and effect relationship between media use and grades, or between media use and personal contentment. If there are such relationships, they could well run in both directions simultaneously.

- Children who live in homes that limit media opportunities spend less time with media. For example, children whose parents do not put a TV in their bedroom, do not leave the TV on during meals or in the background when no one is watching, and do impose media-related rules spend substantially less time with media than do those who are not limited in the choices they make about screen time.

- Over the past five years, young people have increased the amount of time they spend consuming media by an hour and seventeen minutes daily, from an already worrying six hours and twenty-one minutes to a staggering seven hours and thirty-eight minutes! Considering that young people use media seven days a week instead of five, this means that they are spending 54 hours a week on media, more time than most adults spend at work!
- Just under half (45%) of all eight to eighteen-year-olds say they live in a home where the TV is left on most of the time, whether anyone is watching or not, and 64% say the TV is usually on in their household during meals. The percentage of young people reporting a TV on most of the time and a TV usually on during meals has remained relatively constant over the last decade.
- In a typical day, 46% of eight to eighteen-year-olds report sending text messages on a cell phone. Those who do text estimate that they send an average of 118 messages in a typical day. On average, 7th–12th graders report spending about an hour and a half engaged in sending and receiving texts.
- The gender difference in computer time only begins to appear in the teenage years. Boys and girls start out spending equal amounts of time on a computer, but a disparity develops over time. Among fifteen to eighteen-year-olds, there is a gap of about 40 minutes between the genders (two hours for boys, and roughly an hour and twenty minutes for girls). One clear reason for the disparity in this age group is that girls lose interest in computer games as they enter their teenage years, while boys do not. Girls go from an average of 12 minutes a day playing computer games when they are in the eight to ten-year-old group, to just three minutes a day by the time they are fifteen to eighteen years old; there is no such decrease among boys.
- Only a relatively small proportion of eight to eighteen-year-olds say they have any rules about music listening: 26% say they have rules about what types of music they are allowed to listen to, and 10% say they have rules about how much time they can spend listening to music. The proportion with rules about which music they can listen to decreases substantially by age, going from nearly half (47%) of all eight to ten-year-olds to 27% of eleven to fourteen-year-olds to just 12% of all fifteen to eighteen-year-olds.

Another noteworthy study was conducted in Singapore, published by the American Academy of Pediatrics (2009), which found the strongest factor associated with early teenage sexual intercourse for male adolescents was viewing pornography between 14 and 19 years of age. This finding agreed with another study conducted in Sweden with boys between 17-21 years of age. In addition, of the boys who viewed pornography, 59% used computers, 19% used videos, and 14% made use of mobile phones.[4]

RR13.2: *Dangers of Excessive Media Exposure*

From a number of national (US-based) surveys, we found the following:

Parent Further, a search institute resource for families, warns of excessive computer and other media exposure.[5]

According to one study, nearly 1 in 10 young gamers displayed behaviour patterns similar to addiction.[6]

According to A.C. Nielsen, the average American watches more than four hours of TV each day (or 28 hours per week, or two months of nonstop TV-watching per year). In a 65-year life, that person will have spent nine years glued to the tube.[7]

Below are some statistics compiled by TV-Free America:

- The number of murders seen on TV by the time an average child finishes elementary school: 8,000
- The number of violent acts seen on TV by age 18: 200,000
- The percentage of Americans who believe TV violence helps precipitate real life mayhem: 79%

In his book, *Take Back Your Kids*, William Doherty wrote:

During the 7-8pm time slot (once defined as family hour), 80% of television shows use four letter words, and 60% refer to sex.[8]

During all the prime time slots, 74% of all TV shows contain sexual content.[9]

Children are exposed to an estimated 10,000 food advertisements per year, mostly on TV.[10]

Media Awareness Network, has this to say about the effects of Media on children:[11]

Rowell Huesmann reviewed studies conducted in Australia, Finland, Poland, Israel, Netherlands and the United States. He reports, "The child most likely to be aggressive would be the one who (a) watches violent television programs most of the time, (b) believes that these shows portray life just as it is, [and] (c) identifies strongly with the aggressive characters in the shows."[12]

A study conducted by the Kaiser Family Foundation in 2003 found that nearly half (47%) of parents with children between the ages of four and six report that their children have imitated aggressive behaviours from TV. However, it is interesting to note that children are more likely to mimic positive behaviours—87% of kids do so.[13]

Recent research is exploring the effect of new media on children's behaviour. Craig Anderson and Brad Bushman of Iowa State University reviewed dozens of studies of video gamers. In 2001, they reported that children and young people who play violent video games, even for short periods, are more likely to behave aggressively in the real world; and that both aggressive and non-aggressive children are negatively affected by playing.[14]

In 2003, two Iowa State University researchers teamed up with the Texas Department of Human Services and reported that violent music lyrics increased aggressive thoughts and hostile feelings among 500 college students. They concluded, "There are now good theoretical and empirical reasons to expect effects of music lyrics on aggressive behaviour to be similar to the well-studied effects of exposure to TV and movie violence and the more recent research efforts on violent video games."[15]

Columbia University professor Jeffrey Johnson has found that the effect is not limited to children who grew up watching violent shows. Johnson tracked 707 families in upstate New York for 17 years, starting in 1975. In 2002, he reported that children who watched one to three hours of any kind of television each day when they were 14 to 16 years old were 60% more likely to be involved in assaults and fights as adults than those who watched less TV.[16]

Researchers have also pursued the link between media violence and real life aggression by examining communities before and after the introduction of television. In the mid-1970s, University of British Columbia professor Tannis McBeth Williams studied a remote village in British Columbia both before and after television was introduced. She found that two years after TV arrived, violent incidents had increased by 160%.[17]

University of Washington Professor Brandon Centerwall noted that the sharp increase in the murder rate in North America in 1955 occurred eight years after television sets began to enter North American homes. To test his hypothesis that the two were related, he examined the murder rate in South Africa where, prior to 1975, television was banned by the government. He found that twelve years after the ban was lifted, murder rates skyrocketed.

In 1998, Professors Singer, Slovak, Frierson and York surveyed 2,000 Ohio students in grades three through eight. They report that the incidences of psychological trauma (including anxiety, depression and post-traumatic stress) increased in proportion to the number of hours of television watched each day.[18]

A number of studies in the 1970's showed that people who are repeatedly exposed to media violence tend to be less disturbed when they witness real world violence, and have less sympathy for its victims. For example, Professors V.B. Cline, R.G. Croft, and S. Courrier studied young boys over a two-year period. In 1973, they reported that boys who watch more than 25 hours of television per week are significantly less likely to be aroused by real world violence than those boys who watch four hours or less per week.[19]

The late George Gerbner conducted the longest running study of television violence that we know of. His seminal research found that frequent TV viewers tend to perceive the world in ways that are consistent with the images on TV. As viewers' perceptions of the world come to conform with the depictions they see on TV, they become more passive, more anxious, and more fearful. Gerbner calls this the "Mean World Syndrome." Gerbner's research, published in 1994, found that those who watch greater amounts of television are more likely to overestimate their risk of being victimised by crime; believe their neighbourhoods are unsafe; believe "fear of crime is a very serious personal problem"; and assume the crime rate is increasing, even when it is not.[20]

The Vortex Of Conflict Escalation

Meeting (and Not Meeting) Expectations

Just as we admit that as parents none of us is perfect, we also acknowledge that our children do not always live up to our expectations—whether or not our expectations are healthy will be left for the chapter on Realistic Expectations. The fact remains that all humans who are connected with each other have expectations in their relationships. When parents (rightly or wrongly) do not feel that children are meeting their expectations, or when children (rightly or wrongly) do not feel that parents are meeting their core emotional needs, there will be conflict. If parents are able to practice the principles of Good Enough Parenting, hopefully the conflicts will be sorted out constructively. However, since the emotional part of our brain seems to work quicker than the rational part, this does not always happen. When this happens, the conflict may escalate, and become destructive, as parent and child enter into what we call a "Vortex of Conflict Escalation" (see Figure 13.1). This Vortex can involve the exchange of harsh words, throwing of tantrums, or stonewalls of silence and sulking, but either way, it will harm the connection, mar the feeling of acceptance, and damage the relationship. Let us consider how a Vortex might occur when dealing with reasonable limits.

Picture a case in which a 13-year-old boy is defiant about obeying rules. He tests his parents' limits to see how far he can go. What may escape unnoticed is the role parents play in teaching limits. Let us suppose that in this case, when the father tries to teach his son reasonable limits by giving instructions, the boy refuses to cooperate, and the father becomes stern. The

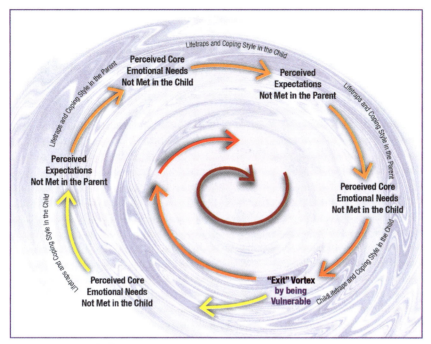

Figure 13.1: Vortex of Conflict Escalation

child debates with the father (the older children are, the better they become at debating). The parent becomes frustrated and raises his voice. The teen also raises *his* voice and walks out. The parent keeps going, following his son out of the room, perhaps issuing threats. The boy retorts with an insult, then both get tired and retreat to their own corners. In the meantime, other family members may witness this scene. Typically, the other parent joins the fray, either against the child or against her spouse. Finally, someone gives in…But is the fault always with the child?

Typically in a situation like this, people will leave thinking that the child has to learn a thing or two about limits. While this may be the case, it is also true that the parents may have been more focused on their own triggers in the vortex of conflict than on the needs of their child. It could be that one or more "exasperation interactions" were hindering the child from learning about limits. These further exacerbate the formation of a vortex between the child and the parent. It then escalates, causing emotional pain and damage. Unnecessary words are used. Name calling or hitting in anger can take place. "Is there another way?" parents often ask. Some parents give up and then the child "wins". Sometimes the parent "wins" and the child develops resentment. In both cases, the parent-child connection is damaged.

> ### ❧ LOUIS LOWDOWN ❧
>
> When our children were in elementary school, we did not allow any television during the week other than appropriate children's shows after homework or something we were watching as a family. Even then, we had times where we didn't allow any during the week, only on weekends. As for computer games, we monitored those as well, and normally only allowed them on the weekends. We made it easy for the kids to be involved in outdoor play, sports, and music, so, add in homework and friends, there wasn't much time left for "screen time". However, when David got a bit older, we found that he would try to sneak in extra computer games. While his grades were not plummeting at school, we were worried more about the deceit and addiction factor, and noticed that it was starting to have a negative effect. I (John) talked with him and made a written agreement on his limits as far as playing computer games. He agreed and for the first few days, it went well. Then one day I caught him red handed—he tried hard to exit the video game, but it was too late. I lost my patience, shouted a rebuke, and went off angrily to my office. David was hurt at my outburst. Later, after my wife's intervention, we talked and I apologised. David also apologised for his lack of seriousness in not sticking to the agreed limits, and for being secretive. Looking back, while I know there was no need for "validation of feelings" considering that he blatantly disregarded a rule we had agreed on earlier, I obviously should not have blown up. I allowed myself to walk straight into a vortex of conflict escalation, which potentially hurt our connection and was counterproductive. What I should have done was, in a firm voice, express my disappointment and then let him reflect, making time to talk later. I did not have to accept his behaviour, but I could have conveyed that differently, in a manner that would have kept us out of the vortex and helped him to learn from his mistake.

Just as children have core emotional needs, parents have normal, healthy expectations. In saying this, we emphasise that this is not about the emotional needs of the parents, but about healthy expectations in a family. (Parents should have their own needs met in their marriage, and in their community, especially in church or with other peer groups. It is not the children's place to meet the emotional needs of the parents.) Just as children can become exasperated when their core emotional needs are not met, parents will not be fulfilled or at peace when their core healthy (not unrealistic) expectations are not met.

So, what reasonable and healthy expectations can and should parents have of their children? Here are some expectations that we think are normal, reasonable, and healthy. These sit well with our experiences, and are parallel with the core emotional needs of children:

1. **Connection:** This involves children responding to the parents, in an age-appropriate manner, as the parents do their best to meet the core emotional need for Connection and Acceptance. Parents want an on-going, life-long connection with their children.
2. **Growth and Performance:** This involves children learning and growing in age-appropriate ways (emotionally, physically, mentally and spiritually). Parents want to see their children living up to their potential and utilizing their God-given strengths and abilities as they respond to the parent meeting the core emotional needs for Healthy Autonomy and Realistic Expectations.
3. **Responsibility and Respect:** This involves children adhering to rules and taking care of themselves in an age-appropriate manner, as parents do their best to meet their children's core emotional need for Reasonable Limits. Parents want to see their children act in honest, helpful and respectful ways and not be entitled and disrespectful.

These three areas define the core expectations of parenting. When children make progress in these three areas, parents will be fulfilled and feel that their parenting amounts to something worthwhile. They will be at peace. Bear in mind, even if a child is not able to make much progress, it is still the responsibility of the parents to accept and love the child unconditionally. Unconditional love is critical to parenting. As God loves us unconditionally, we are called to love our children unconditionally. Many parents get disappointed when expectations and limits are not to a certain mark. They may have unrealistic expectations and impose unreasonable limits, as opposed to realistic expectations and reasonable limits. Parents need to take stock of each child's potential and inclinations, and be grateful for the individuality and gifts of each child. (This will be discussed more in Chapters 15-17 in the section on Realistic Expectations.)

In the beginning of this book, we discussed the different exasperation interactions that were uncovered in our research and experience. We described them and gave examples of statements that parents make when unintentionally sabotaging their parenting. To fully understand the causes of vortexes and the harm they produce, we need to be familiar with the various exasperation interactions.

As a reminder, here they are again: Belittling, Perfectionistic and Conditional, Controlling, Punitive, Emotionally Depriving and Inhibiting, Overprotective, Pessimistic, and Overly Permissive. Each of the above can contribute greatly to the development of a Vortex and also cause our children to experience frustration or exasperation arising from not having their core emotional needs met.

What we would like to do below is to show how both sides contribute to the formation of a Vortex. Parents may, unintentionally and subtly, trigger an interaction that causes frustration on the part of the child, which then prevents the child from listening and obeying. In some cases, the defiant nature of the child can quickly diminish the firmness of the parents in staying committed to their expectations. Please review Chapters Two and Three briefly, then come back and read through these stories of frustration and exasperation. The interplay between meeting the core emotional needs of children and the expectations of parents has to be harmonised and balanced, failing which, parent and child will trigger each other, and a Vortex of Conflict Escalation will emerge, leading to exasperation. *The following vignettes will illustrate*:

Sam and Alice, siblings aged 10 and 12 respectively, are having a tiff. It begins when Alice comes home from school frustrated because she has a lot of homework and several projects due soon. She goes to her room. Sam, her brother, comes into her room without knocking. She gets mad, yells at him and says, "Get out of my room!" He lashes back, then says "sorry" but in a sarcastic tone. She senses that and says, "You are insincere and always disrespectful!" He then brings out examples of how she was disrespectful, too.

Their parents hear the exchange and the father tells Alice to settle down, which is his normal response whenever the kids have an argument. Alice responds angrily to her father for always taking Sam's side. The two children continue to call each other names. The father goes into the room, raises his voice and says, "Why can't you both just get along for once! Even animals behave better than you! Your arguments are so stupid. The house was a lot more peaceful before you two showed up!" As he blows up, they become quiet. The father then commands them both to apologise. They do so, but silently still resent each other and their dad. The dad then calls them names and issues threats as he storms out of the room. At dinner, they do not speak to each other and the atmosphere is uncomfortably quiet and unpleasant.

Later in the evening the father blurts out the good news that he got an email from his boss to say he got a promotion at work. Sam congratulates him, but Alice does not say anything and walks up to her room. The father is disappointed but does not say anything back to her, leaving the issue unresolved.

The Spade family is about to leave the house. Mr. Spade has an appointment and is in a hurry. He tells everyone to hurry up and get dressed. Sarah, 16, takes her time, is on the phone and does not really pay attention. Her dad gets frustrated and yells at her to hurry up. She responds, "Two minutes." Five minutes later, she is still not in the car. Mr. Spade loses it and says he is leaving, but only starts the engine. A few minutes later she comes down. Sarah apologises in the car, but her father refuses to talk to her and withdraws. Everybody becomes quiet for the entire one-hour journey, except for Mr Spade, who lectures Sarah non-stop about her recent behaviour and tells her off sharply. After that, he stops speaking to her and avoids being affectionate. He continues the silent treatment for part of the next day. Sarah then feels bad about herself and retreats into her room, skipping the movie on family night. Even though the parents try to persuade her to join, she refuses. They feel disappointed that she does not prioritise spending time with the family. In the ensuing days, the issue does not get resolved. Both the father and daughter drop the matter and act like nothing happened.

Jack, age 15, comes home from school and talks with his mother. After a few minutes, they begin to watch a TV show together. While this is going on, the father comes home and says in a raging tone, "I thought you were not to watch any TV during school days—what the heck is this? You are so unreliable. You can't be relied upon to follow one single rule". The mother looks at Jack and winks at him to signal that he should not worry about the father who is out of control. The mother defends the son since they are spending time together. Jack then says to the father, "What's the matter, Dad? Did you get up on the wrong side of the bed? It is not a school night. It is Friday, after school, so the weekend rules, where I am allowed to watch TV, apply." The father sarcastically says, "I guess you forgot our agreement. Technically, it is still not the weekend. You'd forget your head if it wasn't attached." The mother gives her husband a stern look. The son rolls his eyes, and says, "We talked about Friday evening being ok the last time and you agreed." The mother joins and concurs. The father refuses to budge. He then senses the divide, and walks away saying, "Seems like you both are always on the same team. Jack, you better hope you don't marry someone who treats you like this," as he storms out. Jack reluctantly turns the TV off and retreats to his room alone. His mother follows and the two spend much of the evening together talking, including about how angry the father has been lately. The following Monday the mother takes Jack to school and the two of them spend many days like this together, conspicuously leaving the father out. He eventually remarks sarcastically to his wife, "You really worship Jack, don't you?" but makes no effort to sort out the conflict.

Maggie, age 13, comes home from school in an extra-excited state of mind—she has been accepted into an after school acting class for which she was on the waiting list. Even though she has been doing well academically, Maggie anticipates that her mother will freak out about the class, seeing as how the girl's final exams are about one month away. When she reaches home a little later than expected, her mother is furious. "Why are you so late, Missy?" Maggie starts apologizing. After an extensive interrogation, Maggie is forced to tell her mother about the class. Her mother flies off the handle, "Your exams are just one month away, and you want to take an acting class? Do you know what people will think of you if all you can do is act? What kind of career is acting? What will your grandparents think? What about your relatives? Look at your cousin—she scored straight As. If you don't do the same, I will not know where to hide my face. Now get changed and do your homework and show it to me when it is all done perfectly. Then start studying for your exams. I have arranged a tutor for you on the weekends." Maggie says, "Yes, mother" but as she walks off, she blames herself and is sad she has disappointed her mother. Her mother hears her mumble and shouts at Maggie, "Stop complaining! You should be grateful that you have opportunities I never had!"

Jayden, seven years old, spreads legos all over the floor of his room. His mother walks in and asks, "Do you know what you are supposed to do when you are finished playing?" Jayden answers dutifully, "I know—clean the room." His mother retorts with, "Yes, but do you ever do what I say?" Jayden responds quickly, "I am sorry, I will this time." Then his mother inquires about his homework. Before he even gets a word out, his mother demands, "Even if you say you finished, there is no way you did a good job. How could you have done it all so quickly?" "The worksheets were easy and the teacher said I am doing well in P1 [first grade]". "That's not important. Your teacher is just trying to be encouraging. I bet today you did not read the homework instructions correctly," says his mother sharply. "Mum, please!" begs Jayden. She raises her voice and says, "Don't you dare be fresh with me." "I wasn't," says the boy. "Oh, yes, you were. You don't even know how to be respectful. Always rude…" She leaves his room. Later when his mother asks him to join her to go to the mall, Jayden refuses. His mother shouts at him, saying he has no respect for her hard work in raising him. The mother never makes amends with Jayden about this particular encounter.

Ryan, aged 10, is told by his mother in the morning to do his household chores. Up to this point he has been good at doing his chores on time, without any reminder. In the evening she reminds him again, but he procrastinates a little, and then goes to his room to rest before dinner. His nap accidentally turns into a deep sleep lasting several hours. His father comes to know about it and blows his top. Ryan gets rudely awakened, comes out of his room, apologises and finishes his chores. His father lectures him before retreating in disgust, and later decides to punish him by grounding him for one week.

Ryan complains to his mother that the punishment is too much, since he has been doing his chores well. The mother agrees and argues with the father, but the father is unbending and says to Ryan, "You need to be punished, only then will you learn to take things seriously. When I say something I mean it. I hope you get the message." Ryan thinks to himself, "I cause a lot of problems in this house. Everyone will be better off if I leave." Ryan's father calls out after him, "If you keep moping around, I will ground you for *two* weeks…" Ryan, feeling exasperated, goes straight to his room.

The next month, Ryan's father tells the family that he would like to take them on a short holiday, but Ryan, fearful of conflict with his dad and unhappy with himself, says, "No thanks, I want to stay at home. I have a lot of work." The father is disappointed at his answer since it was only going to be a short vacation, so he takes the opportunity to bring up more instances of how irresponsible Ryan is over the next few days.

Tabitha, aged 5, is all excited to go to her year-end kindergarten party. When it comes time to go, Tabitha is not able to quite get her dress on by herself. Her mother comes into her room and says, "Honestly, sometimes, I feel that you are a three-year old. Why can't you do this? Here, let me do it for you." Tabitha bursts into tears. About the time they arrive at school, her shoelaces come loose. Tabitha's friends come running to greet her. Just as she is about to tie her shoelaces, her mother says loudly and angrily, in front of the girl's friends, "You still can't do it right! Let me do it." Later on after the school party, her friends make fun of her for not being able to tie her shoelaces. She feels embarrassed as well as resentful of her mother. When they are having dinner together at home, Tabitha purposefully has poor table manners, is rude to her parents and gives her food to the dog under the table. Her mother, guilty for her earlier outburst, cleans up and lets her daughter watch TV until she falls asleep on the couch.

Ben comes home from school and plays computer games, as he always does. His mother reminds him about his promise to be reliable at his new part-time job and to go to work on time, but he ignores her. She pleads with him and he agrees to go to work, but procrastinates and leaves the house late, as usual. Later that week, Ben gets fired. His mother works up her courage to ask, "Honey would you like to talk about your discipline?" Ben gets angry and says, "Why don't you just give me a break? I'm old enough to choose what I like and if I don't like something, why should I do it?" In addition to the above, Ben hardly eats what the mother cooks at home, preferring to eat the junk food he purchases when out with his friends. He plays computer games until the wee hours of the morning; He frequently does not get enough sleep and falls sick. His parents know what is going on, but are afraid to say anything. Her mother, in particular, blames herself and eventually falls into depression.

In all the above examples, the interactions escalated into a Vortex. The children fall short of their parents' expectations in some way. The parents' response is more about how the situation makes them feel than about addressing the situation as a parent who is mindful of the child's core needs. It does not matter which one came first, the child not cooperating or the parent exasperating the child. Either way, each situation quickly evolves into a Vortex of Conflict. Bear in mind that it does not take long for a Vortex to form and escalate.

Exercise: Using the eight examples mentioned above, look at the table in Appendix 4 and identify the perceived unmet core emotional needs in the child, the unmet expectations in the parent, and their respective coping styles. All of these come together and contribute to the formation of a Vortex of Conflict Escalation. (We are using the word "perceived" because sometimes a child or a parent's evaluation of their core emotional need or expectations may not be accurate and or realistic. It is just their perception of what was not met.)

How do we stay

out of the vortex?

CHAPTER FOURTEEN

Avoiding the Vortex

A big part of avoiding "the Vortex" is related to setting things up right. Therefore, the first seven of these ten steps are about what parents should do to lay a good foundation. Once the foundation is in place, parents will usually find that conflict escalates much less often.

1. Give Clear Instructions from the Beginning

Children need clear instructions, especially when it comes to limits. Clarity even helps with infants—around eight months old, babies are able to learn "No". Parents can give them a disappointed look, take their hand and say, "No, don't do that." If the baby persists, the parent can take her away from that particular place to show disapproval, and, in a few days, after repeating this countless times, she will get the message. Somewhere in their second year, they can be expected to greet others, give a "high five", and say "Hi" and "Goodbye". Once children begin walking, they should help their parents pick up toys, books and dirty clothes. This fosters responsibility and a sense of mutuality in the parent-child relationship, little by little, from a young age.

(While parents should not wait until children are older to start expecting some sense of responsibility, they should not be thinking about instilling morals and discipline in their newborn. Babies cry because of hunger, irritation and tiredness, and parents need to attend to them constantly to assure them they are cared for and that their needs will be met. After the age of three months, parents do not have to run to their *every* cry, but they should never neglect or discipline their babies.)

Having strategies in place during known and predictable times of stress can be very helpful in avoiding a Vortex. To this end, 150 families in California allowed researchers to place audio recording devices in their house for a sixteen-month period in hopes of discovering the most frequent times for conflict. No surprises on their findings—most arguments took place during the morning rush to get out of the house for school/work, during the time right before bed, and at the end of the month when finances were getting tight![1] Therefore, it makes sense to have some strategies in place so that you are not setting yourself up for a fight even before it happens.

With the benefit of hindsight, we can surmise that the "hot spots" picked up by that study are the times when the pressure of parents' expectations and children's core needs are most likely to be in conflict. For example, the parent expects the child to be responsible and mindful of the need for everyone to get out of the house quickly in the morning, but the child may need time to get ready quietly and methodically, or to feel connected before beginning the day. The parents' rushing triggers the child's anxieties and prevents emotional needs from being met. Some parents have found that they can keep emotions in check by bringing up limits in the context of regular family meetings. Especially as children hit the secondary/middle school years, family meetings promote clarity and mutual understanding regarding household chores, limits, discipline, and responsibilities.

Different children have different issues and needs—not all children need limits for all things, only those that pertain to them personally (the areas in which they tend to be led into temptation—Matthew 6:13). For example, the subject of how much time to spend playing computer games does not seem to come up in conversations with our daughter, and budget concerns seldom come up with our son. Some issues are age-sensitive. Here are some issues you may want to discuss with your children, depending on your values and their ages:

	Issues	Expectations
1	Tidying toys away	How tidy?
2	Having friends over	How often and expected behaviour?
3	TV on school nights	Allowed? How much? Which shows?
4	Bedtime	During weekdays vs. weekends?
5	Pocket money	Allowance?
6	Phone bills	Limits?
7	Morning	Waking up, leaving house on time?
8	Computer games	Which and how often?
9	Chores	Which and how often?
10	Family dinners	Regularity? (We recommended five times a week.)
11	Curfews	Weeknights vs. weekends?
12	Movies/TV	Age-appropriate?
13	Music lyrics	Acceptable?
14	Internet access	What kind and how much?
15	Teenagers rooms	How tidy?
16	Moodiness and temper tantrums	Tolerance level? (Feelings are acceptable but not necessarily behaviour—see Chapter Seven, section on accepting behaviour vs. accepting feelings)
17	The big NOs	Decide what they will be for your family

When children disobey because parents were not clear about the limits, frustration sets in, and a Vortex might be right around the corner. With some children, it may help for both parties to write out an agreement and keep a copy each, as a point of reference. (This is not meant to be legally binding!) When something is written down, it is amazing how it shuts down potential ambiguities. With the proliferation of smartphones, tablets and other gadgets, there is no reason why agreements about instructions and limits cannot be easily recorded.

2. Be United

When trying to prevent a vortex, it is really important to make sure that mum and dad are on the same page. Since most of us seem to marry our opposite, this will take planning ahead and lots of discussion. At times, getting united on training and disciplining our children will feel a strategic battle discussion. Do not be discouraged. Persevere—it is worth it. Children are very smart; they know which parent is weak in a particular area and some kids will milk that weakness for all it's worth, so be united!

◁ MASTER CLASS ▷

Al and Gloria Baird found that the most helpful aspects of their parenting had to do with limits, "When our children were very young, Gloria's parents gave us two keys to effective parenting that have been invaluable. These keys are simple yet very challenging to put into practice. The first one is for the parents to be united. It is amazing how quickly kids will try to divide their parents as in going to mom for a 'Yes' when dad has already said 'No'. If parents allow this pattern of disunity to develop, the children will be insecure. The second key is for the parents to be consistent. In other words, for parents to mean what they say. The rules should not be constantly changing." Gloria says, "Staci, my oldest, and I recently taught a parenting class together. While preparing, I asked Staci what she remembered from her childhood that helped her presently with her own children. Staci replied, 'You and Dad were the same away from home as you were at home.' She also remarked that she didn't like it when I would answer a request with, 'I'll talk to Dad about it.' It is interesting to see that her answers had to do with unity and consistency." Al adds, "Our other daughters mentioned the consistency of our times with God and our family times, so it seems the unity and consistency principles have been passed from generation to generation....and on to every parenting class we teach!"

---

3. Be Optimistic and Encouraging

What we are specifically trying to get across is be optimistic *when setting limits* and encouraging *when limits are followed*. It is important to convey confidence and to recognize success at every opportunity, since sincere praise is more reinforcing than criticism. On the topic of correcting children's mistakes, Shinichi Suzuki, founder of the world-famous music school, said, "Notice everything, focus on a few, mention one."[2] Suzuki's advice helped us in countless ways over the years!

Here are some examples of the way we can encourage our children as they show signs of improvement in accepting limits:

Look what a great job you are doing with the household chores—it really shows how much you care about our home.

You did such a good job cleaning your room. I bet you are proud of yourself.

The way you handled that conflict was brilliant. You showed a lot of empathy and humility but you also spoke the truth in love.

Thanks for doing your chores. It encourages me when you show you care about all of us pulling together.

Your mum and I have noticed how much effort you are putting in to developing an excellent character and we are so proud of you.

You put so much effort into doing your bit even though I know that this was a particularly busy week for you—that means a lot.

I noticed you washed the dishes without any reminder. Great job!

The focus is not on the actual achievement, but on the effort and what it shows about their character and level of responsibility.

4. Role Play in Family Devotionals

Another idea for pre-empting mistakes and teaching limits in a pro-active way is to role-play in family devotionals. We particularly recommend this for children between ages two and eight.

Experts have stated that role-play helps children:
- Explore imagination
- Think in the abstract
- Acquire language skills
- Build social skills
- Problem solve
- Understand someone else's perspective
- Learn essential life skills from adults
- Discover leadership skills
- Safely explore the world beyond
- Acquire confidence and a sense of self.[3]

Children love to role-play mummy, daddy, teacher, fire fighters, and so forth. When role-play is based on biblical principles such as honesty, obedience, or on biblical characters who have real-life struggles, the role-play becomes "the spoon full of sugar that helps the medicine go down". If your children are below ten, do not let this opportunity slip away—buy a children's Bible, or a Bible in simplified language, and take advantage of this natural lesson planner. Using a myriad of different scenarios from God's words, you can role-play topics such as obedience, learning to say "No" properly, being polite, being respectful, not hitting but requesting politely, ignoring troublemakers instead of fighting, working together to get chores done, being hospitable with guests, and a host of other topics for your family.

In role-play you can demonstrate the proper and the improper, the godly and the ungodly. Sometimes you can have your children act out both parts; kids especially love to give feedback when mum and dad play the "bad-guy" roles! You will have lots of fun and the kids will get the picture about limits. (Role-play may come in handy again in the teenage years, when questions about what to do get the response, "I don't know.")

◄ LOUIS LOWDOWN ►

> I (John) can't remember how many times I lead the Good Samaritan devotional from Luke 10 over the years. We took turns playing all the roles—the kids especially loved it when they got to beat me up! We explored many lessons, especially about loving others and not being hypocrites. During her pre-teen years, Sonia, asked, "Why does it seem like family devotionals are more about what we need to change than they are about God?" After considering this, we realised that, now that the kids were older, the devotionals needed to be less issue-oriented and more about how awesome God and His Word are. Thereafter, we came up with a plan to alternate between having family devotionals and family meetings. During the family meeting, we could talk about discipline, training and expectation issues, and everyone in the family felt great about the division. However, I still believe that when the children were younger, it was extremely effective to teach all sorts of issues through devotionals, as is fitting for implementing Deuteronomy's teaching on "impressing".

5. Engage Cooperation

Here is another helpful tip from Adele Faber and Elaine Mazlish's book, *How To Talk So Your Kids Will Listen and Listen So They Will Talk,* on the topic of engaging cooperation.[4] As long as parents are already consistently practising the steps mentioned above, they will find that "engaging cooperation" works most of the time, and helps parents to avoid exasperation interactions. As in Chapter Seven, we have obtained permission from Faber and Mazlish to use their teaching points,[5] and have made our own cartoons for the sake of illustration.

A. Describe the Problem

Rather than nagging, lecturing, or falling into an exasperation interaction, parents should try describing the problem to their children. When the tone of the home is "we are a family and families love, respect, serve and cooperate", children *usually* want to help solve the problem (see Figures 14.1 and 14.2).

Figures 14.1 & 14.2: Describe the problem

B. Give Information

As with the skill above, giving information prevents parents from sounding harsh, judgmental, and accusatory. This makes it easier for children to respond with a good attitude (see Figures 14.3 and 14.4).

Figures 14.3 & 14.4: Give information

C. Say It with a Word

How often do children tune out the parents because of sensory overload? Parents who struggle with going on *ad nauseum* would do well to switch to a "less is more" mind-set (see Figures 14.5 and 14.6).

Figures 14.5 & 14.6: Say it with a word

D. Talk about Your Feelings

When we have a great connection with our children, they will not want to see us be sad or in pain. While we should not manipulate our children with our emotions, it is fair that we sometimes help them to see things from our point of view (see Figures 14.7 and 14.8).

Figures 14.7 & 14.8: Talk about your feelings

6. Maintain an Excellent Connection

Our experience in working with families has shown us that children get exasperated and discouraged but may not know that they are discouraged or why. How could this be? One reason is that their vocabularies are limited. Four and five-year-olds may not even know the words to describe their feelings. Even when they do, they may be able to recognize their discouragement only with the help of an adult. (Adults who are depressed often take several counselling sessions before they recognize the source of their depression.) When parents do not have a good connection with their children, their kids may not be open to discussing things with them that will help to uncover areas of discouragement. That will bring even more discouragement, and children will know that emotionally something is amiss.

We return again to the first core emotional need. When the connection is high, children want to please their parents, because, in the words of Elkind, the parents have fulfilled their part of a "loyal-commitment contract" and the children want to reciprocate.[6] When parents expect children to comply with limits but do little to enhance their emotional connection, they are inadvertently saying that this contract applies to the children, but not to them. In essence, the parents do not need to follow the rules, but the children must. This becomes a problem for two reasons, the first being that when the children feel the "contract" is broken, they will feel exasperated and this may result in rebellion and retaliation. Often this will show up in their refusal to accept the limits they are given, especially later on in their adolescent years, which inevitably leads to the vortex. When a father, for example, hardly spends time with his children, yet stays on top of them about their school work, their computer usage or their bed times, the children will rebel (either inwardly or outwardly), because inherently they will feel exasperated and discouraged and know that something is amiss. Often when asked, they will not even know where their rebellion comes from. Maintaining a deep connection will inhibit this kind of rebellion from taking root in their hearts.

Secondly, this kind of role modelling will become a breeding ground for the development of the entitlement lifetrap, in which mutual reciprocity is not respected. This lack of reciprocity may come out in their relationship with their teachers and even with peers. So we say again, ensure that connection is always high. Be in touch with their highs and lows, have dinners regularly, play with them and spend time with them, including regular one-on-one time with each child. When parents make a connection from the beginning, and keep it up consistently through the years, children will want to please them and will be much more open to listening and being impacted by their values. Passing down limits is so much easier when the connection is healthy. (Remember, this is about "good enough" parenting, and mistakes of the past can usually be healed by careful attention to the need for connection and acceptance as children develop.)

7. Revise the Rules Periodically

Children must learn to abide by rules and limits until they are ready to go out in the world and spread their own wings. Parents should be aware that some rules will need to be amended as time goes by, as children grow older, and as they demonstrate good behaviour. Children need to feel that they are able to earn their parents' trust and that with greater trust they will enjoy greater privileges and more freedom. This is also related to meeting the core emotional need for healthy autonomy and performance. Examples may include extending curfews, not being as strict with bedtimes, and giving more pocket money, to name a few.

Sometimes rules need to be revisited because parents may have been too rigid with both limits and consequences and children may have been afraid to speak up in support of themselves. At other times, this may not be the case— the child may simply be chafing against the consequences of reasonable expectations and limits, which is a part of the learning experience.

8. Give Options and a Second Chance

When children misbehave, it is helpful for parents to give them awareness by alerting them to the undesirable act and saying, "Would you like to give this another go?" or "Would you like to try that again?" This gives children a chance to pause and take stock of what they have done, and then make a decision to correct themselves. It is like Round Two of engaging cooperation. If the children still choose not to, consequences should come into play. However, before they even get there, give them a chance. (The exceptions to this would be if they were caught stealing, lying, being disrespectful or doing something in your "absolute No list", as well as making sure they know that some obedience issues are safety related and there is no second chance, i.e., holding mummy's hand when crossing the street, etc.) Two vignettes below will illustrate:

Eight-year-old Shirlena comes through the door and drops her bag on the living room floor. Daydreaming about trying out the new pen she just purchased at the school stationery shop, she heads for the stairs. As she makes her way hurriedly, her mother begins a conversation that goes something like this:

    Mother (*smiling*): Hello, sweetheart, how was your day?

    Shirlena (*quickly*): Not now, Mum, I'm in a hurry.

    Mother (*politely*): Rushing for the bathroom?

    Sheila (*impatiently*): No, Mum, I wanna' try out my new pen!

    Mother *(kindly):* Did you forget something, dear?

Shirlena looks confused. The mother stares directly at the bag, and then smiles back at her daughter.

Shirlena (*rolling her eyes just a bit*): But Mum, I'm in a hurry—I can get it later.

Mother (*still kind and smiling*): Would you like to try that again?

Shirlena (*surrenders*): Yes, Mummy…I'm sorry…

Shirlena got the point, came back to where she left her bag, picked it up and took it upstairs to her room. No drama. She was reminded to not leave her things all over the common areas of the house. Two minutes later she was in her room, at her desk, doodling with her new pen, and humming a song she learned in Sunday school. If this is a common situation, it could be the subject of a month of devotionals on the topic of cooperating to make the house a home, or something to that effect.

Constant repetition of this simple, yet powerful principle makes a big difference. Children forget all the time. If consequences are imposed immediately, it causes tension in the house and strains the relationship between parent and child. Parents who tend to exasperate their children—especially by belittling, being punitive, being perfectionistic, or being controlling—should take note. Give them at least one other chance. Learn to be patient. Do not resort to consequences straight away, unless they are older and the misbehaviour is something very serious.

Sometimes, asking them to make another attempt is not all they need. Children get stuck and need help in exploring options. So, if they are stuck, help them to use their imagination. Exploring together shows respect to the children.

A mother discovers that six-year-old Donovan needs to buy some more crayons, even though she just bought him a pack the previous week. Don, as she sometimes calls him, lets this information slip as he shares "highs and lows" with his mother while she drives him home after school.

Don: I have a low.

Mother: What is it, sweetheart?

Don: Stuart borrowed my crayons, and he still hasn't given them back.

Mother: Sounds like you are feeling sad.

Don: Yes, I thought he was my friend.

Mother: What do you think you would like to do now?

Don: I can ask him to give them back.

Mother: Yes, and he might. Any other suggestions?

Don: I don't know…

Mother: Well use your imagination—I'll help you.

Don: I could take some of his things.
Mother: Ok, what else?
Don: I could tell the teacher that he stole my crayons.
Mother: Good, any more ideas?
Don: Maybe I could just forget about it this time since we have more crayons at home anyway...
Mother: Okay, but you might remember to think twice about loaning him your things in the future.
Don: I'll think about it.
Mother: Great! Let's talk more after dinner and you can tell me which plan you think is best.

Such conversations are incredible learning times for children about how to draw boundaries and respect limits. Rather than getting angry, this is a much healthier strategy and one that does not ruin the atmosphere between parent and child. In addition, asking the children about the different options gives parents a window into how much the child has learned. Sometimes their answers can be very encouraging and it would amaze even the parent. Imagine if the mum had just exploded about having to buy more crayons, or how irresponsible the boy was—she would have never learned that there was a kid stealing her son's things, and she would not have been able to help her son through his discouragement.

Exception: If something serious is happening, such as another child molesting or bullying your child, one of the parents needs to intervene immediately.

MOVIE MOMENT – *I Not Stupid Too*[7]

In the top-selling Singapore film *I Not Stupid Too*, the parents become angry at their children for stealing and being disrespectful. The parents had no idea that their children had resorted to the bad behaviour while trying to arrange to spend more time with the parents, who were not listening to their kids at all. This movie is very well done, highlighting how easy it is for busy working parents who actually do love their children to cause exasperation in their kids, and enter a Vortex!

9. Allow Consequences to Take Effect

A consequence is a result or an outcome. In the context of teaching children discipline, the consequence should be related to undesirable behaviour or attitudes that can either cause harm to the children or to others. Learning from natural consequences helps children to be responsible. Rudolf Dreikurs highlighted both natural and logical consequences in his ground-breaking book entitled, *Children: The Challenge*.[8] The series of Cloud and Townsend books called *Boundaries* explains ingeniously the spiritual principles laid out in the Bible related to consequences.[9] And even though we have mentioned it several times, it is worth mentioning again—John Rosemond's book, *Teenproofing,* is one of our all-time favourites for helping teens with limits.[10] In short, the Bible teaches that we reap what we sow; it is a law of nature. When parents do not allow their children to reap what they sow, by jumping in to protect their children from consequences, or by failing to provide consequences, they are doing untold harm to the character of the child.

We believe that consequences have the following effect if used properly:
- Halting undesirable behaviour
- Preventing being drawn into a Vortex of Conflict Escalation
- Helping children realise how serious their misbehaviour is to themselves and others
- Improving children's overall behaviour
- Helping children to take their parent's words and instructions seriously.

Consequences work with adults, too. Have you ever received a speeding ticket? How did that affect your driving thereafter? Have you ever paid a credit card bill late only to have a hefty penalty imposed? Have you ever been taken in by a "get rich quick" scheme only to get burned? Consequences work for people of all ages. However, we generally prefer for our children to learn the lessons when they are young, before the consequences become more serious.

Natural Consequences vs. Logical Consequences

Natural consequences are about children reaping immediately what they have sown as a result of their own behaviour, not as a result of a penalty or consequence imposed by a parent. Here are some scenarios to illustrate:
- If children lose their mobile phones, they have to face the natural consequence of not having one until they are able to afford to buy a new one themselves.
- If children do not study for their exams, they will face the natural consequence of getting poor grades.
- If children are not ready on time, they will face the natural consequence of not getting a ride with their parents (for cities with public transportation).
- If children do not get up on time in the morning, they will face the natural consequence of not being able to arrive at school on time.
- If children are mean or bossy to their friends, there is the natural consequence that no one will like to play with them.
- If children spend all their pocket money, they will have to face the natural consequence of having no money to spend until they receive their next allowance.

- If they return borrowed books late, they will have to face the natural consequence of having to pay the fine from their own allowance.
- If children do not eat what is on the table, they will have to face the natural consequence of going to bed hungry.

⋦ LOUIS LOWDOWN ⋧

> During one of the seasons of life when we were helping our children to focus on going to bed on time and waking up on time, we noticed that our children preferred being driven to school by us rather than taking public transportation. Therefore, we used this natural setting to teach discipline: Mum's 'taxi' would leave on time no matter what. If they missed it, they had no choice but to take public transportation. After it happened once or twice, they realised they had better wake up on time.
>
> When our children entered high school, we gave them their allowance on a weekly basis, which included train (subway) fare, lunch money, and a bit for extras. We told them if they ran out before the week was over, they would have to pack their own lunch. Sure enough, after making sandwiches for several weeks, they got the picture.

Fairly Obvious Exceptions: Do not use natural consequences when the outcome of the undesired behaviour will harm the child. For example:
- Crossing the street without holding the parent's hand—when young children are about to do this, parents should intervene immediately. (Seems like common sense but you never know.)
- Babies touching an electrical wall socket—learning from natural consequences can cause harm and it would be wise to prevent them from doing them in the first place by introducing logical consequences.

As opposed to natural consequences, logical consequences result in children having to face the music when they break a rule, in ways previously established by the parents and children, perhaps in a devotional or family meeting. Such consequences should be talked about and decided collectively with the children. In this way, parents cannot be accused of being unfair later. For logical consequences, the consequences do not follow naturally (automatically), like missing a ride when late, but come when parents intervene and offer discipline as a result.

Here are more scenarios to illustrate:
- If children have heated arguments, they both have to face the agreed logical consequence of taking time-outs and going to their rooms for 10-20 minutes. The more severe the fight, the longer the time outs. (Note: Physical violence should not be tolerated. Just because it is typical for siblings to beat each other up, doesn't mean it is acceptable.)

- If children watch TV or play computer games when they are not supposed to, they will have to face the logical consequence of having their "screen time" privileges removed for a period of time.
- If children play songs with illicit lyrics or illegally download songs, they will face the logical consequence of having their music-playing gadget taken away for a period of time.
- If children cause a disturbance in a restaurant or other public places, they will face the logical consequence of going and sitting somewhere quiet for a while (as long as safety is considered) and not joining the rest of the family.
- If children are rude or extremely disruptive at dinner, they shall leave the table.
- If children leave their toys all over the floor repeatedly, they will have to give a toy away or put the toys aside for a few weeks while they learn.
- If children ride bikes where they are not supposed to, they are not allowed to ride for a week (or longer if they were in danger).
- If children stay out later than the agreed hour, either they are grounded for a while, or their curfew will be earlier in the future.
- If children are disrespectful, parents shall have the right to end the conversation and not respond or continue in a dialogue with them again until the child speaks respectfully.
- If children destroy property, they shall pay for it with their own allowance, or at least for a portion of it.

The following are real examples:

Jim, age 14, was extremely fond of computer games, to the point that he would play them at the expense of doing his work at school. At one point, teachers commented on his underachieving performance to his parents. His parents had a discussion with him and established rules for playing within the limits of only a certain time allocated and only after his schoolwork was satisfactorily done, failing which, his laptop would be taken away for a period of five days. Jim was deceitful and his father caught him in the act. The father followed through with the promised consequences. While it came as a shock to Jim that his father meant what was agreed upon, subsequently his behaviour greatly improved.

Karla, age 10, was invited to the birthday party of one of her friends. While playing in the swimming pool, another girl made some catty remarks to Karla about how stupid her bathing suit looked and how dumb her little brother was. Karla felt humiliated, ashamed, and angry, and lost her temper. She pulled the rude girl's hair, got out of the pool and threw the girl's handbag into the water. The birthday girl's parents quickly intervened, and told Karla's parents about it when they arrived. After hearing Karla's side of the story and empathising with the humiliation, her parent's gave her a stiff challenge—they would decide the consequences after thinking and praying about it, but certainly she would pay to replace the handbag and the contents with her allowance, which would probably take four months. This was a wake up call for Karla, who found it hard to control her temper; her self-control greatly improved after that incident. (Effort was made to help the other girl apologise and the two were reconciled.)

Sometimes parents will be able to predict that a child is about to make a mistake and face a consequence. At those times, it is wise for the parents to intervene and offer alternatives, as we discussed earlier, to help them think through the process before going further with their undesirable behaviour. If children choose to misbehave, then logical consequences will have to be put into effect. However, there are times when a reminder will do the trick.

There will be other occasions when the parents will not be able to see what is about to happen and arrive at the scene after the misbehaviour, in which case consequences must be imposed immediately without any drama.

Other points to take note of while administering consequences:

a. Watch Your Tone
A proper tone is not just a good idea—it is *crucial* in communication. It is okay to show disappointment when misbehaviour is demonstrated, but the tone can easily get out of hand and move from one of righteous anger to one of rage and contempt. Usually when this happens, the child will face the added component of shame and humiliation followed by feelings of resentment and bitterness. This will complicate the dynamic even more. Parents need to avoid having an unhelpful tone and to be mindful which of the different types of exasperation interactions they tend toward using, such as Belittling, Punitiveness, or Pessimistic.

b. Exercise the Consequence Immediately
This is especially important for younger children. When parents see a behaviour that needs correcting, they should first inquire as to what happened and let the children explain. It is possible the parent missed out on something or interpreted the event wrongly. If there was negative behaviour, the consequences should be put into effect immediately. Again, make an agreement of what the consequences should be in your family meetings, writing them down if necessary. (Writing reinforces what everyone in the family has agreed on, and creates a reference point when disagreements occur in the future.) When misbehaviours occur, it is important to exercise the consequence quickly and calmly.

c. Persevere if Change Does Not Happen
Often parents give up when change does not happen, in which case they need to revise the consequences and perhaps even intensify them. Eventually, if administered correctly, consequences will have an effect. Parents who are conflict avoiders who tend to exasperate their children with Overly Permissive interactions tend to not persevere and think their children will change (magically) when they grow up.

d. Consequences Must Fit the Misbehaviour
This is an important principle that parents need to understand when deciding on possible consequences in family meetings. If the level of seriousness is small, then the consequence should also be small. Parents who tend to exasperate their children with Punitive, Controlling or Belittling interactions often come up with consequences that are out of proportion to the level of misbehaviour. Those who tend to exasperate by being Overly Permissive will have the opposite problem.

When a serious offence is committed, it is important to consider the imposition of several consequences to highlight the seriousness of what occurred. Examples of this would be lying, stealing or being deceitful. Again, if all of these are discussed ahead of time, accusations of parents being unfair are minimised and (while probably not liked) the consequence will ultimately be a supportive limit for the child.

Please note: on the issue of "spanking", we do not have the space needed to write all that we would like to convey about the topic. Suffice it to say that we are completely against all forms of abuse; we believe that any abuse done to children in the name of Christianity or the Bible is repugnant to God. In the future, we hope to write a supplementary booklet filled with research on this topic.

10. Meaning Attribution and Proper Reconciliation Needed

We like to say that God is "The God of Why". Look at Exodus and Deuteronomy. God wants children to know why their parents worship Him in the way they do. God wants children to "get it". In the same way, when we have to administer consequences, we must not take it personally but be able to love our children unconditionally and help them understand afterwards. This is part of fulfilling Deuteronomy 6 and Ephesians 6. After unpleasant behaviour is noticed and consequences administered, there should be a time for parent and child to sit down and evaluate the entire scenario. Repair must be done satisfactorily and this must lead to forgiveness and reconciliation. Without proper closure emotionally, resentment and bitterness will set in and can cause disconnection between the parent and child (see Chapter Twenty-Two on Repair and Reconnect). As mentioned before, research has shown that if repair is done well, then conflict between parent and child will have a benign effect on the mental and emotional health of both the children and the parents.

Positive Ending: Isn't it exciting to know that by meeting this core emotional need, you will be able to influence your children, at least to a degree, to be self-controlled and self-disciplined, and to practice reciprocity, fairness, equality and mutuality in their relationships? And the better you get at meeting this core emotional need, the better you will be able to minimize the development of lifetraps such as entitlement, insufficient self-control, and approval-seeking. Even better, you'll be better at avoiding "the Vortex!"

SECTION FIVE

The Core Emotional Need for
Realistic Expectations

How do we know which expectations are healthy and which are not?

CHAPTER FIFTEEN

Realistic Expectations

The Core Emotional Need for Realistic Expectations can be defined as helping our children to understand what is expected of them, while giving them the freedom to be themselves. It involves fine tuning expectations so that they inspire and motivate our children. Expectations that are too high can cause undue pressure and anxiety; expectations that are too low will be uninspiring and can convey a lack of appreciation of and belief in our children's strengths and capacities. In order for the core emotional need for realistic expectations to be met satisfactorily, children need to *consistently* and *on an emotional level* hear and believe the following messages from and about their parents:

> *They have realistic expectations and they know my strengths and weaknesses.*
>
> *They encourage me to do my best, while letting go of perfectionistic expectations.*
>
> *They help me to achieve balance between work and play.*
>
> *Their love for me is not based on the outcome of my achievements at school.*
>
> *They value my strengths and aspirations even though they may be different from theirs and not as recognised by society.*
>
> *They give me the benefit of the doubt when something goes wrong.*
>
> *They guide me in taking care of myself and endeavour to ensure that I enjoy life.*
>
> *They truly forgive me when I mess up.*

Fifteen-year-old Lori grew up in a family of "old money" and over-achievers. While her mother was a professor, her father was a successful investment banker and a former super-athlete who had earned his master's degree at the age of 22. In addition, her aunts, uncles, and grandparents had similar pedigrees. For this young woman, the weight of expectations on her shoulders felt as heavy as the anchor of her father's yacht.

Her parents, who had become Christians in their 20s, recognised perfectionistic tendencies in Lori even while she was still in kindergarten. They deliberately put her in a non-competitive academic situation in order to defuse her stress. However, the unintended atmosphere in the home only served to reinforce Lori's high expectations of herself. Not only did the girl feel depressed if she failed to make all A's on her report card, but she also felt the need to come in first whenever she participated in sports or debates. Nothing less was good enough for her. By the time she was in high school, she began having trouble sleeping before major exams and belittled her younger brother for not having the same drive and determination to excel. Eventually Lori realised that, although surrounded by a loving church family, she had no friends. She sought help when she was able to acknowledge that her ambition had turned into an obsession. (She eventually studied the Bible and became a Christian.

Melvin's parents dedicated their lives to Christ while attending university. His mother says she does not want to put pressure on Melvin; that she does not expect him to be "the best of the best". However, she emphasises academic performance by prioritising homework and after-school classes above Christian relationships and commitments and makes disparaging remarks about children who are not up to speed. The parents *say* that they hope Marvin will choose to become a Christian and that church is important. However, there is a "but"… "But right now our son must put all of his effort into his studies." In addition, Melvin's parents do not allow him to play sports, go to the mall with friends, or play video games.

It is little wonder that Melvin feels a great deal of stress when he is not able to meet his own or his parents' expectations. He feels that he will never be good enough. At the same time, he has virtually no relationships at church even though he has grown up in the same city all his life. (Teens don't really want to hang out with someone who always complains that, "No one *gets* me", "No one loves me because they didn't give me the gift I wanted," "*They* aren't the kind of teens I like," "*The group* is stupid," along with other judgmental comments.)

In fact, Melvin learned to make these kinds of comments from his mother who applies her own unrelenting standards to her opinion of what a youth mentor or a teen Bible study should be and conveys her perceptions to her son. Melvin confided to an adult at church that he feels that his family, school, and church are controlling, unloving, and unaccepting. As a result, he has spoken of suicide on several occasions. Though Melvin told that same adult that he wanted to see a counsellor, his mother has opted to wait until his year-end exams are over.

In Lori's family, the atmosphere plus the girl's temperament caused exaggerated expectations; in Melvin's family, it was caused by his parents' fixation on him rising to his potential.

What are Realistic Expectations?

All of us have expectations. We *expect* our spouses to be faithful. We *expect* the sun to come up tomorrow. We *expect* our friends to return our calls.

We *expect* our children to grow, attend school, do the best they can in their studies, make friends, explore hobbies, learn to take care of themselves, and enjoy a close relationship with the family over the years while becoming their own person. If we consider ourselves to be a Christian family, we will also expect our children to develop their own faith and hope that they would eventually choose a relationship with Jesus for themselves (see Chapter Thirteen for our discussion of normal parental expectations which sometimes lead to a Vortex.)

In some families there are few, if any, expectations. This can leave children adrift. Conversely, in other families, there are too many expectations, spoken or unspoken, for the child to bear. Hence, the name of this core emotional need is *realistic* expectations.

(Since we are assuming that most parents reading this book probably err in the direction of having exaggerated expectations, we will speak mostly of the need to temper expectations. However, we will, from time to time, address those who tend toward over-permissiveness.)

We live in a world where both adults and children are experiencing increasing stress. Demands and expectations at work and school are pushing people to the limit. Fifty years ago in America, for example, husbands were the main breadwinners, while wives cared for their homes, prepared nutritious meals, served as a confidante to their kids after school, and did housework while their kids played outside before dinner. Husbands worked eight hours and were home in time for the family to have dinner, do chores, and possibly watch television together. In nations recovering from the devastation of war in the 20th century, circumstances were not as idealistic, but at least for the middle class, family togetherness was valued.

However, things have changed—although we are surrounded by time-saving devices, we do not seem to have more time. Online social networking keeps us from spending time with our real friends in each other's homes and the demands of life and the expectations of families seem to get more and more intense. We notice that since we first moved to Singapore 25 years ago, parents get home from work two hours later every night. Our friends in the US have told us that recently, the number of women in the workforce has surpassed that of men. Children have not escaped the fallout—they are either at home unsupervised or involved in a plethora of afterschool activities. Families eat together less frequently. Parents also have to rush home to make sure that the homework is done. For some children, this activity can take several hours every night. In addition, there are teens who are busy practising sports for many hours a day (or playing an instrument, honing debate skills, etc.) and sometimes these activities are pursued primarily to improve their resumes or help them get into college on a scholarship, leading to even more pressure.

Children at an increasingly younger age are expected to do more and learn more difficult concepts, beyond what is age-appropriate. Moreover, competitiveness in schools discourages students from helping one another and produces an "every-man-for-himself" mind-set. Pressure does not come only from schools but also from parents. More and more parents are pressuring their children to get into the best schools and universities, causing households to be rife with tension. Children cringe when their parents make comparisons ("Your cousin went to Harvard"), deliver lectures ("When I was your age, I understood the value of hard work…"), and nag them about being number one in class or in a sport.

Parents striving to bring out the best in their children are not helped by parenting philosophies such as those espoused in the "Tiger Mother" article published by the Wall Street Journal on January 8, 2011:

> A lot of people wonder how Chinese parents raise such stereotypically successful kids. They wonder what these parents do to produce so many math whizzes and music prodigies, what it's like inside the family, and whether they could do it, too. Well, I can tell them, because I've done it. Here are some things my daughters, Sophia and Louisa, were never allowed to do,
> - Attend a sleepover
> - Have a play date
> - Be in a school play
> - Complain about not being in a school play
> - Watch TV or play computer games
> - Choose their own extracurricular activities
> - Get any grade less than an A
> - Not be the No. 1 student in every subject except gym and drama
> - Play any instrument other than the piano or violin
> - Not play the piano or violin.[1]

It is unfortunate that the above principles have become a loud voice for parents on which to base their parenting. In our opinion, these parenting principles are unhelpful, and go against the findings of good research on how to raise children to become healthy adults emotionally, spiritually and psychologically.

Many parents these days, even without reading such extremist urgings, overreact out of fear and worry, and force their children to attend extra classes during the weekends, or sign up for multiple sports activities. Even school holidays are filled up with make-up classes and camps. As a result, parents have fewer blocks of time during which they can just relax and talk with one another. In fact, researchers at the University of Michigan found that children's free time, play time, and unstructured outdoor activities have fallen significantly, while the quantity of homework has increased over a 16-year period.[2]

─── ⟨⟩ **RESEARCH REVEALS** ⟨⟩ ───

RR15.1: *Children's Free Time Declining, Homework Increasing*

A study by Sandra Hofferth of the Survey Research Centre at the University of Michigan, entitled "Changes in American Children's Time, 1981-1997", revealed that:

- Children's overall free time had declined by about 12 hours per week in overall free time for children.
- Playtime for children had decreased by three hours per week from 16 hours per week to 13.
- Unstructured outdoor activities had fallen by about 50%.
- Studying (homework) had increased by almost 50% during this 16-year period.

Where does all the competitiveness lead?

To the hospital – some doctors estimate that 75% of all medical conditions begin with stress.
To the mental hospital – it is well-known that stress causes anxiety and depression.
To the divorce court – many divorces are caused by neglect due to lack of work-life balance, arguments about the lack of it, or lack of unity regarding expectations for the children.

However, it is not just adults who are the primary victims. More and more children are also seeing psychiatrists for stress and anxiety. According to the Singapore Institute of Mental Health, 1 in 10 children suffered from some sort of emotional or behavioural issue in 2010.

─── ⟨⟩ **RESEARCH REVEALS** ⟨⟩ ───

RR15.2: *Singapore Children Have High Rate of Mental Illness*

According to the Singapore Institute of Mental Health, many children in Singapore are likely to face depression, which is the most common mental illness here. Others succumb to alcohol abuse, or end up with obsessive-compulsive disorder (OCD), which is anxiety characterised by obsessions, compulsive rituals, and intrusive thoughts and impulses. Another surprising finding is that Singapore has the world's highest rate for OCD—3% of the population. (The figure in the U.S. is 2.3% and 1.1% in Europe.) Mental and chronic physical illness such as cancer, heart conditions, diabetes and high blood pressure often go hand in hand. Over 14% of people with chronic physical illness also have a mental illness. Among those with mental illness, over half have a chronic physical illness. [3]

It is time to wake up! Al Baird, one of our Master Class elders, believes that parents' worries about their children's academic work and extra-curricular pursuits is one of the main causes of families becoming less spiritual and more worldly in the 21st century. This reminds us of a quote attributed to William Sloane Coffin, chaplain of an Ivy League school in the 1950s, "Even if you win the rat race, you're still a rat."[4]

Some encouragement from God's word is appropriate here. Let us examine what Jesus and the Apostle Paul had to say about the rat race:

> *So do not worry, saying, 'What shall we eat?' or 'What shall we drink?' or 'What shall we wear?' For the pagans run after all these things, and your heavenly Father knows that you need them. But seek first his kingdom and his righteousness, and all these things will be given to you as well. Therefore do not worry about tomorrow, for tomorrow will worry about itself. Each day has enough trouble of its own.* (Matthew 6:31–34)

> *Still others, like seed sown among thorns, hear the word; but the worries of this life, the deceitfulness of wealth and the desires for other things come in and choke the word, making it unfruitful.* (Mark 4:18–19)

> *These are the things you are to teach and insist on. If anyone teaches otherwise and does not agree to the sound instruction of our Lord Jesus Christ and to godly teaching, they are conceited and understand nothing. They have an unhealthy interest in controversies and quarrels about words that result in envy, strife, malicious talk, evil suspicions and constant friction between people of corrupt mind, who have been robbed of the truth and who think that godliness is a means to financial gain. But godliness with contentment is great gain. For we brought nothing into the world, and we can take nothing out of it. But if we have food and clothing, we will be content with that. Those who want to get rich fall into temptation and a trap and into many foolish and harmful desires that plunge people into ruin and destruction. For the love of money is a root of all kinds of evil. Some people, eager for money, have wandered from the faith and pierced themselves with many griefs. But you, man of God, flee from all this, and pursue righteousness, godliness, faith, love, endurance and gentleness.* (I Timothy 6:2b–11)

❖ MASTER CLASS ❖

Ron Brumley wrote, "It was very important to us to have Linda home when the kids got home from school, to the point that we sacrificed having a lot more "stuff". A caregiver, no matter how loving, can never take the place of a loving, involved parent. To paraphrase a Proverb, it's more desirable for a teen to come home after school to a small apartment where mom is waiting to listen than to an empty mansion. There is so

> much to be discussed after school, and moms and dads do it best! Though I realise that others may consider our arrangement to have been a luxury, I believe, however, that a lot more families could achieve it for themselves, if they were convicted about its importance and willing to have 'realistic expectations' in the area of material possessions."

Socrates, the Greek Philosopher who lived in the 5th Century BC, offered this interesting piece of advice: "Beware the barrenness of a busy life."[5] A wise man who lived a few hundred years earlier stated something even more profound:

> *Of making many books there is no end, and much study wearies the body. Now all has been heard; here is the conclusion of the matter: Fear God and keep his commandments, for this is the duty of all mankind. For God will bring every deed into judgment, including every hidden thing, whether it is good or evil.* (Ecclesiastes 12:12b–14)

The drive to improve and be better is not wrong. The Bible says that we should work at things with all our heart as if working for the Lord, not for men. But the motives of greed, selfish ambition, and pride are all sinful and not from God. We must take care not to justify our sinfully unrelenting or excessive expectations by cloaking them in a religious robe.

⊰ LOUIS LOWDOWN ⊱

> Our children began learning tennis when they were very young, while we were living in Australia. (We knew that we would eventually move back to Asia so we figured that we should make the most of living in such a sporty nation!) When Sonia, our oldest, turned eight, she insisted on entering tournaments. We are not sure if she was born with a perfectionistic temperament and naturally competitive nature, or if I (John) passed it all to her, but my wife and I decided to intervene early on. We sought advice from fellow tennis parents, Keith and MaryAnn Rose. They taught their children that winning isn't determined by the score—in their family, a match would be considered a "win" if the player had given his best effort, behaved like a good sport, and acted like a gracious winner or loser. Conversely, when the child had won solely in terms of the score, the parents would consider the match to be a loss. By helping Sonia to have healthy expectations, she not only enjoyed her matches, she also grew in her character.

There is tremendous interplay between the core emotional need for realistic expectations and the other core emotional needs. Specifically, we cannot fully meet the need for realistic expectations without ensuring that the core emotional need for connection and acceptance is also adequately met.

When our children are feeling low and unmotivated, we as parents need to take stock of the quality of our connection with and acceptance of our children. We must work on the connection rather than get irritated and turn on the pressure even more, which only pushes our children further and further away. Doing the latter leads to either rebellion or withdrawal and discouragement, which increases the risk of our children going completely against the very values that we hold dear.

*What are the lifetraps
associated with this
core emotional need?*

CHAPTER SIXTEEN

Realistic Expectations: What's at Stake?

Advantages of Meeting this Need

When parents meet the core emotional need for realistic expectations, the child will develop some or all of the following traits/beliefs: realistic standards, graciousness, and self-sacrifice with boundaries.

Realistic Standards

Children who have had the core emotional need for realistic expectations met have healthy standards. They are able to remind themselves, *"It is good to have high standards, but sometimes, good enough is good enough. I am comfortable doing my best without fear of being criticised. Hard work and efficiency are noble, but not nobler than connecting with people or caring for my health. I believe that there is a time to relax and have fun."*

Because of this mind-set, they will be more likely to have good friends and grow up to have healthy families themselves. While they may not appear to have the inner drive that accompanies the unrelenting standards lifetrap (see below), they will certainly be more at peace, and will avoid the accompanying sleepless nights and stomach aches. These children have parents who provide healthy motivation, and who help them to enjoy the process, not just the desired result. It is important to point out that children with healthy standards will enjoy winning as much as anyone else, though they will usually prioritise fairness to others over being "number one".

Graciousness

Children who have had the core emotional need for realistic expectations met have a sense of graciousness. Deep down in their being, they understand this reality: *"Everyone makes mistakes; no one is perfect."* They also appreciate that *"While it is certainly true that we will often reap what we sow, it feels great when others are gracious with me, and therefore, I should extend grace both to myself and others."*

Children who know how to give grace and act with forgiveness will probably experience less stress as adults and be blessed with many friends! It is thus a wonderful mind-set to inculcate in your children: when your children consider discipline to be training and helping, rather than retribution, they would be less likely to be punitive themselves. Notwithstanding that there is a time for other measures, discipline, training, teaching, and giving lots of grace will go a long way towards helping your child develop a Christ-like outlook on life.

Self-Sacrifice with Boundaries

Children who have had the core emotional need for realistic expectations met have a sense of self-sacrifice *with boundaries*. They understand that loving your neighbour as yourself means that you do need to love yourself. They do not feel guilty for thinking, *"I will meet the needs of others without ignoring my own needs at the same time. It is normal to expect that my needs should also be met, although there will be many times when it is good to serve others without expecting anything in return."* Most children possess an inherent sense of fairness: they know when they are being made to do more than their share of the work around the house. Of course, there are kids who love to serve: in this case, it is important that parents do not take advantage of a child with a compliant temperament and nurture the maladaptive side of this lifetrap, instead of the healthy adaptive side. While selflessness and a sense of service are commendable qualities, they should be nurtured appropriately in children. Hence, parents must help such children set boundaries for service and recognise when they are being exploited. Essentially, a child should be trained to genuinely serve, while knowing how to say "No".

Disadvantages Of Not Meeting This Need

The extent to which parents fail to meet the core emotional need for realistic expectations will affect the likelihood of their children's development of some, or all, of the following lifetraps: unrelenting standards, punitiveness, and self-sacrifice.

The Lifetrap of Unrelenting Standards / Hypercriticalness

The core message of the unrelenting standards lifetrap is: *"I must work very, very hard to meet very high standards, or I will be criticised. I do not have time to relax, or have fun. I must always be efficient."* The driving words for this lifetrap are *"I should ..."*

Children who develop this lifetrap are propelled by their incessant need to push themselves. They are constantly striving to work harder in order to get to a better place because their present position is never good enough. In fact, this lifetrap is related to the lifetrap of defectiveness—for contentment is always going to be one position away, within sight, but unreachable.

As they grow older, they develop standards that must be in place, thus making them critical of people who fail to meet these standards. These self-made rules accompany them everywhere they go as they impose them on everyone. They frequently look down on others who do not live up to their exceedingly high expectations and pick on small issues that no one else

Realistic Expectations: What's at Stake? ■ 287

Figure 16.1: The Lifetrap of Unrelenting Standards / Hypercriticalness (Francois as a child)

would have noticed. Moreover, they show a lack of grace towards others who have made mistakes. For instance, they may be hard on their spouse for being late, or lament that the house is not clean enough; they may even comment that their friend's clothing style is not up to scratch.

People with the lifetrap of unrelenting standards actually think the standards they impose are normal and that others are stupid, shoddy, careless, lazy, unkempt, inept, or slow. (Of course, those with the unrelenting standards lifetrap do not notice that they only have these standards in certain areas but that in other areas, they fall short; for example, the no-nonsense academic whose desk is a mess, or the doctor who works tirelessly but has no time for his children.) They are completely unaware of the fact that their reactions to situations, along with their opinions and condemnation of others, are usually out of proportion with the reality of the situation.

They are usually not only hard on others, but also on themselves. They push themselves so hard that taking time off makes them feel guilty. They find it difficult to relax, and all of these factors combine to take a toll on

Figure 16.2: The Lifetrap of Unrelenting Standards / Hypercriticalness (Francois as an adult)

their health. While they may achieve success in life, it usually occurs at the expense of relationships. Because they constantly expect others to comply with their rules, they are difficult companions. Essentially, when they or others fail to meet their standards, they react as though it were a very big deal (see Figures 16.1 & 16.2).

A quick glance at what might have happened to an adult with this lifetrap during childhood:

- One or both parents had very high standards in areas such as cleanliness, academic achievement, and good manners. Even though the parent might not have directly imposed these standards on the child, the child might still have modelled the trait.
- The love of one, or both, of the child's parents was performance-based; thus the child did not experience unconditional love from either, or both, of them. Their approval and acceptance was based on the child's achievements.

- The parents' spoke frequently about what the child should achieve, what others were achieving, and how the child measured up. Character was defined more in terms of achievement than inner qualities.
- The parents were hypercritical of others and showed it.
- When the child did not achieve, she was criticised and shamed. Nothing was ever good enough for her parents (or possibly a teacher or a coach). She hardly received any encouragement.
- The child developed these standards to soothe inner pain (from an inability to forge deep relationships with others) in order to feel good.

Case Study

Charlene and Rebecca's father is a highly successful individual who hails from an established family in the USA—their grandparents have a second mansion exclusively for holidays and are well-connected politically and socially. Status and achievement are highly valued in their extended family. As much as the girls' parents have tried to infuse Christian values in their parenting, they have not been able to protect their daughters from the ongoing scrutiny of their relatives, who constantly compare them with their cousins: "Freddie got a 2300 on his SATs, but I heard that Charlene only got a 2100!" "I know... I bet she doesn't get accepted to riding camp this summer either!"

Although Charlene and Rebecca are doing well academically (both are attending an Ivy League university), they are struggling in several areas of emotional intelligence. Harbouring anger issues, they lack empathy and do not relate to others well. They view themselves as superior and feel that many are below them academically. They do not want to have much to do with those who do not meet their expectations. All in all, they are not that pleasant to be around. Fortunately, the parents have begun to get counselling in order to learn about repair and reconnection with the girls, and how to help their daughters have better relationships with others.

Exercise: Please refer to the Exasperation Interactions worksheet (Appendix 1) and identify the exasperation interaction(s) in Figure 16.1.

The Lifetrap of Punitiveness

The core message of the punitiveness lifetrap is: *"Mistakes have consequences. I should be punished for making mistakes and so should everyone else. It is not okay to make mistakes. We should constantly strive for and demand perfection."*

Children who develop this lifetrap have usually been brought up by parents who do not show grace or mercy either to themselves or to others for mistakes. The parents have a "justice at all costs" mentality and inculcate the same mindset in their children.

Figure 16.3: The Lifetrap of Punitiveness (Kong as a child)

As with their parents, these children grow up to become adults who do not forgive easily. Rather, they see all mistakes as misdemeanours that should be punished. With a rigid sense of justice, they tend to see things in black and white. Mistakes are mistakes, whether committed unintentionally or deliberately. Thus, they are quick to assign blame when they see a mistake. In fact, with the passage of time, they may even come to consider people who show mercy as weak.

Sometimes (not always), they are punitive towards themselves and do not forgive themselves for their past mistakes. They allow their past mistakes to haunt them and refer to them repeatedly. Then again, some people with this lifetrap are hard on others, but soft on themselves. They mask their punitiveness as seeking justice and being "fair". Children with this lifetrap do not have a good understanding of forgiveness. They do not understand that the best way to change people is not through punishment, but the extension of grace and forgiveness (see Figures 16.3 & 16.4).

Figure 16.4: The Lifetrap of Punitiveness (Kong as an Adult)

A quick glance at what might have happened to an adult with this lifetrap during childhood:

- The child's parents blamed him for things and used a condemning tone when they berated him and his siblings. Consequences were usually disproportionate to the mistakes made. Even in adulthood, his parent's voice is still in his head.
- The child attended a school where others were punished frequently for their mistakes. Little grace was shown. Forgiveness was hardly talked about.
- The child's parents did not talk much about grace or forgiveness. They had a negative view of people who held such perspectives.
- The child's parents were either always right and blamed others, or held grudges.
- The child's parents got hurt growing up and ruminated on memories of this hurt. They took it out on others, especially their child.
- The child was brought up in a very negative religious atmosphere in which hellfire and brimstone, and the wrath of God, were used as deterrents of undesirable behaviour.

Exercise: Please refer to the Exasperation Interactions worksheet (Appendix 1) and identify the exasperation interaction(s) in Figure 16.3.

Case Study

Jack and Jill were born one year apart in a European country, and have attended church since they were born. Their mother, who loves them very much, had an unhappy childhood herself, and is often extremely controlling and punitive, which causes frustration in the children.

Their parents' marriage has been deteriorating for a long time; a year ago, their dad moved out. Jack, now 15, has responded to this event by withdrawing from friends and becoming punitive whenever anyone disappoints him. He blows up easily, keeps his room untidy, sports uncombed hair, and rebels against any form of control.

Jill's exasperation has led her down a different road—she has become obsessed with being perfect in every way, and punitive with herself. Her mother responded by becoming even more controlling until Jill developed an eating disorder: now she has to be hospitalised and force-fed. Jill is getting help from counsellors and church mentors. The parents are now trying to reconcile because they can see that their poor marriage has contributed to their children's state. Unfortunately, they may not be able to help Jill before it is too late.

The Lifetrap of Self-Sacrifice

The core message of the self-sacrifice lifetrap is: *"I must meet the needs of others before my own. I do not want to feel selfish, or cause any pain to others."* While this pattern of thinking and behaving seems altruistic, it can create problems in the long run, as it results in imbalanced relationships, and problems with unmet needs.

Typically, children who develop this lifetrap are endearing. Being in tune with others' pain and feelings, they empathise and genuinely care for others. They take on responsibilities in order to relieve others of discomfort. In fact, they would prefer to suffer, rather than allow others to be inconvenienced. Ultimately, they strive to make other people feel better.

Their decision to help others does not come from a desire to please, or to avoid conflict or a threat. Rather, these children genuinely empathise with others so much that they actually feel that it is their responsibility to provide relief for others. When they do not sacrifice for others, they feel guilty. However, such a selfless mind-set becomes a danger and a lifetrap when these self-sacrificing people give and give without getting their own needs met; eventually, they experience burnout. As a consequence, they may experience physical and/or mental health problems such as depression or breakdown. The sad thing is that such individuals are often compassionate people who

Realistic Expectations: What's at Stake? ■ 293

Figure 16.5: The Lifetrap of Self-Sacrifice (Daniella as a child)

feel guilty when they meet their own needs; thus, without intervention, they will almost always prioritise others' needs above their own.

Special Note to parents who are in caring occupations: If you are a health care provider, a counsellor/therapist, a minister, or any helping professional, you probably already struggle with balancing your work and family life. Should you choose to go the extra mile for others, as many noble individuals do, make sure that you do not demand the same of your children: it may not be what they want to do—maybe they will be happier and more productive doing research alone in a laboratory inventing a cure for cancer or finding the replacement for plastic, or taking care of trees in a National Park (see Figures 16.5 & 16.6).

Exercise: Please refer to the Exasperation Interactions worksheet (Appendix 1) and identify the exasperation interaction(s) in Figure 16.5.

Figure 16.6: The Lifetrap of Self-Sacrifice (Daniella as an adult)

A quick glance at what might have happened to an adult with this lifetrap during childhood:

- The child's parents were unable, for whatever reason, to take care of her and/or her younger siblings. So she stepped in and assumed this responsibility, going beyond what should have been expected of a young person.
- The child's parents role-modelled self-sacrifice for her. Perhaps, they were working in one of the helping professions such as nursing, counselling, or church leadership, or highly involved with volunteer work.
- The child had to work, or help out, in her parents' business early on in life because of her parents' financial problems, or poor health.
- The child assumed the role of the parent (parenting the parent) at too early an age, instead of the other way round. For example, one of the child's parents might have been an alcoholic, or might have been abused severely by the other parent, or other relatives.

Case Study

Henry and Henrietta are twins in a family that is run like an army camp. Their father is a policeman (formerly in the military) who expects everything to be ship-shape at all times. Discipline is expected in all areas. Respect for your elders is a must. Talking back is not permitted. Showing weakness is not acceptable. Dad's word is law and "family problems don't exist". Henry and Henrietta's mother works long hours in a factory and their bed-ridden grandmother live with them. Thus, the twins have spent their childhood years serving others, including doing much of the housework, grocery shopping, and getting medicine for their grandmother.

When Henry and Henrietta were little, their parents would slap them for being disobedient or disrespectful. As they got older, they were belittled for the slightest infraction. Consequently, they learnt to stay in line and behave like model children—extremely polite and respectful, but having no emotional connection with the parents.

As adults, Henry and Henrietta are emotionally inhibited, extremely self-sacrificing, and approval-seeking. While Henrietta has become a Christian, she still struggles to be emotionally close to God and others. Henry is still working out his salvation "with fear and trembling", so to speak. Though he knows he should be a Christian and strives to conform to the expectations, his heart still feels far from God.

THE CORE EMOTIONAL NEED FOR REALISTIC EXPECTATIONS AMONG THE PATRIARCHS

Now that we have examined the advantages of meeting the core emotional need for realistic expectations, as well as the dangers that come from not meeting this need, let us study out how the core emotional need for realistic expectations was not met in the family of the patriarchs in Genesis 29:14b–30:1–24; Genesis 32:1–33:1–20; and Genesis 35:16–20.

Questions for Discussion:
- Rachel said, "Give me children, or I'll die." Is it wrong to be desperate to have children?
- What message did she believe about not having children?
- What happened to her in Genesis 30:1? Was this connected to her earlier statement?
- Compare the lives of the first-born (Reuben) and the fourth-born (Judah). From whose line of descendants did Jesus and David come?
- What does this show about how God works?
- Was the first-born that much more special?
- Was God able to work through Leah, even though she was not favoured by Jacob in the same way as Rachel?

Insights:

Dysfunction is the gift that keeps on giving. In the following discussion, we move from the generation of Isaac and Rebekah to the descendants of their children—the family of Jacob himself many years later.

This was a period after Jacob had fled from his own family, after deceiving his brother, Esau. He took his mother's advice and went to his uncle, Laban, who took him under his wing. He worked for Laban for seven years, the price set by his uncle for being able to marry Rachel. However, Laban deceived him by forcing him to marry Leah instead. Uncle Laban made him work an additional seven years for Rachel, although he allowed them to get married a week later (Genesis 29:30) So Jacob ended up with two wives.

As Jacob had grown up in an environment where favouritism was the norm, he himself took on this dysfunctional behaviour by showing favouritism towards his wives: he loved Rachel more than Leah and it was obvious (Genesis 29:30). This favouritism in turn bred deep-seated competitiveness between Rachel and Leah, even though they were sisters.

God worked through the dysfunction and opened Leah's womb and she gave birth to four children. Rachel felt so provoked that she declared to Jacob in Genesis 30:1, "Give me children, or I will die." Rather than let life take its natural course based on trust in God, Rachel perceived life to be a fierce competition. She probably experienced little enjoyment, as much of her life was consumed with proving that she was not a defective wife because of her apparent barrenness.

Though Jacob's wealth was increasing by leaps and bounds, it was a different story on the family front. Wealth was not able to bring the peace and acceptance that he surely wanted. If only Leah and Rachel could have been vulnerable with each other and with Jacob about what they needed, they would have identified each others' wants, which would have enabled them to make amends.

Instead, the sisters engaged in a fierce competition. First, Rachel forced her maidservant, Bilhah, to sleep with Jacob and have children on Rachel's behalf. Bilhah bore two children, Dan and Naphtali. Leah then responded by having Jacob sleep with her maidservant, Zilpah, who bore two sons named Gad and Asher.

Then Rachel made an agreement and allowed Jacob to sleep with Leah in return for some mandrakes. Leah became pregnant again with a child named Issachar, followed by Zebulun and Dinah, a daughter. Finally, God opened Rachel's womb and she bore Jacob a son called Joseph. Much later on, Rachel was again with child, and gave birth to another son who was named Benjamin. Ironically, she had told her husband that if he did not give her children that she would die. In a bizarre twist, having children caused her death. Perhaps a lesson could be drawn here that God may be doing things for a reason, and if we demand our way, He will let us have it, but it might not be the best thing for us…

As you can see from this biblical story, the sisters competed with each other for Jacob's attention by having babies. It meant everything to them. Did God ever say that the number of children is a reflection of one's righteousness? Throughout the Scriptures, there were righteous women who were barren for a long time such as Sarah, Rebekah, Rachel, Hannah, and Elizabeth, to name a few. Though it was never a law, the prevailing culture at the time put forth the erroneous thinking that the more children one has, the better is one's standing before God and man, or at least the more value a woman had.

Clearly, this thinking also permeated the family to the extent that the two sisters spent the rest of their lives competing with each other. Imagine their interactions with each other at home. How did Leah feel when Rachel played with her children? Leah probably did not allow that and kept a close eye on her children for fear that Rachel would harm them out of spite. Likewise, how did Leah take it when Rachel finally had her own children? In fact, the competition escalated to the point that even the names of the children were selected to send a clear message of provocation to the other sister. Imagine the lack of peace and joy in a life driven almost exclusively by competition?

Ultimately, God showed that His workings do not fit within the framework of man's ideas and expectations. Though the firstborn was Reuben, Jesus did not come from his line of descendants. It was the fourth son, Judah (Genesis 29:35), who was Jesus' ancestor, not the first son Reuben nor the favourite son Joseph, who would probably have been most people's pick. Sometimes God meanders and accomplishes His will through the most unlikely people and circumstances. Our thoughts are not His thoughts, and our ways are not His ways.

Another fact to ponder—whose son was Judah? He was the son of the unloved woman, Leah (Genesis 29:35). Again, if it were up to us to decide from whose line David or Jesus should originate, we would probably have picked Rachel as she was the wife whom Jacob loved. However, God chose the unloved wife.

The competitiveness between Jacob and Esau a generation earlier also echoed this rivalry. The twin brothers should have enjoyed fun times together; however, it was not to be. Their parents' favouritism led to sibling rivalry for the blessing and birthright.

While God did mention in Deuteronomy 21:17 that the first-born should be given a double portion of the inheritance of his father, it did not mean that the other children should be deprived of everything. Getting this teaching wrong caused the quality of their lives to deteriorate significantly. What could have been a wonderful life of fun, togetherness, and love turned into painful years of competition, deceit, and turmoil. Eventually, Jacob had to flee his home in guilt and pain.

Unfortunately, the lives of so many people follow this script. The focus may not be over the number of children these days, but a similar competitiveness exists about the kind of education the children are getting, the jobs one has, or the home that one owns. The pursuit of these material things has driven many parents to neglect the core emotional needs of their children. There is no doubt that an unhealthy drive and unrelenting standards causes us to pay a steep price.

It is hard to know why, later on in life, Jacob insisted on receiving a blessing from the man of God in Genesis 32:22–30. Perhaps, all this while, he knew that he had gotten his earlier blessing through deception and fraud. The second time round, he wanted a sincere blessing from God himself—one obtained without double-dealing, but through righteous wrestling. The positive side of Jacob's character was that he was a man who pursued what he wanted wholeheartedly. This time, what he wanted was to be godly: he did not resort to sinful means, or shortcuts. Instead, he fought for what he wanted by wrestling with God, the way Jesus wrestled in his prayer at Gethsemane. In the end, Jacob was blessed, but it came with a limp: his blessing in life would also remind him of his utter dependence on God.

God's providence allowed the two brothers to meet up, in Genesis 32:1–6. When Jacob heard that Esau was coming to meet him, the former trickster was prepared to receive Esau's wrath, but instead he was welcomed into his older brother's arms. After 20 years of separation, they were finally united. Those 20 years apart had done them both a world of good: they had both graduated from the school of "hard knocks", gained some self-awareness, and recognised their shortcomings. Jacob made restitution and Esau accepted it. The deep and wonderful reconciliation endured till the end. Despite their troubled past, neither Jacob nor Esau succumbed to the lifetrap of punitiveness. This positive ending is encouraging and shows how we can circumvent lifetraps that potentially prevent us from giving grace to people who have hurt us in the past.

If we allow Him to do so, God will always work something out for us to come face to face with our past so that we can deal with it and then move on in life in a more secure, settled, and humble state. Unfortunately, Jacob would pass his problems down through his 12 sons by showing favouritism towards some of them, thus causing the cycle to be repeated.

*I only want to help

my children—what

should I do?*

CHAPTER SEVENTEEN

An Asset or a Liability?

At the risk of sounding like broken records, we will start our chapter on how to meet this core emotional need with a reminder to meet the first core emotional need. Check out this Research Reveals about how connection and acceptance helps kids to be better off academically and socially.

RESEARCH REVEALS

RR17.1: ***Good Connection with Parents Means Higher Grades***

One US study published by The Heritage Foundation in 2008 revealed that parents who adopt a sensitive, warm, and responsive type of parenting and engage in play activities with their young children bolster their kids' social and emotional development, communication skills, and ability to focus. Beyond academics, teens whose parents are more involved and who feel they receive more support from their parents are more likely to participate in structured after-school activities that, in turn, are positively correlated with achievement and social competence.[1]

Researchers from Penn State University (in 2005, using data from the Adolescent Health Survey) compared students from three generations of Asian, Hispanic and US born Caucasian families. Regardless of ethnicity, this study showed a significant but independent association between parenting styles and students' grades, as well as positive relationships with others in the community. Thus youths who bonded with their parents and enjoyed good communication with them tended to have higher grades and better physical and emotional well-being.[2]

The core emotional need for connection and acceptance is not unique to a particular gender—research indicates that a father's approval is important for the development of healthy self-esteem in both boys and girls.[3]

Basic Safety

Parents are responsible for protecting their children's welfare. By meeting the core emotional need for realistic expectations, they will be keeping them safe in the following areas: ensuring adequate sleep combined with mental wellness; doing their best to give them freedom from future back pain; and being proactive in the area of preventing near-sightedness.

Sleep Deprivation

One of the world's leading medical journals, *The Lancet*, revealed that among developed countries, Singapore has the lowest mortality rate for young males (the US has the highest) and attributes this to several factors: virtually no access to guns, drugs, or gangs for Singaporean teens; no "ghetto-type areas"; a good education system that mandates participation in extra-curricular activities; and limiting driver's licences to those 18 and over.[4]

However, the increased expectations placed upon them by parents and teachers have resulted in Singaporean children and teenagers experiencing sleep deprivation. It seems that all over the world, pre-schoolers, school-age children, and adolescents are not getting sufficient sleep to enable them to function properly during the day. In fact, research has proven that sleep deprivation can cause significant impairments in cognitive functioning—so no point in staying up night after night studying! Beyond children being crankier and displaying shorter tempers, long-term sleep deprivation can lead to serious mental health issues. Sleep-deprived children can grow up to become adolescents with suicidal thoughts, or adults with anxiety issues.

--- ❈ **RESEARCH REVEALS** ❈ ---

RR17.2: *Sleep Deprivation on the Rise in the Developed World and Endemic in Singapore*

The increased expectations placed upon them by parents and teachers is resulting in many children and teenagers experiencing sleep deprivation, which results not just in crankier children, or shorter tempers, but also in serious mental health issues. *The Wall Street Journal*, on January 18, 2011, reported the following:[5]

- According to America's National Sleep Foundation's 2004 "Sleep in America poll" of 1,473 adults with children aged 10 and younger in the home, 13% of school-age children had difficulty falling asleep at bedtime and 26% of pre-schoolers seemed sleepy or overtired during the day, at least a few days a week. About 45% of adolescents aged 11 to 17 got less than eight hours of sleep a night.

- A 2010 study of 392 boys and girls in the US, published in the *Journal of Psychiatric Research*, showed that those who had trouble sleeping at 12 to 14 years old were more than twice as likely to have suicidal thoughts at ages 15 to 17 as those who didn't have sleep problems at the younger age.

- Another study in the US of 1,037 children revealed that 46% of those who were considered to have a persistent sleep difficulty at age nine had an anxiety disorder at age 21 or 26. By comparison, of the children who didn't have sleep problems at age 9, 33% had an anxiety disorder as young adults. This study was published in 2005 in the Journal of Abnormal Child Psychology.

In yet another study, published in 2010 by Science Translational Medicine, neurologists at Harvard Medical School highlighted that staying awake for 24 hours in a row is on par with legal intoxication with alcohol (in driving) in impairing performance. Sleeping only six hours per night for two weeks causes a similar level of impairment as staying awake for 24 hours.[6]

And finally, in findings that strike close to home, *The Straits Times* of Singapore reported in the April 20, 2012 issue that Singaporean children get an average of two hours less sleep than their peers in Switzerland. Paediatricians from Singapore's National University Hospital studied 372 children aged two to six. The doctors were disturbed to find that the children's parents thought that their children's sleep patterns were fine. One of the professors said, "My personal experience is that many children and teenagers (in Singapore) are quite sleep-deprived. They see me in the clinic for headaches, dizziness and poor attention in class." He also said that after the children took his advice to get more sleep, many of their physical problems improved, and some of the children and teens showed "markedly improved academic ability."[7]

Unfortunately, when researchers confirmed the trend of inadequate sleep among Singaporean children, the parents surveyed actually perceived that their children's sleep patterns were fine. Clearly, they are unaware of the long-term effects of sleep deprivation, in combination with other stressors, on the mental well-being of their children. This may partially explain why Singapore leads the world in mental illnesses among youths: studies have shown that a significant minority would suffer from depression and others are likely to develop a serious mental illness in their lifetime.

◈ RESEARCH REVEALS ◈

RR17.3: *Mental Illness Epidemic among Singapore Youth*

Unfortunately, Singapore leads the world in mental illness among youth, according to an article in *The Straits Times* "Mind Your Body" health magazine.[8] Not surprisingly, with the extra demands at school and after-school tuition, along with reduced sleep, 1 in 14 youths succumb to depression, and 1 in 23 suffer from OCD.[9] It's no wonder that a 2010 study of 6,600 Singaporean adults projected that that 1 in 10 would suffer from a serious mental illness in their lifetime.[10]

We believe that much of the mental anguish is a result of the three lifetraps that we had discussed in the previous chapter. So please take this issue seriously: we owe it to our children and the future of our societies not to let our exaggerated expectations inflict physical and mental harm on the next generation!

Thankfully, it's not all gloom and doom—one Singaporean mother, a Madam Poh, responded to the aforementioned newspaper article on sleep by sharing her family's schedule, which we consider to be a recipe for healthy parenting, albeit difficult to follow in today's climate. Nevertheless, we have included it as a good example for which to strive. In short, Madam Poh wrote that she and her husband, who both work full-time, have three girls aged five, seven, and ten. They have breakfast with their daughters, put them on the school bus, and then head straight to work; thus, they are able to start work by 7:30am at the latest. Their daughters come home by school bus and do their homework before their parents get home, supervised by a caregiver. On a typical day, Madam Poh and her husband leave work by 5pm to have dinner with their girls by 6pm and address any homework questions after dinner. They play together or watch a bit of television. By 7:30pm, they are reading a storybook with their girls and lights are off by 8pm. The older two wake up at 5:50am after ten hours of sleep. The five-year-old wakes up at 6:30pm and takes a one-hour nap in the afternoon. Thus, all the Poh children meet the requirements stated in the National Sleep Foundation's suggested sleep guide.[11]

Heavy Backpacks

Sleep and mental wellness are not the only aspects of our children's Basic Safety and health that are put at risk by exaggerated expectations. Research has also revealed the dangerous effects of excessive expectations of educational institutions on the *physical* well-being of young children. Specifically, students in many countries are carrying backpacks that exceed the recommended weight of 15% of their normal body weight. Moreover, carrying these heavy backpacks exerts an adverse impact on their bodies by undermining their lung volume and causing chronic back pain.

◆ RESEARCH REVEALS ◆

RR17.4: *Heavy Backpacks Cause Lasting Damage*

The Italian Backpack Study done in 1999 found that the average load students carried amounted to 22% of their body weight, thus exceeding the recommended 15%. They also found that 34.8% of students carried more than 30% of their normal body weight at least once during the week.[12]

Researchers in Hong Kong studied students' lung volume. Scientists found that the *average* weight of school students' backpacks was equivalent to

15% of their body weight. However, in the case of those who were carrying up to 20% of their body weight, their lung volume was significantly compromised.[13]

Another study compared the backpack weight of students in India with their counterparts in Houston, Texas. Almost 60% of students aged nine to 20 years old from both countries suffered from chronic back pain! And the percentage of students with back pain who carried backpack loads that constituted only 15% of their body weight regularly was drastically lower.[14]

Myopia

How does eyesight fit into this discussion? Myopia has emerged as a major health issue in parts of Asia, affecting the majority of school children. The causal factors include the over-emphasis on education and inadequate time spent outdoors. In fact, parents need to ensure that their children spend two or three hours a day in the sunlight. No wonder our family GP, Dr Malcolm Lim, told us his biggest grouse with Singapore parents—not protecting their kids' eyesight!

❖ RESEARCH REVEALS ❖

RR17.5: *High Rate of Myopia Linked with Lack of Outdoor Light*

A study published in *The Lancet* in May 2012 revealed that myopia has emerged as a major health issue in parts of Asia, affecting 80–90% of graduating school children compared to 10–20% of those completing secondary schooling in other parts of the world: "The higher prevalence of myopia in east Asian cities seems to be associated with increasing educational pressures, combined with lifestyle changes, which have reduced the time children spend outside."[15]

A BBC report also confirmed the findings of this research study: "According to the research, the problem is being caused by a combination of factors—a commitment to education and lack of outdoor light."[16] The researchers said children who spend two to three hours outdoors a day are "probably reasonably safe" from getting myopia. This could include time spent on the playground and walking to and from school.[17]

Children are increasingly being deprived of an enjoyable childhood, balanced between work and play. This situation has been exacerbated by the two-working parent arrangement that is more common than ever. Most of these jobs do not come with flexible hours or enable parents to meet the needs of their children, but they do manage to exhaust the parents with rising demands.

Even when parents do strive to spend time with their children, they focus almost exclusively on academics, especially in the Asian context. Children from all over Asia are adversely affected by their parents' excessive expectations in the area of academics: societies like Japan, Korea, and India are facing alarming suicide rates that stem from worry over scoring lower than anticipated grades.[18] It is sad to think that young children and adolescents are experiencing mental and physical stress from the ever-rising expectations of parents and educational institutions.

Most parents will say that they love their children, no matter what they do. Unfortunately, whether their children perceive it is an entirely different matter. When parents with lifetraps in this domain say that they absolutely love their children, their kids will feel, at an emotional level, that their parents' love is based on their achievements. This is what happens when children's core emotional need for realistic expectations is not met.

Kids sense this in very subtle ways, often from their parents' non-verbal communication. It may take the form of disappointment on a mother's face when her son has obtained a less-than-desirable grade. Maybe a teenager will notice that his father does not attend basketball games anymore, now that he is no longer on the starting team. It may appear in the withholding of affection when a daughter has decided not to embrace Christianity as soon as the parents had hoped.

Children are sensitive and they are able to read emotions, especially their parents'. They can put two and two together: if they only get praised when they do exceedingly well, they will conclude that their parents' approval is linked to their performance. Depending on their temperament, they may "perform" well, or they may not. But their emotional health will certainly suffer.

Toward the end of November, P6 parents in Singapore wait in agony for their children's PSLE results. (This is a national standardised test that every child takes at the end of primary school, similar to leaving the 6th grade, hence the name—the Primary School Leaving Exam). For years, we have been advising parents not to get so worried over exam results. However, this is no mean feat, as this particular exam determines which "high school" their children will attend. Students are ranked according to their score and only those with the highest scores are eligible for the more sought-after schools.

One year, we happened to run into four mothers after a midweek lesson, all of whom had children who had tested well above the national average and had scores that would get them into very good schools. During our conversations, as they told us about their children's results, we could tell that these parents were dissatisfied; they felt that their children should have done better. (Apparently the mothers expected their offspring to get into elite and prestigious schools, rather than just very good schools.) We ended up having extended fellowship with them because we felt that their exaggerated expectations were endangering their children's mental health, not to mention ruining any connection they might have with their children.

Later that evening, we dropped by the preteen class and saw the children. It was obvious that they, too, were disappointed by their results and felt that they had let their parents down. Even if their parents had not *said* anything negative, the parents' facial expressions and body language had revealed it all. We are absolutely not saying that parents should have no expectations for their children—it is all about *what kind* of expectations and *how* the expectations are communicated. That is why this core emotional need is called "*realistic* expectations." Fortunately, we were able to intervene with three of the four families and they are seeing improvements in their connection.

Parental Involvement—An Asset or a Liability?

When looking at outcomes in the areas of academic achievement, sports achievement, spiritual growth, and all-round success, parental involvement can be either a liability or an asset. Research has shown that parental involvement can produce positive or negative outcomes in terms of their children's academic achievement. Whether it ends up being positive or negative largely depends on *how* parents go about meeting this core emotional need for realistic expectations. Based on the huge amount of expenses, worry, and anxiety which accompany parents' expectations over their children's academic performance, we will speak mostly about academic expectations. Feel free to apply our discussion to other types of expectations.

What helps parents to be an asset?

When parents are meeting the first three core emotional needs already discussed in previous chapters, and especially when the connection is strong, parental involvement can be an asset. Examples of what an involved parent should do include: monitoring children's activities outside the home and school; setting rules; engaging in conversations about and helping children with school work and school-related issues; establishing educational expectations; discussing future planning with children and helping them with important decisions; participating in school-related activities such as meeting with teachers and volunteering in the classroom; and reading to children, as well as doing other enrichment and leisure activities together.

Research has established that parental expectations play a significant role in their children's academic performance, attitude towards their work, and participation in extracurricular activities. Moreover, when parents convey the proper attitude towards schoolwork—effort above competition—their children excel in their studies. In fact, what these studies show in general is that helpful parental expectations appear to be even more influential than peer influence.

─────────────── ⇜ **RESEARCH REVEALS** ⇝ ───────────────

RR17.6: *Parental Expectations*

A meta-analysis of 77 studies, done in the US, published by the Harvard Family Research Project in 2005, consisting of 300,000 elementary and secondary students, found that *parental educational expectations* are a particularly important aspect of parental involvement.[19] Outcomes were affected by how much time parents spent reading to children, whether or not they tried to avoid encounters which produce frustration, (such as "exasperation interactions"), and, to a lesser extent, parents' participation in school-related activities. Furthermore, parental involvement was associated with multiple measures of student achievement for the entire student population, as well as minority and low-income student populations. Overall, "the academic advantage for those children whose parents were highly involved in their education averaged about 0.5–0.6 of a standard deviation for overall educational outcomes, grades and academic achievement."[20]

At the secondary education level, high parental expectations continue to yield significant schooling benefits.[21] In one study of high school seniors, parental expectations played the primary role in shaping the students' academic achievement, attitude towards their work, and participation in extracurricular activities. In yet another study, researchers found that "parental expectations for achievement stand out as the most significant influences on [their] achievement growth, high school credits completed, and enrolment in extracurricular academic high school programs."[22] High parental educational expectations are also associated with better mathematics and reading scores, interest in school, academic self-discipline, future planning, and motivation for schoolwork.[23] In fact, in one highly specific 2006 study conducted with African-American families living in low income areas, researchers found that *when parents taught that success originates from effort rather than surpassing peers, it had a strong positive effect on the math grades of eighth- and ninth-graders.*[24]

What causes parents to be a liability?

Parental involvement must take into account the parent's dynamics with the child. For example, when some parents hear about the positive outcomes of parental involvement, they decide to monitor their children several times a day, and/or push their children to achieve at exceptional levels, while being critical of their children's mistakes. These parents, all in the name of loving their children, are unaware of the harm they are inflicting on their children in the form of anxiety! The manner in which parents interact with their children makes a huge difference. Children learn from their parents. And as we have said over and over in the chapters about lifetraps, we pass both positive and negative traits down to our offspring.

How parents convey their expectations, the quality of their relationship with their children, whether the child still feels accepted after making mistakes, and the level of criticism from parents all make a huge difference in their children's academic performances. Unrealistic expectations of parents and a desire to please others may foster the belief that parental love and social acceptance are contingent upon high achievement—a belief that can increase the risk of developing emotional difficulties.

The rest of this chapter contains strategies about how parental involvement can be an asset, rather than a liability.

Parents Must Prioritise Their Marriage

The first think parents can do to make sure their involvement is an asset to their children and not a liability is to ensure they have a good marriage. As we have said many times in this book already, a healthy marriage is crucial for children's well-being.

The Heritage Foundation, a US-based research and educational institution, offered important insights about changes in the American family. Their 2008 study of American households and the overall well-being of children documents the decline in the number of American children growing up in households with both biological parents, as well as the sharp increase in the proportion of children born to unmarried mothers.[25] They issued the following statement from sociologist Paul Amato:

> "Perhaps the most profound change in the American family over the past four decades has been the decline in the share of children growing up in households with biological parents."[26] [The report went on to state] Studies have shown that children raised in intact families, i.e., with two continuously married parents, tend to fare better in cognitive, emotional, and behavioural areas than children living in other family forms.[27]

---————— ⋞ **RESEARCH REVEALS** ⋟ —————

RR17.7: *Family Structure*

The mission of the Heritage Foundation is to perform timely, accurate research on key policy issues and market these findings to their primary audiences: members of Congress, key congressional staff members, policymakers in the executive branch, the nation's news media, along with the academic and policy communities. In 2008, when they issued the statement above, they accompanied it with the following statistics:[28]

In 1960, 88% of all children lived with two parents, compared to 68% in 2007.[29] In 1960, 5% of all children were born to unmarried mothers. That figure rose to 38.5% in 2006.[30] Demographers have estimated that, overall, one child in two will spend some portion of his or her childhood in a single-parent family.[31] Not surprisingly, the changes

> in family structure over the last 40 years have affected the well-being of children and adolescents. In 2002, nearly seven million children between the ages of 12 and 18 repeated a grade. *Based on this figure, Professor Amato estimates that if the share of two-parent families had remained unchanged between 1980 and 2002, some 300,000 fewer teens would have repeated a grade.*[32]

On the whole, young children from intact families have higher reading achievement test scores on average than their peers living in cohabiting, or step-parent, families. Primary and secondary school children living in conventional households tend to achieve higher academic scores in individual subjects, or grade point averages, than their peers in non-traditional families. Moreover, children living with their biological parents were also less likely to engage in negative and disruptive behaviours than children from other types of households. Finally, at the college level, students from non-intact families also lagged behind their peers from intact families, in terms of the number of years they attended college and their likelihood of graduation.

❖ RESEARCH REVEALS ❖

RR17.8: *Two-Parent Families Better for Education*

It comes as no surprise that reading to young children aids their literary development. However, a study released by the US Census Bureau in 2008 showed that toddlers and preschool-age children in married-parent families are read to more often than peers in non-intact families.[33] Another US study published in 2007 found that of 11,500 kindergarteners living with two parents or parent figures, accounting for parental education and income, children living with married parents achieved higher reading achievement test scores on average than peers living in cohabiting, or step-parent, families.[34]

The National Institute of Child Health & Human Development conducted a study of Early Child Care and Youth Development in the USA. From a sample of 1,015 children, the study found that first-graders whose mothers were married when they were born are less likely to engage in disruptive behaviour with peers and teachers than those whose mothers were single, or cohabiting, at the time of their birth.[35]

All findings below were taken from FamilyFacts.org. All studies were done in the US unless stated otherwise.[36]

- A study published in 2006 showed children between the ages of 3-12 who live in intact families have higher average math scores than peers whose mothers live in cohabiting relationships.[37]
- The association between family structure and nine-year-olds' science and math achievement appears to be cross-national. This study was published in 2003.[38]

- Children between the ages of 7-10 who live in continuously intact families tend to score higher on reading tests than peers who have lived in other family structures. This research was published in 2001.[39]
- Children between the ages of 6-11 who live in intact families tend to be more engaged in their schoolwork than peers in other family structures. This study was published in 2004.[40]
- A study published in 1997 showed that eighth-graders from two-parent families perform better on average in math and science tests than peers from single-parent, or step-parent, families.[41]
- The predominant family structure of a school's student population appears to be linked to the individual science and math scores of eighth-graders, i.e., middle schools whose students come mostly from intact families as a rule have higher math and science scores. This work was published in 1997.[42]
- Ninth-graders whose mothers were married when they were born are more likely to complete an algebra course than peers whose mothers were single when they were born. This study was published in 2006.[43]
- A study published in 2003 found that on average, compared with peers from intact families, adolescents living with a single mother or with mothers who were remarried or cohabiting experience more behavioural problems and lower levels of academic performance. Compared to children living in intact families, peers living in single-mother families, single-mother families with cohabiting partners, and married families with stepfathers were more likely to have been suspended or expelled from school; more likely to have engaged in delinquent activities in the past 12 months; more likely to have problems getting along with their teachers, doing homework, or paying attention in school; and more likely to have lower grade point averages.[44]

The overwhelming research indicates that divorce has a significantly negative effect on children's academic performance. In fact, children whose fathers have *died* do better in school than children whose parents are divorced.[45] It is speculated that children are able to attribute a more positive meaning from a death, however painful, than when their parents go through a divorce. In the case of divorce, children have been known to blame themselves, which usually does not happen in the event of a parent's death. In fact, children from divorced families are statistically less likely to graduate from higher education and more likely to have difficulties obtaining employment.[46]

In simple terms, this means that parents who tried to keep their marriage together "for the sake of the children", as long as the home did not have repeated destructive conflict, did the right thing. We would add that if parents would go the extra mile and proactively work on their marriage for the sake of Love Connection, they and their children would be even better off. Thus, there is ample evidence to suggest that the structure of an intact family in which parents are married, and we would like to add *happily* married, has a positive impact on their children's education.

In addition to improving education and job prospects, another important consequence of a healthy marriage is that parents will be able to put up a united front about what to expect from the child, thus ensuring consistency, as mentioned in the section on Reasonable Limits. It is better for children when they hear similar expectations from both parents. When parents are not united and convey different expectations, children may become confused. Eventually they will figure out which parent is the "weaker link" and either side with the parent that advocates their point of view or play the parents off of each other.

Please note: we are making a big deal out of all of these marriage statistics not to shame single parents—in fact, we salute you for your hard work and perseverance. To you we say, beat the odds! These are just statistics, not prophesies! What we are trying to do is to impress upon readers who are married the importance of prioritising their marriage.

Set Learning-Oriented Goals, Not Performance-Oriented Goals

World-renowned Stanford psychologist, Dr Carol Dweck, has been studying motivation for decades. Her work about academic expectations distinguishes between two kinds of orientations: parents who encourage their children to focus on learning for learning's sake, and parents who push their children to attain high grades.[47] Dweck and her colleagues used the term "learning-oriented" to refer to parents who were more concerned with their children learning *per se* and found that learning-oriented parents tend to (a) emphasise the need to enjoy learning, (b) encourage progress towards their child's potential, (c) inspire their child to seek out challenges, and (d) reward effort over results.

In contrast, parents who were more concerned with high grades and outcomes were identified as being "performance-oriented". These parents tend to (a) believe that success in performance signifies competence and a high degree of intelligence, (b) feel that having a highly intelligent child brings personal recognition, (c) have a desire for that kind of recognition, and (d) expect their child to secure a prestigious job and earn a high salary.[48]

Let's put 2+2 together to see how these orientations affect children!

Sixth-grade students (12-year-olds) at the Johns Hopkins University's Center for Talented Youth were measured for perfectionistic tendencies and then divided into two groups—healthy perfectionists and dysfunctional perfectionists.[49] "Healthy perfectionists" were defined as children who had high scores on being unusually organised and driven, but had relatively low scores in areas related to fear of making mistakes, concern about parents' criticism and self-doubt after taking action. Conversely, the "dysfunctional perfectionists" had high scores in all the aforementioned areas, and were more likely to describe themselves as defensive, anxious, moody, and socially detached—characteristics that hinder academic achievement and lead to social and emotional problems.[50]

⟨ LOUIS LOWDOWN ⟩

Back in 1989, when we had lived in Singapore for a year, John's youngest brother, Elgin, moved in with us at the age of 10. He was attending third grade in the Singapore school system (which was a year ahead of his previous Malaysian school system) and was working hard to catch up. I (Karen) was working from home one day when Elgin walked into the living room during a small staff meeting. I paused to ask him about his day; Elgin grinned shyly and showed me his math test. When I saw the paper, I exclaimed, "Wow, Elgin, you made a 90!" Then I turned to the others and said, "Hey guys, look at that, Elgin made a 90 on his math test!" I gave him a hug, told him where he could find a snack, and returned to the meeting. To me, it was a very ordinary interaction. However, one of the Singaporean sisters commented, "Elgin is so lucky to have such an encouraging big sister like you." I was puzzled and queried, "Wasn't that normal? Isn't that what anyone would say to a child who made a 90 on a test?" "Well, that's not what my mother would have done." "Which was?" "She would have asked me how many other kids made a 90, because if most of the class made a 90, then mine wouldn't have mattered. The next thing she would do would be to take my paper, look through it for the mistakes, and scold me for being so stupid—after all, 90% is not 100%." The other women in the room said their experiences were similar. I was speechless. I now understand that this is not a uniquely Singaporean mind-set—many cultures produce performance-oriented parents. But that was the first time I had witnessed it on a grand scale.

We have chosen to highlight all of these statistics to everyone instead of putting them into Research Reveals boxes because this information is so relevant in the 21st Century! We have seen far too many parents with the performance-oriented disposition, who are freaked out and overly anxious. (This is such a common state of mind in Singaporeans that there is actually a local slang word for it: *"kan cheong"*.) Whether it's over grades or entrance into a choice school, or their kids' participation in sports, music and other hobbies, or even how their kids are doing spiritually—the performance-oriented disposition almost always brings disastrous results!

Special note from John: Those of us from Asian backgrounds need to listen up—research has proven that, compared to Caucasian parents, significantly more Asian parents have performance-oriented goals. And children of performance-oriented parents tend to exhibit more perfectionistic tendencies than their peers with learning-oriented parents, which often causes them to be socially withdrawn, which in turn leaves them vulnerable to social and emotional problems.[51] This is not Good Enough Parenting.

How many children have we seen who struggle with the aforementioned conditions, along with migraines and digestive system malfunctions, all because of parent-generated anxiety? Remember what we said earlier about basic safety—we should not let our unrealistic expectations put our children in harm's way!

⌇ RESEARCH REVEALS ⌇

RR17.9: *Asian Parents More Likely to Have Children with Dysfunctional Perfectionism*

A 1997 Johns Hopkins study by Ablard and Parker found that:

Of Asian parents, 69% had performance-oriented goals compared to only 25% of Caucasian parents.

The researchers also discovered that children of performance-oriented parents were significantly more likely to fall into the dysfunctional perfectionism group than children of parents with learning-oriented goals. These children were likely to be concerned about the following three components: concern over mistakes, parental criticism, and doubts about action.[52]

(Dysfunctional) Perfectionism has also been linked to the following:
- Depression that results from the perceived inability to reach excessive and externally-defined goals;[53]
- Anorexia Nervosa;[54]
- Bulimia;[55]
- Obsessive Compulsive Disorder;[56]
- Migraine;[57]
- Procrastination;[58] and
- Suicidal tendencies.[59]

⌇ LOUIS LOWDOWN ⌇

During our daughter's first two years of elementary school, I (John) was a performance-oriented/kan cheong parent: when Sonia didn't perform up to "my standard" in math, I assumed that she was not trying hard. Period. It did not occur to me that her strengths might lie in other areas, or that she might need some extra work or have a different learning style than I have. My wife challenged me about the way I was speaking to Sonia and showed

> me the folly of my ways. During my "road to Damascus moment", I saw my daughter really, really trying, and it moved me. In fact, one day she told me that she felt "stupid" in her class. My heart went out to her and I realised that I had contributed to her feelings. From then on, I focused only on her effort. Once, we even celebrated when she got a 'C' in Math. It was an occasion that I truly enjoyed. I did not just go with the flow. I changed, and I was happy that I had changed. Even better, Sonia was encouraged and became more joyful. (And she didn't run away when it was time to do mathematics with Dad!)

Do Not Use Praise and Reward, or Punishment, as a Control Style

In our discussion of the core emotional need for autonomy and performance in Chapter Eight, we introduced Dr Edward Deci, a professor well-known for his numerous studies on human motivation. Deci's research led him to conclude that the most powerful and healthy form of motivation is *intrinsic motivation*—"the process of doing an activity for its own sake, of doing an activity for the reward that is inherent in the activity itself."[60]

Deci has spent years studying all different ages, including young children. His research shows that most of the learning done by preschool children is done not because it is instrumental for achieving something else, but because the children are curious: they want to know. Clearly, their learning is intrinsically-motivated.[61]

Children love to learn from a young age. A child's level of curiosity will drive him or her to investigate, ask questions, or make numerous attempts at one task. They appear to have tremendous energy in the way that they go at a certain task over and over again with a singular desire to master it. In fact, they often perceive their work as play, not a chore that has to get done. The bottom line is that they are enthusiastic: they are driven to explore, learn, and grow. It comes naturally to them. Like a sponge, they absorb everything around them as they play and work at the same time. Young children do not distinguish between the two as they are having so much fun playing and working at the same time.

Considering children's natural propensity for work-play, what causes their attitudes to change as they grow older? As Deci put it, "What has happened? Why is it that so many of today's students are unmotivated, when it could not be more clear that they were born with a natural desire to learn?"

This question weighed in Deci's heart and he began to perform many experiments to evaluate the effect of reward and punishment on motivation. What he found was that motivation through rewards over time actually did not promote an excited state of learning, but a sad state of apathy.[62]

For instance, in his many experiments using money as a reward, Deci observed that once the participants started getting paid, they lost interest in the activity and did not do as well. Rewards, he concluded, turn the act of playing into something controlled from the outside. When this happens, play becomes work and the player, a pawn. Deci deduced that rewards have a negative effect on people's intrinsic motivation.

Not surprisingly, Deci obtained even worse results when he used punishment as a motivator. Deadlines, goals, and tight surveillance are frequently-used methods that are supposed to help people to get results. Deci strongly believes that both materialistic rewards and threats of punishment ultimately destroy children's (and adults') enthusiasm and interest.

☙ RESEARCH REVEALS ❧

RR17.10: *Conditional Parenting Causes Schemas*

In 2012, Assor and Tal, two Israeli experts in the field of motivation, published a study in the Journal of Adolescence. They set out to see the negative effect of perceived parental affection and esteem when the child meets the parents' expectation in academic achievement situations. Their sample: Israeli 10th and 11th grade students (approximately 16 1/2 years old). What they found was that parents' conditional positive regard, PCPR, as they called it, correlated with adolescents' self-aggrandizement following success and self-derogation and shame following failure. The outcome was unhealthy behaviour as a result of becoming puffed up after "success" and filled with self-loathing after "failure". The fluctuations between the two, self-aggrandizing and self-derogation, is a reflection of an unstable self-esteem, based primarily on the perceived view of the parents on the outcome of the adolescents' achievements. The self-aggrandizing emerges as a response to the missing unconditional parental regard of "Connection and Acceptance" which was discussed at length previously. Although showing positive regard only when there is an achievement looks seemingly harmless, its effect can be extremely harmful, as this study has indicated.[63]

According to the research above and in our opinion as counsellors, it makes sense that withholding affection conditional parenting would lead to self-aggrandizing and or self-derogation. In schema language, this is about the development of lifetraps such as:

- Entitlement – With this lifetrap, children have a grossly inflated view of themselves without sober judgement. This will sow the seeds of narcissistic behaviour (see lifetrap of "Entitlement" in Chapter Twelve).
- Unrelenting Standards – With this lifetrap, children overcompensate for their perceived failure or lack of successes by swinging to the other extreme and become workaholics and overachievers. This leaves little time for relaxation and drives them to be highly critical of themselves and others (see lifetrap of "Unrelenting Standards" in Chapter Sixteen).

- Defectiveness, Failure, Social Isolation – With these lifetraps, children have a deflated view of themselves and often listen to their inner voices which puts them down. Often these voices carry messages of their parents talking to them when they were young (see lifetraps in the domain of "Disconnection and Rejection" in Chapter Five).

Of course we are not saying to forget about encouraging and praising your children, or that rewards are always bad—just that we should consider how we go about doing it and to what end. Deci and his colleague, Richard Ryan, have noticed that while many parents rely on what they think are effective short-term strategies, the progress made based on their threats and rewards rarely lasts. They argue that rewards given with a controlling style have a substantially negative effect on intrinsic motivation and leave people feeling more pressured and less interested. *On the other hand, when rewards are extended in a non-controlling way as an acknowledgment of good work, they will not produce detrimental effects.* Their perspective seems to suggest that it is the *controlling* intent of rewards that sabotages one's attempts to motivate others, by destroying the very motivation that they had been intended to promote.[64]

So the next time you consider saying, *"If you get all As, then I will give you...."*, *"If you are a good boy, I will give you..."*, *"If you get first place, I will give you..."*, *"If you get into this school, then I will give you..."*, *"If you eat all of your food, then I will give you..."*, or even *"If you don't make an A, you'll be grounded..."*, change your mind, reject these so-called motivational techniques and decide to be an asset, instead of a liability. Strive to help your children be intrinsically motivated. Your kids will be happier and thank you for it one day!

Beware of Exasperation Interactions

Here are some examples of the exasperation interactions in the context of (Un)Realistic Expectations:

Belittling
I hope that you have the intelligence to finish your assignment after all the money I have spent on you.
Your mum and I went to Ivy League schools—what's wrong with you?
Please don't act so stupid.
The least you can do is follow our example.
Look at Auntie Betsy—her sons all made the baseball team. Why am I stuck with such losers?
I don't feel like talking to you right now—you don't even try.

Perfectionistic and Conditional
> *I want this stuff done 100% right, especially when we have others coming over to see how well-behaved our family is.*
>
> *What kind of a family are we if we don't pass our exams?*
>
> *Where will I show my face if you don't have your verses memorised?*
>
> *The Smith men always get football scholarships— it's what we do.*

Controlling
> *I doubt if you can do this for yourself; we'll wait and see.*
>
> *When I was your age, I would have loved it if someone had helped me to choose my classes.*
>
> *I'm so glad we always like the same sports and that you want to do as well as I did in everything.*

Punitive
> *If you mess up, you are going to regret it!*
>
> *If you don't make As (make the team, get a job, etc.), you will hear it from me.*
>
> *If you don't make a high GPA, then just see how long I'll let you have your car.*

Emotionally Depriving and Inhibiting
> *Why are you complaining and making such a fuss? Just do your work and get on with it!*
>
> *Please don't get emotional—it's just a test.*
>
> *It's easier for me to love your brother; at least he tries at school.*

Overprotective
> *Don't worry darling, I will help you to do your homework (says the mother as she actually does the homework).*
>
> *Here, sweetheart, let me type your book report.*
>
> *You don't need to try out for the basketball team, honey. You may get an injury.*

Pessimistic
> *If you actually pass, I will be shocked.*
>
> *I'm just waiting for you to mess up this week.*
>
> *Let's face it: there's a black sheep in every family.*

Overly Permissive
> *(These parents often don't say anything, but when they do...)*
>
> *Don't worry, honey, it's ok if you don't study at all—you can always live with us when you get older.*

Rather than accidentally causing exasperation in their children, parents need to learn how to motivate them properly to enable the kids to realise their potential. Instead of focusing on results that can be damaging, they should place their emphasis on areas related to intrinsic motivation and ensure that the quality of the relationship with their children is strong and deep.

In doing so, parents are sending the following healthy message: "You are special enough to me that I care to spend time with you. I want you to enjoy doing what you are cut out to do." Children who hear such messages will learn to concentrate better on their activities, enjoy their life as they are grow up, and maintain a high level of motivation that will not nose-dive as they grow older. When parents convey confidence in their children, it is amazing how much it can do for their connection with their children.

When parents praise their children in front of visitors, from time to time (not constantly), it sends a positive message. Even if children are pretending that they are not listening, parents should do it anyway. I (John) remember a time when my dad encouraged me in front of my siblings for having a tidy desk. I was doing terribly at school, and two of my brothers were A students, but my dad noticed my desk. That did a lot to cement the connection with my dad, and eventually my grades turned around anyway. Now, it is important to note that we are not talking about boorish parents who boast about their children's achievements non-stop; rather, we are highlighting a way of encouraging tentative children and letting them know that they are believed in.

Another fun yet indirect way that parents can encourage their children in front of others is to try "Resource Gossip"—a tool devised by Mark McKergow, a Solution-Focused consultant based in the UK. He recommends "gossiping" positively about a person in front of them with colleagues, or in the case of a child, with the family.[65] You speak as though the child were not there, and say, for example, in the case of a family encouraging an eight-year-old girl, "Honey (wife to husband), do you know what I heard about Janie? She is kind to the girls at school, even though that sometimes upsets the popular girls." "Really? Wow, I bet she is proud of herself for having her own convictions." "I bet she is, too. Wonder how she is able to do that?" "Freddie, what did you notice about your little sister recently?" "Well, I'm happy that she doesn't come into my room and take my stuff so often." "Hmmm… looks like she is growing up to be a considerate and caring young lady." Just watch little Janie beam and blush as she hears sincere comments from her favourite people!

However, there are some parents and teachers who resort to aggravating children with pessimism, an approach that they call "Negative Psychology". Essentially, they use negative threats in order to induce fear, and tell the children that they are not good enough, in an effort to motivate the latter to do better. These adults genuinely believe that negative messages and fear will offer greater motivation than positive messages!

> ### ⇜ LOUIS LOWDOWN ⇝
>
> Our son, David, experienced the negative psychology approach with his Physics teacher, who kept telling him that he would never score an 'A' on his 10th-grade national exam because he gets distracted too easily. I (John) worked with David on this issue for months, but the teacher was still determined to be a prophet of doom. However, David ended up getting an 'A star' for Physics! The next time I met the teacher, he told me that all this while, he had been using "negative psychology to motivate David." I wasn't very happy with that answer, but I didn't mind because David was encouraged, not so much because of his grade, but because he had put in such effort to get the grade. I see so many parents who think that putting their children down will motivate them. Even when others say nice things about their children, the parents minimise the kind words. And their children never learn how to accept compliments, mainly because their parents have taught them to dismiss positive messages. How sad!

Where does this leave the kids? If they do well, parents will attribute it to one of the following: the exam was easy; the teacher or the extra tuition teacher was good; or since many others did well, it was not a big deal. Conversely, if they don't do well, they will be criticised. The bottom line is that there is no room for encouragement. This is sheer craziness! No wonder the kids feel exasperated! When parents and teachers alike are so stingy with encouragement, such that a kid has to distinguish himself on a supersonic level just to get any encouragement, what kind of message is the child receiving? After all, how often in life does that kind of achievement happen? Once a year? Once a decade? What are the parents thinking?! Parents, let's have empathy for our children and be assets rather than liabilities!

> ### ⇜ LOUIS LOWDOWN ⇝
>
> In Elgin's last year of high school, one of his teachers was also very down on him. As his older brother, I (John) attended the parent/teacher conference and heard the teacher tell him that he would never make it to university. Fortunately, Elgin was not discouraged by his teacher. He would go on to obtain a degree from one of the top universities in Australia and become a high school teacher and "head of department" at an international school in Singapore. Because he is great at motivating youngsters, he has now been placed in charge of helping International Baccalaureate students with their community service work. Not bad for someone whose teacher bought into the "Negative Psychology" nonsense.

Focus on Who Your Children Are, Not What They Do; Focus on the Inside, Not the Outside

Do you truly appreciate effort, instead of grades? One mother we know who has a son with learning difficulties threw her child a party after he received his PSLE / end of elementary school grades, not because they were "high" compared to the other kids, but because she appreciated the work and effort that he had put into his studies. She wanted him to know that she was very proud of him. We hold her up as a mum who understands how to be an asset in her child's academic life, not a liability.

When we praise our children for doing something well because of the effort they put in, we should do so without making any comparison with others. Thus, we should *avoid making statements* such as:

You made us proud by becoming first in the class.

You made us happy by doing what you should, like we expected.

You made us look good because you scored straight A's.

You were the best actor/actress in the entire play.

If your encouragement is based on what they had actually achieved, what happens when they do not achieve the same results the next time round? Then no matter what you say, it will have little effect on them.

Rather, you should direct praise at their personal effort, and avoid making comparisons with others:

You worked so hard for your exam…

You gave it your best and I am proud of you.

I really admire the heart and spirit you put into playing basketball.

Wow, you were amazing in the musical! You are really good at acting.

Look out for other praiseworthy qualities that you may not have noticed or thought were important. This list will get you started:

- helpfulness—helping siblings, classmates
- empathy—putting self in another's shoes
- cooperativeness—cooperating with others in the house
- effort—making the effort to do well in their studies, not just getting good grades
- tidiness—in own room or in whole house
- joyfulness—showing joy and being fun
- forgiveness and compassion—with family members or others
- sense of humour—being funny
- patience—waiting without grumbling
- politeness—having manners, being kind
- caring—having a heart for others.

When you witness these qualities, take your child aside and tell them how much you appreciate them. This is much more effective than just praising the outcome of an exam or a competition. Our children do a lot of good things, but we do not always notice; we should not miss the opportunity to acknowledge the good in our children.

Furthermore, when you encourage your children, be specific. General and ambiguous praise can have a negative effect on children because they may think their parents are insincere. Just saying, "Great job", or "You are awesome", without referencing any specific actions, will not necessarily lift their spirits.

One of the children we have known in the Singapore church since he was born has developed anxiety and stress issues. His mother has hounded her son year in and year out to the point that we were worried for him. He had even talked about suicide. I (John) had a counselling session with the boy who told me that his number one source of stress was the fact that he stopped getting first place in his class (just that year). He cried and said, "I do not have any other talents and by not getting first, I feel useless."

In fact, research has repeatedly shown that parents who give conditional approval, based on their children's performance, may be able to elicit compliance from their children. *However,* their children also suffer from pressure and unhappiness for they are always trying to live up to their parents' expectations. Moreover, the adverse effects of conditional parenting apply not only to high school and college students, but also to adult children.

⌞ RESEARCH REVEALS ⌝

RR17.11: *Conditional Parenting Is Damaging*

A *New York Times* article published in September 2009 featured more of Deci's research, including highlighting several studies done in 2004. Deci and his colleagues asked more than 100 college students whether the love they had received from their parents had seemed to depend on any of the following factors: whether they had succeeded in school; practised hard for sports; been considerate toward others; or suppressed emotions like anger and fear. It turned out that children who received conditional approval were indeed somewhat more likely to act as the parent wanted. However, the children's compliance came at a steep price. First, these children tended to resent and dislike their parents. Second, they were apt to say that the way they acted was often due more to "strong internal pressure" than "a real sense of choice." Moreover, their happiness after succeeding at something was usually short-lived, and they often felt guilty or ashamed.

In a companion study, Dr Assor and his colleagues interviewed mothers of grown children. With this generation, too, conditional parenting proved damaging. Those mothers who, as children, sensed that they were loved

> only when they lived up to their parents' expectations, now felt less worthy as adults. *Yet despite the negative effects,* these mothers were more likely to turn around and use conditional affection with their own children.[66] Dysfunction is truly the gift that keeps on giving!
>
> The article stated further that the same researchers published two replications and extensions of the original study. This time the subjects were Israeli adolescents. The study distinguished between giving more approval when children did what parents wanted and giving less approval when they did not.
>
> The studies found that both positive and negative conditional parenting were harmful, but in slightly different ways. The positive kind sometimes succeeded in getting children to work harder on academic tasks, but at the cost of unhealthy feelings of "internal compulsion." Negative conditional parenting didn't even work in the short run; it just increased the teenagers' negative feelings about their parents.[67]
>
> What these and other studies tell us is that praising children for doing something right in an area that is not meaningful to them, although better than withholding affection or punishing, will still feel to the children like conditional parenting. All of these approaches will eventually prove to be counterproductive.[68]

Contrary to popular belief, most parents of gifted students do not have unrealistic high expectations, or focus extensively on performance outcomes of achievement. Instead, these parents place a great deal of emphasis on:
- Encouraging their children to do well in school—they don't place unrelenting standards on their children, or focus on performance and results
- Getting personally involved in educational activities
- Providing stimulating opportunities so that their children can be challenged and develop their talent.[69]

When parents do not take this approach, their children will very likely conclude that they are not accepted and loved by their parents unconditionally. Their negative thinking will slowly erode their emotional security towards their parents and undermine their self-esteem. In addition, their level of motivation will decline as they grow older, especially when they reach their adolescent years. This is why we have heard so many adolescents say:

> *I'm not going to college.*
> *I don't care about my exams, why should I?*
> *I am just working to get my parents off my back.*
> *I need to do well so that I can get a job that pays me a lot one day.*
> *I can't wait to be on my own one day.*

These children have very little natural drive (intrinsic motivation). They lack spark and joy, and project a flat demeanour. They are sometimes knows as underachievers—a subject that we will now discuss in greater detail.

Learn to Motivate Underachievers

Underachievement relates to the discrepancy between some measure of the child's ability and his or her actual achievement.[70] Underachievers tend to be disorganised, lose assignments, misplace books, daydream, and forget to do their homework. They spend most of their time and energy on television, computer games, and phones. Underachievers often blame their teachers or school for their poor grades, and prioritise sports, hobbies and social life but fail to prioritise academics.

However, beneath this facade of carefree living hides some of the following perceptions:

- Underachievers don't believe that they can reach their goals, even if they were to work hard. Their feelings of defectiveness and failure are triggered at the thought of trying harder. If they have a surrendered coping style, they fulfil the prophecy of their inner voice that says that they cannot reach healthy goals.
- If underachievers do not think that they can win, they will not bother trying. Essentially, they would rather not try then to try and be disappointed out of fear that their flaws will be exposed. Instead, they opt to brag about the low grade that they had managed to achieve without studying.
- While this attitude helps them to feel better about themselves temporarily, there is a constant inner voice that tells them to counterattack their sense of defectiveness and failure. As this voice grows stronger, they will become even more afraid of losing. What underachievers should realise is that, even when they lose, they can still learn valuable lessons that will enable them to triumph at other times.
- There are also underachievers that are driven by the lifetrap of Dependence. They do not feel confident about performing their own tasks and feel that they always need someone beside them to guide them and to succeed. They have low self-esteem about their ability to perform tasks by themselves.
- Some underachievers have magical thinking: they believe that, later in life, things will suddenly change for the better and that they will become extremely well off. Indulging in magical thinking helps them to alleviate their sense of defectiveness by reassuring themselves that everything will turn out alright even when they make no effort.
- They struggle with insufficient self-control because they have not learnt how to persevere through a task. They do not know what it means to really make an effort; thus, they have an unrealistic view of what it takes to perform a task well.

In the case of underachievers, giving them realistic expectations will help them to gain confidence at performing tasks. As they learn to complete tasks and even excel at them, they will increase in their confidence and motivation. Many parents do not know how to scale down to the level of the child, moving them upward gradually. Instead, many parents insist that their children jump through hoops, usually because others are doing the same. However, when their children are unable to match these expectations and fail, it only confirms the voice in their head that tells them there is no point trying. They then lose motivation and talk about giving up.

Parents are usually dumbfounded by such statements. Very often, these parents will state that they have simply been reminding their children to do their school work and pass their exams with high marks—no different than their peers with their children. However, such a strategy will backfire. This kind of intense and unyielding focus on results and performance, along with constant criticism, robs children of their natural motivation. In fact, in their research of parenting practices, Kindlon and colleagues found that the children who perceived that they were not achieving their full potential also felt pressured by their parents to succeed.[71]

Our advice is that if children are not motivated, parents should allow natural consequences to take effect; in other words, let teachers and school counsellors sort it out. Children are more likely to apply themselves with determination when they receive less pressure and criticism from *parents*. They are more likely to understand where they went wrong when the feedback comes from another source like their teachers.

◈ RESEARCH REVEALS ◈

RR17.12: *Motivating Underachievers*

In a study entitled "Parenting Practices at the Millennium (PPM)" conducted in the United States, Dr. Dan Kindlon and his colleagues surveyed hundreds of children and their parents. They found that children (both boys and girls) who stated that they were not working to their intellectual potential were also the very ones who felt that their parents were pushing them too hard academically. And interestingly, the study also revealed that the opposite parent sex tended to exert the greatest influence on the children. Essentially, the only factor related to boys' underachievement was their mothers' pressure, while for girls, the most significant factor was the level of their fathers' expectations.[72]

Learn about Multiple Intelligences and How to Identify Your Children's Gifts

We do not have the space here to do this subject justice, but we implore you to read Howard Gardner's books, especially if you are struggling with having realistic expectations for your children. Dr Gardner, from Harvard University, is the pioneer on the subject of multiple intelligence. For several decades, he and his team of researchers and scientists have validated his theory of the existence of different intelligences in the brain. Gardner advocates exposing children to different experiences, media, and learning styles so that all children have the possibility to be at their best.

When we teach this part of our workshop, we describe the eight intelligences that Gardner has proven to date: logical/mathematical, verbal/linguistic, musical, spatial, environmental, kinaesthetic, interpersonal, and intrapersonal.[73] Based on his theory, we try to help parents see that statistically, it is not possible for children to be gifted in all subject areas, nor is it possible for all children to be good in mathematics! We urge parenats to consider that there are other paths to success and happiness, and we explain how to nurture all eight intelligences to see which ones their children seem to gravitate toward naturally.

MOVIE MOMENT – *Dead Poets Society*,[74] *Happy Feet*[75]

We show scenes from the movie, *Dead Poets Society*, which illustrates how a father with unrelenting standards and exaggerated expectations failed to meet his son's core needs, ultimately ending in tragedy. This is a great film to watch as a group of parents to spur on discussion, but not recommended for children unless they are in the later high school years. However, *Happy Feet* is fine for a younger audience. Our son saw this movie while he was still in elementary school and said, "Mum, you need to use that for movie therapy to help parents who need to learn to accept their kids!"

LOUIS LOWDOWN

My mum taught me to read when I (Karen) was four and I devoured everything in my small town school's library by the time I finished elementary school. Reading always came so easily to me (don't ask about math and science) that I'd always assumed that my daughter would be a voracious reader as well. We read to her since she was born, and her room was filled with books—bought and borrowed. However, when Sonia still didn't get into reading that much by the time she was in the fourth grade, I felt like the world's worst mother. I had followed all the tips, but still, she just wasn't like me, and my narcissistic parent self couldn't help but feel disappointed! Thankfully, my wonderful husband, who had already repented of being a freak-out math dad a year earlier, opened my eyes by pointing out that Sonia had won a tennis trophy when she was just nine years old—how many trophies had I won at nine? Or ever? "Let Sonia be Sonia and she will develop her own strengths, and don't be so egotistical that you think she has to be just like you!" That was very sound advice. I stopped worrying about Sonia's reading. Ultimately, she did well at everything she put her heart in, and God even played a practical joke on me—she's now majoring in English Literature!

Don't Let Yourself Jump to the Worst Case Scenario

Such a mind-set can make meeting your children's core emotional needs difficult, because it is hard to have realistic expectations when you are always in a worst-case scenario mode. Below are case studies of two adults we counselled who are still traumatised by memories of their parents' overreaction to relatively small issues.

⇜ LOUIS LOWDOWN ⇝

> After an elementary school performance, one of the other families invited us for a picnic. The kids rode bikes, while the parents set out the lunch. Everything looked set for a pleasant day, except for the fact that the other mum was a stickler for impeccable table manners. The kids took a while to settle down after returning from their bike ride. They chattered away, laughing and yelling, when suddenly the mother slammed her hand down on the table and shouted at the top of her lungs, "WOULD YOU PLEASE HAVE SOME SELF-CONTROL?!" While the four children had admittedly been a bit noisy, the mother's reaction was completely over the top. My children were shocked—they had never witnessed an adult acting this way in public. I half-expected my daughter to make a wise crack about "who's the one who needs self-control", but luckily, she kept her mouth shut. The woman's husband and children were embarrassed. Needless to say, we didn't go on any more picnics with that family... All that drama over table manners!

Sterling, who is around 40 years old, remembers that when she was young, her mother expected everything to be perfect; so Sterling was petrified of doing anything wrong. One evening, as the family was getting ready to go out for dinner, Sterling's mother yelled at her for taking too long to put on her shoes. In a panic, Sterling put her shoes on the wrong feet. In the car, the yelling continued because her mother then berated her not only for being slow, but also for being stupid enough to confuse her left foot with her right. Sterling was so upset and traumatised by the event that to this day, she can still remember how she felt. Her belittling and controlling mother had completely overreacted to Sterling's "mistake", if indeed anyone could call that a "mistake".

Each day, after coming home from work, Marco's father would watch his son do his homework. After Marco completed it, his dad would test him to see if he knew his work. On several occasions, when Marco did not quite grasp the material, his father would beat him. Marco ended up hating school, studying only to please his father and escape punishment. Due to burnout, Marco eventually dropped out of school, traumatised by his father who overreacted when it came to homework.

So many parents overreact to their children's mistakes—you would think their entire world were coming to an end. A good question to ask would be, "What's the worst thing that can happen?" Really, what concerns are worth worrying about? Is the child's well-being or health in jeopardy, for example? Is he very sick? Does he have to be admitted to a hospital? Does the child have to be taken to the police? Has the child committed grievous hurt against another? Most of the time, 90% of our worries and concerns do not even come true. Even if they do, what is the worst possible outcome?

Let's look back at our examples: What would be the worst-case scenario of a child taking a bit more time to get dressed? You might be a bit late for dinner! And if you have to catch a flight, one of the parents could help dress the child on the way. Is that such a bad thing? The parents could use the car ride to have a great time singing as a family, or if the appointment were not so urgent, the parents could have allowed time for the child to get dressed herself and then praised her for doing a great job. A wonderful experience is lost because the parent's reaction is disproportionate to the mistake made.

What is the worst-case scenario if a child cannot remember all the material he has studied? Not to worry—he just needs to keep working and eventually he will get there. And should he fail a test, he will learn how to do better next time. Is this situation worth imprinting a negative emotional scar on your child?

What is the worst-case scenario of making too much noise at a picnic lunch? This was not a sit-down Christmas dinner at a five-star hotel! A wonderful time of interactions, picture-taking, and laughter during lunch was all spoilt by an end-of-the-world attitude. Having perfect manners was a huge issue for that mother; there was very little room for mistakes, grace, or a learning curve in her household.

⟨ LOUIS LOWDOWN ⟩

When I (John) was young, I was not a good student at all. I often got red marks in my report card (that's local for "Failure"). Once I was so petrified that my parents would see it that I practised signing my dad's signature and forged it so that my dad wouldn't see how badly I had done. Unfortunately, my mother asked to see the report card. (Why does that always happen?) When I showed it to her, she asked my dad if he had signed it and he denied it. I knew I was in trouble. My dad took a look at the card, but instead of shouting at me, he marvelled at how well I had copied his signature! I heard him laugh, which also helped my mother's mood, who then joined in. Though my dad did confront me later and challenge me to do better, it was nothing more than that. I appreciated the way my dad handled the situation; I decided to change, and I certainly never forged his signature again!

Children will make mistakes; so will adults. The "damage" that these kids cause is typically nothing compared to the damage that the parents inflict on their children, considering the fact that the latter will still remember these incidents as adults while the former will not.

There are many reasons why adults overreact. One aforementioned reason is that they have issues themselves—lifetraps that get triggered. Moreover, parents think that only by making a big deal about the mistakes will their children learn from them. Yet, the opposite is true—parents acting in a way that is completely disproportionate to their children's mistakes discourages children. The good news is that when parents choose to remain calm and non-judgmental, it is astounding how much children can learn.

As any entrepreneur or inventor knows, mistakes are an opportunity for teaching, bonding, and connecting. Mistakes, when not viewed negatively by parents, can lead both sides to engage in meaningful conversation, with everyone reflecting together. Both parent and child can turn the entire situation into laughter (not laughing *at* the child); a potentially heavy moment is transformed into a light moment. This approach is so much more effective than turning small mistakes into lifelong scars.

So let us seek to transform day-to-day mistakes into discussions in which the child learns; at times, the very nature of these discussions may even lead to laughter and light moments. Through mistakes and taking calculated risks here and there, our children will learn to spread their wings. They will be boys and girls, and eventually adults, who are neither compliant nor defiant; they will acknowledge their strengths and limitations, be intrinsically motivated, and embrace life with zest and enthusiasm.

─── ❦ **LOUIS LOWDOWN** ❧ ───

> I (Karen) attended a small West Texas farming community high school with a graduating class of 40 kids. In my sophomore year, I took Chemistry, even though I had absolutely no interest in the subject whatsoever. When the end-of-quarter exam came, the teacher gave all the top students an exemption, so only a few other non-science types and I took the test. I scored 57/100 (the passing grade was 60), and I worried about how I would tell my dad. My parents had always encouraged us to do well in school, but they were not overbearing in the least. However, since I had never flunked any exam before, and since my dad had always made good grades himself, I approached telling my father about the "F" with trepidation. The ensuing conversation went like this:
>
> Karen (with a hopeful smile): *Dad, we got our exams back this week. I've got some good news and some bad news.*
>
> Dad: *Tell me the good news.*

Karen: *The good news is that I scored the highest grade in the class on my Chemistry final.*

Dad (with a surprised look): *Well, that is good news. And what's the bad news?*

Karen (looking a bit sheepish): *It was a 57.*

Dad (silence): *...Well, I've only got one thing to say.*

Karen (hesitatingly): *What's that?*

Dad (with a cheeky smile): *When you go to college one day, you'd better major in business so you don't have to take any science classes!*

Karen (relieved): *Thanks, Dad!*

What a wonderful story of a father with realistic expectations (in this case, extremely realistic!) and a daughter who benefited from having her core emotional needs met. (I've said many times before that my first question to God one day will be "Why did I get such nice parents?")

The sequel to this story is that, years later, while pursuing my Master's degree in counselling, I attended a lecture about helping children deal with stress. The Australian lecturer asked for volunteers from the audience to share a personal story of how they dealt with failure. I shared the story above, and when I got to the punch line, *"Well, I've only got one thing to say... When you go to college one day, you'd better major in business so you don't have to take any science classes!"*, the crowd of over 100 people burst into spontaneous applause! The moral of this story is: most mistakes are definitely not the end of the world.

SECTION SIX

The Plus-One Core Emotional Need for
Spiritual Values and Community

So that's the four core emotional needs. What's the Plus One?

CHAPTER EIGHTEEN

Spiritual Values and Community

Meeting the Plus One Core Emotional Need for Spiritual Values and Community in a *Christian* context can be defined as helping our children have a connection with God The Father, God The Son, and God The Holy Spirit based on the teachings of the Bible, as well as a connection with like-minded people in the family of God, the body of Christ, which is His church.

❖ MOVIE MOMENT – *Sister Act 2*[1] ❖

A fun visual for this core emotional need is a scene from the movie *Sister Act 2*. Whoopi Goldberg plays a nightclub singer-turned-nun who is helping the kids in a Catholic school get their groove on for the purpose of winning a singing contest so they can keep the school open for another year. The teenagers perform a hip-hop version of the classical hymn, *Joyful Joyful*, with rap and break dancing included which, combined with the meaningful lyrics of praise to God, is an audio-visual delight, and a real representation of what spiritual values and community might look like.

In order for the core emotional need for spiritual values and community to be met satisfactorily, children need to *consistently* and *on an emotional level* hear and believe the following messages from and/or about their parents:

- *They love God and their relationship with God is their number one priority.*
- *They base their lives on God's word and the principles therein, and they expect my siblings and me to do the same.*
- *They want me to have a relationship with God because they love me and want the best for me, but they want me to do that with my own personal convictions.*
- *My parents love and truly enjoy being part of the church community.*
- *They make sure that I get to spend lots of time with my friends from church as well as letting me go for sleepovers with trustworthy and safe families.*
- *They encourage me to go to Christian camps and meet Christian kids from other cities and even other countries.*

> *They encourage me to help the less fortunate, read my Bible and pray, and share about God with my friends if I am comfortable doing so.*

Sherry grew up going to church and loved being a part of the kids' class on Sundays. She enjoyed visiting with everyone who came to their home for small group Bible discussions, and listened from the next room when her mum did Bible studies with women from the neighbourhood. The older of two children, she was happy when the whole family moved to be a different state to be part of a mission team. Sherry is a sweet girl who loves people and loves connecting. Her father is uncomfortable with emotions; he tends to be distant with Sherry and does not spend much time with her. Sherry's mother is a no-nonsense straight-talker who prefers logic to feelings. Therefore, Sherry finds it difficult to connect with her parents and in her teenage years, sought intimate relationships elsewhere. Unfortunately, there were not any teens in the mission team so she eventually lost her zeal for going to church and began hanging out with friends from school who were not all that interested in what the Bible had to say. She became sexually active before leaving high school. Her mother confided, "It never dawned on me that Sherry would not just naturally love God. I have loved God in my heart since I was a little girl."

Robert's parents are zealous Christians who love God and the Bible. They gave up their jobs in the secular world to be full time ministers when Robert was young, and they truly try to practise what they preach. After Robert hit puberty, he and his father clashed almost daily, partially because of some unresolved issues in Robert's father's life, and partially because of the strife that usually occurs when children grow up and "become sinners." Everything that Robert said seemed to trigger his dad's lifetraps. Since they both tend toward the overcompensation coping style, Robert and his dad entered into vortexes very quickly. The day he turned eighteen, Robert declared himself "free" and moved out, preferring to sleep in a tent on the beach rather than be near his father. Everyone at church felt sorry for the dad, but Robert's mother would cry herself to sleep at night, knowing that it was not just Robert's fault, and fearing for her son's safety and salvation.

Immeasurable heartache and confusion hit us when we read stories like those above. As we said in the introduction, kids are not science projects. Inasmuch as there is no equation that will ensure your kids are successful (whatever that may mean to you) or even emotionally healthy, there is also no guarantee that your children will choose to make Jesus their Lord. In fact, parents whose children are faithful followers of Christ will tell you that it happened mostly because of the grace of God, and that they are just grateful that they did a few things well. However, that is not what young parents want to hear. They want to know what to do. All we can say is that by meeting *all* of the core needs, you are giving your child the best possible chance to be all they can be, have great relationships with you and others, and become a Christian. If things are getting rocky, seek help from others who have made it through difficult times as well as ask yourself (or maybe have someone ask your child) where is harm being caused in the relationship. Then, after reading this chapter, read Chapter Twenty-Two about Repair and Reconnect. We believe that by doing that, you will *eventually* be able to meet this final core need, the plus one core emotional need for spiritual values and community.

(Whether or not your child responds in the way you hope, you as the parent should try to meet all the needs, and let God do the rest. Honestly, some children may just need to follow Jesus later in order to really get it—only God knows. Being down on yourself, down on your child, or down on others because of their situation goes against the very idea of meeting core emotional needs!)

What do we know about the core emotional need for spiritual values and community? Both in the Old and New Testament, God commands us to impart spiritual values to our children that encompass every facet of life. This takes being purposeful and committed. When parents are passive, their children's sinful natures are allowed to be controlled by the world and their lives are led by the flesh instead of the Spirit.

> *So I say, live by the Spirit, and you will not gratify the desires of the sinful nature. For the sinful nature desires what is contrary to the Spirit, and the Spirit what is contrary to the sinful nature. They are in conflict with each other, so that you do not do what you want. But if you are led by the Spirit, you are not under law.* (Galatians 5:16-18)

We want our children to live lives that are free, not under law, but in accordance with the Spirit of God. The best way we know to help them get there goes back to the days of Moses, the teaching that Jewish families literally posted on their doorframes.

> *These are the commands, decrees and laws the Lord your God directed me to teach you to observe in the land that you are crossing the Jordan to possess, so that you, your children and their children after them may fear the Lord your God as long as you live by keeping all his decrees and commands that I give you, and so that you may enjoy long life. Hear, O Israel, and be careful to obey so that it may go well with you and that you may increase greatly in a land flowing with milk and honey, just as the Lord, the God of your fathers, promised you. Hear, O Israel: The LORD our God, the LORD is one. Love the LORD your God with all your heart and with all your soul and with all your strength. These commandments that I give you today are to be upon your hearts. Impress them on your children. Talk about them when you sit at home and when you walk along the road, when you lie*

> *down and when you get up. Tie them as symbols on your hands and bind them on your foreheads. Write them on the doorframes of your houses and on your gates.* (Deuteronomy 6:1-9)

In the New Testament, Jesus encapsulated this teaching succinctly, as related in Mark 12:29-31, after he was asked about the greatest commandment:

> *"The most important one," answered Jesus, "is this: 'Hear, O Israel, the Lord our God, the Lord is one. Love the Lord your God with all your heart and with all your soul and with all your mind and with all your strength.' The second is this: 'Love your neighbour as yourself.' There is no commandment greater than these."*

The apostle Paul referred back to the Torah when by the Holy Spirit he wrote:

> *Children, obey your parents in the Lord, for this is right. "Honour your father and mother"—which is the first commandment with a promise—"that it may go well with you and that you may enjoy long life on the earth." Fathers, do not exasperate your children; instead, bring them up in the training and instruction of the Lord.* (Ephesians 6:1-4)

We will be referring to these passages over and over again in this section. Raising children up in the Lord is not about getting them to go through a course. As God says in Deuteronomy, meeting this core emotional need has to do with our lives and lifestyle—it may sound cliché, but it is true that values are "caught" more than "taught". God gives us innumerable opportunities during the limited years we have with our children. We must mindfully and intentionally make use of these opportunities as they present themselves in order to mould our children's thinking and impart godly values so that they can be inoculated against the onslaught of the world as early as possible. If you think we sound dramatic, please reflect on modern pop culture of the second decade in the new millennium and tell us there is no onslaught. For the rest of this section, we will look at teaching from Deuteronomy plus the passages above from Mark and Ephesians for some invaluable parenting insights.

Deuteronomy was God's second chance with the Hebrews. He had given them the Ten Commandments in Exodus as they left Egypt, but because of the peoples' rebellion, chronicled in Number 14, Moses had to influence a new generation. The book is Moses giving the second telling of God's plan, with added stories of things that had happened over the past 40 years. Written as a summation of recent history and the books of the law, with a view toward instructing the adults who had just been children when leaving Egypt, it is filled with some of Moses' private memories, and also has some beautifully expressed sentiments about our divine romance with God.[2]

Moses begins by reminding the younger generation what he had told the faithless spies and their followers who had all died in the desert during their forty years of wandering (cf. Numbers 14):

And the little ones that you said would be taken captive, your children who do not yet know good from bad—they will enter the land. I will give it to them and they will take possession of it. (Deuteronomy 1:39)

Using our kids as an excuse for not leading a sacrificial life may well lead us to separation from God. In the case of the Israelites, most of their kids did eventually make it, but how sad that it was without mum and dad!

In Deuteronomy 5-8, God repeats some of the laws one more time for this new generation. Moses would be dead one month later. This is his second address in a week to the new generation and you can tell he feels the burden to "impress these things on their hearts." This is a book imploring the people to remember! We have the Bible in so many forms. We can take it in our handbags, briefcases, laptops, tablets, and smart phones. They didn't have such luxury. They had to remember!

Take a few minutes to read Deuteronomy 5 and then take a look at a modern day version of the Ten Commandments that we wrote for Singapore (but if the shoe fits where you live…)

1. I am the Lord your God who brought you out of darkness and your slavery to sin. Therefore, don't love anything more than me in your heart, mind, speech and/or actions.

2. Don't make an idol or worship an image in the form of anything, whether it is a bank account, a monetary note, an apartment or house, a "branded" school, a particular job, a football team, a relationship, a car, or any other object of desire. Why? Because I the Lord am a jealous God, punishing the children for the sin of the fathers to the third and fourth generation but showing love to a thousand generations of those who love me and keep my commands.

3. Don't take my name in vain, either as a joke, or as an expression of surprise, shock or anger, not even in a foreign tongue. It is rude and I won't hold anyone guiltless who misuses my name.

4. Remember that you cannot serve both God and money. Work is not supposed to take up your time and thoughts 24/7. Set apart time that is sacred just for me and for your family. Use that time for reflection and for your loved ones, and use your home as a way to love others. This is a trust issue—you must believe that you will be okay as long as you work hard during the time you do spend at work.

5. Give honour to your parents. If you are a child at home, obey them! If your parents are older, love them, forgive them and spend time with them. Listen to them and never neglect them. If you are a young adult, please show respect to your parents even though you now know that they are not "perfect". They brought you up and they deserve your honour. I am a God who believes in giving honour where honour is due. (And you really will live longer!)

6. Don't commit murder, and don't make excuses and give in to the temptation to follow the world on issues like euthanasia and abortion. I am a God who respects life, and only I have power to give life and take it away.

7. Don't commit adultery. Be true to your spouse. Don't lust after others or flirt, whether it is at work, with friends or on the computer. Don't be easy on yourself if this area, and be open when you are tempted. If you are married, be giving to each other emotionally and sexually. If you are having marriage problems, work out your differences, get counselling if you need to, but don't cheat on each other—and remember that all cheaters eventually get caught! If you are single, train yourself now to be faithful in the future. I am watching, and I am a faithful God.

8. Don't steal. Whether it's money or possessions, time, or intellectual property rights, just don't steal. Be honest and have integrity. I am a God of Truth.

9. Don't lie about others, especially to cause them harm or get them in trouble! You will be judged harshly if you do this, for I am a just God.

10. Last but not least, don't be jealous and envious of what your fellow Singaporeans have (or what your fellow global citizens have, for that matter). Pluck out your jealous, envious, greedy, ungrateful eye and realize that you actually have a great life. Appreciate My blessings and be grateful!!!

After Egypt, the Israelites had had the right response, but they had not changed deeply enough to make it stick. They had not gone through what Paul would later call (in Ephesians 4:22-24) "being made new in the attitude of your mind". Maybe God decided the younger generation needed forty years in the wilderness to transform their "world view" or "belief system." As a parent, are you really making God your number one priority? Do your kids see God's "**Ten**(der) **Commandments**" being lived out in your home?

Moses closed out chapter five with heart-rending words:
> The LORD heard you when you spoke to me and the LORD said to me, "I have heard what this people said to you. Everything they said was good. Oh, that their hearts would be inclined to fear me and keep all my commands always, so that it might go well with them and their children forever ...

So be careful to do what the LORD your God has commanded you; do not turn aside to the right or to the left. Walk in all the way that the LORD your God has commanded you, so that you may live and prosper and prolong your days in the land that you will possess..."

What is God's will for parents? That our hearts would always be inclined to fear Him and keep His commands, and that we would pass this down to our children. He knows if we are like this as individuals and as a married couple, then our lives and our children's lives will be blessed. This is in essence the theme of Deuteronomy, Moses' last hurrah, so to speak. Now we come to our theme verse, 6:4-9.

Hear, O Israel: The Lord our God, the Lord is one. Love the Lord your God with all your heart and with all your soul and with all your strength.

Isn't it fun to read this famous passage in context? The Jews call this "the *Shema*" which means, "Hear" or "Listen up", since it's their most famous passage and begins with that as its first word. Obviously Jesus uses it as the first part of his answer to the question, "What's the greatest commandment?" Loving God with our heart, our soul, our mind and our strength is the basis for all that we do as disciples of Jesus; part of meeting this core emotional need is helping our children to get to the same place with God.

These commandments that I give you today are to be upon your hearts. Impress them on your children. Talk about them when you sit at home and when you walk along the road, when you lie down and when you get up. Tie them as symbols on your hands and bind them on your foreheads. Write them on the doorframes of your houses and on your gates.

We are literally supposed to be constantly meditating on God, talking about God, helping our children to "feel" and experience God; making God alive in our kids' lives. It's common knowledge that people talk about the things that are on their hearts. When we were growing up, our parents talked about many things, especially education and religion (John) and politics and handling finances (Karen). These topics came out during dinner, while they were reading the paper, as we watched television together, and when we were driving in the car as a family. These conversations were not necessarily planned, but they were certainly effective in shaping our worldviews. All the more when we are talking about the number one love of our lives—the Creator of the Universe, the Lamb of God, the Alpha and Omega, the Ancient of Days, the Lord of All. As parents, we must always ask ourselves if our conversations with our children reflect this. What of our speech and lifestyle is being impressed on our kids? If we want to meet the core emotional need for spiritual values, it must be our relationship with God.

> ### ⸙ MASTER CLASS ⸙
>
> Jeanie Shaw says, "I never questioned that God was first in my parents' lives. I felt loved and secure in that. My dad had a demanding job, but his love and preoccupation was for God, his family, and the church." Bill and Sally Hooper's son, David, who serves as an evangelist in a congregation in Texas, said the word he would use to describe his parents is "authentic". When he was growing up, he said he saw that, "their faith was 'authentic'; it was real. They lived what they believed." Kevin, son of John and Nancy Mannel, said that he knew his parents' priorities, "I never doubted their love for me and my siblings, and I never doubted that they would do anything including quitting their jobs and moving or even getting out of the full-time ministry, if it meant the best for our family's spiritual well-being. They prioritised their relationship with God, their marriage, and their kids way more than their jobs." All three of the Baird daughters told their parents that they were influenced by the priority that Al and Gloria put on their walk with God and their marriage.

When parents are meeting the four core emotional needs, and combine that with meeting the plus one core emotional need for spiritual values and community, the child will develop some or all of the following fruit of the Spirit as listed in Galatians 5:22-23: "...*love, joy, peace, patience, kindness, goodness, faithfulness, gentleness and self-control...*"

If children are connected with their parents, they will *usually* want to imitate the values of their parents. Children who see their parents modelling the fruit of the Spirit will admire those qualities themselves. Parents sometimes feel like this process is endless but eventually, the kids will get it.

If parents *are not* meeting the other core emotional needs, it will be hard to meet the plus one need. Why? *Because the child will feel exasperated; he will therefore have a hard time respecting his parents' faith and values, and being drawn to the community.* Worse still, the child will be more inclined to develop some or many of the lifetraps already discussed in this book, which somewhat reflect the acts of the sinful nature from Galatians 5:19-21 or those seen in 2 Timothy 3:1-5.

> *The acts of the sinful nature are obvious: sexual immorality, impurity and debauchery; idolatry and witchcraft; hatred, discord, jealousy, fits of rage, selfish ambition, dissensions, factions and envy; drunkenness, orgies, and the like. I warn you, as I did before, that those who live like this will not inherit the kingdom of God.* (Galatians 5:19-21)
>
> *But mark this: There will be terrible times in the last days. People will be lovers of themselves, lovers of money, boastful, proud, abusive,*

disobedient to their parents, ungrateful, unholy, without love, unforgiving, slanderous, without self-control, brutal, not lovers of the good, treacherous, rash, conceited, lovers of pleasure rather than lovers of God—having a form of godliness but denying its power. Have nothing to do with them. (2 Timothy 3:1-5)

Case Study

Growing up in California, Rose was her mother's pride and joy. When she enrolled in a preschool, everyone there as well as at church thought she was adorable and ahead of her peers developmentally. Rose's mother later confessed that she looked down on the other children at church for not being as smart as her daughter, and assumed it was the parents' fault for only caring about spirituality instead of educational pursuits. Because of this attitude, she was not urgent about making sure her daughter spent time with other children from their church family. However, as Rose started elementary school, she had some behavioural problems and began acting up in class. Rose's teacher complained consistently to Rose's mum about the daughter's disruptive behaviour. Rose's mother felt helpless but also felt that the school did not cater enough for her child's needs.

When the teachers in her church's Sunday school programme expressed their concerns, she pulled Rose out from Sunday School instead of working through her issues. She felt the teachers were singling Rose out unnecessarily, and that the lessons were not captivating enough for her exceptionally bright daughter. Rose is now a teenager, has no friends at church and does not see the need to be a part of the church family and events. She feels closer to the kids she hangs out with at school, most of whom have unfortunately given up on academics and are close to dropping out. However, this is one circle of friends with whom Rose feels that at least she belongs.

Harry is an only child. His parents have always been active at church, including serving as Sunday school coordinators, and Harry has grown up going to church several times a week. Harry's father has always adored him and been completely dedicated to him. When Harry was younger, his father drove him everywhere upon demand, never hesitating to buy the boy his favourite snack or surprise him with the latest gadgets. Whenever Harry complained about anything, his father gave in immediately, since Harry's happiness was his top priority.

When Harry entered his teen years, he was heavily involved in school activities and started drifting away from his church friends. Harry's father did not seem concerned, since he was glad to see his son excelling academically. The dad felt it would be fine for his son to get serious about God in college, since that is when he himself had become a Christian. Eventually, Harry also became moody and withdrawn, even distancing himself from his dad, and had absolutely no interest in attending church services at all. Before his father knew it, Harry had become a Goth, completely changing his appearance and his friends. Harry's father felt helpless as he could no longer reach his son, and there were no other kids in church with whom Harry wanted to spend time. He has not been in touch with the church community for a while and feels that no one can relate to him now.

In these examples, the parents were passing down their own dysfunction, instead of spiritual values. In the next chapter we will spell out what we feel are the spiritual values we should teach, model for, and impress on our children from birth. And now we will revisit the patriarchs one last time, keeping in mind the phrase, "Dysfunction is the gift that keeps on giving".

⟨ DYSFUNCTION IN THE PATRIARCHS ⟩

When we look at the dysfunction in Abraham's family life, in Isaac's, in Jacob's and in his sons', we can clearly see that the dysfunction was passed down through four generations. This dysfunction indicates the ways in which the parents in each generation deprived their own children of the core emotional needs, and the way these children then imitated their parents and repeated the dysfunctional cycle.

1. Favouritism

Let's see how favouritism developed and was passed down from the first generation through the fourth.

First Generation: Abraham (Genesis 21:8-11)

The child grew and was weaned, and on the day Isaac was weaned Abraham held a great feast. But Sarah saw that the son whom Hagar the Egyptian had borne to Abraham was mocking, and she said to Abraham, "Get rid of that slave woman and her son, for that slave woman's son will never share in the inheritance with my son Isaac." The matter distressed Abraham greatly because it concerned his son.

Second Generation: Isaac (Genesis 25:27-28)

The boys grew up, and Esau became a skilful hunter, a man of the open country, while Jacob was a quiet man, staying among the tents. Isaac, who had a taste for wild game, loved Esau, but Rebekah loved Jacob.

Third Generation: Jacob (Genesis 37:3-4)

Now Israel loved Joseph more than any of his other sons, because he had been born to him in his old age; and he made a richly ornamented robe for him. *When his brothers saw that their father loved him more than any of them, they hated him and could not speak a kind word to him.*

Fourth Generation: Joseph (Genesis 48:17-18)

When Joseph saw his father placing his right hand on Ephraim's head he was displeased; so he took hold of his father's hand to move it from Ephraim's head to Manasseh's head. Joseph said to him, "No, my father, this one is the firstborn; put your right hand on his head."

Favouritism was passed down all the way, from one generation to the next, and in each generation they paid the price for it. The families got involved in conflict, husband and wife, siblings with one another, all fighting to get the most attention and approval.

2. Strain on the Marital Relationship

In each generation, it seems that marital relationships were fine until children entered into the picture.

First Generation: Genesis 21:10-11

"Get rid of that slave woman and her son, for that slave woman's son will never share in the inheritance with my son Isaac." The matter distressed Abraham greatly because it concerned his son.

Second Generation: Genesis 27:5-10

Now Rebekah was listening as Isaac spoke to his son Esau. When Esau left for the open country to hunt game and bring it back, Rebekah said to her son Jacob, "Look, I overheard your father say to your brother Esau, 'Bring me some game and prepare me some tasty food to eat, so that I may give you my blessing in the presence of the LORD before I die.' Now, my son, listen carefully and do what I tell you: Go out to the flock and bring me two choice young goats, so I can prepare some tasty food for your father, just the way he likes it. Then take it to your father to eat, so that he may give you his blessing before he dies."

Third Generation: Genesis 30:1-3

When Rachel saw that she was not bearing Jacob any children, she became jealous of her sister. So she said to Jacob, "Give me children, or I'll die!" Jacob became angry with her and said, "Am I in the place of God, who has kept you from having children?" Then she said, "Here is Bilhah, my maidservant. Sleep with her so that she can bear children for me and that through her I too can build a family."

The arrival of children changed the dynamics of their marriage. Abraham and Sarah were holding down the fort, even though Sarah was barren for years, but when children arrived, conflicts ensued.

The early days between Isaac and Rebekah were romantic. Isaac really loved Rebekah, as we see in Genesis 24:67, which tells us, *"Isaac brought her into the tent of his mother Sarah, and he married Rebekah. So she became his wife, and he loved her; and Isaac was comforted after his mother's death."*

It is speculative, but seems logical that their marriage would have suffered at least a bit as a result of each of them taking sides with their respective favourite children and not getting this repaired. If this is true, then their lack of marriage harmony, in turn, would have affected their relationships with their children. For Isaac and Rebekah, this conflict split the family. We do not get the impression that this issue got settled. In fact, Rebekah disappeared from the pages of the Bible thereafter.

And consider the conflicts Jacob had with Rachel and Leah, which were centred on the number of children each sister was able to have.

3. Handling Conflict

<u>First Generation: Abraham (Genesis 21:10-11,14)</u>

...and she said to Abraham, "Get rid of that slave woman and her son, for that slave woman's son will never share in the inheritance with my son Isaac." The matter distressed Abraham greatly because it concerned his son. Early the next morning Abraham took some food and a skin of water and gave them to Hagar. He set them on her shoulders and then sent her off with the boy. She went on her way and wandered in the desert of Beersheba.

<u>Second Generation: Isaac (Genesis 27:42-43)</u>

When Rebekah was told what her older son Esau had said, she sent for her younger son Jacob and said to him, "Your brother Esau is consoling himself with the thought of killing you. Now then, my son, do what I say: Flee at once to my brother Laban in Haran."

<u>Third Generation: Jacob (Genesis 37:26-27)</u>

Judah said to his brothers, "What will we gain if we kill our brother and cover up his blood? Come, let's sell him to the Ishmaelites and not lay our hands on him; after all, he is our brother, our own flesh and blood." His brothers agreed.

Unresolved conflicts ensued which were not dealt with satisfactorily. If it happened at all, it took years before some of the conflicts were repaired and forgiveness rendered by both sides. For example, Esau and Jacob were reconciled after being estranged for twenty years! It took even longer for the rift between Joseph and his brothers to be settled, and that took divine intervention. How many years of close intimacy had been lost as a result of unresolved conflict? When people refuse to take responsibility for their issues, they are alienating themselves from the other members of their family. It is a huge price to pay. As a result of unresolved conflicts, even the relationships between each parent and his or her favourite child was affected, at least in Rebekah's case, since she never saw Jacob again. We also see that Jacob's relationship with Joseph, his favourite, also was affected greatly as a result of tension between the siblings. Unresolved conflict is just not worth it.

4. Children Living in Hostility

First Generation: Abraham (Genesis 25:18b)

His descendants settled in the area from Havilah to Shur, near the border of Egypt, as you go toward Asshur. And they lived in hostility toward all their brothers.

Second Generation: Isaac (Genesis 27:41)

Esau held a grudge against Jacob because of the blessing his father had given him. He said to himself, "The days of mourning for my father are near; then I will kill my brother Jacob."

Third Generation: Jacob (Genesis 45:4-5)

Then Joseph said to his brothers, "Come close to me." When they had done so, he said, "I am your brother Joseph, the one you sold into Egypt! And now, do not be distressed and do not be angry with yourselves for selling me here, because it was to save lives that God sent me ahead of you.

The siblings in each generation, as mentioned above, took years before they repaired their relationships. In the case of Ishmael and Isaac, there never seems to have been any reconciliation. Separation as a result of such hostility took away the joy that can come from being together. How many wonderful years of closeness and intimacy can get lost as a result?

As parents, we need to break the unhealthy cycle that we may unwittingly continue by imitating what our parents may have modelled for us. This comes when we take steps to be spiritual instead of imitating the dysfunction in our family of origin. In the end, when we surrender to God's will, it will be our spirituality that will unleash the power to effectively break our dysfunction and sinful nature with all of its lifetraps and unhealthy coping styles. Transformation that is rooted in our relationship with God and bolstered by meaningful relationships with other spiritual people is what will give us the power to put an end to generations of unhealthy cycles that continue to be passed on from one generation to the next.

We were all born with the inclination to sin, which was passed on to us, starting from Adam. Unless there is intervention, we will pass these on to our offspring, some to a greater extent than others. We are bent towards sinning. No one has to teach us how to sin, we all just naturally know how to do so. As we age, we follow the course of our sinful nature. If we allow our sinful nature to take charge, then we will turn further and further away from God. Sin will then master us and control our lives with disastrous effects. Only the power of God through the Holy Spirit can truly rescue us from this unhealthy cycle that causes us and others harm. So we need to heed the instructions given in His word to change the natural course of ourselves and that of our children. It is our God-given duty as stated both in the New Testament (Ephesians 6:4) and in the Old Testament (Deuteronomy 6:4-9). Considering both Scriptures together, we see how clearly the responsibility is with the parents to break unhealthy cycles, embrace spiritual values, and raise our children up in a godly way.

*How do I know

which spiritual values

are the most important?*

CHAPTER NINETEEN

Spiritual Values

After researching the topic "What Do Parents Want?" for 10 years (1973-1983), therapist and best-selling author Peter Levine found that the top three qualities that most parents want in their children are honesty, having good sense and good judgment, and being obedient to their parents —only 3% chose being studious.[1] It looks like in the deep recesses of their hearts, parents value values! It is interesting that both honesty and obedience stem from teaching children proper limits, moral limits as well as being able to follow rules and instructions.

In a more recent survey (March 2012) done on a cross section of Singapore's population, analysts asked over 800 residents what virtues were most important to them. In order of priority here were the results: Honesty, kindness, gratitude, fairness, forgiveness, empathy, love of learning, principle, hope, self-control, humility, perseverance, open-mindedness, energy, humour, courage, spirituality, creativity, appreciation of beauty and excellence, and curiosity.[2] We were encouraged to see in a nation that prides itself on excellence and achievements, the virtues with the highest rankings had to do with traits accompanying good character.

Parents used to know inherently that if children learned to obey when they were young, they would reap the benefits later in life; they knew that children who had little respect for limits would end up becoming adults who had little respect for anyone. Nowadays, for many parents, teaching their children values, and the limits that come with having values—even getting children to obey simple rules at home and at school—has been made confusing by modern culture, and has brought its own set of heartaches, stress and frustrations.

When some parents think of spiritual values, they think the goal is to raise "good children." Dr. Diana Baumrind, best known for coining the terms "authoritarian, permissive and authoritative parenting styles", believes that the goal of parenting is to develop character and a sense of competence.[3] We agree with her; however, when we think about the goals in the Christian context, the bar is a lot higher. Here we are not just talking about being good, but being godly, and there is a marked difference between the two.

> *"Love the Lord your God with all your heart and with all your soul and with all your mind and with all your strength.' The second is this: 'Love your neighbour as yourself.' There is no commandment greater than these."*
> (Mark 12:30-31, quoting Deuteronomy 6:5 and Leviticus 19:18b)

There are many good people who are simply not interested in God, but they are very good moral people. They believe in being faithful to their wives, they love their children, they work hard at their jobs, and they volunteer to help the poor and needy. They are good people, but God is far from their minds. As Christian parents, our goal is different. We have to help our children to not just become good people but also to embrace God and the Scriptures; to love God with all of their heart, soul, mind and strength and to love their neighbours as themselves. This is a high calling and it is not easy.

Again, it is not about raising up children to be good. As Christians, we ultimately want our children to be like Jesus. We do not want to "settle" for them having the conviction to "be good"—to not lie, steal, cheat at school, or hit other children when they are unhappy. Instead, we want to see them loving what God loves and hating what God hates. Right and wrong must stem from the Scriptures, not from what is not acceptable to others. They must be drawn to the gospel. As their parents, we must creatively find ways to make spirituality attractive to them, more attractive than the world. We believe that if we live out these principles ourselves, and practice "impressing these things on our children", they will eventually be able to salvation and live "life to the full" as put forth by our Creator in the Scriptures.

We put forward seven spiritual values that we feel parents need to impart to their children if they are going to be able to meet the plus one core emotional need for spiritual values and community. These values are the way that children view God, God's word, themselves, right and wrong, others, conflict and forgiveness, repentance. *The Toddler's Bible* by V. Gilbert Beers[4] is a wonderful way to introduce these values at a very young age, and his accompanying book for parents, *Teaching Toddlers the Bible*,[5] is a classic book on shaping our children's belief systems.

1. The Way Our Children View God

How our children learn to view God will set the foundation for how much they will fall in love with Him. An accurate view of God and His qualities will help children to find the Creator to be endearing. Many adults often have a one-dimensional view of God, e.g., that He is "only" punitive or "only" compassionate. As parents, we need to present the biblical and well-rounded view of God to our children from the time they are born, specifically in (but not limited to) the following areas:

God as Creator

Telling our children about God being the Creator of everything is so exciting. We can take them on nature walks, talk to them about everything that God made, and in light of Deuteronomy 6:4-9, talk about this throughout the day. We can do this in our own backyards, in a garden or park, when we are looking out a window, even when we take them to the zoo. The important thing is that we transfer our *excitement*. Our children will pick up quickly on our conviction and eventually make their own connections about how God is the Creator. Even as they grow older, we should enjoy reminding them of this over and over again. Whether on an everyday run to the grocery store or soccer practice, or on a family holiday in a gorgeous spot, the beauty of creation is a great launching pad from which to talk about the Almighty.

⟨ LOUIS LOWDOWN ⟩

Between the two of us, we have lived in seven countries, and have visited many more as part of our work. Naturally our children have often accompanied us. Over the years, we have shared many times with our children about God's creation from 30,000 feet above the earth, or how God seems so real when the sun shines though an opening in the clouds. One time Karen's father picked us up from the Lubbock, Texas, airport at midnight just as a meteor shower was due. He drove us back to his home on a dark, flat, country road, and stopped just so we could all get out and take a look at God's fireworks show. How many times have we quoted Psalm 14:1, in one form or another, that only a fool would say there is no God? Even when the children were babies, we had nature prayer walks with them in their baby strollers, where we would let them feel the tall grass, rub up against the bark of a tree, crush and smell leaves, sniff the flowers, and clap in wonder when they saw a butterfly. Our goal was to help them be in awe of the God of creation before they could talk. According to our friends who picked us up at an airport one evening, the first words out of our kindergarten-aged son were, *"You should have seen the sunset from the airplane. It's hard to imagine that some people don't believe in God!"*

God Is Good

Luke 11:11-13, Acts 17:24-25 and James 1:17 all refer to the good gifts that God gives. Our heavenly Father is inherently good, both in His qualities and in the way that He treats those whom He loves. Let us go back to Deuteronomy.

> *When the Lord your God brings you into the land he swore to your fathers, to Abraham, Isaac and Jacob, to give you—a land with large, flourishing cities you did not build, houses filled with all kinds of good things you did not provide, wells you did not dig, and vineyards and olive groves you did not plant—then when you eat and are satisfied, be careful that you do not forget the Lord, who brought you out of Egypt, out of the land of slavery.* (Deuteronomy 6:10-12)

We might well rewrite that passage today along the following lines, "If and when God gives you a Christian spouse, amazing children, an education, a house, a car, and so much more, be careful that you do not forget the Lord, who brought you out of the world in the first place!" Notice how the concepts of remembrance and gratitude continue to recur. It seems that they are related, i.e. the more we remember how sinful, empty, meaningless and selfish our lives were without God, and the more we focus with gratitude on His blessings, the easier time we have loving, fearing and obeying God.

Continuing in Chapter 6 of Deuteronomy we read as follows:

> *In the future, when your son asks you, "What is the meaning of the stipulations, decrees and laws the Lord our God has commanded you?" tell him: "We were slaves of Pharaoh in Egypt, but the Lord brought us out of Egypt with a mighty hand. Before our eyes the Lord sent miraculous signs and wonders—great and terrible—upon Egypt and Pharaoh and his whole household. But he brought us out from there to bring us in and give us the land that he promised on oath to our forefathers. The Lord commanded us to obey all these decrees and to fear the Lord our God, so that we might always prosper and be kept alive, as is the case today. And if we are careful to obey all this law before the Lord our God, as he has commanded us, that will be our righteousness."* (Deuteronomy 6:20-25)

This passage illustrates how God is "The God of Why". It's true that sometimes God wants us to obey, no questions asked, but more often, He cares about the reasons. He wants us to understand and care about the "why" behind things as well. Especially with our children, we should be making meaning out of conversations like this, explaining *what* happened, telling stories about the heroes, the *who* (as in with whom we have been involved), and sharing the *why*. This helps make God real. It is a good thing when our kids ask questions about our faith. And when they do, we should have the answers (1 Peter 3:15). We will have those answers if we are walking with God in His word.

Deuteronomy 10:17-19 reads:

> *For the LORD your God is God of gods and Lord of lords, the great God, mighty and awesome, who shows no partiality and accepts no bribes. He defends the cause of the fatherless and the widow, and loves the alien, giving him food and clothing. And you are to love those who are aliens, for you yourselves were aliens in Egypt.*

If I were the Creator of the Universe, about to write my own book, would I describe myself this way? God is a good God. When we see God's goodness, we trust Him to love us unconditionally and to want what is best for us. This understanding helps us throughout our Christian lives, e.g., one of the reasons we should love our enemies is so that we can be like God.

> *But I tell you: Love your enemies and pray for those who persecute you, that you may be sons of your Father in heaven. He causes his sun to rise on the evil and the good, and sends rain on the righteous*

and the unrighteous. If you love those who love you, what reward will you get? Are not even the tax collectors doing that? And if you greet only your brothers, what are you doing more than others? Do not even pagans do that? Be perfect, therefore, as your heavenly Father is perfect. (Matthew 5:44-48)

As we pray with our children, thanking God for His gifts, we are not only helping them see God's goodness, which will no doubt help them navigate life's difficulties, but we will also be inculcating gratitude. Gratitude is one of the most important qualities for sound mental health as well as perseverance in being a disciple of Jesus. Without it, our vision gets warped, and we forget all the amazing things that have happened to us so far in our Christian life. The following passage comes to mind:

His divine power has given us everything we need for life and godliness through our knowledge of him who called us by his own glory and goodness. Through these he has given us his very great and precious promises, so that through them you may participate in the divine nature and escape the corruption in the world caused by evil desires. For this very reason, make every effort to add to your faith goodness; and to goodness, knowledge; and to knowledge, self-control; and to self-control, perseverance; and to perseverance, godliness; and to godliness, brotherly kindness; and to brotherly kindness, love. For if you possess these qualities in increasing measure, they will keep you from being ineffective and unproductive in your knowledge of our Lord Jesus Christ. But if anyone does not have them, he is near-sighted and blind, and has forgotten that he has been cleansed from his past sins. Therefore, my brothers, be all the more eager to make your calling and election sure. For if you do these things, you will never fall, and you will receive a rich welcome into the eternal kingdom of our Lord and Saviour Jesus Christ. (2 Peter 1:3-10)

◈ LOUIS LOWDOWN ◈

When our children were babies and toddlers, we usually just prayed prayers of thanksgiving to God, and didn't really do much asking. We felt that if they could just get the gratitude part down first, human nature would help them figure out the asking part later. We talked often of God's goodness, and we applied "impressing these things on our children" by practicing something known as meaning attribution. That means we attributed positive and biblical meaning to different life events. This happened almost all the time—we are a very talkative family! We saw this bearing fruit on one occasion when we were spending time with some of Sonia's very "unchurched" school chums and their parents. We were telling a story about friends of ours in California whose entire street had burned in a forest fire but their house was left standing, and Sonia burst out, "That's so God!"

God is Love

As Gene Edwards put it so aptly in his book, *The Divine Romance*, the whole of Deuteronomy is a love letter from God to Israel and us by extension, wooing us to fall in love with Him, so that we would be His Bride.[6]

Consider God's expressiveness and vulnerability in the following passage from Deuteronomy:

The LORD did not set his affection on you and choose you because you were more numerous than other peoples, for you were the fewest of all peoples. But it was because the LORD loved you and kept the oath he swore to your forefathers that he brought you out with a mighty hand and redeemed you from the land of slavery, from the power of Pharaoh king of Egypt. Know therefore that the LORD your God is God; he is the faithful God, keeping his covenant of love to a thousand generations of those who love him and keep his commands. (Deuteronomy 7:7-9)

God is totally a loving God. He doesn't need us to serve Him, but made us so He could love and care for us—even when we cannot see it. Having this understanding will help our children attribute positive meaning to life's uncertainties.

◈ LOUIS LOWDOWN ◈

We knew we had managed to help our daughter feel that God loved her after a rather humorous event during her turbulent preteen years. She was really mad at us for taking away some privileges, and she sat in her room shouting, "Why did God put me in this family? Nobody loves me but God!" We were relieved that at the moment of having such intense and negative emotions, she still had the clarity to remember that God loved her. Now we can all laugh about those times!

God Is to be Feared

All throughout Deuteronomy, Moses exhorts the Hebrews to fear God.

Fear the Lord your God, serve him only and take your oaths in his name. Do not follow other gods, the gods of the peoples around you; for the Lord your God, who is among you, is a jealous God and his anger will burn against you, and he will destroy you from the face of the land. Do not test the Lord your God as you did at Massah. Be sure to keep the commands of the Lord your God and the stipulations and decrees he has given you. Do what is right and good in the Lord's sight, so that it may go well with you and you may go in and take over the good land that the Lord promised on oath to your forefathers, thrusting out all your enemies before you, as the Lord said. (Deuteronomy 6:13-19)

Here is that theme again, that we are to fear God and serve him with all our heart. It is not very popular in Christian circles these days to talk about fearing God and the notion of the joy of fearing God seems oxymoronic. However, Moses seemed to think it was essential for staying faithful. We feel that it is at least as hard to stay faithful these days with the world assaulting us from every direction every day. Holy fear of God is right, and Solomon said in Proverbs 1:7 that it is the beginning of knowledge!

Fearing God is *not* about being so afraid that we do not want to go near Him, as if He were a monster that wants to punish and consume us. Fearing God is about having a healthy sense of fear that comes from realising who and what He is, and then respecting His commands and decrees. God will judge us, and we will have to teach this to our children. God has the right to hold us accountable, and we need to be careful to instil an appropriate sense of respect for Him as the ultimate authority, as well as a healthy respect for God-given authority figures.

2. The Way Our Children View God's Word

◁ MASTER CLASS ▷

> Walter Evans is a big believer in consistent Bible study—he made sure their family had Monday night devotionals every week, no matter what chaos was reigning in the neighbourhood at the time. The Mannel kids remember Monday night devotionals as well. The Hooper kids remember that their father studied the Bible with them when he got home after work; the two older Brumley children related that the foundation of after school Bible studies with mum and the family devotionals led by dad have helped them all their lives to make right decisions and after periods of rebellion, to be drawn back to what was right. The Baird girls have some great stories about memorising Scriptures during dinner, and Jeanie Shaw can still remember doing the same, plus seeing her dad read the Bible every morning. In fact, she says that he spoke so much Bible to her that it became like a first language.

Their Own Bible Study and Prayer Times

Children will need to be trained to have prayer and Bible study time, separate and apart from devotionals. They can start at a young age using children's versions of the Bible and then move to an adult version later when they are older.

These separate personal devotional times can be done at times with the help of their parents. For example, a parent may go through a particular book in the Bible with their child and teach them on a daily basis, and at other times, the child can read on their own and perhaps journal their own thoughts. Mixing it up will help them to feel like they are at times being guided and at other times left on their own. Guiding them too much does not enable them to spread their wings and dig deeper by themselves. So a balance needs to be struck, and parents must use their judgment to decide which is best since every child is different.

─────────────── ⟨ **LOUIS LOWDOWN** ⟩ ───────────────

> Our children memorized many Bible verses growing up, which we would review during family devotionals. While rote learning was not the main activity of our family devotionals, we did train them to learn these Scriptures and explained their meanings over and over again. Children do not get tired of repetition. As the children got older, we had deeper and even more meaningful talks. Sonia and I (Karen) have always had great talks about her quiet time insights. When she was baptised, I wrote the verse from Acts 17:10-11 about the noble Bereans in her Bible. Even though we are now separated by many time zones, she still calls me from time to time to talk about her insights. Now that David is an only child of sorts, he and I felt that we should do something different, so we decided that we would like to read through the Bible together slowly over the next two years of high school and two years of mandatory service in the Singapore Army. We've been reading on average a chapter a day, and have had a blast discussing all sorts of insights. (We recently covered Deuteronomy, and after David read the first half of chapter six aloud, he paused and said, "Oh, so *that's* what you guys have been doing...") We have made up several evangelistic Bible studies together, come up with Scripture related ice-breakers, and once he even composed a song! I have loved studying the Bible since I became a Christian when I was seventeen, and I can't think of anything more worthwhile to pass down to my children than the same love.

Obeying the Word

Obedience to God's word and to parents must be taught. *"Children, obey your parents in the Lord for this is right,"* (Ephesians 6:1) was the first memory verse we taught our children. It's important for kids to know that we are not just making this stuff up!

> *Observe therefore all the commands I am giving you today, so that you may have the strength to go in and take over the land that you are crossing the Jordan to possess, and so that you may live long in the land that the Lord swore to your forefathers to give to them and their descendants, a land flowing with milk and honey...So if you faithfully obey the commands I am giving you today—to love the Lord your God and to serve him with all your heart and with all your soul—then I will send rain on your land in its season, both autumn and spring rains,*

so that you may gather in your grain, new wine and oil. I will provide grass in the fields for your cattle, and you will eat and be satisfied. (Deuteronomy 11:8-9, 13-15)

As we teach our children to obey God's word, we are laying a lifelong foundation for which they will always be grateful. But we will also be helping them to obey us as well. After all, we (supposedly) have good reasons for what we ask our children to do (see point four on Right and Wrong). Therefore, we need to help our children grasp the concept that God expects obedience from them, and part of that means obeying their parents. There are not many direct teachings on parenting in the New Testament, and the few there are include this commandment being repeated twice, so clearly God wants us as parents to teach and expect obedience from our children.

As children get more independent, they need to have a healthy respect for God's word for many reasons, one of which being that there will be times when they do not feel like obeying their parents at all. However, if they fear God and know they must obey his word, they will (hopefully at least) not do anything *too* stupid! Dr Michael Popkin of Active Parenting suggests that parents hold out obedience to God and His word (or any set of values) as something that benefits the child, not them. Otherwise, when teenagers want to rebel and reject the parents' values, they may end up rejecting God at the same time.[7] Parents must try very hard to help their children see that it is *their* (the kids') life, *their* choices, and *their* relationship with God that is at stake and that the parents are merely pointing things out because they want the kids to think about what is in front of them. (I.e., I am not telling you this for *my* benefit—this is *your* life. I am telling you this because I love you and I want you to have all the information and make the best choices, hopefully better than I may have done…)

3. The Way Our Children View Themselves

For you are a people holy to the LORD your God. The LORD your God has chosen you out of all the peoples on the face of the earth to be his people, his treasured possession. (Deuteronomy 7:6)

This is a beautiful and comforting scripture. When we wrote about the first four core needs, we spoke about how parents influence their children's self-esteem. In this core need, we are showing how God influences their self-esteem. If we can help our children understand that they are God's treasured possession, they will receive an affirmation much greater than what we can give them!

Parents will have a better chance influencing their children's self-esteem if they understand their children well. This can happen when parents have a deep, honest and vulnerable connection with their children, and the children feel safe and not "controlled". Studies have shown that children who don't feel controlled are much more willing to share their personal information with their parents, even when it concerns involvement in sexual behaviour.[8] Parents who give their children space, spend time with them consistently, and meet the core emotional need for connection and acceptance are the ones who will be invited into the private thoughts of their children. We should set the pace in openness—when children see their parents model vulnerability from a young age, the children will likely follow. When this becomes a two-way relationship, parents will have a window into their children's hearts and an opportunity to shape the way they view themselves.

The power of community, which we will cover in the next chapter, can also help your child's view of himself. When your adolescent child has other adult friends whom they like and respect, they will also be willing to share with them about their inner thoughts and issues. It is amazing how much a difference this will make in helping your child view himself in a healthy way.

❧ LOUIS LOWDOWN ☙

When our children were three and five years old, I (Karen) began talking to them about the need to be open and share their thoughts and feelings regularly. This was partly so that they wouldn't get in the habit of hiding things from us that may have happened during the day, such as when they were at kindergarten. But with Sonia, I had a second motive. I worked with her on having positive thoughts about herself and the way she viewed herself in relation to the world around her, because from a very early age, she would sometimes tell herself negative messages. She would actually say them aloud, but under her breath, and I could hear a kind of mumbling coming out of her. I would ask her what she was saying; at first she wouldn't tell me. Eventually it would come out, "I'm saying I am stupid" or something to that effect. I seem to remember these conversations happening when I was driving her home from school, so I would stop the car, park somewhere safe, turn around, look her in the eye, and tell her positive messages to counter the negative ones she was telling herself. I would tell her that those negative thoughts were not true, and that God made her and He knows better, thoughts like, "You are my treasured possession." When she was older, there was one occasion during the preteen turmoil years when she had been ranting and raving, and then switched gears and asked me what was wrong with her. I got her to climb into bed with me and we read this passage from Isaiah together:

> *But now, this is what the Lord says—*
> *he who created you, O Jacob, he who formed you, O Israel:*
> *"Fear not, for I have redeemed you; I have summoned you by name; you*
> *are mine. When you pass through the waters, I will be with you;*
> *and when you pass through the rivers, they will not sweep over you.*
> *When you walk through the fire, you will not be burned;*
> *the flames will not set you ablaze.*

> *For I am the Lord, your God, the Holy One of Israel, your Saviour...*
> *Since you are precious and honoured in my sight,*
> *and because I love you,*
> *I will give men in exchange for you, and people in exchange for your life.*
> *Do not be afraid, for I am with you...Bring my sons from afar*
> *and my daughters from the ends of the earth —*
> *everyone who is called by my name, whom I created for my glory,*
> *whom I formed and made." (Isaiah 43:1-7)*
>
> Sonia cried and asked, "Does God really love me this much?" I was crying, too, and replied, "Yes, sweetheart, He loves us all this much." We held each other and she said, "Mum, from now on, Isaiah 43 is gonna be my favourite verse." Teaching our children to talk sense to themselves with God's word will help them to view themselves through God's eyes.

4. The Way Our Children View Right and Wrong

In Deuteronomy 11:26 and 30:11-20, Moses speaks for God to the people and gives them a choice: They can choose blessings or curses, life or death. God is a God of free will and He would even let them choose to send spies in when that might not have been his original plan. Similarly, we must help our kids learn how to make wise choices and to see that there are consequences for choosing unwisely.

☙ LOUIS LOWDOWN ❧

> When I (John) was 15 years old, my parents sent me from Malaysia to England to attend boarding school. As you can imagine, the boys there got into all sorts of trouble, including sexual sins, bullying, using bad language, lying, stealing, you name it. However, rather than address issues that could potentially scar the boys for life, the school focused on what we have been referring to in this book as "the conventional domain". Looking back, I am amazed the rules they required teenagers to obey. For example, when we spoke to our teachers, we were not allowed to place our hands in our pockets, even in the dead of winter, because it was construed as being disrespectful. If we forgot, we would be punished by getting up 45 minutes earlier the next morning and reporting to a prefect. Here are some of the other rules which we were required to follow:
>
> - Cheering on the rugby field while facing the winds from the Atlantic Ocean with a very high wind chill factor (and no hands in pockets!)
> - Writing letters to our family members at set times
> - Going for walks in the open farm fields at set times (Sunday afternoons)
> - Holding our knives and forks the proper (British) way; we were told off if we did it in the American style.

> While I am not against conventional rules, it strikes me as very skewed that we had the same severe punishment meted out by kids practically our age (prefects) just for "improperly" holding a fork as we had for being disrespectful to our teachers. We were punished for breaking arbitrary rules. Needless to say, I developed a lot of attitudes towards the prefects' authority while schooling there—until I became one myself, of course!

Nucci (please review the subject of the different domains of morality in Chapter Two) observed that disputes over issues in the conventional, prudential and personal domains make up the majority of adolescent-parent disputes.[9] Disciplining and training children about issues within the Moral Domain, which are truly about right and wrong, is always correct. Protecting their safety with boundaries within the Prudential Domain is also a must for parents. However, when parents argue with and discipline their children for "offenses" within the Conventional and Personal Domains, they are on slippery ground. As parents fight with their children about arbitrary and personal issues that are not truly a matter of right and wrong, their children will become exasperated and will experience frustration of their core emotional needs.

Below are some examples of issues that tend to get parents frustrated. Some are related to our children's spiritual values of right and wrong, i.e., the Moral Domain, and some are not. Look at the list below and put them into the four domains mentioned above. Some may fit into more than one category:

- Poor table manners
- Bad language when frustrated or irritated
- Dishonesty about use of money
- Dishonesty about grades achieved
- Hairstyle, hair colour
- Having a tattoo
- Type of earrings
- Type of clothes combination (which match and which don't)
- Wearing revealing or provocative clothing
- Keeping room tidy
- Doing chores at home
- Type of nail polish
- Type of extra curricular activity
- Type of musical instrument
- Type of wall decoration in bedroom
- Type of movie they like to watch
- Personal hygiene
- Disrespect to parents
- Going to school friends' parties
- Going on a holiday with school friends
- Coming home late

- Reading fashion magazines
- Listening to rap or heavy metal music
- Listening to any music with sexually explicit lyrics
- Not getting top grades after trying hard
- Not being naturally gifted at certain subjects
- Not being as smart as another sibling or cousin
- Type of computer games

Think about the disputes that you frequently have with your children. Are they about making you look good, helping you to save face in front of others? Are they about conventional issues? Are they really old enough to be deciding some of these things themselves? Or are they about helping your children develop morally? It was said earlier that it is unlikely that children will disclose their private behaviour to parents who are too controlling. Controlling parents (eg., who do not give their children control over the personal domain) have less chance of knowing their children intimately, especially those at an adolescent stage. Parents can expect a rude awakening about the secret behaviour of their children when they sabotage their children with exasperating behaviour such as belittling, being punitive, perfectionistic, or controlling. Trying to control the outside of their children will only lead to their children keeping them in the dark about their personal struggles and challenges.

When parents overly focus on conventional and personal issues in teenagers and reprimand them for not complying, it will cause a divide, either outwardly, if your child is a counterattacker type with the overcompensation coping style, or inwardly, if they have the avoiding or surrendered styles. Forget the peripherals and focus on the issues about which God cares.

◈ LOUIS LOWDOWN ◈

We knew that as children of church leaders, our kids would feel extra pressure to publically make known their faith. So we went out of our way to encourage our kids to think for themselves and question everything, and we figured that wouldn't be too hard since were living in such a multicultural city. (One year, Sonia's class at school had children from seven world religions and 14 different nationalities!) When Sonia was about seven years old, she asked me, "Mum, how do we know that our religion is right?" My answer: "Well, sweetie, that's what you will have to figure out for yourself as you get older—and I am so proud of you for thinking of such deep questions. Well done!" We kept this in the back of our minds and found appropriate and helpful times to point out things, and eventually she made her own decision. If we had tried to tell her what was right and wrong without letting it be obvious and logical to her, I think it would have backfired. As Sonia got older, she would at times make shocking statements about whether or not certain activities were or were not sinful, to get a reaction—at least that's what it felt like to me. I

> would take a deep breath, and then say, "Well, that's interesting sweetheart. What makes you say that?" I learned this technique from John Rosemond, the brilliant and funny author of Teenproofing, one of the most helpful parenting books I ever read. He calls it "giving them enough rope to hang themselves." Rosemond's point is that if you give your kids the freedom to make a mistake, you can help them figure it out afterwards, provided it is not too dangerous, of course. Sonia would usually rattle on about her reasons, but as she heard herself, she would eventually come to her senses, all without me saying a word. Biting my lip, at least on good days, I would manage to say, "I figured you would come to that conclusion," and then change the subject!

5. The Way Our Children View Others

The Bible makes it clear that we cannot separate love for God and love for our fellow man. Recorded in 1 John 4:19-20, the apostle of love wrote:

> We love because he first loved us. If anyone says, "I love God," yet hates his brother, he is a liar. For anyone who does not love his brother, whom he has seen, cannot love God, whom he has not seen.

As part of impressing God into our kids' hearts, we want our children to imitate the way Jesus feels for, empathises with, and shows compassion to others. When genuine care overflows from their hearts, they will be able to love all kinds of people, and will be a pleasure to all who know them.

More from Nucci (2008), who has this to say about moral development and relationships:

> ...a child's moral development is affected by experiences (including conversations) having to do with feelings and thoughts about the way actions affect people. Parental statements focusing on actions and perspective taking such as, "That really hurt Mike," "How would you feel if someone called you a name like that?" "Do you think it is fair for you to get two toys when everyone else gets one?" are viewed by children as effective and appropriate adult responses to moral transgressions.[10]

Focusing on feelings is crucial, as opposed to labelling an act "sinful". A home atmosphere where pointing out transgressions and labelling others dominates the way parents teach their children would feel negative and be counerproductive to what we are trying to teach about the heart of God.

Create a Home Environment That Fosters Empathy

Besides making it a topic of conversation, we can impress the need to care for others by bringing our children to the elderly, the needy and less fortunate. In addition, parents can influence the way their children view others by guiding them to take people's views and feelings into account in their daily interactions and decisions. Parents must explain things *as they are happening* so that children are able to attribute positive meaning to situations. This takes time and being very thoughtful and purposeful. When our children see us caring for others and when we explain to them specifics about how to do that, with follow-up, it will become part of their belief system.

◈ LOUIS LOWDOWN ◈

> My (Karen) mother was practically a saint in the area of gossip—if my brother or I said something bad about someone, our mum would say, "If you can't say anything nice, don't say anything at all." (Perhaps that's where my love of Movie Therapy came from, because she would tell me, "That's what Thumper's mother said in the Bambi movie!") My mum never spoke ill of another person, and I can't remember her ever complaining about anything when I was living at home. If some guy did do something wrong or annoying, she would smile and say understandingly to my brother and me, "His shoes are probably too tight." Needless to say, the atmosphere of my home was so positive when I was growing up that I don't remember ever getting a bad attitude toward anyone (until I hit puberty, of course). I'm not so sure I have been able to replicate that, but I am ever so grateful for the example my mom set on the positive way to view others.

In Chapter Seven, we talked about the need for parents to show empathy to their children, and not dismiss them or put them down. We mentioned that by listening to their children's hurts and showing empathy, parents are modelling what they want their children to do as well, and exhibited a wide array of good that comes when parents show empathy to their children. Sadly, there are some parents who show little empathy to other family members but they expect their children to become people who care. When adults do not show empathy in the home, it is doubtful that it will be deeply embedded in the hearts of their children.

Focus on Cause and Effect

On occasions when our child inflicts pain or wrongs someone else, our discipline needs to include helping them focus on how the other person feels (after we have validated their feelings). This will help them to respect others and be concerned for their welfare.

We stress the need to keep talking about the manner in which our children's actions affect other people's feelings. If we just point out our children's sins and say, "God does not like this", and tell them how much they are messing up, they may eventually get fed up with anything having to do with "God". Many parents exhibit this kind of missionary zeal in their parenting and quote Scriptures all the time, but do not take the time to explain and process the effect of the misbehaviour. Such opportunities should not be missed. They can be turned into valuable life lessons instead of times when we as parents are just trying to "teach them a lesson" by disciplining them.

On the flip side, when they do positive things, we should focus on the positive way they made others feel, or the positive effect their actions had. Incidentally, this also helps them with their "view" of right and wrong, because children learn best about right and wrong when they see how their right and wrong actions affect other people.

This is essentially what Jesus said when He gave what has come to be known as The Golden Rule:
> *So in everything, do to others what you would have them do to you, for this sums up the Law and the Prophets.* (Matthew 7:12)

Do to others... One way we can impress this principle into our children's hearts is by highlighting situations in which we did well showing empathy, and also when we did not do so well. And, since one of the most important "others" in the lives of us as Christian parents are our very own children, this would also include getting feedback on whether or not we speak to our children in the way that we wish people would speak to us, correct our children in the way that we would like to be corrected, giving our children the benefit of the doubt in the way that we wish others would give us the benefit of the doubt, and encouraging our children in the way that we wish others would encourage us.

We can relate this idea of cause and effect to the Galatians 6 law of sowing and reaping (Galatians 6:7-10) that was discussed in the section on Reasonable Limits—if we sow the seeds of treating others with kindness and respect, we can expect generally to be treated well ourselves. We can also discuss the good tree, good fruit, bad tree, bad fruit principle, also of Matthew 7. Children are very smart; not much gets by them. When they see their parents who go to church having a good marriage (not perfect but always working things out and loving each other), and feel that they are treated with love, respect, kindness, and firmness and given appropriate freedom as well as limits, they will start putting two and two together. They will notice that most of their friends' parents are not as affectionate, that some of their cool teen friends are actually sad, lonely, and have no purpose in life, and that most of their teachers do not in fact have all the answers.

Parents as Role Models

In Deuteronomy 6:4-9, Moses commanded the adults to love the Lord their God and keep His commands in their hearts, *before* they pass it on to their children. Often we miss this part of the commandment. Some have said, "Live It to Give It". Such an example is extremely powerful, and can become a legacy that we will leave behind for our children.

Our children see us through the good times and the bad, witness our highs and lows, and our "normal" days. As our children process this "data", they will connect the dots and see what is really number one in our hearts, who we are on the inside, and what values we hold dear. It goes without saying that our example will be permanently etched in their minds and hearts. They will carry that memory with them till they themselves become adults. It is amazing what they pick up from our behaviour on a daily basis. For example, they will notice how we:

- Talk to and about others
- Treat waiters, cashiers, the respected members of the society, and the "ordinary" people
- Treat our spouse
- Act at work (as in our work ethic and integrity issues)
- Treat and talk about our own parents (as in their grandparents), and our siblings
- View money, wealth and status
- Sacrifice (or not)
- See others spiritually, including those who do not yet know Christ
- See them as children
- Handle conflict
- Handle anger
- Forgive (or not)
- Apologise and humble ourselves (or not).

The list goes on and on—our lives are like a movie to them. There is no way around it. If there is duplicity between what we preach and what we practise, it will have an impact on them. No doubt, we have weaknesses, but there is a difference between parents who are all still works in progress and parents whose Christian lives are riddled with hypocrisy and duplicity.

Not only should we practise what we preach, we need to also preach or teach what we practise. (This is also part of the "impressing these things" on our children that Deuteronomy 6 tells us to do.) Look at the way God tells us to talk to and teach our children, i.e., over and over again whenever we can as opportunities present themselves. Practising what we preach and preaching what we practise go hand in hand according to this Scripture. So, being good examples is crucial but we also need to teach them our beliefs, why we believe them, and make sure there is no disconnect with our actions.

In their book *The Altruistic Personality*, Samuel and Pearl Oliner tell how they interviewed 406 persons who rescued Jews from the Nazi Holocaust and 126 people who lived in the same parts of Nazi-occupied Europe but who did not get involved in helping the Jews.[11] They found that of the people they interviewed, 52% helped because of the moral code of the social group and they responded to an authority figure of that group. Of this group, 19% of them had a strong internal socialised norm so that their helping action appeared to be independent of any authority, and 37% had an empathic orientation, a response of the heart to people in pain.

However, the rescuers were much more likely than the non-rescuers to say that:

- Their parents modelled caring values. In contrast, parents of non-rescuers were more likely to have emphasised economic values, such as getting a good job. (This should make us really consider what kind of conversation we have around the dinner table!)
- Non-rescuers also said that their parents were much more likely to have used harsh punishment. Rescuers instead cited that their parents would occasionally punish them but more often, they would teach and explain principles and attribute meaning to situations.
- Rescuers' parents also were much more likely to have explicitly taught a positive attitude and tolerance towards people from different cultures and religions.

Our takeaway from this research—if we love others and live the Golden Rule, our children are more likely to be empathic and show compassion to others themselves, are more likely to know the difference between right and wrong, and will have Jesus' heart for others. Wow!

MASTER CLASS

> Jeff Mannel, evangelist, said of his parents that they made the Christian life attractive, and they also made loving and helping others attractive. Jeff attributes week in, week out, seeing people coming to their home to meet his parents, and leaving loved, helped, and changed, as one of the contributing factors for why he chose to go into the full time ministry.

6. The Way Our Children View Conflict, Forgiveness and Reconciliation

When we forgive, the bitterness, resentment, and anger are swept away. The negative emotional energy is gone and is replaced by feelings of light-heartedness, freedom, and peace. Indeed, forgiveness *is* the corner stone for healing in relationships.

Defining Forgiveness

The Scriptures take an unambiguous stand on forgiveness. God allows us to choose to forgive, just like He gives us the choice to accept His grace and come to Him in repentance. In the parable of the lost son, also known as the prodigal son (Luke 15), the father allowed the son to come to his senses of his own accord. The father waited patiently at home, looking at the horizon every day, longing to see his son make his way back in humility. When the son made the first move, the father ran and embraced him! (Luke 15:20)

Even with all this compassion waiting to burst from the father's heart, he still gave his son the choice to return. God is the same way. Forgiveness is our choice, but the consequences are grave with regards to our salvation if we choose *not* to forgive:

> Then Peter came to Jesus and asked, "Lord, how many times shall I forgive my brother when he sins against me? Up to seven times?" Jesus answered, "I tell you, not seven times, but seventy-seven times. Therefore, the kingdom of heaven is like a king who wanted to settle accounts with his servants. As he began the settlement, a man who owed him ten thousand talents was brought to him. Since he was not able to pay, the master ordered that he and his wife and his children and all that he had be sold to repay the debt. "The servant fell on his knees before him. 'Be patient with me,' he begged, 'and I will pay back everything.' The servant's master took pity on him, cancelled the debt and let him go. But when that servant went out, he found one of his fellow servants who owed him a hundred denarii. He grabbed him and began to choke him. 'Pay back what you owe me!' he demanded. His fellow servant fell to his knees and begged him, 'Be patient with me, and I will pay you back.' But he refused. Instead, he went off and had the man thrown into prison until he could pay the debt. When the other servants saw what had happened, they were greatly distressed and went and told their master everything that had happened. Then the master called the servant in. 'You wicked servant,' he said, 'I cancelled all that debt of yours because you begged me to. Shouldn't you have had mercy on your fellow servant just as I had on you?' In anger his master turned him over to the jailers to be tortured, until he should pay back all he owed. This is how my heavenly Father will treat each of you unless you forgive your brother from your heart." (Matthew 18:21-35)

The last verse in the section above (verse 35) lets us know that God is not just *making a suggestion* when He tells us to forgive. Here are three more passages that are crucial to our understanding of forgiveness and resolving conflict:

> You have heard that it was said to the people long ago, "Do not murder, and anyone who murders will be subject to judgment." But I tell you that anyone who is angry with his brother will be subject to judgment. Again, anyone who says to his brother, "Raca," is answerable to the Sanhedrin. But anyone who says, "You fool!" will be in danger of the fire of hell. Therefore, if you are offering your gift at the altar and there remember that your brother has something against you, leave your gift there in front of the altar. First go and be reconciled to your brother; then come and offer your gift. (Matthew 5:21-24)

If your brother or sister sins, go and point out their fault, just between the two of you. If they listen to you, you have won them over. But if they will not listen, take one or two others along, so that "every matter may be established by the testimony of two or three witnesses." If they still refuse to listen, tell it to the church; and if they refuse to listen even to the church, treat them as you would a pagan or a tax collector. (Matthew 18:15-17)

Do not judge, and you will not be judged. Do not condemn, and you will not be condemned. Forgive, and you will be forgiven. Give, and it will be given to you. A good measure, pressed down, shaken together and running over, will be poured into your lap. For with the measure you use, it will be measured to you." (Luke 6:37-38)

When defining forgiveness, researchers make a distinction between the genuine and the superficial. Dr. Everett Worthington and Dr. Robert Enright are among the foremost experts on forgiveness in North America.

Dr. Worthington writes:

In genuine forgiveness, one who has suffered an unjust injury chooses to abandon his or her right to resentment and retaliation, and instead offers mercy to the offender.[12]

Dr. Enright tells us:

People, upon rationally determining that they have been unfairly treated, forgive when they wilfully abandon resentment and related responses (to which they have a right), and endeavour to respond to the wrongdoer based on the moral principle of beneficence, which may include compassion, unconditional worth, generosity, and moral love (to which the wrongdoer, by nature of the hurtful act or acts, has no right).[13]

Using both these definitions, combined with the Scriptures on forgiveness, we can accurately say that forgiveness is made up of several components:
- We are aware that the offense was unfair.
- We acknowledge that we have the right to feel angry.
- We give up the right to revenge and retaliation that may cause injury to the offender because God has done that for us.
- We replace the feelings of resentment with compassion, benevolence and love, just as God did for us through the death of His Son, Jesus Christ.

Enright says when people truly forgive someone who has hurt or sinned against them, they reduce or eliminate negative feelings, thoughts and behaviours toward the offender, and develop:
- Positive *feelings or affect* toward the offender
- Positive *behaviour* toward the offender
- Positive *thoughts or cognitions* toward the offender.[14]

(We like to substitute the counselling words "affect" for feelings, and "cognition" for thoughts, thus giving us Affect, Behaviour, Cognition: The ABC's of Forgiveness).

Forgiveness vs. Reconciliation

According to Enright, forgiveness is *not* condoning the offender's actions, excusing the offender's actions, justifying the offender's actions, or just calming down.[15] Forgiveness is also not necessarily the same thing as reconciliation.

As Dr. Enright puts it:

> Reconciling is the act of two people coming together following separation. Forgiving, on the other hand, is the moral action of one individual that starts as a private act, an unseen decision within the human heart.[16]

Reconciliation involves both parties coming together, both rendering forgiveness and asking for forgiveness, and both parties are willing and even desire to still continue in a relationship with each other. However if one party feels unsafe being in a relationship with the other party who is not remorseful over his or her actions, then the injured party, after forgiving, may decide to not get reconciled and have only a limited relationship with the other party. For reconciliation to take place, there must be forgiveness beforehand. It cannot take place unless forgiveness is rendered. However, one can forgive without getting reconciled. We may stay away from unsafe, unrepentant and unremorseful individuals or groups, even after forgiving. (For example, if bullies at school beat up your eight year old, you will hopefully want him to forgive them, but you will surely not expect him to become best friends right away.) Depending on the degree of their lack of remorse and/or repentance, we may decide to never see these people again, or to limit our interaction with them. Having said that, Jesus taught clearly about what to do when we have unity problems, as seen in Matthew 5:23-26 and Matthew 18:15-18. In addition, the Bible commands that we make every effort to live at peace with everyone (Romans 12:16, 18), accept one another as the Lord accepts us (Romans 15:7), and forgive and bear with one another as God bears with all of us (Colossians 3:13), so holding back from reconciling is not to be taken lightly! To give you encouragement, here are some findings about how forgiveness positively affects relationships and mental health.

─────── ⬧ **RESEARCH REVEALS** ⬧ ───────

RR19.1 *Forgiveness Is Good for Health*

- A recent study done by Paleari, Regalia and Fincham has shown that forgiveness is directly related to marital quality. The higher the level of forgiveness, the higher the marital quality.[17]

- Fincham also concluded that forgiveness and marital satisfaction were related. He went on to show that forgiveness affects the overall behaviour of a spouse towards the partner, and that it is not independent of marital satisfaction.[18]
- Orathinkal and Vansteenwegen did studies among married couples in Belgium and concluded that forgiveness and marital satisfaction are linked.[19]
- Unforgiveness is shown to correlate highly with anger, which in turn has been linked to decreased immune functioning.[20]
- Activity in the brain during unforgivenesss is consistent with brain activity during stress, anger and aggression. There may even be a neurophysical basis to label unforgiveness as a separate emotion.[21]
- Seybold et al. examined physical markers in patients at a Veteran Administration Medical Centre and found that people who were chronically unforgiving had blood chemistry assays that were similar to those of people under stress.[22]
- Testing blood pressure and heart rates, Lawler et al. found that high trait forgivers showed the least cardiovascular reactivity and best recovery patterns, whereas low trait forgivers in unforgiving states showed the highest levels of reactivity and poorest recovery patterns.[23] Unforgiving people put their health in harm's way by inducing stress and impairing heart recovery each time they are triggered by thoughts of unforgiveness. On the other hand, forgiving people quell these responses by nurturing forgiving thoughts.
- Lack of forgiveness has shown a strong correlation with anxiety in developmentally appropriate contexts of hurt (e.g., college students hurt by friends or romantic partners; parents hurt by children; spouses hurt by infidelity).[24]
- On the other hand, there is a positive correlation between forgiveness and measures of well-being.[25] In other words, the more forgiving a person is, the less anxiety, depression and/or anger will remain, even after experiencing a great deal of hurt. When we refuse to forgive, the stakes are high. It affects our mental health, our marriage relationships and most importantly, our salvation. When we do not forgive parties who have hurt us, we are not "punishing" them, rather, *we are actually putting ourselves in harm's way.*

Clearly, teaching children about forgiveness is extremely important. One just has to think about how many instances of pain that children carry with them all the way into adulthood. Often, most of these instances relate to areas that were never brought to a proper closure. There was no reconciliation and no forgiveness rendered. For the most part, parents and children do not even know the proper meaning of forgiveness. For many, it is about "pushing it under the carpet", or just trying to "forget about it," or simply saying "sorry".

Since arguments and tension do cause a lot of hurts that get carried into adulthood, we should protect our children from going through such an experience. Why let them ruminate unresolved issues and let these cause a negative effect on their mental and emotional health?

Dr. Enright and his colleagues conducted two studies on forgiveness with children and they came to the conclusion that younger children thought about forgiveness differently than older children.[26]

◁ RESEARCH REVEALS ▷

RR19.2 *Older and Younger Children View Forgiveness Differently*

The findings of Dr. Enright and his colleagues are as follows:[27]

- Children ages 9-10 equate forgiveness with revenge. In other words, children at this age would not naturally want to forgive an offender until he were punished.
- Young children also desire an apology before they are able to forgive. As mentioned in the definition of forgiveness, this should not be a requirement for adults; but for youngsters, this matters. Even for adults, apologising paves the way for reconciliation. Parents who apologise for mistakes that were their fault (both in front of and to their children) are not only getting reconciled, but also being good role models for their children. I have heard many adults say that their parents have never apologised to them. Dr. Enright found that children whose parents modelled forgiveness ended up practicing it themselves.
- When it comes to who they should forgive, adolescents tend to listen to trusted authorities, such as a teacher. It is important for parents and teachers to collaborate and send a consistent message to their children on this subject. Ideally, teachers and parents should discuss and be clear about their understanding of forgiveness. When there is a clear, consistent message about the value of forgiveness, children will be more likely to internalise it and make it part of their belief system.
- Older adolescents usually focus on what will happen *after* the forgiveness is extended, such as whether or not it will lead to restored relationships.
- Some adults take a loving and unconditional view of forgiveness, in that when forgiveness is offered, they have no resentment towards the offender, even though they disapprove of his actions. They separated the offense (the behaviour of the offender) from the offender himself, making forgiveness easier.

Teaching children the importance of forgiveness from a young age is extremely important. Children, as mentioned in the research above, do see forgiveness differently than adults. They also need to learn the difference between forgiveness and reconciliation. The following are important points for parents to note when teaching children forgiveness.

All people, regardless of colour, religion or race, have feelings and they all deserve respect. The world practices showing respect, but only to "important people". When children are rude to their teachers or to a parking attendant or someone in a grocery store, they need to extend apologies. In Singapore, we sometimes see children being very disrespectful to foreign domestic helpers, and their parents simply ignore this. Then we see the same parents scolding their children for showing disrespect towards the school principal. This inconsistency sends a very strong message—that not everyone deserves respect. It is sad to see anyone from any background looking down on others (eg., manual labourers from neighbouring countries) or treating them badly (evident by the number of abuse cases reported). Children need to be taught to respect people regardless of differences.

If children learn about forgiveness as they grow, forgiving and getting reconciled will become a habit for them as an adult. They will figure out that in other families, not everyone apologises or responds to apologies, or agrees to reconciliation. They will then appreciate their family even more and understand that giving and receiving mercy and grace exists in their family and is not just spoken and lectured about. Talk about equipping your children for real life!

Resolve conflicts quickly in the family and between siblings. When conflicts go unresolved, they cause anger, bitterness and resentment. These layers of emotions become barriers that make it difficult for future acts of love and kindness to penetrate. Family members can become numb and lose empathy for the person they are in conflict with—they become less concerned even if the other party is still in pain over the tension or about something else. However, when issues are sorted out quickly, it teaches our children sensitivity to the feelings of others; that they should take into account what others are concerned about (Philippians 2:3-4) and not just focus on their own emotions. When tension is allowed to linger, our children will become immune to the pain and feelings of others. When children lose their ability to empathise, they will become adults who are not able to empathise. This will affect their own marriage and relationships with others.

For young children especially, using well known children's books and various popular media can be very helpful in teaching this concept. For older children, seeing movies and then discussing them together with the parent is extremely useful. Parents should ask open-ended questions when discussing concepts and if the answers do not sit right with the parents, they should dig deeper, but not turn the discussion into another lecture. ("You missed the point of the movie, blah blah...") Respect should be shown to the children's view points. Parents should ask questions and guide the children to a healthy understanding of forgiveness.

7. The Way Our Children View Repentance

> *When you are in distress and all these things have happened to you, then in later days you will return to the LORD your God and obey him. For the LORD your God is a merciful God; he will not abandon or destroy you or forget the covenant with your forefathers, which he confirmed to them by oath.* (Deuteronomy 4:30-31)

God told the Hebrews through Moses that he already had a plan for them to repent. That is how amazing our God is. He is the God of second chances and He always honours repentance. If there is anything we should model for our children, it should be how to repent. Children make mistakes, and so do parents, which just means that everyone needs to be good at repenting. One powerful concept that parents should teach their children is that it is normal to make mistakes, but that it is also right to own up to our mistakes and make amends for what we did wrong. Having a remorseful and contrite attitude about what we did that has hurt others is a very crucial value we need to inculcate in our children.

As highlighted earlier, the more parents are connected with their children and the less they try to control them, the easier it would be for children to come forward to talk about their struggles and sins. They feel confident to approach their parents because they feel accepted and loved despite their mistakes.

Children should be taught from the time they are young to admit their wrongs and apologise. They should also be taught (and shown) that repentance brings joy to the heart and a feeling of being refreshed. It is also important for them to understand that when they choose to hide their sins, they will end up feeling guilty and miserable, which is a sign of an emotionally healthy and tender heart.

> *He who conceals his sins does not prosper, but whoever confesses and renounces them finds mercy.* (Proverbs 28:13)
>
> *Repent, then, and turn to God, so that your sins may be wiped out, that times of refreshing may come from the Lord,* (Acts 3:19)

When children find the courage to confess their struggles, parents should in turn respond with forgiveness, acceptance and reconciliation. We should refrain from being judgemental, negative and punitive. The "I told you so" and "How many times have I told you and you have not listened?" all convey our disbelief in them and will only turn them away from confiding in us further.

From the time they begin to speak their first words, children should be taught to take responsibility for their disobedience. After disciplining them, they should learn to say "I'm sorry" from the heart, which should be followed by forgiveness from parents and assurance of our love for them with hugs and kisses.

Accepting our children's mistakes does not mean we will let them get away with murder as long as they say "sorry". We may have to give them certain appropriate consequences. When children have the right view of repentance, they will be truly remorseful of what they've done and have the courage to confess and face up to the consequences, as well as be able to accept forgiveness and learn from their mistakes. Such a child is not afraid to make mistakes, but learns from them because they know they are given hope to change.

It is important for parents, again, to be role models in this area. Children will experience the power of repentance, forgiveness and reconciliation when they see their parents live that out. How humble are the parents towards each other in managing their conflicts or conflicts with others? How ready are parents to apologise sincerely when they have done something wrong to the children, e.g., yelling at them or hitting them out of anger? How open are parents to feedback and input from their own children or from others? These are all noted by the watchful eyes of our little ones who will only learn repentance from what they see in our lives, not from what we merely preach to them.

❖ MASTER CLASS ❖

> The Brumleys said that their teens were inspired when they saw their parents making changes. Meredith, their second child, said that seeing her parents repent later in life and make the changes they did, inspired her that she too could get open and get her life right with God.

Is Anger Ever Wrong in Parenting?

One question that is often posed to us, related to the issue of frustration of core emotional needs, "Is it wrong or harmful to ever show anger to our children?" Especially in this day and age when many parents are overly permissive, people seem to accept children being angry, but not parents. Some 50 years ago, it was the other way round. Children would not dream of being rude to or angry with their parents. The tables have turned. No doubt we are not advocating that parents be abusive (and being abusive starts with not controlling anger). Far from it! However, does this mean that parenting should be void of all forms of anger?

Anger is a God-given emotion. Getting angry means we are experiencing some kind of injustice, real or perceived. The Bible says that on God was provoked to anger by the people's repeated sins. God sometimes found it necessary to demonstrate His anger to His people; therefore, not all forms of anger are wrong. Paul wrote about anger in his epistles:

In your anger do not sin. Do not let the sun go down while you are still angry. (Ephesians 4:26)

According to this verse, "feeling anger" and "letting anger cause us to sin" are two different matters. We can and should at times be angry, but if our anger leads us to ungodly behaviour then we have clearly crossed the line. We need to control our anger and not sin. Uncontrolled anger, also called "fits of rage", is sin (Galatians 5:20); so are pouting, withholding affection, and sarcasm. All of these aspects of sinning in anger demand repentance. If parents frequently sin in anger, they will cause frustrative and traumatic experiences through their exasperation interactions. However, if parents are not provoked to anger when children have committed outrageous offenses, children may not be aware of the seriousness of some of their actions and they will probably not learn to respect healthy and reasonable limits.

The following examples are stories of families who attend church and who came to us for counselling:

CCTV cameras caught an adolescent boy stealing during a church service—he took money from a wallet that had been left unattended. When confronted, he lied about it until told that his crime had been caught on camera. Imagine if his parents did not get indignant with him about his behaviour.

A seven-year-old boy shouted at his father in front of others, "You have a smelly mouth and a stupid brain," because his father would not allow him to wander around a mall unsupervised. His father brushed that comment aside and refused to see that his son was out of place.

In spite of her parents' pleading, a teenager continued to use her computer for hours non-stop. When her mother finally unplugged the unit, the girl hit her mother in the face and then attacked her father who came to intervene. Both the parents were shocked and dumbfounded, and did not know what to do; all three are receiving ongoing counselling.

While we can acknowledge that some core emotional needs were surely not adequately met in the lives of these children, at the same time, their actions warranted anger being shown. Let's call it "healthy indignation". Why is indignation sometimes healthy?

- Indignation gets their attention – We need to call attention to the unpleasant and abusive behaviour right after it has taken place. Certain acts call for a strong response with a stern tone, from the father (or mother); something like, "You stop that right now—that is unacceptable!" If need be, the parent should intervene, take the child in question somewhere where they can be alone, find out why the child was committing such an act, and give a reprimand. When a parent reacts this way, he will get the attention of the child, which is what is needed for him to gain awareness of his outrageous behaviour.

- Indignation shows them the seriousness of the offense – When a parent is angry in a healthy way, and at the same time does not go overboard and resort to destructive ways of dealing with anger such as physical violence, the use of abusive language, belittling, and name calling, this will show the child how serious the offense was. Often the child has no awareness—he will after the parent makes this known.
- Indignation allows the parents to process his feelings – If a parent keeps his or her feelings in for too long, then at some point the parent will blow up at the child and this time it may be an explosion that will hurt both sides. Many parents who are subjugated or avoiders will end up blowing up like a volcano when they keep suppressing their feelings of anger for long periods of time.
- Indignation and reconciliation lead to repair – After a parent expresses indignation, both parent and child should take time to think (and cool off if necessary), then it is time for repair. When dealt with in this manor, the child will learn how to handle conflict spiritually and constructively. (See the last page of Chapter 14 regarding "Meaning Attribution" and Chapter Twenty-two, the chapter that specifically explains how to repair and reconnect.) By this time, the child should be ready to apologise, and further repair can commence as needed.

In short, healthy indignation should surface infrequently and be reserved for occasions when the offense is highly inappropriate. In any case, it should neither last for an extended time nor be used as a punitive measure (Ephesians 4:26 recommends not longer than a day). Repair, forgiveness and reconciliation should follow as quickly as possible, otherwise parents are giving the devil a foothold and endangering their ability to connect.

We close out this chapter on spiritual values with a story illustrating the joy and sense of peace parents feel when they see their values, rather than their dysfunction, being passed down.

⋞ LOUIS LOWDOWN ⋟

When David was in first grade, or Primary One (P1), as it is known in Singapore, he had a nice circle of friends, including a boy named Jonathan who had a permanent disability and needed a walker. During the school's annual Sports' Day, for which I (Karen) was a volunteer organiser, the P1 kids took part in simple relay races and were allowed to choose their own team, six to a team. One of the relays was a beanbag race which involved walking to a marked spot and back while balancing a small bean bag on one's head and then placing it on the next chap's head. David ended up being on a team with all of his buddies, except for Jonathan, who had not been allowed to participate in any relay. For whatever reason, David's team had supersonic speed and was a full lap ahead of all the other teams by the time the sixth boy took off—victory was eminent! However, right at that moment, Jonathan's mother, holding her crippled child in her arms, shyly asked David if he would allow her son to race for their team, since he had not been allowed to participate in any other race all morning. I saw the conflict on David's face—they were seconds away from first place; if he said "No" to his friend, he would feel lousy, but if he said "Yes", Jonathan would be happy, but they would surely come in last and his teammates might be angry. In that split second, he decided. *"Yes, Jonathan, you can join."* Seeing the look of absolute ecstatic joy on the boy's face probably helped David to feel a little bit better, especially as he watched the mum carry her son across the finish line. Jonathan was beaming, so glad to be part of a team. I was holding back tears, so proud of my son, and suffering for him, too, because I knew it was killing him to give up the trophy. After the hullabaloo died down and the kids were getting refreshments, David walked over to me and said, *"Well, Mum, we may have come in last place in the bean bag race, but I bet in God's eyes, we came in first."* I hugged him and told him that he had made me the happiest mum on the planet, and that I bet God would never forget what he did.

Why does a community

make such a

big difference?

CHAPTER TWENTY

The Power of Community

The Old Testament is filled with inspiring passages about how "community" worked (and sometimes did not work) for the Hebrews. However, for the purposes of this chapter, we will focus on the concept of community found in the New Testament, which offers us an incredible illustration of relationships in the church, also referred to as the body of Christ.

> *The body is a unit, though it is made up of many parts; and though all its parts are many, they form one body. So it is with Christ. For we were all baptized by one Spirit into one body—whether Jews or Greeks, slave or free—and we were all given the one Spirit to drink. Now the body is not made up of one part but of many. If the foot should say, "Because I am not a hand, I do not belong to the body," it would not for that reason cease to be part of the body. And if the ear should say, "Because I am not an eye, I do not belong to the body," it would not for that reason cease to be part of the body. If the whole body were an eye, where would the sense of hearing be? If the whole body were an ear, where would the sense of smell be? But in fact God has arranged the parts in the body, every one of them, just as he wanted them to be. If they were all one part, where would the body be? As it is, there are many parts, but one body. The eye cannot say to the hand, "I don't need you!" And the head cannot say to the feet, "I don't need you!" On the contrary, those parts of the body that seem to be weaker are indispensable, and the parts that we think are less honourable we treat with special honour. And the parts that are unpresentable are treated with special modesty, while our presentable parts need no special treatment. But God has combined the members of the body and has given greater honour to the parts that lacked it, so that there should be no division in the body, but that its parts should have equal concern for each other. If one part suffers, every part suffers with it; if one part is honoured, every part rejoices with it.* (I Corinthians 12:12-26)

> *For by the grace given me I say to every one of you: Do not think of yourself more highly than you ought, but rather think of yourself with sober judgment, in accordance with the measure of faith God has given you. Just as each of us has one body with many members, and these members do not all have the same function, so in Christ we who are many form one body, and each member belongs to all the others. We have different gifts, according to the grace given us. If a man's gift is prophesying, let him use it in proportion to his faith. If it is serving,*

let him serve; if it is teaching, let him teach; if it is encouraging, let him encourage; if it is contributing to the needs of others, let him give generously; if it is leadership, let him govern diligently; if it is showing mercy, let him do it cheerfully. Love must be sincere. Hate what is evil; cling to what is good. Be devoted to one another in brotherly love. Honour one another above yourselves. Never be lacking in zeal, but keep your spiritual fervour, serving the Lord. Be joyful in hope, patient in affliction, faithful in prayer. Share with God's people who are in need. Practice hospitality. Bless those who persecute you; bless and do not curse. Rejoice with those who rejoice; mourn with those who mourn. Live in harmony with one another. Do not be proud, but be willing to associate with people of low position. Do not be conceited. Do not repay anyone evil for evil. Be careful to do what is right in the eyes of everybody. If it is possible, as far as it depends on you, live at peace with everyone. Do not take revenge, my friends, but leave room for God's wrath, for it is written: "It is mine to avenge; I will repay," says the Lord. On the contrary: "If your enemy is hungry, feed him; if he is thirsty, give him something to drink. In doing this, you will heap burning coals on his head." Do not be overcome by evil, but overcome evil with good. (Romans 12:3-21)

As a prisoner for the Lord, then, I urge you to live a life worthy of the calling you have received. Be completely humble and gentle; be patient, bearing with one another in love. Make every effort to keep the unity of the Spirit through the bond of peace. There is one body and one Spirit—just as you were called to one hope when you were called—one Lord, one faith, one baptism; one God and Father of all, who is over all and through all and in all. But to each one of us grace has been given as Christ apportioned it ... It was he who gave some to be apostles, some to be prophets, some to be evangelists, and some to be pastors and teachers, to prepare God's people for works of service, so that the body of Christ may be built up until we all reach unity in the faith and in the knowledge of the Son of God and become mature, attaining to the whole measure of the fullness of Christ. Then we will no longer be infants, tossed back and forth by the waves, and blown here and there by every wind of teaching and by the cunning and craftiness of men in their deceitful scheming. Instead, speaking the truth in love, we will in all things grow up into him who is the Head, that is, Christ. From him the whole body, joined and held together by every supporting ligament, grows and builds itself up in love, as each part does its work. (Ephesians 4:1-7, 11-16)

Comparing the human body to the church is a powerful analogy. We can all appreciate how much the different parts of our body work together, and that the head rules everything. We are aware of how the different parts are dependent on each other. We would not give up one single part because we know how much we need all of our body parts. We also know that those parts only work when they are connected to the body. A severed finger or arm has to be thrown away if it is not almost immediately reattached to the body. What a meaningful visual for every Christian about how much we need each other. Think about it: When people connect with one another and when each person has the interest of others at heart, then something supernatural happens. Through that emotional connection, our deepest hurts get healed. We rejoice together, we mourn together. We love together, we laugh together, and we cry together. We are all weak at different points in our lives. In the church/body, love, connection, care and acceptance flow from the more healthy to the more needy individuals, and vice versa—that is when healing takes place. Not instantly, but through a steady, slow and consistent process, people do get better. No wonder God planned for his people to live in "community".

Unfortunately we live in a day and age when the responsibility for this kind of connection rests on counsellors, educators and therapists. A *New York Times* article from May 2012 spoke of how we are losing the ability to connect and be intimate as we feel the need to outsource our private lives to specialists and no longer seek help from friends and family.[1]

Interestingly, research shows that, more than the *skill* of the therapist, the most helpful and healing ingredient when seeing a therapist is the *connection* between counsellor and client.[2] Close friends, such as those in a committed small group of fellow believers in a church, should be able to provide that essential, most important emotional healing ingredient. Why should this connection be delegated to a paid person, when we can get it from the community of the church? In the fast paced world where couples have to schedule in love making and friends have to plan a month in advance to meet for coffee, people feel too awkward to show this kind of love and connection. Many times they do not even know how to go about it. Sometimes they feel ill-equipped and out of place. Sometimes it is because of a lack of trust. There exists a lot of hype about the global village and the social network keeping people connected, but for the most part, people in the world seem shallower and have few deep relationships—if any. People rarely talk about their deepest pain with one another, and if they do, it's not unusual for their circle of friends to advise them to see a counsellor or a therapist. We are professional counsellors in Singapore, so obviously we believe in these professions. We respect those skilled, trained and gifted professionals who pour themselves out in trying to bring emotional healing to others.

We do not want to play down the need to be adequately trained, but we wonder if professionals understand and appreciate the healing power that can come when people just connect with one another? When Christians combine being vulnerable with the power of God in His word, people can change. If the quality of the relationship is the most important factor in predicting the outcome of "therapy", and if we are part of a community that practises New Testament "love one another" principles, then we should all be able to help each other in small groups. Jesus Christ, the doctor of all doctors, the counsellors of all counsellors and the psychologist of all psychologists, knows that the quality of our relationships with one another is paramount to winning others, as he teaches in John 13:33-34. But it is more than just being a winning witness to a lost world—loving each other the way Jesus loves us has the power to heal one another—if we allow it to happen. We can be surrounded by good, healthy and caring people, who want to take an interest in our lives, but if we refuse to let them in, we will not be healed, and it will be to our detriment. We are the ones who will get lonely and feel isolated as a result. Think back to Ephesians 4—God's plan is for us to be healed through the church. This means each of us has the ingredient to heal someone else by giving of ourselves and by pouring out our hearts to one another. Yes, insight and direction from professionals are of great value; we need to tap into them whenever we are in a situation that is beyond the normal capacity of disciples. In fact, we believe that all ministry leaders should be familiar with the different helping professions and bodies in their communities so that they will have a protocol worked out in emergency situations. However, if we are going to have the church that Jesus meant to leave behind, and help others be healed, we must function as a community.

When we feel truly connected, we feel accepted for who we are, even though we are different, we feel joyful, being believed in given our limitations and gifts, and we feel peaceful, knowing we are forgiven. These friendships add so much spiritual depth and blessing to our lives. Imagine what all these qualities can do for our well-being? Contemporary research points to the health and mental well-being benefits of a closely, connected community.

◈ RESEARCH REVEALS ◈

RR20.1: *Strong Relationships Promote Overall Health!*

Back in the 1970s, Berkman and Syme studied 9,000 people over a nine-year period to determine the major causes of living and dying in a single county (Alameda) in California. With controlled factors such as diet, exercise, and serum cholesterol, they found that the people who lived the longest had friends or were married. They also found that immigrant populations had a more trusting community and closer family ties than non-immigrants. While some of these groups did have a healthier diet, the strong factors for Americans enjoying better health were trusting relationships in community and family.[3]

In today's world there are many valuable institutions that include universities, schools, child-care centres, Boy Scout movements, sports teams, and others.

But only two organisations are designed and instituted by God in His word, and this is our own family and His church. Both institutions need and feed each other constantly. Both supply what the other lacks. They complement one another. If our families tap into the power of the church, the synergy will be incredible. First, our own families will grow. Second, our churches will also benefit as a result of the part we all play. This is God's wonderful plan. Both our families and the church become better when they rely on one another.

We feel that many of the small groups in our churches lack the depth and level of trust and love that real connection and being vulnerable requires. Jesus taught us about this in Matthew 18 when he told us to be humble like little children if we want to be in the kingdom (v.1-4), how to deal with problems in relationships (v.15-17), and the critical importance of forgiveness (v.21-35). *Why are we emphasising this in a parenting book?* We believe that if we are going to meet the last "plus one" core need of our children, we cannot do it alone. We can only do it if we are part of a healthy community, and if we get our children immersed in that healthy community.

We have already seen statistics that show how much influence parents have on their children. Make no mistake about it—parents are the primary influence of their children. However, because we are all dysfunctional to a degree, we can only go so far. This is why the most we are able to be is "good enough". **The church is intended to supply what is lacking in our parenting.**

───── ⸙ **MASTER CLASS** – *Promoting Connection begins at Home* ⸙ ─────

> When their children were all living at home, the Mannel family had a weekly family night on Mondays, with no calls and no appointments allowed. They would have a brief devotional and prayer, then the kids would chose what they would do as a family. Sometimes a movie (not often because nobody talks during a movie), but most of the time family activities like miniature golf or bowling, activities that would promote conversation and more than a few laughs. Holly Mannel's response as to what was her greatest memory of the Mannels parenting was quick and to the point. "Monday family night meant more to me than I can express. Even when I was struggling spiritually, the glue that held me together was knowing that Monday, every Monday, was all about family. We had fun, we laughed, and we were together."
>
> Sam and Geri Laing quoted *"How good and pleasant it is when brothers live together in unity!"* (Psalm 133:1) and said one of the top three things they focused on (in hindsight) was to build a close relationship among their children. "One of the most important but rewarding tasks of parents is to help the children to learn to love, like and respect each other. Just as Jesus had to work to build humility and mutual acceptance among His

'family' of Peter, John, James and the rest of the Twelve, so parents will have to put in the effort to help children get along and genuinely come to love and understand each other. Teach them to 'speak the truth in love,' to communicate their problems and issues without sarcasm and rudeness. Stuffing feelings about one another is not good, but neither is unkindness in how they express them. A large part of this is to make sure the kids are not carrying hurt feelings and anger towards one another and towards you as parents. Help them fully resolve their problems and conflicts. This will take work, oftentimes on a daily basis, but the resulting close, happy family dynamic is one the sweetest blessings on earth! In addition, when the kids are doing well spiritually and with each other, they will have learned lessons about how to have great relationships with others."

The Baird's daughters, Kristi and Keri, remembered the family times, including the way they all memorised Scriptures and shared them during family dinner, as well as the consistency, which built great memories—they had family game nights, fondue by the fireplace and family devotionals. The sense of community began with the family and extended to others. Keri shared, "We knew you loved us, but we also knew you loved others. I remember having lots of people in our home...sometimes they even moved in and lived with us."

Greg Brumley said of his parents that he always felt they truly enjoyed attending church services. He felt that his positive attitudes were formed from years of going to church to be with his and his parents' best friends. Ron and Linda Brumley believe that kids need to see their parents enjoying their interactions with others. They always tried to include their kids when they had people into their home, and teach that relationships within a family should be an attractive feature in the process of sharing one's faith.

When our children are weak physically, we take them to a doctor. When they want to improve in a sport, we get them a coach. When they are not doing well in their relationships with us as a parent, what do we do? Normally, we just let time pass by and usually relationships and conflicts come to a standstill, and no progress is made. Whom do we call for help? Talking to our spouse, attending parenting seminars, and reading a book will all get us started, along with praying. However, do we tap in to the power of our small group? Why don't more people rely on the power of community that is available in a church setting?

A study that was originally conducted in 1982 evolved into a book published in 1987 that describes why Catholic schools in the 80s in the US outperformed public schools in several areas, such as having a higher percentage of students that graduated, enrolled into college and continued college once they were enrolled. The authors of this work, Coleman and Hoffer, attribute these successes to the kind of communities that these Catholic schools built. In particular, they distinguished between two kinds of communities, value communities and functional communities.[4]

◈ RESEARCH REVEALS ◈

RR20.2: *Functional Communities Have Proven Outcomes*

In 1982 a study called *High School Achievement was published*.[5] In its day it was probably the most comprehensive research done on American high schools. Its crucial findings were that students in private Catholic high schools consistently outperformed public school students in several areas such as students from Catholic schools were more likely to graduate, more likely to enrol in college, and more likely to continue their college studies once enrolled. This stirred the curiosity of many. These positive outcomes were partly attributed to the kind of community that was built in these Catholic schools. It was the first study that showed that school dropout rates were related to the aspect of community. Two of the original authors, James Coleman and Thomas Hoffer, detailed and revised their original work and wrote a book, which was published in 1987, entitled, *Public and Private High Schools: The Impact of Communities*.[6] This book describes the kind of *functional communities* among the parents and students of different families that provided support and brought about the positive outcomes in the students of Catholic schools. This stood in contrast with the less effective *value communities* that were prevalent in the other private high schools.

A *value community* in a school is formed as a result of parents choosing a particular school because of a shared value that a particular school has to offer, such as a high passing rate or a high number of students entering top universities. A *functional community* in a school has a common sense of values and shared relationships among those who choose a particular school. In other words, parents and students interact at places of worship, at school, and in each other's homes when they visit one another. Such interaction takes place between parents of a student's friend and that student himself. So the community is functional and relationships at multiple levels take place. This level of community was one of the main causes of the lower dropout rates in the Catholic schools versus the other schools.

Community makes a difference. If this can work with them, it can certainly work with us. We simply do not realise the power other adults can have on our children. Take, for example, the results of research conducted in 2007, which found:

Teens who had at least one adult from their church make a significant time investment in their lives were more likely to keep attending church services. More of those who stayed in church by a margin of 46% to 28%

said five or more adults at church had invested time with them personally and spiritually.[7]

> ◈ **MASTER CLASS** ◈
>
> Steve Hooper said that he is so grateful for the opportunities he had as a child and as a teen to be with strong spiritual adults: "My parents provided us with the opportunity to be around people who would call us higher spiritually through lots of hospitality and making kingdom-first decisions. I was able to go to Russia to visit my brother and sister in the Moscow/St. Petersburg mission teams as well visit the churches in the Philippines and South Africa. My parents' financial sacrifice to make this happen has definitely paid dividends in my life."

To have five or more adults getting involved in the lives of your teens at some time or other is a profound demonstration of the power of community. The power of community within the church is breath-taking. This is part of God's plan, which is surely one of the reasons He instituted the body concept in which we are to grow and change along with our families.

> ◈ **MASTER CLASS** ◈
>
> Ron and Linda Brumley added, "Teens are fascinating, bright, talented and fun loving creatures. Parents who are worried, fearful and uptight about their kids often don't see the goodness that is within them. We needed, and we believe most parents of teens need, other disciples who are much more objective and can help us see and appreciate and enjoy our children." Go, youth workers!!!

The use of the word "community" for many people carries a range of meanings. It can imply being part of a social club where people come together primarily for social reasons. Their friends are there, and so they feel comfortable there. The meaning of community in the sense of what the Bible says carries a different meaning altogether. In his book entitled, *Community: The Structure of Belonging*, Peter Block describes well what community is:

> *Community* as used here is about the experience of belonging. We are in community each time we find a place where we belong. The word belong has two meanings. First and foremost, to belong is to be related to and a part of something. It is membership, the experience of being at home in the broadest sense of the phrase. It is the opposite of thinking that wherever I am, I would be better off somewhere else. Or that I am still forever wandering, looking for that place where I belong. The opposite of belonging is to feel isolated and always (all ways) on

the margin, an outsider. To belong is to know, even in the middle of the night, that I am among friends.

The second meaning of the word belong has to do with being an owner: Something belongs to me. To belong to a community is to act as a creator and co-owner of that community. What I consider mine I will build and nurture. The work, then, is to seek in our communities a wider and deeper sense of emotional ownership; it means fostering among all of a community's citizens a sense of ownership and accountability.[8]

This idea of belonging and of emotional ownership is really an accurate way for all of the church's members to see their respective church communities. Some attend but refuse to develop relationships with others. They do not feel safe, and have issues relating to their mistrust. While they need time to work through this, they need to make it their goal to feel a certain level of belonging. On the other hand, others do feel that they belong but refuse to have any sense of emotional ownership and refuse to submit to any form of healthy accountability. Having a sense of ownership means caring about the community, playing a role in it, and constantly looking for ways to improve the practice of the biblical values that they hold dear. This includes giving feedback and attending meetings. Both of these concepts, the sense of belonging and emotional ownership, need to be grasped by all members, and to the extent that this is understood and practised will be the extent of the health of that community.

Feel free to check out the Singapore church website www.seachurches.org for more information about how the churches in the SEA region help foster a better community connection between children and their churches.

Spiritual Values and Community for Different Age Groups

We believe that we are never too young to begin experiencing community. But with children, this has to be balanced with safety. Whenever couples are allowing their children to be with others, they must ensure that the people are trustworthy. Do not make the mistake of thinking that just because someone attends the same church or "got baptised" that they are necessarily safe to be around children. We hope this does not sound mean, but we have seen the damage done when parents were not vigilant.

Having said that, we encourage parents to have great vacations and retreats with other families from their church community. We think it is a great idea to combine family devotionals, host parties, arrange outings and facilitate sports activities. Parents would be wise to ensure that their children to develop relationships with the children of other parents they know well—that is where community begins. It is not just about children knowing other children, but parents also knowing and having relationships with other parents and their children. Many parents do not know the parents of their children's friends at church and this is a mistake. Friendships must take place at both levels, children with children and parents with parents. This constant interaction is what will help develop the sense of community and will build a wonderful set of memories based on Christian values and community.

Parents should communicate spiritual values repeatedly—adults don't learn spiritual lessons on the first go, so why do we expect our kids to get it the first time? When kids get older, parents can try teaching things from different angles and using different Scriptures. But when they are young, they will not mind the repetition. Parents may get tired of repeating these lessons, but the children at this age usually will not get tired of being taught—unless the parents make it boring, which must be avoided!

The constant time spent with other children and their parents is important and should not be minimised. This will help children learn to fall in love with their church community, rather than just "attend services". Meeting with the body of Christ should surely be more exciting than their school experiences! Having relationships with other children and adults is the gateway to them embracing the spiritual values and community.

⇜ LOUIS LOWDOWN ⇝

> When our children were young, we got priceless input on their behaviour whenever we would hang out with more experienced parents. Maybe because we were older than most everyone in our congregation (when we were 30!), we felt a burning desire to ask for advice whenever we travelled or had visiting speakers over. We telephoned friends in the USA for advice about breastfeeding or how to put our children to sleep—usually at 3am Singapore time! We learned how to do Family Devotionals from our friends in India; they also helped us with discipline, scheduling, and specifically taught us the importance of not allowing our children to moan and whine. We got input from older couples in England and Australia about making sure we did not back down from limits for our children or foster entitlement, sometimes unsolicited, but always helpful. We will be forever grateful for this feedback. However, we notice that in the 21st century, the googling generation does not necessarily have this same sense of community and propensity to learn from older couples. We have heard of young couples searching the Internet rather than telephoning or dropping by the homes of elders who live down the street. We would hope that this book could change that mind-set and get young married couples to seek out help from older folks in their churches who can give them real-time advice and feedback for and about their children.

Preteen aged children have an especially keen sense of right and wrong. They are really listening! Parents should both practise what they preach and preach what they practise. Let them know when you are reaching out to people, who you are helping and why. They will be able to see your morals and values, not just hear you talk about them. The best way to teach them, according to Walker and Taylor,[9] is to ask for your children's opinion, discuss issues with them, seek clarification and understanding, and avoid ordering or lecturing them. To paraphrase Al Baird, once your children hit the preteen years, if you have allowed your relationship with God to drift into lukewarmness and you are practicing "Churchianity" instead of Christianity, it is time for a "second baptism"—figuratively, speaking!

Service for Others

One of the activities that young people really look forward to is being able to participate in acts of service. Teens love helping people! We have seen adolescents completely turn their lives around after getting involved in something bigger than themselves. Some of the teens that had not yet become Christians came back from these outings deciding to make Jesus the Lord of their lives. It is exciting to see how helping kids to get involved in acts of service has such a ripple effect of good outcomes. Parents need to understand that everyone "gets God" in a different way—if your child is going to be drawn to God by helping others, than make it happen! For some teens, coming to church on Sundays, having an adult in their life, or being in a small group just doesn't do it. Some young people may need to see a different side of life in order to eventually realize what an amazing opportunity they have to know God and be a part of His church. (A "Kingdom Kid" once told me, "Have you ever noticed how children do not seem to learn gratitude by being told by their parents how grateful they should be?")

⟨ MASTER CLASS ⟩

> Jeanie Shaw remembers that her parents were always very generous to others in their church community, "I noticed my parents' generosity and a lack of materialism. I was trained to be responsible and generous. My parents were fairly well off financially, but I did not know it. They loved to give to God the first fruits, and taught us as children that with every gift, our thankfulness should result in us giving a portion to God. No matter what situations they found themselves in, they did not get bitter but trusted God. I never heard criticalness from their mouths. The way they lived life became etched into my own heart, so that I looked forward to being married and becoming a parent."

⟨ LOUIS LOWDOWN ⟩

> When our children were born, we were living in Jakarta, Indonesia. We saw poverty everywhere, and we didn't worry about our children taking anything for granted. But by the time they were in kindergarten, we had moved out of the developing world, and we were concerned that the children would

forget to be grateful living in Sydney and Singapore. We brought them to the Jakarta orphanage annually for a few years, and when they were 12 and 10, respectively, we brought them to India for a week. They spent one day each at three different HOPE sites in Delhi. This had a great impact, and Sonia vowed not to buy any new clothes for a year! When she was 16, we let her go back on her own to stay with our dear friends, Mark and Nadine Templer and their children. She volunteered to teach at the HOPE slum schools for a few days with the Templer kids, and learned some great lessons about life while she was there. We believe these opportunities really helped our children's hearts to lean toward Jesus. Later, both Sonia and David were blessed with the opportunity to join about 50 kids from around the world to take part in a HOPE Youth Corps in South India—life-changing doesn't even begin to describe that experience!

Peer Relationships

It is important for parents to encourage their children to spend time with other kids from the community. We, the parents, must make the sacrifices necessary to facilitate this—we must make this happen. Organise your home so that it becomes the centre of activity if at all possible. This helps teens become closer to one another while providing a safe environment.

❖ MASTER CLASS ❖

Ron and Linda Brumley wrote, "Gretchen, our third child, felt that one of the things that helped her the most to become a disciple and stay faithful was the efforts we expended to insure that she had abundant time with her friends from church. San Diego was a smaller, growing church in those days, and the families were fairly spread out. She had no other disciple kids in her high school. We had strong convictions that we needed to do everything we could to get the kids from church together, a lot. Before our kids could drive, this meant that we did the taxi thing, a lot. We were happy to oblige as we realized how important good relationships were for our kids (and us as well)."

Involvement of Other Non-Family Adults

In addition to great peer relationships, the value of having other non-family adults involved in the lives of our children cannot be overstated. Part of why community needs to be fostered from young is that this will help your children have relationships with safe adults they can trust when they get to the age where your words do not carry as much weight. Once this happens, you will be glad that they get along with friends from your Family Group, or enjoy the annual holiday with your Sunday School class.

◁ LOUIS LOWDOWN ▷

> Looking back, we realise that one thing we did that helped our children spiritually was to give them lots of spiritual heroes. We boasted about Christian friends from all walks of life. If someone in our congregation was a cleaner or janitor, and perhaps lost their job because they refused to miss church for work or because they shared their faith with a co-worker, we would tell the kids about it over dinner. If we heard about a wealthy Christian standing up for righteousness at work, we would boast about their integrity. If we knew of someone who used their opportunities to reach out to another person in an unusual way, we boasted about their creativity. We made a big deal about answered prayers, about things people gave up for God—you name it, we boasted about it. This helped our children to admire many adults in our congregation and around the world, to have an idea of what it means to live the Christian life in season and out of season, to treasure relationships, to see God's hand in many circumstances, and to think like a disciple from young.

We believe that it is particularly helpful to have volunteers at church serve in the youth ministry as "mentors". While we believe in the idea that parents should primarily be the ones helping their children spiritually, we also believe that many kids, for various reasons, need outside intervention. If a teen ministry has 30 children, and only one full time youth worker, in our opinion, this ministry is set up for failure. We plead with parents to be vigilant about making sure their church has a thriving youth ministry—your children's futures may depend on it! These wonderful servants can be married couples, young parents, parents of teens, singles, or even campus kids in some cases, as long as they are strong Christians, reliable, willing to take input themselves, and willing to give of their time. Mentors do not necessarily need to be young single adults. It is our opinion that other parents can and should play this role instead of constantly depleting the resources of other singles and campus students. We strongly encourage church leaders to move in this direction, in addition to finding healthy and gifted singles for this important role.

A nationwide sample of USA adolescents were surveyed in 2005 and those who were involved in positive mentoring relationships were more likely to have completed high school, to have attended university, be employed afterwards, have positive mental health in the areas of self esteem and life satisfaction, avoid problem behaviour (gang membership, physical fighting, risk taking), enjoy good health, and have good relationships with their parents, peers, and other adults such as teachers.[10] Wow! The way we see it, youth mentors at church are a "God-send" in the true meaning of the word. Parents, let's make sure we take advantage of this positive by-product of church membership and make things happen for our children as we meet the core emotional need of spiritual values and community, as well as show gratitude to their mentors, which we will discuss more below.

◁ RESEARCH REVEALS ▷

RR.20.3 *What Kind of Mentoring Works?*

Rhodes and DuBois published an article on mentoring in 2006 for the US based Society for Research in Child Development. They found that mentoring relationships were helpful if they had the following components:[11]

Connection – Being close is the foundation of the youth-mentor relationships. In fact, in line with one of the main themes of this book, studies are showing that close bonds between the mentor and the youth are likely to promote positive outcomes. The authors noted that a crucial condition for the mentoring relationship to be effective was for the two people involved to feel connected. Rhodes and DuBois said that there should be a sense of mutual trust between the mentor and mentee; they should like and understand each other, and treat each other with respect. The basic connection between mentor and youth is so powerful that ethnic and or racial background of the mentor and youth did not appear as a significant factor. (Our own experience in a multiethnic church community has shown that to be the case over and over again—the connection between people transcends culture, race and ethnicity.)

Skills – When a mentor possesses specific skills and knowledge in helping youth, there is a greater chance that an effective mentoring process will take place. (We feel that mentors should receive initial and on-going training in order to be equipped. For Christian mentors, this would involve biblical discipleship training as well as listening and other leadership skills.)

Role-modelling – The mentor needs to be a respectable role model. (This is one of the reasons we like to use parents as mentors—they are usually older Christians and not as likely to leave the youngster in the lurch.)

Unselfishness – The mentor needs to work towards helping the youth, as opposed to serving his own interests. (We believe that mentors should be monitored by seasoned leaders to keep motives in check.)

Goals – Mentor and youth should set goals for the relationship and for the mentee that are mutually agreed upon (not just decided by the mentor.)

Consistency – Studies have shown that regular contact has been linked to positive youth outcomes, as this provides emotional support, feelings of security and attachment in interpersonal relationships. (We recommend a weekly one-on-one time, or at least every two weeks, and every other day by social media just to keep in touch.)

Duration – According to this research, the benefits of mentoring appear to accrue with time. They found that positive effects became stronger, provided the relationship remained intact. It was also highlighted that a mentoring relationship lasting less than six months caused a decline in functioning. (In other words, kids who were set up with a mentor relationship that did not even last six months presented as being in a worse position than they were before the mentoring relationship began, and worse off than kids who were not in mentoring relationships at all! This underscores the importance of mentors being willing to persevere, and, unless harm is being caused, the relationship should not be changed quickly.)

Group Settings – The final component of youth mentoring that showed up as being helpful is mentoring in groups. Group mentoring provides motivation from peers and offers alternative solutions. It also improves the relationships among peers. This interaction, along with constructive feedback from the mentor, serves as an upward call and can be useful in inspiring mentees to make positive changes in their lives. (The regularity of group and one-on-one relationships should be balanced and one should not be done at the expense of the other; both should take place. We recommend a group setting of at least once a month. Again there is no "one size that fits all"; the schedule of both mentors and youth should be taken into account when this is planned.)

Partnership Between Parent and Teens Leaders

We think it is particularly helpful for parents and mentors to be on the same page and not work at cross-purposes, rather, they should both work together for the benefit of the youth in question (see Figure 20.1).

We encourage parents to ensure that a healthy relationship is built between their teenagers and their youth ministry mentors. Ideally, we think parents

Unleashing the Power of Community

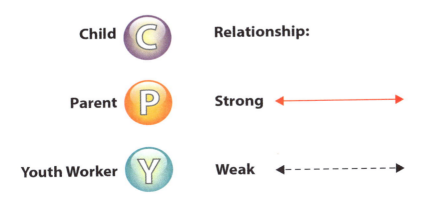

394 ■ Good Enough Parenting

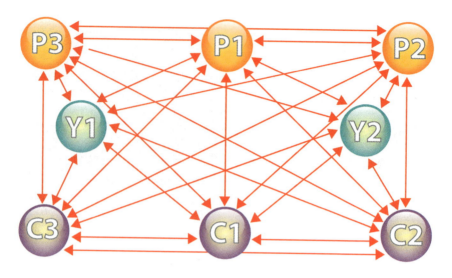

A Functional Community - Strong

Figure 20.1: Functional Community—A strong community
(strong relationships between parents and youth workers)

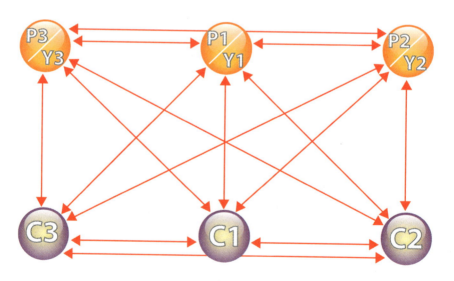

**A Functional Community - Strong
(Parents As Youth Workers)**

Figure 20.2: Functional Community—A strong community
(parents as youth workers)

The Power of Community ■ 395

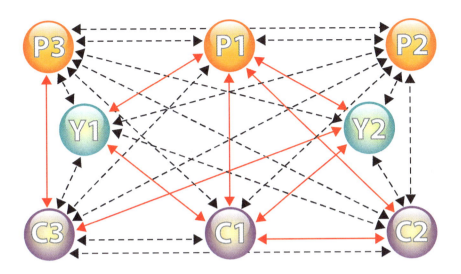

A Value Community - Weak

Figure 20.3: Value Community—A weak community
(weak relationships between parents and youth workers)

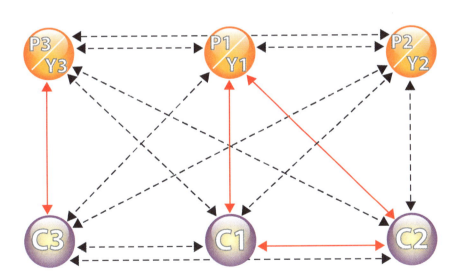

**A Value Community - Weak
(Parents As Youth Workers)**

Figure 20.4: Value Community—A weak community
(parents as youth workers)

should invite their children's mentors over for dinner from time to time. Parents and teen workers/mentors can exchange information on how they feel the teens are doing, using the four plus one core needs as the basis for conversation, which helps ensure a consistency throughout the ministry. (We know of one family with three teen girls whose teen mentor felt so at home with their family that she left a pair of "house shoes" in their basement!) Mentors should experience our gratitude, not just a verbal thank-you, but gratitude that can be felt. Think about it: Someone cares enough to invest in the well-being of your child! It is helpful for the teen to see both the parents and teen workers get along and be partners rather than being suspicious and dismissive of each other. A functional community calls for this kind of a relationship. A value-only community is one where such closeness rarely exists, and where issues remain unresolved.

One more item to consider here is confidentiality. Teens need to "feel safe" with their mentor; i.e., they do not want to feel that what they share in confidence with their youth worker will make its way back to their parents. Youth workers will need to get permission from the teens to convey things to their parents so as to not hurt the trust of the teen toward the mentor. *There are only two conditions upon which confidentiality should be broken, as in the counselling profession: When the teen is potentially causing harm to themselves or others or to another's property.*

In many churches, the teen leaders and parents are not friends. They usually sit on opposite sides of the fence, each having issues or concerns towards how the other is helping, or impeding the growth of the teen spiritually. Too often they do not talk but allow issues and concerns to take their "natural" course. Attitudes are left dangling and never brought to a healthy closure such that both the teen worker and parent feel united and on the same page. This should not be. If parents are going to trust the youth workers, they have to be close. And for youth workers/mentors to have an impact, the parents must be willing to listen to feedback.

When relationships are solid on all fronts, the bonds becomes strong and the community is functional. A value-based community has weak relationships between parents and the teen workers. The diagrams above (see Figures 20.1 to 20.4) help illustrate our point.

Parents, it is exciting to think that by meeting the core emotional need of Spiritual Values and Community, we will be able to influence, at least to a degree, the way our children view God, His word, others, themselves, right and wrong, conflict, and repentance! These essential values that define and shape our children are further impressed into their hearts when they are part of a God-fearing, loving, connected community that continues to bring out the best in them as they grow up to be loving, godly adults.

SECTION SEVEN

Final Thoughts

As a father,

what do I bring

to the table?

CHAPTER TWENTY-ONE

Fatherhood

Many fathers feel, from the time a child is in the mother's womb to the time the baby is born, that the role they play in nurturing and raising the child stands in stark contrast to the role played by mothers. Certainly this was how I (John) felt when both my children were born. My wife carried each of them in the womb, then she delivered both the children after many hours of painful labour. Next came breast-feeding. As a father, the part I played in the actual process seemed so insignificant. No doubt, I ensured that we had the resources, a good hospital, a good doctor, and a relatively well-stocked nursery, but still, I felt a bit left out. Was my role important? Sure we both celebrated together as our children were born, but it seemed a bit out of balance. (Interestingly enough, new research has found that fathers contribute even from the time of conception way more than anyone knew—for example, the diet of a boy shortly before he enters puberty has an impact on up to four generations of his offspring; lifestyle choices and stressors in his life, all pre-pregnancy, also have a very significant impact! The same research has concluded that aging male sperm has an impact on children born to older fathers.[1]) No doubt, I would come to realise the significance of my role later on, and become very much involved in parenting my children. But it is easy for us as fathers to feel emotionally left out, perhaps even defective and insignificant, compared to the role our spouses play.

The sad fact is that many fathers continue to have this distorted thinking long after their children are born, believing that their role is mostly that of providing for the material well-being of the family. They delegate the responsibility of parenting to their wives, who feel overwhelmed. With the majority of mothers also working outside the home, and few jobs offering flexible working hours, many women are exhausted. This fatigue then affects their marriage, spills over into their parenting, which in turn affects their work, and so the cycle goes. The bottom line is that too few fathers have the conviction that parenting is a shared responsibility. There is such a need for husbands to get involved and *own* their vital role as fathers.

The good news is there are those who do understand the importance of the father's involvement, and this trend is growing—the study below highlights that a new generation of dads are more committed to fathering than previous generations.[2]

◈ RESEARCH REVEALS ◈

RR21.1: *The Trend of Involvement by Fathers*[3]

The US-based National Center for Fathering (NCF) and the National Parent Teacher Association (PTA) have partnered together to assess the degree of involvement and support that fathers provide to their school-age children. The findings of this survey, conducted in 2009, expand upon a similar survey originally conducted in 1999, providing an assessment of the changes in father engagement over the last ten years. Both sets of data were collected through a single-stage, random dial, national phone survey of 1,000 individuals ages 18 and over.

Key Findings

Over the last ten years, a number of key gains were made that show fathers have significantly increased their involvement with their children at school. Increases were made in the following areas:

- Walking/taking their child to school 38% to 54%, an increase of 16%
- Attending class events 28% to 35%, an increase of 11%
- Visiting their child's classroom 30% to 41%, an increase of 11%
- Volunteering at their child's school 20% to 28%, an increase of 8%

Fathers also significantly increased their interaction with teachers, school officials and other parents. Fathers increased their engagement by:

- Attending parent-teacher conferences 69% to 77%, an increase of 8%
- Attending school meetings 28% to 35%, an increase of 7%
- Attending school-based parents meetings 47% to 59%, up 12%

The single largest gain over the past ten years was a 20% gain in meeting with other dads for support. Well done, fathers!

Even though the good news above is encouraging, significant opportunities for increased father involvement remain as measured by the percentage of dads answering that they *"never"* engage in the following activities:

- 39% Never read to their child
- 32% Never visit their child's classroom
- 54% Never volunteer at their child's school
- 74% Never have lunch with their child at school

So while the involvement of fathers has been growing steadily, there is still a tremendous need for many fathers to be engaged with their children both at home and in school, and all the more as we see families deteriorating. Sadly, it is expected that only 50% of children in the USA today will spend their childhood in an intact family.

◁ RESEARCH REVEALS ▷

RR21.2: *Percentage of US Children Living Apart from Their Fathers*

Of students in grades one through twelve, 39% of U.S. teens (17.7 million) live in homes where their biological fathers are absent.[4]

Racial demographics divide up as follows: 63% of black children, 35% of Hispanic children, and 28% of white children are living in homes with their biological father absent.[5]

Rural vs urban demographics: 33% of teens in rural areas live away from their father, while 43% of urban teens live away from their father.[6]

Children who were part of the "post World War II generation" could expect to grow up with two biological parents who were married to each other and 80% did. Today, only about 50% of children will do so.[7]

With the increasing number of premarital births and a continuing high divorce rate, the proportion of children living with just one parent rose from 9% in 1960 to 28% in 1996. As of 2009, 57.7% of all black children, 31.8% of all Hispanic children, and 20.9% of all white children were living in single-parent homes.[8]

Although there are differing expectations for fathers from culture to culture, clearly the rate of absent fathers is a global concern. Some experts have

◁ RESEARCH REVEALS ▷

RR21.3: *Absentee Fathers around the Globe*

A study done by Engle and Breaux in 1998 stated the percent of female-headed households in developing countries at any one time is between 10% and 25% and has increased gradually over the last decade.[9]

The highest rates of female headship are reported in the African countries of Botswana (46%), Swaziland (40%), Zimbabwe (33%), and the Caribbean countries such as Barbados (44%) and Grenada (43%). In the developed countries, rates are equally high; for example, 38% in Norway and 30% in Germany.[10]

attributed this to the increase of urbanisation, scarce jobs, and poor economies; others to the rising number of women in the workforce, enabling women more freedom of choice to escape painful marriages.[11] While there may be truth to these suppositions, the rigid mind-set in some cultures does not help. For example, one study found that in some countries in Africa, fathers have great social status and a big presence in the family, but have little parental involvement.[12] According to friends of ours from that continent, if fathers *are* involved, it is in the area of teaching their children to respect authority, not in the day to day parenting of children. Our experience in Asia has been similar, but we are happy to see things starting to change. research has shown that fathers make a *huge* contribution to the wellbeing of their children. Thus to be an absent father is to deprive one's children of a huge potential resource that can affect their lives for the better in a wide array of outcomes, and also deprive the father of the joy of connection.

The Impact Fathers Can Have

The research into the importance of fathers is relatively new, but more and more findings are showing that many positive psychological and emotional outcomes are linked with a father's involvement. The truth is, there is no substitute for having fathers be involved—no nanny, grandfather, uncle or older siblings can make up the difference. We have already shown in the section called, "How Marriage Affects Parenting" (see Chapter One) that the health of a marriage can directly affect the health of a child, both through their parenting and also by providing emotional security to the child. Below are more statistics that leave no doubt of the importance of dads in their children's lives!

RESEARCH REVEALS

RR21.4: *Fathers Make a BIG Difference!*

The following statistics are taken directly from the Child Welfare Information Gateway website:[13]

The quality of the marriage relationship affects the parenting behaviour of both parents. For couples who report a good marriage when surveyed, both father and mother are more responsive, affectionate, and confident with their infants; more self-controlled in dealing with defiant toddlers; and better confidants for teenagers seeking advice and emotional support than those who do not.[14]

Fathers who treat the mothers of their children with respect and deal with conflict within the relationship in an adult and appropriate manner are more likely to have boys who understand how to treat women and are less likely to act in an aggressive fashion toward females. Girls who have involved, respectful fathers see how they should expect men to treat them and are less likely to become involved in violent or unhealthy relationships. In contrast, research has shown that husbands who display anger, show contempt for, or who stonewall their wives (i.e., "the silent treatment") are more likely to have children who are anxious, withdrawn, or antisocial.[15]

Children with involved, caring fathers have better educational outcomes. A number of studies suggest that fathers who are involved, nurturing, and playful with their infants have children with higher IQs, as well as better linguistic and cognitive capacities.[16]

Toddlers with involved fathers go on to start school with higher levels of academic readiness. They are more patient and can handle the stresses and frustrations associated with schooling more readily than children with less involved fathers.[17]

The influence of a father's involvement on academic achievement extends into adolescence and young adulthood. Numerous studies find that an active and nurturing style of fathering is associated with better verbal skills, intellectual functioning, and academic achievement among adolescents.[18] For instance, a 2001 U.S. Department of Education study found that highly involved biological fathers had children who were 43% more likely than other children to earn mostly A's and 33% less likely than other children to repeat a year at school.[19]

Even from birth, children who have an involved father are more likely to be emotionally secure, be confident to explore their surroundings, and as they grow older, have better social connections with peers. These children also are less likely to get in trouble at home, school, or in the neighbourhood.[20]

Infants who receive high levels of affection from their fathers (e.g., babies whose fathers respond quickly to their cries and who play with them) are more securely attached; they can explore their environment comfortably when a parent is nearby and can readily accept comfort from their parent after a brief separation. *A number of studies suggest they also are more sociable and popular with other children throughout early childhood.*[21]

The way fathers play with their children also has an important impact on a child's emotional and social development. Fathers spend a much higher percentage of their one-on-one interaction with infants and pre-schoolers in stimulating and playful activity than do mothers. From these interactions, children learn how to regulate their feelings and behaviour. For example, roughhousing with dad can teach children how to deal with aggressive impulses and physical contact without losing control of their emotions.[22]

Generally speaking, fathers also tend to promote independence and an orientation to the outside world. Fathers often push achievement while mothers stress nurturing, both of which are important to healthy development. As a result, children who grow up with involved fathers are more comfortable exploring the world around them and more likely to exhibit self-control and pro-social behaviour.[23]

One study of school-aged children found that children with good relationships with their fathers were less likely to experience depression, exhibit disruptive behaviour, or lie, and less likely to exhibit anti-social behaviour.[24] This same study found that boys with involved fathers had fewer school behaviour problems and that girls had stronger self-esteem.[25] In addition, numerous studies have found that children who live with their fathers are more likely to have good physical and emotional health, achieve academically, and avoid drugs, violence, and delinquent behaviour.[26]

The National Center for Fathering in the USA also released a study that systematically reviewed fathers' involvement for one year before measuring an offspring's outcomes. In particular, positive outcomes were related to the fathers' engagement with their children. The term engagement that the experts adopted meant "direct contact, such as play, reading, outings or care giving activities." In the end they chose 24 papers, comprising sixteen longitudinal studies involving approximately 22,000 individuals, from new-born babies to young adults. Here were some of their findings from fathers who were engaged with their offspring:[27]

- Boys with highly engaged fathers had less behavioural problems during the early school years than boys with less engaged fathers during the preschool years.
- High father engagement in poor families (with stable marriages) predicted lower incidence of delinquency during the early adult years for both sexes.
- For adolescents already engaging in rather high rates of delinquency at baseline, higher rates of father involvement had a protective effect against criminality 1-2 years later.
- The risk of psychological morbidity during adulthood for women was decreased by their father's engagement with them at the age of seven (e.g., reads to the child) and at age sixteen (e.g., interested in the child's education).
- Engaged fathers in socially more advantaged families had a protective effect against emotional distress in young adulthood.
- Father engagement reduces the frequency of behavioural problems in boys and psychological problems in girls; it also enhances cognitive development while decreasing criminality and economic disadvantage in low socioeconomic status families.

NOT TO BE MISSED: Below are excerpts from an April 2012 article in *The Straits Times* about a survey on fathers' involvement done by Adrienne Burgess, Policy Advisor to the US-based Fatherhood Institute:[28]

- High-quality and substantial father involvement from one month following birth is connected with a range of positive outcomes in babies and toddlers, including better language development and higher IQs at 12 months and three years old.
- The IQ effect continues: A significant relationship is found between positive father engagement at age six, and IQ and educational achievement at age seven, and between high father involvement at age seven and IQ seven and at age eleven.
- A high level of father involvement at age seven to 11 is linked with better national examination performance at age 16.

Let us look now at what research has identified as the three main ways fathers should get involved with their children:[29]

1. Engagement – Fathers should have direct contact with their children such as playing, reading, going on outings or care-giving activities.
2. Accessibility – Fathers should make themselves available to their children even when they are not in physical contact, for example, speaking on Skype when away on a business trip or living in another city.
3. Responsibility – Fathers should take responsibility for their children's care and welfare, such as choosing clothes, diapers and sleeping arrangements, again regardless of physical proximity.

If a father makes the effort to meet all the four plus one core emotional needs of his child, he will be doing the above. Fathers do not necessarily have a different broad goal from the mother, but fathers should take into account their unique gifts and gain awareness of their unhelpful tendencies.

One recurring pattern we see with fathers is that many dads are involved with their young children but they lose the connection when their kids enter adolescence. When children are ten years old and below, the relationship between father and child, except for severe cases of abuse and neglect, is normally positive. After all, children at this stage adore their dads. They love playing with them, and, to a large extent, obeying them as well. It is during the adolescent years when the relationship gets tested and things go awry.

Understanding the Changes in the Adolescent Stage

Before we talk about the challenges during the adolescent stage, let us spend some time understanding this important yet trying period of their lives. The adolescent period is a succession of stages that occurs during the years from puberty to adulthood (see Chapter Six). The American Academy of Paediatrics divides this period into three stages:[30]

a. Early adolescence, generally ages 12 and 13
b. Middle adolescence, ages 14 to 16
c. Late adolescence, ages 17 to 21.

These are some of the most difficult years for parents, especially for fathers. It is a time of testing, a time when dads may feel that everything in their lives is going well except for their relationships with their teens. Yet, if fathers are educated about what to expect, and gain awareness about the kinds of exasperation interactions to which they are prone (see Chapters Two and Three), they will be able to turn this around and these years can be filled with many pleasant memories. This period can also bring about awareness and insights into the father's own life. Going through difficult times together, collaborating on projects, having deep conversations, plus fathers realising and apologising for their shortcomings, if handled well, can set a foundation for connection and acceptance for years to come, and provide great memories for future interactions.

When children hit the early adolescent stage, most parents are stunned at the dramatic changes that have taken place in their child. The child may change from a wonderfully compliant young boy or girl to someone who now argues and will not cooperate. The atmosphere at home becomes tense and the "new normal" includes arguments that ensue at least several times a week. Some parents feel guilty and blame themselves for this change, others blame their teen; almost no one knows what to expect and how to handle this stage.

While a good deal of this journey is something that teens have to make on their own, fathers being there to do their job may determine how the teen arrives at the end of adolescence and continues into young adulthood. Some adolescents are able to handle this better than others. Depending on the amount of turmoil, the parents' marriage may also be put to the test. Parents need to brace themselves for this difficult period, be educated about what is about to happen, put on their seat belts and stay involved with their children. It is a difficult period for the child, too. If both parents and child work through this difficult time together, rather than react to each other, they will experience a time of bonding.

Let us examine the changes adolescents go through in context with the four plus one core emotional needs. Three developments are taking place at the same time:
- Going through puberty
- Accelerated autonomy
- The desire to feel accepted for who they are.

During puberty, teenagers hit "the stage of adolescence in which an individual becomes physiologically capable of sexual reproduction."[31] This biological change affects adolescents' moods, perspectives on the opposite gender, tastes for clothes, styles, music, and how they view themselves. Usually they do not know how to see themselves. They have an innate desire to be independent. This is not something strange or unhealthy. This is actually part and parcel of growing up and spreading their own wings and developing autonomy. It's just that they also have a fear of growing up; this explains some of the confusion!

As they start trying to stand on their own two feet, they will resist some of the direction and guidance of their parents. Such resistance is natural at this stage. If parents are prepared, they will not be caught off guard and they will be in a better position to deal with this change. However, it's not unusual for fathers in particular to ask, "What happened to Daddy's little girl?" or suddenly feel competitive with their sons. Fathers can be unsure of how they are feeling during this time and not react well, which can contribute to potential tension between father and child or father and mother. Expecting hiccups, understanding how to deal with this change, talking to the child, and managing the "resistance" will improve the chance of a positive outcome, whether it is the self-esteem of the child or the atmosphere in the house. Rather than getting frustrated as their adolescents develop autonomy and identity, fathers "in the know" increase involvement. Training and getting properly equipped will help.

Stay Involved Through Thick and Thin

Why is this period particularly difficult for fathers? Let us go back to the idea that the early years with an involved father are fantastic. The child usually admires the father, loves playing with him, and listens to him. When fathers leave for work, their young children ask if they can follow. (Our son's first words, directed at John, were literally, "I want to go with you.") The father is the child's hero and he can do no wrong. This in turn, lifts the father's spirits, and a wonderful connection is built. When young children misbehave, parents can easily put an end to such undesirable behaviour since they are so small. For example, parents can literally pick them up from a squabble with another child, and take them away. Parents can give looks of disapproval, which can be effective at times, and they will be able to react accordingly. Discipline can lead to positive outcomes. However, in the adolescent age, parents now have to rely on reasoning, drawing out feelings, debating, arguing, listening attentively, listening without giving off strong non-verbal signals, and apologising; all of which are a lot more difficult and challenging than just picking up and moving a three-year-old.

Then there is the issue of the way the desire for autonomy accelerates during the adolescent period. So now, "Daddy's little girl" is ready to take a stand, voice her own opinions, criticise her parents, and even start distancing herself from them physically as well. This has a way of triggering negative emotions in many fathers, and they can feel rejected by their own offspring. Fathers will often feel it more than mothers. When men feel rejected, they generally withdraw, even those who tend toward overcompensation by nature. These fathers may counterattack in the beginning, but then they will shift into a different mode and start to feel detached from their children. Fathers tend to pull back and let mothers take control, and only in a crisis do they come to the scene. Fathers whose temperaments give rise to the avoidance coping style will naturally avoid conflict from the start and stay distant from their adolescent. In both situations, after distancing themselves from their adolescent children, they put their energy into something else, like their work. This puts an unfair burden on the mothers. Wives tend to stick with their teenagers longer since, in general, women bear with difficult relationships longer than men do.

Herein lies the challenge for fathers when children hit the adolescent stage. In the adolescents' quest for more autonomy and acceptance, they resist, debate, argue, question and reason more than any time previously. This triggers fathers because they likely sees this as being a challenge to their authority, and in turn they exert themselves. This triggers their teens, who reciprocate, and a Vortex develops between fathers and teenagers. The relationship temporarily gets disconnected, and since fathers tend to be more function-oriented and less relationship-oriented, they are at a loss. So over time, with repeated instances of this kind, fathers eventually retreat. They get detached as a form of protection and thus, the connection gets eroded slowly.

⟨ LOUIS LOWDOWN ⟩

Karen shares about this stage of life from a Mother and Wife's point of view: Seeing our 12-year-old daughter go through puberty and begin clashing with her dad was scary. Sonia was determined to prove she could win, and John was determined not to back down. I was afraid that Sonia and John's intense debates would end up driving Sonia away, and I also resented the tense atmosphere in the house. David, 10, also felt uncomfortable. In fact, during one loud encounter, he grabbed me by the hand and pulled me toward his room. I asked him where we were going, and he said, "Follow me!" He brought me to his room and we got onto his bed. He then pulled the covers completely over both of our heads and he whispered, "Someday, I'm going to write a book called *I Survived My Family*." Not too long after that, John and I had some good talks, and his relationship with Sonia began to improve drastically.

John shares: When Sonia was below 11 years of age, she was generally an obedient girl. She had her ups and downs, but I felt that she listened to me on most occasions. When she hit adolescence, there was a noticeable shift. She had always been feisty, but now she was super opinionated. (I wonder where she got that?) I remember our first heated debate. It was right after dinner. My wife and son left the table and went upstairs, leaving the two of us to sort out our issues. I was starting to be impressed by the depth of Sonia's reasoning, but I was also hurt. I should have conveyed that I was proud of her, but I wanted to show her that I had a point, too. I also felt that she should show respect to me as her father. But this was not to be the case. We went on and on. Eventually, I realized that neither of us was giving in, and feeling disappointed and angry, I terminated the conversation abruptly. I remember thinking, "My daughter is growing up. My goodness, is this what growing up means?" The next day, I initiated with her and we patched up the tension. A few days later, I suggested we go out for a date and she said she didn't want to. I started to feel the tug to pull away because I did not want to get hurt again. Fathers, it is easy to get hurt and withdraw, which is how I was feeling. But I hung in there and even though

> she was not excited when I said I wanted us to spend some time together, I persevered. We did end up spending some time together, and eventually our dates became a fun-filled routine, as I recounted in Chapter Six. The moral of this story: don't pull back when your teens give off signals that you are no more the awesome dad they once thought you were.

Here are some examples of comments from adolescents who are beginning to challenge their father's authority:

I'll do it, but not now.
Why do I have to do what I don't like?
I never said I would do it.
I thought you meant something else.
Who made up these stupid rules anyway?
What are you going to do about it?
Just leave me alone.
Nobody understands me.
Why are there are so many rules?

Any of the above will most likely aggravate fathers, as they will hear such statements as challenges to their authority. Their first thought may then be, "Who do you think you are?" If fathers respond with anger towards their adolescents, and later on detach and pull away, the connection will be affected. Eventually if no repair is done, the connection will erode.

Let us look at the following changes from childhood to adolescence:

A child tends to be more...	An adolescent tends to be more...
• Admiring of parents	• Critical of parents
• Respectful	• Disrespectful
• Compliant about limits	• Argumentative about limits
• Affectionate	• Distant
• Cooperative	• Resistant
• Honest	• Deceitful
• Drawn to teacher and school	• Critical of teacher and school
• Enthusiastic about spending time with parents, even more than with friends	• Reluctant to spend time with parents, and would much rather be with friends

In looking at the above list on the right side, it is easy to see why this would trigger parents, especially fathers, as these behaviours lead adolescents to not "doing the right thing". This goes against the tendency of fathers who are more focused on this aspect of their adolescents' behaviour than the mothers. Many fathers suffer from "shell shock" and it takes time for them to accept that their child has changed for what appears to be the "worse". It takes continual involvement, perseverance and courage to stay connected to their adolescent children during this challenging period, because believe it or not, more than ever at this time in their lives, teens need our acceptance! So, fathers, when the going gets tough, the tough stay connected. We must be strong and not allow ourselves to be frustrated by resistant and sometimes defiant teenagers; we are not to take their lack of cooperation personally! (Easier said than done!) Sometimes their words can cut like a dagger into the heart, but fathers, we have to take this in our stride. Talking with our spouses will help us to calm down. Afterwards, we will need to do the really important step, which is to speak vulnerably with our teenager. Hopefully, as the connection gets mended, the vulnerable communication will be two way, with each side sharing weaknesses, feelings and needs, gently and with a respectful tone. But fathers, we have to be "the man" and get it started. Being vulnerable breaks the cycle of the Vortex that typically results when emotions are allowed to flare up uncontrollably (see Chapter Twenty-Two for specifics on being vulnerable).

❖ LOUIS LOWDOWN ❖

When David was eight or nine years old, he was extremely compliant and obedient. Once he became an adolescent, I realized that he often did not keep his side of the bargain when it came to agreeing on responsibilities. I would talk to him about expectations, only to feel at the end of the day that I had not been thorough enough when we went through all the conditions. I told him that he was good at finding loopholes in our agreements and that I sometimes felt like I needed a lawyer. We had to hash things out. There were times when I felt like I wanted to not battle with him about such issues and would rather leave him alone. However, if I did leave him alone, then who was going to guide him? And if I did engage, what was the potential risk of conflict? There really was only one way out, to talk in such a way so as to not "put him down" and gently lead us to where we could both be on the same page. This was what I chose to do, and yes, I made mistakes along the way. I blew up at him several times, but we always patched up and eventually we reached an understanding. We bump heads a lot less often, and we are doing very well, staying connected, while he allows me to guide him as his father during his final year of high school.

Fathers, do not withdraw or let your hurts dictate the depth of the relationship with your adolescent. It takes effort to maintain a deep connection with them, and it takes both sides learning and asking for forgiveness on many occasions.

Let us remember the exhortations about fatherhood from the Scriptures:

> *"Which of you fathers, if your son asks for a fish, will give him a snake instead? Or if he asks for an egg, will give him a scorpion? If you then, though you are evil, know how to give good gifts to your children, how much more will your Father in heaven give the Holy Spirit to those who ask him!"* (Luke 11:11-13, NIV)

> *Fathers, do not exasperate your children; instead, bring them up in the training and instruction of the Lord.* (Ephesians 6:4, NIV)

> *Fathers, do not embitter your children, or they will become discouraged.* (Colossians 3:21, NIV)

> *Fathers, don't exasperate your children by coming down hard on them. Take them by the hand and lead them in the way of the Master.* (Ephesians 6:4, The Message)

> *Fathers, do not exasperate your children, so that they will not lose heart.* (Colossians 3:21, NAS)

Know the Father's Unique Contribution

Let us now focus on the general strength of fathers. Please let us qualify that in some families, it is the mother who tends to have the strengths that are outlined below. This does not mean that the married couple got it backwards, or that they are bizarre. It means that these mothers have talent and skills in an area that men usually have, and that makes them special, not strange. So it is totally fine if the mother is more driven to performing tasks and the father is the more sensitive one and better at relationships. What follows is the general pattern that we have seen in the given population.

The Apostle Paul wrote the following about the strengths of mothers and fathers:

> *Just as a nursing mother cares for her children, so we cared for you. Because we loved you so much, we were delighted to share with you not only the gospel of God but our lives as well. Surely you remember, brothers and sisters, our toil and hardship; we worked night and day in order not to be a burden to anyone while we preached the gospel of God to you. You are witnesses, and so is God, of how holy, righteous and blameless we were among you who believed. For you know that we dealt with each of you as a father deals with his own children, encouraging, comforting and urging you to live lives worthy of God, who calls you into his kingdom and glory.* (1 Thessalonians 2:7b-12)

Here, as Paul reminisced about his relationship with the Christians in Thessalonica, he talked about ways he and his companions treated them as a mother and as a father. While this passage does not talk about parenting *per se*, it does give us an outline of the way a godly man felt that mothers and fathers should normally relate to their children. Mothers would be nurturing, and would relate very much on a relationship level, sharing their lives with their children, building a bond and an attachment. For most families, mothers are superior to their counterpart husbands in building relationships. No doubt we are speaking of this in general terms, and there is absolutely nothing wrong with the opposite situation, but in most cases, mothers do the nurturing better than fathers.

But look what Paul says about dads—the father is the one who encourages, comforts and urges the children. Remember the three ways that research says that fathers need to be involved with their children—engagement, accessibility and responsibility, probably very similar in nature to what Paul was talking about. Fathers tend to be better at helping children with tasks, and motivating them to help them move forward in life. In summary, we generally find these differences between fathers and mothers:

- A father tends to be more focused on "doing" and a mother tends to be more focused on relationships within the family.
- A father tends to talk about achievement in school (although in Asia this trend is changing) while a mother tends to be more focused on the children building healthy friendships with others.
- A father tends to be involved in "rough and tumble" activities and a mother tends to be more focused on talking, so a mother tends to stay in conversation longer than a father.
- A father tends to give solutions to problems while a mother tends to be focused on what the problem is about.
- A father is less comfortable persevering with a difficult relationship than a mother.

It is important to bear these differences in mind as we outline the steps that parents can take to bring out the best in their children. Fathers and mothers need to collaborate and together meet the core emotional needs of their children. Fathers should not compete with mothers, but work together as partners. Given the natural strengths that Paul through the Holy Spirit attributed to dads, consider some specifics.

Fathers Are Awesome at Play

Who is usually better at playing with the children? Fathers or mothers? When the family goes swimming, who does what? When our kids were young, and we went to a pool, I (Karen) would think of all the safety issues—sunscreen, hats, floaties, depth of pool, lifeguards, you name it. I would play and make sure the kids were having fun, but primarily I was thinking of protecting. As the kids got older, I might swim a few lengths, follow the kids if they were swimming underwater, carry them on my back, help them with their diving or let them swim under my legs now and again. I would also sit near the side of the pool talking and kicking; sometimes I would get out of the pool and read. What was John doing? I (John) would carry the kids piggy back, play Marco Polo, and throw them up in the air over and over again to the point of exhaustion, although the kids never seemed to get tired of it! Who do the kids want to go to the pool with? Honestly, they love their dad playing "rough" with them. This is part of how children and fathers get bonded. Who do children like to play hide and seek with? Mothers or fathers? Dads run faster than their wives (at least most of us do), we are louder and we make scarier sounds. Many fathers do not value the wonderful impact their crazy antics have with their children. Remember the research we quoted earlier, that simple rough and tumble acts have a very positive effect on the children.

In Chapter Six, we cited many ways a father's play can help children—in areas such as reading other people's emotions, being able to regulate their own emotions, and how to generate their own exciting play. These areas in turn help children to develop social skills and get along well with their peers. The benefits of such interaction between fathers and their children is literally priceless. (There is a caveat to this—the father must keep the tone of the interaction positive and not resort to one of the exasperation interactions, such as being belittling or controlling, which would end up having the opposite effect.[32]) How sad many fathers continue to be absent and deprive their children from reaping such a wide array of advantages.

Fathers Provide a Voice of Reason

While emotions are good, emotions do not rule the day in every decision that needs to be made. After empathising, a father's practical approach to life can come in handy so that emotions do not take complete control, and so that children more inclined to go with their feelings can be guided.

⟨ LOUIS LOWDOWN ⟩

> I (John) think about the time when Sonia was 17 years old, and had worked very hard for her upcoming exams. Sonia tends to be a perfectionist and feel easily stressed (or maybe I passed down the unrelenting standards lifetrap?) so we talked before exam time about not worrying about the outcome, doing her best, letting God do the rest, getting enough sleep, etc. Sonia was positive when her exams began, but became discouraged when she thought that she did not do particularly well on the first of two biology tests. She felt lousy and had no confidence that she would do well on the second exam. She spoke to Karen, and then late at night, sensing that she was not settled, I went into her room to see how she was. She began crying and started pouring out her heart about feeling that she would not do well. I listened and told her how I had noticed she had worked so hard and that

> she knew more than she was giving herself credit for. I also told her that she probably had done better than she thought, and reminded her that her teacher thought very highly of her work. All in all, the talk lifted her up and in the end, she was able to go into the next exam with confidence. I remember that it was a late night, but it was worth it; we both remember that talk with fondness. She needed to hear a rational voice, a voice that would give her the confidence to go forward.

Adolescents need this kind of rational perspective, sometimes because they are too negative and cannot see the possible victories up ahead, and other times because they do not see past their noses when it comes to long-term consequences. Many of them seem to think that life will turn out well even when they sit on their laurels. A father's voice of reason, giving evidence to the contrary, can often wake them up to the reality that they may be headed for trouble down the road.

⋖ LOUIS LOWDOWN ⋗

> When David was younger, he was not achieving the kind of grades he was capable of achieving. No, this was not a case of a dad's unrelenting standards, just a case of a child's lack of reasonable standards. It took me going through his report card, and showing him evidence, especially focusing on the "effort" grade. As a father, I had to talk to him about the practicals of what would happen in his future if he didn't do his best now. I persuaded him that if he worked hard and used his God-given talents now, then he would have so many more options when he was older and would be able to make more choices in life. However, if he goofed off now and did not live up to his potential, he might one day regret it. (Note: This discussion was in regards to the national exam given to students in countries with a British Commonwealth history, the grades for which sometimes show up on job interviews at 40 years of age.) Having talks on such a practical level made the difference and eventually he got the point, developed his own convictions about doing things with all of his heart to please God, and did his best on the exams.

The voice of reason can also help boys see that placing too much weight on the outward beauty of a girl is shallow. Long-term quality of a healthy relationship is not solely about how beautiful a woman is. While it is natural and normal for boys to be attracted to girls physically, putting all of their focus on this can lead them down a dangerous path. As brothers in Christ, my son and I have had many discussions about purity and struggles with lust. I am proud of my son for feeling comfortable talking to me about such things. (For single mums, if their sons feel awkward, they can arrange for other older male mentors to talk to their sons about such issues.) As for talking about what kind of Christian sister would make a good wife, one of our favourite verses is, *"Charm is deceptive, and beauty is fleeting, but a woman who fears the Lord is to be praised…"* (Proverbs 31:30a) Fathers, please don't hold back —talk with your sons about such things and help them to build conviction in these areas.

◁ RESEARCH REVEALS ▷

RR21.5: *Teenagers and Sexuality*

(The following data is taken from the website for the US Center for Disease Control and Prevention/CDC.[33])

Many young people engage in sexually risky behaviours that can result in unintended outcomes. For example, among American High School students surveyed in 2009, the following came to light.

- 46% had engaged in sexual intercourse
- 34% had engaged in sexual intercourse within three months prior to the survey, and of these
- 39% did not use a condom the last time they had sex
- 77% did not use birth control pills or Depo-Provera, a three-month birth control injection, to prevent pregnancy the last time they had sex
- 14% had "had sex" with four or more people during their brief life.

Consider a sobering study conducted in Singapore published by the American Academy of Pediatrics in 2009, which included the following findings among adolescents between 14 and 19 years of age:[34]

- The strongest factor associated with early sexual intercourse for adolescent males was viewing pornography. This finding agreed with another study conducted in Sweden with boys between 17 and 21 years of age.
- Most of the boys viewed pornography on a computer (59%); other popular sources were videos (19%) and mobile phones (14%).

Given the rampant exposure to pornography, how could this not be a topic that a father and son talk about on a regular basis? How can fathers leave this to chance and expect their adolescents to come out of this unscathed in today's day and age? Unless fathers (and mothers) are involved in the lives of their sons and daughters, they will statistically fall prey to Internet pornography and who knows what else.

Fathers who are not involved with their adolescents offering the guidance and advice they so much need may one day regret it. As mentioned in the Basic Safety section of Chapter Thirteen on Reasonable Limits, fathers need to actively be involved and know if proper Internet filters are installed in the computers, phones and tablets of their adolescents.

Other times when a voice of reason can help:
- Taking on too much with a limited schedule – A father's voice of reason can help a child with time management, to sort out priorities and to know when to say "No" to a certain task or activity, for example, spending too much time on sports at the expense of other things or having an imbalanced schedule.
- Handling difficult relationships at school – When an adolescent has disagreements with friends or fellow students, good practical sound advice from a father *who is involved* goes a long way. There will be times when they will feel that others are gossiping about them, not treating them fairly, and/or teasing them about their values as a Christian. At times like these, having a dad to lean on gives kids confidence.
- Living within their means – Some children have a way of not sticking to spending limits. A father's voice reminding the family to not go over budget can help prevent emotions ruling the day with certain purchases. (While saying all this, if a father comes across as a "know it all" or as miserly, it also does not help, and he will meet with resistance.)

Fathers Can Help Children to Avoid Abusive Relationships

Suppose you have a child with the subjugation lifetrap. Imagine that this subjugated child is in a dysfunctional friendship with a bully or is a teen and has a crush on someone who is verbally abusive toward him or her. Typically, those with the subjugation lifetrap will continue to stay in such relationships and will always put the needs of the other person before their own needs. Imagine if your child is constantly getting abused, but denies that the other person is an abuser. This is where the voice of an involved father can help the child to see the truth. Talking about feelings alone might not lift the fog in the eyes of a subjugated or a surrendered adolescent. The voice of a strong father will. We should protect our daughters from falling prey to such abuses from other boys and men, and teach our boys and girls how to deal with bullies in a Christ-like manner. The following case studies from our youth ministry may help to illustrate this point:

Francine, one of the teen sisters in our youth ministry, was being pursued by a young man from her school named Zack. He tried over and over to get Francine to go out with him. Even though they were friends and got along well in class, she told him she was not interested in anything more. Zack became angry when she rejected his advances. He began to tease and taunt her, saying rude things to Francine at school in front of others, and the girl went home crying on more than one occasion. Her father had a talk with the whole family, and Francine's older brother, Fred, decided to get involved. Fred had been on the same tennis team as Zack and they got along well, so Fred stepped up and called him. They had a polite discussion, with the brother helping Zack to see that the way he was treating Francine was not right. Fred told him that Francine appreciated their friendship but would not be able to be his friend if this behaviour continued. Fortunately, Zack got the message, and nothing negative happened further. Francine and her brother continued to be friends with Zack and brought him to their church several times. This positive outcome would not have been possible if Francine's dad had not intervened in the beginning. We have witnessed teenage girls being stalked, and it is important for girls to feel that they have a dad who will help to keep them safe.

The Applebys are Christian parents who love reaching out to the lost and evangelising. On one occasion, when their two children were preteens, the Applebys invited a boy from their church to come and play in their home. Little did the parents know that he had been exposed to pornography and had decided to try out some new "activities" on their son. This continued for several years; the boy would come over to play, the two boys would go into the attic, and all sorts of things happened behind closed doors. Sadly, this led to incest between the siblings, which (of course) damaged the relationships in the family, although the parents only knew about it much later. By the time this "family secret" came out in the open, there were many scars in the kids' lives. If the parents knew then what they know now, the father would have been more watchful and protective in general, and more careful about allowing the kids to be in a room with the door closed.

When Aisha was eight years old, her parents arranged for a male tutor to help her with some school-work. This tutor took advantage of Aisha and molested her. Thankfully the girl knew something was wrong and reported this to her parents the same day. In hindsight, it could have been prevented if the parents had arranged for tutoring in a room with a parent present. Parents need to be vigilant and not leave things to chance. Some trauma occurs only after repeated frustration of needs, but recurrence is not necessary in the case of sexual abuse—once can be enough. Fathers, protect your daughters, and your sons.

RESEARCH REVEALS

RR21.6: *Teenage Girls and Sexuality*

The same American Academy of Pediatrics study of Singaporean 14-19 year olds that found boys affected by pornography found that the strongest factor associated with early sexual intercourse for female adolescents was their having a history of sexual abuse. It was also found that sexually abused girls had more partners than non-abused. [35]

Fathers Can Be a Positive Male Role Model

A father is in a position to affect his children by being a positive male role model. When a daughter has a healthy connection with a father who is a great role model in many areas, it not only boosts her self-esteem, but also keeps her from looking for connection and acceptance in unhealthy places. Boys need healthy role models, too; not just in the area of relationships and marriage, but in having good character, a strong work-ethic, a love of adventure and a healthy view of their masculinity. What a great gift to the family when the father models all of these qualities, plus is a good provider, an honest businessman or worker, a kind son to his own parents, and enthusiastic about his relationships with God and the church.

> **◁ LOUIS LOWDOWN ▷**
>
> I (Karen) would love to share this story here about dad's being role models. As the captain of the Badminton team at his school, David got in a tricky situation during a tournament. A player on the opposing team did something that was unsportsmanlike, which caused David's teammate to lose his match. David was torn between avoiding conflict by keeping quiet or bringing the issue up to the coach of the other team, who happened to be the principal of the school they were playing against. He plucked up his courage, and in the end, the match was replayed, David's teammate won, and everyone (except for the player on the other team) was happy about how David handled it. He was even sent a letter of commendation by his own principal. I praised David for his grace under fire, and asked, "How were you able to do that?" He replied that he just kept thinking to himself, "What would Dad do in this situation? How would Dad handle this?" As a mum, I couldn't have been prouder.

Fathers Encouragement May Mean More

Depending on their particular dynamics, in some families, the mother is quite encouraging, and the father is not as vocal. Interestingly, this sometimes means that when the children become teens, they will take the father's encouragement more seriously. (When mum says it, they think, "Aw, that's just mum…") Our teens need constant encouragement, especially in regards to the following areas:

- For having a heart for people
- For being well regarded and worthy of respect
- For being smart and intelligent
- For being attractive
- For being hard working.

Constant encouragement in front of others goes a long way in building up a teen's self-esteem. We both take the opportunity, from time to time, to brag about our kids in front of our best friends. Sometimes they feel embarrassed about it, but we know it has also encouraged them a lot when they know what we think of them deep in *our* hearts. Nothing encourages them like knowing how proud we are of them. There is something about encouragement from a father that goes a long way in building up the kids' self-worth and security.

When a dad does not over-encourage, and when the connection with his teens is strong, there is a higher chance that the kids will believe his encouragement. A son will feel it when his father does not show that he is proud of him. As young males go from boys to men, it is healthy for fathers to move toward not just being proud of their sons but respecting them as well. Many adult sons are still waiting to hear their father's say, "I am proud of you," and "I respect you, son."(Daughters, too.)

◈ LOUIS LOWDOWN ◈

I (John) once asked David to take a few days to think about what I would have to do to affect his relationship with God in a negative way. He came back to me with the following:

"If you never really cared for me and did not spend time with me, and If you were a control freak."

As it has been said, love is not spelled "t-h-i-n-g-s"; love is spelled "T-I-M-E". Spending time conveys that your child is special and that he/she is a gem!

Ensure Your Marriage Is Healthy

At the risk of sounding extremely repetitive, we must harp on the importance of marriage yet again. The way a father treats his wife will set the tone for how his adolescent son views women, and how he will one day treat his girlfriend and eventually, his wife. A father also models for his daughter how women are to be respected by their boyfriend/husband. It is amazing how many people try and separate marriage from parenting, yet over and over again, research shows otherwise. Seeing her father look lovingly at her mother will make a daughter look forward to being married to a good man. If the home does not provide security, they will look for it elsewhere. (For more on this topic, please see Chapter One and refer to the Introduction of our book on marriage, *I Choose Us*.[36])

Find Similarities with Your Adolescents

Consider the potential impact of how a father and child's temperaments compare, whether they are alike or different. Consider first the case where the adolescent son or daughter may be like the father. If the father is an overcompensator as well as the daughter, the father will provide an excellent example for the daughter. She will think that both her dad and she are a lot like each other. This helps the father to know how to empathize with the daughter in some ways better than the mother if she is not an overcompensator. The same argument of course can be made of the mother and son. In our family my son and wife have similar temperaments, while my daughter and I are similar, and so when she has a little tiff with my wife, and my help is solicited, my daughter responds well when I say, "I think when mum said this, you actually felt this..." Usually because we are so alike she says, "Yes, that is exactly right." This helps me show empathy and in the end she then becomes more open to my feedback. The same goes with my son and my wife. Obviously there are many possible combinations—the point is that we want to look for what we might have in common with our adolescents and take advantage of that for the sake of connection.

If a father is involved with the children, then when the children have arguments with each other or with their mother, the father will be able to relate and offer his perspective, which will be valued. Too often, fathers check out when they come home after work, thinking that they should only be roped in when disciplinary action is needed. If the father sees this as his role, he will always be the "bad guy" since he will only be involved when some kind of consequence is needed for the children.

Fathers, while your son will look up to you tremendously when you meet the core emotional needs, you have to also remember that as he grows, he will be his own man and may develop aspirations different from those of you, his father. When this happens, be proud of his choices and get behind him 100%.

Make the Transition as a Parent as Children Get Older

Please remember "exasperation interactions", and recall the ways parents can cause frustrative and traumatic experiences in their children (see Chapters Two and Three). When children are young, up to the age of nine or ten, before they hit the young adolescent stage, most of them will succumb to the authority of their parents. Children have not yet reached a stage where they value their autonomy and their separateness as an individual. When they reach puberty and their adolescent characteristics kick in, they will resist and show disapproval for the lack of connection, acceptance, respect, space, freedom, spiritual depth, and confidence. They will start speaking up. This changes in the adolescent stage and will continue to change as they age. So for a good few years, from the age of ten all the way till they are in the early twenties, they will continue to grow. Fathers spend these years getting baffled, and as explained, fathers especially then tend to become detached and stop getting really involved. Some fathers will try more than others, but unless fathers make a decision to be engaged with their children in the battle and in their relationship, eventually these fathers will also get detached. A lack of awareness of the ways in which they engage in exasperation interactions will result in the core emotional needs not being met, and adolescents will eventually rebel. Fathers then put it all down to having difficult children, luck, fate and sometimes spiral downwards into self-pity and think that God has punished them for their own rebellion when they were teenagers. At other times, they send their children for therapy.

Yet so much can be repaired if only parents would gain awareness of their tendency to exasperate their children. Parents are not the only cause of frustrative and traumatic experiences in children, but they are the cause if they repeatedly engage in any of the exasperation interactions, intentionally or not. Most children, while going through frustrative and traumatic experiences even at a very young age, will still be relatively obedient, simply because at that age children have no choice. Even when they are aware that their parents have made mistakes, they still would not know what to do. Some harbour resentment. After all, what can they do if the parents are in the wrong? Who is going to give the parents consequences? Who is going to tell the parents what to do? So kids bite the bullet, move on and hope for better days. However, this will all catch up when the children hit the adolescent stage. If fathers continue with their unhealthy styles and tighten the screws so to speak, this will not result in a positive outcome but only in hurts, arguments, debates, resistance, and rebellion. So it is important that fathers make a shift from engaging in exasperation interactions to making the effort to meet the core emotional needs. Of course, this takes hard work and involves fathers:

- Being humble to unlearn and relearn healthy parent-child interactions
- Being able to apologise and repair a relationship when it gets strained and to do so quickly, not letting it fester and produce bitterness
- Being able to have long talks with their spouse and get feedback.

I (John) know from experience that getting feedback from a spouse and others who are able to help us is extremely helpful. Fathers, it takes swallowing our pride but it is worth it!

A father's humility and vulnerability can set the tone of how the children respond when they are in the wrong. A father who is unwilling to apologise will pass this trait on to his children. The good news is that children in their heart of hearts desire to be close to their parents and when they see them being vulnerable and humble, especially their fathers, it encourages them to draw near and respond in kind.

I know I've made mistakes... How can I make amends?

CHAPTER TWENTY-TWO

Repair and Reconnect

During the course of parenting, it is not unusual to have arguments, experience the occasional tense moment, and even encounter a temporary breakdown or two in the connection between parent and child—sometimes between husband and wife! It is natural for parents to feel frustrated when their children act out over and over again after many reminders. Mums and dads rightfully take issue with their children for talking back, being rude to others, lying, spending too much money, not taking schoolwork seriously, and the list goes on. Even when trying to be Good Enough Parents, mums and dads sometimes become frustrated, slip into exasperation interaction mode and stay there for a while. When this happens, the parent-child relationship gets disconnected and repair is needed. If you find yourself at this stage, or if things are worse and there has been no connection for a while, *and you have already read the rest of this book,* then you are ready for this chapter called "Repair and Reconnect".

Don't be deceived by the philosophy of "let's just cool down", or "let's forget the episode", believing that, in time, everything will get back to normal and that you will experience connection again. That is doubtful. When heated arguments take place, and unhelpful words are spoken by one or both parties, the result is hurt feelings that need to be dealt with. If the relationship is repaired quickly, all will be forgotten—by nature, children are resilient and forgiving. If these hurts are not processed well, however, children or parents or both will ruminate, replaying the hurtful words over and over and getting more and more negative. When we ruminate, our thoughts get distorted and the pain gets worse, affecting our concentration level. We could be talking to someone else, but be thinking about the painful argument we had with our child. We could be driving or eating or replying to emails, but still be preoccupied. For some parents, the disconnection becomes an obsession and even affects their sleep. How many times have we heard people say, "If only I had talked with them earlier, I would have spared my family a lot of pain and suffering."

When children do not get reconnected with their parents quickly, they feel abandoned, alone, unloved or misunderstood. Shame and guilt set in. Sometimes parents and children process these pains differently. Children may feel hopeless, while parents may feel that things will get better. Young children especially look at hurts and pain differently than adults. For example, the parent may feel angry, but the child may feel humiliated and shamed.

Such emotions, felt repeatedly, lead to exasperation and discouragement, which affects not only the way the child feels about the parent but also the child's physical and mental health. So, when parent and child become disconnected, it is important to get reconnected as quickly as possible. To this end, it is in the interest of every parent to know how to effectively repair the relationship with his child. Repairing and reconnecting will bring the relationship between the parent and child to a new level of intimacy.

On the positive side, if a connection already existed before the disruption, both sides will usually want to come back to the state of connection again by being reconciled. However, if the practice of one or both parties was to deny any hurtful feelings, and to simply "move on" or avoid, reconnecting will be more difficult; still, it is never too late. The process of getting reconnected involves both parent and child being vulnerable. The child will have to be old enough to talk about her feelings to be able to understand and do this effectively. If need be, the other parent or a safe adult can help to coach the child. Before describing how to be vulnerable, let us spend some time explaining this concept even further.

MOVIE MOMENT – *Chicken Little,*[1] *Freaky Friday,*[2] *Divine Secrets of the Ya-Ya Sisterhood*[3]

> When working on connection with your younger children, a great film to watch together is the animated *Chicken Little*. The father had doubted his son and been a bit embarrassed by how different his son was. The son finally confronted his dad and in a moment of stress, all of his attitudes came pouring out. The father offered a heartfelt apology and proved his repentance in the remaining moments of the story. After your family has watched the show for entertainment/family time, parents can replay the scene described above—perhaps during a family devo or family dinner. Then the parents can ask the children, either together or one at a time, if the children have ever wanted to speak up to the parents the way Chicken Little did, or if the parents have ever made the kids feel the way the Papa Chicken made his son feel. They may say "No", but they may think of it at a later time, or they may be glad you asked. For older children, try watching *Freaky Friday*, which was mentioned in the chapter on empathy (see Chapter Seven). This is a great movie for discussion and repentance. If you are trying to get reconnected with adult children, you may find it helpful to watch *Divine Secrets of the Ya-Ya Sisterhood*, first by yourself and later with your adult child. You can also buy your adult children the film so that they can watch on their own, or you can just watch by yourself and try to "repent" first.

Healing Comes from Being Vulnerable

When we are vulnerable with anyone, we allow ourselves to be known in a much more intimate way. We move toward healing as we vulnerably discuss our lifetraps, our coping styles, and their origins. We are assuming that most of you feel safe enough with someone to do this; ideally with your spouse. Alternatively, find someone else to talk to with whom you can feel safe.

As we mentioned earlier (see Chapter Twenty), one of the findings in the field of counselling is that treatment has the greatest chance of success in an atmosphere where the client feels safe and respected.[4] In fact, this is rated to be a more successful predictor than the skill of the therapist or the type of therapy employed. Therefore, a safe environment with a person, or even with a group of supportive church friends or a like-minded group of people can lead to some kind of emotional healing. When we feel safe enough to remove our "masks", we may discover a deep inner feeling of hurt, disappointment or fear, which we did not realise was there; we are getting into the deep recesses of our soul. This is what experts call the "child side". We believe that Jesus was at least partly talking about this concept in the following passage:

> *At that time the disciples came to Jesus and asked, "Who is the greatest in the kingdom of heaven?" He called a little child and had him stand among them. And he said: "I tell you the truth, unless you change and become like little children, you will never enter the kingdom of heaven. Therefore, whoever humbles himself like this child is the greatest in the kingdom of heaven."* (Matthew 18:1-4)

What exactly did Jesus mean when He taught that we should be like little children? Certainly being childish, immature and undisciplined were not the traits He had in mind. We think that Jesus meant for us to imitate the godly qualities of a child—the side where we do not put up a front but are transparent about how we really feel and what we really need. This is what we see in children. Children are genuine in their demeanour. If they are angry, they let you know. If they are happy, it shows! Jesus admires these qualities in children and teaches us to bring out those innocent, genuine feelings that have been tucked away. We believe Jesus values this kind of humility, brokenness, and vulnerability and finds it endearing.

Different experts have seen the value of getting in touch with our child side. Drs Alice Miller, Donald Winnicott, and Emmet Fox, early experts in the field of child development, taught that we should experience the child side of ourselves, or our true self.[5] Dr Charles Whitfield defines the child side as "who we are when we feel most authentic, genuine or spirited."[6]

Our child side experiences the feelings of joy and pain. It wants and needs to express these feelings without fear or judgment. This is seen clearly in young children and is one of the reasons why they are so endearing. As adults we do not completely lose our child side; we only become good at hiding it. This child side is who we *truly* are. It is the side that expresses what we need, when we are weak, when we are happy and contented, when we are sad, and when we are afraid. When children start experiencing unhealthy guilt or shame or fear at a young age, they are usually at a loss, not knowing how to cope with these emotions. Often, the people who induce such feelings of unhealthy shame, guilt and fear are the parents, and some of them are grossly ignorant about healthy parenting skills and principles. As a result many people grow up with feelings of unhealthy guilt, shame or fear from a young age, which erodes their child side. Then as needs are not met, a child develops a false sense of who he is.

Children rely on their parents to meet their core needs. When a child does not feel loved and accepted by his parents, or when the messages he receives are negative, the child is powerless to know that these messages are false. Since these negative messages get repeated over and over, the child comes to believe them. When he accepts them as the truth about himself, lifetraps develop. In order to manage the pain and fear these lifetraps cause us, the child develops a false front in the form of unhealthy coping styles that hide real needs and desires. The child then grows into an adult who is so in the habit of using his coping style to respond to his fears that he no longer knows he is shutting himself off from his innermost thoughts and feelings. Eventually, with repetition, the child side gets completely hidden and comes out only here and there, and the false side has now become a very natural part of the person's makeup and personality. It is deeply embedded, and the more a person relies on this side of himself, the less he will be in touch with his child side. Moreover, the adult vocabulary is more extensive so as the child grows up, he will subconsciously know what to say to deter others from getting to his child side. The end result is that if the child side is not nurtured, the false unhealthy coping style takes over and little healing can take place.

This coping style is not our true inner self. When Jesus tells us to be like a little child, we believe that He is calling on us to bring out our child side, which is genuine, sincere and teachable. It takes humility and courage to expose our child side, and when it does come out, we are finally being vulnerable. Believing the false truth of our lifetraps and covering up our real selves with our coping styles only prolongs the pain and keeps us from healing. For example, when a parent loses his temper and quarrels with his child, he might act tough rather than be vulnerable. He might pretend that he does not need anyone and that he is fine, which is the avoidance coping style. He may cope by being busy, but in doing so may keep himself detached from his true child side. The coping style of avoidance may even put him on the path of getting involved in an addiction or being a workaholic. Whatever it is, it will prevent him from being in touch with his real self, his child side. When feelings of guilt or shame arise, he may overcompensate or counterattack in order to protect himself. Since he is not being vulnerable, the child side is hidden, but a false angry side comes out instead by way of the overcompensation coping style. Then there are those who surrender because they hear a critical parent voice and give in, thinking that everything is their fault. While this may not lead to a volatile quarrel the way an overcompensation coping style would, they are still not vulnerable, so the child side stays tucked away. Some people mistakenly think this is a sign of humility, but true humility focuses on God, not self, therefore a truly humble person would be able to let the child side be exposed. Whatever the coping style, when parents respond to triggers by hiding their inner selves/child side, they will eventually become accustomed to the façade.

Speaking from personal experience, when we start being vulnerable, we will suddenly feel confusion, fear, excitement, sadness and even anger. When this happens, it is actually good news. However, many people will give up at this point because they feel awkward and hurt. It is easier to stay in touch with their old, false self and the coping style to which they have been accustomed for so long. They would rather stay with the *familiar* than move towards something that is *healthier*.

As we practice being vulnerable, we should not let the awkward feelings dissuade us from pressing on. We should not give into our fear, rather, we should allow ourselves to feel our old fears, and look to our spouse to help us feel safe and comfortable. This can be a place of real healing rather than the false place of relating through our lifetraps and coping styles. If we feel more comfortable writing instead of talking and sharing, it is fine to do so, as long as we are being vulnerable. When we get there, we will feel a real connection.

With humility and courage, we can take responsibility for our own healing. It may take a while. We may need to have a "do over" now and again, but with each attempt, we will get closer to being healed—emotionally, mentally, and spiritually, and as a result, attaining a sense of peace. All of us, from every corner of the globe, yearn for this kind of peace, whether we are rich, poor, young or old. The alternative is holding in our unhealthy feelings until they become unbearable. How is that a better option? Our feelings have a way of coming out, whether we like it or not, through our present unhealthy coping style. This may lead to all sorts of self-destructive behaviour, including dependence on alcohol, smoking, over-eating, sexual promiscuity, or through counterattacking others which damages relationships around us. While this is happening, we may numbly go about our routine, feel less alive, less engaged, and less "present" when we are with our children. But our child side, the energetic side, is waiting to come out, and it has to be drawn out carefully, through being vulnerable.

Men are notorious for frowning at the thought of being vulnerable with anyone, let alone their children. Usually men view conversations in the realm of hurts and feelings as something belonging to the opposite gender. They laugh, and look down on such things, but truthfully, it is their avoidant side that is reacting. Little do they realise that suppressed feelings lead to stress, distress and illness, simply because this part of them is not liberated. They end up experiencing less personal growth, and miss out on how wonderful it is to get in touch with their child side. As comfortable as we may be with our false self (coping style), our false self cannot help us get healed. Only the child side, the true self, can take us to a healthier place. Staying with the false messages of our lifetraps through our coping styles will only prolong the pain and hold back the healing—they function to hide our child side. So, let us get our child side out and be vulnerable! Whitfield says that most of us expose our child side for only about 15 minutes a day![7] Whether with our spouse, or children, or with other safe friends, it is time to get started.

We should be patient with each other and help each other go through this process. This is what love for each other is all about; making the effort to help ourselves and others change, as Dr M. Scott Peck defines love in his book *The Road Less Travelled*:

> (Love is) the will to extend one's self for the purpose of nurturing one's own or another's spiritual growth.[8]

Having explained how being vulnerable is related to meeting the needs of our child side, let's get specific and talk about *how* to be vulnerable.

How To Be Vulnerable

When it comes to communicating in a vulnerable way, we like to think of being vulnerable as having three or four components: sharing our weakness, our feelings, our need, and apologising where necessary. We would like to present different scenarios to which parents and adolescents can refer as a guide to help stay engaged with each other.

Suffice it to say that it is usually difficult for both parents and adolescents to enter into a vulnerable exchange. Often one side will get defensive and trigger the other, who may very well counterattack as a result. If, after hearing each other's perspectives, one side is still not satisfied, it is best not to escalate the exchange and enter into a Vortex (see Chapters Thirteen and Fourteen). Instead, take a little time out, and then initiate to restart the dialogue. Being vulnerable instead of just letting out feelings and anger can be very helpful and reconciliatory.

You will need to say as a parent, "You know, I think if we keep talking it will get worse. I really want both of us to take time to think about what happened and when both sides are more calm, we will be able to better understand each other." Be very aware of how you are coming across—remember that in communication, words are not nearly as important as tone and body language.[9]

Being vulnerable with each other helps a parent to know what the child is feeling when he says, "Mum, I am really angry at you for saying this", or "Dad, you just don't understand what I am thinking and feeling", or, "I am not seeing things the way you are" or "I don't agree with you". These are all common statements and with vulnerability something very powerful takes place—both the parent and the child will be able to truly understand and connect, and this will have an unbelievable effect on the parent-child relationship. There is something about exposing your weakness, feeling understood and voicing out your needs that draws us closer to one another. Usually these messages are hidden deep within a person, and what comes out is our coping style, which is not helpful, and often leads us into the Vortex of Conflict Escalation. Instead, when we are vulnerable, our hidden child side comes out, and healing takes place at an emotional level, which can be very powerful for reconciliation and connection.

When these hidden emotions are not let out in a healthy way, they will come out eventually in some unhealthy manner, usually in the form of rage, or in the form of emotional inhibition, where over time, the person becomes very numb and rigid. In one way or other, these coping styles fall in one of three ways we have outlined previously—surrender, avoidance or overcompensation. Whatever the coping style, relying on any of them is not healthy and damages the parent-child relationship. Parents must learn how to put their finger on the emotions behind the coping styles (or identify how the child side is feeling), and that is what being vulnerable is all about—bringing our child side out into the open.

In Appendix 5, we have presented different scenarios between a parent and an adolescent, and there are exercises on how both parties can practise being vulnerable. We choose to say parent and adolescent, rather than parent and child, as most fights and quarrels take place when children become adolescents. Further, when a child reaches this point in life, they will be able to grasp written instruction about being vulnerable, which might be challenging for younger children. (This is not meant to be an excuse for parents to not be humble to their younger children.)

Bear in mind that after the child has been vulnerable, a lecture should not take place. What better way to shut down anyone's child side? Remember, the listening party should validate the other's feelings, summarise, identify the other's emotions, and speak in a gentle tone, not in a judgmental or lecturing tone, which many parents tend to do (see Chapter Seven on Empathy). You will make incredible strides in getting reconnected when you put these steps into practise.

Follow the steps outlined on how to validate and listen to your children. If the listening party disagrees with anything stated, this should also come from a vulnerable point of view. In this way both sides are entering into a state where they are attempting to understand and know each other's weaknesses and needs. Being vulnerable comprises four main areas:

- Weakness and fears – Usually related to your unhealthy coping styles or lifetraps
- Apologising if necessary – Stating how you were triggered and how you responded in an inappropriate manner, if this was indeed the case, and apologising for it.
- Feelings – What you are feeling but not in an accusing way
- Needs – Core emotional needs for children and other needs and expectations for parents

In all the examples in Appendix 5, we treat the components of being vulnerable separately. Please take time to do this exercise. These four components are essential and need to be memorised. A friend of ours noted the similarity between the four steps of being vulnerable with the biblical account of the Pharisee and tax collector:

> *To some who were confident of their own righteousness and looked down on everybody else, Jesus told this parable: "Two men went up to the temple to pray, one a Pharisee and the other a tax collector. The Pharisee stood up and prayed about himself: 'God, I thank you that I am not like other men—robbers, evildoers, adulterers—or even like this tax collector. I fast twice a week and give a tenth of all I get.' But the tax collector stood at a distance. He would not even look up to heaven, but beat his breast and said, 'God, have mercy on me, a sinner.' I tell you that this man, rather than the other, went home justified before God. For everyone who exalts himself will be humbled, and he who humbles himself will be exalted." (Luke 18:9-14)*

The one who was *connected* to God showed the four qualities of being vulnerable: Weakness and Apology (posture, "I am a sinner"), Feeling (beating of his breast as a sign of sorrow), Need (mercy). Given his humility, the tone of his voice would have surely been penitent, gentle, and soft spoken. The Pharisee, on the other hand, was not connected to God, nor probably anyone except himself. His tone was probably arrogant and self-righteous.

Principles that Parents Should Consider When Repairing Parent-Child Relationships

When an argument ensues, do you as a parent take the time to reflect and gain awareness of your own issues? The following are some questions you can ask:

a. What triggered me? Parents need to gain awareness of their own issues.
b. Why did this trigger me? Did I get angry because my own agenda was not met, or did I get angry because I really want what is best for my child? For example, if an argument came about because the parent wanted the child to stick to a certain spending limit, then the parent's agenda is to help train the child to be more disciplined. However, if the parent was angry because the child did something the parent did not approve of (eg. got a certain hair style for teenagers, or bought a certain dress) then perhaps the parent's reactions may be associated with shame on their part, in which case this is more an issue that the parent has to come to terms with. On the other hand, did the child not adhere to healthy limits that were imposed by the parents? Did the child not cooperate with an earlier agreement? Did the child not honour family values, such as integrity and purity?
c. Was there a sudden change in rules? If parents have been allowing children to get away with very few healthy limits and have all of a sudden come to the realisation of their mistakes, then they should first have a discussion about this. Often parents make such changes suddenly and this abrupt change will cause a huge reaction on the part of the children and inevitably a fight will result. Parents should say something to the effect, "Honey all this while, we realise that we have made mistakes in our parenting. We need to take responsibility for that. This part is not your fault. We have a new awareness of ourselves as parents. Especially after seeing this pattern in your behaviour, we would like to discuss with you some changes that we are going to implement. We know that this is not going to be easy for you, and it is also not easy for us, but we have talked about it and we want to go over it with you." Then implement the new limits and this time stick to your convictions. When the child sees your new stance, he will eventually come to respect it, although initially he may be upset or even show his temper.
d. Did I listen to my child empathically or did I jump to conclusions and start making judgments?
e. Discuss with the other parent, if he or she was not involved in the argument. Ask them objectively and let them give you their feedback. Avoid turning this interaction into another fight, as this can make resolving the other previous one with the child even more difficult. Be vulnerable with each other.
f. After reflecting on the above, be calm and be ready to be vulnerable with the child. When children are young, parents especially need to initiate. Children process tension in a very negative way and this can be detrimental to their mental health over the long haul if issues are not resolved quickly.

g. Usually, if resolving conflicts quickly is a habit in the family then as the children get older they will also initiate to resolve issues. This is a good sign. If parents are still initiating this with adolescents, then this can also be an issue that parents bring up with the child, but do so after the argument is resolved. Both sides need to be in the practice of initiating. There should not be such an imbalance that only one side initiates most of the time.

Forgiveness

Since we are all sinners, understanding forgiveness and knowing how to extend it to each other is a very crucial component of a healthy family. Yet we have noticed how little emphasis forgiveness is given in major approaches to therapy. Experts and writers come up with all kinds of attending, assessment and intervention skills, but only in rare cases is forgiveness given the attention it deserves. Sadly, even many Christians do not know the correct biblical definition of forgiveness. We strongly believe that unless it is properly understood and rendered, the possibility of relapse will be high and families will not grow and change as part of their journey together. It is no doubt difficult, but it is still essential. When we forgive, all the bitterness, resentment, and anger are swept away. The negative emotional energy is gone and is replaced by feelings of light-heartedness, freedom, and peace. Indeed, forgiveness *is* the corner stone for healing in our family relationships.

For more help on repairing and reconnecting, please review the teaching on forgiveness in the discussion of shaping our children's values (see Chapter Nineteen). And make sure you review the huge section on meeting the core emotional need of Connection and Acceptance one more time (see Chapters Four to Seven).

Ron and Linda Brumley's 40-year-old son, Matthew, their youngest, wrote this letter in response to our question about what in the Brumley's parenting helped him. In many ways, his letter sums up so much of what we have tried to say about meeting the four plus one core emotional needs. It especially highlights Ron's example as a dad, how his parents pointed him to God, and their ability to Repair and Reconnect.

⊰ MASTER CLASS ⊱

"When you break down our walk with God, it's really about gratitude, isn't it? It is not a matter of do's and don'ts. As a child growing up in church, it was hard for me to distinguish this because, while I was under my parents' control as I should have been, my life felt *to me* like a series of do's and don'ts and consequences (rewards and punishments). So, as I started to work on a personal relationship with God, it was very difficult for me. My rebellious nature made me feel like I was being deprived of what I 'wasn't allowed' to do as a disciple. In reality, if I had been able to grasp all the incredible gifts I had and the ultimate sacrifice God made for me, I would have had a different outlook on being a disciple. In short, I would have been more grateful.

The greatest help in my life as a disciple has been seeing the gratitude of my parents for God and what He has done for them. Through the hard times I never saw my parents complain or worry about what was in front of them spiritually or physically. Believe me, regrettably so, I gave them plenty to worry about. Instead, I saw them face adversity with faith and humility. Of anything in my walk with God, this has been the greatest example.

During times of spiritual challenges, I've seen my parents mature, and, respected as they are, get humble and ask what they can do to change, instead of getting prideful and depending on themselves to figure it out. When I walked away from God a few years back, my parents asked what they did wrong or what they could change, instead of listing off the numerous things that I was doing wrong and needed to change. This had an incredible impact on me and was one of the strongest outside influences on my being restored to God.

In times of physical trouble I've watched my parents stare in the face of death and be able to say thank you to God for what they have. I remember talking to my dad the night before he was to have open-heart surgery. I never heard him once complain about his situation. I didn't hear a fear of dying but rather sadness in the possibility of leaving behind the people he loved the most. (I think I was more scared than he was!) Dad's attitude was due to the security he had and still has in his relationship with God. Having a father that is able to live life with that kind of security with God has been a great example for me. I think kids need to be able to brag about their parents, as to how they live their lives, and I've enjoyed being able to brag about mine."

EPILOGUE

We hope you have enjoyed the journey of *Good Enough Parenting*. You have been introduced to "lifetraps" and "coping styles", and learned how to avoid "exasperation interactions". You became extremely familiar with the four plus one core emotional needs, and you got up close and personal with real families through the Master Class and Louis Lowdown sections. You read more research than you knew was out there, you picked up a few movie titles, and then you got deep with the Bible and the Patriarchs. You learned about the unique gifts of fathers, how to be vulnerable, and how to repair and reconnect when the need arises.

Our dream is for parents everywhere to grow in their self-awareness, break the cycle of dysfunction, and raise loving families. We want to help mums and dads meet their children's core emotional needs, and create a legacy that leads to every successive generation becoming healthier. Hopefully you will be able to come back to these pages for reminders—"What was that second core emotional need again?" "Which one of the exasperation interactions did I do this time?" "How can I avoid the Vortex?!" Perhaps some of you will form *Good Enough Parenting* support groups in your hometowns and work with other parents, or organise workshops for church, communities, or schools. Remember we said in the Introduction that your children are not science projects, they are more like works of art…So hopefully, whether you are working on a Van Gogh, a Rembrandt or a Picasso, your masterpieces will be unique and beautiful, and will one day turn around to you and say, "Thanks for being Good Enough Parents!"

Appendix 1

Exasperation Interactions Worksheet

Identify the exasperation interaction(s) based on the cartoon illustration of each lifetrap. (For a larger, printable version, visit www.gep.sg)

Exasperation Interactions / LIFETRAPS	Belittling	Perfectionistic and Conditional	Controlling	Punitive	Emotionally Depriving and Inhibiting	Overprotective	Pessimistic	Overly Permissive
Disconnection & Rejection								
Mistrust								
Defectiveness								
Emotional Deprivation								
Social Isolation								
Emotional Inhibition								
Failure								
Impaired Autonomy & Performance								
Vulnerability to Harm or Illness								
Dependence								
Enmeshment								
Abandonment								
Subjugation								
Negativity								
Impaired Limits								
Entitlement								
Insufficient Self-Control								
Approval-Seeking								
Exaggerated Expectations								
Unrelenting Standards								
Punitiveness								
Self-Sacrifice								

Copyright © 2012, Louis Counselling & Training Services Pte. Ltd. • www.gep.sg

Appendix 2

Exercise on Processing Difficult Emotions

Answering the following questions will help you to gain insight into the way you react and respond to your child's feelings:

1. Think of some of the common types of emotions—joy, excitement, happiness, contentment, longing, anger, loneliness, embarrassment, fear, shame, sadness; feelings of betrayal, helplessness, depression; feeling unwanted or rejected. When you see any of these in your children, which ones make you feel uncomfortable?
2. What about these feelings makes you uncomfortable?
3. Which of the three broad coping styles (surrender, avoidance and overcompensation/counterattacking) are triggered when you see these emotions in your children?
4. How does your coping style manifest when you see these feelings in your children? For example, do you blame yourself, avoid talking and leave, or get short-tempered with your children? Or perhaps you may let your spouse deal with these uncomfortable emotions, or think it is your fault, retreat by yourself and feel sad?
5. Do you behave in a similar way each time your child experiences these feelings?
6. Can you remember specific incidents involving these feelings from *your* childhood? (Maybe you experienced these emotions or someone around you did.)
7. Did your parents welcome these feelings?
8. In general, how did your parents deal with *your* emotions?
9. When your parents dealt with you this way, how did that make you feel?
10. Is there anything you wish that your parents had said or done instead?
11. What did you want from them?
12. In the end, how did you cope with these feelings when you were a child? What do you remember doing specifically?
13. Is this similar or different to how you deal with your child when he experiences the same feelings?
14. What do you think your child wishes you would do or say instead?
15. If you were to do that, how would you be feeling now?
16. Do you see that not talking about feelings with your child can be harmful to your child?

Copyright © 2012, Louis Counselling & Training Services Pte. Ltd. • www.gep.sg

Appendix 3

Exercise on Connecting with Your Child (Ages 2-4)

A 3-year-old child feels rejected by his peer group at nursery school

Child: I don't want to go…(*or possibly won't say it out loud but will be expressed non-verbally*)

Write down what would be your typical response:

_____

_____

Suggested response:

Mum: I'm sorry that you don't feel like going to school. Can you tell me why, sweetheart? Mummy wants to know…I won't be angry – just tell me…
Child: I don't want to talk about it, Mummy.
Mum: (waits for child to be ready, with a kind and patient face)
Child: (finally) Yesterday, I tried to play with some kids at the playground and they told me to go away…
Mum: That must have made you feel sad…
Child: Yes…(*child looks very sad and stops talking…*)
Mum: You know what? That would make me feel sad, too…(*is affectionate while saying this*)
Mum: (*waits for a while before speaking, just allows the child to be silent and holds the child*) What did you do when they did not want to play with you?
Child: I sat by myself.
Mum: Did you also feel angry?
Child: Yeah…
Mum: Well, I think I would have felt angry, too. *(Child sobs a bit)*
Mum: Did Tim say that as well?
Child: No, Tim wasn't there.
Mum: I bet Tim will be at school today and that he would like to play with you…You two are very good friends, right? Don't you have fun when you play together?
Child: Umm…
Mum: What game did you play with him on Monday? Red Rover, right? Yeah…that was fun, wasn't it? Do you think Tim will play with you today? I think he will…
Child: OK, I think, or I'll play with Tim…
Parent: All right, give me a hug…

Exercise on Connecting with Your Child (Ages 5-8)

With older children, parents should spend more time talking about feelings.

Mum: You don't seem to be as excited about going to school as you were a few weeks ago...
Child: I don't feel well.

Write down what would be your typical response:

_____

_____

Suggested response:

Mum: OK, well, if I didn't feel well I don't think I would want to go to school. Do you have a fever or is it a stomach thing?
Child: A stomach thing...
Mum: Oh my, when did it start?
Child: Just now when I was eating breakfast.
Mum: Do you think you caught a bug...or could it be a worry tummy ache?
Child: Well, it is true that I'm a bit worried. You see, some of the kids don't want to play with me during recess.
Mum: Well, I can see why that would make you feel sad...Tell me more about your sadness, what does that sadness feel like?
Child: Well it feels like I have no friends and I am all alone.
Mum: That makes you also feel lonely, right? Well, I love you and I don't want you to feel lonely.
Mum: Do you think that the kids who did not want to play with you might have had a hard day?
Child: I don't know...
Mum: How about Tim? He seems to enjoy playing with you and he is very kind when he comes over to our house. What about playing with him for a while?
Child: OK...
Mum: If that doesn't go well, we can talk more later. You know that I like playing with you, and spending time with you, right?
(Child smiles.)
Mum: In fact, I can't wait for you to come home! And when Daddy gets back, he will play what?
Child: Hide and Seek!
Mum: Hooray!

Exercise on Connecting with Your Child (Ages 9-12)

Dad: Hey buddy how is school?
Child: Whatever…

Write down what would be your typical response:

_____

_____

Suggested response:

Dad: I know that feeling. Sometimes things just don't go our way…
Child: Yeah. It ticks me off. The kids at school are so mean. You know – they don't want me to join them. I really hate them!
Dad: Well, I am sorry. Sounds like you feel sad *and* angry. Did anything in particular happen?
Child: Well, it was recess and then they all wanted to play catch and when I wanted to join in they said they had too many people but when Jack joined after that they let him. It's so unfair!
Dad: That doesn't sound very nice…
Child: Exactly!
Dad: Do you think there are some possible reasons why they may have done this?
Child: They're mean!
Dad: Can you think of another possible reason?
Child: They have something against me.
Dad: Could be…Did I ever tell you a story of how this happened to me when I was about your age?
Child: That happened to you?
Dad: Yes…I was playing a card game with my friends, and I was very good at it and kept winning. After a few days, one of my friends decided to kick me out. I think they were afraid I would keep winning, you know…
Child: Yes, maybe my friends are like that, too.
Dad: Hey, where was Tim during all of this?
Child: Tim was absent today – he was getting his braces on.
Dad: Oh, no wonder. Well, I have an idea. Why don't you and Tim play Frisbee? You and Tim always have fun playing, right?
Child: Yeah…
Dad: Is there anything else you would like to tell me about?
Child: Well, I told them that they were losers!
Dad: Hmmm…Anything else?
Child: (*embarrassed*) I used a bad word, and then walked away.
Dad: And did that make you feel better?
Child: Not really.

Copyright © 2012, Louis Counselling & Training Services Pte. Ltd. • www.gep.sg

Dad: What do you think happened there?
Child: I let my anger win.
Dad: Is that helpful, when we let our anger win?
Child: No
Dad: I tell you what. I'm sure you would like to talk to me more, but you might need some time to think about what happened, and you also need to do your homework, right? So why don't we spend some time tonight talking, before you go to sleep, ok? I really love you and I am sorry you had a hard day…but I know that you will do the right thing and not let those bullies get you down. I love you, little man, give me a hug.

(Later that night…)

Child: Hey Dad can we talk now?
Dad: Sure, buddy, I'm all ears.
Child: Well, I know I shouldn't have said that word at school, and I know that I need to face the consequence, but I don't know how to get over this angry feeling.
Dad: Thanks for owning up to your mistake. I think we better have a No Television rule this weekend. And instead, let's spend some extra time thinking of things to do in the future when we are up against bullies, ok?
Child: Ok…

Exercise on Connecting with Your Child (Adolescent Years – 12 and above)

Teen (girl): Gosh, school again. When will this stop.
Parent: You seem down today.
Teen: Well, I have so much going on…

Write down what would be your typical response:

_____

_____

Suggested response:
Parent: Is all that stressing you out?
Teen: Yeah. I just wish I didn't have to go to school, you know. I wish I could change schools.
Parent: I know that feeling. Did I ever tell you a time when I felt like the teachers were against me?
Teen: No, what happened?
Parent: Well, we had an exam and they accused me of cheating. Actually my friend wanted to copy my answers, and he started to talk to me and I answered and said, "No".
Teen: Wow, then what did you do?
Parent: Well, what I did was not very nice…
Teen: What?
Parent: After my exam, I yelled at the teacher and walked off. Then they just dropped the matter…
Teen: (*laughs loudly*)
Parent: So tell me sweetie, what's getting you down?
Teen: Well, I was talking with Asha, you know, my close friend, and a boy named Sammy made fun of me and said I was fat. I hate him.
Parent: That's rude! Old Sammy, huh? Is he a fitness coach? Humph! I would be mad if someone said that to me. I can just imagine how that made you feel.
Teen: I stared back at him.
Parent: Then what did he do?
Teen: He kept making fun of me, in front of others. I hate him. I hate him.
Parent: What did Asha do?
Teen: She told him off, too.
Parent: Asha is a good friend. You guys have been buddies a long time. I am wondering why Sammy really did that? What do you think?
Teen: Easy, he is a jerk. I can't wait to leave that school!
Parent: This probably won't make you feel any better, but when I was your age, I had people make fun of me, too, and I hated it!
Teen: Really? What did you do?

Parent: My friends and I just ignored him, but it wasn't very fun!
Teen: Seriously.
Parent: Hey, didn't Sammy ask you out recently and you turned him down?
Teen: Yes.
Parent: Do you think maybe he likes you and he felt hurt when you did not want to go out with him, and he wants to get back at you?
Teen: Maybe…
Parent: So sweetie, are you gonna' be ok?
Teen: Yes, I'll be fine…
Parent: Anyway, do you want me to have a talk with the teachers?
Teen: No way! Stay out of this! I can handle it!
Parent: (*Affectionately*) OK. I won't. It's just that I'm sad when you're sad, you know. Just out of curiosity, what are some of your ideas of how you might handle this?
Teen: I am going to tell Sammy privately what I think and we'll see how it goes from there.
Parent: That is a very good idea. I think you'll be fine. Would you like to pray about this?
Teenager and parent pray for wisdom, godliness, or whatever might be needed…
Parent: Let's talk more about this after dinner, ok?
That night or next morning, they do a bible study on the topic.

Appendix 4

Exercise on the Vortex of Conflict Escalation

Fill in your answers in the blanks below. We have given our suggested answers for Example 1. (For a larger, printable version, visit www.gep.sg)

Example	Perceived Core Emotional Need Not Met in Child	Type of Exasperation Interaction Experienced by the Child	Coping Style of Child	Perceived Expectation Not Met in Parent	Coping Style of Parent
Sam and Alice	Connection and Acceptance (favouritism shown by father); Reasonable Limits (throwing tantrums)	Belittling (harsh words from father); Overly Permissive (felt free to be enraged); Emotionally Depriving and Inhibiting (cold quiet dinner atmosphere)	Overcompensation (Alice resented her father and her brother)	Responsible and Respectful; Connection	Overcompensation (with occasional threats and then being quiet - an "intimidating pout"); Avoidance (issue was never resolved)
The Spade Family					
Jack					
Maggie					
Jayden					

Copyright © 2012, Louis Counselling & Training Services Pte. Ltd. • www.gep.sg

Example	Perceived Core Emotional Need Not Met in Child	Type of Exasperation Interaction Experienced by the Child	Coping Style of Child	Perceived Expectation Not Met in Parent	Coping Style of Parent
Ryan					
Tabitha					
Ben					

Exercise on the Vortex of Conflict Escalation (Suggested answers)

(For a larger, printable version, visit www.gep.sg)

Example	Perceived Core Emotional Need Not Met in Child	Type of Exasperation Interaction Experienced by the Child	Coping Style of Child	Perceived Expectation Not Met in Parent	Coping Style of Parent
Sam and Alice	Connection and Acceptance (favouritism shown by father); Reasonable Limits (throwing tantrums)	Belittling (harsh words from father); Overly Permissive (felt free to be enraged); Emotionally Depriving and Inhibiting (cold quiet dinner atmosphere)	Overcompensation (Alice resented her father and her brother)	Responsible and Respectful; Connection	Overcompensation (with occasional threats and then being quiet – an "intimidating pout"); Avoidance (issue was never resolved)
The Spade Family	Reasonable Limits (not respectful of time leaving); Connection and Acceptance (father refuses to speak, not affectionate)	Punitive (father not speaking); Emotionally Depriving and Inhibiting (withholding affection and not speaking)	Avoidance (going to her room and withdrawing from family night)	Responsible and Respectful; Connection	Overcompensation (brought up the same subject again the next day); Avoidance (not wanting to get reconciled)
Jack	Realistic Expectation (father changed his mind)	Controlling (father rules were rigid and not clear); Belittling (father attacked Jack's character); Overprotective (mother spent more time with Jack)	Overcompensation (Jack's sarcasm)	Responsible and Respectful; Connection (Jack was overly attached with his mum and not at all with his dad)	Overcompensation (constant "put-downs" to his son and mother); Avoidance (no reconciliation)
Maggie	Realistic Expectation; Healthy Autonomy and Performance; Connection and Acceptance	Perfectionistic and Conditional (doing well was not enough, constant comparing); Belittling; Controlling; Pessimistic	Surrender (blamed herself)	Responsible and Respectful	Overcompensation (putting the daughter down)
Jayden	Connection and Acceptance (not believed in); Realistic Expectation	Belittling (was put down); Pessimistic (Mother did not give son benefit of doubt); Emotionally Depriving and Inhibiting (was not listened to); Controlling	Avoidance (went to his room and later did not want to follow the mother)	Responsible and Respectful (supposedly did not take school work seriously); Connection (did not want to go on family holiday)	Overcompensation (mother put the son down); Avoidance (no reconciliation)

Copyright © 2012, Louis Counselling & Training Services Pte. Ltd. • www.gep.sg

Example	Perceived Core Emotional Need Not Met in Child	Type of Exasperation Interaction Experienced by the Child	Coping Style of Child	Perceived Expectation Not Met in Parent	Coping Style of Parent
Ryan	Realistic Expectation; Connection and Acceptance	Punitive; Controlling; Belittling; Emotionally Depriving and Inhibiting; Perfectionistic and Conditional	Surrender (thought it was his fault for causing problems in the house); Avoidance (fearful of conflict with his dad)	Connecting; Responsible and Respectful	Overcompensation (brought up the same issues in a punitive manner)
Tabitha	Healthy Autonomy; Connection and Acceptance	Belittling (was put down by mother); Overprotective (had to depend on parent); Emotionally Depriving and Inhibiting (strained relationship and no reconciliation); Overly Permissive (left to sleep alone)	Overcompensation (making a mess at dinner)	Growth and Performance (child not able to perform tasks like her peers)	Overcompensation (put daughter down when she was not able to perform age-appropriate tasks)
Ben	Reasonable Limits	Overly Permissive (Parents did not follow through on tasks delegated)	Overcompensation (blamed others when things went wrong)	Responsible and Respectful; Growth and Performance (did not take care of his health, too much time on the computer, etc)	Surrendered (mother thought it was her fault and was afraid to bring issue up with son)

Appendix 5

Exercise on Being Vulnerable

Make an attempt to write down your vulnerable statements and compare them with the suggested ones.

I) Parent Being Vulnerable with Adolescent (after cooling down)

a. Adolescent does not come home on time and doesn't call to inform the parents of the reason. When teen arrives an hour late, with a valid excuse, the parent doesn't listen and accuses in a loud voice.

Weaknesses and Fears

Needs

Other Feelings, Apologising if Necessary

Remember that the listening party should validate these feelings, summarise them back, identifying all the emotions of the other person, and say them back in a gentle tone, as opposed to lecturing.

b. Adolescent does not give full attention to the parents when they are talking to him/her.

Weaknesses and Fears

Needs

Other Feelings, Apologising if Necessary

Remember that the listening party should validate these feelings, summarise them back, identifying all the emotions of the other person, and say them back in a gentle tone, as opposed to lecturing.

c. Adolescent is not being honest and gives excuses instead for not doing a chore.

Weaknesses and Fears

Needs

Other Feelings, Apologising if Necessary

Remember that the listening party should validate these feelings, summarise them back, identifying all the emotions of the other person, and say them back in a gentle tone, as opposed to lecturing.

d. Adolescent does not disclose his/her relationships with those of opposite gender.

Weaknesses and Fears

Needs

Other Feelings, Apologising if Necessary

Remember that the listening party should validate these feelings, summarise them back, identifying all the emotions of the other person, and say them back in a gentle tone, as opposed to lecturing.

II) Adolescent Being Vulnerable with Parent (after cooling down)

a. Parent pushing the adolescent to do better in the area of studying when he/she is already working hard in this area.

Weaknesses and Fears

Needs

Other Feelings, Apologising if Necessary

Remember that the listening party should validate these feelings, summarise them back, identifying all the emotions of the other person, and say them back in a gentle tone, as opposed to lecturing.

b. Parent controls the schedule too much and aggravates the adolescent.

Weaknesses and Fears

Needs

Other Feelings, Apologising if Necessary

Remember that the listening party should validate these feelings, summarise them back, identifying all the emotions of the other person, and say them back in a gentle tone, as opposed to lecturing.

c. Parent's marriage is tumultuous and causing concern to the adolescent.

Weaknesses and Fears

Needs

Other Feelings, Apologising if Necessary

Remember that the listening party should validate these feelings, summarise them back, identifying all the emotions of the other person, and say them back in a gentle tone, as opposed to lecturing.

d. Parent compares the adolescent with a sibling or someone else.

Weaknesses and Fears

Needs

Other Feelings, Apologising if Necessary

Remember that the listening party should validate these feelings, summarise them back, identifying all the emotions of the other person, and say them back in a gentle tone, as opposed to lecturing.

Exercise on Being Vulnerable (Suggested Responses – There could be any number of responses so we are just providing one viewpoint.)

I) **Parent Being Vulnerable with Adolescent (after cooling down)**

a. *Adolescent does not come home on time and doesn't call to inform the parents of the reason. When teen arrives an hour late, with a valid excuse, the parent doesn't listen and accuses in a loud voice.*

Weaknesses and Fears (in this case, apologise in the beginning)

Suggested response:
Sweetheart, first let me say that I am sorry I exploded and didn't listen when you first came home. My weakness is that when you are out late, I get worried, and when you don't call, I get scared. I kept looking at my watch over and over again, and I thought maybe something happened to you. So, I called several times, and when you didn't answer, I felt even more anxious. But anyway, I am very sorry that I attacked. I know I need to be more trusting of you.

Feelings

Suggested Response:
I do feel that it would be more considerate if you could just remember to call or text. People do have accidents, and I was very worried about you.

Needs

Suggested response:
What I need from you is to keep me updated. I don't want you to update me throughout the day, as I think that is over the top. But, when you don't come home in the evening as planned, and show up an hour later, that is cause for me as a parent to worry. I know you are having fun, and I need you to know that I want you to have fun, but I need to be informed and be respected as a parent.

Apologising if Necessary

Suggested response:
Again, I am sorry for my outburst and I hope you can forgive me.

Remember that the listening party should validate these feelings, summarise them back, identifying all the emotions of the other person, and say them back in a gentle tone, as opposed to lecturing.

b. Adolescent does not give full attention to the parents when they are talking to him/her.

<u>Weaknesses and Fears</u>

Suggested response:
During our interaction earlier, when we spoke, I really felt that I had something important to say. When you kept your fingers on the keyboard and didn't look at me, I felt you did not think that what I was saying was important. I react when you do that and I start to have negative thoughts about you, assuming that you are disrespectful. I fear that others will also have this kind of impression of you. I also felt that I was a lousy parent when you did that and I wanted to punish myself. This is my surrendered way of coping, and I have to work on this.

<u>Needs</u>

Suggested response:
As your parent I need you to give me your full attention, especially when I say that I have something important to tell you. I need to feel that you will respect my words. It matters a lot to me when you do that since you are my son/daughter. I love you a lot.

<u>Other Feelings, Apologising if Necessary</u>

Suggested response:
I am sorry that I walked away while I was talking. That was not respectful and I apologise for that. I was irritated but I could have been more in control of my reactions.

Remember that the listening party should validate these feelings, summarise them back, identifying all the emotions of the other person, and say them back in a gentle tone, as opposed to lecturing.

c. Adolescent is not being honest and gives excuses instead for not doing a chore.

Weaknesses and Fears (in this case, apologise in the beginning)

Suggested response:
My weakness is that when I feel people are being dishonest with me, I want to keep probing and digging, and this can be very irritating. I have a fear that you are not being honest with me. I promise that I will react better if you tell me the truth. I know that in the past I must have done this to you, and counterattacked. This must have been difficult for you. I have to keep working on this weakness. I am sorry for my part in this conflict and for being obnoxious.

Needs

Suggested response:
I need our relationship to be based on honesty and humility. When I feel that our relationship is not based on that it saddens me and I won't feel close to you. When I heard you give the reasons you gave for not doing the chore, I had a negative reaction. I was sad because I felt that you did not come clean and tell me everything. I know that I need to do better when you do confess that you haven't done your chores yet, but I know that as a parent, I can tell you that I prefer that you own up rather than give excuses. I want us to be close, and it bothers me when we are not. I want our relationship to be built on trust for one another.

Other Feelings, Apologising if Necessary

Suggested response:
Again, I am sorry for being really angry when I found out that you did not do your chores. This must have made it difficult for you to feel that you can tell me everything. I will try to do better.

Remember that the listening party should validate these feelings, summarise them back, identifying all the emotions of the other person, and say them back in a gentle tone, as opposed to lecturing.

d. Adolescent does not disclose his/her relationships with those of opposite gender.

Weaknesses and Fears

Suggested response:
One of my biggest fears is that you are developing close relationships with someone of the opposite sex that I do not know anything about. There is nothing wrong if you are just friends—I want you to have friends of the opposite gender. However when it becomes more than just friends, it can lead you to doing things together that you may regret, like acting on your impulses.
I want to give you my word that I will not react if you tell me you have a boyfriend/girlfriend. Perhaps I have made it difficult for you to approach me, and I can understand this. If you choose not to tell me, then I will really get worried and I will become very suspicious of you. I do not want there to be secrets between us, especially about something like this. I am very worried about you and where this will take you. I have lost sleep as a result of this. There is part of me that also wants to avoid talking about this issue, but I know avoidance is wrong. I have not been able to concentrate on my work either. Please understand that you mean a lot to me, and I need to work on not being carried away worrying all the time.

Needs

Suggested response:
I long for our relationship to be based on honesty, the way it used to be. When it's not, it hurts both of us. Having someone special is a new thing for you, and as a parent, I need you to tell me so that I can guide you. We may not agree on everything, but that is something we can work on together later. But for now, I need to know what is going on. I want to be respected as a parent, and to be able to talk about difficult issues, instead of avoiding them.

Other Feelings, Apologising if Necessary

Suggested response:
This is such an important period of your life and I really want you to build relationships right so you do not have any regrets later. I am sorry if I have made you feel uncomfortable talking about this.

Remember that the listening party should validate these feelings, summarise them back, identifying all the emotions of the other person, and say them back in a gentle tone, as opposed to lecturing.

II) Adolescent Being Vulnerable with Parent (after cooling down)

a. Parent pushing the adolescent to do better in the area of studying when he/she is already working hard in this area.

<u>Weaknesses and Fears</u>

Suggested response:
When you keep pushing me, it makes me feel that you don't really care about how much I have tried and how I feel. This makes me angry, and this is my weakness. When I get angry, then I think about avoiding you, which is wrong. It is so hard to keep hearing that I need to do better and better when I have already given my best. At times, I get negative thoughts and think that I am a disgrace to you. I certainly do not feel that you are happy about where I am right now and I know I am not dealing with this well. I fear that, if I keep working harder just for you, my motives will be all muddled up. I will not try hard because of my own passion and love for studying. I am not strong enough for our relationship to go on like this. Sometimes I get tempted to lie about my results just to make you feel happy but I know this is not right. It is a weakness that I have and I find myself getting tempted to do this.

<u>Needs</u>

Suggested response:
I need you to know that I am trying my best. I need you to support me, not to criticise me. I don't know how much better I can do. I want you to be proud of me, even if this is my best and I can't go any further. I do not want our relationship to be based on results, or how it makes you look as a parent to other parents. I need to know that you value me for who I am.

<u>Other Feelings, Apologizing if Necessary</u>

Suggested response:
I also feel ashamed of myself when I do not make you feel proud of me. This has caused me to feel sad many times, and sometimes I get anxious to the point that I am not even able to concentrate. Some of my friends also feel the same way, and many of them have plans to give up and even lie to their parents about their results. I do not want to do that.

Remember that the listening party should validate these feelings, summarise them back, identifying all the emotions of the other person, and say them back in a gentle tone, as opposed to lecturing.

b. Parent controls the schedule too much and aggravates the adolescent.

<u>Weaknesses and Fears</u>

Suggested response:
It feels like every time I come home, I can predict what you will ask. I feel like avoiding you these days, and I know this is wrong, but that this is my tendency—to avoid conflict. I am afraid that if my schedule is not exactly right that you will be mad at me. I hate this feeling. Sometimes when you have a business trip away I actually think to myself that this is good news because I will finally get you off my back. This is not a positive feeling and I want to change this. I fear that you are terribly unhappy with me and that you think I am such a failure. This is probably not true but this is what I am thinking.

<u>Needs</u>

Suggested response:
I need you to trust me. I need you to treat me like you have confidence in me, not like a child, who does not know right from wrong. It is hard for me to feel trusted when I feel you are a nag. I want a great relationship with you, and when my relationship with you goes well, I feel encouraged. It matters more to me that you trust me, even more than having anyone else trust me, including my teachers at school.

<u>Other Feelings, Apologising if Necessary</u>

Suggested response:
I am sorry if I have made you feel that I cannot be trusted. Perhaps it would help me if you can tell me how I have done that. I know that I need to get better at this, and I want to. I hope we can start again on a clean slate and move forward from here.

Remember that the listening party should validate these feelings, summarise them back, identifying all the emotions of the other person, and say them back in a gentle tone, as opposed to lecturing.

c. Parent's marriage is tumultuous and causing concern to the adolescent.

Weakness and Fears

Suggested response:
Whenever I hear you both fighting, it makes me sad. Sometimes I worry that it is my fault, and I surrender to these accusing thoughts, especially when I hear you arguing about me or what I have done. I feel useless and insecure, and many nights I go to bed and pray for God to help you both. I do not know what to do; it has made me very anxious most days. Even when I am out I think about how you are both getting along.
It has also made me feel that I should never get married, as I do not want a marriage where we fight all the time. Sometimes I feel that I have to be the parent to you when you tell me how mum/dad treats you, and honestly, I feel at a loss. I do not know what to say other than to beg you to both get help. I feel helpless and I fear that you will separate one day, sooner rather than later.

Needs

Suggested response:
I need you and mum/dad to get along with one another the way you tell us to. I need you to be an example in this area. It makes me feel happy when the two people I love the most in the world are getting along, rather than fighting. I hope this can be something that you think about. I do not want to come across like I am telling you what to do as your son/daughter. I just want you to know that I need us all to get along and be a happy family once again.

Other Feelings, Apologising if Necessary

Suggested response:
Maybe I have also done something wrong. Sometimes when you both fight, I bite my nails and get distracted. I am sorry if I have done things to cause you both to be upset. I love you both very much.

Remember that the listening party should validate these feelings, summarise them back, identifying all the emotions of the other person, and say them back in a gentle tone, as opposed to lecturing.

d. Parent compares the adolescent with a sibling or someone else.

<u>Weaknesses and Fears</u>

Suggested response:
Most of the time, when I disappoint you, you compare me to_____ (name). This has made me feel jealous towards _____ . I know that this is wrong because _____ has not done anything to me. I know that this is my weakness, and I do not want to feel this, but I guess I feel that I am a failure. Then, when I see _____ , I counterattack him/her and then you in different ways. I wish sometimes you had a different kid instead of me. Sometimes I want to run away. I do not want to have this kind of negative thinking. I don't like feeling this way and I guess I am so fragile and this is something I have to work on.

<u>Needs</u>

Suggested response:
I need you to accept me for who I am. I am not saying that if I misbehave that you should also accept my wrongdoing. I need you at these times to tell me what I need to change and do better. Perhaps I did not respond the way I should but I know in my heart I want to feel guided and also accepted. I feel so special when you can accept me for who I am, instead of getting upset with me when I am not as talented or as good as _____ . I long for us to be close even when I grow up and become an adult. I hope we can move forward from here.

<u>Other Feelings, Apologising if Necessary</u>

Suggested response:
I feel angry when comparisons are being made. Then I also feel worthless and do not think that I deserve to be your child. Sometimes I want to get back at you. I know this is all wrong and I am sorry for having these feelings.

Remember that the listening party should validate these feelings, summarise them back, identifying all the emotions of the other person, and say them back in a gentle tone, as opposed to lecturing.

NOTES

Introduction

1. Moore, K. A., & Zaff, J. F. (2002, November). Building a better teenager: A summary of "what works" in adolescent development, research brief. *Child Trends*, 1-5.
2. Ibid.
3. Johnson, J. G., Cohen, P., Kasen, S., Smailes, E., & Brook, J. S. (2001). The association of maladaptive parental behavior with psychiatric disorder among parents and their offspring. *Archives of General Psychiatry, 58*, 453-460.
4. Whitfield, C. L. (2004). *The truth about mental illness: Choices for healing*. FL: Health Communications, Inc. 4-7, 253; Whitfield, C. L. (2001). *Not crazy: You may not be mentally ill*. Pennington: Muse House Press.
5. Winnicott, D. (1953). Transitional objects and transitional phenomena. *International Journal of Psychoanalysis, 34*, 89-97.

Chapter One

1. Young, J. E., Klosko, J. S., & Weishaar, M. E. (2003). *Schema therapy: A practitioner's guide*. NY: The Guilford Press.
2. *Stress: The fight or flight response*. (n.d.). Retrieved May 30, 2012, from Psychologist World: http://www.psychologistworld.com
3. Maslow, A. H. (1987). *Motivation and personality, Third Edition*. New York: Harper & Row, Publishers, Inc. 27-28.
4. Ibid., 18.
5. Ibid., 31.
6. Lockwood, G., & Perris, P. (2012). A new look at core emotional needs. In M. B. van Vreeswijk, *Handbook of schema therapy: Theory, research and science* (pp. 41-66). West Sussex, UK: Wiley-Blackwell.
7. Louis, J. P., & Louis, K. M. (2010). *I choose us: A Christian perspective on building love connection in your marriage by breaking harmful cycles*. Singapore: Louis Counselling & Training Services.
8. Young, Klosko & Weishaar (2003), *Schema therapy*, 10.
9. Young, J. E., & Brown, G. (1999). *Young Schema Questionnaire: Short version*. New York: Cognitive Therapy Centre of New York.
10. Schmidt, N. B., Joiner, T. E., Young, J. E., & Telch, M. J. (1995). The Schema Questionnaire: Investigation of Psychometric Properties and the Hierarchical Structure of a Measure of Maladaptive Schemas. *Cognitive Therapy and Research, 19*(3), 295-321; Cecero, J. J., Nelson, J. D., & Gillie, J. M. (2004). Tools and tenets of schema therapy: toward the construct validity of the early maladaptive schema questionnaire-research version (EMSQ-R). *Clinical Psychology & Psychotherapy, 11*, 344-357; Samuel, D. B., & Ball, S. A. (2012). The Factor Structure and Concurrent Validity of the Early Maladaptive Schema Questionnaire: Research Version. *Cognitive Therapy and Research*. Online publication date: 15-Feb-2012.
11. Lee, C. W., Taylor, G., & Dunn, J. (1999). Factor Structure of the Schema Questionnaire in a Large Clinical Sample. *Cognitive Therapy and Research, 23*(4), 441-451.
12. Hoffart, A., Sexton, H., Hedley, L. M., Wang, C. E., Holthe, H., Haugum, J. A., Nordahl, H. M., Hovland, O. J., & Holte, A. (2005). The Structure of Maladaptive Schemas: A Confirmatory Factor Analysis and a Psychometric Evaluation of Factor-Derived Scales. *Cognitive Therapy and Research, 29*(6), 627-644.
13. DiClemente, R. J., Santelli, J. S., & Crosby, R. A. (Eds.). (2009). *Adolescent health: Understanding and preventing risk behaviors*. San Francisco, CA: Jossey-Bass. 378.
14. Rostosky, S. S., Wilcox, B. L., Wright, M. L. C., & Randall, B. A. (2004). The impact of religiosity on adolescent sexual behavior: A review of the evidence. *Journal of Adolescent Research, 19*(6), 677-697; Michalak, L., Trocki, K., & Bond, J. (2007). Religion and alchohol

in the U.S. National Alcohol Survey: How important is religion for abstention and drinking? *Drug and Alcohol Dependence, 89*(2-3), 268-280; Wong, Y. L., Rew, L., & Slaikeu, K. D. (2006). A systematic review of recent research on adolescent religiosity/spirituality and mental health. *Issues in Mental Health Nursing, 27*(2), 161-183.

15 Cummings, E. M., & Davies, P. T. (2010). *Marital conflict and children: An emotional security perspective.* New York: The Guilford Press. 8.
16 Ibid., 10.
17 Ibid., 28.
18 Ibid., 64-65.
19 Ibid., 65-66.
20 McCoy, K., Cummings, E. M., & Davies, P. T. (2009). Constructive and destructive marital conflict, emotional security and children's prosocial behavior. *Journal of Child Psychology and Psychiatry, 50*(3), 270-279.
21 Goeke-Morey, M. C., Cummings, E. M., & Papp, L. M. (2007). Children and marital conflict resolution: Implications for emotional security and adjustment. *Journal of Family Psychology, 21*(4), 744-753; Grych, J. H., & Fincham, F. D. (1990). Marital conflict and children's adjustment: A cognitive-contextual framework. *Psychological Bulletin, 108,* 267-290; Cummings, E. M., Ballard, M., & El-Sheikh, M. (1991). Responses of children and adolescents to interadult anger as a function of gender, age, and mode of expression. *Merrill-Palmer Quarterly, 37,* 543-560.
22 Cummings, E. M., & Wilson, A. G. (1999). Contexts of marital conflict and children's emotional security: Exploring the distinction between constructive and destructive conflict from the children's perspective. In M. Cox, & J. Brooks-Gunn (Eds.), *Formation, functioning, and stability of families* (pp. 105-129). Mahwah, NJ: Erlbaum; Winter, M. A., Davies, P. T., Hightower, A. D., & Meyer, S. (2006). Relations among family adversity, caregiver communications, and children's family representations. *Journal of Family Psychology, 20,* 348-351.
23 El-Sheikh, M., Cummings, E. M., Kouros, C. D., Elmore-Staton, L., & Buckhalt, J. A. (2008). Marital psychology and physical aggression and children's mental and physical health: Direct, meditated, and moderated effects. *Journal of Consulting and Clinical Psychology, 76,* 138-148.
24 Cummings & Davies (2010), *Marital conflict and children,* 31.
25 Ibid., 31, 81.
26 Ibid., 102.
27 Avnet, J., Kerner, J. (Producers), Bass, R., Franken, A. (Writers), & Mandoki, L. (Director). (2002). *When a man loves a woman* [Motion Picture]. United States: Touchstone Pictures.
28 Cummings & Davies (2010), *Marital conflict and children,* 128.
29 Ibid., 75-76.
30 Ibid., 82.
31 Ibid., 87.
32 Ibid., 89.
33 El-Sheikh, M., Buckhalt, J. A., Mize, J., & Acebo, C. (2006). Marital conflict and disruption of children's sleep. *Child Development, 77*(1), 31-43.
34 Cummings & Davies (2010), *Marital conflict and children,* 157.
35 Ibid., 180.
36 Gottman, J., & Declaire, J. (1998). *Raising an emotionally intelligent child—The heart of parenting.* New York: Simon & Schuster. 142.
37 Hetherington, E. M. (1992). Coping with marital transitions: A family systems perspective. *Monographs of the Society for Research in Child Development, 57*(2-3), 1-14; Gottman & Declaire (1998), *Raising an emotionally intelligent child,* 141.
38 Louis & Louis (2010), *I choose us.*
39 Sandberg, J. G., Yorgason, J. B., Miller, R. B., & Hill, E. J. (2012). Family-to-work spillover in Singapore: Marital distress, physical and mental health, and work satisfaction. *Family Relations, 61,* 1-15.
40 Cummings & Davies (2010), *Marital conflict and children,* 35.

⁴¹ Scripture quotations marked NLT are taken from the *Holy Bible, New Living Translation*, copyright 1996, 2004, 2007 by Tyndale House Foundation. Used by permission of Tyndale House Publishers, Inc., Carol Stream, Illinois 60188. All rights reserved.
⁴² Scripture quotations marked NAS are taken from the *New American Standard Bible®*, Copyright © 1960, 1962, 1963, 1968, 1971, 1972, 1973, 1975, 1977, 1995 by The Lockman Foundation. Used by permission.
⁴³ Scripture quotations marked NT Greek are taken from *The New Testament in the Original Greek,* Copyright © Robinson & Pierpont. MA: Chilton Book Publishing. Used by permission.
⁴⁴ Scripture quotations marked KJV are taken from *The Holy Bible: King James Version.* Dallas, TX: Brown Books Publishing, 2004.
⁴⁵ Smalley, G., & Trent, J. (1996). *The blessing*. New York: Pocket Books.

Chapter Two

¹ Scripture quotations marked The Message are taken from *The Message.* Copyright © by Eugene H. Peterson 1993, 1994, 1995, 1996, 2000, 2001, 2002. Used by permission of NavPress Publishing Group.
² Baumrind, D., Berkowitz, M. W., Lickona, T., Nucci, L. P., & Watson, M. (2008). *Parenting for character: Five experts, five practices*. (D. Streight, Ed.) Oregon: CSEE. 11.

Chapter Three

¹ Young, J. E. (2003). *Young Parenting Inventory.* (Cognitive Therapy Center of New York) Retrieved October 4, 2011 from Schema Therapy: http://www.schematherapy.com/id205.htm
² Louis, J. P., Sexton, H., Lockwood, G., Hu, Y., Hoffart, A., & Chong, W. (2012). *A cross cultural exploration of the associations between the latent structures of the Young Schema Questionnaire and the Young Parent Inventory.* In process of being published.
³ Sheffield, A., Waller, G., Emanuelli, F., Murray, J., and Meyer, C. (2005). Links Between Parenting and Core Beliefs: Preliminary Psychometric Validation of the Young Parenting Inventory. *Cognitive Therapy and Research, 29*(6), 787-802.
⁴ Baumrind, D. (1967). Child-care practices anteceding three patterns of preschool behavior. *Genetic Psychology Monographs, 75*, 43-88.
⁵ Teicher, M. H., Samson, J. A., Polcari, A., & McGreenery, C. E. (2006). Sticks, stones, and hurtful words: Relative effects of various forms of childhood maltreatment. *The American Journal of Psychiatry, 163*(6), 993-1000.
⁶ Hartt, J., & Waller, G. (2002). Child abuse, dissociation, and core beliefs in bulimic disorders. *Child Abuse and Neglect, 26*, 923-938.
⁷ Crawford, E., & O'Dougherty Wright, M. (2007). The impact of childhood psychological maltreatment on interpersonal schemas and subsequent experiences of relationship aggression. *Journal of Emotional Abuse, 7*, 93-116.
⁸ Cukor, D., & McGinn, L. K. (2006). History of child abuse and severity of adult depression: the mediating role of cognitive schema. *Journal of Child Sexual Abuse, 15*, 19-34; Harris, A. E., & Curtin, L. (2002). Parental perceptions, early maladaptive schemas, and depressive symptoms in young adults. *Cognitive Therapy and Research, 26*, 405-416; Shah, R., & Waller, G. (2000). Parental style and vulnerability to depression: The role of core beliefs. *Journal of Nervous and Mental Disease, 188*, 19-25; Wright, M. O., Crawford, E., & Del Castillo, D. (2009). Childhood emotional maltreatment and later psychological distress among college students: the predicting role of maladaptive schemas. *Child Abuse and Neglect, 33*, 59-68.
⁹ van Hanswijck de Jonge, P., Waller, G., Fiennes, A., Rashid, Z., & Lacey, J. H. (2003). *Reported sexual abuse and cognitive content in the morbidly obese. Eating Behaviors, 4*, 315-322.
¹⁰ Messman-Moore, T. L., & Coates, A. A. (2007). The impact of childhood psychological abuse on adult interpersonal conflict: the role of early maladaptive schemas and patterns of interpersonal behavior. *Journal of Emotional Abuse, 7*, 75-92.

[11] Cecero, J. J., Nelson, J. D., & Gillie, J. M. (2004). Tools and tenets of schema therapy: toward the construct validity of the early maladaptive schema questionnaire-research version (EMSQ-R). *Clinical Psychology & Psychotherapy, 11*, 344-357.

[12] Louis, J. P., & Louis, K. M. (2010). *I choose us: A Christian perspective on building love connection in your marriage by breaking harmful cycles.* Singapore: Louis Counselling & Training Services.

[13] Khan, A. (Producer), Gupte, A. (Writer), & Khan, A. (Director). (2007). *Taare Zameen Par* [Motion Picture]. India: Amir Khan Productions.

[14] Hyler, S., Rieder, R. O., Spitzer, R. L., & Williams, J. (1987). *Personality Diagnostic Questionnaire-Revised.* New York: New York State Psychiatric Institute; Specht, M. W., Chapman, A., & Celluci, T. (2009). Schemas and borderline personality disorder symptoms in incarcerated women. *Journal of Behavior Therapy and Experimental Psychiatry, 40*, 256-264; Ball, S. A., & Cecero, J. J. (2001). Addicted patients with personality disorders: traits, schemas, and presenting problems. *Journal of Personality Disorders, 15*, 72-83; Petrocelli, J. V., Glaser, B. A., Calhoun, G. B., & Campbell, L. F. (2001). Early maladaptive schemas of personality disorder subtypes. *Journal of Personality Disorders, 15*, 546-559; Arntz, A., & van Genderen, H. (2009). *Schema therapy for borderline personality disorder.* Chichester: Wiley; Lobbestael, J., Arntz, A., & Sieswerda, S. (2005). Schema modes and childhood abuse in borderline and antisocial personality disorder. *Journal of Behavior Therapy and Experimental Psychiatry, 36*, 240-253; Young, J. E., Klosko, J. S., & Weishaar, M. E. (2003). *Schema therapy: a practitioner's guide.* NY: The Guilford Press; Hoffart, A., Versland, S., & Sexton, H. (2002). Self-understanding, empathy, guided discovery, and schema belief in schema-focused cognitive therapy of personality problems: A process-outcome study. *Cognitive Therapy and Research, 26*, 199-219.

[15] Welburn, K., Coristine, M., Dagg, P., Pontefract, A., & Jordan, S. (2002). The Schema Questionnaire-Short Form: Factor analysis and relationship between schemas and symptoms. *Cognitive Therapy and Research, 26*(4), 519-530; Pinto-Gouveia, J., Castilho, P., Galhardo, A., & Cunha, M. (2006). Early maladaptive schemas and social phobia. *Cognitive Therapy and Research, 30*, 571-584.

[16] Lumley, M. N., & Harkness, K. L. (2007). Specificity in the relations among childhood adversities, early maladaptive schemas, and symptom profiles in adolescent depression. *Cognitive Therapy and Research, 31*(5), 639-657; Rijkeboer, M. M., & de Boo, G. M. (2010). Early maladaptive schemas in children: Development and validation of the schema inventory for children. *Journal of Behavior Therapy and Experimental Psychiatry, 41*, 102-109.

[17] Schmidt, N. B., Joiner, T. E., Young, J. E., & Telch, M. J. (1995). The Schema Questionnaire: Investigation of Psychometric Properties and the Hierarchical Structure of a Measure of Maladaptive Schemas. *Cognitive Therapy and Research, 19*(3), 295-321; Beck, A. T., Freeman, A., & Associates. (1990). *Cognitive therapy of personality disorders.* New York: Guilford Press.

[18] Rittenmyer, G. J. (1997). The relationship between early maladaptive schemas and job burnout among public school teachers. *Dissertation Abstracts International, 58*(5-A), 1529; Rijkeboer, M. M., & van den Bergh, H. (2006). Multiple group confirmatory factor analysis of the Young Schema-Questionnaire in a Dutch clinical versus non-clinical population. *Cognitive Therapy and Research, 30*(3), 263-278.

[19] Leung, N., Waller, G., & Thomas, G. (1999). Core beliefs in anorexic and bulimic women. *Journal of Nervous and Mental Disease, 187*, 736-741; Rijkeboer & van den Bergh (2006), Multiple group confirmatory factor analysis.

[20] Ibid.

[21] Dobrenski, R. A. (2001). Romantic jealousy: Symptoms, schemas, and attachment. *Dissertation Abstracts International, 62*(6-B), 2954; Rijkeboer & van den Bergh (2006), Multiple group confirmatory factor analysis.

[22] Decouvelaere, F., Graziani, P., Gackiere-Eraldi, D., Rusinek, S., & Hautekeete, M. (2002). Hypothese de l'existence et de l'evolution de schemas cognitifs mal adaptes chez l'alcool-dependant [Hypothesis of existence and development of early maladaptive schemas in alcohol-dependant patients]. *Journal de Therapie Comportementale et Cognitive, 12*, 43-48; Rijkeboer & van den Bergh (2006), Multiple group confirmatory factor analysis.

²³ Braitman, K. A. (2002). Relationships among body satisfaction, appearance schemas, early maladaptive schemas, and sociocultural attitudes towards appearance. *Dissertation Abstracts International, 62*(10-B), 4835; Rijkeboer & van den Bergh (2006), Multiple group confirmatory factor analysis.
²⁴ Louis, Sexton, Lockwood, Hu, Hoffart & Chong (2012), *A cross cultural exploration*.

Chapter Four
1. Mehrabian, A. (1971). *Silent messages* (1st ed.). Belmont, CA: Wadsworth.
2. Rosemond, J. (2001). *Teen-Proofing: Fostering responsible decision making in your teenager*. Kansas City: Andres McMeel Publishing.
3. Gottman, J., & Declaire, J. (1998). *Raising an emotionally intelligent child—The heart of parenting*. New York: Simon & Schuster.
4. Smith, C., & Denton, M. L. (2005). *Soul searching: The religious and spiritual lives of American teenagers*. New York: Oxford University Press. 56; Myers, S. (1996). An interactive model of religiosity inheritance: The importance of family context. *American Sociological Review, 61*, 858-866; Kieren, D., & Munro, B. (1987). Following the leaders: Parents' influence on adolescent religious activity. *Journal for the Scientific Study of Religion, 26*(2), 249-255; Nelson, H. (1980). Religious transmission versus religious formation: Preadolescent-Parent Interaction. *Sociological Quarterly, 21*, 207-218; Ozorak, E. W. (1989). Social and cognitive influences on the development of religious beliefs and commitment in adolescence. *Journal for the Scientific Study of Religion, 28*(4), 448-463; Stott, G. (1988). Familial influence on religious involvement. *The Religion and Family Connection: Social Science Perspectives, 3*, 258-271; Smith, C., & Sikkink, D. (2003). Social predictors of retention in and switching from the religious faith of family of origin. *Review of Religious Research, 45*(2), 188-206.
5. Menehan, K. (2006). *Tiffany Field on massage research*. Retrieved May 20, 2012, from Massage Magazine exploring today's touch therapies: http://www.massagemag.com/News/2006/January/125/Tiffany.php
6. Russek, L. G., & Schwartz, G. E. (1997). Perceptions of parental caring predict health status in midlife: a 35-year follow-up of the Harvard Mastery of Stress Study. *Psychosomatic Medicine, 59*(2), 144-149.
7. Ginott, H. G. (2003). *Between parent and child: The bestselling classic that revolutionized parent-child communication*. New York: Three Rivers Press.
8. Dreikurs, R., & Soltz, V. (1990). *Children: The challenge: The classic work on improving parent-child relationships—Intelligent, humane & eminently practical*. New York: Plume. 36-37.
9. Ibid., 57-67.
10. Elkind, D. (2006). *The hurried child: Growing up too fast too soon*. MA: Da Capo Press. 205.
11. Ibid., 211.
12. Faber, A., & Mazlish, E. (1980). *How to talk so kids will listen and listen so kids will talk*. New York: Avon Books, Inc. 18.
13. Gottman & Declaire (1998), *Raising an emotionally intelligent child*, 25.
14. Ibid., 67.

Chapter Five
1. U.S. Department of Health and Human Services, Administration for Children and Families, Administration on Children, Youth and Families, Children's Bureau. (2010). *Child Maltreatment 2009*. Available from http://www.acf.hhs.gov/programs/cb/stats_research/index.htm#can
2. *How to prevent sexual abuse of your child?* (2009, February 19). Retrieved May 30, 2012, from The Parents Zone: http://www.TheParentsZone.com
3. National Center for Victims of Crime. (1997). *Child sexual abuse*. Retrieved August 31, 2012, from Network of Victim Assistance - NOVA: http://www.novabucks.org/childsexualabuse.html

468 ■ Good Enough Parenting

4   American Humane Association Children's Division. (1993). *Child sexual abuse: AHA fact sheet #4*. Englewood, CO: American Humane Association.
5   Sgroi, S. (1989). Stages of recovery for adult survivors of child sexual abuse. *Vulnerable populations: Sexual abuse treatment for children, adult survivors, offenders, and persons with mental retardation Volume 2*, S. Sgroi, Ed. Lexington, MA: Lexington Books.
6   Male survivors of childhood sexual abuse. (1990). *Virginia Child Protection Newsletter*, 31: 1-12.
7   Widom, C. S. (1992). *The cycle of violence*. Washington, D.C.: National Institute of Justice, U.S. Department of Justice.
8   Widom, C. S. (1995). *Victims of childhood sexual abuse—Later criminal consequences*. Washington, D.C.: National Institute of Justice, U.S. Department of Justice.
9   American Humane Association Children's Division (1993), *Child sexual abuse*.
10 Childhelp. (n.d.). *National child abuse statistics*. Retrieved May 30, 2012, from Childhelp: http://www.childhelp.org/pages/statistics#abuse-conseq
11 United States Government Accountability Office, 2011. *Child maltreatment: strengthening national data on child fatalities could aid in prevention* (GAO-11-599). Retrieved from http://www.gao.gov/new.items/d11599.pdf
12 U.S. Department of Health and Human Services (2010), *Child Maltreatment 2009*.
13 U.S. Department of Health and Human Services Administration for Children and Families Administration on Children, Youth and Families Children's Bureau. *Child abuse and neglect fatalities 2009: Statistics and interventions*. Retrieved from http://www.childwelfare.gov/pubs/factsheets/fatality.pdf
14 Snyder, H. N. (2000, July). *Sexual assault of young children as reported to law enforcement: victim, incident, and offender characteristics*. Retrieved from http://bjs.oup.usdoj.gov/content/pub/pdf/saycrle.pdf
15 Child Welfare Information Gateway. (2008). *Long-term consequences of child abuse and neglect*. Washington, D.C.: U.S. Department of Health and Human Services. Retrieved May 31, 2012 from http://www.childwelfare.gov/pubs/factsheets/long_term_consequences.cfm
16 Ibid.
17 Fang, X., Brown, D. S., Florence, C. S., & Mercy, J. A. (2012) The economic burden of child maltreatment in the United States and implications for prevention. *Child Abuse & Neglect, 36*(2), 156-165.
18 Harlow, C., U.S. Department of Justice, Office of Justice Programs. (1999). *Prior abuse reported by inmates and probationers* (NCJ 172879) Retrieved from http://bjs.ojp.usdoj.gov/content/pub/pdf/parip.pdf
19 Ibid.
20 Child Welfare Information Gateway (2008), *Long-term consequences of child abuse and neglect*.
21 Ibid.
22 Ibid.
23 *Parental substance abuse*. Retrieved May 31, 2012 from http://www.childwelfare.gov/can/factors/parentcaregiver/substance.cfm
24 Ibid.
25 Swan, N. (1998). Exploring the role of child abuse on later drug abuse: Researchers face broad gaps in information. *NIDA Notes, 13*(2). Retrieved May 31, 2012 from the National Institute on Drug Abuse website: www.nida.nih.gov/NIDA_notes/NNVol13N2/exploring.html
26 Jones, S., Jones, B., & Nystrom, C. (1984). *God's design for sex*. CO: Navpress.
27 Jones, S., & Jones, B. (1993). *How and when to tell your kids about sex: A lifelong approach to shaping your child's sexual character*. CO: Navpress.

Chapter Six
1   Bruckeimer, B., Lowry, H. (Producers), Wells, R., Andrus, M., Khouri, C. (Writers), & Khouri, C. (Director). (2002). *Divine secrets of the Ya-Ya Sisterhood* [Motion Picture]. United States: Warner Bros. Pictures.

2 YMCA. (2000). *Talking with teens: The YMCA parent and teen survey final report*. New York: The Global Strategy Group, Inc.; Doherty, W., & Carlson, B. (n.d.). *Overscheduled kids, underconnected families: The research evidence*. Retrieved May 21, 2012, from Putting Family First: www.puttingfamilyfirst.org

3 Fiese, B., & Schwartz, M. (2008). Reclaiming the family table: Mealtimes and child health and wellbeing. *Social Policy Report: Giving Child and Youth Development Knowledge Away, 22(4)*, 1-19.

4 Fiese, B. H., Foley, K. P., & Spagnola, M. (2006). Routine and ritual elements in family mealtimes: Contexts for child wellbeing and family identity. *New Directions for Child and Adolescent Development, 111*, 67-90.

5 Gillman, M. W., Rifas-Shiman, S. L., Frazier, A. L., Rockette, H. R. H., Camargo, C. A., Field, A. E., Berkey, C. S., & Colditz, G. A. (2000). Family dinners and diet quality among older children and adolescents. *Archives of Family Medicine, 9*, 235-240.

6 CASA. (2007). *The importance of family dinners III*. New York: Columbia University.

7 O'Connor, D. B., Jones, F., Conner, M., McMillan, B., & Ferguson, E. (2008). Effects of daily hassles and eating style on eating behavior. *Health Psychology, 27*, 20–31.

8 Lin, B., Guthrie, J., & Frazao, E. (1999). Quality of children's diets at and away from home: 1994-1996. *Food Review, 22*, 2-10.

9 Fiese, Foley & Spagnola (2006), Routine and ritual elements in family mealtimes.

10 Beals, D. E. (2001). Eating and reading: Links between family conversations with preschoolers and later language and literacy. In D. K. Dickinson & P. O. Tabors (Eds.), *Beginning literacy with language: Young children at home and school*. (pp. 75-92). Baltimore, MD: Paul H. Brookes Publishing; Fivush, R., Bohanke, J., Robertson, R., & Duke, M. (2004). Family narratives and the development of children's emotional well-being. In M. W. Pratt & B. H. Fiese (Eds.), *Family stories and the life course across time and generations* (pp. 55-76). Mahwah, NJ: Erlbaum.

11 Hersey, J. C., & Jordan, A. (2007). *Reducing Children's TV Time to Reduce the Risk of Childhood Overweight: The Children's Media Use Study*. Final report. Prepared for the Centers for Disease Control and Prevention and The Association of Preventive Medicine Teaching and Research. Washington, DC: Research Triangle Institute International.

12 Halford, J. C. G., Boyland, E. J., Hughes, G., Oliveira, L. P., & Dovey, T. M. (2007). Beyond-brand effect of television (TV) food advertisements/ commercials on caloric intake and food choice of 5-7-year-old children. *Appetite, 49*, 263-267; Harris, J. L. (2008). *Priming obesity: Direct effects of television food advertising on eating behavior and food preferences*. PhD thesis, Yale University, New Haven, CT.

13 Putting Family First: www.puttingfamilyfirst.org

14 Doherty & Carlson (n.d.), *Overscheduled kids*.

15 Hofferth, S. L. (1999). *Changes in American children's time, 1981-1997*. University of Michigan's Institute for Social Research, Center Survey; Hofferth, S. L. (2001). How American children spend their time. *Journal of Marriage and the Family, 63*, 295-308.

16 Putnam, R. (2000). *Bowling alone: The collapse and revival of American community*. New York: Simon & Schuster.

17 RGA Communications, The 1995 Kentucky Fried Chicken Family Dinner Survey.

18 Putnam (2000), *Bowling alone*.

19 Hofferth (1999), *Changes in American children's time*; Hofferth (2001), How American children spend their time.

20 U.S. Department of Health and Human Services. (1999). *Trends in the well-being of America's children and youth, 1999*. Washington, DC: U.S. Department of HHS.

21 Hofferth (1999), *Changes in American children's time*; Hofferth (2001), How American children spend their time.

22 Council of Economic Advisers to the President. (2000). *Teens and their parents in the 21st century: An examination of trends in teen behaviour and the role of parental involvement*. Washington, DC: Council of Economic Advisors to the President.

23 YMCA (2000), *Talking with teens*.

24 Levine, M. (2008). *The price of privilege: How parental pressure and material advantage are creating generation of disconnected and unhappy kids*. New York: HarperCollins.

25. Forthofer, M. S., Markman, H. J., Cox, M., Stanley, S., & Kessler, R. C. (1996). Associations between marital distress and work loss in a national sample. *Journal of Marriage and Family, 58,* 597-605; Muella, R. (2005). The effect of marital dissolution on the labour supply of males and females: Evidence from Canada. *Journal of Socio-Economics, 34,* 787-809; Turvey, M. D., & Olson, D. H. (2006). Marriage & family wellness: Corporate America's business? MN: Life Innovation, Inc. 11-12; Louis, J. P., & Louis, K. M. (2010). *I choose us: A Christian perspective on building love connection in your marriage by breaking harmful cycles.* Singapore: Louis Counselling & Training Services. 4.
26. Bowlby, J. (1988). *A secure base: Parent-child attachment and healthy human development. Tavistock professional book.* London: Routledge. 24.
27. Ibid.
28. Bowlby, J. (1969). *Attachment. Attachment and Loss: Vol. 1. Loss.* New York: Basic Books. 194.
29. Bowlby (1988), *A secure base.*
30. Rutter, M. (1995). Clinical implications of attachment concepts: Retrospect and Prospect. *Journal of Child Psychology & Psychiatry, 36* (4), 549-571.
31. Berlin, L. J., Cassidy, J., & Appleyard, K. (2008). The influence of early attachments on other relationships. In *Handbook of attachment, theory, research, and clinical applications.* New York: The Guilford Press.
32. Pearce, J. W., & Pezzot-Pearce, T. D. (2007). *Psychotherapy of abused and neglected children (2nd ed.).* New York & London: Guilford Press. 17-20.
33. Colin, V. L. (1991, June 28). *Infant attachment: What we know now.* Retrieved May 21, 2012, from Office of the Assistant Secretary for Planning and Evaluation, U.S. Department of Health and Human Services: http://aspe.hhs.gov/
34. Anderson, S. (2000). *The journey from abandonment to healing: Surviving through—and recovering from—the five stages that accompany the loss of love.* New York: Berkley Books.
35. Winnicott, D. W. (1965). Ego distortion in terms of true and false self. In *The maturational process and the faciliating environment: Studies in the theory of emotional development* (pp. 140-152). New York: International UP Inc.
36. Elkind, D. (2006). *The hurried child: Growing up too fast too soon.* MA: Da Capo Press. 122.
37. Elkind, D. (2007). *The power of play: How spontaneous, imaginative activities lead to happier, healthier children.* Cambridge, MA: Da Capo Press. 3.
38. Ibid., 3.
39. Bowlby (1969), *Attachment,* 194.
40. Elkind (2007), *The power of play,* 3.
41. Child Development Institute, LLC. *"Play is the work of the child" Maria Montessori.* Retrieved September 14, 2012, from Child Development Institute Parenting Today: http://www.childdevelopmentinfo.com
42. Elkind (2007), *The power of play,* 3.
43. Ibid., 3-13.
44. Sweeney, D. (n.d.). *The Mozart effect: Classical music and your baby's brain.* Retrieved May 20, 2012, from BabyCenter: http://www.babycenter.com/0_the-mozart-effect-classical-music-and-your-babys-brain_9308.bc
45. Barber, N. (2000). *Why parents matter: Parental investment and child outcomes.* New York: Bergin & Garvey. 18.
46. Gottman, J., & Declaire, J. (1998). *Raising an emotionally intelligent child—The heart of parenting.* New York: Simon & Schuster. 143.
47. Tan, H. Y. (2011, October 19). No enrichment classes? Good parenting works too. *The Straits Times,* A14.
48. Ibid.
49. Elkind (2006), *The hurried child,* 124; Erikson, E. H. (1950). *Childhood and society.* New York: Norton.
50. Tan (2011, October 19), No enrichment classes? Good parenting works too.
51. Koestner, R., Franz, C. E., Weinberger, J. (1990). The family origins of empathic concern: A 26 year longitudinal study. *Journal of Personality and Social Psychology, 58,* 709-717.

52   MacDonald, K., & Parke, R. D. (1986). Parent-child physical play: The effects of sex and age of children and parents. *Sex Roles, 7-8,* 367-379.
53   Gottman & Declaire (1998), *Raising an emotionally intelligent child,* 170-171.
54   Toh, K., Chia, Y. M., & Lua, J. M. (August 28, 2012). 'Without extra lessons, our kids may lose out'. *The Straits Times,* A7.
55   Parker-Pope, T. (2012, August 23). Simon says don't use flashcards. *The New York Times.* Retrieved September 14, 2012, from http://well.blogs.nytimes.com/2012/08/23/simon-says-dont-use-flashcards/
56   McClelland, M. M., Acock, A. C., Piccinin, A., Rhea, S. A., & Stallings, M. C. (2012). Relations between preschool attention span-persistence and age 25 educational outcomes. *Early Childhood Research Quarterly;* Parker-Pope (2012, August 23), Simon says don't use flashcards.
57   Gottman & Declaire (1998). *Raising an emotionally intelligent child,* 199.
58   Hartup, W., & Moore, S. (1990). Early peer relations: Developmental significance and prognostic implications. *Early Childhood Research Quarterly, 5,* 1-7.
59   Elkind (2007), *The power of play,* 149; Piaget, J. (1950). *The moral judgement of the child.* London: Routledge & Kegan Paul.
60   Nieboer, G. (1995, May 14). *Kids games.* Retrieved April 23, 2012, from Kids Games: http://www.gameskidsplay.net
61   Elkind (2006), *The hurried child,* 126, 127.
62   Seuss. (n.d.). *Dr. Seuss Quotes (Author of Green Eggs and Ham).* Retrieved May 20, 2012, from Goodreads: http://www.goodreads.com/author/quotes/61105.Dr_Seuss
63   Elkind (2006), *The hurried child,* 127.
64   Ibid., 131.
65   Bennett, W. J. (Ed.). (1995). *The children's book of virtues.* New York: Simon & Schuster.
66   Kohn, A. (1986). *No contest: The case against competition.* Boston: Houghton Mifflin.
67   *HealthyChildren.org - Stages of Adolescence.* (2011, May 10). (American Academy of Pediatrics) Retrieved May 20, 2012, from healthychildren.org: http://www.healthychildren.org
68   Baumrind, D., Berkowitz, M. W., Lickona, T., Nucci, L. P., & Watson, M. (2008). *Parenting for character: Five experts, five practices.* (D. Streight, Ed.) Oregon: CSEE. 11.

Chapter Seven
1   Pratt, C. A. (Producer), Conroy, P., Carlino, L. J. (Writers), & Carlino, L. J. (Director). (1979). *The Great Santini* [Motion Picture]. United States: Warner Bros. Pictures.
2   Kazan, E. (Producer), Steinbeck, J., Osborn, P. (Writers), & Kazan, E. (Director). (1955). *East of Eden* [Motion Picture]. United States: Warner Bros. Pictures.
3   Gunn, A. (Producer), Rodgers, M. (Writer), & Waters, M. (Director). (2003). *Freaky Friday* [Motion Picture]. United States: Buena Vista Pictures.
4   Reiner, R., Zweibel, A. (Producers), Zweibel, A. (Writer), & Reiner, R. (Director). (1994). *North* [Motion Picture]. United States: Castle Rock Entertainment.
5   Ngiam, E., Kim, C. (Producers), Ngiam, E. (Writer), & Ngiam, E. (Director). (2003). *Crammed* [Short Film]. Singapore: Ellery Ngiam Pte. Ltd.
6   Gottman, J., & Declaire, J. (1998). *Raising an emotionally intelligent child—The heart of parenting.* New York: Simon & Schuster. 20.
7   Gottman & Declaire (1998), *Raising an emotionally intelligent child,* 16, 38.
8   Baron-Cohen, S. (2011). *Zero degrees of empathy: A new theory of human cruelty.* London: Allen Lane.
9   Ibid., 4-5.
10 Ibid., 16, 29.
11 Baron-Cohen (2011), *Zero degrees of empathy,* 42, 160; Bryer, J. B., Nelson, B. A., Miller, J. B., & Krol, P. A. (1987). Childhood sexual and physical abuse as factors in adult psychiatric illness. *American Journal of Psychiatry, 144,* 1426-1430.
12 Ibid.
13 Baron-Cohen (2011), *Zero degrees of empathy,* 105.

14. Gottman & Declaire (1998), *Raising an emotionally intelligent child*, 132.
15. Ginott, H. G. (2003). *Between parent and child: The bestselling classic that revolutionized parent-child communication.* New York: Three Rivers Press; Gottman & Declaire (1998), *Raising an emotionally intelligent child*; Faber, A., & Mazlish, E. (1980). *How to talk so kids will listen and listen so kids will talk.* New York: Avon Books, Inc.
16. Faber & Mazlish (1980), *How to talk so kids will listen and listen so kids will talk.*
17. Ginott (2003), *Between parent and child*, 118; Gottman & Declaire (1998), *Raising an emotionally intelligent child*, 128-134.

Chapter Eight

1. Miserandino, M. (1996). Children who do well in school: Individual differences in perceived competence and autonomy in above-average children. *Journal of Education Psychology, 88*(2), 203-214.
2. Deci, E. L., & Flaste, R. (1996). *Why we do what we do: Understanding self-motivation.* New York: Penguin Books. 30.
3. *Self-determination theory: An approach to human motivation & personality.* Retrieved September 14, 2012 from http://www.selfdeterminationtheory.org/
4. Deci & Flaste (1996), *Why we do what we do*, 220; Lepper, M. R., & Greene, D. (1975). Turning play into work: Effects of adult surveillance and extrinsic reward on children's intrinsic motivation. *Journal of Personality and Social Psychology, 31*, 479-486; Lepper, M. R., Greene, D., & Nisbett, R. E. (1973). Undermining children's intrinsic interest with extrinsic reward: A test of the 'overjustification' hypothesis. *Journal of Personality and Social Psychology, 28*(1), 129-137.
5. Deci & Flaste (1996), *Why we do what we do*, 66.

Chapter Nine

1. Walters, G., Gotoh, J., Lasseter, J. (Producers), Stanton, A. (Writer), Stanton, A., & Unkrich, L. (Directors). (2003). *Finding Nemo* [Motion Picture]. United States: Walt Disney Pictures.
2. Louis, J. P., & Louis, K. M. (2010). *I choose us: A Christian perspective on building love connection in your marriage by breaking harmful cycles.* Singapore: Louis Counselling & Training Services.
3. Burghes, L., Clarke, L., & Cronin, N. (1997). *Fathers and fatherhood in Britain.* London: Family Policy Studies Centre; Bradshaw, J., & Millar, J. (1991). *Lone parent families in the UK.* Department of Social Security Research Report No 6. London: HMSO.
4. Louis & Louis (2010), *I choose us*, 8.
5. Waite, L., & Gallagher, M. (2000). *The case for marriage: Why married people are happier, healthier, and better off financially.* New York: Doubleday. 128.
6. Louis & Louis (2010), *I choose us*, 9.
7. O'Neill, R. (2005). *Does marriage matter?* London: Civitas, Institute for the Study of Civil Society. 10.
8. Office for National Statistics. (2001). *Work and worklessness among households.* London: The Stationery Office; Office for National Statistics. (2002, May). *Family resources survey, Great Britain, 2000-01.* London: The Stationery Office.
9. McLanahan, S., & Sandefur, G. (1994). *Growing up with a single parent.* Cambridge, MA: President and Fellows of Harvard College. 167-168.
10. Office for National Statistics. (2002). *Social trends 32.* London: The Stationery Office. Table 5.25, 103.
11. Cockett, M., & Tripp, J. (1994). *The Exeter family study: Family breakdown and its impact on children.* Exeter: University of Exeter Press. 21.
12. Amato, P. R. (2000). Consequences of divorce for adults and children. *Journal of Marriage and the Family, 62,* 1269-1287; Simons, R. L., Lin, K-H., Gordon, L. C., Conger, R. D., & Lorenz, F. O. (1999). Explaining the higher incidence of adjustment problems among children of divorce compared with those in two-parent families. *Journal of Marriage and the Family, 61*(4), 1020-1033.
13. O'Neill (2005), *Does marriage matter?*, 27.

14 Daly, M., & Wilson, M. (1996). Evolutionary psychology and marital conflict: The relevance of stepchildren. In Buss, D. M., & Malamuth, N. M. (Eds.), *Sex, power, conflict: Evolutionary and feminist perspectives*. Oxford: Oxford University Press. 9-28.
15 Cawson, P. (2002). *Child maltreatment in the family*. London: NSPCC. 10.
16 Lum, S. (2008, January 16). Paedophile jailed 22 yrs for sex acts on 2 boys. *The Straits Times*. Retrieved September 14, 2012, from asiaone news: http://www.asiaone.com/News/AsiaOne%2BNews/Crime/Story/A1Story20080116-45304.html

Chapter Ten
1 Deci, E. L., & Flaste, R. (1996). *Why we do what we do: Understanding self-motivation*. New York: Penguin Books. 33.
2 Ibid., 149.
3 *ParentFurther*. (n.d.). (Search Institute) Retrieved April 23, 2012, from ParentFurther: A Search Institute resource for families: http://www.parentfurther.com
4 Ibid.
5 Ibid.
6 Rosemond, J. (2001). *Teen-proofing: Fostering responsible decision making in your teenager*. Kansas City: Andres McMeel Publishing.
7 Popkin, M. H. (1998). *Active parenting of teens*. Georgia: Active Parenting.
8 Bryce, I., Ziskin, L. (Producers), Lee, S., Ditko, S., Koepp, D. (Writers), & Raimi, S. (Director). (2002). *Spiderman* [Motion Picture]. United States: Columbia Pictures.
9 Fishburne, L., Ganis, S., Ganis, N. H., Llewelyn, D., Romersa, M. (Producers), Atchison, D. (Writer), & Atchison, D. (Director). (2006). *Akeelah and the Bee* [Motion Picture]. United States: Lions Gate Films.
10 Louis, J. P., & Louis, K. M. (2010). *I choose us: A Christian perspective on building love connection in your marriage by breaking harmful cycles*. Singapore: Louis Counselling & Training Services.

Chapter Eleven
1 *Dictionary and Thesaurus—Merriam-Webster Online*. (n.d.). Retrieved May 20, 2012, from http://www.merriam-webster.com/thesaurus/boundary
2 *Dr. Phil.com – advice – parenting*. Retrieved September 14, 2012, from http://drphil.com/articles/category/4/
3 Henner, M., & Sharon, R. V. (1999). *I refuse to raise a brat: Straightforward advice on parenting in an age of overindulgence*. New York: HarperCollins. xvii.
4 Szalavitz, M. (2011, January 24). *The key to health, wealth and success: Self-control*. Retrieved May 20, 2012, from Time.com Healthland: http://healthland.time.com; Moffitt, T. E., Arseneault, L., Belsky, D., Dickson, N., Hancox, R. J., Harrington, H., et al. (2010, December 21). A gradient of childhood self-control predicts health, wealth, and public safety. *Proceedings of the National Academy of Sciences of the United States of America*.
5 Margulies, S., Wolper, D. L. (Producers), Dahl, R. (Writer), & Stuart, M. (Director). (1971). *Willy Wonka & the Chocolate Factory* [Motion Picture]. United States: Paramount Pictures.
6 Solomon, G. *Cinemaparenting*. http://www.cinemaparenting.com
7 Hotchkiss, S. (2002). *Why is it always about you? The seven deadly sins of narcissism*. New York: Free Press.
8 Cloud, H., & Townsend, J. (1998). *Boundaries with kids*. Michigan: Zondervan.

Chapter Twelve
1 Szalavitz, M. (2011, January 24). *The key to health, wealth and success: Self-control*. Retrieved May 20, 2012, from Time.com Healthland: http://healthland.time.com; Moffitt, T. E., Arseneault, L., Belsky, D., Dickson, N., Hancox, R. J., Harrington, H., et al. (2010, December 21). A gradient of childhood self-control predicts health, wealth, and public safety. *Proceedings of the National Academy of Sciences of the United States of America*.

2   Duckworth, A. L., & Seligman, M. E. P. (2005). Self-discipline outdoes IQ in predicting academic performance of adolescents. *Psychological Science, 16*(12), 939-944.
3   Ibid.
4   Duckworth, A., Quinn, P., & Tsukayama, E. (2011). What *No Child Left Behind* leaves behind: The roles of IQ and self-control in predicting standardized achievement test scores and report card grades. *Journal of Educational Psychology.*

Chapter Thirteen
1   Steyer, J. P., & Clinton, C. (2002). *The other parent: The inside story of the media's effect on our children.* New York: Atria Books.
2   *Kids-in-mind: Movie ratings that actually work.* (n.d.). Retrieved May 29, 2012, from Kids in mind: http://www.kids-in-mind.com
3   Rideout, V. J., Foehr, U. G., & Roberts, D. F. (2010). *Generation M²: Media in the lives of 8- to 18-year olds—A Kaiser Family Foundation study.* The Henry J. Kaiser Family Foundation, California.
4   Wong, M. L., Chan, K. W., Koh, D., Tan, H. H., Lim, F. S., Emmanuel, S., & Bishop, G. (2009). Premarital sexual intercourse among adolescents in an Asian country: Multilevel ecological factors. *Pediatrics*; Haggstrom-Nordin, E., Hanson, U., & Tyden, T. (2005). Associations between pornography consumption and sexual practices among adolescents in Sweden. *International Journal of STD and AIDS, 16*(2), 102-107.
5   *ParentFurther.* (n.d.). (Search Institute) Retrieved April 23, 2012, from ParentFurther: A Search Institute resource for families: http://www.parentfurther.com
6   Douglas, G. (2009). Pathological video game use among youth 8 - 18: A national study. *Psychological Science, 20*(5), 594-602.
7   *Television & Health.* (n.d.). Retrieved May 30, 2012, from California State University Northridge: http://www.csun.edu/science/health/docs/tv&health.html
8   Doherty, W. J. (2000). *Take back your kids: Confident parenting in turbulent times.* Notre Dame, Indiana: Sorin Books. 138-142.
9   Ibid.
10 Ibid.
11 *Research on effects of Media Violence* (n.d.). Media Awareness Network: http://www.media-awareness.ca
12 Huesmann, L. R. (1982). Television violence and aggressive behavior. In: D. Perl, L. Bouthilet, & J. Lazar (Eds.), *Television and behavior: Ten years of programs and implications for the 80's* (pp. 126-137). Washington, DC: U.S. Government Printing Office.
13 Rideout, V. J., Vandewater, E. A., & Wartella, E. A. (2003). *Zero to six: Electronic media in the lives of infants, toddlers and preschoolers—A Kaiser Family Foundation report.* The Henry J. Kaiser Family Foundation, California.
14 Anderson, C. A., & Bushman, B. J. (2001). Effects of violent video games on aggressive behavior, aggressive recognition, aggressive affect, physiological arousal, and prosocial behavior: A meta-analytic review of the scientific literature. *Psychological Science, 12*, 353-359.
15 Anderson, C. A., Carnagey, N. L., & Eubanks, J. (2003). Exposure to violent media: The effect of songs with violent lyrics on aggressive thoughts and feelings. *Journal of Personality and Social Psychology, 84*(5), 960-971.
16 Johnson, J. G., Cohen, P., Smailes, E. M., Kasen, S., & Brook, J. S. (2002). Television viewing and aggressive behavior during adolescence and adulthod. *Science, 295*(5564), 2468-2471.
17 Williams, T. M. (Ed.). (1986). *The impact of television: A natural experiment in three communities.* New York: Praeger.
18 Singer, M. I., Slovak, K., Frierson, T., & York, P. (1998). Viewing preferences, symptoms of psychological trauma, and violent behaviors among children who watch television. *Journal of the American Academy of Child and Adolescent Psychiatry, 37*, 1041-1048.
19 Cline, V. B., Croft, R. G., & Courrier, S. (1973). Desensitization of children to television violence. *Journal of Personality and Social Psychology, 27*(3), 360-365.
20 Gerbner, G. (2004). TV violence and the art of asking the wrong question. In *The World & I; A Chronicle of Our Changing Era*, July, 1994, pp.385-397. Retrieved September 14,

2012, from Center for Media Literacy: http://www.medialit.org/reading-room/tv-violence-and-art-asking-wrong-question

Chapter Fourteen

1. Cynaumon, G. (2003). *Discover your child's D.Q. factor: The discipline quotient system*. Brentwood, TN: Integrity Publishers. 20-22.
2. Suzuki, S. (1983). *Nurtured by love: The classical approach to talent education*. Miami, FL: Warner Broz. Publication Inc.
3. *Pretend play: The magical benefits of role play*. (n.d.). Retrieved May 29, 2012, from One Step Ahead: http://www.onestepahead.com
4. Faber, A., & Mazlish, E. (1980). *How to talk so kids will listen and listen so kids will talk*. New York: Avon Books, Inc.
5. Ibid.
6. Elkind, D. (2006). *The hurried child: Growing up too fast too soon*. MA: Da Capo Press. 157.
7. Chan, P. Y., Seah, S. Y. (Producers), Leow, R., Neo, J. (Writers), & Neo, J. (Director). (2006). *I Not Stupid Too* [Motion Picture]. Singapore: Mediacorp Raintree Pictures.
8. Dreikurs, R., & Soltz, V. (1990). *Children: The challenge: The classic work on improving parent-child relationships—Intelligent, humane & eminently practical*. New York: Plume.
9. Cloud, H., & Townsend, J. (1998). *Boundaries with kids*. Michigan: Zondervan.
10. Rosemond, J. (2001). *Teen-Proofing: Fostering responsible decision making in your teenager*. Kansas City: Andres McMeel Publishing.

Chapter Fifteen

1. Chua, A. (2011, January 8). *Why Chinese mothers are superior - WSJ.com*. Retrieved April 23, 2012, from The Wall Street Journal: http://www.online.wjs.com
2. Hofferth, S. L. (1999). *Changes in America children's time, 1981-1997*. University of Michigan's Institute for Social Research, Centre Survey.
3. Chang, A. L. (2011, November 19). 1 in 10 will suffer from mental illness: Study. *The Straits Times*, 1, A10, B4.
4. Maggio, R. (Ed.). (1998). *The new beacon book of quotations by women*. Beacon Press.
5. *Socrates quotes*. (n.d.). Retrieved May 28, 2012, from Goodreads: http://www.goodreads.com/author/quotes/275648.Socrates

Chapter Sixteen (No Notes)

Chapter Seventeen

1. Kim, C. C. (2008). Academic success begins at home: How children can succeed in school. *Backgrounder (Published by The Heritage Foundation), 2185*, 1-12; Wimer, C., Simpkins, S. D., & Dearing, E., et al. (2008). Predicting youth out-of-school time participation: Multiple risks and developmental differences. *Merrill-Palmer Quarterly, 54*(2), 179-207.
2. Kim (2008), Academic success begins at home; Pong, S., Hao, L., & Gardner, E. (2005). The roles of parenting styles and social capital in the school performance of immigrant Asian and Hispanic adolescents. *Social Science Quarterly, 86*(4), 928-950.
3. Kindlon, D. (2001). *Too much of a good thing: Raising children of character in an indulgent age*. New York: Hyperion. 84.
4. Goh, C. L. (2012, April 26). Singapore 'has lowest youth death rate' among rich nations. *The Straits Times*; Patton, G. C., Coffey, C., Cappa, C., Currie, D., Riley, L., Gore, F., … Ferguson, J. (2012). Health of the world's adolescents: A synthesis of internationally comparable data. *The Lancet, 379*(9826), 1665-1675.
5. Petersen, A. (2011, January 18). *How much sleep do children and teenagers need? Grown-up problems start at bedtime*. Retrieved February 10, 2012, from The Wall Street Journal: http://online.wsj.com

6. Cohen, D. A., Wang, W., Wyatt, J. K., Kronauer, R. E., Dijk, D.-J., Czeisler, C. A., & Klerman, E. B. (2010). Uncovering residual effects of chronic sleep loss on human performance. *Science Translational Medicine, 2*(14), 14ra3.
7. Khalik, S. (2012, April 20). Not enough sleep? Kids in S'pore sleep less than those in Switzerland: Study. *The Straits Times*, C1.
8. Wee, L. (2012, May 3). Young & disturbed. *The Straits Times. Mind Your Body.* 12.
9. Ibid.
10. Chang, A. L. (2011, 19 November). '1 in 10 will suffer from mental illness': Study. *The Straits Times*, 1, A10.
11. Poh. (2012, April 22). *The Straits Times.* Forum page.
12. Negrini, S., & Carabalona, R. (2002). Backpacks on! Schoolchildren's perceptions of load, associations with back pain and factors determining the load. *Spine, 27*(2), 187-195.
13. Lai, J. P., & Jones, A. Y. (2001). The effect of shoulder-girdle loading by a school bag on lung volumes in Chinese primary school children. *Early Human Development, 62*(1), 79-86.
14. Iyer, S. R. (2001). An ergonomic study of chronic musculoskeletal pain in schoolchildren. *Indian Journal of Pediatrics, 68*(10), 937-941.
15. Morgan, I. G., Ohno-Matsui, K., & Saw, S. M. (2012). Myopia. *The Lancet, 379* (9827), 1739-1748.
16. BBC News. (2011, October 25). *Lack of outdoor play linked to short-sighted children.* Retrieved May 29, 2012, from BBC News: http://www.bbc.co.uk/news/health-15427954; McGrath, M. (2012, May 4). *Massive rise in Asian eye damage.* Retrieved May 29, 2012, from BBC News: http://www.bbc.co.uk/news/health-17942181
17. Feng, Z. (2012, May 5). *Myopia in kids: Spend more time outdoors.* Retrieved May 29, 2012, from The Straits Times: http://www.straitstimes.com
18. Lien Centre for Social Innovation. (2010). *The world that changes the world: How philanthropy, innovation, and entrepreneurship are transforming the social ecosystem.* (W. Cheng, & S. Mohamed, Eds.) Singapore: John Wiley & Sons. 57.
19. Jeynes, W. H. (2005, December). *Parental involvement and student achievement: A meta-analysis.* Family Involvement Research Digests. Retrieved May 30, 2012, from Harvard Family Research Project: http://www.hfrp.org
20. Ibid.
21. Toney, L. P., Kelley, M. L., & Lanclos, N. F. (2003). Self- and parental monitoring of homework in adolescents: Comparative effects on parents' perceptions of homework behavior problems. *Child & Family Behavior Therapy, 25*(1), 35-51; Zhan, M. (2006). Assets, parental expectations and involvement, and children's educational performance. *Children and Youth Services Review, 28*, 961–975; Catsambis, S. (2001). Expanding knowledge of parental involvement in children's secondary education: Connections with high school seniors' academic success. *Social Psychology of Education, 5*(2), 149–177; Jeynes, W. H. (2003). A meta-analysis: The effects of parental involvement on minority children's academic achievement. *Education and Urban Society, 35*(2), 202–218; Trusty, J. (2003). Modeling Mexican Americans' educational expectations: Longitudinal effects of variables across adolescence. *Journal of Adolescent Research, 18*, 131–153.
22. Catsambis (2001), Expanding knowledge of parental involvement; Kreider, H., Caspe, M., Kennedy, S., & Weiss, H. (2007). Family involvement in middle and high school students' education. *Harvard Family Research Project*, 1-12.
23. Zhan (2006), Assets, parental expectations and involvement; Spera, C. (2006). Adolescents' perceptions of parental goals, practices and styles in relation to their motivation and achievement. *Journal of Early Adolescence, 26*(4), 456–490; Marchant, G. J., Paulson, S. E., & Rothlisberg, B. A. (2001). Relations of middle school students' perceptions of family and school contexts with academic achievement. *Psychology in the Schools, 38*, 505–519.
24. Gutman, L. M. (2006). How student and parent goal orientations and classroom goal structures influence the math achievement of African Americans during the high school transition. *Contemporary Educational Psychology, 31*, 44–63.
25. Kim (2008), Academic success begins at home.

26. Amato, P. R. (2005). The impact of family formation change on the cognitive, social and emotional well-being of the next generation. *The Future of Children, 15*(2), 76.
27. Ibid.
28. Kim (2008), Academic success begins at home.
29. U.S. Census Bureau, Historical Time Series. (2008). Living arrangements of children under 18 years old: 1960 to the present, Table CH-1. http://www.census.gov/population/socdemo/hh-fam/ch1.xls .
30. Ventura, S. J., & Bachrach, C. A. (2000). Nonmarital childbearing in the United States, 1940-99. *National Vital Statistics Reports, 48*(16), Table 1; Brady, E. H., Martin, J. A., & Ventura, S. J. (2007). Births: Preliminary data for 2006. *National Vital Statistics Reports, 56*(7), Table 1.
31. Bumpass, L. L., & Sweet, J. A. (1989). Children's experience in single-parent families: Implications of cohabitation and marital transition. *Family Planning Perspectives, 21*(6), 252-260.
32. Amato (2005), The impact of family formation change, 88-89.
33. U.S. Census Bureau. (2008, September 1). *A child's day, 2004. Table D9*. Retrieved May 29, 2012, from United States Census Bureau: http://www.census.gov/population/socdemo/well-being/2004_detailedtables/04tabD09.xls
34. Artis, J. (2007). Maternal cohabitation and child well-being among kindergarten children. *Journal of Marriage and Family, 69*, 222-236.
35. Cavanagh, S. E., & Houston, A. C. (2006). Family instability and children's early problem behavior. *Social Forces, 85*(1), 551-581.
36. The Heritage Foundation. *Strong beginnings: How families bolster early educatonal outcomes*. Retrieved September 14, 2012, from FamilyFacts.org: http://www.familyfacts.org/briefs/23/strong-beginnings-how-families-bolster-early-educational-outcomes
37. Hofferth, S. L. (2006). Residential father family type and child well-being, *Demography, 43*(1), 53-77.
38. Pong, S. L., & Hampden-Thompson, G. (2003). Family policies and children's school achievement in single- versus two-parent families. *Journal of Marriage and Family, 65*(3), 681-699.
39. Carlson, M. J., & Corcoran, M. E. (2001). Family structure and children's behavioral and cognitive outcomes. *Journal of Marriage and Family, 63*(3), 779-792.
40. Brown, S. L. (2004). Family structure and child well-being: The significance of parental cohabitation. *Journal of Marriage and Family, 66*(2), 351-367.
41. Pong, S. L. (1997). Family structure, school context, and eighth- grade math and reading achievement. *Journal of Marriage and Family, 59*(3), 734-746.
42. Ibid.
43. Cavanagh, S. E., & Schiller, K. S. (2006). Marital transitions, parenting, and schooling: Exploring the link between family-structure history and adolescents' academic status. *Sociology of Education, 79*(4), 329-354.
44. Manning, W., & Lamb, K. (2003). Adolescent well-being in cohabitating, married, and single-parent families. *Journal of Marriage and Family, 65*, 876-893; The Heritage Foundation. *Family and adolescent well-being*. Retrieved September 14, 2012, from FamilyFacts.org: http://www.familyfacts.org/briefs/34/family-and-adolescent-well-being
45. Biblarz, T. J. (2000). Family structure and children's success: A comparison of widowed and divorced single-mother families. *Journal of Marriage and the Family, 62*(2), 533-548; Louis, J. P., & Louis, K. M. (2010). *I choose us: A Christian perspective on building love connection in your marriage by breaking harmful cycles*. Singapore: Louis Counselling & Training Services. 11.
46. Ely, M., West, P., Sweeting, H., & Richards, M. (2000). Teenage family life, life chances, lifestyles and health: A comparison of two contemporary cohorts. *International Journal of Law, Policy and the Family, 14*, 1-30; Ross, C. E., & Mirowsky, J. (1999). Parental divorce, life course disruption, and adult depression. *Journal of Marriage and the Family, 61*, 1034-1045; Amato, P. R., & Booth, A. (1997). *A generation at risk: Growing up in an era of family upheaval*. Cambridge, MA: Harvard University Press. 173-175; Louis & Louis (2010), *I Choose us*, 11.

47. Dweck, C. S., & Leggett, E. L. (1988). A social-cognitive approach to motivation and personality. *Psychological Review, 95,* 256-273; Ablard, K. E., & Parker, W. D. (1997). Parents' achievement goals and perfectionism in their academically talented children. *Journal of Youth and Adolescence, 26*(6), 651-667.
48. Hills, T. W. (1987). Children in the fast lane: Implications for early childhood policy and practice. *Early Childhood Research Quarterly, 2,* 265-273.
49. Parker, W. D. (1997). An empiracal typology of perfectionism in academically talented 6th graders. *American Educational Research Journal, 34,* 545-562.
50. Ibid.
51. Ablard & Parker (1997), *Parents' achievement goals and perfectionism.*
52. Ibid.
53. Blatt, S. J. (1995). The destructiveness of perfectionism: Implications for the treatment of depression. *American Psychologist, 50,* 1003–1020.
54. Lask, B., & Bryant-Waugh, R. (1992). Early-onset anorexia nervosa and related eating disorders. *Journal of Child Psychology and Psychiatry, 33*(1), 281-300.
55. Axtell, A. & Newton, B. J. (1993). An analysis of alderian life themes of bulimic women. *Journal of Alderian Theory, Research and Practice 49*(1), 58-67.
56. Rasmussen, S. A., & Eisen, J. L. (1992). The epidemiology and clinical features of obsessive compulsive disorder. *Psychiatric Clinics of North America, 15*(4), 743-758.
57. Brewerton, T. D., & George, M. S. (1993). Is migraine related to eating disorders? *International Journal of Eating Disorders, 14,* 75–79.
58. Adderholt-Elliot, M. (1989). Perfectionism and underachievement. *Gifted Child Today, 12,* 19–21.
59. Adkins, K. K., & Parker, W. D. (1996). Perfectionism and suicidal preoccupation. *Journal of Personality, 64,* 529–543.
60. Deci, E. L., & Flaste, R. (1996). *Why we do what we do: Understanding self-motivation.* New York: Penguin Books. 21.
61. Ibid., 21.
62. Ibid., 22.
63. Assor, A., & Tal, K. (2012). When parents' affection depends on child's achievement: Parental conditional positive regard, self-aggrandizement, shame and coping in adolescents, *Journal of Adolescence, 35,* 249-260; Roth, G., Assor, A., Niemiec, C. P., Ryan, R. M., & Deci, E. L. (2009). The emotional and academic consequences of parental conditional regard: comparing conditional positive regard, conditional negative regard, and autonomy support as parenting practices. *Developmental Psychology, 45,* 1119–1142.
64. Deci & Flaste (1996), *Why we do what we do,* 38.
65. McKergow, M., & Clarke, J. (2007). *Solutions Focus Working: 80 real life lessons for successful organisational change.* Glasgow: SolutionsBooks. 54.
66. Assor, A., Roth, G., Israeli, M., Freed., & Deci, E. (2007). *Parental conditional positive regard: Another harmful type of parental control.* Paper presented at the Society for Research in Child Development (SRCD), (Boston USA).
67. Roth, Assor, Niemiec, Ryan & Deci (2009), *The emotional and academic consequences of parental conditional regard.*
68. Kohn, A. (2009, September 14). *When a parent's 'I love you' means 'Do as I say'.* Retrieved May 31, 2012, from The New York Times: http://www.nytimes.com
69. Bloom, B. S. (1985). Generalization about talent development. In B. S. Bloom (Ed.), *Developing talent in young people.* New York: Ballentine Books; Gottfried, A. W., Gottfried, A. E., Bathurst, K., & Guerin, D. W. (1994). *Gifted IQ: Early developmental aspects.* New York: Plenum Press.
70. Rimm, S. (2006). *When gifted students underachieve: What to do about it.* Waco, TX: Prufrock Press Inc. 3.
71. Kindlon (2001), *Too much of a good thing.*
72. Ibid., 127.
73. Gardner, H. (1993). *Frames of Mind: The Theory of Multiple Intelligences.* New York: Basic Books.
74. Henderson, D., Witt, P. J., Haft, S., Thomas, T. (Producers), Shulman, T. (Writer), & Weir, P. (Director). (1989). *Dead Poets Society* [Motion Picture]. United States: Touchstone Pictures.

75   Miller, B., Miller, G., Mitchell, D. (Producers), Coleman, W., Collee, J., Miller, G., Morris, J. (Writers), Miller, G., Coleman, W., & Morris, J. (Directors). (2006). *Happy Feet* [Motion Picture]. United States: Warner Bros. Pictures.

Chapter Eighteen
1   Rudin, S., Steel, D. (Producers), Orr, J., Cruickshank, J., Mason, J. A. (Writers), & Duke, B. (Director). (1993). *Sister Act 2: Back in the habit* [Motion Picture]. United States: Touchstone Pictures.
2   Edwards, G. (1984). *The divine romance*. Illinois: Tyndale House Publishing Inc.

Chapter Nineteen
1   Levine, P. (2006, February 8). *What do parents want*. Retrieved May 30, 2012, from Peter Levine: A blog for civic renewal: http://www.peterlevine.ws
2   Tan, H. Y. (2012, March 3). What matters most? *The Straits Times*, D2.
3   Baumrind, D., Berkowitz, M. W., Lickona, T., Nucci, L. P., & Watson, M. (2008). *Parenting for character: Five experts, five practices*. (D. Streight, Ed.) Oregon: CSEE. 18.
4   Beers, V. G., & Boerke, C. (1992). *The toddlers bible*. CO: David C Cook.
5   Beers, V. G. (1993). *Teaching toddlers the bible*. Victor Books.
6   Edward, G. (1984). *The divine romance*. Illinois: Tyndale House Publishing Inc.
7   Popkin, M. H. (1998). *Active parenting of teens*. Georgia: Active Parenting.
8   Smetana, J. C., Metzger, A., Gettman, D. C., & Campione-Barr, N. (2006). Disclosure and secrecy in the adolescent-parent relationships. *Child Development, 77*, 201-217.
9   Baumrind, Berkowitz, Lickona, Nucci & Watson (2008), *Parenting for character*, 84.
10 Baumrind, Berkowitz, Lickona, Nucci & Watson (2008), *Parenting for character*, 83.
11 Baumrind, Berkowitz, Lickona, Nucci & Watson (2008), *Parenting for character*, 47.
12 Worthington, E. L., Jr. (1998). *Dimensions of forgiveness: Psychological research & theological perspectives*. Radnor, PA: Templeton Foundation Press. 140.
13 Enright, R. D., & Fitzgibbons, R. P. (2000). *Helping clients forgive*. Washington, DC: American Psychological Association. 29.
14 Enright, R. D. (2001). *Forgiveness is a choice: A step-by-step process for resolving anger and restoring hope*. Washington: APA LifeTools. 34.
15 Ibid., 28-30.
16 Ibid., 31.
17 Paleari, F. G., Regalia, C., & Fincham, F. D. (2005). Marital quality, forgiveness, empathy, and rumination: a Longitudinal analysis. *Journal of Social Behaviour and Personality, 3*, 368-378.
18 Fincham, F. D. (2000). The kiss of porcupines: From attributing responsibility for forgiving. *Personal Relationships, 9*, 239-251.
19 Orathinkal, J., & Vansteenwegen, A. (2006). The effect of forgiveness on marital satisfaction in relationship to marital stability. *Contemporary Family Therapy, 28*, 251-260.
20 Herbert, T., & Cohen, S. (1993). Stress and immunity in humans: a meta-analytical review. *Psychosomatic Medicine, 55*, 364-379.
21 Pietrini, P., Guazzelli, M., Basso, G., Jaffe, K., & Grafman, J. (2000). Neural correlates of imaginal aggressive behavior assessed by positron emission tomography in healthy subjects. *The American Journal of Psychiatry, 157*, 1772-1781.
22 Seybold, K. S., Hill, P. C., Neumann, J. K., & Chi, D. S. (2001). Physiological and psychological correlates of forgiveness. *Journal of Psychology and Christianity, 20*, 250-259.
23 Lawler, K. A., Younger, J. Y., Piferi, R. A., Billington, E., Jobe, R., Edmondson, K., Jones, W. H. (2003). A change of heart: cardiovascular correlates of forgiveness in response to interpersonal conflict. *Journal of Behavioral Medicine, 26*, 373-393.
24 Fitzgibbons, R. P. (1986). The cognitive and emotive use of forgiveness in the treatment of anger. *Psychotherapy, 23*, 629-633; Park, Y., & Enright, R. D. (1997). The development of forgiveness in the context of adolescent friendship conflict in Korea. *Journal of Adolescence, 20*, 393-402; Subkoviak, M. J., Enright, R. D., & Wu, C. (1992, October). *Current developments related to measuring forgiveness*. Paper presented at the annual

meeting of the Midwestern Educational Research Association, Chicago, IL.; Subkoviak, M. J., Enright, R. D., Wu, C., Gassin, E. A., Freedman, S., Olson, L. M., & Sarinopoulos, I. C. (1995). Measuring interpersonal forgiveness in late adolescence and middle adulthood. *Journal of Adolescence, 18*, 641-655.

25. Coyle, C. T., & Enright, R. D. (1997). Forgiveness intervention with postabortion men. *Journal of Consulting and Clinical Psychology, 65*, 1042-1046; Sarinopoulos, I. C. (1996). *Forgiveness in adolescence and middle adulthood: Comparing the Enright Forgiveness Inventory with Wade Forgiveness Scale*. University of Wisconsin-Madison.
26. Enright (2001), *Forgiveness is a choice*, 218-224.
27. Ibid., 220.

Chapter Twenty

1. Hochschild, A. R. (2012, May 5). *The outsourced life*. Retrieved May 31, 2012, from The New York Times. Sunday Review: http://www.nytimes.com
2. Clients, not practitioners, make therapy work - British Association for Counselling & Psychotherapy. (2008, October 17). *Medical News Today*. Retrieved May 28, 2010, from http://www.medicalnewstoday.com; Crabb, L. (1997). *Connecting: Healing for ourselves and our relationships, a radical new vision*. Nashville, Tennessee: Word Publishing; Lambert, M. J., & Barley, D. E. (2001). Research summary on the therapeutic relationship and psychotherapy outcome. *Psychotherapy: Theory, Research, Practice, Training, 38*(4), 357-361.
3. Berkman, L., & Syme, L. (1979). Social networks, host resistance, and mortality: A nine-year follow-up study of Alameda County residents. *American Journal of Epidemiology, 109*(2), 186-204.
4. Coleman, J. S., & Hoffer, T. (1987). *Public and private high schools: The impact of communities*. New York: Basic Books Inc.
5. Coleman, J. S., Hoffer, T., & Kilgore, S. (1982). *High school achievement: public, Catholic, and private schools compared*. New York: Basic Books Inc.
6. Coleman & Hoffer (1987), *Public and private high schools*.
7. Kelly, M. (2007, August 7). *LifeWay research finds parents churches can help teens stay in church*. Retrieved May 31, 2012, from LifeWay Biblical Solutions for Life: http://www.lifeway.com
8. Block, P. (2008). *Community: The structure of belonging*. San Francisco: Berrett-Koehler Publishing, Inc. xii.
9. Walker, L. J., & Taylor, J. H. (1991). Family interactions and the development of moral reasoning. *Child Development, 62*, 264-283; Schaefer, C., & DiGeronimo, T. F. (2000). *Ages and stages: A parent's guide to normal childhood development*. New York: John Wiley & Sons, Inc. 212.
10. Rhodes, J. E., & DuBois, D. L. (2006). Understanding and facilitating the youth mentoring movement. Social Policy Report: Giving Child and Youth Development Knowledge Away, 20(3), 1-19.
11. Ibid.

Chapter Twenty-One

1. Shulevitz, J. (2012, September 15). Why fathers really matter. *The Straits Times*, D14-15; Shulevitz, J. (2012, September 8). Why fathers really matter. Retrieved October 16, 2012, from *The New York Times*, Sunday Review: http://www.nytimes.com
2. *1996 Gallup Poll on Fathering*. (n.d.). Retrieved June 6, 2012, from The National Center for Fathering's Gallup Poll: http://www.fact.on.ca/rel_supp/gallup.htm
3. National Center for Fathering, National PTA. (2009). *Survey of fathers' involvement in children's learning: Summary of study findings*. Retrieved September 14, 2012, from National Center for Fathering: http://www.fathers.com/documents/research/2009_Education_Survey_Summary.pdf
4. Nord, C. W., & West, J. (2001). *Fathers' and mothers' involvement in their children's schools by family type and resident status, NCES 2001-032*. Washington, DC: U.S. Department

of Education. National Center for Education Statistics. Table 1. Retrieved September 30, 2012, from http://fatherhood.hhs.gov/pdf/nces-2001032.pdf

5. Kreider, R. M., & Fields, J. (2005). Living arrangements of children 2001. *Current Population Reports*. Washington, DC: U.S. Census Bureau. 70-104. Table 1.
6. Youthviews, Gallup Youth Survey 4 (June, 1997)
7. Poponoe, D. (1993). American family decline, 1960-1990: A review and appraisal. *Journal of Marriage and Family, 55*.
8. Saluter, A. F. *Marital status and living arrangements: March 1994*. US Bureau of the Census, Current Population Report. 28-484. Washington, DC: GPO, 1996. US Bureau of the Census. Statistical Abstract of the United States 1997, Washington, DC: GPO, 1997.
9. Engle, P. L., & Breaux, C. (1998). Fathers' involvement with children: Perspectives from developing countries. *Social Policy Report, XII*(1), 1-24; Bruce, J., Lloyd, C. B., & Leonard, A., with Engle, P. L., & Duffy, N. (1995). *Families in focus: New perspectives on mothers, fathers and children*. New York: Population Council.
10. Engle & Breaux (1998), Fathers' involvement with children; United Nations. (1995). *The world's women 1995: Trends and statistics*. New York: United Nations.
11. Engle & Breaux (1998), Fathers' involvement with children.
12. Ibid.
13. Rosenberg, J., & Wilcox, W. B. (2006). *The importance of fathers in the healthy development of children*. U.S. Department of Health and Human Services. Administration for Children and Families. Administration on Children, Youth and Families. Children's Bureau. Office on Child Abuse and Neglect.
14. Lamb, M. E. (2002). Infant-father attachments and their impact on child development. In C. S. Tamis-LeMonda & N. Cabrera (Eds.), *Handbook of father involvement: Multidisciplinary perspectives* (pp. 93–118). Mahwah, NJ: Erlbaum; Cummings, E. M., & O'Reilly, A. W. (1997). Fathers and family context: Effects of marital quality on child adjustment. In M. E. Lamb (Ed.), *The role of the father in child development* (3rd ed., pp. 49–65, 318–325). New York, NY: John Wiley & Sons; Lamb, M. E. (1997). Fathers and child development: An introductory overview and guide. In M. E. Lamb (Ed.), *The role of the father in child development* (3rd ed., pp. 1–18, 309–313). New York, NY: John Wiley & Sons.
15. Gable, S., Crnic, K., & Belsky, J. (1994). Co-parenting within the family system: Influences on children's development. *Family Relations, 43*(4), 380–386.
16. Pruett, K. (2000). *Father-need*. New York, NY: Broadway Books; Sternberg, K. J. (1997). Fathers, the missing parents in research on family violence. In M. E. Lamb (Ed.), *The role of the father in child development* (3rd ed., pp. 284-308, 392-397). New York, NY: John Wiley & Sons
17. Pruett (2000), *Father-need*.
18. Goldstine, H. S. (1982). Fathers' absence and cognitive development of 12–17 year olds. *Psychological Reports, 51*, 843–848; Nord, C., & West, J. (2001). *Fathers' and mothers' involvement in their children's schools by family type and resident status*. Retrieved September 30, 2012, from http://fatherhood.hhs.gov/pdf/nces-2001032.pdf
19. Nord & West (2001), *Fathers' and mothers' involvement*.
20. Yeung, W. J., Duncan, G. J., & Hill, M. S. (2000).Putting fathers back in the picture: Parental activities and children's adult outcomes. In H. E. Peters, G. W. Peterson, S. K. Steinmetz, & R. D. Day (Eds.), *Fatherhood: Research, interventions and policies* (pp. 97–113). New York, NY: Hayworth Press; Harris, K. M., & Marmer, J. K. (1996). Poverty, paternal involvement, and adolescent well-being. *Journal of Family Issues, 17*(5), 614–640; Pleck, J. H. (1997). Paternal involvement: Levels, sources, and consequences. In M. E. Lamb (Ed.), *Th e role of fathers in child development* (3rd ed., pp. 66–103). New York, NY: John Wiley & Sons.
21. Pruett (2000), *Father-need*; Lamb (2002), Infant-father attachments.
22. Parke, R. D. (1996). *Fatherhood*. Cambridge: Harvard University Press.; Lamb (2002), Infant-father attachments.
23. Parke (1996), *Fatherhood*
24. Mosley, J., & Thompson, E. (1995). Fathering behavior and child outcomes: The role of race and poverty. In W. Marsiglio (Ed.), *Fatherhood: Contemporary theory, research, and social policy* (pp. 148–165). Thousand Oaks, CA: Sage.

25 Mosley & Thompson (1995), Fathering behavior and child outcomes.
26 Horn, W., & Sylvester, T. (2002); U.S. Departmentof Health and Human Services, Substance Abuse and Mental Health Services Administration (SAMHSA). (1996). *The relationship between family structure and adolescent substance abuse*. Rockville, MD: National Clearinghouse for Alcohol and Drug Information; Harper, C., & McLanahan, S. S. (1998). *Father absence and youth incarceration*. Paper presented at the Annual Meeting of the American Sociological Association, San Francisco, CA; Brenner, E. (1999). *Fathers in prison: A review of the data*. Philadelphia, PA: National Center on Fathers and Families.
27 Sarkadi, A., Kristiansson, R., Oberjlaid, F., & Bremberg, S. (2007). Fathers' involvement and children's developmental outcomes: a systematic review of longitudinal studies. *Acta Paediatrica, 97*(2), 153-158.
28 Why dad should be more involved in children's lives. (2012, April 24). *The Straits Times*, B6.
29 Sarkadi, Kristiansson, Oberjlaid & Bremberg (2007), Fathers' involvement and children's developmental outcomes.
30 *HealthyChildren.org - Stages of adolescence*. (2011, May 10). (American Academy of Pediatrics) Retrieved April 23, 2012, from healthychildren.org: http://www.healthychildren.org
31 *puberty - definition of puberty by the Free Online Dictionary, Thesaurus and Encyclopedia*. (2009). Retrieved April 23, 2012, from The Free Dictionary: http://www.thefreedictionary.com
32 MacDonald, K., & Parke, R. D. (1986). Parent-child physical play: The effects of sex and age of children and parents. *Sex Roles, 7-8*, 367-379.
33 *Sexual risk behavior: HIV, STD, & teen pregnancy prevention*. (2011, July 12). Retrieved June 7, 2012, from Centers for Disease Control and Prevention: http://www.cdc.gov/HealthyYouth/sexualbehaviors
34 Wong, M. L., Chan, K. W., Koh, D., Tan, H. H., Lim, F. S., Emmanuel, S., & Bishop, G. (2009). Premarital sexual intercourse among adolescents in an Asian country: Multilevel ecological factors. *Pediatrics*; Haggstrom-Nordin, E., Hanson, U., & Tyden, T. (2005). Associations between pornography consumption and sexual practices among adolescents in Sweden. *International Journal of STD and AIDS, 16*(2), 102-107.
35 Ibid.
36 Louis, J. P., & Louis, K. M. (2010). *I choose us: A Christian perspective on building love connection in your marriage by breaking harmful cycles*. Singapore: Louis Counselling & Training Services.

Chapter Twenty-Two
1 Del Vecho, P., Fullmer, R. (Producers), Dindal, M., Kennedy, M. (Writers), & Dindal, M. (Director). (2005). *Chicken Little* [Motion Picture]. United States: Walt Disney Pictures.
2 Gunn, A. (Producers), Rodgers, M. (Writers), & Waters, M. (Director). (2003). *Freaky Friday* [Motion Picture]. United States: Buena Vista Pictures.
3 Bruckeimer, B., Lowry, H. (Producers), Wells, R., Andrus, M., Khouri, C. (Writers), & Khouri, C. (Director). (2002). *Divine secrets of the Ya-Ya Sisterhood* [Motion Picture]. United States: Warner Bros. Pictures.
4 British Association for Counselling & Psychotherapy. (2008, October 17). Clients, not practitioners, make therapy work. *Medical News Today*. Retrieved May 28, 2010, from http://www.medicalnewstoday.com
5 Whitfield, C. L. (2006). *Healing the child within*. FL: Health Communications, Inc. 1.
6 Ibid., 9.
7 Ibid., 11.
8 Scott Peck, M. (1978). *The road less travelled*. NY: Touchstone. 81.
9 Mehrabian, A. (1971). *Silent messages* (1st ed.). Belmont, CA: Wadsworth.

BIBLIOGRAPHY

1996 Gallup Poll on Fathering. (n.d.). Retrieved June 6, 2012, from The National Center for Fathering's Gallup Poll: http://www.fact.on.ca/rel_supp/gallup.htm

Ablard, K. E., & Parker, W. D. (1997). Parents' achievement goals and perfectionism in their academically talented children. *Journal of Youth and Adolescence, 26*(6), 651-667.

Adderholt-Elliot, M. (1989). Perfectionism and underachievement. *Gifted Child Today, 12,* 19–21.

Adkins, K. K., & Parker, W. D. (1996). Perfectionism and suicidal preoccupation. *Journal of Personality, 64,* 529–543.

Amato, P. R. (2000). Consequences of divorce for adults and children. *Journal of Marriage and the Family, 62,* 1269-1287.

Amato, P. R. (2005). The impact of family formation change on the cognitive, social and emotional well-being of the next generation. *The Future of Children, 15*(2).

Amato, P. R., & Booth, A. (1997). *A generation at risk: Growing up in an era of family upheaval.* Cambridge, MA: Harvard University Press. 173-175.

American Humane Association Children's Division. (1993). *Child sexual abuse: AHA fact sheet #4.* Englewood, CO: American Humane Association.

Anderson, C. A., & Bushman, B. J. (2001). Effects of violent video games on aggressive behavior, aggressive recognition, aggressive affect, physiological arousal, and prosocial behavior: A meta-analytic review of the scientific literature. *Psychological Science, 12,* 353-359.

Anderson, C. A., Carnagey, N. L., & Eubanks, J. (2003). Exposure to violent media: The effect of songs with violent lyrics on aggressive thoughts and feelings. *Journal of Personality and Social Psychology, 84*(5), 960-971.

Anderson, S. (2000). *The journey from abandonment to healing: Surviving through—and recovering from—the five stages that accompany the loss of love.* New York: Berkley Books.

Arntz, A., & van Genderen, H. (2009). *Schema therapy for borderline personality disorder.* Chichester: Wiley.

Artis, J. (2007). Maternal cohabitation and child well-being among kindergarten children. *Journal of Marriage and Family, 69,* 222-236.

Assor, A., & Tal, K. (2012). When parents' affection depends on child's achievement: Parental conditional positive regard, self-aggrandizement, shame and coping in adolescents, *Journal of Adolescence, 35,* 249-260.

Assor, A., Roth, G., Israeli, M., Freed., & Deci, E. (2007). *Parental conditional positive regard: Another harmful type of parental control.* Paper presented at the Society for Research in Child Development (SRCD), (Boston USA).

Avnet, J., Kerner, J. (Producers), Bass, R., Franken, A. (Writers), & Mandoki, L. (Director). (2002). *When a man loves a woman* [Motion Picture]. United States: Touchstone Pictures.

Axtell, A. & Newton, B. J. (1993). An analysis of alderian life themes of bulimic women. *Journal of Alderian Theory, Research and Practice 49*(1), 58-67.

Ball, S. A., & Cecero, J. J. (2001). Addicted patients with personality disorders: traits, schemas, and presenting problems. *Journal of Personality Disorders, 15,* 72-83.

Barber, N. (2000). *Why parents matter: Parental investment and child outcomes.* New York: Bergin & Garvey.

Baron-Cohen, S. (2011). *Zero degrees of empathy: A new theory of human cruelty.* London: Allen Lane.

Baumrind, D., Berkowitz, M. W., Lickona, T., Nucci, L. P., & Watson, M. (2008). *Parenting for character: Five experts, five practices.* (D. Streight, Ed.) Oregon: CSEE.

BBC News. (2011, October 25). *Lack of outdoor play linked to short-sighted children.* Retrieved May 29, 2012, from BBC News: http://www.bbc.co.uk/news/health-15427954.

Beals, D. E. (2001). Eating and reading: Links between family conversations with preschoolers and later language and literacy. In D. K. Dickinson & P. O. Tabors (Eds.), *Beginning literacy with language: Young children at home and school.* (pp. 75-92). Baltimore, MD: Paul H. Brookes Publishing.

Beck, A. T., Freeman, A., & Associates. (1990). *Cognitive therapy of personality disorders.* New York: Guilford Press.

Beers, V. G. (1993). *Teaching toddlers the bible.* Victor Books.

Beers, V. G., & Boerke, C. (1992). *The toddlers bible.* CO: David C Cook.

Bennett, W. J. (Ed.). (1995). *The children's book of virtues.* New York: Simon & Schuster.

Berkman, L., & Syme, L. (1979). Social networks, host resistance, and mortality: A nine-year follow-up study of Alameda County residents. *American Journal of Epidemiology, 109*(2), 186-204.

Berlin, L. J., Cassidy, J., & Appleyard, K. (2008). The influence of early attachments on other relationships. In *Handbook of attachment, theory, research, and clinical applications.* New York: The Guilford Press.

Biblarz, T. J. (2000). Family structure and children's success: A comparison of widowed and divorced single-mother families. *Journal of Marriage and the Family, 62*(2), 533-548.

Blatt, S. J. (1995). The destructiveness of perfectionism: Implications for the treatment of depression. *American Psychologist, 50,* 1003–1020.

Block, P. (2008). *Community: The structure of belonging.* San Francisco: Berrett-Koehler Publishing, Inc.

Bloom, B. S. (1985). Generalization about talent development. In B. S. Bloom (Ed.), *Developing talent in young people.* New York: Ballentine Books.

Bowlby, J. (1969). *Attachment. Attachment and Loss: Vol. 1. Loss.* New York: Basic Books.

Bowlby, J. (1988). *A secure base: Parent-child attachment and healthy human development. Tavistock professional book.* London: Routledge.

Bradshaw, J., & Millar, J. (1991). *Lone parent families in the UK.* Department of Social Security Research Report No 6. London: HMSO.

Brady, E. H., Martin, J. A., & Ventura, S. J. (2007). Births: Preliminary data for 2006. *National Vital Statistics Reports, 56*(7), Table 1.

Braitman, K. A. (2002). Relationships among body satisfaction, appearance schemas, early maladaptive schemas, and sociocultural attitudes towards appearance. *Dissertation Abstracts International, 62*(10-B), 4835.

Brenner, E. (1999). *Fathers in prison: A review of the data.* Philadelphia, PA: National Center on Fathers and Families.

Brewerton, T. D., & George, M. S. (1993). Is migraine related to eating disorders? *International Journal of Eating Disorders, 14,* 75–79.

British Association for Counselling & Psychotherapy. (2008, October 17). Clients, not practitioners, make therapy work. *Medical News Today.* Retrieved May 28, 2010, from http://www.medicalnewstoday.com

Brown, S. L. (2004). Family structure and child well-being: The significance of parental cohabitation. *Journal of Marriage and Family, 66*(2), 351-367.

Bruce, J., Lloyd, C. B., & Leonard, A., with Engle, P. L., & Duffy, N. (1995). *Families in focus: New perspectives on mothers, fathers and children.* New York: Population Council.

Bruckeimer, B., Lowry, H. (Producers), Wells, R., Andrus, M., Khouri, C. (Writers), & Khouri, C. (Director). (2002). *Divine secrets of the Ya-Ya Sisterhood* [Motion Picture]. United States: Warner Bros. Pictures.

Bryce, I., Ziskin, L. (Producers), Lee, S., Ditko, S., Koepp, D. (Writers), & Raimi, S. (Director). (2002). *Spiderman* [Motion Picture]. United States: Columbia Pictures.

Bryer, J. B., Nelson, B. A., Miller, J. B., & Krol, P. A. (1987). Childhood sexual and physical abuse as factors in adult psychiatric illness. *American Journal of Psychiatry, 144*, 1426-1430.

Bumpass, L. L., & Sweet, J. A. (1989). Children's experience in single-parent families: Implications of cohabitation and marital transition. *Family Planning Perspectives, 21*(6), 252-260.

Burghes, L., Clarke, L., & Cronin, N. (1997). *Fathers and fatherhood in Britain.* London: Family Policy Studies Centre.

Buss, D. M., & Malamuth, N. M. (Eds.). (1996), *Sex, power, conflict: Evolutionary and feminist perspectives.* Oxford: Oxford University Press.

Carlson, M. J., & Corcoran, M. E. (2001). Family structure and children's behavioral and cognitive outcomes. *Journal of Marriage and Family, 63*(3), 779-792.

CASA. (2007). *The importance of family dinners III.* New York: Columbia University.

Catsambis, S. (2001). Expanding knowledge of parental involvement in children's secondary education: Connections with high school seniors' academic success. *Social Psychology of Education, 5*(2), 149-177.

Cavanagh, S. E., & Houston, A. C. (2006). Family instability and children's early problem behavior. *Social Forces, 85*(1), 551-581.

Cavanagh, S. E., & Schiller, K. S. (2006). Marital transitions, parenting, and schooling: Exploring the link between family-structure history and adolescents' academic status. *Sociology of Education, 79*(4), 329-354.

Cawson, P. (2002). *Child maltreatment in the family.* London: NSPCC.

Cecero, J. J., Nelson, J. D., & Gillie, J. M. (2004). Tools and tenets of schema therapy: Toward the construct validity of the early maladaptive schema questionnaire-research version (EMSQ-R). *Clinical Psychology & Psychotherapy, 11*, 344-357.

Chan, P. Y., Seah, S. Y. (Producers), Leow, R., Neo, J. (Writers), & Neo, J. (Director). (2006). *I Not Stupid Too* [Motion Picture]. Singapore: Mediacorp Raintree Pictures.

Chang, A. L. (2011, 19 November). 1 in 10 will suffer from mental illness: Study. *The Straits Times.*

Child Development Institute, LLC. *"Play is the work of the child" Maria Montessori.* Retrieved September 14, 2012, from Child Development Institute Parenting Today: http://www.childdevelopmentinfo.com

Child Welfare Information Gateway. (2008). *Long-term consequences of child abuse and neglect.* Washington, D.C.: U.S. Department of Health and Human Services. Retrieved May 31, 2012 from http://www.childwelfare.gov/pubs/factsheets/long_term_consequences.cfm

Childhelp. (n.d.). *National child abuse statistics.* Retrieved May 30, 2012, from Childhelp: http://www.childhelp.org/pages/statistics#abuse-conseq

Chua, A. (2011, January 8). *Why Chinese mothers are superior - WSJ.com.* Retrieved April 23, 2012, from The Wall Street Journal: http://www.online.wjs.com

Clients, not practitioners, make therapy work - British Association for Counselling & Psychotherapy. (2008, October 17). *Medical News Today*. Retrieved May 28, 2010, from http://www.medicalnewstoday.com

Cline, V. B., Croft, R. G., & Courrier, S. (1973). Desensitization of children to television violence. *Journal of Personality and Social Psychology, 27*(3), 360-365.

Cloud, H., & Townsend, J. (1998). *Boundaries with kids*. Michigan: Zondervan.

Cockett, M., & Tripp, J. (1994). *The Exeter family study: Family breakdown and its impact on children*. Exeter: University of Exeter Press.

Cohen, D. A., Wang, W., Wyatt, J. K., Kronauer, R. E., Dijk, D.-J., Czeisler, C. A., & Klerman, E. B. (2010). Uncovering residual effects of chronic sleep loss on human performance. *Science Translational Medicine, 2*(14), 14ra3.

Coleman, J. S., & Hoffer, T. (1987). *Public and private high schools: The impact of communities*. New York: Basic Books Inc.

Coleman, J. S., Hoffer, T., & Kilgore, S. (1982). *High school achievement: public, Catholic, and private schools compared*. New York: Basic Books Inc.

Colin, V. L. (1991, June 28). *Infant attachment: What we know now*. Retrieved May 21, 2012, from Office of the Assistant Secretary for Planning and Evaluation, U.S. Department of Health and Human Services: http://aspe.hhs.gov/

Council of Economic Advisers to the President. (2000). *Teens and their parents in the 21st century: An examination of trends in teen behaviour and the role of parental involvement*. Washington, DC: Council of Economic Advisors to the President.

Cox, M., & Brooks-Gunn, J. (Eds.). (1999). *Formation, functioning, and stability of families*. Mahwah, NJ: Erlbaum.

Coyle, C. T., & Enright, R. D. (1997). Forgiveness intervention with postabortion men. *Journal of Consulting and Clinical Psychology, 65*, 1042-1046.

Crabb, L. (1997). *Connecting: Healing for ourselves and our relationships, a radical new vision*. Nashville, Tennessee: Word Publishing.

Crawford, E., & O'Dougherty Wright, M. (2007). The impact of childhood psychological maltreatment on interpersonal schemas and subsequent experiences of relationship aggression. *Journal of Emotional Abuse, 7*, 93-116.

Cukor, D., & McGinn, L. K. (2006). History of child abuse and severity of adult depression: the mediating role of cognitive schema. *Journal of Child Sexual Abuse, 15*, 19-34.

Cummings, E. M., & Davies, P. T. (2010). *Marital conflict and children: An emotional security perspective*. New York: The Guilford Press.

Cummings, E. M., & O'Reilly, A. W. (1997). Fathers and family context: Effects of marital quality on child adjustment. In M. E. Lamb (Ed.), *The role of the father in child development* (3rd ed., pp. 49–65, 318–325). New York, NY: John Wiley & Sons.

Cummings, E. M., & Wilson, A. G. (1999). Contexts of marital conflict and children's emotional security: Exploring the distinction between constructive and destructive conflict from the children's perspective. In M. Cox, & J. Brooks-Gunn (Eds.), *Formation, functioning, and stability of families* (pp. 105-129). Mahwah, NJ: Erlbaum.

Cummings, E. M., Ballard, M., & El-Sheikh, M. (1991). Responses of children and adolescents to interadult anger as a function of gender, age, and mode of expression. *Merrill-Palmer Quarterly, 37*, 543-560.

Cynaumon, G. (2003). *Discover your child's D.Q. factor: The discipline quotient system*. Brentwood, TN: Integrity Publishers.

Daly, M., & Wilson, M. (1996). Evolutionary psychology and marital conflict: The relevance of stepchildren. In D. M. Buss, & N. M. Malamuth (Eds.), *Sex, power, conflict: Evolutionary and feminist perspectives* (pp.9-28). Oxford: Oxford University Press.

Deci, E. L., & Flaste, R. (1996). *Why we do what we do: Understanding self-motivation.* New York: Penguin Books.

Decouvelaere, F., Graziani, P., Gackiere-Eraldi, D., Rusinek, S., & Hautekeete, M. (2002). Hypothese de l'existence et de l'evolution de schemas cognitifs mal adaptes chez l'alcool-dependant [Hypothesis of existence and development of early maladaptive schemas in alcohol-dependant patients]. *Journal de Therapie Comportementale et Cognitive, 12,* 43-48.

Del Vecho, P., Fullmer, R. (Producers), Dindal, M., Kennedy, M. (Writers), & Dindal, M. (Director). (2005). *Chicken Little* [Motion Picture]. United States: Walt Disney Pictures.

Dickinson, D. K., & Tabors, P. O. (Eds.). (2001). *Beginning literacy with language: Young children at home and school.* Baltimore, MD: Paul H. Brookes Publishing.

DiClemente, R. J., Santelli, J. S., & Crosby, R. A. (Eds.). (2009). *Adolescent health: Understanding and preventing risk behaviors.* San Francisco, CA: Jossey-Bass.

Dictionary and Thesaurus—Merriam-Webster Online. (n.d.). Retrieved May 20, 2012, from http://www.merriam-webster.com/thesaurus/boundary

Dobrenski, R. A. (2001). Romantic jealousy: Symptoms, schemas, and attachment. *Dissertation Abstracts International, 62*(6-B), 2954.

Doherty, W. J. (2000). *Take back your kids: Confident parenting in turbulent times.* Notre Dame, Indiana: Sorin Books.

Doherty, W., & Carlson, B. (n.d.). *Overscheduled kids, underconnected families: The research evidence.* Retrieved May 21, 2012, from Putting Family First: www.puttingfamilyfirst.org

Douglas, G. (2009). Pathological video game use among youth 8 - 18: A national study. *Psychological Science, 20*(5), 594-602.

Dr. Phil.com – advice – parenting. Retrieved September 14, 2012, from http://drphil.com/articles/category/4/

Dreikurs, R., & Soltz, V. (1990). *Children: The challenge: The classic work on improving parent-child relationships—Intelligent, humane & eminently practical.* New York: Plume.

Duckworth, A. L., & Seligman, M. E. P. (2005). Self-discipline outdoes IQ in predicting academic performance of adolescents. *Psychological Science, 16*(12), 939-944.

Duckworth, A., Quinn, P., & Tsukayama, E. (2011). What *No Child Left Behind* leaves behind: The roles of IQ and self-control in predicting standardized achievement test scores and report card grades. *Journal of Educational Psychology.*

Dweck, C. S., & Leggett, E. L. (1988). A social-cognitive approach to motivation and personality. *Psychological Review, 95,* 256-273.

Edward, G. (1984). *The divine romance.* Illinois: Tyndale House Publishing Inc.

Edwards, G. (1984). *The divine romance.* Illinois: Tyndale House Publishing Inc.

El-Sheikh, M., Buckhalt, J. A., Mize, J., & Acebo, C. (2006). Marital conflict and disruption of children's sleep. *Child Development, 77*(1), 31-43.

El-Sheikh, M., Cummings, E. M., Kouros, C. D., Elmore-Staton, L., & Buckhalt, J. A. (2008). Marital psychology and physical aggression and children's mental and physical health: Direct, meditated, and moderated effects. *Journal of Consulting and Clinical Psychology, 76,* 138-148.

Elkind, D. (2006). *The hurried child: Growing up too fast too soon.* MA: Da Capo Press.

Elkind, D. (2007). *The power of play: How spontaneous, imaginative activities lead to happier, healthier children.* Cambridge, MA: Da Capo Press.

Ely, M., West, P., Sweeting, H., & Richards, M. (2000). Teenage family life, life chances, lifestyles and health: A comparison of two contemporary cohorts. *International Journal of Law, Policy and the Family, 14,* 1-30.

Engle, P. L., & Breaux, C. (1998). Fathers' involvement with children: Perspectives from developing countries. *Social Policy Report, XII*(1), 1-24.

Enright, R. D. (2001). *Forgiveness is a choice: A step-by-step process for resolving anger and restoring hope.* Washington: APA LifeTools.

Enright, R. D., & Fitzgibbons, R. P. (2000). *Helping clients forgive.* Washington, DC: American Psychological Association. 29.

Erikson, E. H. (1950). *Childhood and society.* New York: Norton.

Faber, A., & Mazlish, E. (1980). *How to talk so kids will listen and listen so kids will talk.* New York: Avon Books, Inc.

Fang, X., Brown, D. S., Florence, C. S., & Mercy, J. A. (2012) The economic burden of child maltreatment in the United States and implications for prevention. Child Abuse & Neglect, 36(2), 156-165.

Feng, Z. (2012, May 5). *Myopia in kids: Spend more time outdoors.* Retrieved May 29, 2012, from The Straits Times: http://www.straitstimes.com

Fiese, B. H., Foley, K. P., & Spagnola, M. (2006). Routine and ritual elements in family mealtimes: Contexts for child wellbeing and family identity. *New Directions for Child and Adolescent Development, 111*, 67-90.

Fiese, B., & Schwartz, M. (2008). Reclaiming the family table: Mealtimes and child health and wellbeing. *Social Policy Report: Giving Child and Youth Development Knowledge Away, 22(4)*, 1-19.

Fincham, F. D. (2000). The kiss of porcupines: From attributing responsibility for forgiving. *Personal Relationships, 9*, 239-251.

Fishburne, L., Ganis, S., Ganis, N. H., Llewelyn, D., Romersa, M. (Producers), Atchison, D. (Writer), & Atchison, D. (Director). (2006). *Akeelah and the Bee* [Motion Picture]. United States: Lions Gate Films.

Fitzgibbons, R. P. (1986). The cognitive and emotive use of forgiveness in the treatment of anger. *Psychotherapy, 23*, 629-633.

Fivush, R., Bohanke, J., Robertson, R., & Duke, M. (2004). Family narratives and the development of children's emotional well-being. In M. W. Pratt & B. H. Fiese (Eds.), *Family stories and the life course across time and generations* (pp. 55-76). Mahwah, NJ: Erlbaum.

Forthofer, M. S., Markman, H. J., Cox, M., Stanley, S., & Kessler, R. C. (1996). Associations between marital distress and work loss in a national sample. *Journal of Marriage and Family, 58*, 597-605.

Gable, S., Crnic, K., & Belsky, J. (1994). Co-parentingwithin the family system: Influences on children'sdevelopment. *Family Relations, 43*(4), 380–386.

Gardner, H. (1993). *Frames of Mind: The Theory of Multiple Intelligences.* New York: Basic Books.

Gerbner, G. (2004). TV violence and the art of asking the wrong question. In *The World & I; A Chronicle of Our Changing Era*, July, 1994, pp.385-397. Retrieved September 14, 2012, from Center for Media Literacy: http://www.medialit.org/reading-room/tv-violence-and-art-asking-wrong-question

Gillman, M. W., Rifas-Shiman, S. L., Frazier, A. L., Rockett, H. R. H., Camargo, C. A., Field, A. E., Berkey, C. S., & Colditz, G. A. (2000). Family dinners and diet quality among older children and adolescents. *Archives of Family Medicine, 9*, 235-240.

Ginott, H. G. (2003). *Between parent and child: The bestselling classic that revolutionized parent-child communication.* New York: Three Rivers Press.

Goeke-Morey, M. C., Cummings, E. M., & Papp, L. M. (2007). Children and marital conflict resolution: Implications for emotional security and adjustment. *Journal of Family Psychology, 21*(4), 744-753.

Goh, C. L. (2012, April 26). Singapore 'has lowest youth death rate' among rich nations. *The Straits Times*.

Goldstine, H. S. (1982). Fathers' absence and cognitive development of 12–17 year olds. *Psychological Reports, 51*, 843–848.

Gottfried, A. W., Gottfried, A. E., Bathurst, K., & Guerin, D. W. (1994). *Gifted IQ: Early developmental aspects*. New York: Plenum Press.

Gottman, J., & Declaire, J. (1998). *Raising an emotionally intelligent child—The heart of parenting* . New York: Simon & Schuster.

Grych, J. H., & Fincham, F. D. (1990). Marital conflict and children's adjustment: A cognitive-contextual framework. *Psychological Bulletin, 108*, 267-290.

Gunn, A. (Producer), Rodgers, M. (Writer), & Waters, M. (Director). (2003). *Freaky Friday* [Motion Picture]. United States: Buena Vista Pictures.

Gutman, L. M. (2006). How student and parent goal orientations and classroom goal structures influence the math achievement of African Americans during the high school transition. *Contemporary Educational Psychology, 31*, 44–63.

Haggstrom-Nordin, E., Hanson, U., & Tyden, T. (2005). Associations between pornography consumption and sexual practices among adolescents in Sweden. *International Journal of STD and AIDS, 16*(2), 102-107.

Halford, J. C. G., Boyland, E. J., Hughes, G., Oliveira, L. P., & Dovey, T. M. (2007). Beyond-brand effect of television (TV) food advertisements/ commercials on caloric intake and food choice of 5-7-year-old children. *Appetite, 49*, 263-267.

Harlow, C. U.S. Department of Justice, Office of Justice Programs. (1999).*Prior abuse reported by inmates and probationers* (NCJ 172879) Retrieved from http://bjs.ojp.usdoj.gov/content/pub/pdf/parip.pdf

Harper, C., & McLanahan, S. S. (1998). *Father absence and youth incarceration*. Paper presented at the Annual Meeting of the American Sociological Association, San Francisco, CA.

Harris, A. E., & Curtin, L. (2002). Parental perceptions, early maladaptive schemas, and depressive symptoms in young adults. *Cognitive Therapy and Research, 26*, 405-416.

Harris, J. L. (2008). *Priming obesity: Direct effects of television food advertising on eating behavior and food preferences*. PhD thesis, Yale University, New Haven, CT.

Harris, K. M., & Marmer, J. K. (1996). Poverty, paternal involvement, and adolescent well-being. *Journal of Family Issues, 17*(5), 614–640.

Hartt, J., & Waller, G. (2002). Child abuse, dissociation, and core beliefs in bulimic disorders. *Child Abuse and Neglect, 26*, 923-938.

Hartup, W., & Moore, S. (1990). Early peer relations: Developmental significance and prognostic implications. *Early Childhood Research Quarterly, 5*, 1-7.

HealthyChildren.org - Stages of Adolescence. (2011, May 10). (American Academy of Pediatrics) Retrieved May 20, 2012, from healthychildren.org: http://www.healthychildren.org

Henderson, D., Witt, P. J., Haft, S., Thomas, T. (Producers), Shulman, T. (Writer), & Weir, P. (Director). (1989). *Dead Poets Society* [Motion Picture]. United States: Touchstone Pictures.

Henner, M., & Sharon, R. V. (1999). *I refuse to raise a brat: Straightforward advice on parenting in an age of overindulgence*. New York: HarperCollins. xvii.

Herbert, T., & Cohen, S. (1993). Stress and immunity in humans: a meta-analytical review. *Psychosomatic Medicine, 55*, 364-379.

Hersey, J. C., & Jordan, A. (2007). *Reducing Children's TV Time to Reduce the Risk of Childhood Overweight: The Children's Media Use Study*. Final report. Prepared for the

Centers for Disease Control and Prevention and The Association of Preventive Medicine Teaching and Research. Washington, DC: Research Triangle Institute International.

Hetherington, E. M. (1992). Coping with marital transitions: A family systems perspective. *Monographs of the Society for Research in Child Development, 57*(2-3), 1-14

Hills, T. W. (1987). Children in the fast lane: Implications for early childhood policy and practice. *Early Childhood Research Quarterly, 2,* 265-273.

Hochschild, A. R. (2012, May 5). *The outsourced life.* Retrieved May 31, 2012, from The New York Times. Sunday Review: http://www.nytimes.com

Hoffart, A., Sexton, H., Hedley, L. M., Wang, C. E., Holthe, H., Haugum, J. A., Nordahl, H. M., Hovland, O. J., & Holte, A. (2005). The Structure of Maladaptive Schemas: A Confirmatory Factor Analysis and a Psychometric Evaluation of Factor-Derived Scales. *Cognitive Therapy and Research, 29*(6), 627-644.

Hoffart, A., Versland, S., & Sexton, H. (2002). Self-understanding, empathy, guided discovery, and schema belief in schema-focused cognitive therapy of personality problems: A process-outcome study. *Cognitive Therapy and Research, 26,* 199-219.

Hofferth, S. L. (1999). *Changes in American children's time, 1981-1997.* University of Michigan's Institute for Social Research, Center Survey.

Hofferth, S. L. (2001). How American children spend their time. *Journal of Marriage and the Family, 63,* 295-308.

Hofferth, S. L. (2006). Residential father family type and child well-being, *Demography, 43*(1), 53-77.

Horn, W., & Sylvester, T. (2002); U.S. Departmentof Health and Human Services, Substance Abuse and Mental Health Services Administration (SAMHSA). (1996). *The relationship between family structure and adolescent substance abuse.* Rockville, MD: National Clearinghouse for Alcohol and Drug Information.

Hotchkiss, S. (2002). *Why is it always about you? The seven deadly sins of narcissism.* New York: Free Press.

How to prevent sexual abuse of your child? (2009, February 19). Retrieved May 30, 2012, from The Parents Zone: http://www.TheParentsZone.com

Huesmann, L. R. (1982). Television violence and aggressive behavior. In D. Perl, L. Bouthilet, & J. Lazar (Eds.), *Television and behavior: Ten years of programs and implications for the 80's* (pp. 126-137). Washington, DC: U.S. Government Printing Office.

Hyler, S., Rieder, R. O., Spitzer, R. L., & Williams, J. (1987). *Personality Diagnostic Questionnaire-Revised.* New York: New York State Psychiatric Institute.

Iyer, S. R. (2001). An ergonomic study of chronic musculoskeletal pain in schoolchildren. *Indian Journal of Pediatrics, 68*(10), 937-941.

Jeynes, W. H. (2003). A meta-analysis: The effects of parental involvement on minority children's academic achievement. *Education and Urban Society, 35*(2), 202–218.

Jeynes, W. H. (2005, December). *Parental involvement and student achievement: A meta-analysis.* Family Involvement Research Digests. Retrieved May 30, 2012, from Harvard Family Research Project: http://www.hfrp.org

Johnson, J. G., Cohen, P., Kasen, S., Smailes, E., & Brook, J. S. (2001). The association of maladaptive parental behavior with psychiatric disorder among parents and their offspring. *Archives of General Psychiatry, 58,* 453-460.

Johnson, J. G., Cohen, P., Smailes,E. M., Kasen, S., & Brook, J. S. (2002). Television viewing and aggressive behavior during adolescence and adulthod. *Science, 295*(5564), 2468-2471.

Jones, S., & Jones, B. (1993). *How and when to tell your kids about sex: A lifelong approach to shaping your child's sexual character.* CO: Navpress.

Jones, S., Jones, B., & Nystrom, C. (1984). *God's design for sex*. CO: Navpress.

Kazan, E. (Producer), Steinbeck, J., Osborn, P. (Writers), & Kazan, E. (Director). (1955). *East of Eden* [Motion Picture]. United States: Warner Bros. Pictures.

Kelly, M. (2007, August 7). *LifeWay research finds parents churches can help teens stay in church*. Retrieved May 31, 2012, from LifeWay Biblical Solutions for Life: http://www.lifeway.com

Khalik, S. (2012, April 20). Not enough sleep? Kids in S'pore sleep less than those in Switzerland: Study. *The Straits Times*, C1.

Khan, A. (Producer), Gupte, A. (Writer), & Khan, A. (Director). (2007). *Taare Zameen Par* [Motion Picture]. India: Amir Khan Productions.

Kids-in-mind: Movie ratings that actually work. (n.d.). Retrieved May 29, 2012, from Kids in mind: http://www.kids-in-mind.com

Kieren, D., & Munro, B. (1987). Following the leaders: Parents' influence on adolescent religious activity. *Journal for the Scientific Study of Religion, 26*(2), 249-255.

Kim, C. C. (2008). Academic success begins at home: How children can succeed in school. *Backgrounder (Published by The Heritage Foundation), 2185*, 1-12.

Kindlon, D. (2001). *Too much of a good thing: Raising children of character in an indulgent age*. New York: Hyperion.

Koestner, R., Franz, C. E., Weinberger, J. (1990). The family origins of empathic concern: A 26 year longitudinal study. *Journal of Personality and Social Psychology, 58*, 709-717.

Kohn, A. (1986). *No contest: The case against competition*. Boston: Houghton Mifflin.

Kohn, A. (2009, September 14). *When a parent's 'I love you' means 'Do as I say'*. Retrieved May 31, 2012, from The New York Times: http://www.nytimes.com

Kreider, H., Caspe, M., Kennedy, S., & Weiss, H. (2007). Family involvement in middle and high school students' education. *Harvard Family Research Project*, 1-12.

Kreider, R. M., & Fields, J. (2005). Living arrangements of children 2001. *Current Population Reports*. Washington, DC: U.S. Census Bureau. 70-104. Table 1.

Lai, J. P., & Jones, A. Y. (2001). The effect of shoulder-girdle loading by a school bag on lung volumes in Chinese primary school children. *Early Human Development, 62*(1), 79-86.

Lamb, M. E. (1997). Fathers and child development: An introductory overviewand guide. In M. E. Lamb (Ed.), *The role of the father in child development* (3rd ed., pp. 1–18, 309–313). New York, NY: John Wiley & Sons.

Lamb, M. E. (2002). Infant-father attachments and their impact on child development. In C. S. Tamis-LeMonda & N. Cabrera (Eds.), *Handbook of father involvement: Multidisciplinary perspectives* (pp. 93–118). Mahwah, NJ: Erlbaum.

Lamb, M. E. (Ed.). (2003). *The role of the father in child development*. New York, NY: John Wiley & Sons.

Lambert, M. J., & Barley, D. E. (2001). Research summary on the therapeutic relationship and psychotherapy outcome. *Psychotherapy: Theory, Research, Practice, Training, 38*(4), 357-361.

Lask, B., & Bryant-Waugh, R. (1992). Early-onset anorexia nervosa and related eating disorders. *Journal of Child Psychology and Psychiatry, 33*(1), 281-300.

Lawler, K. A., Younger, J. Y., Piferi, R. A., Billington, E., Jobe, R., Edmondson, K., Jones, W. H. (2003). A change of heart: cardiovascular correlates of forgiveness in response to interpersonal conflict. *Journal of Behavioral Medicine, 26*, 373-393.

Lee, C. W., Taylor, G., & Dunn, J. (1999). Factor Structure of the Schema Questionnaire in a Large Clinical Sample. *Cognitive Therapy and Research, 23*(4), 441-451.

Lepper, M. R., & Greene, D. (1975). Turning play into work: Effects of adult surveilance and extrinsic reward on children's intrinsic motivation. *Journal of Personality and Social Psychology, 31*, 479-486.

Lepper, M. R., Greene, D., & Nisbett, R. E. (1973). Undermining children's intrinsic interest with extrinsic reward: A test of the 'overjustification' hypothesis. *Journal of Personality and Social Psychology, 28*(1), 129-137.

Leung, N., Waller, G., & Thomas, G. (1999). Core beliefs in anorexic and bulimic women. *Journal of Nervous and Mental Disease, 187*, 736-741.

Levine, M. (2008). *The price of privilege: How parental pressure and material advantage are creating generation of disconnected and unhappy kids.* New York: HarperCollins.

Levine, P. (2006, February 8). *What do parents want.* Retrieved May 30, 2012, from Peter Levine: A blog for civic renewal: http://www.peterlevine.ws

Lien Centre for Social Innovation. (2010). *The world that changes the world: How philanthropy, innovation, and entrepreneurship are transforming the social ecosystem.* (W. Cheng, & S. Mohamed, Eds.) Singapore: John Wiley & Sons. 57.

Lin, B., Guthrie, J., & Frazao, E. (1999). Quality of children's diets at and away from home: 1994-1996. *Food Review, 22*, 2-10.

Lobbestael, J., Arntz, A., & Sieswerda, S. (2005). Schema modes and childhood abuse in borderline and antisocial personality disorder. *Journal of Behavior Therapy and Experimental Psychiatry, 36*, 240-253.

Lockwood, G., & Perris, P. (2012). A new look at core emotional needs. In M. B. van Vreeswijk, *Handbook of schema therapy: Theory, research and science* (pp. 41-66). West Sussex, UK: Wiley-Blackwell.

Louis, J. P., & Louis, K. M. (2010). *I choose us: A Christian perspective on building love connection in your marriage by breaking harmful cycles.* Singapore: Louis Counselling & Training Services.

Louis, J. P., Sexton, H., Lockwood, G., Hu, Y., Hoffart, A., & Chong, W. (2012). *A cross cultural exploration of the associations between the latent structures of the Young Schema Questionnaire and the Young Parent Inventory.* In process of being published.

Lum, S. (2008, January 16). Paedophile jailed 22 yrs for sex acts on 2 boys. *The Straits Times.* Retrieved September 14, 2012, from asiaone news: http://www.asiaone.com/News/AsiaOne%2BNews/Crime/Story/A1Story20080116-45304.html

Lumley, M. N., & Harkness, K. L. (2007). Specificity in the relations among childhood adversities, early maladaptive schemas, and symptom profiles in adolescent depression. Cognitive Therapy and Research, 31(5), 639-657.

MacDonald, K., & Parke, R. D. (1986). Parent-child physical play: The effects of sex and age of children and parents. Sex Roles, 7-8, 367-379.

Maggio, R. (Ed.). (1998). *The new beacon book of quotations by women.* Beacon Press.

Male survivors of childhood sexual abuse. (1990). *Virginia Child Protection Newsletter, 31*: 1-12.

Manning, W., & Lamb, K. (2003). Adolescent well-being in cohabitating, married, and single-parent families. *Journal of Marriage and Family, 65*, 876-893.

Marchant, G. J., Paulson, S. E., & Rothlisberg, B. A. (2001). Relations of middle school students' perceptions of family and school contexts with academic achievement. *Psychology in the Schools, 38*, 505–519.

Margulies, S., Wolper, D. L. (Producers), Dahl, R. (Writer), & Stuart, M. (Director). (1971). *Willy Wonka & the Chocolate Factory* [Motion Picture]. United States: Paramount Pictures.

Marsiglio, W. (Ed.). (1995). *Fatherhood: Contemporary theory, research, and social policy.* Thousand Oaks, CA: Sage.

Maslow, A. H. (1987). *Motivation and personality, Third Edition.* New York: Harper & Row, Publishers, Inc.

McClelland, M. M., Acock, A. C., Piccinin, A., Rhea, S. A., & Stallings, M. C. (2012). Relations between preschool attention span-persistence and age 25 educational outcomes. *Early Childhood Research Quarterly.*

McCoy, K., Cummings, E. M., & Davies, P. T. (2009). Constructive and destructive marital conflict, emotional security and children's prosocial behavior. *Journal of Child Psychology and Psychiatry, 50*(3), 270-279.

McGrath, M. (2012, May 4). *Massive rise in Asian eye damage.* Retrieved May 29, 2012, from BBC News: http://www.bbc.co.uk/news/health-17942181

McKergow, M., & Clarke, J. (2007). *Solutions Focus Working: 80 real life lessons for successful organisational change.* Glasgow: SolutionsBooks. 54.

McLanahan, S., & Sandefur, G. (1994). *Growing up with a single parent.* Cambridge, MA: President and Fellows of Harvard College.

Mehrabian, A. (1971). *Silent messages* (1st ed.). Belmont, CA: Wadsworth.

Menehan, K. (2006). *Tiffany Field on massage research.* Retrieved May 20, 2012, from Massage Magazine exploring today's touch therapies: http://www.massagemag.com/News/2006/January/125/Tiffany.php

Messman-Moore, T. L., & Coates, A. A. (2007). The impact of childhood psychological abuse on adult interpersonal conflict: the role of early maladaptive schemas and patterns of interpersonal behavior. *Journal of Emotional Abuse, 7,* 75-92.

Michalak, L., Trocki, K., & Bond, J. (2007). Religion and alchohol in the U.S. National Alcohol Survey: How important is religion for abstention and drinking? *Drug and Alcohol Dependence, 89*(2-3), 268-280.

Miller, B., Miller, G., Mitchell, D. (Producers), Coleman, W., Collee, J., Miller, G., Morris, J. (Writers), Miller, G., Coleman, W., & Morris, J. (Directors). (2006). *Happy Feet* [Motion Picture]. United States: Warner Bros. Pictures.

Miserandino, M. (1996). Children who do well in school: Individual differences in perceived competence and autonomy in above-average children. *Journal of Education Psychology, 88*(2), 203-214.

Moffitt, T. E., Arseneault, L., Belsky, D., Dickson, N., Hancox, R. J., Harrington, H., et al. (2010, December 21). A gradient of childhood self-control predicts health, wealth, and public safety. *Proceedings of the National Academy of Sciences of the United States of America.*

Moore, K. A., & Zaff, J. F. (2002, November). Building a better teenager: A summary of "what works" in adolescent development, research brief. *Child Trends,* 1-5.

Morgan, I. G., Ohno-Matsui, K., & Saw, S. M. (2012). Myopia. *The Lancet, 379* (9827), 1739-1748.

Mosley, J., & Thompson, E. (1995). Fathering behavior and child outcomes: The role of race and poverty. In W. Marsiglio (Ed.), *Fatherhood: Contemporary theory, research, and social policy* (pp. 148–165). Thousand Oaks, CA: Sage.

Muella, R. (2005). The effect of marital dissolution on the labour supply of males and females: Evidence from Canada. *Journal of Socio-Economics, 34,* 787-809.

Myers, S. (1996). An interactive model of religiosity inheritance: The importance of family context. *American Sociological Review, 61,* 858-866

National Center for Fathering, National PTA. (2009). *Survey of fathers' involvement in children's learning: Summary of study findings.* Retrieved September 14, 2012, from National Center for Fathering: http://www.fathers.com/documents/research/2009_Education_Survey_Summary.pdf

National Center for Victims of Crime. (1997). *Child sexual abuse.* Retrieved August 31, 2012, from Network of Victim Assistance - NOVA: http://www.novabucks.org/childsexualabuse.html

Negrini, S., & Carabalona, R. (2002). Backpacks on! Schoolchildren's perceptions of load, associations with back pain and factors determining the load. *Spine, 27*(2), 187-195.

Nelson, H. (1980). Religious transmission versus religious formation: Preadolescent-Parent Interaction. *Sociological Quarterly, 21*, 207-218.

New American Standard Bible®, Copyright © 1960, 1962, 1963, 1968, 1971, 1972, 1973, 1975, 1977, 1995 by The Lockman Foundation.

Ngiam, E., Kim, C. (Producers), Ngiam, E. (Writer), & Ngiam, E. (Director). (2003). *Crammed* [Short Film]. Singapore: Ellery Ngiam Pte. Ltd.

Nieboer, G. (1995, May 14). *Kids games.* Retrieved April 23, 2012, from Kids Games: http://www.gameskidsplay.net

Nord, C., & West, J. (2001). *Fathers' and mothers' involvement in their children's schools by family typeand resident status, NCES 2001-032. Washington, DC: U.S. Department of Education. National Center for Education Statistics.* Retrieved September 30, 2012, from http://fatherhood.hhs.gov/pdf/nces-2001032.pdf

O'Connor, D. B., Jones, F., Conner, M., McMillan, B., & Ferguson, E. (2008). Effects of daily hassles and eating style on eating behavior. *Health Psychology, 27*, 20–31.

O'Neill, R. (2005). *Does marriage matter?* London: Civitas, Institute for the Study of Civil Society.

Office for National Statistics. (2001). *Work and worklessness among households.* London: The Stationery Office.

Office for National Statistics. (2002, May). *Family resources survey, Great Britain, 2000-01.* London: The Stationery Office.

Office for National Statistics. (2002). *Social trends 32.* London: The Stationery Office.

Orathinkal, J., & Vansteenwegen, A. (2006). The effect of forgiveness on marital satisfaction in relationship to marital stability. *Contemporary Family Therapy, 28*, 251-260.

Ozorak, E. W. (1989). Social and cognitive influences on the development of religious beliefs and commitment in adolescence. *Journal for the Scientific Study of Religion, 28*(4), 448-463.

Paleari, F. G., Regalia, C., & Fincham, F. D. (2005). Marital quality, forgiveness, empathy, and rumination: a Longitudinal analysis. *Journal of Social Behaviour and Personality, 3*, 368-378.

Parental substance abuse. Retrieved May 31, 2012 from http://www.childwelfare.gov/can/factors/parentcaregiver/substance.cfm

ParentFurther. (n.d.). (Search Institute) Retrieved April 23, 2012, from ParentFurther: A Search Institute resource for families: http://www.parentfurther.com

Park, Y., & Enright, R. D. (1997). The development of forgiveness in the context of adolescent friendship conflict in Korea. *Journal of Adolescence, 20*, 393-402.

Parke, R. D. (1996). *Fatherhood.* Cambridge: Harvard University Press.

Parker-Pope, T. (2012, August 23). Simon says don't use flashcards. *The New York Times.* Retrieved September 14, 2012, from http://well.blogs.nytimes.com/2012/08/23/simon-says-dont-use-flashcards/

Parker, W. D. (1997). An empiracal typology of perfectionism in academically talented 6th graders. *American Educational Research Journal, 34*, 545-562.

Patton, G. C., Coffey, C., Cappa, C., Currie, D., Riley, L., Gore, F., ... Ferguson, J. (2012). Health of the world's adolescents: A synthesis of internationally comparable data. *The Lancet, 379*(9826), 1665-1675.

Pearce, J. W., & Pezzot-Pearce, T. D. (2007). *Psychotherapy of abused and neglected children (2nd ed.)*. New York & London: Guilford Press. 17-20.

Perl, D., Bouthilet, L., & Lazar, J. (Eds.). (1982). *Television and behavior: Ten years of programs and implications for the 80's*. Washington, DC: U.S. Government Printing Office.

Peters, H. E., Peterson, G. W., Steinmetz, S. K., & Day, R. D. (Eds.). (2000). *Fatherhood: Research, interventions and policies*. New York, NY: Hayworth Press.

Petersen, A. (2011, January 18). *How much sleep do children and teenagers need? Grown-up problems start at bedtime*. Retrieved February 10, 2012, from The Wall Street Journal: http://online.wsj.com

Petrocelli, J. V., Glaser, B. A., Calhoun, G. B., & Campbell, L. F. (2001). Early maladaptive schemas of personality disorder subtypes. *Journal of Personality Disorders, 15*, 546-559.

Piaget, J. (1950). *The moral judgement of the child*. London: Routledge & Kegan Paul.

Pietrini, P., Guazzelli, M., Basso, G., Jaffe, K., & Grafman, J. (2000). Neural correlates of imaginal aggressive behavior assessed by positron emission tomography in healthy subjects. *The American Journal of Psychiatry, 157*, 1772-1781.

Pinto-Gouveia, J., Castilho, P., Galhardo, A., & Cunha, M. (2006). Early maladaptive schemas and social phobia. *Cognitive Therapy and Research, 30*, 571-584.

Pleck, J. H. (1997). Paternal involvement: Levels, sources, and consequences. In M. E. Lamb (Ed.), *The role of the father in child development* (3rd ed., pp. 66–103). New York, NY: John Wiley & Sons.

Poh. (2012, April 22). *The Straits Times*. Forum page.

Pong, S. L. (1997). Family structure, school context, and eighth- grade math and reading achievement. *Journal of Marriage and Family, 59*(3), 734-746.

Pong, S. L., & Hampden-Thompson, G. (2003). Family policies and children's school achievement in single- versus two-parent families. *Journal of Marriage and Family, 65*(3), 681-699.

Pong, S., Hao, L., & Gardner, E. (2005). The roles of parenting styles and social capital in the school performance of immigrant Asian and Hispanic adolescents. *Social Science Quarterly, 86*(4), 928-950.

Popkin, M. H. (1998). *Active parenting of teens*. Georgia: Active Parenting.

Poponoe, D. (1993). American family decline, 1960-1990: A review and appraisal. *Journal of Marriage and Family, 55*.

Pratt, C. A. (Producer), Conroy, P., Carlino, L. J. (Writers), & Carlino, L. J. (Director). (1979). *The Great Santini* [Motion Picture]. United States: Warner Bros. Pictures.

Pratt, M. W., & Fiese, B. H. (Eds.) (2004). *Family stories and the life course across time and generations*. Mahwah, NJ: Erlbaum.

Pretend play: The magical benefits of role play. (n.d.). Retrieved May 29, 2012, from One Step Ahead: http://www.onestepahead.com

Pruett, K. (2000). Father-need. New York, NY: Broadway Books.

puberty - definition of puberty by the Free Online Dictionary, Thesaurus and Encyclopedia. (2009). Retrieved April 23, 2012, from The Free Dictionary: http://www.thefreedictionary.com

Putnam, R. (2000). Bowling alone: The collapse and revival of American community. New York: Simon & Schuster.

Putting Family First: www.puttingfamilyfirst.org

Rasmussen, S. A., & Eisen, J. L. (1992). The epidemiology and clinical features of obsessive compulsive disorder. Psychiatric Clinics of North America, 15(4), 743-758.

Reiner, R., Zweibel, A. (Producers), Zweibel, A. (Writer), & Reiner, R. (Director). (1994). *North* [Motion Picture]. United States: Castle Rock Entertainment.

Research on effects of Media Violence (n.d.). Media Awareness Network: http://www.mediaawareness.ca

RGA Communications, *The 1995 Kentucky Fried Chicken Family Dinner Survey.*

Rhodes, J. E., & DuBois, D. L. (2006). Understanding and facilitating the youth mentoring movement. *Social Policy Report: Giving Child and Youth Development Knowledge Away, 20*(3), 1-19.

Rideout, V. J., Foehr, U. G., & Roberts, D. F. (2010). *Generation M²: Media in the lives of 8- to 18-year olds—A Kaiser Family Foundation study.* The Henry J. Kaiser Family Foundation, California.

Rideout, V. J., Vandewater, E. A., & Wartella, E. A. (2003). *Zero to six: Electronic media in the lives of infants, toddlers and preschoolers—A Kaiser Family Foundation report.* The Henry J. Kaiser Family Foundation, California.

Rijkeboer, M. M., & de Boo, G. M. (2010). Early maladaptive schemas in children: Development and validation of the schema inventory for children. *Journal of Behavior Therapy and Experimental Psychiatry, 41*, 102-109.

Rijkeboer, M. M., & van den Bergh, H. (2006). Multiple group confirmatory factor analysis of the Young Schema-Questionnaire in a Dutch clinical versus non-clinical population. *Cognitive Therapy and Research, 30*(3), 263-278.

Rimm, S. (2006). *When gifted students underachieve: What to do about it.* Waco, TX: Prufrock Press Inc.

Rittenmyer, G. J. (1997). The relationship between early maladaptive schemas and job burnout among public school teachers. *Dissertation Abstracts International, 58*(5-A), 1529.

Rosemond, J. (2001). *Teen-Proofing: Fostering responsible decision making in your teenager.* Kansas City: Andres McMeel Publishing.

Rosenberg, J., & Wilcox, W. B. (2006). *The importance of fathers in the healthy development of children.* U.S. Department of Health and Human Services. Administration for Children and Families. Administration on Children, Youth and Families. Children's Bureau. Office on Child Abuse and Neglect.

Ross, C. E., & Mirowsky, J. (1999). Parental divorce, life course disruption, and adult depression. *Journal of Marriage and the Family, 61*, 1034-1045.

Rostosky, S. S., Wilcox, B. L., Wright, M. L. C., & Randall, B. A. (2004). The impact of religiosity on adolescent sexual behavior: A review of the evidence. *Journal of Adolescent Research, 19*(6), 677-697.

Roth, G., Assor, A., Niemiec, C. P., Ryan, R. M., & Deci, E. L. (2009). The emotional and academic consequences of parental conditional regard: comparing conditional positive regard, conditional negative regard, and autonomy support as parenting practices. *Developmental Psychology, 45*, 1119–1142.

Rudin, S., Steel, D. (Producers), Orr, J., Cruickshank, J., Mason, J. A. (Writers), & Duke, B. (Director). (1993). *Sister Act 2: Back in the habit* [Motion Picture]. United States: Touchstone Pictures.

Russek, L. G., & Schwartz, G. E. (1997). Perceptions of parental caring predict health status in midlife: a 35-year follow-up of the Harvard Mastery of Stress Study. *Psychosomatic Medicine, 59*(2), 144-149.

Rutter, M. (1995). Clinical implications of attachment concepts: Retrospect and Prospect. *Journal of Child Psychology & Psychiatry, 36* (4), 549-571.

Saluter, A. F. *Marital status and living arrangements: March 1994.* US Bureau of the Census, Current Population Report. 28-484. Washington, DC: GPO, 1996. US Bureau of the Census. Statistical Abstract of the United States 1997, Washington, DC: GPO, 1997.

Samuel, D. B., & Ball, S. A. (2012). The Factor Structure and Concurrent Validity of the Early Maladaptive Schema Questionnaire: Research Version. *Cognitive Therapy and Research.* Online publication date: 15-Feb-2012.

Sandberg, J. G., Yorgason, J. B., Miller, R. B., & Hill, E. J. (2012). Family-to-work spillover in Singapore: Marital distress, physical and mental health, and work satisfaction. *Family Relations, 61,* 1-15.

Sarinopoulos, I. C. (1996). *Forgiveness in adolescence and middle adulthood: Comparing the Enright Forgiveness Inventory with Wade Forgiveness Scale.* University of Wisconsin-Madison.

Sarkadi, A., Kristiansson, R., Oberjlaid, F., & Bremberg, S. (2007). Fathers' involvement and children's developmental outcomes: a systematic review of longitudinal studies. *Acta Paediatrica, 97*(2), 153-158.

Schaefer, C., & DiGeronimo, T. F. (2000). *Ages and stages: A parent's guide to normal childhood development.* New York: John Wiley & Sons, Inc.

Schmidt, N. B., Joiner, T. E., Young, J. E., & Telch, M. J. (1995). The Schema Questionnaire: Investigation of Psychometric Properties and the Hierarchical Structure of a Measure of Maladaptive Schemas. *Cognitive Therapy and Research, 19*(3), 295-321.

Scott Peck, M. (1978). *The road less travelled.* NY: Touchstone.

Self-determination theory: An approach to human motivation & personality. Retrieved September 14, 2012 from http://www.selfdeterminationtheory.org/

Seuss. (n.d.). *Dr. Seuss Quotes (Author of Green Eggs and Ham).* Retrieved May 20, 2012, from Goodreads: http://www.goodreads.com/author/quotes/61105.Dr_Seuss

Sexual risk behavior: HIV, STD, & teen pregnancy prevention. (2011, July 12). Retrieved June 7, 2012, from Centers for Disease Control and Prevention: http://www.cdc.gov/HealthyYouth/sexualbehaviors

Seybold, K. S., Hill, P. C., Neumann, J. K., & Chi, D. S. (2001). Physiological and psychological correlates of forgiveness. *Journal of Psychology and Christianity, 20,* 250-259.

Sgroi, S. (1989). Stages of recovery for adult survivors of child sexual abuse. In S. Sgroi (Ed.),*Vulnerable populations: Sexual abuse treatment for children, adult survivors, offenders, and persons with mental retardation Volume 2.* Lexington, MA: Lexington Books.

Sgroi, S. (Ed.). (1989).*Vulnerable populations: Sexual abuse treatment for children, adult survivors, offenders, and persons with mental retardation Volume 2.* Lexington, MA: Lexington Books.

Shah, R., & Waller, G. (2000). Parental style and vulnerability to depression: The role of core beliefs. *Journal of Nervous and Mental Disease, 188,* 19-25.

Sheffield, A., Waller, G., Emanuelli, F., Murray, J., and Meyer, C. (2005). Links Between Parenting and Core Beliefs: Preliminary Psychometric Validation of the Young Parenting Inventory. *Cognitive Therapy and Research, 29*(6), 787-802.

Shulevitz, J. (2012, September 15). Why fathers really matter. *The Straits Times,* D14-15.

Shulevitz, J. (2012, September 8). Why fathers really matter. Retrieved October 16, 2012, from *The New York Times,* Sunday Review: http://www.nytimes.com

Simons, R. L., Lin, K-H., Gordon, L. C., Conger, R. D., & Lorenz, F. O. (1999). Explaining the higher incidence of adjustment problems among children of divorce compared with those in two-parent families. *Journal of Marriage and the Family, 61*(4), 1020-1033.

Singer, M. I., Slovak, K., Frierson, T., & York, P. (1998). Viewing preferences, symptoms of psychological trauma, and violent behaviors among children who watch television. *Journal of the American Academy of Child and Adolescent Psychiatry, 37,* 1041-1048.

Smalley, G., & Trent, J. (1996). *The blessing*. New York: Pocket Books.

Smetana, J. C., Metzger, A., Gettman, D. C., & Campione-Barr, N. (2006). Disclosure and secrecy in the adolescent-parent relationships. *Child Development, 77*, 201-217.

Smith, C., & Denton, M. L. (2005). *Soul searching: The religious and spiritual lives of American teenagers.* New York: Oxford University Press.

Smith, C., & Sikkink, D. (2003). Social predictors of retention in and switching from the religious faith of family of origin. *Review of Religious Research, 45*(2), 188-206.

Snyder, H. N. (2000, July). *Sexual assault of young children as reported to law enforcement: victim, incident, and offender characteristics.* Retrieved from http://bjs.ojp.usdoj.gov/content/pub/pdf/saycrle.pdf

Socrates quotes. (n.d.). Retrieved May 28, 2012, from Goodreads: http://www.goodreads.com/author/quotes/275648.Socrates

Solomon, G. *Cinemaparenting.* http://www.cinemaparenting.com

Specht, M. W., Chapman, A., & Celluci, T. (2009). Schemas and borderline personality disorder symptoms in incarcerated women. *Journal of Behavior Therapy and Experimental Psychiatry, 40*, 256-264.

Spera, C. (2006). Adolescents' perceptions of parental goals, practices and styles in relation to their motivation and achievement. *Journal of Early Adolescence, 26*(4), 456–490.

Sternberg, K. J. (1997). Fathers, the missing parents in research on family violence. In M. E. Lamb (Ed.), *The role of fathers in child development* (3rd ed., pp. 284-308, 392-397). New York, NY: John Wiley & Sons

Steyer, J. P., & Clinton, C. (2002). *The other parent: The inside story of the media's effect on our children.* New York: Atria Books.

Stott, G. (1988). Familial influence on religious involvement. *The Religion and Family Connection: Social Science Perspectives, 3*, 258-271.

Stress: The fight or flight response. (n.d.). Retrieved May 30, 2012, from Psychologist World: http://www.psychologistworld.com

Subkoviak, M. J., Enright, R. D., & Wu, C. (1992, October). *Current developments related to measuring forgiveness.* Paper presented at the annual meeting of the Midwestern Educational Research Association, Chicago, IL.

Subkoviak, M. J., Enright, R. D., Wu, C., Gassin, E. A., Freedman, S., Olson, L. M., & Sarinopoulos, I. C. (1995). Measuring interpersonal forgiveness in late adolescence and middle adulthood. *Journal of Adolescence, 18*, 641-655.

Suzuki, S. (1983). *Nurtured by love: The classical approach to talent education.* Miami, FL: Warner Broz. Publication Inc.

Swan, N. (1998). Exploring the role of child abuse on later drug abuse: Researchers face broad gaps in information. *NIDA Notes, 13*(2). Retrieved May 31, 2012 from the National Institute on Drug Abuse website: www.nida.nih.gov/NIDA_Notes/NNVol13N2/exploring.html

Sweeney, D. (n.d.). *The Mozart effect: Classical music and your baby's brain.* Retrieved May 20, 2012, from BabyCenter: http://www.babycenter.com/0_the-mozart-effect-classical-music-and-your-babys-brain_9308.bc

Szalavitz, M. (2011, January 24). *The key to health, wealth and success: Self-control.* Retrieved May 20, 2012, from Time.com Healthland: http://healthland.time.com

Tamis-LeMonda, C. S., & Cabrera, N. (Eds.). (2002). *Handbook of father involvement: Multidisciplinary perspectives.* Mahwah, NJ: Erlbaum.

Tan, H. Y. (2011, October 19). No enrichment classes? Good parenting works too. *The Straits Times*, A14.

Tan, H. Y. (2012, March 3). What matters most? *The Straits Times*, D2.

Teicher, M. H., Samson, J. A., Polcari, A., & McGreenery, C. E. (2006). Sticks, stones, and hurtful words: Relative effects of various forms of childhood maltreatment. *The American Journal of Psychiatry, 163*(6), 993-1000.

Television & Health. (n.d.). Retrieved May 30, 2012, from California State University Northridge: http://www.csun.edu/science/health/docs/tv&health.html

The Heritage Foundation. *Family and adolescent well-being*. Retrieved September 14, 2012, from FamilyFacts.org: http://www.familyfacts.org/briefs/34/family-and-adolescent-well-being

The Heritage Foundation. *Strong beginnings: How families bolster early educatonal outcomes*. Retrieved September 14, 2012, from FamilyFacts.org: http://www.familyfacts.org/briefs/23/strong-beginnings-how-families-bolster-early-educational-outcomes

The Holy Bible, New Living Translation, copyright 1996, 2004, 2007 by Tyndale House Foundation.

The Holy Bible: King James Version. Dallas, TX: Brown Books Publishing, 2004.

The Message. Copyright © by Eugene H. Peterson 1993, 1994, 1995, 1996, 2000, 2001, 2002. NavPress Publishing Group.

The New Testament in the Original Greek, Copyright © Robinson & Pierpont. MA: Chilton Book Publishing.

Toh, K., Chia, Y. M., & Lua, J. M. (August 28, 2012). 'Without extra lessons, our kids may lose out'. *The Straits Times*, A7.

Toney, L. P., Kelley, M. L., & Lanclos, N. F. (2003). Self- and parental monitoring of homework in adolescents: Comparative effects on parents' perceptions of homework behavior problems. *Child & Family Behavior Therapy, 25*(1), 35-51.

Trusty, J. (2003). Modeling Mexican Americans' educational expectations: Longitudinal effects of variables across adolescence. *Journal of Adolescent Research, 18*, 131–153.

Turvey, M. D., & Olson, D. H. (2006). *Marriage & family wellness: Corporate America's business?* MN: Life Innovation, Inc.

U.S. Census Bureau, Historical Time Series. (2008). Living arrangements of children under 18 years old: 1960 to the present, Table CH-1. *http://www.census.gov/population/socdemo/hh-fam/ch1.xls* .

U.S. Census Bureau. (2008, September 1). *A child's day, 2004. Table D9*. Retrieved May 29, 2012, from United States Census Bureau: http://www.census.gov/population/socdemo/well-being/2004_detailedtables/04tabD09.xls

U.S. Department of Health and Human Services Administration for Children and Families, Administration on Children, Youth and Families Children's Bureau.Child abuse and neglect fatalities 2009: Statistics and interventions. Retrieved from http://www.childwelfare.gov/pubs/factsheets/fatality.pdf

U.S. Department of Health and Human Services, Administration for Children and Families, Administration on Children, Youth and Families, Children's Bureau. (2010). Child Maltreatment 2009. Available from http://www.acf.hhs.gov/programs/cb/stats_research/index.htm#can

U.S. Department of Health and Human Services. (1999). *Trends in the well-being of America's children and youth, 1999*. Washington, DC: U.S. Department of HHS.

United Nations. (1995). *The world's women 1995: Trends and statistics*. New York: United Nations.

United States Government Accountability Office, 2011. *Child maltreatment: strengthening national data on child fatalities could aid in prevention* (GAO-11-599). Retrieved from http://www.gao.gov/new.items/d11599.pdf

van Hanswijck de Jonge, P., Waller, G., Fiennes, A., Rashid, Z., & Lacey, J. H. (2003). Reported sexual abuse and cognitive content in the morbidly obese. *Eating Behaviors, 4*, 315-322.

van Vreeswijk, M. B. (2012). *Handbook of schema therapy: Theory, research and science.* West Sussex, UK: Wiley-Blackwell.

Ventura, S. J., & Bachrach, C. A. (2000). Nonmarital childbearing in the United States, 1940-99. *National Vital Statistics Reports, 48*(16).

Waite, L., & Gallagher, M. (2000). *The case for marriage: Why married people are happier, healthier, and better off financially.* New York: Doubleday.

Walker, L. J., & Taylor, J. H. (1991). Family interactions and the development of moral reasoning. *Child Development, 62*, 264-283.

Walters, G., Gotoh, J., Lasseter, J. (Producers), Stanton, A. (Writer), Stanton, A., & Unkrich, L. (Directors). (2003). *Finding Nemo* [Motion Picture]. United States: Walt Disney Pictures.

Wee, L. (2012, 3 May). Young & disturbed. *The Straits Times. Mind Your Body.* 12.

Welburn, K., Coristine, M., Dagg, P., Pontefract, A., & Jordan, S. (2002). The Schema Questionnaire-Short Form: Factor analysis and relationship between schemas and symptoms. *Cognitive Therapy and Research, 26*(4), 519-530.

Whitfield, C. L. (2001). *Not crazy: You may not be mentally ill.* Pennington: Muse House Press.

Whitfield, C. L. (2004). *The truth about mental illness: Choices for healing.* FL: Health Communications, Inc.

Whitfield, C. L. (2006). *Healing the child within.* FL: Health Communications, Inc.

Why dad should be more involved in children's lives. (2012, April 24). *The Straits Times*, B6.

Widom, C. S. (1992). *The cycle of violence.* Washington, D.C.: National Institute of Justice, U.S. Department of Justice.

Widom, C. S. (1995). *Victims of childhood sexual abuse—Later criminal consequences.* Washington, D.C.: National Institute of Justice, U.S. Department of Justice.

Williams, T. M. (Ed.). (1986). *The impact of television: A natural experiment in three communities.* New York: Praeger.

Wimer, C., Simpkins, S. D., & Dearing, E., et al. (2008). Predicting youth out-of-school time participation: Multiple risks and developmental differences. *Merrill-Palmer Quarterly, 54*(2), 179-207.

Winnicott, D. (1953). Transitional objects and transitional phenomena. *International Journal of Psychoanalysis, 34*, 89-97.

Winnicott, D. W. (1965). Ego distortion in terms of true and false self. In *The maturational process and the faciliating environment: Studies in the theory of emotional development* (pp. 140-152). New York: International UP Inc.

Winter, M. A., Davies, P. T., Hightower, A. D., & Meyer, S. (2006). Relations among family adversity, caregiver communications, and children's family representations. *Journal of Family Psychology, 20,* 348-351

Wong, M. L., Chan, K. W., Koh, D., Tan, H. H., Lim, F. S., Emmanuel, S., & Bishop, G. (2009). Premarital sexual intercourse among adolescents in an Asian country: Multilevel ecological factors. *Pediatrics.*

Wong, Y. L., Rew, L., & Slaikeu, K. D. (2006). A systematic review of recent research on adolescent religiosity/spirituality and mental health. *Issues in Mental Health Nursing, 27*(2), 161-183.

Worthington, E. L., Jr. (1998). *Dimensions of forgiveness: Psychological research & theological perspectives*. Radnor, PA: Templeton Foundation Press.

Wright, M. O., Crawford, E., & Del Castillo, D. (2009). Childhood emotional maltreatment and later psychological distress among college students: the predicting role of maladaptive schemas. *Child Abuse and Neglect, 33*, 59-68.

Yeung, W. J., Duncan, G. J., & Hill, M. S. (2000).Putting fathers back in the picture: Parental activitiesand children's adult outcomes. In H. E. Peters, G. W. Peterson, S. K. Steinmetz, & R. D. Day (Eds.), *Fatherhood: Research, interventions and policies* (pp. 97–113). New York, NY: Hayworth Press.

YMCA. (2000). *Talking with teens: The YMCA parent and teen survey final report.* New York: The Global Strategy Group, Inc.

Young, J. E. (2003). *Young Parenting Inventory.* (Cognitive Therapy Center of New York) Retrieved October 4, 2011 from Schema Therapy: http://www.schematherapy.com/id205.htm

Young, J. E., & Brown, G. (1999). *Young Schema Questionnaire: Short version.* New York: Cognitive Therapy Centre of New York.

Young, J. E., Klosko, J. S., & Weishaar, M. E. (2003). *Schema therapy: A practitioner's guide.* NY: The Guilford Press.

Youthviews, Gallup Youth Survey 4 (June, 1997)

Zhan, M. (2006). Assets, parental expectations and involvement, and children's educational performance. Children and Youth Services Review, 28, 961–975.

INDEX

Page numbers in *italics* refer to illustrations.

A

Attachment, 109-112

C

Community, 333-396
Connect, work, play, 112-136, *114*
Connection and acceptance, 65-100
    patriarchs, 97-100
Controlling, 54-55
Coping styles, 13-18
    avoidance, 15-17
    overcompensation, 17-18 surrender, 14-15
Core emotional need, 18-22
    definition, 19

E

Emotionally depriving and inhibiting, 56-58
Exasperation
    interactions, 49-62
    interaction worksheet, 435
    new testament, 41
    pathway, *23*
Expectation of parents, 244-245

F

Fatherhood, 399-421
Forgiveness, 366-373, 432

H

Healthy autonomy and performance, 163-194
    patriarchs, 190-194

G

Good enough parenting model, *25*

L

Lifetraps, 13-14, 62,
    abandonment, 179-181
    approval-seeking / recognition-seeking, 226-228
    defectiveness / shame, 80-83

    dependence / incompetence, 174-176
    emotional deprivation, 83-85
    emotional inhibition, 88-90
    enmeshment / undeveloped self, 176-179
    entitlement / grandiosity, 220-223
    failure, 90-92
    insufficient self-control / self-discipline, 223-226
    mistrust / abuse, 77-79
    negativity / pessimism, 184-187
    punitiveness, 289-292
    self-sacrifice, 292-295
    social isolation, 85-88
    subjugation, 181-184
    unrelenting standards / hypercriticalness, 286-289
    vulnerability to harm and illness, 171-174

M

Master Class, 7-11
    baird, 255, 280, 340, 355, 384, 389
    brumley, 42, 167, 187, 280-281, 355, 374, 384, 386, 390, 432-433
    evans, 71, 158, 211, 235-236, 355
    fontenot 84-85, 135-136, 156
    hooper, 109, 340, 355, 386
    laing 6, 67, 383-384
    mannel, 122, 340, 355, 366, 383
    shaw, 20, 71, 340, 355, 389
Marriage affects parenting, 24-32, 187-188, 309-312, 402, 419
Movie moment,
    akeelah and the bee, 202
    chicken little, 424
    crammed, 142
    dead poets society, 326
    divine secrets of the ya-ya sisterhood, 103, 424
    east of eden, 141
    finding nemo, 169
    freaky friday, 141, 424
    happy feet, 326
    i not stupid too, 265
    north, 141-142
    when a man loves a woman, 29
    sister act 2, 333
    taare zameen par, 61

Index ■ 503

the great santini, 141
willy wonka and the chocolate factory, 213

N

Natural and logical consequences, 266-270
Nucci's domains, 45-46

O

Overly permissive, 59-60
Overprotective, 58-59

P

Perfectionistic and conditional, 52-54
Pessimistic, 59
Plus one core emotional need, 333-396
  patriarchs, 342-346
Processing emotions, 147-160
  worksheet, 436
Punitive, 56

R

Realistic expectations, 275-298
  patriarchs, 295-298
Reasonable limits, 209-230
  patriarchs, 229-230
Repair and reconnect, 423-433
Research reveals
  absentee fathers around the globe, 401
  abuse in childhood increases likelihood of mental disorders, 144
  affects of marriage on a child's well-being, 31
  adolescent well-being is strongly related to the quality of the parent-child relationship, 4
  an extensive look at media and youth, 238-240
  asian parents more likely to have children with dysfunctional perfectionism, 314
  attachment research and connection, 110-111
  changing the protocol for premature babies, 69
  childhood games better than flashcards, 126
  children's free time declining, homework increasing, 279
  conditional parenting causes schemas, 316-317
  conditional parenting is damaging, 322-323
  connect, work, play defined, 113-115
  dangers of excessive media exposure, 240-242
  dealing with sexual abuse, 94-96
  decline in time spent between parents and children, 106-108
  Elkind's belief in play, 112
  family structure, 309-310
  fathers make a big difference, 402-404
  forgiveness is good for health, 369-370
  functional communities have proven outcome, 385
  good connection with parents means higher grades, 301
  heavy backpacks cause lasting damage, 304-305
  high rate of myopia linked with lack of outdoor light, 305
  honouring your parents really does bring long life, 70
  how marriage affects work, 32
  important aspects of family time, 105-106
  marital conflict and children, 27-28
  mental illness epidemic among singapore youth, 303
  motivating underachievers, 325
  older and younger children view forgiveness differently, 371
  origin of the four plus one, 21-22
  parental expectations, 308
  percentage of US children living apart, 401
  relevance between people's present lifetraps with pathologies, 62
  schema in new testament, 33-35
  sleep deprivation on the rise in the developed world and endemic in singapore, 302-303
  self-discipline more important than IQ, 218-219
  singapore children have high rate of mental illness, 279
  strong relationships promote overall health, 382
  teenage girls and sexuality, 417
  teenagers and sexuality, 415
  teens secretly want parents in their

lives, 69
traumatic experiences during childhood cause lifetraps, 60
trend of involvement of fathers, 400
two-parent families better for education, 310-311
unhealthy parenting promotes mental illness, 4-5
what exasperates children, 49-50
what kind of mentoring works, 392-393
working on marriage benefits children, 187-188

S

Schema, *see also* Lifetraps
new testament, 32-36

Spiritual values, 333-377
see also Plus one core emotional need

V

Vortex of conflict escalation, 242-250
exercise, 443-446

Vulnerable, 425-430
exercise, 447-462